# VIRGINIA
## and her
## QUAKER MEETINGS

Meetings existing
in 1993
are underlined

# THE FRIENDLY VIRGINIANS

## America's First Quakers

Jay Worrall, Jr.

HERITAGE BOOKS
2019

# HERITAGE BOOKS
*AN IMPRINT OF HERITAGE BOOKS, INC.*

**Books, CDs, and more—Worldwide**

For our listing of thousands of titles see our website
at
www.HeritageBooks.com

Published 2013 by
HERITAGE BOOKS, INC.
Publishing Division
5810 Ruatan Street
Berwyn Heights, Md. 20740

Copyright © 1994 Jay Worrall, Jr.

All rights reserved. No part of this book may be reproduced or transmitted in any form or by any means, electronic or mechanical, including photocopying, recording or by any information storage and retrieval system without written permission from the author, except for the inclusion of brief quotations in a review.

International Standard Book Numbers
Paperbound: 978-0-7884-5513-1
Clothbound: 978-0-7884-5512-4

## THE FRIENDLY VIRGINIANS
## CONTENTS

| | | |
|---|---|---|
| Photos and Credits | | vi |
| Preface | | vii |
| I. | The Quaker Way Comes to Virginia, 1655-1660 | 1 |
| II. | Virginia's Quakers and the Right to Worship as One Wishes, 1660-1663 | 19 |
| III. | In Which the Truth is Crushed to Earth, 1664-1677 | 43 |
| IV. | The Friendly Virginians Become Somewhat Respectable, 1677-1700 | 67 |
| V. | At Last within the Law, 1700-1733 | 91 |
| VI. | West of the Blue Ridge, 1733-1750 | 123 |
| VII. | The Quaker Way Alters Course, 1750-1763 | 145 |
| VIII. | Farewell, Britannia, 1763-1775 | 163 |
| IX. | The Friendly Virginians and the American Revolution, 1775-1781 | 191 |
| X. | After So Many Ages, 1782-1800 | 225 |
| XI. | To the Westward Waters, 1800-1820 | 265 |
| XII. | The Blood of Christ, 1820-1833 | 331 |
| XIII. | On Laying Down Virginia Yearly Meeting, 1833-1850 | 351 |
| XIV. | O, Virginia! Virginia! 1850-1865 | 397 |
| XV. | They Leap the Hedge, 1865-1900 | 439 |
| XVI. | Thee Interests Me, 1900-1950 | 479 |
| XVII. | I Think of the Great Work, 1950-Now | 507 |
| Appendix A: Quaker meetings in Virginia | | 537 |
| Acknowledgements | | 540 |
| Bibliography | | 541 |
| End Notes | | 563 |
| Index | | 575 |

# DEDICATION

*First*

for Carolyn
who has welcomed so long
the shades of old time Friends
journeying through her life

*Then*

for Jay, Caidya and Emilie
Sara and Laura

## PHOTOS AND CREDITS

Fox at Carlisle Market Cross--Robert Spence/Friends Library, London.
Governor William Berkeley--Virginia Historical Society.
George Fox--Robert Spence/Friends Library, London.
Stratton Manor--reproduced from *Virginia's Eastern Shore* by Ralph T. Whitelaw.
George Keith--Quaker Collection, Havenford College.
Hopewell Friends' Meeting house--from *Hopewell Friends History* by Hopewell Friends Meeting,
Abram's Delight, Winchester--Winchester-Frederick Historical Society
Edward Stabler's House, Petersburg--*Southside Virginian*.
Jim Lincoln at His Forebears' Graves--John Kirkpatrick.
Christopher Johnson's House, Lynchburg--from *Lynchburg an Architectural History*, by S. Allen Chambers, Jr.
Virginia's Old Capitol--from *Richmond, Virginia in Old Prints* by Alexander W. Weddell,
Back Creek Friends Meeting house--*Hopewell Friends History*.
Quaker Meeting house, Arden--from *Berkeley County. U.S.A.*, by William T. Doherty.
Elias Hicks--Quaker Collection, Havenford College.
Stephen Grellet--Quaker Collection, Havenford College.
The Peaceable Kingdom at The Branch--Abby Aldrich Rockefeller Folk Art Center.
John B. Crenshaw--from *Quaker Biographies*, by Philadelphia Yearly Meeting.
Samuel M. Janney--from his *Memoirs*.
Young Quaker Woman--Janney Wilson.
Anna Jeanes--Stapeley Hall.
Virginia Randolph--Virginia Randolph Educational Center.
Waiting for the Trade, Urbanna--W. Lincoln Highton/Virginia Writers' Project of the U.S. Works Progress Administration
Map of the Virginia Friends Meetings--John Vogt       End Papers

## PREFACE

Respected Reader,

You can find a few sentences in most Virginia histories about the Friends or Quakers. Likewise, history books about Quakers touch briefly on their rise and progress in Virginia.

The following account comes largely from a putting together and sorting out of all these touchings. It is a mosaic from which emerges the picture of a people plain and plain-spoken, good neighbors who became law-breakers at times, often hard to understand, downright peculiar.

They viewed and view war as a curse from hell. Their heroes' characters are the obverse of warrior heroes'. They are a religious people with practically no theology except the conviction that there is some thing of God in you and me and every man and woman, boy and girl.

Contrary to popular wisdom, American Quakers did not first appear in Pennsylvania, the Quaker State, in 1682. Rather they appeared in 1655 in Virginia. In the 330-odd years thereafter, the Friendly Virginians, as I have come to call them, have stood for peace and against violence, for religious freedom, civil rights and womens' rights. They have striven to end war, change the penal system and aid Native Americans. Their world view has affected their lives and characters and also, as you will read, the ways of the larger society.

                                                Jay Worrall, Jr.
                                          Charlottesville, Virginia 1994

The first Friends' ministers in England, having no meetinghouses, spoke out-of-doors. This print depicts George Fox at the Market Cross in Carlisle, 1653. The sheriff's men (lower right) are trying to break through George's hearers to arrest him. Elizabeth Harris in Virginia evidently preached out-of-doors too, but was not troubled by government authorities.

I

## THE QUAKER WAY
## COMES TO VIRGINIA (1655 -1660)

> The Friend who went to Virginia is returned in a pretty condition. There she
> was gladly received by many who met together, and the Governor is convinced.
> -- Gerard Roberts of London
> writing to George Fox, July 1657

This history about Virginia and Virginians begins far from Virginia on a street corner in the city of London in the summer of 1654. Two men stand there on the street corner haranguing the passers by. Elizabeth Harris, a young London housewife, stands among the listeners.

The men belong to the loose new movement called the Children of the Light or the Friends of God, jokingly known as "Quakers." Francis Howgill in his early thirties and Edward Burrough, 22 made a bizarre impression standing there on the late summer street corner. For one thing, they came from the country far north of London and they looked countrified to the Londoners. For another, they were enthusiasts and revolutionaries with passion in their words. The news spread through London's coffee houses "that there was a sort of people come there that went by the name of plain North Country plowmen, who did differ in judgment to all other people in the city."[1]

They were declaring things never heard in London before: The mighty day of the Lord is here...you of London, be not satisfied with outward ceremonies and old forms...no longer look outward for sermons and hymns, organs, whistles and pipes, bells, cushions, altars and fonts to change your lives...come away...come away...there is some thing of God in *you*. turn your mind *within*...examine your heart...try your ways, with the Light Christ Jesus has enlightened *you*.[2]

Elizabeth Harris, feminine and firm-chinned, about 26, a woman who wore warm colors and red petticoats, was caught and held by the street corner message. She began to attend the brand-new Quaker meeting in Robert Benbricke's downtown London parlor. She learned that the words of a woman who feels inspired to stand up in the silence and speak in meeting are as welcome as a man's words. She began to speak in meeting, and soon she, Elizabeth Harris, was out in the streets urging Londoners to join the Children of the Light.

Later in 1655 Francis Howgill and Edward Burrough left the street corners and rented the large room of an ancient house in Aldersgate. The house was known as "The Bull and Mouth" or "The Mouth" from the sign of the tavern that occupied one corner of it.* It was well known as a place where Londoners came to hear speakers for the Levellers and other radical political parties.[3] Here Howgill and Burrough regularly held "threshing meetings." These threshing meetings were held on weekdays to persuade members of the public to "come out of the world" and to join the Friends. "Retired meetings," on the other hand, were held on First Days (Sundays) when Friends met together for worship. Elizabeth Harris was often there.

The English people of 1655 had come through more than a century of religious turmoil, ever since King Henry the Eighth declared in 1534 that the churches of England were no longer answerable to Pope Clement the Seventh. Many were put off by the class-conscious and aristocratic Anglican churches, by surplices and stained glass windows, prescribed prayers and collects. Then in 1649 King Charles and the Anglican church were deposed; Oliver Cromwell became Lord Protector of the land; and black-gowned Dissenter preachers whose sermons dwelt on hellfire and brimstone, election and reprobation, and the salvation of a chosen few appeared in the church pulpits. Neither Anglican or Puritan approaches satisfied everyone.

From 1647 when George Fox, the first Quaker, first began "to publish the Truth" until 1652, a few people left the "steeple houses" to join the Quaker movement. After 1652 the trickle turned to a torrent. North Country English began coming to the new Quaker meetings by the thousands. In 1654 there came a second expansion when a company of recently convinced Quakers--"Sixty from the North"--moved down to London and the south of England, preaching to crowds, "holding threshing meetings to gather the harvest."

Some clergymen and county magistrates became alarmed, and several of the frockless Quaker ministers were jailed as heretics and blasphemers. Nevertheless the movement of the Friends of God kept growing. By 1655 there were about twenty thousand Quakers in England. Most of them came from the working classes and from the left wing Puritan sects. They met in

---

* Probably the Bull and Mouth sign preserved in London's Guildhall Museum.

little groups and circles all up and down the country, in homes and barns and out-of-doors, waiting in silence for guidance from God.

Money came in dribs and drabs and then in sizable sums to foster the movement. It was funnelled to two treasurers: Margaret Fell of Swarthmore Hall in Lancashire and Gerard Roberts, wine cooper at the sign of the Fleur-de-Lys in Watling Street, London. By 1655 the Quaker leaders had the money--the "outward means" they called it--to take abroad their vision of the inward way to God, to bring the whole world into the movement. George Fox--he of the piercing gaze, long hair and leather breeches--wrote that year from his cell in Cornwall's Launceston Jail:

> "Let all nations hear the sound by word or writing. Spare no place, spare not tongue nor pen. But be obedient to the Lord God and go through the work. And be valiant for the Truth upon earth, and tread and trample all that is contrary."[4]

Elizabeth Harris, Quaker for less than a year, was one of many who were ready to go "for the service of the Truth" abroad. She set out across the Atlantic Ocean, leaving her husband William and their baby son in London.

The old records do not reveal the manner of Elizabeth Harris's going--excepting one letter that Francis Howgill wrote to Margaret Fell, 21 May, 1655:

> "And wisdom begins to grow among Friends [in London] and divers are moved to go forth in the ministry. Two young men and two young women are moved to go to Barbados, out of the city; and another young man, a Scotchman, is moved to go for Scotland; and other two young women are gone to Wales and other two go to Oxford--all these are citizens [of London]."[5]

It is a fair guess that Elizabeth is one of the two young London women who sailed that May to Barbados. That green island was a way-point for the ships of the tobacco fleet from London to Virginia. It is likely that Elizabeth sailed from England in June, stopped on Barbados for a little time, and then travelled on. She may have arrived in Virginia as early as September 1655.

Mary Fisher, Quaker, single and 32 years old, also travelled from England to Barbados, about November 1655. Mary spent some six months in Barbados, promoting the new Quaker faith. Then she sailed for Boston with Ann Austin, mother of five children. The two women arrived at Boston in July 1656.[6] So it appears that the first three Quaker messengers to America--Elizabeth Harris, Mary Fisher and Elizabeth Austin--all were women."[7][8]

That the first three were women tells something about the mindset of Quakers. Their central idea was and is that some thing of God is borne in every human being, male and female; that all are equal, brothers and sisters, children of God. In the 17th century, when men and men alone ruled the churches all across Christendom, Quaker women stood out uniquely in their leading roles. This was only one aspect of the Quaker movement that shocked the British establishment.

Elizabeth Harris arrived in Virginia before disturbing news about the Quakers had time to cross the ocean. Gerard Roberts mentioned her in a letter he wrote from London to George Fox, July 1657:

> "The Friend who went to Virginia [evidently E Harris] is returned in a pretty condition. There she was gladly received by many who met together, and the Governor is convinced."[9]

From these two sentences in a crumbling letter, we learn that Elizabeth Harris was the first to publish Quakerism successfully on the American mainland, and that it was published first in Virginia.

The two women Friends who sailed to Boston were not successful. Mary Fisher and Ann Austin sailed in to Boston harbor aboard the ship *Swallow*, on 11 July, 1656.

The authorities in Boston by that time had received anti-Quaker warnings from England. They took Mary and Ann right away to Boston's jail and burned the Quaker literature in their baggage. In jail they stripped the women and searched for tokens of witchcraft on their bodies. On 7 August

---

* One Quaker family and one Quaker man arrived in America before 1655: Joseph Warner, his wife, and son John came from Blockley in Worcestershire to settle in the Schuylkill Valley a little west of now Philadelphia in 1653. The Warners are the first English people known to settle in Pennsylvania. They probably became Quakers before leaving England. Richard Smith of Southampton, Long Island, went to England on a visit in 1654, came under the influence of William Dewsbury--one of the Valiant Sixty--and returned to Long Island a convinced Friend. Neither the Warners nor Richard Smith, however, are known to have been Quaker "messengers" or spreaders of the word.

they shipped Mary and Ann back to England on the *Swallow* with a warning not to return.[10]

\* \* \*

What was Virginia when Elizabeth Harris arrived? The civilized part of the colony lay wholly on the Eastern Shore and in the Tidewater, around Chesapeake Bay. A flat and sandy land, the Tidewater, with four tide-streaked violet-and-silver rivers, swamps full of shadows and shy furry wild creatures, and dark-looping slowflowing streams.

The English, in that land in those years, lived lonely, close to the river and stream banks. They lived on clearings along the water banks, each with a clapboarded high peaked little house, a few outbuildings and a scattering of tobacco and corn fields and pastures hacked out of the woods.

About eighteen thousand English people lived in Virginia then, some two or three thousand of them on the Eastern Shore, some fifteen or sixteen thousand on a mainland Virginia that reached 90 miles inland and 160 miles north to south. Many were recently arrived immigrants, including quite a few Cavaliers--aristocrats who had stood for Charles I and his losing cause. They had come to Virginia to escape Oliver Cromwell's retribution.

For every newcomer who lived to become a Virginian, eight or nine died. The ships that sailed to Virginia out of the Thames and the Medway took six weeks to six months crossing the Atlantic. Aboard those ships often were "stench, fumes, vomiting, many kinds of sicknesses--fever, dysentery, scurvy, the mouth-rot and the like--all of which come from old and sharply salted food and meat, also from bad and foul water." For those who survived the ocean passage, some four out of five died of "the seasoning fever" once they reached Virginia. Governor Berkeley wrote in 1671 that "there is not oft unseasoned hands (as we term them) that die now, whereas heretofore not one of five escaped the first year."

No wonder some convicted men in England, when offered a choice of hanging or being sent to Virginia, answered "Hang me."

More than half of the population were indentured servants, men and women who signed papers to work for a certain master three to seven years in Virginia in exchange for their ship passage. For each servant brought into Virginia, the master was granted fifty acres.

Some five thousand African slaves lived in Virginia then and perhaps four thousand Indians-Nansemond and Nottaway tribesmen south of the James; Powhites and Chickahominies between the James and York Rivers; Mattaponi and Pamunkeys on the Middle Peninsula between York and

Rappahannock Rivers; Wicomico on the Northern Neck between the Potomac and Rappahannock; and Occahannocks and Accomacks on the Eastern Shore, to name a few. The Virginia Indians were reduced in numbers and harmless in the settled parts of the colony in 1655, but the settlers feared the Indians who roamed the woods north of York River and west of the fall line.

Almost every home had a boat landing and some kind of a boat. There were only four or five hundred horses and donkeys and practically no wagons for there were no wagon roads. But there were more than twenty thousand bulls, cows and calves; five thousand goats; three thousand sheep, and hogs beyond counting. Deer visited the clearings. On winter nights wolves prowled the pigpens and chicken coops.

The woods pressed close around Virginians' dwellings in the 1650s--great pines, black walnuts, red and white oaks, cypress and gum, cedar, juniper, hickory and chestnut trees. In the spring, white dogwoods splashed the tender green woods. Virginians in the 1650s lived with trees--with the leaves shining wet in rain, with crimson and yellow leaves in autumn--living lonely, a little homesick as dwellers of all new lands must be, living by their own hands and brains. There were few enslaved among them then.

\* \* \*

Elizabeth Harris certainly knew something of conditions when she arrived in Virginia. She evidently landed at Kickatan (Hampton) off some ship of the tobacco fleet, then crossed Hampton Roads to the sparsely settled country south of James River in Norfolk, Nansemond, and Isle of Wight Counties. A good many of the settlers there were plain people of a Puritan inclination who were dissatisfied with the high church, formal kind of religion that the law then mandated in Virginia. Very few Cavaliers lived among them. Governor Berkeley had harassed these southside people over their failure to support the established church until hundreds of them abandoned their farms in 1649 and moved north to Maryland. This was only six years before Elizabeth came. She must have gone straight from her ship to the Dissenting remnant south of the James, those who had not moved to Maryland, for the first Virginians to become Quakers lived there.

The governor "convinced" by Elizabeth can only be Richard Bennett (1608-1676). He had been a leader of the south-of-James River Dissenters who moved to Maryland in 1649. Bennett came back to Virginia in 1652 when Oliver Cromwell named him governor, after Cromwell deposed Charles

I as King of England. Bennett finished his three-year term as the governor at Jamestown on 1 April 1655. He probably returned to his plantation on Nansemond River and met Elizabeth Harris later in 1655 when she spoke in some Nansemond church or home. Richard Bennett remained a friend of the Friends for the rest of his life. When he died in 1676 he willed 2,000 pounds of tobacco to each of four Nansemond Quaker neighbors. Two Quakers were among the executors of his will. His daughter, Anne Bennett, also became a Quaker.[11]

Elizabeth Harris went on up Chesapeake Bay from Nansemond to the dissenters in Maryland who had been chased there from Virginia in 1649. There were two communities of them--one settled on farms along the Patuxent River led by Richard Preston, the other on Severn River near present-day Annapolis.[12] Elizabeth convinced quite a few people in both Maryland communities of the power of the Inward Light. Then she sailed home to London, having sojourned in Virginia and Maryland about a year and a half.

Very little has been written about the flesh and blood woman Elizabeth Harris. She is mentioned randomly in bits and pieces of letters, books, and old manuscripts. None of the pieces proves directly that she is "the Friend who went to Virginia" and returned to London "in a pretty condition." But collectively they provide internal evidence to show that Elizabeth was that woman.

Fitting these pieces in their places, the following picture emerges: She was born right by the Tower of London about 1629, named Elizabeth Bache. Her father was Humphrey Bache, a goldsmith at the Sign of the Snail on Tower Street. Elizabeth was the Bache's oldest child. Her mother died after her fifth child's difficult birth, and then her father gave up goldsmithing. He got work as a foreman on the fortifications around London during England's Civil War and later worked in the Customs House. He embezzled £150 in these two jobs, by padding payrolls and taking kick-backs.

Elizabeth helped to bring up her motherless brothers and sisters and did not get much schooling. In 1649 she married William Harris in London's St Mary's Abchurch[13] and had her own baby, Will Harris the younger. Then in the summer of 1654 the first Quaker messengers came to London, and Elizabeth Harris was among the first to be convinced by them. She left their little boy with her husband when she set sail for Virginia in 1655. Before she sailed, however, she spoke earnestly with her father about her new faith. In 1656 he too joined Friends. He repented his dishonesty and repaid £160 for the money he had taken as graft.[14]

The next information comes from Gerard Roberts' letter reporting that the Friend who went to Virginia had returned to London. He wrote it in July 1657. But Elizabeth stayed home in London only a few months. Then she journeyed to Venice with another woman Friend, Elizabeth Cowart, to plead with the citizens of that city of canals to turn to the Inward Light. They got back to London in April 1658.[15]

While Elizabeth Harris was in Italy, Robert Clarkson wrote to her from Anne Arundel County, Maryland. He was one of those who were convinced of the Quaker Truth during Harris's trip to America:

> Eleventh Month 14, 1657 [14 January 1658 according to the modern calendar*] Elizabeth Harris, Dear Heart, I salute thee in the tender love of the Father which moved thee toward us, and I do own thee to have been a minister by the will of God to bear the outward testimony to the inward word of Truth in me and others.

He then reports that his wife has joined him as a convinced Friend and mentions twenty and more Marylanders who "abide convinced." Ann Dorsey and her husband, the first he mentions as convinced, are most likely Elizabeth Harris's aunt and uncle--for Humphrey Bache mentioned his sister Ann Dorry (or Dorsey) in his will.[16] Ann and Edward Dorsey came to Maryland from southside Virginia in 1649, among the dissenting families harassed by Governor Berkeley.[17]

Robert Clarkson also mentions letters written by Elizabeth to the Maryland Friends. He writes that "The two messengers thou spoke of in thy letters [Josiah Coale and Thomas Thurston] have not yet come" being probably in jail in Virginia. He tells Elizabeth that "the books that were sent" have been received and distributed to seven places in Maryland where Quakers live. And he closes:

> With my dear love I salute thy husband and the rest of Friends; and rest with thee in the Eternal Word which abideth forever. Farewell. Robert Clarkson[18]

---

* In 1752 Great Britain changed the calendar from Julian Year to Gregorian Year. The Julian year began on March 25 and ended March 24 while the Gregorian begins on January 1, ends December 31. Until 1752 Friends called March "the First Month."

Margaret Fell of Swarthmore Hall, who was to marry George Fox in 1668, wrote to Elizabeth Harris in 1659 or 1660, although what she wrote or why is not known. For Margaret Fell, Jr., who was in London to get treatment for her ailing knee, wrote to her mother then that "Thy letters which thou [wrote] to Friends came safe here. That to E. Harris, I sent with R. Ben[bricke] and the others were sent as directed."[19] Robert Benbricke, who was entrusted with the letter, was a Friend whose home in downtown London was a place where Friends held retired meetings.[20]

On 5 April 1660, Elizabeth was one of five women--two with babies at their breasts--who, visiting imprisoned Friends in Salisbury Prison, were themselves locked up there for a time.[21] That summer, John Stubbs wrote to George Fox from London. His letter reveals something of Elizabeth Harris's commitment, her determination, and her emotional side:

> Here is Elizabeth Harris who sometimes goes forth to steeple-houses in sackcloth and she hath much peace in this service. There was some seemed rather to be against it, which troubled her a little. She spoke to me with many tears about it several weeks ago, and I said I thought I might write to thee about it, and she desired I might. After she had been at Cambridge, it came to her that she must go to Manchester the sixth month. And so she would be glad to have a line or two from thee about it before she go, as soon as can be, the time draws near of her passing.[22]

Elizabeth's father, Humphrey Bache, suffered for his new-found faith along with Elizabeth. He was imprisoned in 1660, and wrote a short manuscript titled "A Few Words in True Love" in his cell. But he contracted tuberculosis in prison and died two years after being released.[23] He named Elizabeth Harris, his oldest daughter, and Elizabeth Harrison, his sister, to execute his will and mentioned Ann Dorry or Dorsey, another of his three sisters.[24]

The Harris family, or at least William Harris and little Will, emigrated from London to Anne Arundel County in Maryland, right after Humphrey Bache died. They settled on 100 acres which they called "Harris' Mount." It was located where Routes 665 and 387 (Severn Ridge Road) meet near present-day Annapolis.[25] Whether Elizabeth came along is not known. If so, she returned after a time to England. On 6 June 6 1665, she was imprisoned again, this time in Northampton Castle, after her third conviction for attending Quaker meetings, and was held there seven years, until 1672.[26]

Elizabeth, wan from jail, made her way to Maryland in 1672, but her husband, faithful William, had died there two or three years earlier. In his will he mentioned some of Elizabeth's clothing which he had kept against her return--including a red petticoat, from which it is inferred that she wore "warm colors and red petticoats." And Elizabeth, now widowed and about 43 years old, was living at Harris' Mount when George Fox visited her there 18 and 19 October, 1672.[27] The next year she married Quaker James Warner in Maryland, but he lived only a year or so after their marriage.[28]

In 1677, the London Quaker, Edward Billing, who was one of the proprietors of West Jersey, granted a tract of land there to Elizabeth Harris.[29] She sold this land in 1688. The deed, in the New Jersey State Library in Trenton, bears her initials "EH," writ large--the only known exemplar of her handwriting. This deed refers to her as "of Westminster in the county of Middlesex," that is, the city of London. It may be that she returned to London late in her life. Or it may be that she died in Maryland and that her remains lie quiet in the old Friends' burying ground near Galesville.

\* \* \*

America was only one far place where the first Quakers sailed. They traveled all across the known world, convinced that they had rediscovered the spiritual well spring of the first Christians, lost during centuries of churchiness and formality. They believed they had found again the existence of a divine light in every man, woman and child, a radiance from God akin to the spirit of Christ. This inward light, they held, if it is turned to as one's guiding star, leads a person to "the Truth."

So they traveled, as the Friends of God, in the service of the Truth:

- Three Friends—William Caton, William Ames, and John Stubbs—crossed the English Channel to Holland.
- Margaret Fell's account book shows payments for journeys to Spain and Jerusalem and "£47.10s for the Friends that went to Venice."
- Friends went to France in 1654 and again in 1657. Nearly all the Catholic countries of the Continent were visited, but to little effect--except that some Quakers wound up in the dungeons of the Inquisition, and John Perrot was chained to the floor of Rome's mad house.
- Three men Friends, who set out for China and Prester John's shadowy country, got no farther than Alexandria in Egypt.

The results of all these travelings were discouraging. Outside Holland there were not many Quaker convincements. By contrast, Elizabeth Harris's visit to Virginia and Maryland was a spectacular success. Perhaps her success was due to her attractive person or perhaps to her early arrival in Virginia before derogatory news about the Quaker movement arrived from England. However it was, "she was gladly received by many who met together" along the south shore of Hampton Roads and James River, and Govenor Richard Bennett was one of the Virginians she "convinced."

\* \* \*

Late in 1657, about two years after Elizabeth Harris, two young Englishmen appeared in Virginia: Josiah Coale, 24 years old, from Bristol and Thomas Thurston, 35, from the countryside near Bristol. Josiah Coale joined the Quakers in 1654 after he heard John Camm and John Audland of "Sixty from the North" speaking in Bristol. He had been locked up in English jails at least once for being a Quaker and was to be jailed many times again. Thurston was on his second trip to America, having been barred from coming ashore in Boston with seven other Quakers, in August 1656.[30]

Josiah Coale wrote to Margaret Fell before he left England that he was going to Virginia with his friend Thomas because "I have been made sensible of the groaning of the seed in that place."[31] This probably means that Josiah had heard of some persecution of the first Virginia Quakers under the Virginia governor who succeeded Richard Bennett. That was Edward Digges, a man not in sympathy with the Quaker outlook; for Coale and Thurston "were soon put in prison and not suffered to pass" when their ship arrived in James River.[32]

They were held in Jamestown jailhouse about six months. Governor Digges's Council, sitting as Virginia's General Court, at first ordered "that they are to be kept in prison till the ship that brought them be ready to depart the country again." But when one or the other of them, Josiah or Thomas, said to the Court "that though they might not be suffered, yet he must come another time," the order to send them home by ship was angrily rescinded.[33] They were released from the jail in spring 1658, then turned out on foot into the vast woods north of York River to find their way as best they could. No doubt it was assumed that the two young men would die there. However, a Virginian named Thomas Chapman volunteered to try to guide them through the forest.[34] It appears that Thomas Chapman grew up near Willoughby's Spit where the city of Norfolk is today.[35] Very likely he was one who had heard Elizabeth Harris when she made the first Quaker convincements in his home neighborhood three years before.

The outcasts headed north toward New England. According to George Bishop, the first Quaker historian, they travelled "in an untrodden path by any English hitherto (as hath been heard of)...through uncouth passages, vast wildernesses and uninhabited countries for near 200 miles together."[36]

They must have been sighted by Indians soon after crossing the York River. Indian eyes certainly watched them through the springtime forest leafery as they trudged north. Governor Digges and Virginians generally feared these Indians, went armed against them and periodically sent the militia to burn their villages. Susquehanna Indians accosted the three Quakers after they had traveled about a hundred miles, and this may be the first time Quakers and Indians ever met--an occurrence with historic overtones. For instead of being tomahawked, the three were given "the most courteous treatment"[37] and helped on their way.

There is no way now to know how the Quakers communicated with the Indians. Perhaps Thomas Chapman was the interpreter. At any rate, Coale, Thurston and Chapman got it across the yawning gap of cultures that they saw the Indians as friends. The three likely would have perished without Indian help. Thomas Thurston hurt his leg after they crossed the Potomac into Maryland. As George Bishop described it, "Thomas Thurston being sick among them many days and that near unto death, the Susquehanna Indians took what care they could of him in all things...and some of the Susquehannas came to visit [Thomas] when they heard he was in prison afterwards in Virginia."[38]

\* \* \*

While Josiah Coale and Thomas Thurston were still in the jail at Jamestown, another Quaker from London appeared among the fishermen and farmers of Virginia's Eastern Shore. William Robinson was his name and he was so devoted to the Quaker cause that it brought his death soon after.

Will Robinson voyaged to America aboard the *Woodhouse*. Many ships have sailed across the pages of American history--the *Susan Constant*, *Godspeed*, and *Discovery*, the *Mayflower* and *Welcome*, all brought pioneering founders to America. But none of these sailing ships carried passengers more passionately committed to the ideals they sailed for. None kept a stranger, more mystical log.

The *Woodhouse* carried eleven passengers. All of them, seven men and four women, were Friends who came to London under a leading "for America." But by spring 1657, word had reached London that any ship captain who brought Quakers to America would run into trouble. The eleven Friends could not find a ship to carry them.

Just at this time, Robert Fowler, a Yorkshire Quaker of four years' standing, happened to be building a little coasting ship at Bridlington Quay. When he heard about the eleven who were trying to get to America, "New England was presented" before him. He drove the last pegs to finish the cutter, named her *Woodhouse*, recruited five men and two boys for a crew, steered for London and took the eleven thankful Friends aboard his "providential ship." He wrote in the log that he took "the Lord's servants aboard, who came with a mighty Hand and an outstretched Arm with them." Then in mid-June the tiny *Woodhouse* tacked down the Thames toward the open Atlantic, "leaving" as her log records "all hope of help as to the outward."

According to the log, Robert Fowler and his friends navigated across the ocean not by compass but by "openings," "drawings," and "leadings". These are entries from Robert Fowler's ecstatic, God-drunk log:

> The Lord caused us to meet together every day, and He Himself met with us and manifested Himself largely unto us, so that by storms we were not prevented from meeting above three times in all our voyage....

> As we were taking council of the Lord, the word from Him was Cut through and steer your straightest course and mind nothing but me,...and we saw the Lord leading our vessel as if it were a man leading a horse by the head, we regarding neither latitude nor longitude but kept to our line....

> When we had been five weeks at sea, when the powers of darkness appeared in the greatest strength against us, having sailed but about 300 leagues [900 miles], Humphrey Norton, falling into communion with God, told me that he had received a comfortable answer and that about such a day we should land in America, which was even so fulfilled....

> Our drawing had been all the passage to keep to the southward until the evening before we made land. Then the word was 'Let them

steer northwards until the day following.' Soon after the middle of the day there was a drawing to meet together before our usual time and it was said to us that we should look abroad in the evening. And as we sat waiting before the Lord, they discovered land....

[We found that we were] in the creek [North River] which led between the Dutch plantations [Manhattan Island] and Long Island.... The power of the Lord came much upon us and an irresistible word came unto us 'that the seed of America shall be as the sand of the sea.'[39]

Thus the *Woodhouse*, according to her captain, sailed by divine guidance from London to the future New York City. She debarked five of her eleven passengers on Manhattan Island. Then she proceeded on through Hell-gate to Newport, Rhode Island, where the other six passengers went ashore on 3 August 1657.

The eleven *Woodhouse* passengers no sooner landed than they scattered all up and down the line of American colonies. In Plymouth Colony, Boston and Martha's Vineyard; New Haven; the Dutch Plantations on Manhattan and Long Island; in Maryland and Virginia, *Woodhouse* passengers came to speak in the streets and invade the churches, urging the people to "wait on the Lord," to "listen within" and to "come away." They did so in bodily peril and inward exaltation: By the end of 1659 every one of the 11 had been imprisoned. Five were dead, four by accidental drowning (Sarah Gibbons, Mary Wetherhead, Richard Doudney and Mary Clark) and one by purposeful hanging (Will Robinson). Two had their right ears cut off (Christopher Holder and John Copeland), one (Humphrey Norton) was branded with the letter H for "Heretic," and two were beaten unconscious with tarred ropes (William Brend in Boston and Robert Hodgson in New Amsterdam). Dorothy Waugh, the eleventh passenger, was jailed and whipped in Boston and jailed again in New Amsterdam.[40]

And in those same two years, by the end of 1659, the eleven passengers succeeded in seeding little meetings of the Friends of God from Massachusetts to Virginia, where none had been before.

Just how Will Robinson came south after landing at Newport on 3 August 1657 is not known. But he did arrive on Virginia's Eastern Shore late in 1657, where about two thousand English and a few Dutch people fished and farmed. He held meetings there, accompanied for a time by Christopher Holder and Robert Hodgson, but mostly on his own; and he did convince some Eastern Shore people to become Quakers.[41]

On 29 January 1657 a constable arrested Will Robinson and brought him before the Northampton County Court. The chief of the justices on the bench that day was Lieutenant-Colonel John Stringer, a physician, politician, and right hand of Colonel Edmund Scarburgh, the great man of the Eastern Shore.

The charges against Will Robinson were "heresy" and being "a seducer of the people to faction." The Quakers believed then--for reasons which will be explained--in keeping on their hats in court and everywhere, except in time of prayer; and Will Robinson's broad-brimmed hat doubtless irritated Justice Stringer. The Quakers also refused--and still refuse--to swear on the *Bible* in court, and Robinson's refusal to swear must have been a second aggravation. Then, when Justice Stringer examined prisoner Robinson on his religious views, he became completely exasperated, found Robinson guilty as charged and also guilty of *denying the humanity of Christ in open court*.[42] This last charge doubtless arose from the Quaker emphasis, then and now, on the concept of God as a Holy Spirit and with corresponding lack of emphasis on the Father and Son aspects of the Trinity.

Justice Stringer ordered the sheriff to transport William Robinson across the Bay to the General Court in Jamestown. William's clothes and chest were sold to pay the costs. The General Court imprisoned him for six months in the jail just vacated by Josiah Coale and Thomas Thurston.

Will Robinson was staying in the home of Henry and Ann Vaux when he was arrested, and Henry Vaux was transported across the Bay too. Whether Henry Vaux was jailed with Will Robinson is not clear. It is clear, however, that Henry Vaux and Thomas Chapman are the first *Virginians* known to have become convinced Quakers. Will Robinson somehow managed to stay on in Virginia after he was released from jail. He held "threshing meetings" through the winter of 1658-59. When he was getting ready to leave Virginia in the spring of 1659 he wrote to George Fox: "There are many people convinced, and some in several parts are brought into the sense and feeling of Truth."[43]

\* \* \*

Thomas Thurston returned to Virginia in the fall of that year 1659. Since leaving Virginia in spring 1658, he had been jailed in Maryland and in

Sandwich, Massachusetts. He was jailed again when he returned to Virginia. Then, as George Bishop noted, some of the Susquehanna Indians who nursed Thomas back to health after he walked out of Virginia in 1658, came to visit him in his Virginia jail. Josiah Coale wrote from New England to Margaret Fell:

> As concerning my dear brother Thomas Thurston...I hear he is returned to Virginia, where he has been imprisoned but is now at liberty again, and the governor of that place [Samuel Matthews, who evidently felt more kindly toward Quakers than his predecessor, Governor Edward Digges] hath promised that he shall have liberty in the country; where there is like to be a great gathering.[44]

Josiah Coale also returned to Virginia, late in 1660. He then wrote to George Fox: "I left Friends in Virginia generally very well and fresh in the Truth."[45]

Seven little circles of Virginians began meeting to worship in the manner of Friends after 1655.

One group, at Corotoman near the mouth of the Rappahannock River in Lancaster County, met from 1656 until 1659. It disrupted after the members refused court orders to pay the Reverend Mr. David Linsey of the established church "in satisfaction for his ministry among them." Most of the Corotoman Friends, including the Dickinson, Powell, Gorsuch and Clapham families, moved up Chesapeake Bay to the Patapsco River, where they were the first settlers on the site of present day Baltimore.[46]

A second group met in David Cuffin's house in Northumberland County, close by the mouth of the Potomac River and about fifteen miles north of the Corotoman Friends. The county court fined the Northumberland Quakers three times for meetings they held during 1660. When they kept on meeting, the court fined David Cuffin £100, seizing his 650 acre plantation and crops of corn and tobacco to pay the fine. Five others were sentenced to whippings of 20 lashes and fines of 125 pounds of tobacco.[47]

The remaining five Quaker groups, all meeting regularly when Josiah Coale wrote his letter in 1660, were:
- At Chuckatuck, in Nansemond County between Nansemond River and Chuckatuck Creeks[48]
- In Norfolk, near the mouth of Elizabeth River[49]
- At Merchant's Hope in Prince Georges County, near the present city of Hopewell[50]

- At Nassawaddox on the Eastern Shore[51]
- In York County[52]

* * *

Friends held a General Meeting in Skipton, Yorkshire, in 1660. A minute from that meeting summarizes all the letters sent home by Friendly messengers traveling outside of England. It reads:

> We have received certain information...of the great work and service of the Lord beyond seas in several parts and regions as Germany, America, *Virginia* and other places, as Florence, Mantua, Palatine, Tuscany, Italy, Rome, Turkey, Jerusalem, France, Geneva, Norway, Barbados, Bermuda, Antigua, Jamaica, Surinam, Newfoundland through all which Friends have passed in service of the Lord.[53]

In all these places no greater work and service had been performed than in Virginia. Elizabeth Harris, Josiah Coale and Thomas Thurston, and Will Robinson had "gone through" their work. In the five years from 1655 to 1660 they planted the Quaker way in Virginia.

Sir William Berkeley began his second term as Virginia's governor in 1660--"a very peevish man and much set against the Truth and Friends."

## II

## VIRGINIA'S QUAKERS AND THE RIGHT TO WORSHIP AS ONE WISHES
## 1660-1663

> Once more I beseech you, gentlemen: to have an exact care of this pestilent sect of ye Quakers.
>
> --Governor William Berkeley
> to the justices of Lower Norfolk, Virginia, 1663

The struggle over the right to worship as you wish began in Virginia in 1642, when William Berkeley became governor. That was thirteen years before Elizabeth Harris's visit.

Virginia had sixteen English governors during its first thirty-five years as a colony, 1607 to 1642. None was an exceptional manager, and nearly all today are mere signatures on faded documents. The Privy Council of King Charles I, looking for a likely man to take charge in Virginia, chose William Berkeley.

Berkeley was a dark-haired and dashing bachelor 35 years old. His family had enjoyed great influence at the English Court for centuries and his brother, Lord John, was Charles I's confidant. Berkeley's father, Sir Maurice Berkeley of Bruton, Somerset, had himself lived in Virginia as an official under Governor Yeardley in 1621. William Berkeley entered Oxford in 1623 and was admitted Master of Arts in 1629. Then he entered the Colonial Office in London and made a reputation for vigor and intelligence. He published a play titled "The Lost Lady" in 1638; acquired polish as a courtier at Whitehall; was knighted in 1639, and joined the Privy Chamber, the King's inner circle of advisors.[1] He left for Virginia late in 1641, with England teetering on the brink of civil war.

Berkeley brought to Virginia a set of thirty-one "Instructions to Sir William Berkeley, One of the Gentlemen of Our Privy Chamber, Governor of Virginia and to the Council of State There." These instructions indicate the priorities of Charles I and his counsellors in the troubled England of 1641. The first of them directs Governor Berkeley "That in the first place you be careful Almighty God may be duly and daily served according to the form of religion established in the Church of England." The remaining thirty require oaths of allegiance to the king, prescribe how Virginia's laws are to be made, her courts of law operated, men from sixteen to sixty armed, liquor sales controlled, and the like.[2]

In this secular and scientific Twentieth Century, it seems odd that Virginia's church affairs should be first on Berkeley's list. In 1642, however, King Charles I and his father James before him had been insisting over thirty years that kings, all kings, are ordained by God to govern their people as the king sees fitting. As Charles saw it, his subjects had no *rights*. They might have had *privileges* granted by royal favor; otherwise they had only duties. Since the King of England is accountable only to God, quite naturally he is the head of the Church of England and all his subjects must worship only in that church.

By 1642, a resistance to the notion of the Divine Right of Kings had built up across England. The resisters were known as Puritans or Dissenters, or Parliament Party people, who believed they *did* have rights and *should* be free to worship as they wished. By 1642, there were almost as many Puritans as Royalists in England and bloody civil war was about to begin. Most Puritans were members of the established Church of England who wanted to reform the church from within. A few were thorough-going Dissenters who broke away from the established church and formed congregations of their own, against the law.

Governor Berkeley of course was a Royalist, a Cavalier, a King's man to his autocratic fingertips. When he arrived in Jamestown, he began to attend the red brick church there, heading a procession of dignitaries and their ladies to the church with pomp and ceremony to sit in the governor's oak-doored pews. Behind them sat the rest of the worshippers, roughly according to their rank in the Jamestown community.

The worship service consisted largely of readings from the *Book of Common Prayer*. These readings, formulated in the time of Henry VIII and Queen Elizabeth, evoked attitudes of deference. When the service ended, the governor and his party left as they came, while the rest of the congregation respectfully stood and waited. Governor Berkeley soon named as his personal chaplain a clergyman from Lower Norfolk, Thomas Harrison.[3]

On his arrival, Governor Berkeley had found quite a few Puritans in the colony already. They were a majority in three parish churches south of Hampton Roads (where Norfolk and Portsmouth now stand): the Elizabeth River church in Lower Norfolk County and East Parish and Chuckatuck Parish churches in adjoining Nansemond County. These Puritans included prominent citizens, like Cornelius Lloyd who represented Lower Norfolk in the General Assembly and Richard Bennett, master of the great Bennett's Welcome plantation on Nansemond River.

Just before Berkeley arrived in Jamestown, the Norfolk Puritans sent Richard Bennett's brother Philip to Boston with a petition asking for three Puritan ministers to serve in Virginia. Governor John Winthrop of Massachusetts Bay soon nominated three divines for this service: John Knowles, 42, of Watertown, Massachusetts, a Cambridge University graduate; William Tompson, 44, of Braintree, an Oxford graduate; and Thomas James, a preacher in New Haven, Connecticut. The three ministers started south in Philip Bennett's pinnace, which "bilged upon the rocks" near present day New York City in a howling, green water storm. They reached Virginia 1 March 1642, nearly five months after leaving Boston.[4]

Governor Berkeley was furious when he heard of the Puritan ministers' arrival. He immediately arranged for the General Assembly to require "that all men whatsoever which shall reside in the Colony are to be conformable to the orders and constitution of Church of England and...all non-conformists...shall be compelled to depart the Colony." So the three New England ministers stayed only a few months, then returned unwillingly to New England.[5]

The Norfolk families left without ministers resented the governor's high-handedness. Somehow, too, it profoundly bothered Thomas Harrison, the governor's chaplain. He left his safe living and went to Norfolk to take the place of the ousted New Englanders. There he became a thorough-going Puritan preacher. Angered, Governor Berkeley called an Assembly in November 1647 which took notice of Thomas Harrison's defection by passing the following law:

> Upon divers information presented to this Assembly against several ministers for their neglect and refractory refusing, after warning given to them, to read common prayer or divine service upon the Sabbath days...be it enacted that...all...ministers...do...read such prayers as are appointed...by the said Book of Common Prayer. No parishioner shall be compelled...to pay any manner of tithes or duties to any unconformist.[6]

Thomas Harrison then fled Virginia for Boston, and the governor took extreme measures to root out non-conformity. He had the doors of the three Norfolk churches nailed shut, and when the parishioners kept on meeting for worship in their homes he had many arrested. Finally he ordered militia men to confiscate the firearms of the disobedient families, leaving them defenseless in their wilderness surroundings. In 1648 and 1649, many of the families moved bag and baggage up Chesapeake Bay. Seventy-seven families settled near present-day Annapolis, and sixty more headed by Richard Preston settled on Patuxent River in Maryland. Not all the Norfolk neighborhood's Puritan families left Virginia but those who remained stayed quiet and did not try to reopen the shut-up churches.[7]

Clearly, the first round of the struggle to make religion a matter of free choice was won by those who believe it should be State-controlled.

\* \* \*

Berkeley's position of loyalty to King Charles and the King's church became wobbly in the 1640s. For in England by 1645 Parliament armies led by Thomas Fairfax and Oliver Cromwell defeated Charles's Royalist gentry. Charles was captured; and one chill afternoon in London in January 1649--just when the Virginia Puritans were moving to Maryland--the great ax of a Puritan executioner beheaded him.

Oliver Cromwell and his Council of State took over the British government in 1649. For two years the new council was too busy with home affairs to worry that Virginia's Governor Berkeley continued loyal to King Charles. Then in the fall of 1651 the Council in London sent a letter to Richard Bennett in his Maryland exile. The letter was followed by a fleet of armed ships and nine hundred soldiers. The fleet arrived in James River in December.[8]

When the Commonwealth's fleet appeared off the Virginia Capes, Berkeley blustered and talked of resistance. In the end he sat down in Jamestown with Cromwell's three commissioners: Richard Bennett and William Claiborne, Puritans of Virginia, and Captain Curtis, the fleet's commander. Berkeley agreed to submit Virginia to the Commonwealth and the commissioners made some concessions to Berkeley. One concession was that nothing should be done to exclude the *Book of Common Prayer* from church services for a year.[9]

Berkeley then retired to his country place at Green Spring three miles inland from Jamestown. Bennett took over as governor.

\* \* \*

Richard Bennett was governor of Virginia under Cromwell from 1652 until 1 April 1655. Two more Commonwealth governors, Digges and Matthews, succeeded him, men of a more or less dissenting way of thinking about religious matters. During the administrations of these last two governors, 1655 to 1660, the Quaker way started up and made a little headway in Virginia. But Oliver Cromwell died in 1658, and the Commonwealth government began to crumble. His son Richard succeeded as Lord Protector, but proved incapable. Parliament then, in the summer of 1659, invited Charles II to come back from exile and be king.

Near the end of 1659, Samuel Matthews, Virginia's governor, died; and the General Assembly, tacking about nimbly in response to the political winds, invited the old Royalist, William Berkeley, whose hair now was gray, to be Virginia's governor again. Charles II was grateful for Berkeley's loyalty and promptly confirmed him as governor. At that time, Charles II spoke of Virginia fondly as "My Old Dominion"--a phrase which has lived through the centuries.[10]

William Berkeley, again governor in 1660, soon received instructions from his new King's Privy Council. One was "that all religious exercises should be according to the profession of the Church of England." And Berkeley, who had rooted out the Puritans during the 1640s, set out briskly in 1660 to evict the new non-conformists, the Quakers, from his colony.[11]

As previously noted, the Quaker movement is based on the conviction that there is some thing of God in every human being. The Friends call this divine thing "the inward light" or "the light of Christ" or "the Christ within" or "the divine seed." The way Quakers worship is to "wait on the Lord;" that is to listen in silence to the still small voice inside each worshiper. They try to live in accordance with what they apprehend during this silent listening. That way of living they call "minding the light" or "walking in the light."

The Quaker way appeals deeply to some when they encounter it, but it infuriates others. For Quakers when they walk in the light are likely to walk right across the conventions of the times.

In England, ministers of the established church, Dissenter preachers, and other writers, excoriated the Quakers in broadsides and pamphlets. By 1664, more than 240 publications had gone on sale with titles like: *The Quaker Quasht and His Quarrel Quelled*; *Quakers Are Inchanters and Dangerous Seducers*; and *A Sad Caveat to All Quakers, Not to Boast Any More That They Have God Almighty by the Hand When They Have the Devil by the Toe*.

The gist of these writings is that the Friends were practicing a kind of Christianity extremely different from any the writers knew. Quakers deny the absolute authority of the *Bible*, that was the principal criticism. Instead, they rely more on a "light within them" which, as scores of writers undertook to prove, was unbiblical.

Quite a few writers deplored Friends' rejection of a whole collection of doctrines and practices that orthodox Christians held dear (often described as "The Faith once delivered by the Saints" or "Particulars that Saints are required to be steadfast in"). These rejected things included John Calvin's doctrine that only a few people selected by God will be saved from damnation, the rituals of baptism and communion, singing psalms in time of worship, the notion that places of worship are especially holy, and even strict observance of the Sabbath Day. Friends' failure to pay tithes or church taxes and their references to reverend ministers as "hireling priests" and "paid teachers" were especially resented.

Others dwelt on more secular singularities. One writer marvelled at the way newly convinced Friends adopted their new society's plain lifestyle. He reported on "the burning of their fine clothes, prints and ribbons which [suddenly] seem to them like so many hellish hags and furies." Several undertook to show how misguided Friends were in refusing to swear or take an oath. Many more inveighed against Friends' refusal to render "the Honour due to Magistrates, Ministers and others according to their Places and Dignities."[12]

In Virginia, Governor Berkeley and his councillors were among those infuriated, for Virginia Quakers collided with the accepted way of doing things at several points:

- They refused to attend the established churches--"steeplehouses" "bellhouses" or "masshouses" Friends called them.
- They refused to swear on the Bible or take any oath in court, saying that all people should tell the truth, swearing or no swearing.
- They insisted on treating rich or poor the same, saying that all are brothers and sisters, equals under the parenthood of God. They did not remove their hats or curtsy in the presence of Cavaliers or before the judges in the courts. They addressed these great personages with the familiar "thee" just as servants were addressed, instead of the deferential "you" which was expected in those days.
- They insisted too that war is evil--since all people as children of God are bound to love, respect, and support one another. So they declined to serve as soldiers or Indian fighters.

When the Grand Assembly met in Jamestown in March 1659-1660, it passed a good many acts. The first of these confirmed the return of William Berkeley, decreeing "that the Honorable Sir William Berkeley be Governor and Captain General of Virginia and that he govern according to the ancient laws of England and the established laws of this country."

The second act, probably suggested by Berkeley, is titled "An Act for Suppressing Quakers." It reads:

> Whereas there is an unreasonable and turbulent sort of people commonly called Quakers who, contrary to law, do daily gather [in] unlawful assemblies...teaching...lies, miracles, false visions, prophecies and doctrines...endeavoring...to destroy religion, laws, communities and all bonds of civil society, leaving it arbitrary to every vain and vicious person whether men shall be safe, laws established, offenders punished and Governors rule....
>
> To prevent and restrain which mischief it is enacted:
>
> That no master...of any ship...do bring into this Colony any...Quakers under penalty of £100...
> That all Quakers...be imprisoned...till they...depart the Colony
> That no person shall entertain any...Quakers...nor permit in or near their house any assemblies of Quakers
> And that no person do presume on their peril to dispose or publish their books, pamphlets or libels....[13]

About the beginning of 1660, when this new law was published, seven men either resigned or were turned out of public office in the counties south of the James. All seven evidently were Quakers, convinced either by Elizabeth Harris or one of the Quaker ministers who followed her into Virginia:

- Major John Bond, 40, was dismissed as a justice in Isle of Wight County. He had served in the House of Burgesses for several years and was county sheriff in 1656. The Assembly resolved that "whereas a complaint has been exhibited to this Assembly concerning the factious and schismatical demeanor of Major John Bond, and the same proved by several testimonies; it is ordered that he hath shown himself unfit to be continued as a magistrate."[14]

- Major Thomas Davis, Robert Lawrence and William Denson all handed in their resignations as justices in Nansemond County.[15]
- Francis Emperor, 32, and two brothers curiously named John Porter, Senior and John Porter, Junior, all were named to the fifteen member court of Lower Norfolk county in 1660, but were scratched off the list by Governor Berkeley in April 1661. John Porter, Senior, a popular man, was elected to the Grand Assembly in 1663, but it was reported that he was "loving to the Quakers and stood well affected toward them and had been at their meetings."[16] So the seat was denied to him.

Governor Berkeley urged on Virginia's sheriffs to enforce the Quaker Act and to wipe out the five illegal Quaker meetings in Virginia as of 1660--the Norfolk, York, Merchant's Hope, Chuckatuck and Nassawaddox "conventicles". He wrote Sheriff Richard Conquest of Norfolk on August 8, 1660, saying:

> I hear with sorrow that you are very remiss in your office in not stopping the frequent meetings of this most pestilent sect of ye Quakers. Whether this be so or not, I do charge you...not to suffer any more of their meetings or conventicles.[17]

And Sheriff Conquest and his successors did their best to comply. They violently disrupted meeting after silent Quaker meeting, in the homes of Richard Russell, Francis and Mary Emperor, Benjamin Forby, and Robert and Isabel Spring, arresting more than fifty Norfolk worshippers in these meetings, some as many as five times. The county court fined some and sent others to Jamestown for heavier penalties and tongue-lashings by Governor Berkeley.

Quaker Thomas Owen of Norfolk stood before Berkeley and his General Court in 1661. Looking levelly at his judges he said, "Tender consciences must obey the law of God, however they suffer." Berkeley or one of the judges roared back "There is no toleration for wicked consciences!"[18]

The governor wrote again to the Norfolk authorities on 27 June 1663: "Once more I beseech you, gentlemen, to have an exact care of this pestilent sect of ye Quakers."[19] The Norfolk sheriff's men increased their efforts accordingly. They were there every time Friends gathered to prevent their illegal worship. Richard Russell was first fined 5,000 pounds of tobacco (enough to buy a large plantation) and later the overwhelming fine of £100 sterling.[20] Ben Forby was jailed and then ordered to pay 25 pounds of tobacco a day until he recanted--which as it appears, he never did.[21] John Porter Junior, and Mary Emperor, the widow of Francis, were fined and fined again for being taken in Quaker meetings. Finally they both were sentenced to be deported from the colony--although this last sentence was never carried out.[22]

These Quakers were fools for God. They never tried, in Norfolk or elsewhere, to meet secretly. After four years of trying to worship in peace, some moved away, and the others stopped trying.

York County's Quakers included Thomas Bushrod, a well-to-do and high tempered merchant in his mid-fifties, his wife Mary Bushrod, and their Pocoson neighbors Edmund and Mary Chisman. In September 1659, the York County Court, Colonel Christopher Calthorpe presiding, noted that "there are several dangerous persons now in the County called Quakers who by their frequent private meetings in the nature of Conventicles have seduced and misled many poor ignorant persons." The court ordered its sheriff to "repair to ye several places of such meetings and there forewarn them from ye like meetings in the future."

However, the next month the court heard again that the "dangerous, turbulent, seditious persons termed Quakers...continue their unlawful meetings." The Reverend Mr. Philip Mallory then came before the court with a letter he had received from Thomas Bushrod "whereby he [Bushrod] certifies of a seeming desire of a conference with him [Mallory] by ye said Quakers." Mr. Mallory declared "free willingness and honest desire for the conference," and Colonel Calthorpe agreed "that such a disputation publicly had with ye said Quakers may (by ye blessing of God) prevent for ye future [Quaker meetings]." Nevertheless, he instructed Mr. Mallory not to answer the letter just yet, since "the Court looking upon this as a matter of high concernment to ye Country do conceive all proceedings therein ought to be from ye Honorable Governor and Council."

Two years later, the York County Court learned of more Quaker meetings, including a meeting on August 25 when "several Quakers met in ye woods, amongst which was Mrs. Mary Chisman and two or three negroes belonging to her husband." Then Mr. Justinian Aylmer, 26, an Anglican clergyman and Philip Mallory's assistant, came before the court to charge that Thomas Bushrod "on Friday last used slanderous, rude, contemptible and mutinous language against the reverend clergy." The court at once issued a warrant for Bushrod's arrest, his incarceration, and his appearance before the Governor.

Before the Governor, Mr. Aylmer testified that he met Thomas Bushrod aboard a ship riding in York River, where they were buying slaves. Aylmer complained that Bushrod called him "a lying knave and ugly blind rogue," and said "that Mr. Philip Mallory (that Reverend Divine) and your petitioner are a 'couple of Episcopal knaves'." Aylmer also testified that Thomas Bushrod was defiant about his Quakerism, declaring that "The Quakers shall and will continue their meetings; they will meet next Sunday; and my wife will be there."[23]

The disposition of the Bushrod case is lost and unknown. But nothing more about Quakers in York County is heard for twelve years after 1661. Thomas Bushrod died in 1676, leaving a somewhat Quakerly direction in his will that he was to be "buried in my garden by the side of my wife Mary without honors, prayers or other customs used at funerals."[24] Edmund Chisman died in prison in 1676. He took part in Bacon's Rebellion against Governor Berkeley and was attainted of high treason.[25]

The Quakers of Merchant's Hope came to the attention of the Charles City County Court in 1663. Merchant's Hope lies on the south shore of the James. It was a port of call for trading vessels, in what is now Prince George County. In those days, however, Merchant's Hope was in Charles City County which encompassed both sides of the James. The Charles City court met at Westover on the James' north bank, then the home of Theodorick Bland, and that is where the Merchant's Hope Friends were prosecuted. The court, ironically, was headed by Theodorick Bland whose young wife Anne, daughter of Richard Bennett, would become a professed Quaker. Other justices of the eight-member court were Captain Robert Wynne and Mr. Stephen Hamlin. Both of them would have grandchildren or great-grandchildren who were to join the Quakers in Virginia. William Byrd, later the owner of Westover, also sat on the court.[26]

Francis Whittington was the first Quaker of Merchant's Hope to be ferried across the James and brought before this court, as it sat around the Blands' dining table in December 1663. The court fined Whittington 1,000 pounds of tobacco "for his contemptuous irreverent coming into His Majesty's court with his hat on his head" and 2,000 more pounds for having "neglected the baptizing of his child contrary to the law."[27]

When the court met the next month, in January, Howell Edmonds, Benjamin Travers and Ed Freeze appeared from Merchant's Hope. The members of the court all knew Howell Edmonds, a white-haired, steady, cheerful old planter. Seven years before in 1656, the court had honored him for his neighborliness and good standing in Jordans Parish. The justices had shaken Howell Edmonds' hand then and exempted him from all public services and taxes.[28] It was hard to picture this venerable man as a law-breaker. Nevertheless, since justice must be served, the court fined Howell Edmonds and each of his two companion culprits 1,000 pounds of tobacco for keeping on their hats. Then it developed "that Howell Edmonds by his own confession and other sufficient evidence hath suffered a meeting of several men called Quakers at his house on the 27th December last under pretense of divine worship, vidzt himself, Benjamin Travers and Ed Freeze with three others commonly known to be such." For this offense Howell Edmonds was fined 5,000 more pounds of tobacco and the others 200 pounds.

But when the court met in February the same four Friends--Edmonds, Whittington, Travers and Freeze--with two more men from Merchant's Hope were brought in again, and again they were fined 1,000 pounds of tobacco for keeping on their hats. Then it was proved, and Howell calmly agreed, that *another* Friends meeting had been held at his home in January, *after* his punishment by the court. Ten persons had been present, including a traveling Friends minister. The justices were ruffled. They fined Howell Edmonds again 5,000 pounds of tobacco, Ben Freeze and Ed Travers 500 pounds and each of the others 200 pounds, and ordered "that all the said Quakers that are strangers or not resident in this County be forthwith conveyed away from constable to constable to the place of their several dwellings. And if they or any of them have no settled abode, such be presented to the next Justice to the place or places where they pretend to abide, to be proceeded against as vagrants according to the laws of England."[29]

At a later session, this Charles City court reimbursed the sheriff for putting the Quakers out of the county. Howell Edmonds and his family were removed to Surry County, Ben Travers (who was a gunsmith) and his family to Henrico.[30] In this way the Quaker meeting at Merchant's Hope was destroyed and Governor Berkeley's will was enforced.

\* \* \*

By the spring of 1663, three of the five Friends' groups in the Virginia Colony had been broken up, in Norfolk, in York County, and at Merchant's Hope. Still, Quaker ministers from England were quietly coming into Virginia to declare their illegal beliefs, and the Governor wanted the county sheriffs to stop them before they could lure more people away from the colony's churches. The sheriffs were not completely successful in this, for ten or more Quaker travelers visited Virginia between 1660 and 1663 without being arrested:

- Richard Pinder wrote to England in August 1660 that "Friends is well in Maryland and Virginia."[31] And Richard's companion, George Rofe, a glazier of Halstead, England, with many jailings behind him, wrote from Bermuda in December 1661: "Many settled meetings there are in Maryland and *Virginia* (emphasis added) and New England and the islands thereabouts and in the island of Bermuda; through all which places I have traveled...having a great and weighty service for the Lord."[32] George Rofe traveled in and about Virginia unimpeded until he drowned in a shipwreck in Chesapeake Bay, 1663.[33] Joseph Nicholson, Jane Liddal and Jane Millard visited Virginia about March 1662, having "many hard travels and sufferings for the Lord."[34]
- John Perrot and two companions came in 1663 without being arrested or jailed.[35]
- Nor were Wenlock Christison and George Preston, on the Eastern Shore in 1663.[36]

It was a different story, however, for George Wilson when he came to visit the Chuckatuck Quakers in the fall of 1661. He came from England's Lake Country, a soldier turned Friend. He had been jailed in England for believing as he did, and just before he came to Chuckatuck he was whipped from constable to constable away from Boston.[37]

George Wilson wrote a letter from Chuckatuck 21 October 1661 to "All the Rulers, Courts and Councils in Virginia--from the Governor who sits upon the throne unto the Constable who is to obey his commands." He wrote it to protest the Act for Suppressing Quakers, saying:

> Come out of the dark in which is the ignorance and errors of this world, and turn your minds to the eternal and true Light...the law of our God, written [in the Scriptures] is just, according to that of God in all consciences. [But you say that you] make other laws

and boasts in them, saying 'We have a law'. But [who] art thou, as said the Apostles, which boasteth of [thy] law? I say unto thee, take heed, lest through breaking of God's law thou dishonor God, by doing or suffering that unto others be done which thou would not have done unto thyself.[38]

This letter was delivered to the Cavalier refugee Francis Moryson, who was occupying the governor's chair while William Berkeley was away in England. Shortly thereafter, George Wilson was arrested in Chuckatuck and jailed in the Jamestown jail in irons. There he wrote four more letters to Moryson and finally in May 1662 he appealed to King Charles, writing that "In prison...I was chained to a post with an Indian which they have hanged for killing an Englishman, our legs was made fast to one bolt. And since, they have caused me to be put into a dungeon with four men more which is arrested for murder." Elsewhere, he reported that his dungeon had no windows "but close made up with brick and lime."[39]

Four Quakers from Maryland--Thomas Taylor, Thomas Hooker, Henry Willcockes, and William Cole--came to Jamestown to protest George Wilson's imprisonment and ended up as prisoners in the jail with him. The first-named three of these Maryland Quakers may have been jailed only briefly--Thomas Taylor became speaker of the Maryland Assembly in later life. But William Cole "never fully recovered from the effects of the imprisonment which he then endured."[40]

As for George Wilson, "here, after being cruelly scourged and heavily ironed for a long period, George Wilson's flesh actually rotted from his bones and within the cold damp walls of the miserable dungeon of James's Town he lay down his life."[41] He must have died after six or seven months in the jail.

Two more Friends were arrested when they reached Virginia late in 1663, a year or more after George Wilson died in the jail. Alice Ambrose and Mary Tomkins had been whipped and jailed in New England and jailed again in New Amsterdam on the way south to Virginia. They had "good service" in Virginia for a month or two, and then were arrested. Their punishment was "32 stripes apiece with a nine-corded whip, three knots in each cord...the very first lash of which drew the blood and made it run down in abundance from their breasts; and having their chests and goods taken away and so expelled [from Virginia]."[42]

Another anti-Quaker action in 1660 has been nearly lost from knowledge now behind the shifting shadows of the years. It appears in the letter written by Richard Pinder on 17 June 1660:

> Friends is well in Maryland and Virginia and the power of the Lord is entered among the Indians and one of them was moved to go abroad in the power to minister and *they did hang him and since four or five of them is moved to go forth and we hear as if they should have hanged them.*[43]

It is not known now whether this hanging (or hangings) happened in Maryland or in Virginia. One possibility is that the victims were those Susquehanna Indians who befriended Thomas Thurston in 1658 when he hiked north through the forest and out of Virginia, for we do know from George Bishop's history that "some of the Susquehanoes came to visit [Thomas Thurston] when they heard he was in prison afterwards in Virginia."

\* \* \*

As the result of the Act for Suppressing Quakers, only two little Quaker groups remained in Virginia when spring came on in 1664; one at Chuckatuck in Nansemond County, the other at Nassawaddox on the Eastern Shore. Chuckatuck is the point of land on the south side of James River between two tributaries, Chuckatuck Creek and Nansemond River. It lies about ten miles up river from Norfolk. Here lived Thomas Jordan, 30, and his bride Margaret, who was 22 years old in 1664. Their plantation at the water's edge up Nansemond River was the center of Quaker convincement in Nansemond and Isle of Wight Counties. That countryside had few roads, bridges or horses. Most of the new Quaker families came to meet in the Jordans' great room on First Days in boats, with the father and sons rowing or sailing to worship.

The Nansemond sheriff tried hard to break up the unlawful meetings of the Chuckatuck Friends. Thomas Jordan wrote:

> I was held in six weeks' imprisonment for being taken at a meeting in my own house and released by the King's proclamation; again taken at a meeting at Robert Lawrence's and bound over to the Court of Nansemond; and for refusing to swear according to

their will and against the command of Christ, was sent up to Jamestown, a prisoner upwards of ten months....Taken by distress by John Blake (sheriff) two feather beds and three feather bolsters...by Thomas Godwin (deputy sheriff) ten head of cattle.[44]

John Grave or Graves boated regularly to the meetings in Chuckatuck. He lived six or seven miles up the James near present day Smithfield. In 1662, when he was 21, he wrote a poem about his new faith and its persecutors, titling it "A Song of Sion--Written by a Citizen Thereof Whose Outward Habitation Is in Virginia":

Be silent now all people, young and old
Give ear all nations, let your eyes behold
How Christ's pure Light, now glorious, doth appear...

O all mankind submit to Him in fear
And let your priests for shame deceive no more

[Christ] truly will reward equal and right
According as each loves or hates his Light

O wretched men, would you *yourselves* enthrone
And seek to rule where Christ should rule alone? ...

Dare you revenge yourselves upon a man
That fears the Lord and not bow to you can?
Or for reproving you of any ill
Will you your cruelty on them fulfill?

And for meeting together in Christ's name
Dare you make havoc of them for the same? ...

And no place else can you to them afford
But prison-holes because they fear the Lord?
Think you the Lord not angry is for this?
Or do you think that ye his stroke shall miss?...

Not else I feel that now to say I have
But that I am your fellow-friend, John Grave.[45]

Thomas Jordan's young wife, Margaret, was jailed with her husband later, and the Nansemond sheriff carted away more of their possessions. Other Chuckatuck Friends suffered too, as John Grave's poem suggests. But they kept on meeting together in spite of the Act for Suppressing Quakers.

The Quakers on the Eastern Shore centered around the mouth of Nassawaddox Creek on Chesapeake Bay. After Will Robinson visited the neighborhood in 1657, one Levin Denwood and others convinced by Will Robinson built a ten-foot-square meeting house in Thomas Leatherbury's field.[46] It seems to have been the first Friends' meeting house built anywhere in America.

The great man of Virginia's Eastern Shore in those days was Colonel Edmund Scarburgh (1618-1671). Like Governor Berkeley, Edmund Scarburgh had a powerful connection in London, for his brother, Sir Charles Scarburgh, was physician to the King. He was a merchant on a grand scale, a tobacco planter, land speculator, operator of a shoe factory employing nine shoemakers, of a brewery, and a salt monopoly, and owner of a fleet of seven vessels. He represented the Eastern Shore in Virginia's House of Burgesses most of his adult years and was Speaker of the House under Governor Berkeley when he was only 27. Scarburgh was a justice of the county court most years and sometimes was Sheriff, and was Virginia's Surveyor General from 1655 to 1671. He lived with his wife and five children on a baronial 3,000 acre place called Occahannock House six miles up the Bay from Nassawaddox; and he kept young Ann Toft for his mistress at Gargaphia, another of his Eastern Shore plantations.[47]

This Edmund Scarburgh was known as a man not to be crossed. He hated the Eastern Shore's Indians and rode out to harry them many times. The Indians feared him and called him "The Conjuror." When Quakers appeared on the Eastern Shore, he expressed great dislike for them too.[48]

Despite Scarburgh's aversion to Indians, one of his ships, the *Sea Horse*, was seized by the New Netherlands government in Delaware Bay in 1651 when in the act of trading guns and ammunition to Indians there. In 1653, Scarburgh was again accused of trading guns to the Indians, and about the same time he tried to declare the Eastern Shore independent of the Colony of Virginia. Governor Bennett ordered his arrest then, and Scarburgh left Virginia for a time in order to escape trial. Bennett disabled Scarburgh from holding public office for these last offenses, and the debarment continued until 1658, when Scarburgh was restored to his former offices by Governor Matthews.[49]

After his restoration, Scarburgh joined zestfully in efforts to rid Virginia of Quakers. He haled Eastern Shore Quakers into court and punished them with fines and the sheriff's whip.[50] He closed up the little Friends' meeting house at Nassawaddox and sent some Quakers over the Bay to Jamestown to be dealt with by Governor Berkeley.

One Quaker never reached Jamestown. The court record for 1660 notes cryptically that

> John Hale, Quaker, refusing to take the Oath of Allegiance and Supremacy and committed into the sheriff's custody was by wind and weather...cast away and lost.[51]

Remarkably, the sheriff that year was *Edmund Scarburgh*, the Conjuror himself.

A Quaker who did reach Jamestown was Henry Vaux, the Friend who was host to Will Robinson in 1657 and 1658, when Will introduced the Quaker way on the Eastern Shore. Henry Vaux was arrested a second and a third time for his Quaker activities in November 1660, and then was taken to Jamestown by Sheriff Scarburgh where he was locked up for quite a while in the jail. Soon after being returned home, Henry Vaux died--probably as the result of treatment in jail. As a macabre after-note, the Eastern Shore court--controlled by Scarburgh--issued an order that he "be paid out of the estate of Mr. Henry Voss [Vaux] for attendance and administration of medicine as physician £50 sterling."[52] But Edmund Scarburgh was no physician. He was an unprincipled man with a heart in darkness.

By 1662, most but not all of the Nassawaddox Quakers had moved north across the Pocomoke River into Maryland to get away from Conjuror Scarburgh and his ministrations. The Conjuror, however, decided to claim as Virginia's the land where they settled, and so get the Quakers again under his authority. As Surveyor General he arbitrarily re-drew the Virginia-Maryland line across the Peninsula and got some backing in Jamestown for the new boundary claim. Then on Monday morning, 12 October 1663, he arrived at Annemessex, the Friends' settlement.

According to Scarburgh's official report he was "accompanied with Colonel Stringer, four of the [Northamptom County, Virginia] commission and about forty horsemen whom I took with me for pomp [and] safety." He arrested Stephen Horsey because Horsey would not acknowledge his authority and marked the "broad arrow" on Horsey's door to indicate that he was confiscating the property by authority of the King. His report continues:

> We went to the house of Ambrose Dixon, a Quaker, where a boat and men belonging to Groome's ship [i.e., the *Dove of London*. Samuel Groom, the master, was a Quaker] and two running Quakers were, also George Johnson and Thomas Price, inhabitants and Quakers. There...briefly demanding their obedience and they all refusing...I set the broad arrow on their door and so marched off to Henry Boston's...."

Scarburgh and his forty horsemen next went to the Manoakin settlement four miles from Annemessex where non-Quakers lived,

> Where I sent summons for all the householders and freemen to appear, who coming most cheerfully and willingly they all subscribed [i.e. promised their obedience--except two Maryland officials] They further desired that in regard to the intermixed neighborhood of Quakers together with the frequent access of boats full of Quakers and the confusion they did and might produce, that officers might be appointed [for their protection]...and to this day...the Quakers bid defiance to the Government of his Majesty's country of Virginia boasting their insolence and forgeries.

Beside the *Dove*, there was a second Quaker vessel in Pocomoke Bay on the day of the Conjuror's visit, for he reports that "one Hollinworth, merchant of a Northern vessel [William Hollingsworth of Salem, Massachusetts] came and presented his request for liberty to trade, which I doubted [suspected] was some plot of the Quakers": As for the five Quakers who defied him that day, Scarburgh described them thus:

> Stephen Horsey...a cooper by profession who lived long in the lower parts of Accomack once elected a Burgess *by the common crowd* and thrown out by the Assembly for a factious and tumultuous person, a man repugnant to all government...that left the lower parts to head rebellion at Annamessecks....

> George Johnson, the proteus of heresy who...is notorious for shifting, schismatical pranks....

Thomas Price, a creeping Quaker, by trade a leather dresser, whose conscience would not serve to dwell amongst the wicked and therefore retired to Annamessecks....

Ambrose Dixon, a caulker by profession, that lived long in the lower parts, was often in question for his Quaking profession, removed to Annemessex there to do what he could not be here permitted. [He] is a prater of nonsense and much led by the spirit of ignorance, for which he is followed. A receiver of many Quakers his house is the place of their resort, and [he is] a conveyor of engaged persons [i.e., Quakers who were supposed to be subjects of Eastern Shore Virginia] out of the County....

Henry Boston, an unmannerly fellow that stands condemned on our records [as] slighting and condemning the laws of the country, a rebel to government and disobedient to authority, for which he received a late reward with a rattan....

These are all except two or three loose fellows that follows the Quakers for scraps whom a good whip is fitter to reform.[53]

Stephen Horsey "the man repugnant to all government" became one of the first justices of Somerset County, Maryland. (Somerset was established when the boundary dispute over the land Colonel Scarburgh tried to take for Virginia was decided in Maryland's favor.) George Johnson, "the proteus of heresy," and Henry Boston, that "unmannerly fellow," also became Somerset County judges.[54]

As for Colonel Scarburgh, his raid into Maryland incensed Maryland's Governor Calvert, who visited Governor Berkeley in Jamestown to protest in person. Governor Berkeley disclaimed any responsibility for the indefensible incident,[55] and Colonel Scarburgh's credibility, already shaky, weakened further. Then in 1670 the colonel finally brought about his own downfall. Indians who lived near Occahannock House stole some of Scarburgh's livestock. Scarburgh then sent a message to the Indian village that the Great Spirit would speak to them if they would assemble in a ditch on his place the following Sunday morning. The Indians gathered as directed. Scarburgh then fired a great cannon loaded with grapeshot, which he brought from one of ships and hid at the end of the ditch. The shot massacred and mangled most of the assembled village.⁵⁶ After this not even the influence of brother Charles in London could save Edmund Scarburgh. He was tried in James City "touching the complaint of the Indians and other matters [and] it is the unanimous judgment of Governor [Berkeley], Council and Burgesses...that the said Colonel Edmund Scarburgh shall from henceforth stand suspended from all offices as well military as civil."⁵⁷ So the Conjuror's sway ended. He died seven months later, in 1671.

A handful of families stayed on at Nassawaddox despite Scarburgh's displeasure: Levin Denwood, Mary his wife, Brownes and Coes, Eyres and Leatherburys and a few others. There is no information about their activities for the ten years from 1663 until 1673. Near the end of 1663, Ambrose London was brought into the Northampton County Court "for not coming to church" and "being brought before the Court demeaned himself insolently and appeared under the notion of a Quaker." For this he was fined 1,000 pounds of tobacco.⁵⁸ Also in 1663, Edmund Scarburgh got the Virginia Assembly to pass a law against plantation owners who allowed Indians to stay on their plantations, a law evidently aimed at Quaker George Truitt and others who were friendly to the Indians.

After these two incidents, nothing more is known about the Nassawaddox Quakers until 1673. George Fox visited the Annemessex Quakers then and noted that his companions "John Cartwright and John Jay went to [Eastern Shore] Virginia where there were desires after the Truth."⁵⁹ So it is uncertain whether the Friends at Nassawaddox managed to keep up their meetings during the ten dark years. However, the meeting was in full swing again by 1677, when John Bowater, an English visitor noted that one George Brickhouse was a leader of the meeting.⁶⁰

At Nassawaddox on the Eastern Shore and at Chuckatuck on the James then: here lived two little bands of neighbors with the calm, raw courage to dispute the State's edict that everyone must worship as the State ordains. At Nassawaddox possibly and at Chuckatuck certainly: the little Quaker groups continued there to worship after the manner of Friends in spite of the Act for Suppressing Quakers. George Wilson, John Hale, and Henry Vaux--and possibly some poor Indians whose names only God knows--were martyrs for religious freedom in Virginia. Levin and Mary Denwood and their friends possibly, and Thomas and Margaret Jordan and their friends certainly, they were the first to hold out successfully in Virginia for the right to worship God their way.

\* \* \*

Governor Berkeley and the Virginia Burgesses continued to make anti-Quaker laws in the years following 1660 and the Act for Suppressing Quakers--five more laws in five years:

- Act XII of the Grand Assembly for 1661 titled "None to Be Married but by Ministers..." makes Quaker marriages invalid, decreeing
    "...That no marriage shall be solemnized nor reputed valid in law but such as is made by the ministers according to the laws of England...and according to the prescription of the rubric of the Common Prayer Book."[61]

- Act III passed by the 1662 session, "Against Persons that Refuse to Have Their Children Baptized," reads
    Whereas many schismatical persons out of their adverseness to the orthodox established religion, or out of the new fangled conceits of their own heretical inventions, refuse to have their children baptized [they] shall be amerced 2,000 pounds of tobacco.

- Act IX of the same 1662 session, "Sundays Not to Be Profaned":
    Quakers who, out of non-conformity to the Church, totally absent themselves, are liable to a fine of £20 for every month's absence from Church. And all Quakers for assembling in unlawful assemblies and conventicles shall be fined and pay, each of them there taken, 200 pounds of tobacco for each time.[62]

- Act I of the 1663 session, "Prohibiting the Unlawful Assembly of Quakers," forbids any group
    ...To assemble themselves in the number of five or more of the age of 16 years or upwards at any one time in any place under pretence of joining in a religious worship not authorized by the laws of England nor this country.

This last law also forbids ships' captains to bring Quakers to Virginia, forbids Virginians to allow Quakers to teach or preach in or near their houses, and makes it a crime for justices or sheriffs to go easy on Quakers. "If," this Act concludes, "any of the said persons, Quakers or other separatists" shall promise to quit meeting with the Quakers, then he or she is to be discharged from all the penalties aforesaid."

- The fifth and final Act in this series, passed in 1666, is "Against Refractory Soldiers" and was written mainly because Quaker men were conspicuously absent from the muster field on days appointed for military exercises.[63]

Virginia's lawmakers were certainly not alone in trying to legislate the Quaker movement out of existence. The Quakers were the radicals and reds of the English-speaking world in the seventeenth century--just as Martin Luther, William Tyndale and the first Protestants against the authority of Mother Church were the radicals of the sixteenth century. Such radicals threaten the established order of things both in the churches and in government. The Quakers' stubborn, unbending, maddening position caused governing officials in England, in the Massachusetts Bay Colony, and elsewhere to oppose them violently.

In England, persecution of Quakers began near the very start of their movement. George Fox was first jailed one Sunday in 1649 in Nottingham after he interrupted the minister's sermon in the church there. He was jailed again in Derby in 1650 for "blasphemy" and a third time in Carlisle after he caused a riot in that city's church.[64] In December of 1653, Mary Fisher and Elizabeth Williams were flogged in Cambridge. From that time on, the number of punished Quakers swelled, slowly through 1654 and early 1655 and faster thereafter, keeping pace with the growth of the movement.[65]

Fox estimated that by 1656 "there were seldom fewer than one thousand in prison in this nation for Truth's testimony--some for tithes, some for going to the steeple houses, some for contempts as they called them, some for not swearing and others for not putting off their hats, etc."[66] By April 1659, more than three hundred Quakers are known to have died martyrs in England's prisons or through ill usage by constables.

The Puritan government of Massachusetts opposed Quakers just as vehemently. In October 1656, soon after Mary Fisher and Elizabeth Austin were turned away from Boston, the Massachusetts General Court decreed that any Quakers who entered the colony were to be jailed, whipped, kept constantly at work and "none suffered to converse or speak with them" before they were expelled from the colony. Any ship captain who brought in a Quaker was to be fined £100. This law did not keep Quakers from coming, and so two more laws were passed in 1657 and 1658:

October 1657--One ear is to be cut from every Quaker male re-entering Massachusetts. Any residents who "entertain or conceal any Quakers" are to be fined "40 shillings for every hour's concealment." Three young Quaker men each lost an ear under this law: Christopher Holder, after he came from Virginia for a second visit to Massachusetts; John Copeland, who became a Virginian in later life; and John Rous.

October 1658--The penalty of *death* was ordained for re-entering Quakers and severe penalties were prescribed for Massachusetts residents who embraced "the horrid opinions of the Quakers."

After passage of the October 1658 law, two Quakers earlier expelled from the colony deliberately re-turned to Boston "to look the new law in the face": Will Robinson and Marmaduke Stephenson. They were accompanied by six recently convinced Quakers of Salem, Massachusetts, who "brought linen wherein to wrap the dead bodies of those who are to suffer." All eight were incarcerated in Boston's jail. And when Mary Dyer, a newly convinced Friend who was the wife of Rhode Island's attorney general, came to visit them she was locked up with them. Will Robinson, Marmaduke Stephenson, and Mary Dyer were then sentenced to be hanged under the new law.

Will Robinson and Marmaduke Stephenson were hanged October 1659. Mary Dyer was led to the gallows with them, her ankles and wrists were tied and she was blindfolded. Then suddenly she was reprieved and hustled out of Massachusetts. But Mary Dyer returned to Boston yet again about six months later, and Governor Endicott reluctantly consented for her to be hanged. Public opposition grew stronger when a fourth Quaker, William Leddra of Barbados, was hanged in March 1661.[67]

George Fox, the first Quaker, spent 57 strenuous days in Virginia and North Carolina in 1672. Somerton Friends Meeting near Suffolk, Virginia, dates from George's stay in the neighborhood.

## III

## IN WHICH THE TRUTH IS CRUSHED TO EARTH
## 1664-1677

> In my old leather breeches
> And my shaggy, shaggy locks
> I am walking in the glory of the Light,
> Said Fox.
> --The George Fox Song
> by Sydney Carter

By the springtime of 1664, only one or possibly two Quaker meetings were left alive in Virginia. The Assembly's anti-Quaker laws had damped out the little brush fires of the new faith elsewhere in the colony. Just before that spring came on, three men, Quakers, arrived in James River. They just about extinguished the new faith *everywhere* in the colony.

John Perrot was the leader of the three. He was a bearded man--most unusual for Quakers of that day--somewhat saintly in his appearance, dressed in simplest clothing, a vegetarian as to diet, sonorous and poetic in the way he expressed himself. This John Perrot was a Baptist in 1655, living near Waterford, Ireland, when he joined the Children of the Light. Edward Burrough and Francis Howgill convinced him--the same who convinced Elizabeth Harris earlier that year in London--and he set out to spread the Quaker message about the same time as Elizabeth. He traveled in England and Ireland and then in June 1657 went with John Love, an Irish Friend of Limerick, and other Friends, for Athens and Jerusalem.

Perrot and his fellow travelers went to Leghorn in Italy, and then to the Turkish island of Zante. From there Perrot visited and preached in Corinth, Athens, Smyrna. From all these places he wrote back to England, and his reputation grew among the Quakers. Then he and John Love went to Venice where they delivered a paper to the Doge. In June 1658 they went on to Rome to speak to the Pope.

The two Irish Friends in Rome called on Father John Crey, an Irishman and chaplain to the Pope. They spread their desire to see the Pope before Father Crey "as an unfolded sheet on a smooth floor." Instead of arranging an audience, however, Father Crey arranged for the Friends' arrest as heretics. They were taken out of bed that night in their inn at the Sign of the Cock in Piazza Formase and incarcerated, first in the city jail and then in the Prison of the Inquisition. John Love died in that prison in a few months, and John Perrot was kept there about eighteen weeks. Then he was taken to Rome's Pazzarella, its Prison for Mad People. There he was kept, amidst screams, gibberish and terrible laughter, often chained and sometimes beaten. He was imprisoned three years, until two Friends from England who carried a letter written on Perrot's behalf by King Charles II, finally got him released. He returned to England in summer 1661 in high repute among his fellow Quakers.[1]

While a prisoner in Rome, John Perrot thought steadily about the Quaker faith for which he suffered. He concluded that Quakers must always follow directly the leading of the Inner Light and, conversely, *must never follow customary and traditional ways of worship*. He reflected that Quaker men in England kept their hats on their heads before dignitaries, in courts of law and in meetings for worship. The hats came off only when a Friend in meeting was moved to pray; and this was the custom and tradition that, Perrot decided, must go. He wrote home, announcing that he had "received by express commandment from the lord God of heaven" an order to "bear a sure testimony against the custom and tradition of taking off the hat by men when they go to pray to God." He wrote:

> If any Friend be moved of the Lord God to pray in the congregation of God [by] fall[ing] down with his face to the ground, without taking off the hat or the shoes, let him do so in the fear and name of the Lord; and if the world be contentious, ask them why...take off your hat without precept and not your shoes, being it was a precept which God commanded Moses, saying 'Take off thy shoes from off thy feet'.

John Perrot began to preach against "hat honor" as soon as he returned to England. He attracted many Friends to his views. George Fox and most other Quaker leaders were, however, repelled. The Quaker movement was only just recovering from James Nayler's extravagances in 1656 when he was tried before Parliament for riding into the city of Bristol while being wildly worshiped by seven companions, like Christ Himself. Fox saw John Perrot as "Nayler all over again." Perrot's increasingly strange writings reinforced this fear. One writing began: "A Wren in the Burning Bush, Waving the Wings of Contraction, to the Congregated Clean Fowls of the Heavens, in the Ark of God, Holy Host of the Eternal Power, Salutation"!

Perrot ignored George Fox's remonstrance. He kept on preaching his enthusiastic views with emphasis on hat honor. Thus he created the first schism among Quakers in their brief fourteen-year history. In January 1662, he sailed for America. He traveled in Barbados and Jamaica, in Maryland, and finally Virginia. Everywhere, he divided the newly convinced Quakers. Joseph Nicholson wrote to George Fox from Barbados in 1663: "Indeed here is sad work and mad work by John P., all upon heaps the like I never saw, they are not the people they were, John's blessing is very black, surely his end I fear will not be good."

John Perrot arrived in Virginia late in 1663, with John Browne, his companion from England, and William Fuller, a prominent Maryland Friend. The embattled Chuckatuck Friends received them with some reserve, having heard word about Perrot's stay in Barbados. However, Perrot overcame their doubts by rescuing two Chuckatuck Quakers, William Yarrett and Edward Jones, from the jail at Jamestown. As William Yarrett reported the incident:

> Soon after [Perrot, Browne and Fuller arrived], I and another were taken prisoners for having a meeting in my house, which meeting was before the said Perrot came in, and we were committed prisoners.... Soon after, the said Perrot and John Browne having business in James Town and hearing that we were in prison, came into the prison and did declare some words in the prison, and we having liberty from the Sheriff went to Edward Jones his house which was my fellow prisoner, and had more words declared there [by Perrot]....

> John being received amongst most of Friends here and being a report that he was received amongst Friends in the Barbados generally, I did reason with the weak fleshly part that it would be better to receive two into my house that was not in the power of the Lord than to deny one that was in the power of the Lord. So weakness came over me and I pleaded that [it] were an indifferent thing to me whether the hat were put on or off in time of prayer.

By the time John Perrot reached Virginia, he had expanded his ideas for abolishing form and ceremony from Quakerism. He preached at Chuckatuck impressively that the custom of holding meetings for worship regularly on First Day (Sunday) was dead and formal. Hold your meetings only as the Spirit leads you, he said. The Inward Light must be trusted hour by hour.

When it is right for Friends to meet at a certain place and time, all will be moved to go there at the time.

And so the Chuckatuck Friends, somewhat confused and divided, stopped boating to Thomas and Margaret Jordan's farm on First Days for worship. All the fines, imprisonments and beatings rained down on them by the sheriff's men had not stopped them; but John Perrot's preaching did.

Early in 1664, Perrot and John Browne left Chuckatuck and its little paralyzed community of Quakers for the West Indies. Browne went home to England; but Perrot stayed on in Barbados, and there he abruptly quit the Quakers. He called on Barbados's governor, Thomas Modyford, and impressed Modyford both with his "good temper, skill and knowledge in merchant affairs" and with the fact that he was known to King Charles--as evidenced by the letters that the King had sent to obtain his release from Rome's madhouse three years before. The governor thereupon offered John Perrot a government position and, when Perrot accepted, wrote a gleeful report to the King, saying

> And really, Sire, it may take off much of that sect's rude temper when they shall find in the newsbooks that John Perrot, an eminent preaching Quaker, was content for His Majesty's Service to appear in a satin suit, with a sword and belt and to be called 'Captain'.[2]

Perrot ran far out from the Quakers. John Taylor, visiting Barbados in 1665, wrote:

> One of the judges of this place told me that he never had seen one who so severely exacted an oath from people as John Perrot did: for he saith, that if any will go to hell he will dispatch them quickly. And another judge that was also present, said that Perrot had altogether renounced his faith and aimed at nothing but his profit.[3]

He died in Barbados September 1665--less than two years after he left Friends and turned back to the world. "Such a one," wrote William Sewel, the Dutch Quaker historian, "was John Perrot, though even some wise men admired him for a time. Whether he ever repented sincerely, I can not tell."[4]

\* \* \*

All through 1664 the Quaker movement in Virginia lay as if dead. Governor Berkeley was satisfied that his anti-Quaker laws had done their work.

Then late in 1665 in the winter, John Burnyeat, 34, a traveller from Lowe's-water in England's Lake Country, came to Chuckatuck. He was a country man raised on a hill farm called Crabtree Beck, a Quaker for twelve years from the day he heard George Fox speak to an out-of-doors crowd at Pardshaw Crag near the farm. John Burnyeat wrote in his Journal:

> In the winter following I went down to Virginia, and when I came there Friends there, the greatest part of them were led aside by John Perrot...and they had quite forsaken their meetings and did not meet together once in a year and had lost the very form and language of the Truth, many of them and were become loose and careless and much one with the world in many things: so that the cross of Christ, for which they had suffered, was shunned by them and so sufferings escaped, and they got into outward ease.
>
> For they had endured very great sufferings for their meetings and did stand faithful therein till he came among them and preached up this notion of his, by which he judged Friends' practice and testimony in the Truth and for the Truth to be but forms, and so pretending to live above such things, drew them far from their zeal for the Truth....And thus, they being seduced or bewitched as the Galatians were into a fleshly liberty, the offence of the Cross ceased and the power was lost.
>
> And when I came there, it was hard to get a meeting among them. And much discourse I had with some of the chief of them, and...I obtained a meeting, and the Lord's power was with us and amongst us, and several were revived and refreshed.[5]

One other English Quaker, Thomas Newhouse, came to Virginia in 1655.[6] He was one of the enthusiasts of those early Quaker years who were called to testify in spectacular ways for the Truth. These earnest first Friends were led by the example of Isaiah of the Old Testament who "walked naked and barefoot" (Isa 20:3); and by the imagery of Jeremiah who wrote "Therefore, behold, the days are coming, says the Lord when I shall...empty their vessels and break their jars in pieces. Then Moab shall be ashamed" (Jeremiah 48:12). So these Friends walked naked in streets and into churches as a portent against the wickedness of the times or as a warning that the world's people were not covered by the Truth:

- Elizabeth Fletcher, a girl of sixteen and "a very modest, grave young woman, yet contrary to her own will or inclination, went naked through the streets" of Oxford.[7]
- Solomon Eccles, a music teacher turned Quaker, went through the fair at Smithfield "naked, with a pan on his head full of fire and brimstone, flaming up in the sight of the people, crying repentance among them, and bade them remember Sodom."[8]
- Margaret Brewster came into a Boston church with her hair down on her shoulders, ashes on her head, her face blackened, dressed in sackcloth, attended by four other Friends "as a sign to warn the bloody town of Boston to end its cruel laws."[9] John Greenleaf Whittier wrote a poem about the episode:

    > She came and stood in the Old South Church
    >     A wonder and a sign
    > With a look the old-time sibyls wore
    >     Half-crazed and half-divine.[10]

- Elizabeth Harris herself, after she returned home from Virginia and Maryland, visited London churches in sackcloth to bid the worshipers repent.

As for Thomas Newhouse, he entered a New England church in 1663 and broke two empty bottles before the congregation "crying out as he did so that thus those who persecuted Friends should be dashed to pieces."[11] There is no direct evidence that Thomas witnessed in this Old Testament way in Virginia. But, he remained in Virginia many years, and some things he said embarrassed Virginia's Quakers, including his assertion before an assembly of people in Norfolk that "a great part of the Bible is false".[12] In 1680 the Assembly passed a law against interrupting church services which may have been occasioned by Newhouse.[13]

John Burnyeat came back to Virginia in spring 1666 to encourage the Chuckatuck Friends. Then he went home to England, but returned to Chuckatuck a third time in July 1671. No other traveling minister visited Chuckatuck in the five years between John Burnyeat's visits as far as is known. Yet, in 1671 Burnyeat wrote:

> I found a freshness among them, and they were many of them restored and grown up to a degree of their former zeal and tenderness; and a great openness I found in the country and had several blessed meetings.[14]

\* \* \*

The first Quaker, George Fox himself, said that he felt a motion from the Lord to visit America, just a few months before John Burnyeat returned to Chuckatuck in July 1671. In that year, 1671, George Fox was a prison-marked, grizzled, thickset kind of man, just turned forty-seven. He grew up in the hamlet of Drayton in Leicestershire:

> ...Brought up in country business; and as he took most delight in sheep, so he was very skilful in them; an employment that very well suited his mind in several respects, both for its innocency and solitude.[15]

He was companionable as a teenager, but he worried his parents when he balked at going to Drayton's parish church with them.

Nathaniel Stephens (1606-1678), an Oxford graduate who followed Calvinist thinking, was the rector of Drayton's Church of St. Michael and All Angels. He preached from Fenny Drayton's high pulpit that God elects some people to salvation and rejects others according to His inscrutable will. No one has a chance of avoiding hell except through the church and the church's rites, Baptism and Communion. Humanity fell from God's grace when Eve bit the apple, and unless you *believe* in Jesus Christ and Him crucified, you are lost, preached Mr. Stephens. His book, *Vindiciae Fundamenti*, was published in 1658. It is "a threefold defence of the Doctrine of Original Sin, together with some other fundamentals of Salvation." Somehow young George could not stomach Mr. Stephens and the things he preached.[16]

Instead of church, George took to walking in the night with his *Bible* and to sitting by the sheep alone on green hillsides and lost in thought. Sometimes he went to ministers in the neighborhood and asked them questions about life and death and ultimate things. Their answers never satisfied him.

Changes worked in him then, this teen-ager, out of the silences and voices of his inner life. He felt despair as he walked the cart-paths at night, because no one helped him to find whatever it was that he was reaching for. And then he had a surge of insight. As he wrote years later:

> When all my hopes...were gone, so that I had nothing outwardly to help me, nor could tell what to do then, oh then, I heard a voice which said, 'There is one, even Christ Jesus that can speak to thy condition,' and when I heard it my heart did leap for joy.

Thereafter, George relied principally on the still small voice and the inward light, which he called the Light of Christ or the Spirit of Christ, to guide him. And this is how the Quakers' movement began.

One morning in 1646, he wrote in his journal, he woke up with the feeling that he "was come up in the Spirit through the flaming sword into the paradise of God. All things were new and all the creation gave unto me another smell than before."

The next spring he went on a walking trip around the Midland counties. Somewhere near Nottingham he met Elizabeth Hooton, mother of three. Elizabeth listened closely to George's talk about the Light of Christ. He convinced her and she became the second person to join the Children of the Light, after George himself. By the time of Elizabeth's death, twenty-four years later, 40,000 people had joined George Fox and Elizabeth Hooton "in the Truth."

George got his first taste in Nottingham of what it is to walk through life by the rocky path and narrow gate. He was arrested there one Sunday morning in 1648, charged with blasphemy and locked up for a few weeks in Nottingham Jail. His police record, after his first offense in Nottingham:

| Year | Term | Facility | Offense |
| --- | --- | --- | --- |
| 1650 | 50 weeks | Derby Jail | Blasphemy |
| 1653 | 10 | Carlisle Jail | Blasphemy, heresy and seducing |
| 1655 | 90 | Launceston in Cornwall | Refusing oath of abjuration |
| 1660 | 20 | Lancaster Jail | Disturbing the peace |
| 1662 | 3 | Leicester Jail | Refusing oath of allegiance |
| 1664 | 100 | Lancaster Jail and Scarborough Castle | Refusing oath of allegiance |
| 1673 | 108 | Worcester Jail | Refusing oath of allegiance |

He was no angel, George Fox, for he had a vindictive streak; he exulted in the misfortunes of his opposers. He was a man of his time, sharing the common English aversion to "Popery," the faith of the Roman Catholics. In fact he judged all other sects harshly. In his younger years, he lapsed occasionally into psychic oversensitivity.* With these failings, he lived an extraordinary life, beaten by mobs, shot at with a pistol that misfired, and stalked by men with drawn rapiers. He was thrown down church steps, over church walls, into mud puddles. He was ridiculed, wondered at, respected, hated, loved, betrayed, and revered by thousands.

All through his career, Fox held to the Inward Light, the Light of Christ as the primary guide for the living of one's life. About the time of the troubles with John Perrot, however, he modified his point of view; for it was borne home to him then that the movement he had founded needed some outward organization, in addition to the inward leading of the Light. He evidently reflected that to be human is to be both an *individual* and also a *social* being. He saw that some cohesion and order were needed to hold the Children of the Light together, and to help individuals distinguish between leadings of the Light and mere "notions."

To this end George Fox began to promote another kind of Friends' meeting in addition to the meetings for *worship*: that is, meetings for *business*. He proposed that local meetings should meet *monthly* for business; that adjacent meetings should meet *quarterly*; and that the quarterly meetings should come together in a *yearly* meeting. Also, he thought that the business meetings should be held as men's and women's meetings since men and women have special capabilities for carrying out certain kinds of church business. With all this, he urged only a bare minimum of organization. The main means for linking the Children of the Light was to be the unity they experienced while "waiting on the Lord" in silence.

William James called George Fox "a religious genius," and this adjustment of the Quaker movement to meet the realities encountered in its first years indicates Fox's genius. The establishing of regular monthly, quarterly and yearly meetings for business was one reason why he came to America in 1671. He also came to heal the division caused by John Perrot.

---

* In the winter of 1651, G.F. reports in his *Journal*, the Lord commanded him to pull off his shoes and walk the streets of Lichfield crying, "Woe unto the bloody city of Lichfield!" As he did so "there ran like a channel of blood down the streets and the market place was like a pool of blood."

George's wife Margaret had been "praemunired" and in and out of jail for the seven years from 1664 to 1671[17]--a praemunired person was one declared by the courts to be out of the protection of the Crown, with all possessions forfeited to the Crown and imprisoned during the King's pleasure. Then as George describes it in his journal:

> I was moved by the Lord to speak to Martha Fisher and Hannah [Salter] to go to the King and his Council and to move them for Margaret's liberty. And they went in the Lord's power. And these two women got Margaret's discharge...of which the like was never heard in England...After [Margaret] came up to London a free woman I began to prepare for America.

George and Margaret celebrated her release at the Yearly Meeting for 1681 in London where "many came from all parts of the nation and a mighty meeting it was and the Lord's power was over all." Then they went down to Gravesend where twelve Friends were waiting to accompany George "towards America and some of the isles thereunto belonging": Thomas Briggs, William Edmundson, John Rous (the same John Rous whose ear was cut off in Boston), John Stubbs, Solomon Eccles, James Lancaster, John Cartwright, Robert Widders, George Pattison, John Hall, Elizabeth Hooton and Elizabeth Miers. On the twelfth of Sixth Month (August) 1671 they boarded a vessel called the *Industry*.[18]

Fox was not well when the *Industry* set sail. Five years of prison and more years of confronting sheriffs and judges, of organizing Friends' meetings, of riding up and down Great Britain, had worn him. When the *Industry* reached Barbados after fifty-two days at sea, he went to bed in Richard Forstall's house in Bridgetown. He was in pain, yet "is cheery and keeps above all." From his bed he dictated several papers.[19]

One of these papers was a letter to Governor Christopher Codrington of Barbados, a letter often described as a complete statement of Friends' beliefs. George Fox did not, however, write it for that purpose, and it is not at all a full statement. It does not even mention directly the key Quaker principle of "that of God in every person." He wrote this letter to the Governor to clear the Barbados Friends of false charges. It affirms Friends' reverence of God, Christ Jesus and the *Bible*, while stressing Friends' conviction that the Bible is not the Word of God; goes on to deny that Friends were inciting the slaves in Barbados to rebel; and urges those who have "negroes and tawny Indians" to teach them to "keep the way of the Lord."[20]

In Barbados in 1671, George Fox first came into direct contact with slavery, but it was something that had concerned him for quite a while. In 1657--before any other religious leader whether Catholic, Anglican or Puritan had published a word about slave-holding--Fox wrote "To Friends Beyond Sea, that Have Blacks and Indian Slaves." He made only a beginning in this, his first discussion of slavery. He did not condemn slave-holding as such but he did set forth the basic Quaker concept that all men and women are equal under God. All nations are of one blood, he wrote, and he urged Friends "to have the mind of Christ, and to be merciful, as your heavenly father is merciful."

George got better after three weeks in bed at Richard Forstall's, and ventured into Barbados's brilliant blue outdoors. His concern revived when he saw the slaves in their rags. He met with great numbers of them and spoke to them of God and Truth, and he exhorted the Barbados Quakers in their meeting house:

> Do not slight them, to wit the Ethiopians, the blacks now, neither any man or woman upon the face of the earth...Christ died for all, both Turks, barbarians, Tartarians and Ethiopians; he died for the tawnies and for the blacks as well as for you that are called whites...and hath enlightened them as well as he hath enlightened you.

The servitude of the blacks should end in freedom just as it did for white servants, Fox declared in Barbados:

> It will doubtless be very acceptable to the Lord, if so be that masters of families here would deal so with their servants, the Negroes and blacks whom they have bought with their money, to let them go free after a considerable term of years, if they have served them faithfully. And when they go and are made free, let them not go away empty-handed. This, I say, will be very acceptable to the Lord.[21]

George and the Friends with him stayed three months on Barbados and then sailed on to Jamaica, where they stayed seven weeks and a day. They established some new Friends meetings for worship and also the new arrangement of regular meetings for business. Old Elizabeth Hooton, the first convinced Quaker, died and her companions laid her tenderly to rest there. Then they sailed on to North America. They sailed for forty-two more days, and while they sailed King Charles II issued a Declaration of Indulgence, temporarily suspending the laws that made worship outside the Established Church a crime. This was providential, for without the King's Indulgence their visits to Virginia and the New England colonies would have been marked by whippings and jailings. Their ship dropped anchor in Maryland's Patuxent River. It was the 20th of Second Month (April) 1672.

They went ashore and rested overnight in the house of Quaker James Preston-the son of Richard Preston who led the Puritan families forced out of Virginia by Governor Berkeley in 1649. Then according to George's journal:

> Then there was a meeting appointed by John Burnyeat [who had just come up to Maryland from Virginia] about three score miles off which held four days which we went to though we were weary...and a glorious meeting we had. After the public meeting [for worship] there were men's and women's meetings [for business] and I opened to Friends the service thereof [he explained what the meetings for business were for and how they were to be conducted] and all were satisfied.[22]

This Meeting, held on West River, Maryland, was the first gathering of the present Baltimore Yearly Meeting of Friends, which has been gathering regularly, year by year, ever since.

After the Meeting, the travelers from England with a few Maryland Friends divided into three parties: William Edmondson and three Friends sailed south to Chuckatuck in Virginia; James Lancaster and John Cartwright went north by sea to New England; and George Fox and some six others crossed Chesapeake Bay to Maryland's Eastern Shore and then went north by land to New England.

* * *

William Edmondson (1627-1712) who went to Virginia, was a man from Westmoreland, who was first a carpenter, then a sergeant in Cromwell's army, and then a storekeeper in Ireland. He was one of several Quaker merchants credited with introducing the single price system of merchandising instead of haggling over each transaction. Convinced by James Nayler in

1653, he and his wife and brother started the first Irish Friends' meeting, in Lurgan, County Armagh.

In Virginia, William Edmondson continued John Burnyeat's efforts to revive the Chuckatuck Quakers. Describing his seven weeks' visit there, he wrote:

> Things were much out of order; but the Lord's testimony and power went over all. When I had got several powerful meetings among them and their minds a little settled, so that Truth had got some hold, I appointed a men's meeting [for business] for settling them in the way of Truth's discipline.
>
> Afterwards, it being upon me, I traveled to Carolina and two Friends accompanied me, it being all wilderness and no English inhabitants or path-ways, but some marked trees to guide people.

Edmondson's visit to North Carolina, which began with a sixty mile horseback ride through the woods in spring rains, was the first visit ever to that colony by any Christian minister. He went to the house of Henry Phillips (Phelps) on Perquimans River where Hertford, the county seat of Perquimans County, stands today:

> He [Henry] and his wife had been convinced of the Truth in New England, and came here to live; and not having seen a Friend for seven years before, they wept for joy to see us. It being a First Day morning when we got there, although I was weary and faint and my clothes wet, I desired them to send to the people thereaway to come to a meeting...about the hour appointed many people came, but they had little or no religion for they came and sat down in the meeting smoking their pipes. In a little time the Lord's testimony arose...and their hearts [were] reached by it...One [Francis] Toms, a justice of the peace, and his wife were at the meeting...and desired to have the next meeting at their house, about three miles off on the other side of the water; so we had a meeting there the next day, and a blessed time it was; for several were tendered with a sense of the power of God, received the Truth, and abode in it.

So "the tender seed of Truth" was planted in raw, brand new North Carolina.

After these two meetings in Hertford, William Edmondson and his two companions rode hard back to Chuckatuck in order to get to the men's meeting for business which William "had appointed...to be on the fifth day of the week," and

> We got...to the men's meeting, and the Lord's power was with us and Friends received Truth's discipline in the love of it, as formerly they had received the doctrine of Truth, for which they were great sufferers in the spoiling of their goods, the Governor [Berkeley] being a very peevish man, and much set against Truth and Friends....
>
> I traveled to several places in the vicinity of Chuckatuck and had comfortable meetings with Friends, and traveled three miles above James Town to a place called Green Spring, where were several convinced people. A meeting had been settled there but was lost, the people being stumbled in their minds and scattered by the evil example of one Thomas Newhouse, who had been a preacher among them....I got them together and settled a meeting; they were glad thereof and much comforted, as sheep that had been astray, and returned again to the shepherd, Christ Jesus....
>
> As I returned, it was laid upon me to visit the governor, Sir William Barclay [Berkeley] and to speak with him about Friends' sufferings. I went about six miles out of my way to speak with him, accompanied by William Yarrett, an honest, and ancient Friend. I told the Governor that I came from Ireland, where his brother [Lord John Berkeley] was Lord Lieutenant, who was kind to our Friends. He was very peevish and bitter, and I could fasten nothing upon him with all the soft arguments I could use....
>
> I came that night to Justice Taverner's house, his wife a Friend [Major Thomas Taberer and his Quaker wife, Margaret, lived in Isle of Wight County on a plantation called Basse's Choice] and he loving to Friends. The next day was the men's [business] meeting at William Wright's house [at Chuckatuck]. The Justice and his wife went to the meeting, about eight or nine miles, and several other persons...particularly Richard Bennett, alias Major General Bennett

[the Governor who was convinced by Elizabeth Harris in 1655] and Colonel Teve [Thomas Dew of Nansemond, who was Speaker of the Virginia House under Governor Bennett and a relative of William Wright's wife Mary], with others and a great many Friends...and a blessed heavenly season it was. Many were tendered by the Lord's power....

We had first a meeting for the worship of God; then Friends drew into a large upper room to the men's meeting, where I was with them in settling the affairs of the Church. Justice Taverner's wife...told me that the Major General, Colonel Teve [Dew] and others were below staying to speak to me; so I went down to them. They were courteous and said they only stayed to see me, and acknowledged what I had spoken in the meeting was Truth. I told them the reason for our Friends' drawing apart from them was, to lay down a method to provide for our poor widows and fatherless children, to take care that no disorders were committed in our Society; and that all lived orderly. The Major General replied, he was glad to hear there was such care and order among us.

He likewise asked me how I was treated by the Governor?, having heard that I was with him....He asked me if the Governor called me dog, rogue etc.? I said 'No, he did not call me so., 'Then' said he, 'you took him in his best humor, those being his usual terms when he is angry, for he is an enemy to every appearance of good.' They were tender and loving and we parted so....

When I had been some time with Friends in Virginia and had many sweet serviceable meetings among them and things somewhat settled, I found my spirit clear of that service and took boat and went back to Maryland....[23]

\* \* \*

While Edmundson visited Virginia, George Fox and six companions traveled from Maryland to New England and back again, holding meetings with English and Indians. They got back to Maryland on September 19 and spent seven weeks on Maryland's Eastern and Western Shores. Then on November 5 at sun-up, George Fox with Robert Widders, James Lancaster, and George Pattison (a sea captain by profession) left James Preston's house on Patuxent River in a small sloop and set sail south on Chesapeake Bay towards Virginia.

The four men slept one night in the wet woods. The second night they happened upon a ship from Plymouth, at anchor, and Fox and one of his companions slept aboard the ship, while the other two slept alongside in the rocking sloop. The third day they rounded Old Point Comfort, sailed a little way up the James and came to Chuckatuck. They must have arrived there soon after first frost when the great Virginia trees were turning reds and yellows.

Following William Edmondson's instructions the four found William Wright's house, where Edmondson had worshiped with the local Friends and talked with the old Governor, Richard Bennett. William Wright had died since Edmondson's departure; but Mary Wright, his widow, welcomed them and put out the word of their arrival. Three days later "there was a great meeting of Friends and people; and there came Colonel Thomas Dew and a justice and a captain with other officers and many of account, and they were much taken with the Truth."

It is interesting that so many people of importance in the world came to this Quaker meeting. The King's Indulgence was in effect then and attending the meeting, technically speaking, was not a criminal act. But William Berkeley, Quaker-hater, was still the governor of Virginia. Colonel Dew, the justice, the captain and others of account who came to the meeting at Mary Wright's must have known that they were flirting with trouble. Yet they came.

James Lancaster wrote in his Journal of events after the meeting at Mary Wright's:

> The 12th day [of November] we passed over the water called Nansemond and went about four miles by land, where we had a precious meeting, and men's and women's meetings settled [so began the Terrascoe Neck Meeting].
>
> From thence we passed 12 miles and boated over...Pagan's Creek to William Yarrow's house [William Yarrett's, where John Perrot had stayed] and on the 17th day we had a very large meeting and two justices of the peace and their wives; and a lieutenant-colonel's wife was there. We were put to meet without the doors for there were so many people, and a great openness in

them to receive the Truth. [This was the beginning of Pagan Creek Meeting near present-day Smithfield]

After the meeting [at Pagan Creek] was done we passed by water about a mile and ten miles by land to one Thomas Jordan's house [the founder of Chuckatuck Meeting]...the noise of the Truth did sound abroad.

The 18th day we passed about eight miles to the Western Branch [of Nansemond River] where we met with Friends and we were refreshed. [The beginning of Western Branch Meeting near present day Isle of Wight Courthouse, where five generations of Friends met for 172 years thereafter.]

And on the 19th day we passed about 30 miles through woods toward Carolina, and a flashy and wet way, and at the night we came to a place called Somerton, to a poor house and there we found a woman that had a sense of God [here began Somerton Friends Meeting which still meets to this day].

George Fox and companions went by canoe down the Chowan River to North Carolina. They spent eighteen days in the wilderness country where William Edmondson had been earlier--Perquimans and Pasquotank Counties nowadays. "The Truth spreadeth," they wrote, and Friends still meet in those counties, in the Piney Woods and Up River Meetings. They had friendly meetings with the Indians there and

A doctor did dispute with us...concerning the Light and the Spirit. And he so opposed it in everyone, that I called an Indian because [the doctor] denied it to be in them, and I asked [the Indian] if he did lie and do that to another which he would not have them do the same to him...was there not something in him that did tell him of it, that he should not do so but did reprove him. And [the Indian) said there was such a thing....in him when he did any such a thing....So we made the doctor ashamed...and he ran so far out that he would not own the Scriptures.

The four men returned to Mary Wright's from North Carolina on December 13. They had spent their first fourteen days in Virginia on the south shore of the James working generally to the west, upriver from

Chuckatuck. Then after twenty days in North Carolina, they used their last twenty days in Virginia to hold six meetings and to visit families eastward and downriver from their base at Mary Wright's home in Chuckatuck.

Some of the six meetings those last twenty days were covered by the Spirit, as Friends say. One at the home of John Porter, Jr., on the eastern branch of Elizabeth River was "a very precious and glorious one, very living and fresh." The sheriffs of the two counties they visited on this swing--Nansemond and Lower Norfolk--both met Fox and, remarkably, neither sheriff tried to interfere. Nansemond's sheriff actually came to a meeting where George Fox spoke on December 5, and "all were reached by the Truth." As for Lower Norfolk, George noted that "in this county, they said the High Sheriff had an order to take me; but I met him by chance and he took me by the hand and was very civil and courteous."

However, the zeal of the Norfolk Quakers, bright in the early 1660s, was pretty well quenched by the time of Fox's visit. Most people who came to the meetings were "of the world"; and among these who were or had been Quakers, George found some "bad walkers and talkers." The Quaker movement did not revive in Lower Norfolk for nearly two centuries after George Fox's visit.

The four travelers started back from Norfolk to Maryland on 30 December 1672. They spent their last night in Norfolk at Sara Willoughby's house on Willoughby's Spit, where the Route 64 Bridge-Tunnel from Norfolk to Hampton starts today. This Sara Willoughby they described as "a very tender widow woman of the world [who] received us with tears kindly."

Hampton Roads in December can be mighty cold and stormy. The four in their open boat had all they could do to cross it on December 31: "The storm and wind being high, towards evening we had much ado to get to the shore, and, our boat being open, the water flashed in and over, and when we had got to the [Newport News] shore we made us a fire to warm us, and there lay by it all that night in the woods, and the wolves roaring about us."

They sailed on the next day, "but the wind being against us we sailed backwards and forwards and we got to the shore called Point Comfort, where yet we found but small comfort" and they slept in the woods again where "it snew and blew so cold that it was hard for some to abide it." Finally on January 3 "the wind was pretty fair and we passed on our way, sailing and rowing north on Chesapeake Bay."

They stopped for the night at Milford Haven by Gwynn's Island, and sailed on to hold meetings for worship at the mouths of Rappahannock River and of Potomac River. They reached James Preston's in Maryland, "about the first hour of the night" on January 5th.[24]

\* \* \*

Governor Berkeley in his later years was a man with a low boiling point. The news that Quakers south of the James had the nerve to reappear again, in the face of all the laws forbidding them in Virginia, upset him. No sooner had Parliament revoked the King's Indulgence allowing worship outside the established church than he resumed his orders for the southside sheriffs to stamp out Quaker activities. His orders appear in the minutes of the Governor's Council in 1674 and again on 15 June 1675:

> The Honorable Governor being informed [again] that there are several [Quaker] conventicles in Nansemond County, it is ordered...that...they be proceeded against according to the laws of England and this country. Colonel Bridger is desired strictly to command the justices of Nansemond, Lower Norfolk and the Isle of Wight Counties to make strict inquiry of the same.[25]

"Colonel Bridger" is Joseph Bridger (1628-1686), one of Governor Berkeley's Councillors and commander of the Colony's militia in the four counties south of the James--Lower Norfolk, Nansemond, Isle of Wight and Surry. He was almost certainly one of the gentry present at Mary Wright's when Fox preached on 17 December 1672.

There are three pieces of evidence that Bridger and some of the county sheriffs, having met with the Quakers in worship, now were reluctant to proceed against them:

- For one, the Chuckatuck Friends felt confident enough of the future that they built a meeting house and began meeting in it by 1675. This house was closed down or destroyed in 1678, for meetings and weddings again were held in Quaker homes after that year which suggests that the Act for Suppressing Quakers was again in full force. That the house was built at all, however, is a sign that official resistance to Friends was softening.
- For another sign, many gentry of Nansemond and Isle of Wight who came to hear George Fox in 1672, were so reached that they openly identified with Friends thereafter. Thomas Godwin, who was Nansemond's sheriff in 1660, and his wife Elizabeth came to hear Fox, and they later joined

the Chuckatuck meeting. So did William and Anna Boddie, Isle of Wight's largest landowners.[26] Thomas Taberer, a justice of Isle of Wight, was friendly to the Quaker cause, and his wife Margaret was a devoted Friend. Isle of Wight Justices Joseph Woory and Barnardo Kearney often came to meetings with their wives. Thomas Dew of Nansemond, who once was Speaker of the Virginia House, also became a Friend.

- And for a final bit of evidence, the Friends of Chuckatuck met regularly after 1672, as did the five new meetings south of James River--Terrascoe Neck, Pagan Creek and Western Branch in Isle of Wight, and Southern Branch and Somerton Meetings in Nansemond. Toward the end of 1672 George Fox sent John Cartwright and John Jay to the Eastern Shore of Virginia, "where there were desires after the Truth"[27] and soon afterward the Nassawaddox Meeting was heard from again, and a new Eastern Shore meeting was established at Guilford Creek. So then, eight Friends' meetings were alive in Virginia in the mid-1670s, in spite of Berkeley's orders to close them down.

Edmondson and Fox mentioned a *ninth* meeting located *north* of the James at Green Spring. This meeting did not survive. William Edmondson wrote that its members were "stumbled in their minds and scattered by the evil example of...Thomas Newhouse who had been a preacher among them."[28] Now Thomas Newhouse, as previously stated, *was* a radical. His extreme behavior may have killed the Green Spring Meeting. Also, Green Spring, which lies between Jamestown and present-day Williamsburg, is the place where Berkeley had his country retreat, and Berkeley's hostile nearness may be another reason for the demise of the meeting there.

\* \* \*

George Fox landed in Bristol on 28 June 1673, upon his return from America to England. He immediately asked the Bristol Friends to correspond with the Friends of Chuckatuck; and a letter from Chuckatuck to Bristol dated 25 June 1674 tells something of the condition of Virginia Friends following Fox's visit:

Dear Friends...We received your loving letters and have had them read in our meetings....We are also greatly refreshed and gladdened to hear that Truth prospers so well amongst you in England....We also in some measure can give you the like intelligence...for since our dear friend G. Fox's departure hence (whose coming among us hath been very prosperous) our meetings which, at that time was not very large are at this time (as we suppose) more than doubled, and several of them (we do believe) are very true and savory Friends; and not only so (but as we judge) a large convincement is upon many who as yet stand off.

And some there is amongst us, as well as amongst you, that through their miscarriages and disobedience doth give advantage to the enemies to speak reproachfully of Truth, which at some time doth cause some dissettlements amongst us...we being not many in number but as the power of God hath...cleared up the understandings of Friends to a new gathering into his Truth...so we trust that by the same power all things that are contrary to Truth and the prosperity thereof shall be brought to nought....

Several other things remarkable hath here fallen out this year, as a priest arrived here in the ship *Samuel and Marie* of Bristol and hanged himself. Also, our Nansemond priest, setting into a railing discourse against the Quakers and making his boast that shortly he would reconvert all the newly convinced Quakers...strangely drowned in a little small creek...all which things have drawn the minds of many into a serious consideration...and makes for the prosperity of Truth, which we trust the Lord will carry on in this perverse and wild place.

We kindly bid you farewell and remain your friends and brethren

Will: Denson
Will: Yarrett
Tho: Jordan[29]

Four Quaker men came from the British Isles to Virginia in the mid-1670s, in the wake of George Fox's visit. Two of these made trouble for the Virginia Friends, while two were helpful.

- First came Richard Gotby (alias Richard Dowell) of Bristol. All known of him is that he behaved badly in Virginia and that he handed in a written apology to the Bristol Mens' Meeting on returning to England in November 1673.[30]
- Then came Edward Beare, also from Bristol, whose "remarkable and sad end" was reported in the letter of 25 June 1674 from Chuckatuck Friends to Bristol. They wrote:

> One Edward Beare last year arrived here in the Katherine of Bristol whose remarkable and sad end we think here to note out...he gave as good a testimony for the Truth as Judas did when he brought back the money and said he had betrayed innocent blood:
> 
> We have been informed that he, the said Beare, did formerly make a profession of the Truth amongst Friends in Bristol or elsewhere, and that some Friends having entrusted him with goods shipped upon the ship Katherine he sought to defraud them...as for any profession of Truth in this place we never saw any from him, but his behavior altogether [that of] a dishonest drunken fellow....
> 
> ...Having spent and embezzled what he had gotten by the voyage he took another voyage to New England and there insinuated himself into the favor of Friends, and through craft and deceit got some Friends to entrust him with goods...that he...was to lade in Virginia for the aforesaid Friends' account...and the New England Friends engaged to send hither a vessel at the [time of the tobacco] crop for the transport of the [tobaccoes to be obtained by Beare in return for the sale of the goods].
> 
> ...In meantime,...Beare comes to Virginia and here marries a wife by the priest (a harlot) and follows strongly his old course of drunkenness and was of great esteem among the drunken rout, but in conclusion, towards the shipping time this Beare buried his wife, and suddenly after fell sick himself, and in the time of his sickness the wrath of God (without all doubt) having seized strongly upon his soul, he

> was sorely distressed in spirit and complained exceeding much of the wrong he had done....
>
> ...And he sent for Thomas Jordan and his wife and complained of his state and told how well it was with him in the days he continued in Truth, and said if God would restore him he hoped to become a new man...and Thomas Jordan told him if he did perform his promise made unto the Lord it might be well with him again--if not, a worse thing might befall him, and so left him at that time....
>
> Within three or four hours after comes the master of the New England vessel for the [tobaccoes] aforementioned which Beare, not being in a capacity of performing, fell into his old anguish of spirit...not long after, there being in the house but one person, his mother-in-law, he bids her fetch him a little warm broth presently, and while the fire was blowing up in the next room...Beare slipped out the running string of his drawers and tied it about his neck and got to the rail of the bed, and so with one knee upon the bed and the other leg upon the ground crouching he hanged himself....[31]

After the two disgraceful visitors, Gotby and Beare, there came two who were more welcome:

- John Bowater (c. 1629-1704) came from Dudley Meeting south of Birmingham. He traveled in America in 1677 and 1678 visiting some thirty-six groups of Friends in New York, New England, Maryland, and Virginia. He held meetings at nine places in Virginia and encountered Indians in Virginia and elsewhere. When he returned home he reported that "he was more kindly used by the poor Indians in America than by some pretended Christians here in England....They entertained me in their wigwams (the best of their habitations or lodgings)...but these Christians in their cold gaols, under confinement."[32]

- William Edmondson returned in 1677 to visit Friends along James River and in North Carolina for a second time, and he is counted as the fourth English visitor of the mid-1670s. After this second visit

William became anxious about the situation of the African slaves whose numbers were increasing rapidly. So he wrote this letter to American Quakers:

> It would be acceptable with God..., if you did consider [the black peoples'] condition of perpetual slavery, and make their condition your own....For perpetual slavery is an aggravation and an oppression...and Truth is that which works the remedy...so it would be well [for them to] see and know the difference between you and other people...many of you count it unlawful to make slaves of Indians and if so, then why the Negroes?[33]

*It is the first known writing by any Briton to suggest that enslaving is an abominable practice.*

Stratton Manor lies on the south tip of Virginia's Eastern Shore. While Benjamin Stratton lived here ca. 1694-1717, the Friends of Magothy Bay Meeting met here for worship. It is the oldest existing gathering place of Friendly Virginians.

## IV

## THE FRIENDLY VIRGINIANS BECOME SOMEWHAT RESPECTABLE 1677-1700

> The finer essence of George Fox's queer teaching...was surely this--that Christian qualities matter much more than Christian dogmas. No Church or sect had ever made that its living rule before.
> -- George Macaulay Trevelyan
> in *English Social History*, 1944

Sir William Berkeley, a strong and decisive governor during his first ten years in Jamestown from 1642 to 1652, was a different man after he returned to power in 1660. Although he was only 54, he behaved in crotchety ways. He flew into rages more and listened less. His "Berklean look," the scowl he used to cow visitors, became famous. He blocked the election of new members to the House of Burgesses, and the House came increasingly under his thumb.

Sir William conducted more and more of the Colony's business from his country place at Green Spring. He demanded a bodyguard of twenty-four men, quartered at Green Spring and costing the tax-payers a whopping 75,000 pounds of tobacco a year. When Indians along the upper Rappahannock River killed some English people, he ordered Major General Smith to slaughter all the men of all the Indian tribes along the river and to bring back the women and children for sale as slaves. He saw to it that his own pay and perquisites increased. In 1670, at 64, he married Frances Culpeper Stephens, the young widow of Carolina's governor. She turned out to be as acquisitive and grasping as Berkeley had become himself.

Charles II, the playboy king in England and his council, did little to supervise Governor Berkeley's activities after 1660. In 1670, however, the Lords Commissioners of Foreign Plantations sent a twenty-three-item questionnaire requiring information about the Colony's legislature and courts, militia, boundaries, population, and the like. Governor Berkeley's responses to the questionnaire are politic and responsible--excepting his answer to the twenty-third question:

> Question: What course is taken about instructing the people within your government in the Christian religion; and what provision is there made for the paying of your ministry?

> Berkeley's Answer: ...We have 48 parishes and our ministers are well paid, and by my consent should be better [paid] if they would pray oftener and preach less...I thank God there are no free schools nor printing, and I hope we shall have none these hundred years; for learning has brought disobedience and heresy and sects into the world, and printing has divulged them and libels against the best government. God keep us from both![1]

Taxes during Berkeley's second administration rose steadily, and mutterings of discontent rose too. In 1673, the Surry County Court prosecuted "a company of rude and seditious people to the number of 14 [who] did unlawfully assemble at the parish church of Lawnes Creek [about twelve miles up the James from Chuckatuck] with intent to declare they would not pay their public taxes." Five of the fourteen men prosecuted were Quakers or soon joined them: Robert Lacy, John Sheppard, John Barnes, William Tooke and John Gregory. By 1676, the discontent came to the boiling point in Bacon's Rebellion, a bloody civil war.[2]

Nathaniel Bacon, Jr., of Henrico County led the rebellion. He first called together a guerrilla force to put down Indian attacks against the frontier farmers, after Governor Berkeley refused to call out the militia. It is not clear whether Berkeley refused because it would have damaged his private fur trade with the Indians, or because he was afraid the militia would turn against him if called out. At any rate Bacon marched on Jamestown after Berkeley declared him an outlaw, defeated Berkeley's militia and burned the town. The rebellion seemed about to triumph, but collapsed when Bacon suddenly died of dysentery.

As previously observed, William Edmondson returned to visit the Chuckatuck Quakers in 1677. Having arrived in the middle of Bacon's Rebellion, he wrote in his journal:

> The country was in great trouble...and the governor Sir William Berkeley, and Col. Bacon at fierce war one against another...only Friends stood neuter and my being there was not in vain on that account...then came frigates from England with soldiers to appease the difference....Col. Bacon died and several of his party were

executed, others fined in great sums, but Friends were highly commended for keeping clear.[3]

Three commissioners and a regiment of soldiers came from England to settle the trouble. They arrived while Sir William now somewhat senile and deaf was taking heated vengeance against the defeated rebels. He had twenty-three of them hanged in spite of the commissioners' protests. They had to send him to England in May 1677 in order to halt the dance of death. When Berkeley reached London, Charles II refused to see him. "That old fool," Charles said, "hath killed more people in that naked country than I did for the murder of my father."[4] Berkeley died soon afterward.

* * *

The passing of Berkeley, their great oppressor, did not change things for Virginia's Children of the Light in one sense. The six anti-Quaker laws remained in effect.

The county justices continued after 1677 to be stern when young couples were brought before them for daring to marry after the manner of Friends. These first Quaker marriages in Virginia were celebrated in homes, barns, orchards or meadows. The bride and her groom sat together with a little party of relatives and friends. No clergyman was there, for the Friends believed that no middleman should stand between themselves and their Maker. A silence fell over the group. Presently the couple rose in the silence, joined hands, looked into one another's eyes, and said their promises to one another in the presence of the God and the assembled company. Quaker brides alone among all the brides of Christendom did not (and do not) promise to obey, for they were (and are) seen to be equals of their husbands.

When the couple finished their promises to be loving and faithful to one another through all their lives, various Friends spoke in prayer or in benediction as the Spirit moved them. After an hour or so two elder Friends shook hands to end the meeting. All rose, shook hands all round, congratulated the bride and groom with smiles, kisses, joyous tears and handshakes, and signed their marriage certificate. In this way they began their life together.

But such marriages were illegal and scandalous under Virginia's Act of 1661, titled "None to Be Married but by Ministers." When Mary Goldsmith of Norfolk married George Johnson by Quaker ceremony in 1679, they were at once brought into court and fined.[5]

Two years later, in 1681, a Quaker child aggravated the Henrico County court by refusing to take the oath as a witness. The case was a rape case and the complainant was Katherine Watkins, who was not a Quaker herself although married to Henry Watkins, Quaker of Malvern Hill--probably his second wife. Katherine accused Mulatto Jack Long, a slave of Thomas Cocke's of throwing her down and ravishing her "at or near the piney slash between the aforesaid Cocke's and Henry Watkins' house." The case, tried by Justices William Byrd and John Farrar, proved difficult, for some witnesses supported Katherine's side of the story, while others said that she had enticed Jack after drinking cup after cup of hard cider in the August sun. A key witness was Henry Watkins' 12-year-old daughter Elizabeth who, however, told the court that she could not testify under oath because oaths and swearing were contrary to her upbringing. The justices threatened Elizabeth with a whipping and actually jailed the little girl for a time, but could not get her to swear.[6]

It is evident then that the anti-Quaker laws were still being enforced after Governor Berkeley left the Colony in 1677; but now the laws were no longer being energetically enforced. Furthermore, Friends had been in Virginia more than twenty years, and they had a better sense of who they were and what they were about.

In 1676, while Bacon's Rebellion still was being fought, Virginia Friends sent their first delegate to meet with other Friends outside the Colony. He was Samuel Groom, a grizzled sea captain. He represented Virginia at a meeting of Friends in London, come together to counsel about "the prospering of Truth." In 1676 Sam'l Groom was master of the *Globe of London*, a great ship of the tobacco fleet. He had been calling at Virginia ports for many years, worshiping with the Chuckatuck and Eastern Shore Friends while his ship loaded tobacco and passengers. He attended the first Maryland Yearly Meeting in 1672 while his ship rode out a storm in Patuxent River. In 1683 he would arrive in Delaware River with 360 Quakers coming to settle Pennsylvania, as master of the *Grayhound*, 550 tons.[7]

In that same year of 1676, a 28-year-old Scot, Robert Barclay of Ury, wrote a systematic explanation of the Quaker way. He wrote it in Latin after he and his friend, George Keith, debated the merits of Quakerism with students of the University of Aberdeen. He titled the book

*An Apology for the True Christian Divinity*
*As the Same is Held Forth and Preached by the People Called in Scorn Quakers*

This *Apology* was published in English in 1678, and Friends' Meetings in Virginia and everywhere soon received copies. It knit together the ecstatic testimonies of George Fox and the earlier Quaker ministers and unified their sometimes rambling insights.

Quakers, Robert Barclay continually explains, are embarked on an inward spiritual adventure led by some thing of God that shines within every man and woman. This Inward Light "shining in and upon the heart" can overcome the dark side of human nature for anyone who is willing to use the Light. The inward way of approaching God, he explains, makes it possible to remain in the world and raise a family, yet live a life of the spirit such as is ordinarily possible only in a cloister.

The *Apology* has fifteen propositions or theses, and Barclay's method is to prove each one in three ways: by citing church authorities; by Scripture; and by reason. By this three-pronged method, he seeks to convince the three great divisions of Christianity. The appeal to the Church Fathers is for the benefit of Catholics, for whom church tradition and doctrine have final authority. The appeal to Scripture is for Protestants, for whom the Bible is the final authority. The appeal to reason is for Socinians and Unitarians who rely finally on common sense.

Having used these three proofs, however, Barclay declares that none of them is the way to "certain knowledge of God." That can be learned only by "the inward immediate manifestation and revelation of God's Spirit, shining in and upon the heart, enlightening and opening the understanding." He is describing here the Quaker way of sitting quietly with one's friends, waiting for guidance from the still small voice within.

As for the Scriptures, Barclay says that "they are only a declaration of the fountain and not the fountain itself...a secondary rule subordinate to the Spirit" by which one can test the leadings and insights received in silent worship. As for reason and common sense, he declares, "When the rational principle sets up itself there above the seed of God, to reign and rule as a prince in spiritual things...there is anti-Christ."[8]

Heeding George Fox's recommendations on the organization of Friends Meetings and having Barclay's *Apology* in hand, Virginia's Quakers began now to regroup and reach out. In Eleventh Month (January) 1679, forty-three Quaker women sent a letter "from our woman's meeting in the Western Branch of Nansemond River--to the womans meetings in England in the north country, at Swarthmore, London, Bristol or elsewhere we may be received in the House of God...."⁹ These forty-three mothers and daughters all lived along the south shore of James River, from Alice Hollowell of Norfolk to Margaret Yarrett of what is now Smithfield. They doubtless were meeting apart from their men, holding a women's quarterly meeting for business.

Equality between men and women has always been a Quaker glory. Elizabeth Hooton of Nottingham was the first to join George Fox in the Quaker adventure, and Elizabeth Harris, the first to bring it to Virginia. Fox and other first Friends debated opponents (male) who held that it was all wrong for women to speak in time of worship. Paul wrote to Timothy, the opponents stressed, that "I permit no woman to teach or to have authority over men; she is to keep silent"* and to the church at Corinth, "The women should keep silence in the churches" and "It is shameful for a woman to speak in church."** But the Friends rebutted, citing Paul's avowal to the Galatians that "There is neither Jew nor Greek, there is neither slave nor free, there is neither male nor female; for you are all one in Christ Jesus."***

There was some disagreement among early Friends whether men and women should meet together for business, or separately. Fox favored separate business meetings for men and women, and separate meetings became the practice. That resulted in an architectural style for many Friends' meeting houses that featured two front doors side by side and a movable partition to divide the meeting room in two for business meetings.

In 1674, Virginia Friends received "An Epistle from Women Friends in London" suggesting the kinds of business best dealt with by women--an epistle, no doubt, referred to frequently by the 43 women who met at "the Branch" in 1679. It lists seven women's activities:

---

\* 1 Timothy 2:12

\*\* Corinthians 14:34-35

\*\*\* Galatians 3:28

- To visit the sick, and the prisoners that suffer for the testimony of Jesus; to see that they are supplied with things needful....

- And relieving the poor, making provision for the needy, aged, and weak that are incapable of work....

- A due consideration for the widows, and care taken of the fatherless children and poor orphans (according to their capacities) for their education and bringing up...; and putting them out to trades in the wholesome order of the creation....

- Also the elder women exhorting the younger, in all sobriety, modesty in apparel and subjection to Truth; and if any should be led aside by the temptations of Satan in any way, endeavoring to reclaim such....

- And to stop tattlers and false reports and all such thing as tend to division amongst us....

- Also admonishing such maids and widows as may be in danger through the snare of the enemy, either to marry with unbelievers, or go to the priest to be married....

- And that maid servants that profess Truth and want places be...settled [and] that the savoury life and good order of Truth be minded between mistresses and maids."[10]

\* \* \*

In 1682, news came that made Virginians see the handful of Quakers among them in a new light. That year on the Delaware River, 270 miles north of Jamestown, a new town arose out of the forest, soon turning into a city. "Philadelphia"--the City of Brotherly Love--it was called according to the seamen of the northern vessels that visited in James River. It was being laid out according to Christopher Wren's rejected plan for rebuilding London after the Great Fire of 1666. And, most amazing news, the city was being built and settled almost entirely by Quakers!

Philadelphia, that dawning Quaker city, was the capital of a vast new province granted by King Charles II to one William Penn. This Penn was the 38 year old son of Admiral Penn of the British Navy and his Dutch wife. The younger Penn, an aristocrat with ruffles at his wrists and a sword at his side, turned Quaker in 1667 when he went into a meeting of the Friends of God in Cork. He heard the Irish minister Thomas Loe there, who spoke on the theme, "There is a faith that overcomes the world and a faith that is overcome by the world." Penn shed tears then and decided that day "rather to suffer affliction with the people of God than to enjoy the pleasures of sin."[11]

Admiral Penn, who died in 1670, never received from the Crown all his salary as a naval officer. He had also loaned the Crown money for naval purposes. This debt now totalled £16,000, and William Penn, the Admiral's heir, petitioned Charles II in 1680 for repayment. Instead of money, for the playboy king always needed money, Penn asked for a tract of land in America lying north of Maryland.[12] Charles granted the petition, and Penn promptly established the new province, Pennsylvania, as a haven for Friends, who were then being locked up wholesale in England's jails.

Shiploads of Quakers began to arrive in Philadelphia during December 1681, in packets that brought them over the Atlantic in eight weeks or so from London and Liverpool, Bristol, and Plymouth. Many of the broad-beamed vessels sailed on to Virginia to load tobacco after they discharged their Quaker passengers on the shores of the Delaware. Three thousand Friends—men, women and children—came in the first two years.[13] They came faster than the carpenters could build them houses. Many families lived for a time in caves dug into the Delaware River bank.

By the end of 1683, Philadelphia had 357 houses, some of clapboard and others red brick. This was ten times the size of any Virginia settlement. Incredibly, Penn met the Indian chiefs of the countryside in June 1683 under an elm tree by the river and insisted on *paying them* for the land! (He said later that Henry Compton, the Episcopal Bishop of London, had suggested it to him.) He sat on the ground with the Indians, ate roast acorns and hominy with them, and joined in a jumping contest with the young men![14] It caused much talk and head-shaking in Virginia.

\* \* \*

In (1681, Virginia's Governor Culpeper informed the Board of Trade that there was a congregation of "Sweet Singers" in the colony.[15] This was the first mention of any worshipers in Virginia beside the Quakers, outside the established church. For twenty-six years, until the Sweet Singers came along, the Quakers had been the only dissenter group. Nothing more is known about the Sweet Singers beyond this single notice of them.

Two years later, in 1683, still another kind of dissenters appeared in the Colony --Presbyterians. Presbyterianism as a form of Christian worship was practiced for three generations before Quakers appeared. The first Presbyterian was thundering John Knox of Scotland (ca. 1505-1572), who was first a Catholic priest, then a minister of the Church of England. He spent the years from 1553 to 1559 in Geneva, Switzerland, where he adopted certain views held by that stern reformer, John Calvin. Knox incorporated these views in a Confession of Faith, which was endorsed by Scotland's Parliament in 1560. He led the revolution that capsized the Catholic Church as Scotland's state church and put the Covenanters, the first Scots Presbyterians, in control of their country. "I fear the prayers of Knox more than an army of 10,000 men" said Mary, the Catholic Queen of Scots, before she was dethroned; and that saying is heard to this day in Presbyterian sermons.

Presbyterians and Quakers united in abhorring the Book of Common Prayer that played such a central part in established church worship. Otherwise, the Presbyterian approach to God varied radically from the Quakers' inward and silent way:

- Calvinist views about the depravity of humankind, of original sin and the fall of man, contrasted decidedly with the optimistic Quaker view of "that of God" in every person.
- Presbyterians retained two of the seven rites of the Catholic Church--baptism and the communion cup--as a means of achieving grace in this life and salvation in the next; whereas the Quakers, abandoning all seven rites, focused on the right living of one's life as the way to grace.
- The attitude toward women in the early Presbyterian church is suggested by the title of John Knox's pamphlet "The First Blast of the Trumpet against the Monstrous Regimen of Women"--a position that opposes the Quaker concept of equality of the sexes.
- Calvin's teaching of election and reprobation--that some people are singled out by God for salvation while all others are doomed--was particularly opposed by the Friends. George Fox, visiting near Loch Lomond in Scotland in 1657, noted in his journal:

> The priests had frightened people with the doctrine of election and reprobation, and said that the greatest part of men and women, let them pray or preach or sing and do what they could, it was all nothing if they were ordained for hell. So I was made to open to the people the folly of their priests' doctrines [by

saying] 'And doth not Christ say, Go preach the gospel to all nations...? He would not have sent them out into all nations to preach the doctrine of the salvation if the greatest part of men was ordained for hell.'"[16]

Francis Makemie (1658-1708) brought the Presbyterian idea to Virginia in 1683. He was a Scots-Irishman born in County Donegal and educated at the University of Glasgow. He formed Presbyterian congregations, first near Norfolk and later in Accomack County on the Eastern Shore. He married Naomi Anderson, daughter of a wealthy Eastern Shore merchant and became wealthy as a millowner and owner of Onancock's general store. Naomi's father gave the Makemies a substantial home called Dicher's Hall in Onancock. It was one of several Eastern Shore preaching points in Virginia and Maryland where Mr. Makemie held divine worship.

In his sermons, he presently began to attack the Quakers' tenets, and in 1691 he wrote a book of *Catechisms* that derided Quaker beliefs. The immediate result was a visit to Dicher's Hall by George Keith (1638-1716), Scottish Quaker and headmaster (then or recently) of the famous school in Philadelphia now called William Penn Charter School.

Now George Keith was no mere schoolmaster for he, like John Perrot, was to cause a schism in the Society of Friends; and his visit to Eastern Shore Virginia was no casual visit, for it seriously affected the course of Quakerism there.

Keith was born near Aberdeen and educated to be a Presbyterian minister. He was well-versed in theology and mathematics. At 25 Keith was a short, active compact man with a Scottish burr to his talk. He joined the Aberdeen Friends, and then for twenty-seven years was a leader among Friends. He associated with Robert Barclay in writing the *Apology*; bravely explained the Quakers' position before convocations of hostile Presbyterian divines; and took his share of beatings and imprisonments. In 1670, while in Aberdeen's prison, the Tolbooth, he wrote his *Benefit, Advantage and Glory of Silent Meetings*. There are immediate revelations nowadays--revelation did not end when the Bible was written is the book's main theme.

In 1684 Keith went with Fox, Penn and Barclay on a visit to Germany. Soon afterward, he was appointed Surveyor-General of East Jersey through William Penn's influence and came to live at Freehold, New Jersey with his wife Elizabeth and their two daughters. He laid out the boundary line between East and West Jersey. In 1689 the family moved to Philadelphia where George Keith became the first master of the Friends Public School.[17]

Until he came to Philadelphia, George Keith was in full unity with Friends. But then he began to voice some different views, tinged with his orthodox Presbyterian upbringing:
- He began to question whether Friends in their devotion to the Inward Christ were neglecting the outward historic Christ.
- The variety of views that Friends held so freely, began to bother him, and he drafted a Confession of Faith for Friends. All new members, he argued, should be required to conform to this Confession by answering yea or nay as each point was put to them.
- And not *all* Friends should be allowed to speak or pray in meeting, he said. That liberty should be reserved for those having "sound knowledge, experience and spiritual ability."[18]

Most Philadelphia Friends rejected these proposals as "downright Popery," but some that approved of them presently formed a distinct party within Philadelphia Yearly Meeting in support of George Keith. By and by they separated from the Yearly Meeting, calling themselves "*Christian Quakers.*"[19]

Notice now the reasons why John Perrot succeeded in leading some Quakers out of the Society of Friends and the reasons why George Keith did the same thing one generation later. They are absolutely different reasons:
- Perrot led his followers toward greater inwardness, saying that one's Inward Teacher should be followed unquestioningly without check or hindrance from any outward authority.
- Keith led in just the other direction, toward orthodox Christianity, the outward way, with its comfortable framework of pre-digested doctrine, and its corps of professional spiritual directors to mediate between the worshiper and God.

Ever since Perrot and Keith, one or the other of the two tendencies--toward inwardness on the one hand or toward outwardness on the other--have periodically appeared in the Society. While some Friends at some times seek universalism and greater personal freedom, some at other times reach toward uniformity and professional leadership.

The split in Philadelphia Yearly Meeting was just developing when George Keith sailed down to Onancock in 1691 to challenge Francis Makemie. John (or Gawen) Drummond, a Friend recently come from Scotland who was clerk of Guilford Creek Meeting near Onancock, joined him there. They knocked at the door of Dicher's Hall on a Saturday afternoon. Mr. Makemie met them, remarking tartly that he had expected them the day before, then led them into his parlor. The Scots dialect was spoken broad and broader, loud and louder, as the three men disputed that afternoon in Makemie's parlor.

At first Mr. Makemie must have been somewhat overwhelmed by the Quakers, for he refused to debate George Keith in public. In Makemie's words,

> He impudently charged me as a false teacher, and challenged me to a public debate before the multitude; which I scorned with sharp retorsion, and that for the following reasons:
>
> First, Their principles were unknown, because never unanimously agreed upon nor fairly published to the world; therefore not to be disputed in words. Second, We would dispute before an ignorant and illiterate multitude who would be most incompetent judges. Third, Because he would run into learning and I must follow, and so what should be delivered would not tend to their edification but fall to the ground and be lost.
>
> But afterward I gave him a challenge to oppose my Catechism and principles in writing.[20]

The tables turned, however, when word reached Mr. Makemie that George Keith was no longer in unity with most Philadelphia Friends. Makemie went to Philadelphia in August 1692 when the dispute between "Keithites" and the Yearly Meeting leaders was raging. On returning home to Onancock he published a gleeful account of the Quaker discord. He reported that the Philadelphia Quakers "fly out against Keith, calling him 'a reviler of the brethren', 'brat of Babylon' 'accuser of the brethren' 'one that always endeavoreth to keep down...Truth,'" and that Keith "pays them home again in the same coin and calls [them] 'fools', 'ignorant heathens', 'silly souls', 'liars', 'heretics', 'rotten ranters', 'Muggletonians', etc."[21]

George Keith's defection embarrassed Quakers everywhere and his visit to Onancock hurt the Eastern Shore Quakers. Hugh Roberts, a Quaker minister of Merion Meeting in Pennsylvania, wrote to William Penn in England:

> Well, let me and others write unto thee what we will, I think thee canst hardly believe that he is gone so bad as he [George Keith] is...Our Friends in Barbados, Virginia, Maryland, East and

# BECOME SOMEWHAT RESPECTABLE, 1677-1700

West Jersey, Long and Rhode Islands have given their judgment against George Keith and his spirit, and some eminent Friends from all these parts came here [to Philadelphia] to visit Friends, and all of us did hear their testimony against George Keith and his spirit [and] their testimony also of their great unity with Friends...."[22]

\* \* \*

Now the two kings during the Restoration of the British monarchy from 1660 to 1688, were the brothers Charles and James Stuart. They were sons of Charles Stuart I, king from 1625 until he was beheaded at Whitehall in 1649. It is well known that Charles I was a fervent Defender of the Faith, that is, of the Church of England. But it is not so well known that Charles I's wife, Henrietta Maria, was a fervent Catholic and the aunt of Louis XIV of France, leading Catholic of Europe in that time.

Before Henrietta Maria married, she wrote from the Louvre in Paris to Pope Urban VIII in Rome:

> Most Holy Father...there is nothing in the world so dear to me as the safety of my conscience and the welfare of my religion...I give you my sincere assurance and word...that if it shall please God to bless this marriage [to Charles of England] and give me children I shall choose none but Catholics to look after and bring up these children....
>
> Most Holy Father
> Your very devoted daughter, Henrietta Maria"[23]

And Henrietta Maria was as good as her word. She and her children celebrated Mass privately in the childrens' formative years; and when her sons grew up to be kings they were, publicly, Defenders of the Faith, that is, of the Church of England, and privately, Catholics!

And this odd arrangement at the very nerve-center of the British kingdom influenced the fortunes of the Virginia Quakers at the ragged far edge of that far-flung kingdom. Three times during the Restoration years, the Stuart brother kings tried to lift the laws that made criminals of Britons who worshipped outside the established Church, as Catholics or as Dissenters:

- In December 1662 Charles II issued a Declaration of Indulgence intended to set aside those laws. When it was sent to Governor Berkeley, Charles II wrote to Berkeley:

> "Because we are willing to give all possible encouragement to persons of different persuasion in matters of religion to transport themselves thither [to Virginia] with their stocks; you are not to suffer any man to be molested or disquieted in the exercise of his religion so he be content with a quiet and peaceable enjoying of it."[24]

Parliament voted down this Declaration two months later and the persecution of the Quakers resumed savagely. However, the two months provided a little temporary relief for Virginia's Quakers--as Thomas Jordan recalled when he wrote that "I was held in six weeks' imprisonment for being at a meeting in my own house *and released by the King's proclamation*."

- March 1672: Charles II tried again ten years later, when he issued a second Declaration of Indulgence. He pardoned 491 Friends then locked up in British jails--an event celebrated in Quaker annals as "the Great Pardon." But Parliament again refused to repeal the penal laws as Charles wished; and Charles was again humiliated. Friends had a second breathing spell, this time eleven months when non-conformity was allowed in England and her colonies. This explains why no one arrested George Fox and his Friends when they visited America and why Governor Berkeley allowed William Edmondson to depart in peace when Edmondson called on him in Jamestown.

James II became King when his brother Charles died in 1685 and

- In April 1687 James published still a third Declaration of Indulgence, which was received in Virginia that October. Virginia's governor then was Lord Francis Howard, Baron of Effingham, who was probably a quasi-secret Catholic himself. The Declaration pleased Lord Howard, for the minutes of his Council of 21 October 1687 record that "His Excellency was this day in Council pleased to acquaint the Council that he had received His Majesty's most gracious Declaration for Liberty of Conscience, which he is pleased to order to be published in James City on Tuesday next with the beat of drum and the firing of great guns."

Six months later, April 1688, the Virginia Assembly met and took up the matter of carrying out King James' Declaration. The House of Burgesses reviewed Virginia's laws that conflicted with the Declaration and actually passed a "Bill for Repealing the Act Prohibiting the Unlawful Assembly of

Quakers." Quakers across Virginia believed then that their long nightmare as outlaws was ending. But the Bill never became a law, for the Governor closed the Assembly before the Upper House could act on it. The legislators were so bitterly opposed to Governor Howard that they agreed with him on nothing.[25]

As it turns out, James II's Declaration of Indulgence ruined him. He announced that he was publishing it "by virtue of our royal prerogative...making no doubt of the concurrence of our two houses of Parliament when we shall think it convenient for them to meet." But James never again had a chance to call Parliament to meet, for England now was thoroughly and negatively aware that he was trying to replace Anglican with Catholic as England's official church.[26]

Seven English nobles in June 1688 visited Mary Stuart, James' Protestant daughter in Holland. They invited her and her husband, William of Orange, to bring an army of liberation to England. William was then the head of government of the Netherlands, and he and Mary were the leading Protestants of Europe. They accepted the invitation, coming to England with an army of 15,000 in November 1688. James fled to France; William and Mary became England's king and queen in February 1689, without a shot fired or a pike bloodied, and this was Britain's "Glorious Revolution."

With William and Mary enthroned, Parliament at last, after twenty-nine years of obstinate refusing, passed an Act of Toleration, May 1689. The act was a curious compromise that fell short of allowing religious liberty. The preamble explained that it provided only "some ease to scrupulous consciences in the exercise of religion...to unite their Majesties Protestant subjects in interest and affection." It excluded Catholics and anyone denying the doctrine of the Trinity from toleration. All tax payers, no matter where they went to church, were still required to pay for the support of the Church of England. And it forbade Quakers or other dissenters to witness in court, serve on a jury or hold Government offices without swearing an oath.[27]

Nevertheless, this Act of Toleration ended persecution under the Quaker Act and allied laws. After hundreds of years the state church in England was no longer required to practice cruelty on principle. In 1689 the British government half-admitted that it is humankind's incorrigible nature to worship God in differing ways.[28]

As for England's Quakers, their meetings were no longer illicit "conventicles" to be raided at the constables' pleasure. Suddenly they found themselves in calmer waters.

\* \* \*

Sadly and perversely, the Glorious Revolution and the Toleration Act brought *less* tolerance for Virginia's Quakers. Late in 1689 Howard of Effingham was replaced as Virginia's governor by Captain Francis Nicholson, 30--a hot tempered, high-handed bachelor, a rake but also a Tory devoted to the established Church. He somehow omitted to announce to Virginia's Assembly the passage of the Toleration Act, and it was not recognized in Virginia in 1689.

Governor Nicholson did, as one of his first acts, present to the Assembly a paper signed by the Bishop of London, which created the post of "Commissary" in Virginia. The Commissary was to be a sort of deputy bishop, to supervise the ministers of Virginia's forty-eight parishes. The man chosen to be Commissary was James Blair, 35, a Scot and a graduate of the University of Edinburgh. He had been in Virginia five years as rector of Varina Church, located near a new little community of Quakers at Curles in Henrico County.

In 1690, England was at war with France (the "War of the League of Augsburg" it was called in Europe, and "King William's War" in America). Governor Nicholson then reported to his Council that the Quakers of Pennsylvania had declared they would not fight if the French and Indians attacked Pennsylvania but instead would welcome them and feed them. He also said that Virginia's Quakers were not reporting their places of worship to the county courts; they were holding secret meetings; no one knew what plots they were hatching. This mixture of rumor and half-truth served to keep up public suspicion of the Colony's Quakers.

James Blair, for his first official communique as Commissary, sent out the following notice:

> Whereas the Right Reverend Father in God, Lord Bishop of London, taking into his consideration the great contempt of religion and dissoluteness of life and manners which are too visible within this Colony...for remedy and redress of the same has...appointed me, James Blair, his Commissary...

> Now know ye that I, the said James Blair...intend to revive and put in execution the Ecclesiastical Laws against all cursers, swearers and blasphemers, all whoremongers, fornicators and adulterers, all drunkards, ranters and profaners of the Lord's Day and contemners of the Sacraments, and against all other scandalous persons....

This was startling. The new Commissary was announcing a plan to resurrect in Virginia the kind of ecclesiastical courts that had long been abandoned in England. He was proposing to take away the county courts' jurisdiction over moral offenses and to transfer such cases to courts manned by judges of his own appointment and answerable solely to himself.[29] The language concerning "ranters," "profaners" and "contemners" meant that he planned to harry Virginia's Quakers in these church courts.

James Blair was a determined man. He remained as Commissary for fifty-three years until his death, and he accomplished many things during that time, including founding the College of William and Mary. He did not, however, succeed in setting up church courts, even with Governor Nicholson's backing. If he had, the cause of religious freedom would have suffered quite a set-back.

A few years later, Mr. Blair examined the mistaken ideas of Presbyterians and Deists, Catholics and Quakers. The Quakers, he explained, "usurp the liberty of following the unguarded dictates of the infallible spirit of God." Any people, he said, who disparage the Bible--meaning Quakers--"strike at the root of all revealed religion."

Some word about Parliament's Toleration Act of 1689 filtered through to Virginia, even though its passage was never announced by Governor Nicholson. In Henrico County, the Act was cited in the Court Order Book for 1690.[30] Gradually, an uneasy feeling developed in some Virginia sheriffs that Quaker-baiting no longer had firm official backing.

\* \* \*

In 1691 two visiting Quakers from England invoked the Toleration Act, perhaps for the first time in Virginia--Thomas Wilson, 37, and James Dickinson, 32, both from England's Lake Country. Thomas Wilson, "a little, dark-complexioned, black-haired, articulate man," was said to be "the most able and powerful [Quaker] minister of the Word of Life in the Age." Both of them wrote accounts of their visit to America, recounting that they spent two months in Barbados, after which they sailed to New York City and met with Friends there on Long Island, in New Jersey, Philadelphia, and Maryland. Then, Thomas Wilson wrote, "We...traveled to Virginia and had many good and comfortable meetings amongst them [and] we found a tender, humble people there." James Dickinson generally agreed in this appraisal of the Virginia Friends; but he also noted that "We warned them against the superfluous fashions of the world which too much prevailed amongst them, and judged against that spirit of [Keithian] separation amongst them."[31]

The two travelers went on from Virginia to North Carolina and "had good service...and hard travel, the country being so full of wild creatures that wolves would come and howl about the houses in the night time." Then they splashed back to Virginia a-horseback through flooded swamps, "and so traveled up James River, having meetings as we went until we came to Curles, where we had some meetings to satisfaction....We went from Curles through the woods to Black Creek [in New Kent County] where we had appointed a meeting...none having been there before."

This meeting at Black Creek was held outdoors in an orchard in the spring of 1691. It was a historic happening, because the two Quaker travelers invoked the Toleration Act that day in Virginia, and also because they convinced some families in that blooming New Kent orchard who remained faithful among the Virginia Friends for generations. As Thomas Wilson described it:

> The sheriff, with some officers, came to break it up. James Dickinson being then declaring, the sheriff asked him, from whom he had his commission to preach? James answered to this effect: 'I have my commission from the Great God, unto whom thou and I must give an account.'
>
> At which words the sheriff seemed much astonished; and after they had some further discourse, the sheriff swore, for which James reproved him....He answered, 'I know I should not swear' seeming then very mild, and said, we had a gracious king and queen [William and Mary] and they had given us our liberty [by the Toleration Act]. I then stood up and asked the sheriff a question: inasmuch as he had said, we had a gracious king and queen who had given us our liberty, which was true, by what law would the sheriff persecute us? He then turned about and went away; whereupon James Dickinson spoke aloud saying 'Let the sheriff answer the question.' But instead of doing this, he took the man of the house a little way off, and sent him back to bid us go off his land.
>
> I told him, we did not come here without his leave, and...had not broken the King's law, but were there upon a religious account,

and if they would have a little patience and hear what we had to say for the Lord, we would go peaceably away.

Most of the people stayed, and we had a heavenly meeting amongst them. Several were convinced, and in a short time after a meeting house was built....

After the said meeting at Black Creek, one Charles Fleming who had not been at any of our meetings before, kindly invited us to lodge with him, which we did; and from his house traveled towards Maryland....[32]

Nearly a year later in March of 1692, some Virginia Quakers sent a petition to the House of Burgesses. It was the first time in their history of thirty-seven years that the Virginia Friends had felt free enough to approach the government in Jamestown in this way. The petition asked the legislators to respect Friends' feelings about war and bloodshed. To us all people are brothers and sisters, the Friends explained. We are called to do to others as we would be done by. Therefore we cannot learn war. Please excuse us from musters and military duty, that was their petition.[33]

Two Friends of the new Curles Meeting brought the petition to Jamestown: John Pleasants, 48, and John Woodson, 34. Pleasants and Woodson were not typical farmer Friends. They were large landowners and merchants with warehouses on the deep water at the mouth of Four Mile Creek where it enters the James. John Pleasants was convinced of the Quaker way about 1680 when he married Jane Larcome Tucker, a sea captain's young widow who lived at Bermuda Hundred. His convincement was as complete as Paul's on the road to Damascus. Only three years earlier, in 1677, he and four other Henrico men had appeared before the King's Commissioners to complain that "the people are betrayed to the perfidy of the merciless Indians" and "it is our desire and request for your Honors that the war against all Indians in general be forthwith prosecuted."[34]

Henrico County's citizens had elected Pleasants to the House of Burgesses only the month before he handed in the Friends' petition to the House. He refused the honor, since it would have required him to take oaths of office. But he was well and favorably known to some Burgesses. The petition was referred to the House's Committee for Grievances and Propositions, and the Committee's chairman, Major Samuel Swann, soon reported back that the petition seemed reasonable! Major Swann recommended a new bill for regulating Virginia's militia which would have eased matters for the Quakers' young men; but the House did not agree. So nothing was done in response to the Quakers' plea in 1692.[35]

But the knowledge that some legislators respected their convictions was encouraging. So in 1696 John Pleasants carried a second Quaker petition to Jamestown, again asking relief from military duties. The Committee for Grievances and Propositions again recommended favorable action, and this time the House agreed and ordered a bill to be drawn up "imposing less fines than in the said Acts" of 1666 and 1684.[36]

\* \* \*

In the years following George Fox's visit, the Virginia Quakers gradually adopted the "good order" of monthly, quarterly and yearly meetings for business. Members of the six little meetings south of the lower James--Chuckatuck, Terrascoe Neck, Pagan Creek, Western Branch, Southern Branch and Somerton--began to meet together every three months, almost at once. Men and women held separate business meetings[37] and then came together for a time of quiet worship on these quarterly occasions. For a little time the quarterly meetings were held in the General Meeting house built at Chuckatuck; but this house, of which the Friends spoke so proudly, evidently was closed by the Nansemond sheriff about 1678.[38] For a good many years thereafter, the quarterly meetings were held in Friends' barns and orchards.

Early in the 1690s, the Friends on the *upper* James also began to meet quarterly with delegates from Curles and New Kent, joined a little later by Friends from Merchant's Hope and Burleigh, White Oak Swamp, Skimino and Warwick Meetings. Then the older, down-river grouping was called "Lower Quarterly Meeting" or "the Lower Quarter," and the newer "the Upper Quarter."

In October 1696 the Upper Quarter sent representatives to a meeting of the Lower Quarter. This, it seems, was the beginning of Virginia Yearly Meeting. The 62-year-old patriarch Thomas Jordan of Chuckatuck was the clerk of this meeting. Friends met on Thomas Tooke's plantation, near James River and near the county line between Isle of Wight and Surry Counties.

No doubt, one item of business was the petition that John Pleasants took to Jamestown that same month in 1696. Another item had to do with Friends' determination not to pay taxes for support of the established

Church. As Thomas Jordan wrote to London: "For the most part, they put the priests, wages into the country [general] taxes, so that it's obscure to Friends what they take per poll for the priests."[39]

\* \* \*

Francis Nicholson governed Virginia from 1690 to 1692 and then was succeeded by Sir Edmund Andros. Sir Edmund's six year tenure in Virginia was uneventful. During his administration in Virginia, Francis Nicholson served as the King's governor in Maryland. When Andros retired in 1698, Nicholson returned to govern Virginia.

Nicholson's first act as governor of Maryland had been to put through a law which made the Church of England the *established* church in the colony. A little later he picked a political fight with William Penn. He corresponded with one Robert Snead, a disgruntled magistrate in Pennsylvania. "Here is no living for those that are not Quakers," Snead wrote, and "I wish I were out of this Government." Snead then related the faults in Pennsylvania's government to Nicholson. And William Penn wrote to Nicholson 22 November 1697, accusing him of spying and sending derogatory information on to London about Pennsylvania's affairs.

One day in May of 1698, shortly before leaving Maryland and returning to Virginia, Governor Nicholson dictated to his secretary seventeen pages of memoranda about colonial problems: the state of the clergy; collecting custom duties at the ports along Chesapeake Bay; the need for a frigate to cruise the Bay and keep order; trouble caused by certain "incendiaries in the [Maryland] House of Delegates" who were "setting up to be lawyers"; "how to prevent the French King's design which apparently tends to compass us in round and to lay an ambush behind all the King's Colonies on ye Continent of America"; and the manufacturing of consumer goods in America, a practice contrary to "the interest of England." About half of the seventeen pages, however, are taken up with problems relating to Maryland's Papists and to Quakers both in Maryland and Pennsylvania:

- As for Papists, Nicholson dictated "that the Papists being our professed enemies and joining together against us...It is proposed that if it can be granted they may not have so large a liberty as now they enjoy."
- As for Maryland's Quakers he spoke of them as "enemies to our church." "Query," he dictated, "Whether their books and papers may not be seized in order to make further discoveries." He also noted that "Richard Johns, a principal Quaker of Maryland [and, incidentally, an

ancestor of Johns Hopkins] when in England this last year...complimented Lord Baltimore about his coming again into Maryland, it being a talk among some of them that he should be again restored ye Governor."

- And as for Pennsylvania's Quakers and William Penn in particular, Governor Nicholson listed many grievances--their harboring of runaway servants and seamen--the manufactures they set up "with which in time they will supply the needs of that Province"--"the partial and foul judgments of the Quaker Justices"--William Penn's efforts to replace Nicholson as governor of Maryland--and the long dispute about the Maryland-Pennsylvania boundary line.[40]

When Nicholson returned to Virginia in 1698 he was greeted cordially in Jamestown by Commissary Blair, who had not gotten along well with Governor Andros. Nicholson and Blair had a falling out in later years, but in the 1690s they were allies. Mr. Blair took a seat in the Governor's Council--the first clergyman to be so honored. He and Governor Nicholson began again their planning to discourage Virginia's dissenters. Mr. Blair soon set up quarterly gatherings of all Virginia's ministers to "exercise their talents by set discourses of every man in his turn, against Popery, Quakerism, or any other prevailing heresy, as also in explications of Scripture."[41]

\* \* \*

Francis Makemie, the Presbyterian minister, boated over from Onancock to Jamestown in April 1699 just at the beginning of that year's General Assembly. He came to petition the Governor for the rights granted to dissenters in England under the Toleration Act of 1689. Mr. Makemie according to the Council's minutes

> Prayed that a proclamation may issue declaring the freedom and liberty of conscience that is allowed by the laws of England, and forbidding all persons whatsoever to interrupt any sect of dissenters in the free and open exercise of religion....
>
> The said Makemie was called into the Council Chamber and His Excellency [Nicholson] by advice of the Council was pleased to let him know that all dissenters under his government shall have such liberty allowed them as the law directs, provided they use it civilly

and quietly...which is all the encouragement they can or should expect from him.[42]

This appearance by Francis Makemie forced the hands of Nicholson and Blair. A few days later, ten years after the fact, Virginia's Assembly finally took notice of Parliament's Toleration Act. Quaker meetings and Presbyterian church services were at last within the law, and Quakers and Presbyterians henceforward were allowed to vote.[43] Clearly the struggle for liberty of worship in Virginia took a new and hopeful turn in 1699.

\* \* \*

In spite of the newly noticed law, Nicholson and Blair continued their Quaker-quashing efforts. From the minutes of the Governor's Council, 30 May 1699:

> Whereas divers complaints have been made of the evil and seditious practices used in several parts of the country by the people called Quakers: therefore ordered, that it be recommended to Mr. Commissary Blair to consider the most proper methods for preventing the like for the future.[44]

Commissary Blair at the June Council meeting urgently recommended another investigation of Quakers. Council then ordered the county sheriffs to obtain "an exact account of what private and public meetings of any other religion than the Church of England as by law established, are kept in their respective counties, where...and what persons resort thereto, what particular religion they are of, how their preachers are qualified; and whether any wandering strangers came in to their counties as preachers or upon any pretense of religion whatsoever?"[45]

But the results of this inquiry appear never to have been reported, and no expose of evil and seditious Quaker practices ever was published.

THE REV. GEORGE KEITH.

George Keith (1638-1716) was a fiery Scot, an early companion of George Fox, who changed his mind about the Quaker way after Fox's death. In 1691 Keith visited Virginia in behalf of the Society of Friends. Eleven years later he re-visited, to promote the Church of England.

# V

# AT LAST WITHIN THE LAW
# 1700-1733

> There is a great opening in the hearts of people here in Virginia, and our Meetings doth increase.
> -- Isaac Ricks and Daniel Sanbourne of Virginia Yearly Meeting
> to London Friends, January 1700

Beginning in 1700, Virginia's Children of the Light no longer were outlaws. They no longer needed to brace themselves for the sheriffs' men come to break up their silent worship. It was a happier, serener thing to sail to worship on a First Day morning, without the chance of being arrested.

Twenty Quaker groups or "meetings" gathered in the Tidewater and on the Eastern Shore in 1700. Most of them met on the home place of some member who lived along a creek or river. The worshipers gathered in the great room of the house, or in the barn, or outside the house on fine days under the blue sky.

The Virginia Quakers of 1700 sat down on First Day mornings in a rough, neighborly circle. No priest or professional religious person was present since, as they said, "Christ sits at the head of the Meeting." A quiet then fell over the circle. The men and women, boys and girls, freed their minds of workaday cares. Sometimes nothing came. Sometimes a leading, an insight, an inspiration, a concern came to a Friend in the circle. Then the Friend broke the silence, speaking to the condition of the others there. The messages out of the silence dealt with God and goodness, temptation and despair, mercy, justice and kindness, simplicity and honesty and freedom and faithfulness, fairness, and what it is to be at peace. Many of the messages related to Bible passages. They came variously from women and men, from oldsters and earnest teen-agers, from mothers and budding maidens. After some messages the quiet somehow deepened, and the circle knit and gathered in a kind of solemn joy. Thus they ministered to one another, in Virginia in 1700.

Their neighbors knew them as people who wore the plainest clothes, said "thee" instead of "you," kept silence or spoke "as the spirit of the heart moved" and held war to be a curse from hell. They were a peculiar, friendly, obstinate, truthful people. They found some thing of God in the people around them and so they made good neighbors. It was hard for their neighbors to understand what made them do as they did, but they did make good neighbors.

\* \* \*

The Virginia Quakers throve after 1700 although they were still subject to quite a few legal penalties. In 1700, seven of their twenty Meetings were brand new, having sprung up about the time the Toleration Act was recognized in the Colony. The seven new meetings were held in the homes of members, on the banks of the great Virginia rivers: Binford's, Butler's, Lawne's Creek, and Weyanoke Meetings along James River; Skimino Meeting on York River; White Oak Swamp Meeting high up the Chickahominy; and William Duff's Meeting up Rappahannock River.

Of the thirteen older meetings, only six had meetinghouses built specifically for Quaker worship: two on the Eastern Shore, called Guilford Creek (or Muddy Creek) and Nassawaddox Meeting houses, and four along James River, the Chuckatuck, Pagan Creek, Merchant's Hope and Curles Meeting houses. The other seven meetings still gathered in members' homes in 1700: Black Creek Meeting in New Kent County, Nansemond Meeting on the south branch of Nansemond River, Somerton, Terrascoe Neck, Warwick, Levin Bufkin's, and Western Branch (of Nansemond River).

The meeting houses were only plain little clapboard and shingle buildings. Curles Meeting house, rebuilt in 1696, was 30 by 20 feet. Two new houses were built in 1702: at Levin Bufkin's Meeting, 20 by 20 feet and at Western Branch, 25 by 20. Western Branch Meeting house cost 3,200 pounds of tobacco.[1] It was built on an acre, "the old field of Francis Hutchins's, by the highway side," near present day Isle of Wight Court House. Abraham and Robert Ricks, sons of Virginia Yearly Meeting's clerk, did most of the carpentry. Frances Denson, Will's widow, and her sons James and John gave 1,300 pounds of tobacco. Francis Bridle supplied the nails.

The little meeting houses were not considered to be sanctuaries or especially holy places. Each of them was, however, the center of a caring community--where friendships were made, young men and women fell in love, where children had first thoughts about high things and all joined in a serious search for the will of God.

This sudden new blossoming after the Toleration Act was shared by the Quaker movement in the colonies north and south of Virginia. Friends' Meetings were established by 1700 in all four New England colonies--Massachusetts, Connecticut, New Hampshire and Rhode Island. The governor of Rhode Island, Walter Clarke, was a Friend. In the Middle Colonies, Pennsylvania's "Holy Experiment" in government was well under way. East and West Jersey were under Quaker control. The Quakers of Maryland and New York, especially on Long Island, had considerable influence. In North Carolina, the Society of Friends was the only organized religious entity, and John Archdale, Quaker, was the governor. In South Carolina there were Quaker stirrings too. Joseph West, the governor there from 1671 to 1684, was a friend of the Friends.[2] About 330,000 colonials lived in America in 1700, and an estimated 30,000 of them were members of the Society of Friends.[3]

Most of the dissenting religious groups that sprang up during the God-drunk 1600s disappeared soon after their founders died. It is noteworthy that the Quaker movement did not fade after George Fox died in London in 1691. In his lifetime George certainly had a major part in inspiring and guiding Friends in England and America. Beside his visit to America in 1672, he wrote two or three letters a year for thirty-two years to various American Friends--eighty-eight letters in all. "Follow the Light," he wrote. "Be valiant for the Truth, spread it abroad. Keep your meetings and live together in unity." And "Let the Light shine among the Indians and Blacks."[4]

He urged Friends in one of his last letters, in 1688, not to use the names of days or months that commemorate the heathen gods. Instead, he advised, say "First Day" for Sunday, "Fourth Day" for Wednesday, "First Month" for January, and so on.[5]

On his deathbed in 1691, nearly the last thing George said was "Mind poor Friends in Ireland and America" and he said it twice over.

\* \* \*

The rise of the Quakers concerned Virginia's upper class. Captain Hugh Campbell visited Governor Nicholson to discuss the situation. The Captain proposed to establish three Anglican churches, at North River in Norfolk, at Somerton in southern Nansemond and at Blackwater in Isle of Wight County. He offered to buy 200 acres for each church and its glebe house (rectory), and a Bible. His purpose doubtless was to counter the rising Quaker influence south of the James. Governor Nicholson for his part promised to allot part of the proceeds from marriage licenses and tavern keepers' licenses in the three counties to the three churches.[6]

In London the Reverend Dr. Thomas Bray persuaded the Bishop of London in 1698 to organize the Society for Propagating Christian Knowledge (SPCK). Dr. Bray had been the Anglican Church's Commissary in Maryland when Francis Nicholson was governor there, and the two men between them had persuaded Maryland's legislature to name the Anglican Church as Maryland's established church. A principal purpose of the SPCK in the colonies, according to Dr. Bray, was to convert "the Quakers who are so numerous in those parts to the Christian faith, from which they are totally apostatized and so may be looked upon as a heathen nation."[7]

The very first missionary recruited by Dr. Bray was George Keith, disowned by the Friends of London Yearly Meeting in 1695 and ordained an Episcopal priest in London in 1700. In summer 1702 Keith came to America, representing a branch of SPCK called the Society for Propagating the Gospel in Foreign Parts (SPG), later known as the Venerable Society. To convert as many Quakers as possible, he traveled the colonies for two years from New Hampshire to Carolina. He distributed anti-Quaker literature and delivered hundreds of sermons laced with anti-Quaker rhetoric. Often he entered Friends' meeting houses along with local Anglicans, challenging the Friends to debate him. The victory in these debates seems to have gone to the side whose account we read.

Keith's usual charge was that Friends believe the Inward Light is a sufficient guide "without anything else." The Friends' usual reply was that they believe all the Scriptures say about Christ, but that the inner experience is the essential thing.[8]

The Reverend Mr. Keith happened upon a traveling Friends' minister, John Richardson of Yorkshire, in Lynn, Massachusetts, in July 1702. The two men debated in the Friends' meeting house there for two hot days, and both wrote about it in their journals:

- Keith says he read "the vile errors" of Edward Burrough, and was answered by John Richardson with "falsehoods and impertinences and gross perversions of Scripture."
- Richardson says he interrupted Keith while Keith was ridiculing Burrough and Fox and "said to him loudly that all the meeting might hear, 'Thee offers violence to that sense and understanding which God has given thee...and [will have] trouble from the Lord in thy conscience.' I spoke in the Lord's dreadful power and George trembled so much as I seldom

ever saw a man do." According to Richardson, another of Keith's outrageous assertions was that Quaker women sometimes "did salute men," that is greet them with a kiss.[9]

Keith came to America with a letter of introduction to Governor Nicholson. The governor welcomed Keith and his companion, the Reverend Mr. John Talbot, when they arrived in Virginia 18 April 1704. The pair are not known to have invaded any Virginia Friends' meetings during their ten weeks' stay, but Governor Nicholson and Commissary Blair arranged for them to preach in many Anglican churches where they doubtless attacked the tenets of Friends. Governor Nicholson paid fifty-six pounds for a supply of anti-Quaker pamphlets for Mr. Keith to distribute. No Virginia or North Carolina Friends are known to have left their meetings at Keith's call. No doubt, however, his visit concerned the Quakers of both colonies.[10]

At the end of his visit in Virginia, Mr. Keith stayed ten days with his daughter Anne and her husband George Walker at Kickatan (Hampton). George Walker was a staunch Quaker. He and Anne had married after the manner of Friends when Keith was still a Quaker in good standing. After Keith turned from Friends to the Church of England, Anne turned too. This caused considerable tension in the Walker household, since George Walker insisted on raising the Walkers' children as Friends.

\* \* \*

Anglicans were not the Quakers' only critics. That summer of 1704, four German-speaking Swiss sisters named Lerber were living at Gloucester Church, across York River from Yorktown. They were recently come from Bern, and one of the sisters had promised to marry young Johan Rudolph Ochs. Ochs also was a Bernese immigrant. He and his bride-to-be were full of plans for their future life. Among other things, they decided to cast their lot with the Quakers. The devout older sister of the bride-to-be, Maria Elisabet Lerber, was disturbed knowing nothing about Quakers. She wrote to Johannes Kelpius living near Philadelphia, to ask his opinion. Maria's letter was dated 23 August 1704, and Kelpius sent his twenty-two-page reply on October 10. Both letters are in German.[11]

Kelpius, 31, came to Pennsylvania with forty-five other young German men to await the Millennium. For a short time after their arrival in 1694 they lived among the German Quakers of Germantown. Then Kelpius led the forty-five a few miles west to live as hermits in the wilderness on the ridge between Wissahickon Creek and the Schuylkill River. "Roxborough," that Philadelphia enclave, is named for Kelpius's anchorite cell or cave, described as a "burrough of rocks." The first oil portrait painted in America depicts Kelpius in 1705, clean-shaven, his hand on his forehead reading, in a monk's robe and a knit cap.* He and his company there by the Wissahickon called themselves the Society of the Woman of the Wilderness, an occult brotherhood.

They were Rosicrucians with an other-worldly view of things--waiting in the forest as bridegrooms for the Woman Clothed in the Sun, the Woman in the Wilderness mentioned in the Book of Revelations,** coming as a harbinger of the world's end. The woman was "to come up from the Wilderness leaning on her beloved," according to Kelpius. So the beloved waited there and "they did well to observe the signs of the times and every new phenomenon of meteors, stars or colors of the skies if peradventure the Harbinger may appear." They kept a watch through every night with a telescope so as to be ready if the Woman came before sunrise.[12] They believed in a three-step progression of holiness--the barren, the fruitful and the wilderness state of the Elect of God. To be Elect it is necessary to dwell in the wilderness. Moses became elect by dwelling forty years in the wilderness; Jesus was tempted forty days in the wilderness; John the Baptist came from the wilderness.[13]

Kelpius began his letter to Maria Lerber by remarking that *all* the sects, the Friends included, have *some* excellence. Then he criticizes the Friends for saying "He is come, Friends, we bide none other!" The truth is he says, "You [Quakers] have indeed received a glimpse of [Christ's] beauty through His spirit in your hearts. But never yet have ye seen the Lord of Glory *himself*." And he asks "If ye be the holy people, God's only people, whence comes it that the number of...sinners among you is far greater than the number of the just?" If you want to join the Elect, he concludes, you must "come into the wilderness."

So then in 1704, here stands the Reverend Mr. George Keith in clerical collar and parson's gaiters, berating Friends for failing to be Bible-based orthodox Christians; and there stands Magister Johannes Kelpius in his monk's robe, calling Friends "to the wilderness." Keith and Kelpius at the two poles of the tension, the dynamic tension that has characterized the Society of Friends through all its history.

---

\* Owned by the Historical Society of Pennsylvania.

\*\* Revelations 12.6 and 12.14

As for Johan Ochs and his bride, they went ahead and married and apparently joined Friends in London in 1705. They lived out their lives in England and in Urbanna, Virginia, and had five sons.[14]

\* \* \*

Virginia was growing at the close of the 1600s. The population stood at about 40,000 in 1670 (including some 2,000 slaves). In 1700, the estimate was 70,000 (with 8,000 slaves). After 31 October 1698, when the State House in Jamestown burned down, Governor Nicholson decided to establish a better capital. Four years earlier he had been praised for moving Maryland's capital from St. Mary's City to Annapolis. Now in Virginia he chose Middle Plantation, seven miles from Jamestown and a higher, healthier spot.

William and Mary College's first building, designed by Christopher Wren, was going up on 330 acres just west of Middle Plantation. James Blair, the Commissary, raised the money for the College in London in 1691, and he was its president from 1693 on for fifty years. Although the Wren building was not completely built in 1699, Governor Nicholson arranged with James Blair for it to house Virginia's legislature and government offices "temporarily" until the colony's new capitol building could be built. But the new capitol was not readied for five years, until 1704. By that time Nicholson and Blair, close friends in 1699, were open enemies. The Wren Building was too small both for college classes and the colony's governance, and five years of stumbling over one another irritated all concerned. The falling out between the two men may explain why Mr. Blair's recommendation, made in 1699, to investigate Virginia's Quakers never was pursued.[15]

Also, Governor Nicholson's attitude toward Friends changed within a year or two after the move from Jamestown to Middle Plantation, now renamed Williamsburg. In May 1699, he still looked upon Friends with dark disfavor. That month he refused to deal with Daniel Akehurst and George Walker, Quakers. They had been sent to Williamsburg by the Quaker deputy governor of North Carolina, Thomas Harvey, to settle the boundary line between the two colonies. Nicholson sent the two emissaries back to Harvey with a note, "We think the gent appointed by you are not sufficiently qualified because it does not appear that they have taken the Oath or been approved by His Majesty, per the Act of 1697."[16]

But in 1701 Governor Nicholson visited Maryland and lodged at the house of Richard Johns--the very same Friend he had called an "enemy" in

1698. John Richardson, the Friends' minister, was a guest there too. As John Richardson tells in his journal,

> I was also in company with the governor of Virginia, at our friend Richard Johns' house upon the west cliffs of Maryland, for we both lodged there one night...I heard that he had been studious in a book against Friends called the Snake and Friends desired he might have the answer called the Switch....I said to him I had heard that he had seen a book called the Snake in the Grass; he confessed he had. I desired he would accept of the answer and be as studious in it as he had been in The Snake; which he promised he would and took the book.*

John Richardson also recounted an incident told him by a Friend in Maryland, which happened "either in his [Nicholson's] or the preceding governor's time in Virginia," and which possibly indicates a dawning respect for Quaker ways in Nicholson's mind:

> The governor wanted a cooper to mend his wine, cider and ale casks, and some told him there was a workman near, but he was a Quaker. [He] said, if he is a workman, it made no matter what he professed; so the Quaker, such as he was, was sent for and came with his hat under his arm.
> The governor was somewhat at a stand to see the man come in after that manner and asked if he was the cooper he had sent for. He said 'Yes.'
> 'Well' said the Governor, 'are you not a Quaker?'
> 'Yes' replied the man, 'I am so called, but I have not been faithful.'
> He then asked 'How long have you been called a Quaker?'
> The poor man said 'About 20 years.'
> 'Alas for you, poor man' said the governor, 'I am sorry for you.'[17]

---

* *The Snake in the Grass* was published anonymously in 1696. It is a collection of writings adverse to Quakers. Joseph Wyeth wrote *A Switch for the Snake* published in 1699 as the Quakers' answer.

Twice more thereafter, Quaker travelers reported friendly interviews with Governor Nicholson. In May 1705 Esther Palmer and Mary Banister visited Virginia from England in Truth's service. Esther noted in her journal,[18] "Called at ye Governor's (at his request) who treated us kindly."[19] For 26 July 1705, Thomas Story, also from England, noted:[20]

> I called at Williamsburg to see Colonel Nicholson, then governor, who was kind beyond expectation. The governor and I discoursed for some time on various subjects...liberty of conscience in matters of religion...that all people who are of opinion they ought to pay their preachers should pay their own, and not exact pay from others...of the Kingdom of Christ on earth, which is in the world but not of the world...that the kingdoms of men ought not to interfere with the kingdom of Christ....Though the Governor was attached to the national church and its interest, he heard with candour and took no offense.[21]

So Francis Nicholson went from enmity to a more tolerant view of Friends during his time as Virginia's governor. His change typifies the changing attitude of many people in the colonies in those years.

\* \* \*

Esther Palmer and Thomas Story were only two of some fifteen Friendly ministers who visited Virginia's twenty meetings in the yeasty years from 1695 to 1705. They were young, these travelers, from the 23-year-old seaman Thomas Chalkley to 41-year-old William Ellis. Most came from old England with a few from New England, Long Island, Pennsylvania, North Carolina. All of them came from the generation after George Fox's. Typically they combined a reverence for the Inward Light with a detailed knowledge of the Bible.

They also combined a serious view of the creation with a kind of solemn humor. John Salkeld (1672-1739), in Virginia in 1701, had an irrepressible sense of humor:

- He once sprang to his feet during meeting for worship after noticing some worshipers dozing. "Fire, fire!" he shouted. Everyone was awake immediately, and many asked "Where?" "In hell!" John responded, "to burn up the drowsy and unconverted."

- As he emerged from his cornfield in Chester County, Pennsylvania, a passer-by named Cloud remarked, "John, thee will have a good crop of corn." Salkeld, afterward relating the incident, said "I heard a voice coming out of a Cloud, saying 'John, thee will have a good crop of corn.'"[22]

Several of the fifteen travelers kept journals. They recorded perilous adventures--capsized in boats, lost in the virgin Virginia forests, and challenged by skeptics:

- William Ellis (1658-1709) wrote in 1699 "About Chuckatuck there are many Friends, and several are under exercise that Truth may increase, but there is too much indifference amongst some."[23]
- John Richardson (1667-1753) recalled the case of a young Puritan woman, the housekeeper of Quaker Matthew Jordan of Chuckatuck, who took offense when she heard Richardson say "something about election," but when the housekeeper came to the next meeting to rebuke Richardson "the Lord's mighty power broke in upon us, to the tendering of many hearts." As for the young woman "her heart was as if it had melted within her'" and she was convinced to join Friends.[24]
- Elizabeth Webb (1663-1726) recounted an insight she had while sitting in the little circle of worshipers at James Howard's Meeting in Charles City County: "Here a great sense of ye great work of God came weightily upon me and I covenanted with ye Lord that if he would be pleased to make way for me and give me a suitable companion I would give up my days in his service." A little later, she reporting having a dream which made her see "that the call of God is to the black as well as the white."[25]

The most complete of these journals was written by Thomas Story (1663-1742). He visited Virginia twice--for three months in 1698 and 1699 and two and a half months in 1705. He was a son of a wealthy Anglican family of Carlisle, England, and brother of an Anglican clergyman. Educated as a lawyer, he stopped wearing his sword and joined Friends when he was 28.

Thomas Story began his first voyage to Virginia with twenty days of waiting for fair weather in Thames River, followed by seventy-two winter days of sailing the Atlantic. The ship was the *Providence of London*, William Cant, a Quaker, her captain. She finally limped through the Virginia Capes and anchored in Mobjack Bay 10 March 1698.

Next morning, Story and his companion Roger Gill took the *Providence's* long boat up York River, sailing and rowing all day and night to reach Bangor House on Queens Creek near Williamsburg. That was the homeplace of Quaker Edward Thomas. Arriving at 5 a.m. on March 12, they rested there a few hours and then took horses to tour Virginia. On the Lower Neck, between York and James Rivers, they held Friends' meetings at Warwick River, Skimino Creek, Black Creek, and at the now-long-gone palisaded town of Martin's Hundred. At Skimino, Thomas Story convinced John Bates and his family "of the Truth," and the Bateses were a power among Virginia Friends for four generations thereafter.

After two weeks on the Lower Neck, three Friends from Chuckatuck came in a boat to ferry Story and Gill south over James River. They stayed first in the Terrascoe Neck Friends' community. Old John Copeland, whose right ear had been cut off by the Boston Puritans thirty years before, was their host. Then they visited Chuckatuck, Western Branch, and Southern Branch Meetings, and Somerton Meeting (which Thomas Story calls "Barbican, being the last meeting in Virginia toward Carolina)."

In North Carolina, Story writes, "we were respectfully received and entertained by the lieutenant-governor [Quaker John Harvey], I having brought letters to the governor [Quaker John Archdale] from England." They held meetings for ten days in North Carolina settlements (which in those days all were located in the six northeastern counties between the Great Dismal Swamp and Albemarle Sound) and were pleased that some black people came to the meetings.

Returning to Virginia, Story and Gill went up James River to Friends at Merchant's Hope and Curles, then north to isolated Friends living high up the Pamunkey and Mattaponi Rivers. They came upon a poor Chickahominy Indian town of eleven wigwams and ministered there, although some tough white men disturbed the worship. Then returning to Yorktown they held a Friends meeting on the evening of 23 May 1699, in the house of a man named Bonger.

Roger Gill died during their travels and Thomas Story was sad. He went on alone to visit Eastern Shore Virginia and was saddened more to find things out of order at Nassawaddox Meeting, with "Friends intermarrying and intermixing with the world." However he was cheered by two large, powerful meetings he attended at Guilford Creek.

In the spring of 1705, Thomas Story came back to Virginia for his second visit. On June 17 he rode eleven miles through a thunderstorm near Somerton--"the fire and water seemed commixed in their descending on us, and the thunder sharp and sonorous and so near as if it had been bombs splitting among us. I...looked back several times to see if any were slain behind...a stifling smell of sulphur." On June 20, he encountered an "opposer," an Anglican minister with a French accent named James Burtell.

This Mr. Burtell came to a Friends' gathering at Terrascoe Neck especially to critique what Thomas Story had to say. Thomas spoke out of the silence that day of "a necessity for freedom from sin in this life in order to fit us for the Kingdom of God"--reflecting George Fox's conviction that a person who obeys the Inward Light will be freed from sin. Mr. Burtell sharply disagreed, arguing instead that all humans are sinners until some of us at death are chosen to enter the kingdom of heaven. Both men quoted numerous Bible texts. The dispute went on until nightfall.

Mr. Burtell was not satisfied. He challenged Thomas Story to another dispute, with the date set for July 5 in Colonel Bridger's house near Chuckatuck. (This was neutral ground, for Colonel William Bridger like his father, Colonel Joseph before him, was both a friend of the Friends and a vestryman of the local Anglican parish. William Bridger's wife, Elizabeth, was so attached to Friends that she refused to swear for legal purposes but rather affirmed after the Quaker manner.)[26]

Thomas Story arrived at Bridger's, at the appointed time, with Joseph Glaister, a local Friends' minister and a shoemaker by trade. They found there a large auditory of all ranks of people...six justices of the peace, several colonels, majors, captains and other military officers, lawyers and others." It was immediately arranged for Joseph Glaister and Mr. Andrew Monro, an elderly Anglican minister and colleague of Mr. Burtell, to engage in a preliminary dispute before the Burtell-Story main event.

The first two points Glaister and Monro argued were water baptism and the possibility of becoming free from sin in this life. When they were about to begin the third argument, whether Christ's apostles ever took money in pay for their ministry, Monro said faintly, "Mr. Glaister. You are a much younger man than I am and stronger. I confess you have a close way of reasoning, though I think I have the truth on my side but can hold out no longer." He then retired from the fray, calling for a pipe of tobacco and a tankard of ale. The afternoon was so far gone then that the two principals, Burtell and Story, did not debate that day.

On July 10 Burtell and Story met again at the house of Thomas Jordan III. (This place also was neutral ground, for Jordan was the eldest of the ten sons of old Thomas Jordan, Jr., the Chuckatuck Friend--the only one of the ten sons who left Friends to "go into the world." Although Thomas III was a politician and magistrate, he was sympathetic to the Quaker way and sometimes entertained traveling Friends in his home. *His* oldest son, Thomas Jordan IV, after being a magistrate and man of the world for a time, joined Friends in later years.)

Many people came to hear the July 10 dispute, arriving at the appointed time of 9 a.m. and waiting until James Burtell arrived at noon. Burtell attacked at once, asking, "Why do not you the people called Quakers use the Lord's prayer in your assemblies? ...They who do not use it are no Christians, but you never use it." To which Thomas Story replied "...though we do not use the very words of that prayer in our meetings, as the manner of some is, yet we *sometimes* use it verbatim, and *often* the sum of it in other terms." Burtell retorted, "I never heard you; and who else ever did?" Then, as Story reports it, "arose a voice and cloud of witnesses, both Friends and others, saying 'I have; I have, I have. 'Oh, then' Burtell said, 'I have nothing more to say on that account.'

Story and Burtell argued next whether Christian ministers should receive pay for their labors in the Anglican manner, or should not, in the Quaker manner. And they ended the day by arguing whether baptism by water or baptism by the Holy Spirit is preferable. The last words were said late in the afternoon, "all the company being very grave and silent."

Two days later, on July 12, Major Jordan told Thomas Story "that he had heard since the last dispute that we had 50 to one on our side among the people, and that it was thought most of them were turning Quakers." Story replied "I am glad, but think I had rather hear they are turned than turning; for the Cross is hard for many...who are truly convinced but not obedient, because of the glory and friendship of the world."

\* \* \*

Virginia's Quakers raised ministers of their own who began to travel in the service of Truth after 1700. These "public Friends" were farmers, or craftsmen like Joseph Glaister, or housewives. They were distinguished among other Friends only because they proved able to rise from their seats and "speak to the condition" of the silent little assemblies. They were not specially trained in accordance with George Fox's insight related in his *Journal* thus:

> As I was walking in a field on a First day morning, the Lord opened it to me that being bred at Oxford or Cambridge was not enough to fit and qualify men to be ministers of Christ."[27]

Friends looked upon their ministers as spiritually gifted persons especially in touch with that of God within them. They were thought less to speak for themselves, than as mouthpieces whose messages came from God. When the meeting was inspired by a speaker, Friends said afterward, "We heard the shout of the King today!"

At first the ministers sat in the circle of worshipers. Then the circle fell out of favor and "facing benches" appeared, elevated on a low platform at one end of the meetinghouse and fronted by a railing. There the ministers sat facing the body of the meeting. Still later, elders began to sit on the facing benches with the ministers. Their duty was to "oversee" the vocal ministry, whether it came from the facing benches or from the body of the meeting. The elders encouraged promising young speakers and restrained or corrected ill-advised ones.[28]

James Bates (1650-1723) of Skimino is the first Virginia minister known to travel outside the colony. John Richardson, the English Quaker, having met James Bates at Virginia Yearly Meeting at Pagan Creek in September 1701, invited James to come along with him; and James journeyed north to Nantucket Island with Richardson. They held a meeting there at Mary Starbuck's in her "large and bright rubbed room...the glass windows taken out of the frames and many chairs placed without...: It was not long before the mighty power of the Lord began to work and in it [James Bates] did appear in testimony in the forepart thereof. While he was speaking, a priest...threw out some reflections upon him." Later in Lynn, Massachusetts, James Bates joined Richardson in combatting George Keith. They visited William Penn at Pennsbury, then sailed to Bermuda and on to England. Bates did not get home to his family near Williamsburg for five years.[29]

Four more Virginians appeared as public Friends about the same time as James Bates:

- Jane Pleasants (c1640-1710) of Curles Meeting began to travel as a Quaker minister soon after husband John Pleasants died in 1690. She rode to the meetings around Virginia on a broad-backed horse, sidesaddle behind her manservant. In 1701, Jane was crossing James River on a ferry on the way to the Yearly Meeting at Pagan Creek. Her horse reared and flung himself halfway into the river, nearly capsizing the ferry.[30]
- Thomas Page (c1653-1720), a tailor, was a member first of Chuckatuck and later of Western Branch Meeting. William Ellis wrote home to England in July 1699 that "One Thomas Paige is a public minister [at

Chuckatuck] and in my sense Truth increases in him. There is a convincement in those countries."[31]

- Nathan Newby (c1660-1728) of Somerton Meeting was a blacksmith and quite a controversial Friend. His slave died in 1699, and there was talk that Nathan had mistreated the man.[32] In 1707 a committee was appointed to investigate because "some do say that they do not receive refreshment from his ministry."[33] Nevertheless Nathan was co-clerk or clerk of Virginia Yearly Meeting in 1702, 1703, and 1705; was friendly with the Indians around Great Dismal Swamp who came to his smithy to have their weapons repaired;[34] and served on many Yearly Meeting committees until his death. Nathan's brother Gabriel who lived fifty miles south of him was the first-known clerk of North Carolina Yearly Meeting, 1698.
- Elizabeth Small (1666-1717), minister of Chuckatuck, possessed "a tender, affectionate and affable disposition...with an excellent and acceptable gift in the ministry." At her life's end she admonished two visitors to her bedside to "be valiant for the Truth and walk steadily therein, and remember my dear love to Friends.[35]

\* \* \*

After the Toleration Act became recognized in Virginia, Virginia Yearly Meeting emerged as a legally recognized entity. Beginning after 1698, the Yearly Meeting was held for six days in September, a little before harvest time. The place was Pagan Creek, near present day Smithfield. Friends from all eighteen of the mainland meetings gathered there "to their great comfort and encouragement" and parted "under the sense of the love and goodness of God."[36]

Friends at these Yearly Meetings first heard reports of the spiritual progress of the eighteen local meetings. Then they worked out decisions on matters such as "the right ordering," of marriages--and always they discussed and discussed such matters until all interested Friends spoke and all aspects of the matter were opened.

They never reached any decision until all were in agreement. They never took a vote. The Truth, Friends believed, is what is in the mind of God. They believed that each one in the meeting for business has some piece of Truth and by putting all these together, the Truth that is in God's mind may be apprehended. The Meeting's clerk sat at the head of the Meeting, whose job was to catch "the sense of the Meeting" and to write a minute describing each decision that the Meeting reached.

In business sessions, the clerk read epistles from London Yearly Meeting and from the five other American Yearly Meetings--New England, New York, Philadelphia, Maryland and North Carolina. A committee of literate Friends wrote replies, and a careful list was drawn up of all Friends' sufferings at the hands of the county sheriffs during the year.

When the business all was settled, Friends sat down again to worship. Attenders who lived some distance away were guests of the Pagan Creek Friends, some sleeping in their barns and garrets. Old friendships renewed when groups gathered in the meeting house yard or around the dinner tables of their hosts.

\* \* \*

When 1700 came, the only dissenting Christians in Virginia were Presbyterians and Quakers, and soon thereafter the Presbyterians disappeared for a while. Mr. Makemie's two Presbyterian "preaching points" in Accomack County died when Mr. Makemie died in 1708, and the only remaining Presbyterian congregations were four little groups near Norfolk served by Reverend Josiah Mackie. All four dissolved when Mr. Mackie died in 1716.[37] The Presbyterians were replaced by two new groups of Protestants--Huguenots and Baptists.

Some 700 French Huguenots arrived in Hampton Roads about 1700. The 700 came from among 500,000 Protestants who fled France after 1685. That year Louis XIV, urged on by his mistress, Françoise d'Aubigne, revoked the Edict of Nantes--which had guaranteed the Protestants of France religious freedom for the previous eighty-seven years. Huguenot refugees appeared in England about the time Britain's Quakers were freed from persecution by the Toleration Act of 1689. Money for the French refugees' relief was about the first corporate gift ever made by the English Quakers to other sufferers.[38]

The 700 were officially encouraged to migrate to Virginia by the British government. They were led by Marquis de la Luce and three pastors who promised in England to use the Church of England's order of worship in Virginia.[39] Governor Nicholson provided fifty acres apiece for each refugee family, on Virginia's western frontier--at Manakin Town, a deserted Indian village twenty miles up James River from Richmond. The Assembly designated the place "King William Parish in Henrico County," and a church was built there where the service was in French.

This use of French language in the church caused Governor Nicholson some concern. He instructed Commissary Blair in 1702 "to take care that the French ministers of Manakin Town conform themselves to the liturgy of the Church of England [since I have] been informed they do not." Later in 1702, however, "Commissary Blair reported he had written Mr. De Joux, French minister at Manakin Town [who] positively affirmed that he constantly every Lord's Day reads the Service of the Church of England and administers the Sacrament as by the liturgy is directed." The governor, satisfied, then allotted an additional 10,000 acres to King William Parish.[40]

As the French children grew up speaking English, King William simply became a small parish of the established Church. Young Huguenots married their English neighbors. Soon Huguenots disappeared as a separate ethnic group.

\* \* \*

The first appearance of Baptists in Virginia was recorded by Quaker Thomas Story in his journal for 23 April 1699. "We had a meeting at York City [Yorktown]," Story wrote, "at the house of a preacher among the General Baptists." The preacher was a Thomas Bonger.[41]

No other record exists of Baptists in Virginia until 1714. That year a Baptist minister, Robert Norden from Warbleton in Sussex, old England, arrived in Prince George County. He arranged with the Quakers of Burleigh Meeting on Ward's Creek to hold Baptist meetings in their meetinghouse on Sunday afternoons. This arrangement lasted nearly a year. Then on 14 June 1715, Reverend Norden appeared before the Prince George court to "take the oaths" required by the Toleration Act. This may have dismayed the Burleigh Friends, for that same day Matthew Marks registered his house as an "anabaptist public meeting house." The Prince George Baptists thereafter worshipped there.[42]

The Baptist persuasion is considerably older than the Quakers'. English refugees in Amsterdam, Holland organized the first known Baptist congregation in 1609--nearly forty years before George Fox began his travels. Fox, when he was 19, visited his Baptist "Uncle Pickering" in London and worshiped for a time with the Baptists there.[43] A people centered on the historical Christ, the Baptists hold that the Bible is an all-sufficient rule and that baptism by water brings about spiritual renewal.

The first Virginia Baptists were *General* Baptists who believed that *all* humankind are capable of being saved. This branch of the church faded in the 1740s and was replaced in Virginia by *Particular* Baptists who believed with Calvin that only God's few elected people may be saved.

* * *

William Byrd II (1674-1744) was one of Virginia's leading gentlemen. Slim and handsome, elegant and humorous, he was known as "The Black Swan." His parents sent him to an English public school and then to learn the law in London's Middle Temple, whence he returned to Virginia sophisticated and ambitious. He appreciated wine, pretty women, and gourmet food. In 1708 he was invited to join the Governor's Council. In 1709 he began a diary which he kept in a secret shorthand. His home was Westover, the great James River plantation seven miles west of Charles City.

Westover was close by four Quaker meetings--Curles Meeting up river, where the Pleasants and Woodson families worshipped; Weyanoke Meeting down river, near Charles City; and Black Creek and Skimino Meetings to the north, where the Fleming and Bates families respectively were faithful Friends. The Black Swan knew some of these Friends. He mentioned them from time to time in his secret diary--along with notes about his wife's insubordinate ways, about Virginia's politics, the "dance" he did every morning by way of calisthenics, the prayer he said at bedtime, troubles with his slaves, his early morning readings in Hebrew, French and Latin and Homer's *Odyssey*, the roast beef he had for dinner and the epsom salts he took for his digestion.

Byrd's attitude toward his Quaker neighbors was half-friendly, half-puzzled. He liked their straight-forwardness and their reliability but did not quite understand them. Why did they stay clear of politics, shun horse races, cock fights and militia days, and fail to compete for the things he, William Byrd, valued? Why did they decline his invitations to stay for dinner? Here are some of his secret diary entries (deciphered in the 1930s by Marian Tinling of the Huntington Library in Pasadena, California):

> November 14, 1709--Before I rose this morning I made a [Quaker] song on John Pleasants.

> March 29, 1711, on his way home from Williamsburg --About 10 I took leave of the Governor and returned...as far as Mr. [Charles] Fleming's where we drank abundance of cider, but could not see his

pretty daughters because they were gone to a [Quaker] meeting. Mr. Fleming himself went with us to show us the way to the bridge.

> June 5, 1711--Young Woodson [a Quaker] brought me a letter from Charles Fleming concerning the quitrents of New Kent and I wrote an answer. Woodson would not stay for dinner.

> February 11, 1712, on a tour of his outlying plantations--I proceeded to Mr. Fleming's where I got about 5 o'clock....We were courteously used here and I saw two pretty daughters of Mr. Fleming. I ate some turkey for supper and ate heartily....Then we talked till about 10 o'clock and then retired.

> February 18, 1712--James Bates [the Quaker minister who traveled abroad five years, 1701 to 1706] came to buy Skimino Mill and at last agreed to take it for £248....When Bates had secured his bargain he went away home not withstanding I would have him stay for dinner. I ate some fricassee of chicken. It continued to snow all day....

William Byrd was less respectful and more contemptuous of the English Quaker seaman, Captain Thompson of the *Pelican* (which ship, very likely, belonged to John Osgood, the Quaker tobacco merchant of London). Captain Thompson came to Westover to solicit Byrd's tobacco crop for transport to England. Evidently his behavior was obsequious and unquakerly. When Byrd went aboard the *Pelican* to look her over, he was saluted with thirty-two guns and plenty of Canary wine, and became "almost drunk" during a ten-hour party. Byrd promised to ship twenty-five hogsheads aboard the *Pelican* alright, but as he wrote:

> January 5, 1712--About 9 o'clock came Major Harrison and the captain of the *Pelican*. I gave them a bottle of sack. In the afternoon we were merry and made the Quaker captain drink the Queen's health, on his knees.

In his official place on the Governor's Council, William Byrd was careful to be severe with Quakers. The Toleration Act recognized in Virginia in 1699 decreed only that dissenters would be *tolerated*. It fell far short of guaranteeing religious *freedom*--Quakers still were haled into court if they refused to pay church taxes or report for militia duty. The Council acted as

Virginia's highest court, and Byrd from his judge's chair confronted many a Quaker offender, hat on, standing quietly before the bar of justice. Why in the world, Byrd wondered, did they insist on getting in such trouble? He wrote:

> September 21, 1711--I was a long time in discoursing with the Governor concerning what should be done with obstinate Quakers....
>
> October 4, 1711--I rose at 7 o'clock and my wife shaved me with a dull razor. About 11 o'clock we went to the militia court....We fined all the Quakers and several others....I spoke gently to the Quakers which gave them a good opinion of me; and several of them seemed doubtful whether they would be arrested or not for the future. I told them they would certainly be fined five times in a year if they did not do as their fellow subjects did. The sun set before we had finished.[44]

\* \* \*

Penalties for Virginia Quakers who got into trouble with the law continued to be severe after the Toleration Act came into effect in 1699. After 1699, however, Friends were in a subtly stronger position. Now they were able to defend themselves more freely than in the days when they were outlaws by definition. John Richardson took part in such a defense in Virginia in the spring of 1701:

> Being at a Friend's house, an ancient widow, I observed several persons of note come into the yard...to make, as appeared afterwards, a seizure for rates [taxes] for the government and priest. Not being distinctly charged, but a mixed rate, it occasioned Friends to be straitened about the payment of them [that is, Friends were willing to pay all taxes excepting those for church and military taxes. But these last were so mixed in with the general taxes, that it was impossible to distinguish among them and Friends were in doubt--'straitened'--about how much of the tax bill to pay and how much to refuse to pay. The problem still prevails today for Friends who refuse payment of war taxes].

Observing the priest to be there, and very busy, I asked 'What has he come about?' The Friend replied 'They are come to make distress for the 40 pounds...of tobacco, payable for every taxable head, all above 16 years old'. There were along with the priest, the sheriff and constable for the government and divers merchants of note as spectators....

I stepped out to the priest, who seemed a topping brisk man, his temper in this case not unsuitable to his name, which was Sharp; and desired him to be careful how he devoured widows' houses. He briskly replied 'I do not'; to which I as closely returned 'I find you do.'

He denied my assertion and said 'The government gave me what I demanded and took'; to which I gave the following answer: 'Inasmuch as you did not do anything for the widow for which you might reasonably require a reward, I believe the government will not insist....' The priest, displeased with this modest reply, tartly replied 'You are no Christians.'[45]

Usually the punishment of Friends after 1700 at the hands of Virginia's authorities was limited to seizure of their possessions: a hogshead of tobacco; a mare; a gun and five pewter dishes; and the like. A few days after Robert Pleasants was born in 1723, the Henrico sheriff came right in to his parents' bedroom at Curles and took away the bed. [This sheriff, it seems, was Thomas Jefferson, whose grandson and namesake was none other than Thomas Jefferson of Monticello.][46]

Sometimes, however, Friends still were jailed. John and Robert Crew with their sons, Andrew and Galley, all of Weyanoke Meeting, spent time in the Charles City jail for "refusing to bear arms." Galley Crew was kept there so long that the meeting took up a collection for his support in jail. Joseph Pleasants was locked up by Sheriff Thomas Jefferson in Henrico jail for refusing to pay fines totalling fifty shillings.[47] And further down the James, practically the whole male membership of Chuckatuck Meeting were jailed ten days apiece.[48]

The wholesale jailing took place in 1711 when the new governor, Alexander Spotswood, heard that a French squadron was sailing to attack Virginia. He mobilized the militia, 15,000 strong, and proceeded to rebuild the crumbling fort on Old Point Comfort called Fort Algernon. Since the Quakers of the lower James clearly would not take up arms, Spotswood ordered them to work on Fort Algernon. When they refused that, he jailed them. He wrote to Lord Dartmouth, the Queen's Secretary of State, on 15 October 1711:

> I have been mightily embarrassed by a set of Quakers. They have not only refused to work themselves, or suffer any of their servants to work on the fortifications, but affirm that their consciences will not permit them to contribute in any manner of way to the defence of the country...at the same time they say that [they are] obliged by their religion to feed the enemies. [So] I have thought it necessary to put the laws of this country in execution against that sect....
>
> I doubt not they will sufficiently exclaim against me on this occasion, and perhaps their brethren in England...may think fit to attack me, but I'm persuaded I shall not incur my Sovereign's displeasure so long as I act by rule of law.
>
> ...It is absolutely necessary to discourage such dangerous opinions...everyone that is either lazy or cowardly would make use of the pretence of conscience to excuse himself from working or fighting...and I fear the Quakers would find too many proselytes on such occasions.[49]

The men of Curles Meeting did not unite with their downriver Friends in regard to fort-building. They did help to repair the Battery at Jamestown in 1711.[50] Nevertheless, Governor Spotswood was displeased with the Curles Friends. They refused to sell him pork that same year, 3,000 barrels of it to provision a contingent of Virginia militiamen about to march against the French in Canada.[51]

\* \* \*

Alexander Spotswood governed Virginia from 1710 to 1722. Like Francis Nicholson his predecessor, he acquired a new attitude toward Friends during his time in office. In 1718 Governor Spotswood took a political risk when he appointed Quaker George Walker, George Keith's son-in-law, to be Naval Officer (Customs Collector) for the Lower District of James River. The House of Burgesses officially deplored this appointment of a Quaker.[52]

Also in 1718, Spotswood revoked the old anti-Quaker law of 1663 that prohibited Quakers from meeting together. He did so after Benjamin Holme, a Friends' minister from Cumberland, England, clashed with Anglican ministers in southside Virginia. As Benjamin Holme told it:

> ...Several people who were not of our Society [were] desirous of having meetings in their houses, which, I suppose, disturbed some of their priests, for it was thought one or more of them wrote to the King's Attorney to acquaint the Governor of it....
>
> And there having been an old Act made against Friends in the year 1663, I believe some of the priests did therewith endeavor to frighten the people from coming to or permitting meetings to be in their houses; which Act, when the Government of Virginia sent it home with others to lay before the present King [George I], the same was rejected by them and made void...and the Governor of Virginia...issued out a proclamation...that the law was repealed....
>
> Some time before the Proclamation came out, I and two Friends more made the Governor a friendly visit, in which he showed himself respectful to us.[53]

Two years later, the Quaker sea captain Luke Knott impressed Governor Spotswood still further. Captain Knott was master of an unarmed Maryland ship, *West River Merchant*, 150 tons, with a crew of twelve, bound home from London. Near Barbados in January 1720, the *Merchant* was brought to by a pirate's cannon ball across her bow. The pirate ship was *Royal Rover*, with a crew of 148 desperadoes under Walter Kennedy, alias "Captain Callifax."

It happened that *Royal Rover*, long at sea, was already loaded with loot. When the pirate boarding party swarmed onto the *Merchant*, amazingly enough they did no violence. Instead, eight of the party surrounded Captain Knott on his quarterdeck. They were sick of pirating, they said, and they offered to keep Callifax from plundering the *Merchant*, if Captain Knott would carry them to Virginia. Knott agreed, and the pirates--although they did filch some food--showered Knott with gifts: ten chests of sugar, ten rolls of Brazilian tobacco, thirty gold pieces and gold dust. Then the *Merchant* sailed on to Virginia with the eight pirates.

Captain Knott landed four of the eight at Kickatan (Hampton) and four in York County, where they squandered money in spectacular sums, including £30 paid to a tavern keeper for the company of his bar maids. They were soon arrested on suspicion of piracy, and six of the eight were executed by hanging.

Governor Spotswood was impressed that the Quaker captain turned over the pirates' gifts, worth £250, saying he wanted no part of stolen goods. "When masters of ships are so honest as to discover and yield up what is thus given them in lieu of their own private losses, I cannot but recommend them to His Majesty's favor", Spotswood wrote.[54]

\* \* \*

After the Toleration Act passed, a remaining stumbling-block for Friends was the swearing of legal oaths. As long as judges required them to *swear* they could not go into court to recover debts or as witnesses. The Quakers' rationale was that Truth is sacred; that all people should speak the truth with no need for oath taking; and that Christ taught "Swear not at all."[*] In 1695 the English Parliament passed an act, the Seventh and Eighth of William, that made it legal for Friends to *affirm* the truth of their testimony in court; and in 1705, finally, Virginia's House of Burgesses recognized this Affirmation Act.[55]

The only trouble was that this Act required Friends to say certain words that troubled them because they sounded much like an oath:

> I, A.B., do declare in the presence of almighty God, the witness of the truth of what I say....

For twenty-seven years, English Friends lobbied the Parliament for a new Affirmation Act which finally passed in 1722. The new form of words generally satisfied Friends:

> I, A.B., do solemnly, sincerely and truly declare and affirm....[56]

Soon after the new Affirmation Act passed, Robert and Joseph Jordan, 29 and 27--Quaker grandsons of Thomas Jordan of Chuckatuck--were called to testify in Nansemond County Court. The brothers insisted on using the new simple form of affirmation; but the Nansemond justices, having never heard of the new form, refused to let them testify and jailed them instead.[57]

---

[*] Matthew 5:33-37.

Presumably they were soon released, but soon thereafter Robert Jordan was jailed again.

This second jailing came in 1723, just after Robert returned to Nansemond from ten months of travel in New England on Quaker service. He was called into court for refusing to pay church taxes and made some statements there about religion that offended the presiding justice. Consequently, he was taken to Williamsburg under guard to appear before Hugh Drysdale (governor of Virginia, 1722 to 1726). In this time of trial, Robert Jordan wrote:

> Some [Friends] forsook me as being ashamed of my testimony and of my sufferings for it...and Truth's adversaries seemed to rejoice, for I was made to stand like a fool for them to glory over me.

He was brought in three times before the governor and Council, where Commissary James Blair closely questioned him. When the Council finally passed sentence of "a year's imprisonment or bond with security for good behavior," Jordan opted for prison, saying "This is a hard sentence and I pray God to forgive mine adversaries." Of his stay in Williamsburg prison, Robert Jordan wrote:

> I was first placed in the debtor's apartment but in a few days was removed into the common side where condemned persons are kept, and for some time had not the privilege of seeing anybody except a negro who once a day brought water to the prisoners. The place was so dark that I could not see to read even at noon without creeping to small holes in the door...the infectiousness brought on me the flux....The Governor [Drysdale] was made acquainted with my condition....The Commissary [Blair] visited me more than once, under a show of friendship but with a view to ensnare me, and I was very weary of him.

> I wrote again to the Governor to acquaint him of my situation, so after a confinement of three weeks I was discharged without any acknowledgment of compliance [by me]...Thus I returned home with praise and thanksgiving in my heart to the Lord who had caused his Truth to triumph....

Robert Jordan was jailed still a third time in 1727-28 for refusing to pay church taxes. After fifteen weeks he was again released without paying the government's demand.⁵⁸

\* \* \*

In spite of buffets from Virginia's sheriffs and justices in the early 1700s, the Friends held on to their conviction that all humans are brothers and sisters under the parenthood of God. They attested to this belief by witnessing against war and by caring for the uprooted Indians around them.

The Quaker men's refusal to take part in military exercises contrasted starkly with the attitude of Virginians as a whole. Out of a population of 85,000 in 1710, the militia was 15,000 strong.⁵⁹ Most young men looked forward to the Saturdays when the militia drilled in the courthouse towns. Drill day was a time to wear a cockade, to get off the farm, to be patriotic, to meet friends in the tavern after the drilling was done.

In 1727 Virginia's Yearly Meeting petitioned William Gooch, the new governor, asking relief "for their sufferings by spoil of goods and imprisonment under militia law." Gooch received the delegation of Quakers kindly and he laid their petition before his Council; but the Council decided that "the said fines being imposed on them for their refusing obedience to the law, they ought therefore not to be relieved."⁶⁰

As for Virginia's Indians, their relationships with the Quakers stayed bright. Nathan Newby, the Quaker blacksmith of Somerton Meeting, befriended the Indians who lived around Great Dismal Swamp. They came to have him mend their guns and stayed to socialize. "They think there is one Divine Being who made all things," Nathan noted, "and that he always beholds all the Indians...and that all bad Indians who will lie, steal, cheat, and do other ill things, when they die, go to a cold country...but the good Indians, who will not do such things, go to a warm country where they have fat pork and roasting ears."⁶¹

Black slaves were another kind of uprooted people: about 8,000 in Virginia in 1700, increasing to 30,000 by 1733. Many of the Virginia Quakers acquired a slave or two to help with the farm work or housework then. But as the slave population increased, so did stories of harsh punishments and maltreatment.

Some Friends became uneasy. They pondered the Bible teaching, "Do to others as you would have others do to you." (One of the uneasy ones was

Levin Bufkin the younger, a fervent Friend of Nansemond. His father had been a white slave in Algiers from about 1679 to 1681.)[62]

In September 1714, this unease touched Friends gathered for Virginia Yearly Meeting. They wrote to London Yearly Meeting asking "whether Friends that have servants or slaves that go to hear the priest ought to pay the priest?"[63] In 1722, Virginia Yearly Meeting discussed slavery again and more urgently. "Are all Friends clear of being concerned with the importation of slaves or purchasing them for sale?," the minute read. "Do they use those well they are possessed of, and do they endeavor to restrain from vice and to instruct them in the principles of the Christian religion?"[64]

\* \* \*

No spiritual movement continues at the breathless pace of its first beginning. A slowing time comes, followed by new speed-ups and slow-downs, peaks and valleys, revival and relapse. After 1700, a slowing time came for Friends. They were affected by three intertwined tendencies which can be described as formality, smug selfrighteousness, and worldly wealth.

Margaret Fox, George's widow, was distressed by the formality. About 1700, nearly 86 years old, Margaret came up to London from her home at Swarthmore Hall. George, her beloved, had brought her a length of scarlet cloth for a cloak from one of his trips in the time of their marriage, and now in London Margaret saw that the London Friends were beginning to dress all in Quaker gray. It seemed to her that the gray symbolized a creeping emphasis on outward uniformity and a lengthening list of formal rules. She wrote in protest:

> Christ Jesus saith that we must take no thought what we shall eat, or what we shall drink, or what we shall put on; but bids us consider the lilies how they grow in more royalty than Solomon. But contrary to this, they [London Friends] say we must look at no colors, nor make anything that is changeable colors as the hills are, nor sell them, nor wear them. But we must all be in one dress and one color. This is a silly poor gospel.[65]

In spite of Margaret's view, Quaker men and women wore gray for 170 years afterward; and there have been times when the Society of Friends' rules and forms have been strict and numerous.

As for self-righteousness, that tendency is pondered by Elton Trueblood, the twentieth century Quaker teacher, thus:

A crusader against evil is himself in danger. Our danger in opposing manifest evil is that, by contrast, we are relatively less evil, and may therefore come to think of ourselves as righteous. The temptation comes somewhat as follows

X is evil
I am opposed to X
Therefore, I am good

Our safety lies in the constant realization that all of us are [human] and that, as [humans], we are in the same fundamental predicament.[66]

Not all Friends fall into this "righteousness" mind-set, but it has been observed in certain Friends at certain times through all their history.

And worldly wealth--ironically, wealth came to quite a few Friends because they pursued the ideal of Truth and Honesty. George Fox wrote "that people at first shied away from doing business with Quaker storekeepers, "but then people came to see Friends' honesty and truthfulness, and 'yea' and 'nay' at a word in their dealing and...they would not cozen or cheat them, and at last they might send any child and be as well-used as themselves at any of their shops." Then people flocked to do business in Quakers' stores and mills.[67]

The children of such Quaker businessmen inherited considerable money. Then it turned out that money and property encumber people and turn them toward worldly pleasures and worldly cares. Most, but not all of the families who came into Quaker money left the Quakers. As the saying went

Ye'll seldom see a coach-and-four
A-stopping at the Meeting's door

Before 1700 these shadows fell only on Friends in the two Quaker capitals, London and Philadelphia. In London, the Gracechurch Street Meeting was made up of worshipers who, during the 1690s, were becoming the richest merchant and banking families in England--Hanburys, Barclays (offspring of Robert Barclay the Apologist), Gurneys, Lloyds (Lloyds of London), and Christys.[68] In Philadelphia, the wry by-word about "God-fearing money-making Quakers" came early.

In Virginia, however, all but a few Quaker families lived a simple farming life. Until 1700 they were still fending off serious persecution. Thereafter, though, many Virginia Friends built mills and warehouses along the rivers and creeks, attracted the trust of their neighbors and made money in spite of the sheriffs' attentions. Then stories sprang up about Quaker rogues. About 1700, "Ebenezer Cook, gent" published a narrative poem in London titled "The Sot Weed Factor." It recounts the writer's adventures as a tobacco trader in America. The villain of the poem is an Eastern Shore Quaker.

> I then began to think with care
>    How I might sell my British ware
> To this intent, with guide before
>    I tript it to the Eastern Shore
> While riding near a sandy bay
>    I met a Quaker, Yea and Nay
> A pious conscientious rogue
>    As e'er wore bonnet or a brogue
> Who neither swore nor kept his word
>    But cheated in the fear of God
> And when his debts he would not pay
>    By Light Within he ran away
> With this sly zealot soon I struck
>    A bargain for my English truck
> Agreeing for 10,000 weight
>    Of Sot weed good and fit for freight
>    Broad Oronooko bright and sound.

The poem goes lugubriously on to tell how Ebenezer entrusted his good English merchandise to the crooked Quaker, who then absconded without paying the 10,000 pounds of tobacco for it[69] (the crook possibly was Edward Beare).

So came these three shadows, formality, self-righteousness, and the pursuit of worldly wealth, to beset Quakerism.

\* \* \*

Until the 1730s the Quaker center in Virginia lay in the colony's southeast corner--where Elizabeth Harris planted the seed. William Byrd pondered why so many Friends lived in southeast Virginia.

Byrd was one among three Virginia and four North Carolina gentlemen commissioned in 1728 to determine the boundary line between the two colonies. The party started out on the Atlantic Ocean beach at Back Bay on March 5, with numerous surveyors and slaves and a chaplain (Peter Fontaine, the rector of Byrd's church). They sighted their line due west along 36° 30" north latitude. On March 14 they reached the Great Dismal Swamp which no one ever had crossed. Sixteen surveyors and assistants with axes, alidades and astrolabes, chains and poles, were ordered into the swamp to run the line across it, while the gentlemen and their body servants rode around the swamp's north end. The gentlemen met the bedraggled surveyors as they emerged from the swamp on March 28.

During their ride around the Great Dismal, Byrd and his companions passed two Quaker meeting houses. One was Nansemond (Southern Branch) Meeting's near Suffolk, the other Somerton Meeting's near Holland, begun when George Fox visited there in 1672. Byrd wrote:

> In our journey we...passed by no less than two Quaker Meeting houses, one of which had an awkward ornament on the west end of it, that seemed to ape a steeple. I must own I expected no such piece of foppery from a sect of so much outside simplicity.
>
> The persuasion prevails much in the lower end of Nansemond County, for want of ministers to pilot the people a decenter [Anglican] way to Heaven.
>
> The ill reputation of tobacco planted in those lower parishes makes the clergy unwilling to accept of them, unless it be such whose abilities are as mean as their pay. Thus whether the churches be quiet [empty] or indifferently filled, the Quakers will have an opportunity of gaining proselytes. People uninstructed in any religion are ready to embrace the first that offers. Tis natural for helpless man to adore his Maker in some form or other.[70]

Two kinds of tobacco were raised in Virginia, "Sweet Scented" and "Oronoco." "Sweet Scented" was milder and brought a higher market price. And since, by Virginia law, each Anglican clergyman received 16,000 pounds of tobacco per year for a salary, the clergymen who had "Sweet Scented" parishes made more money. The "Sweet Scented" parson's tobacco pay was worth £80 to £100 sterling, the "Oronoco" parson's £40 to £65. In 1728, eleven of Virginia's thirty counties were Sweet Scented, and only two of them had Quaker meetings--New Kent and Hanover.[71]

But nothing remains the same. While William Byrd was riding through Nansemond that March of 1728, Virginia and Virginia's Quakers were shifting west and westward. There were several reasons: Tobacco crops wore out the fields after three years and the planters went west to find fresh. Some roadways and bridges became wide enough in the 1720s for wagons, which appeared for the first time,[72] making the business of moving one's household goods easier. The main reason, though, lay in the attraction of new land for adventurous men and women.

As the population moved west, so did the Quaker meetings. Three meetings, all in eastern Virginia, closed their doors from 1700 to 1733--Guilford Creek Meeting on Virginia's Eastern Shore and Lawne's Creek and Warwick Meetings. Eleven new meetings sprang up, six east of the Fall Line--Binford's, Blackwater, Hunnicutt's, Murdaugh's, Picquinoqui Swamp, and Surry--and five west--Amelia, Genito, Cedar Creek, Fork Creek, and Camp Creek.

In 1700 the Blackwater River marked southside Virginia's frontier.[73] But by 1733 the frontier had pushed far west of the Blackwater, far west of the Fall Line and the Tidewater and far up the Piedmont toward the mountains, looming hazy blue and mysterious across the sunset.

Hopewell Friends began to meet at the site of this their meeting house six miles north of Winchester by 1734.

# VI

## WEST OF THE BLUE RIDGE
## 1733-1750

> Dear Friends who inhabit the Shenandoah and Opequon--....I desire that you be very careful (being far and back inhabitants) to keep a friendly correspondence with the native Indians.
> -- Thomas Chalkley, 1738

The Blue Ridge Mountains stood as a barrier against the Virginians for four generations. Only a few young men had climbed into them. On winter nights around the fireplaces, and in summer in the dooryards while families took the breeze and watched the fireflies, they speculated on what might be there beyond the Mountains. Rumors, about Indians, game herds and rich land, were told.

Governor Spotswood organized an exploring party in the summer of 1716, to cross the Mountains and find out for sure what lay beyond. A troop of horsemen clattered out of Williamsburg that August with the 40-year-old governor at the head. They rode to the foot of the Blue Ridge and climbed it (along present day Route 33 from Stanardsville west), contending with hornets, blackberry thickets and the late summer sun. They reached the summit on September 5, then peered down at the grand sweep of the Valley of Virginia. John Fontaine, the expedition's chaplain, noted that "We drunk King George's health here and all the Royal Family." Then they descended into the Valley (near present day Elkton) and camped two nights by the Shenandoah River.[1] Once back in Williamsburg, Spotswood advertised the Valley. He gave each member of the expedition a pin, a miniature golden horseshoe engraved "Sic Juvat Transcendere Montes" (What a Pleasure It Is to Cross the Mountains). So he dramatized the Valley and created a wave of interest. Presently a few brave families dared to move there.

The very first of these families was Quaker connected. They were the Stovers or Staubers,[2] Jacob and Sarah and their children who moved in 1727 from their farm near present-day Reading, Pa. They settled in sight of Massanutten Mountain in what is now Page County. The families of Adam Miller and eight more German-speaking families from the Pennsylvania Colony either accompanied the Stovers or followed them there. Jacob

Stover, born in Switzerland and a kind of German Baptist by religion, married Sarah, the Quaker daughter of George Boone in 1715.[3] The Stover children were reared under the influence of both parents' religious backgrounds, for their son Daniel, when he testified in a Caroline County court case in 1742, refused to swear on the Bible. He explained that he was a Baptist but a kind of Baptist who professed the same tenets as the Quakers; after which the court allowed him to *affirm* the truth of his testimony.[4*]

The next Valley settlers, who came in 1729, were out-and-out Quakers--43 year old Abraham and Anne Hollingsworth, their four children and niece Lydia. They came from the New Ark Meeting in Delaware to Virginia, settling near an Indian camp at the Shawnee Spring, in what is now the south end of Winchester.

\* \* \*

Ever since the Huguenots had been seated in Manakin Town, Virginia's politicians favored the idea of inducing "societies" to settle on the Western frontier, to be "buffers" against Indian attacks. In September 1701, the Burgesses had passed an act "For the Better Strengthening of the Frontiers and Discovering the Approaches of an Enemy."[5] This law empowered the Governor to allot 10,000 to 30,000 acres of unclaimed frontier land to any suitable "society."

The law was little used for 26 years, until William Gooch became Virginia's governor in 1727. Governor Gooch immediately began to promote the Valley as a place to live. He was acting on instructions from London, where there was growing concern that the French in the Mississippi Valley might be planning some military move against England's Colonies.

The new governor was not troubled at all that the Indians, ancient inhabitants of the Valley, were the real owners of the land. But his effort to people the Valley was somewhat impeded by the fact that hundreds of square miles of the northern Valley were already claimed as private property by an Englishman. This was Thomas, sixth Lord Fairfax, Baron of Cameron, a 34 year old bachelor who lived in a towered castle in Kent. King Charles II, in exile in 1649, had given outright the whole Northern Neck of Virginia

---

[*] The Stovers are an important family in America's history, the forebears of Ida Stover, mother of President Eisenhower. Daniel Boone, the famous nephew of Sarah Boone Stover, may have been named for Daniel Stover.

--all the land between the Potomac and Rappahannock Rivers--to some of his "right trusty and well beloved" companions in exile; and the patent to this mighty tract had come down to Lord Fairfax through his mother.

Robert "King" Carter was Fairfax' land agent in Virginia and he was also the senior member of Governor Gooch's Council. He objected strenuously to Gooch's plan to grant away the Valley land claimed by Fairfax.[6] But the Lords Commissioners in London, fearing the French, pressed Gooch to get on with it. And so, between 1728 and 1736 the Governor signed Orders in Council which granted 15 or more huge virgin tracts of Valley land to various applicants. The grants ranged in a magnificent arc north to south, from large "Fairfax" acreage along the Potomac taken by Richard ap Morgan of Pennsylvania, to 105,000 acres taken by William Byrd around the present-day city of Roanoke. Typically the grantees paid 10 shillings per 100 acres for the land and also promised to settle a given number of families on their tracts -- usually one family on each 100 acres.

Four of the huge grants involved Quaker applicants --
- Alexander Ross, 48, a Friend of the Nottingham Meeting in southern Chester County, Pa, and his Scotch-Irish partner, Morgan Bryan, went to Williamsburg in October, 1730. There they obtained an Order in Council for 100,000 acres of beautiful land on both sides of Opequon Creek just north of present day Winchester.[7]
- Robert McKay, also a Nottingham Meeting Friend and his German partner, Yost Hite, went to Williamsburg a year later in October 1731. They obtained 100,000 acres to the south of Ross and Bryan's grant. They also bought 40,000 acres allotted to the Van Meter brothers north of present-day Front Royal.[8]
- Jacob Stover, the first settler, acquired two Quaker partners - Johan Ochs the Younger and Ezekiel Harlan of Kennett Square, Pa. The three went to Williamsburg in 1730 to ask for an enormous wedge of Fairfax-claimed land along the Potomac where they proposed to establish a colony of Protestants from Switzerland. When they were turned down by Governor Gooch and King Carter, they went on to London. There they appealed to His Majesty's Commission for Trade and Plantations. They were opposed there, however, by Lord Thomas Fairfax in person and were turned down again. Ezekiel Harlan died in London during the hearings. Stover and Ochs later were granted parcels totalling about 14,000 acres further south in the Valley.[9]

- Benjamin Borden (1692-1743), a Friend from Freehold, New Jersey, was an ambitious businessman with his eye on the main chance. When King Carter died in 1732, Borden sailed to England and applied to Lord Fairfax to succeed Carter as Fairfax' land agent. When Borden did not get the job, he promptly returned to Freehold, moved his family to Virginia and finally, in 1736, got a patent for a "Great Tract" of 99,129 acres around present-day Lexington.[10]

\* \* \*

Borden, and William Beverly who owned the patent north of Borden's, around present-day Staunton, induced many Scotch-Irish families, Presbyterians from Pennsylvania, to settle their land--and the middle Valley remains to this day dotted with Presbyterian churches. Stover and Ochs attracted Germans. But Alexander Ross and Robert McKay persuaded many Quaker families to people their patents, and so five Friends' Meetings sprang up north and south of Winchester beginning in 1733.

These Friends were the grandchildren of the immigrants who came with Penn to Pennsylvania. They came from farms around Philadelphia, from Chester and Bucks Counties in Pennsylvania and Burlington County in New Jersey--very few from Philadelphia itself. The families began to come in the summer of 1732, bringing furniture and farm tools on strings of packhorses. Fathers walked and mothers rode, carrying the baby. Frisky small fry explored the path sides, while the oldest son tailed the pack horse string or drove along the family cow.

They came by the wagon road from Philadelphia to the frontier town of Lancaster. Then they struck the Indian path, the Great Warriors Path, one horse wide, that ran southwest through virgin woods to the Susquehanna River. Only God knows now how they forded or swam or rafted across the Susquehanna. By the evening camp fires they thanked God for His care. A hundred miles after the Susquehanna they splashed across the Potomac at Pack Horse Ford. Then the Valley of Virginia came into their view.

It was and is a kind of green Eden.[11] The land was open and park-like; for the Indians had periodically burned it over to make hunting easier.[12] Great mountains loomed blue on either side, east and west. The spring comes a few days earlier here than in Chester County, Pa. Presently, somewhere about Opequon Creek, Alexander Ross or Robert McKay would meet them, gravely smiling, and lead them to their new home sites.

Six days in the week, those first Friends in the Valley, fathers and mothers, sons and daughters, worked hard--raising log houses and barns, breaking the sod for new corn fields, planting kitchen gardens. On Sunday or First Day, however, they gathered with their neighbors to tend the spiritual dimension of their lives.

The five Quaker meeting places established in the Valley in the 1730s were these:

- Providence Meeting was the northern-most, on Richard and Charity Beeson's place along Tuscarora Creek (two miles west of present day Martinsburg, West Virginia).[13]
- Hopewell Meeting held in a log house near Alexander and Catherine Ross' farm (about six miles north of Winchester). Hopewell, was the largest meeting and the headquarters of Quaker activities in the Valley. The meeting house when it was built in 1734 was the first building for Christian worship west of the Blue Ridge. No other denomination is known to have put up a church building west of the Blue Ridge until Opequon Presbyterian Church was built in 1736.
- Hollingsworth's (or Parkins' Meeting), now called Centre Meeting, met at Abraham and Anne Hollingsworth's, or in Isaac Parkins' house, just south of Winchester.
- Crooked Run Meeting held in Robert McKay's home, three miles north of Front Royal. The home built of squared chestnut logs still stands, in Cedarville on U.S. Route 522.[14]
- Linville Creek, later Smith's Creek, met at first on land owned by Robert McKay, about where Broadway is now located -- some 70 miles south of Providence Meeting and furthest south of the five Valley meetings. John Churchman of Nottingham Meeting made a rather critical judgment about these Friends when he visited them in fall 1739: "I went to a few families settled up Shenandoah, above the Three-Topt Mountain," he wrote. "I believe that the delight in hunting and a roving idle life drew most of them under our name to settle there."[15]

\* \* \*

Friends eventually were out-numbered in the Valley by Germans and Scotch-Irish. Both these ethnic groups also came south from Pennsylvania. Both groups had been attracted to Pennsylvania because William Penn welcomed persecuted people to settle in the Quaker colony:

- The Germans came mostly from Protestant communities along the Rhine River. They were savaged there by French Catholic troops who occupied the Rhine Valley after 1685.[16]
- The Scotch-Irish were descendants of lowland Scots families which moved to northern Ireland early in the 1600s. Beginning in the 1660s, however, Irish industries were deliberately crippled by the English, and there was a slow economic decline. After 1700, a large part of Ireland's people emigrated, the Catholics to Spain and France and the Scotch-Irish Protestants mostly to Pennsylvania.[17]

Valley Germans were a clean, orderly and hard-working people. They settled all up and down the Valley but generally a little south of the Quakers in what are now Shenandoah, Page, Warren and Rockingham Counties. They were mostly Lutheran and Reformed Church members with some Moravians, Mennonites and Brethren. The first German church building in the Valley was "the Dutch Chapel," Lutheran, built about 1747 on Cedar Creek, the southern border of Frederick County.[18]

The Mennonites and Brethren were close-related with the Friends in their spiritual outlook. They saw themselves as gemeinde (communities) of brothers and sisters committed to following Christ, with a commitment that goes beyond preaching, hymns and prayer on Sunday mornings.[19] With the Friends they held that war and violence are evil.

Scotch-Irish in the Valley were uniformly Presbyterian. Their first church building was the Opequon Church, built 1736 on the Valley Pike at Kernstown.[20] They were a rugged, determined and unwavering sort, characterized by the Presbyterian elder who is said to have prayed, "Thou knowest, Lord, I am unco' hard to turn...." Unlike the Friends they were aggressive and war-like, good soldiers and willing Indian-fighters. Some of them held that "the only good Indian is a dead Indian."

\* \* \*

Friends in the Valley in 1730s were isolated. The living was primitive and dangerous. While old Thomas Hollingsworth from Delaware was visiting his son at the Shawnee Spring, he was killed by a charging woods buffalo. Friends came to their meetings for worship carrying guns against wild animals. One Quaker woman riding home from meeting sidesaddle with her baby in her arms was chased by wolves right to her cabin door.[21]

Yet these back country Friends did enjoy their lives. They had good times while helping one another to build cabins and raise barns. They were just settled in their new homes and hardly had time to build Hopewell Meeting House before young couples fell in love, and married after the manner of Friends. The whole Quaker community gathered to witness these weddings and to celebrate them. First Quaker bride in the Valley was Hannah McKay, Robert's daughter. She married in 1734 to George Hollingsworth, 22. He was Abraham and Anne's oldest child.[22]

Quaker ministers criss-crossed and knit together the Quaker world on both sides of the Atlantic in those days. The first minister to reach the Valley was Joseph Gill, 60, of Dublin, Ireland. he visited the meetings on "old" Virginia during the summer of 1734 and then came right across the trackless Blue Ridge, accompanied by Samuel Jordan and William Duff, Virginia Friends. Joseph Gill wrote cheerfully in his journal that he found the Valley Friends in a thriving way, with divers young ministers appearing among them. He was enthused about four brothers, Thomas, John, Hur and Henry Mills, who "one after the other appeared in the ministry in wilderness Virginia." But Hannah McKay was about to be married when Joseph arrived at Hopewell Meeting, and he was dubious about "the great preparation for a marriage entertainment and the crowds (sic) which assembled to partake of it." He spoke closely to Friends about the need for moderation and temperance.[23]

* * *

The Valley was still Indian country when the first white settlers came. A treaty was in effect, made in 1722 at Albany between the chiefs of the Five Nations and the governors of New York, Pennsylvania and Virginia. By this treaty the Iroquois and their allies agreed to stay west of the Blue Ridge with the east side reserved for the whites.[24] So the Valley Quakers and the other whites in the Valley were trespassers in terms of the Albany Treaty. In the 1730s it appears that no particular tribe was based in the northern Valley, but rather it was a hunting ground visited periodically by hunters of several tribes. Nevertheless the white settlers had moved west of the Treaty line.

Clearly, however, the tribes welcomed the coming of Pennsylvania Quakers to the Valley.[25] Were these not the children of Onas, of William Penn, whose loving justice had been told around the council fires of the tribes now for two generations?[26] Indians feared and avoided the few families from old Virginia who moved to the Valley. "Long Knives" or

"Tuckahoes" the Indians called them[27]--but the Friends they welcomed. The Great Warrior's Path running north and south along the Valley floor--now Route 11--went close by four of the five Quaker meeting places (all except Crooked Run Meeting's).

Stories have come down about the visits of Indian hunters to Quaker homes in the Valley of Virginia:

- The Hollingsworths of Seneca Spring lived right by a major Indian camping place and kept up friendly relations with the Seneca families who sojourned there.
- Joseph Carter and his family came from Bucks County, Pa., to settle on Spout Spring on Opequan Creek about five miles east of Winchester. Across the creek was a grove, where two or three hundred Indians at a time would stay for weeks. Joseph Carter was a shoe maker and as the story goes, two Indians visited his shop one day. One of the men slipped a pair of new shoes under his blanket, but Joseph saw him do it and recovered the shoes before the culprit left the shop. The Indian's companion reported the incident to the chiefs and that evening the culprit was being severely chastised. Joseph, however, waded across the Opequon and asked for the punishment to cease.[28]
- William and Joseph Lupton, brothers, came from Buckingham Meeting in Bucks County in 1740 and passed the winter sheltered under a fallen tree. They built a cabin there near a spring on the edge of a wide meadow two miles west of Winchester, and Joseph Lupton, 54, brought his wife Mary and eight children to set up housekeeping there. The spring was an Indian camping place and many came to camp there near the Lupton's cabin.[29]
- Benjamin Allen and family settled on the Great Warrior's Path where it crosses Smith's Creek, about 1734. An aged man of the Senedo tribe frequently visited the Allens. He told that their farm was the place of a great slaughter in his boyhood where the southern Indians (Catawbas) "killed my whole nation" excepting only himself and another boy. A great burial mound on the Allen farm was the grave site of the slaughtered Senedos.[30] The extinction of that tribe may explain why no tribe was based in the northern Valley when Quakers arrived there.

The Hollingsworths, when they moved to the Valley in 1729, found some Senecas and paid them for the land.[31] When Alexander Ross and Robert McKay brought more Friends families there three years later, however, no particular tribe could be found who claimed the soil. This failure to pay the Indians weighed hard on the Quakers' consciences. Thomas Chalkley, now 63, a Philadelphia Friends' minister who often visited the Virginia meetings, wrote a letter about this failure on July 21, 1738:

> Dear Friends who inhabit the Shenandoah and Opequon--...I desire that you be very careful (being far and back inhabitants) to keep a friendly correspondence with the native Indians....
>
> As nature had given them and their forefathers the possession of this continent of America (or this wilderness), they had a natural right thereto in justice and equity; and no people...according to the...glorious gospel of our dear and holy Jesus Christ, ought to take away or settle on other men's lands or rights without consent, or purchasing the same...which I suppose in your case is not yet done.
>
> Therefore my counsel and Christian advice to you is, my dear friends, that the most reputable among you do with speed endeavor to agree with and purchase your lands.... Take example of our worthy and honorable late proprietor, William Penn....
>
> Consider you are in the province of Virginia...and the Virginians have made an agreement with the natives to go as far as the mountains and no farther; and you are over and beyond the mountains....
>
> ...my good will to you and to your new little settlement, that you may sit every one under your own shady tree, where none might make you afraid...In the love of our holy Lord Jesus Christ, your real friend,
>
> T.C. [32]

\* \* \*

Loudoun County lies east across the Blue Ridge from the Valley of Virginia. Catoctin Creek waters the west part of Loudoun; and a few families from

Bucks County, Pa., members of Falls Meeting--at the Falls of the Delaware River across from Trenton, New Jersey--moved to land along Catoctin Creek in 1733. They arrived in Virginia about the same time as the Valley Friends. The Indians had been gone ten years or so from Catoctin by 1733, but otherwise the situations of the two Friends' groups were much the same--isolated and primitive.

Amos and Mary Janney, Francis and Jane Hague and John and Sarah Hough was among the first Quaker settlers on Catoctin.[33] They worshipped in their homes until 1741, then built a log meeting house near Amos Janney's mill on Catoctin Creek. They named Amos Janney, 40, and Jane Hague, 33, to be their first clerks. Their meeting was named "Fairfax" since the Catoctin area was located in Fairfax County until Loudoun was split off from Fairfax in 1757.

Amos Janney's younger brother Jacob followed Amos to Virginia in 1743. Jacob Janney had just married a 16-year-old Philadelphia girl named Hannah Ingledue and a remarkable wife Hannah turned out to be. The couple settled near Goose Creek, six miles southwest of Fairfax Meeting. There, according to tradition child bride Hannah immediately started Goose Creek Friends Meeting, sitting alone on a log in the unbroken forest for an hour each First Day.[34] She and Jacob raised eight sons and three daughters at Goose Creek, made a farm on 96 acres and built a mill. The Goose Creek Friends, Janneys, Nichols' and Walkers, built their log meeting house in 1750.[35]

From their beginnings the Fairfax and Goose Creek Friends were in close touch with the Friends of the five Valley meetings. They were linked as a quarterly meeting under the care of Philadelphia Yearly Meeting along with the Monocacy and Bush Creek Meetings north across the Potomac River in Frederick County, Maryland. Betrothals among the young people of the nine Quaker communities were frequent. These nine "backwoods" meetings (ten meetings after 1745, when the Fawcett family began the Mt. Pleasant Meeting on Cedar Creek in southern Frederick County) were only loosely in touch with the older Virginia meetings east of the Blue Ridge which formed Virginia Yearly Meeting.

\* \* \*

The older Virginia meetings continued to increase. Four new meetings opened on mainland Virginia east of the Blue Ridge between 1733 and 1750--Bennett's Creek Meeting, Caroline, Fine Creek, and Sugar Loaf

Mountain in Albemarle County. On the Eastern Shore, Nassawaddox Meeting--the meeting that built the first Friends Meeting House in America--was laid down, but the Mifflin family opened a new little house meeting at Swansgut. The number of Virginia Friends' meetings overall grew from 20 in 1700, to 28 in 1732, to 40 meetings in 1750.

Virginia Yearly Meeting continued to petition the General Assembly to stop punishing Friends for refusing to support the Established Church and the military establishment. The petitions met with varying responses, reflecting the ambiguous and shifting attitudes of Virginia's politicians toward the Quakers in their midst--a people who were scrupulously honest citizens on the one hand and maddeningly obstinate law-breakers on the other. A petition in 1736 seemed to result in kinder treatment by the sheriffs,[36] and so the next year the Yearly Meeting sent a memorial of thanks.[37] The memorial apparently enraged some legislators and *increased* Friends' sufferings. In 1738 and 1739 the Yearly Meeting handed in two more petitions.[38] The 1738 petition reads:

> To the Honourable the Governor and Council and Burgesses met in General Assembly at Williamsburg, the humble petition of the People called Quakers.
>
> We...beseech you...to consider the case of our Society in this Dominion who...have been subject to great loss and detriment in our substance and employment by annual seizures and distresses upon our goods and persons.... We humbly conceive it is in your power to relieve us [for] in most of the provinces under the British Government our Friends sit easy in this behalf....
>
> We pay all taxes for support of government...the public are not charged in the least for our poor; and we nevertheless willingly contribute to the public poor, and endeavor to follow peace with all men....
>
> We hope it will please the almighty God to put it into your hearts to say 'Amen' to the prayer of our petition....

\* \* \*

The public's good opinion of Quakers was certainly hurt by a few wealthy members whose life styles were at odds with the Quaker ideal of simple living. Best known in Virginia of these wealthy Quakers was John Hanbury of London.

The Hanbury family first appear in Quaker records in 1657 when George Fox held a threshing meeting at Richard Hanbery's place at Pontymoil in Wales "and a great convincement there was."[39]. John Hanbury (1700-1758) was Richard's great-grandson. He came from Wales to London and married Anna, the daughter of Quaker tobacco merchant John Osgood. Then he inherited Osgood's business and built it up until he, John Hanbury, was the world's greatest tobacco merchant.[40]

Hanbury's name was familiar all across Virginia. He was the agent and banker in London for many famous Virginia families including the Washingtons and Custises--George Washington and widow Martha Custis received a note of congratulations from Hanbury and Co. when they married.[41] John Randolph of Matoax owed £11,000 to the Hanburys in 1759 and finally had to mortgage all his property "excepting my favorite body servant, Syphax" to them after a series of poor tobacco crops.[42] Isham Randolph wrote his will so as "to prevent my great creditor, John Hanbury of London, merchant, from being put to my difficulty in recovering the money I owe him."[43]

Ships flying the Hanbury ensign--the *Anna*, *Osgood*, *Dunkirk* and *Fishborn*--called in James River annually to carry the tobacco crop to England. The Quaker merchants in James River who were Hanbury's correspondents, Pleasants', Woodsons and Jordans, became wealthy in their own right. Virginia Yearly Meeting[44] and Maryland Yearly Meeting[45] sent money "for the general stock" to London Yearly Meeting by captains of Hanbury ships. John Hanbury was a friend of Robert Dinwiddie,[46] the London merchant who was governor of Virginia from 1751 to 1758. Eventually both the Virginia and Maryland colonies appointed Hanbury their trustee to safeguard their assets in the Bank of England--for which Hanbury and Co. received six percent commissions or about £330 a year from each Colony.[47]

John Hanbury was a man of absolute integrity, widely trusted. In this respect he was exemplary. His business activities, however, led him to betray his Quaker heritage. In 1739 Hanbury's ship, the *Anna*, named for his wife, brought 380 Africans from Guinea to the upper James to be sold into slavery. And the *Anna* was armed with ten cannon. In 1755 John Hanbury took great interest in the success of Braddock's expedition in America. He wrote the Duke of Newcastle to advise the employment of Indian scouts (which, if General Braddock had taken the advice, might have saved Braddock from disaster).[48]

Such behavior gave cause to criticize Quakers as hypocrites. One such critic was "W.W." who sent a letter to the *Virginia Gazette*, after the *Gazette* published the petition sent by Virginia Yearly Meeting to the Assembly in 1738.

> 24 Nov. 1738: Mr. Parks--I see by our last Gazette that you have oblig'd the people call'd Quakers by publishing their petition to the Assembly, to be exempted from paying parish levies. I hope therefore you'll publish the following Composition for Making a Quaker....
>
> First, take a handful of the herb of Deceit, and a few leaves of Folly and a little of the rose of Vain-Glory, with some of the buds of Envy and a few blossoms of Malice with a few Formality flowers and a sprig or two of idle Conceit;
>
> Take some of the seeds of Pride, and some of the seeds of Hypocrisy, and some seeds of Forbidden Pleasure, and some of the bark of Self-Will, and put them together into a mortar of Defiance and pound them with a pestle of Head-Strong wood:
>
> Also take an ounce of Ill-Manners and three quarters of an ounce of Cheat-Seed, a good quantity of the roots of Ambition, and the pith of Self-Conceit, together with some plums that grow on Runagate hill, and some of the grapes that grow in the suburbs of Sodom and some of the spice of Babylon;
>
> And then take those twenty sorts, and strew them altogether in a Stony-hearted jug, over the fire of Cold Zeal, and pour in a little of the water of Wild Fountain; and when they are all simmered and soaked together enough, grate in a little Folly powder, and strain it through a cloth of Vanity, and suck every morning through a spout of Ignorance,
>
> And in a little time it will raise the Spirit, and you will quake and shake and smite on your breast, and so you will become a perfect Quaker. [49]

"W.W." was not the only Virginian who disliked Quakers in 1738. On the other hand they had some admirers. The Reverend Mr. Anthony Gavin of St. James Parish in Goochland County reported to the Bishop of London August 5, 1738, that "I struggle with many difficulties from Quakers who are countenanced by high-minded men."[50] Four years later someone sent a petition to Governor Gooch protesting the growing "countenance of Quakers by men in high station."[51]

\* \* \*

The spiritual history of our race runs in tides, waves and ripples. Sometimes the faces of humankind turn toward high spiritual things, then turn back again to the secular, material world. In the 12th century, cathedral spires pointing to heaven were built all over Europe. In the 16th came the Reformation when men and women tried to reach a new level of understanding of this mysterious universe and how to live in it. The 17th saw the Quaker movement born. In the 1730s, nearly a hundred years after the Quaker beginning there came a new movement--the Great Awakening--in England and America.

The new movement began in 1733, the year when Quakers came to settle in the Valley of Virginia. It was started by a few earnest students at Oxford University, who called themselves the Holy Club. The club members, led by the brothers John and Charles Wesley, proposed to save their souls by being good and doing good in a *methodical* way.[52] The Great Awakening was brought to Virginia in 1739 by George Whitefield. He was a 24 year old alumnus of Oxford and of the Holy Club and an ordained Anglican minister.

At 24 George Whitefield was a blazing phenomenon. He was an enthusiastic, deeply pious young man with a gift for drama, a magnificent voice and a message that swayed the whole Protestant world. Soon after leaving Oxford, he began preaching outdoors in England to crowds so large that no church could hold them. He delivered his sermons with emotion and sweep, never reading them and never dividing his points into dry Firstlys, Secondlys and Thirdlys as the custom then was. His voice reached for a Philadelphia street block according to Benjamin Franklin.[53] In his lifetime George Whitefield *preached to more people than had any man alive, probably to more than any man in history.*[54]

Mr. Whitefield brought "evangelistic" or "new light" or "new side" Christianity to America in 1739. It is an approach to Christianity that has continued to be vital and compelling from his day to ours. Virginia has famous television preachers today carrying on George Whitefield's tradition. The authority of the Bible; the primacy of John 3.16 as a Bible text; salvation from eternal hell fire through faith without much reference to good works; the three aspects of God; the deity of Christ and His vicarious atonement for the sins of depraved human beings; periodic revival services in the churches; calls to come to the altar and be saved--these typify evangelical Christianity, then and now.

In England before his first trip to America, Mr. Whitefield encountered 20 or more Friends at various places in his travels. He wrote in his Journal that these Friends "glorified God in my behalf" and "entertained me...in a most Christian manner."[55] A Quaker minister sailed with him on the ship to America and Whitefield invited the Quaker to use his cabin for a meeting after the manner of Friends. "He spoke with much earnestness," Whitefield wrote, "but in my opinion his foundation was wrong. He seemed to make the light of conscience and the Holy Spirit one and the same thing, and represented Christ *within* and not Christ *without* as the foundation of our faith: whereas the outward righteousness of Jesus Christ imputed to us, I believe, is the sole foundation and cause of all the inward communications which we receive from the Spirit of God."[56]

Here the divergence between Quakerism and Evangelicalism comes clear. The Quaker emphasizes the inward working of the Holy Spirit, a touch of Christ in each person's soul; the Evangelical rests his faith on the flesh and blood historic Christ and His vicarious atonement. The Quaker looks to the *Spirit* of Christ; the Evangelical looks to Christ *and him crucified*.[57]

Mr. Whitefield and his retinue of 16 people arrived at Philadelphia on Friday, November 2. That Sunday, he

> ...went in the evening to the Quakers' meeting and felt somewhat in sympathy with the man that spoke. but I heartily wish they would talk of an outward as well as an inward Christ; for otherwise we make our own holiness and not the righteousness of Jesus Christ the cause of our being accepted by God.[58]

He stayed in Philadelphia, making friends with Ben Franklin and with several Quakers including Anthony Benezet. Franklin recalled that:

> Mr. Whitefield...was at first permitted to speak in some of our churches; but the clergy, taking a dislike to him, soon refus'd him

their pulpits and he was oblig'd to preach in the fields. The multitudes of all sects and denominations that attended this services were enormous.[59]

Whitefield depicted in his sermons the tortures which unsaved people could expect and he mightily convinced his hearers of the folly of risking hell fire. People were so wrought up that they wept and cried for mercy, and Whitefield wept with them. Hundreds were converted and the membership of many churches multiplied.[60]

From Philadelphia Whitefield and his party traveled south to Georgia, where he planned to build an orphanage with slave labor. He reached Williamsburg Saturday, December 15, 1739, and was received courteously by Governor Gooch and Commissary Blair. He preached the sermon in Bruton Church that Sunday.[61] It was the only time he preached in Virginia that visit, but this one appearance had a great effect on future events in the Colony.

So George Whitefield brought the Great Awakening to America. There was considerable opposition to his methods, in Virginia and elsewhere. An ordained Anglican clergyman, he disregarded the orders and canons of his church. His emotional approach and the extravagant conduct of his converts outraged Anglican decorum.[62] His insistence on fine theological distinctions alienated him from the Wesley brothers and other religious leaders. It was said that many of Whitefield's converts slid back into indifference after the excitement wore off. Nevertheless, he planted Evangelicalism in America, and he planted so well that the concept is alive and well to this day.

John Greenleaf Whittier (1807-1892), the Quaker poet, wrote a four-page poem titled "The Preacher," a meditation on George Whitefield and what Whitefield accomplished from a Quaker's point of view. Whittier calls him

> A homeless pilgrim with dubious name
>     Blown about on the winds of fame;
> Now as an angel of blessing classed,
>     And now as a mad enthusiast.

Whitefield had faults, but so has everybody, Whittier decides--

> No perfect whole can our nature make
>     Here and there the circle will break...

So, incomplete by his being's law
    The marvellous preacher had his flaw;
With step unequal, and lame with faults,
    His shade on the path of History halts.

One fault is Whitefield's use of fear to sway his listeners--

    Wisely and well said the Eastern bard
        Fear is easy, but love is hard

And another fault is Whitefield's focus on Heaven and Hell, ignoring the here and now--

    Thus he--to whom in the painful stress
        Of zeal on fire from its own excess,
    Heaven seemed so vast and earth so small
        That man was nothing, since God was all--
    Forgot as the best of times have done,
        That the love of the Lord and man are one.

He had no concern for the evils of war or of slavery--

    So by Savannah's banks of shade
        The stones of his mission the preacher laid
    On the heart of the negro crushed and rent,
        And made of his blood the wall's cement
    Bade the slave-ship speed from coast to coast
        Fanned by the wings of the Holy Ghost...

    Father of Light! How blind is he
        Who sprinkles the altar he rears to Thee
    With the blood and tears of humanity!

But nevertheless, George Whitefield left the world a better place--

    So in light and shadow the preacher went,
        God's erring and human instrument...

    The flood of emotion deep and strong
        Troubled the land as it swept along

> But left a result of holier lives,
> > Tenderer mothers and worthier wives.
> The husband and father whose children fled
> > And sad wife wept when his drunken tread
> Frightened peace from his roof-tree's shade...
> > In a strength that was not his own began
> To rise from the brute's to the plane of man.

Whittier thought that the Society of Friends, alone of all the denominations, was unaffected by George Whitefield's "flood of emotion"--

> In silent protest of letting alone
> > The Quaker kept the way of his own,--
> A non-conductor among the wires,
> > With coat of asbestos proof to fires....
> And vague of creed, and barren of rite,
> > But holding, as in his Master's sight,
> Act and thought to the Inner Light,
> > The round of his simple duties walked,
> And strove to live what the others talked.

The fact is, however, that the Society of Friends *was* affected. The coat of asbestos was *not* fireproof, as we shall presently see.

\* \* \*

At the time of Mr. Whitefield's visit, December 1739, Friends were the only organized dissenters in Virginia--excepting only the Presbyterians of Opequon Church and a few new Scotch-Irish Presbyterian backwoods congregations. The Presbyterians on the Eastern Shore and the Baptist church at Burleigh were long gone. Within a few years after 1739, however, Presbyterians and Baptists re-appeared in Virginia in force. Their re-appearance was a direct result of the Great Awakening.

The Presbyterian's return began when the Morrises, the Hunts and two other families in Hanover County became dissatisfied with the services in their parish church. In 1739 they heard that Mr. Whitefield was coming to Williamsburg 60 miles away, but he left before they could hear him. However, they obtained a book of Whitefield's sermons, and read them together instead of going to church. Then they began reading Martin Luther's works. Their numbers increased and they built a "Reading House" on Samuel Morris's land. This caused them to be cited to appear before Governor Gooch and Council.[63]

In Williamsburg they showed the Governor a book, the Confession of Faith of the Presbyterian Church of Scotland. This book, they declared, expressed their views on religion. And "Governor Gooch, himself of Scotch origin and education, upon looking at the volume, pronounced the men Presbyterians...the men were dismissed with a gentle caution from the Governor not to excite any disturbance in His Majesty's Colony."

In July 1743, a traveling Presbyterian Evangelical came to Morris's Reading House, the Reverend Mr. William Robinson. He was the son of an English Quaker physician, pock-marked and blind in one eye. He preached four successive days to successively larger audiences: the text of his first sermon--"I tell you nay: but except ye repent ye shall likewise perish" (Luke 13.3). So he established the New Side Presbyterian way--and Evangelicalism--permanently in central Virginia.

After Mr. Robinson's four days a good many people in Hanover and surrounding counties began to attend Presbyterian meetings. Most of the new Presbyterians came over from the Established Church, but at least one was a Quaker of Curles Meeting, Thomas Watkins. The first Presbyterian meeting house in Henrico County was built on Thomas Watkins' farm at Malvern Hill in 1747.[64] Visiting Evangelicals--including George Whitehead himself--visited the new congregations and kept new converts coming.

In August 1747 Reverend Samuel Davies, 24, arrived in Hanover from Pennsylvania to be the Presbyterians' first permanent minister. He visited Williamsburg repeatedly to get licenses for new Presbyterian places of worship, encountering much hostility from Peyton Randolph, the colony's Attorney-General, and a good degree of sympathy from Scottish Governor Gooch. Mr. Davies was careful to stay within the limits of the Act of Toleration as it had been recognized in Virginia in 1699. For a time Peyton Randolph denied that the Act was in force in Virginia, but Davies insisted it was in force and eventually made his point.

Finally in 1754, after eleven years of struggle, the Presbyterians' troubles were resolved by the coming of the French and Indian War. Mr. Davies toured Virginia delivering war sermons based on gory Old Testament texts. He persuaded whole battalions of Scotch-Irishmen to turn out against the French and Indian enemies. Official opposition to the Presbyterians of Virginia then disappeared.[65] Hanover Presbytery was established in 1755 with Mr. Davies as its first Moderator.

Presbyterians of Virginia contended from 1743 to 1754 for *toleration* of their way of worship. They did not join the Friends in the struggle for absolute *freedom* of religion, and they did not suffer as the Friends did seizures of their goods for refusing to support the Established Church. Friends stood alone as freedom fighters until Baptists re-appeared in the Colony.

Baptists began to return in 1743. That year 14 or 15 families from New Jersey[66] settled on Mill(s) Creek at present day Garrardstown, West Virginia. They built Mill Creek Baptist Church, on land either given or sold to them by Quaker John Mills (John Mills--1688-1760--was father of the four Mills brothers, who were early ministers of the Hopewell Friends). In 1754, they were joined by elder Shubael Stearns and his family from Tolland, Connecticut--fervent Evangelical converts of George Whitefield.[67]

When war came in 1754, the Mill Creek congregation was shepherded east by elder John Gerrard to Loudoun County for a time, out of the way of Indian attacks. The Stearns', however, moved to Guilford County, North Carolina, where Shubael established the Sandy Creek Church. It soon grew from 16 members to more than 600 and became the brood hen church for Baptist Churches of North Carolina and southside Virginia.[68] Dan River Baptist Church was the first of this brood in Virginia, launched during revival services in August, 1760.[69]

In contrast to Presbyterian ministers, who were educated and trained, the Baptist preaches were untrained although many of them were able speakers, well-versed in the Bible. Their approach was emotional and their appeal was to plain farming families. They believed absolutely in separating the Church from the State. Unlike the Presbyterians they largely ignored the Toleration Act and generally refused to apply for preaching licenses.[70]

Like the Quakers they were criticized and ridiculed. The *Virginia Gazette* for October 31, 1771, published a contribution titled--

A Receipt to Make an Anabaptist Preacher

Take the herbs of Hypocrisy and Ambition...of the seed of Dissention and Discord one ounce...one ounce of the Spirit of Self-Conceitedness....

\* \* \*

Now we have come to the middle years of the 1700s. Sixteen times more men, women and children live here in Virginia now than a hundred years earlier--about 173,000 white and 120,000 black people in 1750. These Virginians have moved their frontier west and west, settling high and higher up the tilt of the Piedmont plateau, clear to the Blue Ridge; with three or four thousand living clear over the Blue Ridge, in the Valley still claimed by the Native Americans (whose numbers are uncountable.) Not only are the Virginians scattered more widely over the landscape in 1750: they are more widely separated also in terms of class and color; of wealth and point-of-view.

John and Rebecca Flower Lincoln are the Quaker great-grandparents of President Abraham Lincoln. They moved south from Pennsylvania to Rockingham County, Virginia in 1750 and rest now in their family's burying ground on Route 42 between Harrisonburg and Broadway. James Lincoln, 92, their descendant, visits their graves in 1990.

# VII

# THE QUAKER WAY ALTERS COURSE
## 1750-1763

> So far as true love influences our minds, so far we feel a desire...to lessen the distresses of the afflicted and to increase the happiness of the creation.
>
> -- John Woolman

By 1750 landowners with mansion-houses and slaves held the river banks of Virginia's four great rivers. "New Nigras" were continually arriving off the slave ships from West Africa. The slaves were to be seen everywhere, a mixed blessing. They freed their owners from drudgery and made many owners rich; but they also imparted a vague sense of unease. For slavery is a kind of deliberate exploitation that offends ideas of justice and shared humanity, impossible to reason away entirely.

Furthermore, though one's "servants" might smile and say "Massa" during the day, one could not really know what they were thinking--or doing at night. Some sultry summer nights at bedtime, white families could just hear the distant pulse of African drums. Were the Nigras only dancing? Were they voodoo drums? Sometimes the drums sounded sinister.

The drums had become worrisome by 1740. The Assembly passed a law requiring militia patrols to ride out at night and break up slaves' gatherings. Friends owning slaves were pressured to join the militia for this special purpose. And this new development was discussed at Virginia Yearly Meeting held at Chuckatuck in September 1740. The minute reads:

> Upon a proposal to this Meeting whether any Friend may go a-patrolling to keep the blacks in subjection: after Friends considered it, it was the opinion of this Meeting that Friends can in no way comply with it.[1]

Following this Yearly Meeting, the clerk sent out a summary of the Meeting's "sense" to Virginia's local meetings:

> Dear Friends--It hath pleased...God that the place of our outward abode is in a land where persecution does attend us for our religious

testimony.... We beseech you therefore in the love of God [to continue your resistance against] paying hire to the priests, and the learning of war....

[Since] the trial of our faith and patience in the latter of these is likely to be greater than for these many years...we exhort that all Friends everywhere bear a concurrent testimony therein [and do not] use any evasions to shun the Cross.

...The general plea and argument used by our adversaries...is that, as the intent of the law is for the country's preservation in case the blacks should make any attempt against it, and as many of us having negroes ought--as they say--be helpful and assistant to defend the country against any attempt of that nature...

Which argument--tho' it may have some color of fleshly reason...ought not to sway us so as to make us lay waste a testimony grounded on...love and peace.

...In order that we may be serviceable in some measure in the case, those who have negroes are advised to use them as fellow creatures and the workmanship of the same all-wise Creator that made and created us, not abusing them....[2]

* * *

Six years later in the summer of 1746, a 26-year-old traveler with a serious, sweet face under a broad-brim Quaker hat, John Woolman of Mount Holly, New Jersey, visited the Virginia Quakers.[3] He came under a religious concern along with his friend Isaac Andrews.

In the years since that summer John Woolman has come to be recognized as one among the finest flowerings of American Quakerism. Charles Sainte-Beuve in his *History of Port-Royal* tries to define what it is to be a saint. His definition fits the man John Woolman. "Such souls," Sainte-Beuve writes, "arrive at a certain fixed and invincible state, a state which is genuinely heroic, and from which the greatest deeds are performed.... Their inner state before all other things is one of love and humility--of infinite confidence in God--of severity to themselves, with tenderness for others."[4]

John Woolman's visit in 1746 prefigured a profoundly important, blessed turn in the course of Virginia's history and the history of the United States of America. There was no indication of the visit's future impact, though, in its beginning. John described the beginning in his *Journal*:

> I...found an enlargement of gospel love in my mind, and therein a concern to visit friends in some of the back settlements of Pennsylvania and Virginia; and being thoughtful about a companion, I expressed it to my beloved friend Isaac Andrews, who told me that he had drawings to the same places.... [So] I opened the case in our monthly meeting, and friends expressing their unity therewith, we obtained certificates to travel as companions--his from Haddonfield and mine from Burlington [New Jersey].

So John and his friend Isaac rode out in the May weather of 1746. They had several meetings in Chester County and one near Lancaster, Pennsylvania. Then they crossed the river Susquehanna and had meetings in a raw new settlement there. They followed blazemarks on the trees to the Friends' settlement on Monocacy Creek, south of Hagerstown, Maryland; splashed across the Potomac and rode clear across Virginia north to southeast, 400 miles. They visited all the Quaker settlements along the way, from Fairfax, Hopewell and Smith's Creek, to the old settlements in Nansemond and Isle of Wight Counties. They went on to Perquimans in North Carolina and "found some openness in those parts and a hopeful appearance among the young people." Afterwards "we turned again to Virginia, and attended most of the meetings which we had not been at before, laboring amongst Friends, in the love of Jesus Christ, as ability was given."

Two conditions impressed John Woolman in Virginia in 1746. One was the hardship of life in a new country. The other impression, which led John directly to the great work of his later life, was the bad consequence to slave-- holding families of living "in ease on the hard labor of their slaves."

Many Quakers in the 1740s owned slaves, in Virginia and around John Woolman's neighborhood in Mount Holly, including John's grandfather Henry Burr.[5] Yet, when John was 21, he clerked in a store where the owner kept a slave and John wrote then that he felt "uneasy" and came to believe that "the practice was not right." John and Isaac Andrews in Virginia saw ragged gangs of black people working under overseers in the fields, including the fields of Friends who invited John and Isaac to stay overnight. These sights brought John's uneasiness to an abhorrence. He wrote:

> When I eat, drank, and lodged free-cost with people, who lived in ease on the hard labor of their slaves...I found...this uneasiness return upon me, at times, through the whole visit.
>
> Where the masters bore a good share of the burthen, and lived frugally, so that their servants were well provided for, and their labor moderate, I felt more easy; but...the white people and their children so generally living without much labor, was frequently the subject of my serious thoughts. I saw...so many vices and corruptions increased by this trade and way of life, that it appeared to me as a dark gloominess hanging over the land; and though many now willingly run into it, yet in future the consequence will be grievous to posterity.[6]

After John returned home from Virginia in 1746, he penned a short manuscript describing his abhorrence of slavery. His father on his deathbed urged John to publish the manuscript, and in 1754 John had *Some Considerations on the Keeping of Negroes. Recommended to the Professors of Christianity of Every Denomination* printed in Philadelphia, Benjamin Franklin the printer. The little book had a devastating logic for Friends, whose basic belief is that there is some thing of God in every person.

Even before *Some Considerations* was published Philadelphia Yearly Meeting quoted from it in its annual epistle to Virginia Yearly Meeting of 1753.[7] Its publication marks the real beginning of anti-slavery in America, a mind-set which spread outward from the Society of Friends like the ripples from a stone thrown in a pond.

John Woolman returned to Virginia in 1757. In the eleven years since his first visit, he had grown from a promising young man to a spiritual leader among the 20,000 Friends living in and around Philadelphia. In those eleven years almost single-handed, he led the Philadelphia Quakers to begin to see that slavery is evil and unChristian. He came to Virginia in 1757 to witness against slavery.

Woolman rode south in 1757 accompanied by his brother Uriah. As they rode, John prayed for strength to speak the truth in love to slaveholders. The custom was for Virginia Quakers to provide free hospitality to visiting ministers, but John decided to insist on paying their slaves in order to "keep clear from the gain of oppression."[8]

On May 11, 1757, the Woolmans crossed the Potomac into Virginia following the Post Road (now Route 301) south. This time John spent about six weeks in Virginia and North Carolina. From what he wrote in his journal, nothing very notable happened in the six weeks. The external record of events, though, tells another story.

According to his journal, John and his brother fell in with a colonel of militia who rode along with them on their way from the Potomac ferry to Port Royal. They talked about slavery, with the colonel justifying slave-holding. He said that "the lives of the negroes were so wretched in their own country, that many of them lived better here than there." John replied "If compassion for the Africans...was the real motive for our purchasing them, that spirit of tenderness...would incite us to use them kindly [but] we manifest by our conduct that our views in purchasing them are to advance ourselves." He went on to predict "if the white people [continue] to prefer their outward prospects of gain to all other considerations and do not act conscientiously toward [black people] as fellow-creatures, I believe that...times [will] change in a way disagreeable to us."[9]

Some Friends of Cedar Creek Meeting rode with John the thirty-five miles from Cedar Creek to Camp Creek Meeting. As they rode, one Friend advanced the theory that blacks are the offspring of Cain that unsavory Old Testament character. "Their blackness," the Friend suggested, "being the mark God set upon [Cain].... It is the design of Providence they should be slaves." John refuted the suggestion, quoting texts from Genesis. Then "in some pressure of spirit," he declared "I believe liberty is their right."

John spoke in Friends' meetings at Camp Creek, at a Friend's house near Charlottesville, at Fork Creek Meeting, Cedar Creek, White Oak Swamp, Weyanoke, Burleigh, Blackwater. Always his topic was slavery. Sometimes he spoke with his face wet with tears. At Cedar Creek he "found a tender seed." In some other meetings "it appeared to me that through the prevailing of the spirit of this world the minds of many were brought to an inward desolation."

From Blackwater Meeting he rode twenty miles to Virginia Yearly Meeting for 1757, held that year in Western Branch Meeting House. When Friends went to business, a set of queries was presented by a committee appointed to update the Yearly Meeting's Book of Discipline. Woolman recognized that the committee had adapted some of these queries from Philadelphia Yearly Meeting's new Book of Discipline which he himself had helped to edit. He was troubled by the alteration of one Philadelphia query which read "Are there any concerned in the importation of negroes, or *buying them after imported*?" The Virginia committee, however, had watered it down to read "Are there any concerned in the importation of negroes, or *buying them to trade in*?" When he heard this, Woolman rose and protested.

It is inconsistent for Friends to buy negroes, he said. They are "captives of war, or taken by stealth...and their being our fellow creatures and sold as slaves adds greatly to the iniquity." John Woolman thought his protest did not make much of an impression. "Friends appeared attentive to what was said" he wrote, "some expressed a care and concern about their negroes; none made any objection by way of reply to what I said; but the query was admitted as they had altered it." He reflected that the altered query did *some* good, since "some of their members have heretofore traded in negroes."[10] And he left the rest to God.

\* \* \*

John Woolman may have thought his whole trip did not make much difference. But one never knows, does one? For the year of his trip, 1757, clearly is the year when Virginia's Friends first "came under the weight of the concern" to do something about slavery. Before 1757 they had been disturbed over the slaves' oppression and concerned to treat their own slaves kindly. After 1757 they moved slowly toward clearness that slavery is evil; and that they, Children of the Light and Friends of God, were called to testify and witness against the evil.

Notice now: until the 1750s the Friends were a people whose great aim was to bring the whole world to their inward way of approaching God. The epistle written by Virginia Yearly Meeting to Philadelphia Yearly Meeting in 1748, puts it this way:

> ...It seems to us that if the faithful among us continue to show forth the work of the Spirit of Christ by humbly walking in the dictates thereof...the borders of Zion will be enlarged in this wilderness land.

Sometime during the 1750s however--about the time John Woolman visited Virginia--Friends' focus changed. They seemed to realize that only certain people, people of a certain mind-set or soul-set, not all, are attracted to the inward way. They may have seen then that the evangelical churches were growing much faster then their own modest increase. Perhaps that was the reason for the change.

Whatever the reason, the Friends made a turning in the 1750s, a hundred years into their history. They lost interest in attracting new members; and where they had been concerned previously to help poor and unfortunate people *within their own society*, now they began to reach out to serve unfortunates in the larger society in an organized way.[11] Attending to the plight of black people was a first step.

In the narrowest sense Friends did not become "humanitarian" in the 1750s. They did not claim then or now that virtue consists solely in acts for the benefit of humankind without any reference to the benefit of God. Christ's second commandment, "You shall love your neighbor as yourself" has never ruled out His first, that "You shall love the Lord your God with all your heart and with all your soul and all your mind." Sometime in the 1750s, though, the second command acquired a new urgency for Friends.[12]

For the first hundred years the Friends' great word was Truth. Then in the 1750s they began to emphasize Love when describing the nature of God and the spirit of Christ. In the 1750s they began to acquire their reputation as "that fellowship of Christians distinguished for their integrity *and incomparable human sympathy*."[13]

\* \* \*

In the human scheme of things, women are the nurturers. The Friends' new humanitarian view somehow gave women a more important part--or, rather, returned women to their original importance among the Children of Light. About this time the Virginia Friends renewed their womens' meetings for business. It happened this way:

Edward Stabler, a young man raised among the York, England, Friends came to America in the mid 1750s. He married Mary Robinson at Providence Meeting in what is now Media, Pennsylvania, and then settled in Petersburg, Virginia, as a merchant. Soon after the Stablers began to worship in Curles Meeting, they noticed that the Curles women were not taking part in the monthly meetings for business. In 1758 Curles Friends requested Edward, 28, to be clerk of a newly organized womens' monthly meeting, to teach the women how to conduct meetings and record minutes.[14] In 1763 Edward agreed to do the same thing for the women of Virginia Yearly Meeting. The next year Mary Stabler succeeded her husband as womens' clerk of the Yearly Meeting.[15]

Womens' meetings for business which had languished in Virginia Yearly Meeting for fifty years thus were renewed. Quaker women after the 1750s emerged as about the only women in Virginia's patriarchal society who were capable of running a business meeting.*

\* \* \*

Slavery was no great concern of the backwoods Friends in the valley of Virginia, in the 1750s. Only a scattering of slaves were to be found there. Rather, the valley Friends' concern was the threat of war. Quakers in Virginia had kept up their peace testimony over the generations by refusing to join the militia. But now a *full* test of faithfulness was coming for the valley's Friends.

And what is this "peace testimony"? It is based on George Fox's declaration that there is "that life and power that takes away the occasion of all wars"; and it is informed by Jesus' teaching, "Do not resist one who is evil but overcome evil with good." As Daniel Hoffman, a modern-day Quaker poet, describes it:

> Of this peculiar people's testimony
> another is, not fighting
> but suffering, since they affirm
> all wars and fightings come of the lusts
> of men's own hearts, not
> the spirit of Christ Jesus[16]

Sometime in the summer of 1754, the Valley settlers noticed that the Indians had disappeared--all gone west overnight, into the Alleghenies. An ominous and scary discovery. Rumors flew. Some said they had seen

---

\* After 1750, the proportion increased of women ministers among all friends' ministers who visited Virginia. This increase may be another indication of womens' revived importance in the Society. According to my count:

| YEARS | MINISTERS' VISITS | |
|---|---|---|
| | All | Women |
| 1700-1749 | 58 | 13 (22%) |
| 1750-1799 | 144 | 36 (25%) |
| 1800-1849 | 106 | 34 (32%) |

strange Indians. It was widely believed that the strangers had brought some secret message from the west to the Indians of the Valley.[17]

For a few years after 1732 when whites began to arrive, the whites and Indians in the Valley had been peaceful neighbors. Then friction developed:

- In the summer of 1738 seven frontier families, none of them Quaker families, were wiped out by Indian raiders from the West -- five families in the Valley, two in what is now Loudoun County.[18] No doubt the raids were intended to discourage further encroachment of whites to the west. Thereafter each summer saw similar incidents, with aggressive retaliation by the frontiersmen.[19]

- In 1739 Thomas Penn, William's son and successor as a proprietor of Pennsylvania, betrayed his father's policy of fair treatment for the Indians. That year he devised the "Walking Purchase," cheating the Minisink tribe of their ancestral woods and causing hot resentment.[20] He was a grasping man, Thomas Penn, who left the Quakers long before 1739.

- In 1744 at Lancaster, Pennsylvania; in 1752 at Logtown near present-day Pittsburgh; and in 1753 in Winchester, Indian chiefs met with colonial officials to make treaties. Both sides soon claimed that each successive treaty had been violated by the other side.[21]

- In 1748 the Ohio Company formed to develop the vast country beyond the Ohio River. The King in Council granted 500,000 acres to the Company, after intensive lobbying in London by Quaker John Hanbury. He stressed the importance of planting the British flag in western America before the French claimed it. The twelve directors of the Ohio Company included Laurence and Augustine Washington, nine other Virginians and Hanbury. Visits by the Company's surveyors to the Ohio Country alarmed both French and Indians.[22]

- By 1753 a French detachment sent from Canada had built Fort LeBoeuf near present-day Erie, Pennsylvania. That October Virginia's Governor Dinwiddie sent Major George Washington, 21, to Fort LeBoeuf to order the French to clear out. The order was ignored of course, and this triggered the bloody French and Indian War.

Both the French and the British immediately began to declare loving friendship for the Indian tribes, wooing their help to crush the enemy.[23] No doubt the Indians, when they vanished from the Valley in 1754, were lured away by French promises.

The King in Council sent a proper task force to rout the French early in 1755--two crack infantry regiments under Major General Edward Braddock, 60, a Scot and a cool professional soldier. Maps were studied in London: Alexandria, Virginia, was chosen for the British base; and Sir John St. Clair of Braddock's staff soon arrived in Alexandria with an advance party.

Sir John plotted routes for the task force to march on Fort Duquesne (present day Pittsburgh) where the French had moved their major base. He employed pioneers to cut a road from Winchester to the Ohio Company's camp at present-day Cumberland, Maryland. He recruited 1,200 American militiamen, including a few young men of Quaker parentage caught up in the war excitement--among them Daniel Morgan of a Crooked Run Meeting family in Virginia and John West, Jr., brother of the famous artist Benjamin West. There would have been more militia, except that the Pennsylvania Assembly, controlled by Friends, absolutely refused its support.[24]

Braddock's two regiments arrived at Alexandria in mid-March 1755, on thirteen transports--two of them owned by John Hanbury. On April 9 they marched out of Alexandria, company by company, one regiment on either side of the Potomac, on the way to Fort Duquesne, 240 mountainous miles away. The 44th Foot under Colonel Sir Peter Halkett, splendid with yellow facings on red coats, marched into Winchester colors flying, officers on horseback leading their companies, sergeants major behind, alert to see that the troops kept step to the fifes and drums. Boots shined, muskets gleaming, cross-belts white with pipe clay, eyes front, ranks dressed and covered. All Winchester and Frederick County felt safe and secure, and grateful to the King. Even the Hopewell Quakers were impressed.

The two regiments met at Cumberland, Maryland, and proceeded west with pioneers ahead hacking the way through virgin forest. Seven miles from Fort Duquesne on July 9, the task force was ambushed and destroyed--Braddock and Halkett killed, 977 dead or wounded, all cannon captured. The survivors limped back toward Philadelphia. Alarm spread up and down the valley of Virginia.

Then terror came, the world turned topsy turvy. Indians, knowing now that the British could be beaten, openly went over to the French. Before July 1755 was out, Indian raiding parties appeared in the valley.[25] The warriors came, avengers, faces streaked red, black and yellow, with scalping knives and French-made muskets. They struck cabins from Winchester to Staunton and on south in the summer nights. When the mornings came, smoke from burning cabins marked the strikes. Corpses of the families, scalped, lay helter-skelter around each ruined home.

That winter the raids stopped awhile. The Indian war parties never went abroad in cold weather. But England formally declared war against France in spring 1756; and now the Indian war parties returned to the valley with French support.[26] One party of fifty braves with a French captain descended on the Tuscarora settlement where Martinsburg, West Virginia, stands today. The settlers there had made a fort, John Evans' fort, and they went into it during the first night raid. Some of the Tuscarora settlers were Friends, members of Providence Meeting on Tuscarora Creek, and some or all of the Providence Friends took shelter in the fort. The Hackney boy, a Quaker boy, beat the drum that called the settlers in to the fort.[27]

The war party did not attack John Evans' fort, but instead stole south from Tuscarora to Opequon Creek, following the Valley Road (now Route 11) down to the neighborhood of Hopewell Meeting.[28] They massacred some families there in the night. Next morning the Opequon families, most of them, fled to nearby forts. But the Quaker families of Hopewell, jaws set, pale and tight-lipped, refused to go into the forts. And marvelous to say, none of them and none of their homes were harmed.[29]

This raid and others like it in 1757 and 1758 panicked the valley. Its population thinned and thinned as families abandoned their farms and fled east. Most of those who stayed went to live in the improvised forts dotted along the frontier line from Hampshire County, now West Virginia, to Halifax County on the North Carolina line. The men left the cramped forts to tend their fields, with lookouts posted against prowling Indians. Everyone looked forward to winter when they could stop "forting" and live in their own homes awhile. Autumns seemed unending, the leaf colors deepening too slowly, seasons of sad beauty. Hope swept the forts when the first frost came, but the families waited on for "Indian summer" to end--that hazy time of year when Indian raiders were most active.

In those terrible years, the valley Quakers emerged as a really peculiar people. By and large they stayed in their homes, tended their farms, and met for worship as usual. They neither went into the forts, retreated east of the Blue Ridge, or took up arms. On one hand they must have been frightened for their lives. On the other, they were trying to witness for the Truth as they saw it.

God is love--there is a life and power that does away with the occasion for fighting--Senecas are God's children, too--let not your heart be troubled, neither let it be afraid. Such quiet, quiet words came out of the First Day silences then. Peace is the way, dear friends, peace. If history does not prove this to be so, it is time now to begin to prove it is so.[30]

So they ministered to one another, even while the smoke of burning cabins hung on the valley air.

Philadelphia Yearly Meeting created a new committee--the Meeting for Sufferings--to look after the emergency needs of Friends living in the Pennsylvania, Maryland, and Virginia war zones. Hopewell Friends wrote to the Meeting for Sufferings on "ye 5th of ye 9th month 1757." Of the valley's hundred-odd Quaker families, they listed eleven living west of Hopewell Meeting house, "driven from their habitations...and we find that some have been drove from home almost two years and are not likely to get home again, and some of them that are got home do stand in need of some help."

The Meeting for Sufferings promptly sent £50 to help the eleven families and asked for further details. Hopewell replied: "You requested to know whether any of them were visited or attacked by the Indians. We answer 'No, nor any Friends' house burnt except one.'"[31]

What was it then that kept Friends so safe in the midst of so much mayhem? One answer may be found in their "settled intention to practice love." Another may be the liking the Indians had for them. Friend James Kenny went west to Pittsburgh in April 1759 to keep store for the Pemberton brothers. He wrote in his journal about Indian feelings for Quakers:

> Here was an Indian who had a white woman. He seemed glad to see Quakers and the woman mentioned she wondered at the esteem the Indians professed for the Quakers.
>
> In Pittsburgh, I met
>
> An old man Indian named Pisquiton (Beaver King's brother) who sometimes called himself a Quaker.... Another old Indian, Daniel, called himself a Quaker too--but Daniel said he could fight and be a Quaker too, when it was surmised that the enemy was coming.[32]

All this is not to say that all the frontier Quakers were faithful or that the Indians recognized all of them for Quakers. Some Friends joined the militia and indeed two of Frederick County's eight militia companies were captained by Isaac Parkins of Centre Meeting and Edward Rogers of Hopewell Meeting (Quakers who evidently were penitent and returned to good standing in their meetings after the war.) One Hopewell Friend's house was burned, and eleven families living west of Winchester found it necessary to move into town for a time. Far to the south in Bedford County a little Quaker group only just settled there pulled back in 1758 to live a while with the South River Friends near present day Lynchburg.[33]

Those Friends were not censured, but the Providence Friends on Tuscarora Creek who fled for refuge into John Evans' Fort were severely censured. Providence Meeting was closed down in 1758, no longer recognized as a Friends Meeting by Philadelphia Yearly Meeting. When it was "allowed" again late in 1760, it re-opened under the new name of Tuscarora Meeting.[34]

The Providence Friends' behavior contrasts with the Luptons'--Joseph 70, and Mary 67. They lived two miles west of Winchester and knew many Indians. One Friday night in December 1756 the Luptons entertained William Reckitt, an English Quaker, and his companion. Reckitt wrote:

> We lodged at Joseph Lupton's, an ancient Friend who with his wife was very loving to us. The Indians had killed and carried away several within a few miles of their habitation; yet they did not seem much afraid, for they said, they did not so much as pull in the sneck-string of the door when they go to bed and had neither lock nor bar.[35]

Virginia's Assembly passed an act for drafting single men into the militia in 1756. A number of young Quakers allowed themselves to be drafted, ignoring the advice of Virginia Yearly Meeting to resist the new law.[36] However, some of the valley Friends' young men were sentenced to Winchester's log jail for refusing to soldier, and some were flogged. George Hollingsworth--the same George who was the valley's first Quaker bridegroom--was also jailed when he took part in a silent meeting of Friends under the jail's windows to protest the incarceration of the draft refusers there.[37]

East of the Blue Ridge seven young Friends absolutely refused to be drafted. They were marched under guard to Winchester--John and William

Ellyson of Black Creek Meeting in New Kent County, Cornelius and John Harris and Archelaus, William and John Stanley of Cedar Creek Meeting, Hanover County. The seven were prodded along 140 miles to Winchester, refusing all the way to take the oath of allegiance, remove their hats, eat the King's rations, or answer their names at roll call. Once in Winchester they were lodged in the guard house, refusing to hold muskets or to work on Fort Loudoun then being built in the town.

George Washington, the militia colonel commanding at Winchester, now 24-years-old, threatened them with flogging. He held off, however, when Edward Stabler of Petersburg and Isaac Hollingsworth of Winchester, Friends' ministers, called on him and asked him to wait until Friends could appeal to Governor Dinwiddie on behalf of the seven.[38] Washington wrote to Dinwiddie for advice, and Dinwiddie's instructions were "to confine them with a short allowance of bread and water till you bring them to reason." But on 4 August 1756, Washington, frustrated, wrote Dinwiddie that:

> I could by no means bring the Quakers to any terms. They chose rather to be whipped to death than to bear arms.

Meanwhile, Edward Stabler and four other Friends visited Governor Dinwiddie in Williamsburg. On August 19, Dinwiddie wrote to Washington:

> A great body of Quakers waited on me in regard to their friends with you, praying they may not be whipped. Use them with lenity, but as they are at their own expense I would have them remain as long as the other draughts.[39]

Finally, in December 1756, Joshua Brown, 39, a minister of West Nottingham Meeting in Maryland, came to Winchester, "having felt a draft of love to visit Friends settled about Hopewell in Virginia." He wrote:

> There were seven young men who had been brought up out of Virginia by militia officers under Colonel George Washington, who had been condemned to imprisonment for six months because they were not free to bear arms. They had suffered much threatening and were taken out to be whipped. This was not done. The great Master had preserved them in faithfulness.

They had gained the favor of the officers. Their time was now out and they requested me and my companion to go with them to Colonel Washington. He was very pleasant and discharged them.⁴⁰

French and Indian attacks continued furious in the valley right through the summer of 1758. Then at summer's end the attacks stopped. This blessed development came through the efforts of certain Pennsylvania Quakers.

In Pennsylvania the legislature was controlled by Quakers for seventy-four years, from 1682 to 1756, while non-Quaker governors controlled the government's executive side most of that time. When Pennsylvania's governor declared war on the Delaware Indians in April 1756, Israel Pemberton, Peter Worrall, and four other Quaker legislators resigned in protest. They immediately organized The Friendly Association for Regaining and Preserving Peace with the Indians by Pacific Measures. Mennonites and Schwenkfelders supported the Friends in this enterprise to right the wrongs done to the Indians.⁴¹

The Friendly Association's members worked for two years. They collected money for gifts to Delawares, Shawnees, and other tribes helping the French. They struggled with inter-tribal politics and with Governor William Denny of Pennsylvania who wrote to England in 1757 that he resented "a body of men [Quakers] who have no more pretensions than any other religious society to concern themselves in a matter of government."⁴² In July 1757 Tedyuscung, King of the Eastern Delawares, agreed to peace, and in October 1758 the Iroquois imposed peace on the rest of the tribes. With that, three years of terror along the frontier ended, and the Friendly Association achieved its purpose.

Governor Denny's resentment went hand in hand with a wide-spread rumor that the Quakers were really interested in peace with the Indians for money-making reasons. There was some basis for the rumor too. Israel Pemberton, 43, was a leading light in the Friendly Association. He was a blunt, driving man, a leader in business, in politics, and in the affairs of Philadelphia Yearly Meeting. His brother John and Friends like Anthony Benezet chided Israel for his devotion to business.⁴³ They urged him to "come out of the world's hurries." Israel, however, argued that his spiritual activities and business activities were compatible.

As soon as the Friendly Association won over the Indian tribes in 1758, Israel opened a fur trading business at Fort Pitt. Isaac Zane, Jr., John Langdale, Samuel Lightfoot and James Kenny, all Quakers, were among Israel's Indian traders. Israel must have made money in this fur business, but he declared that he was in it to gain "the Indians to the English interest."[44] He probably did that too, for his traders treated the Indian hunters fair and friendly. Israel Pemberton: an exemplar of the Quaker who does well by doing good.

Pontiac, Chief of the Ottawas, rallied the Western tribes in 1763 and tried once more to push back the whites. There were more night raids and massacres in the valley until Pontiac subsided in 1766.[45] Then for a time there was peace in the valley of Virginia.

\* \* \*

The thoroughfare running south into the valley and along the valley floor was wide enough for wagons after 1750, clean down to Linville Creek in now Rockingham County--although tree stumps in the right of way were high enough to "stump" a wagon. It was no longer called the Great Warrior's Path but now the Great Philadelphia Wagon Road. Increasing numbers, Quaker and otherwise, came down the Wagon Road to find new homes.

Most of the moving families liked the looks of the green northern valley and considered settling there--until they asked about acquiring land. Then they found that the terms were no longer attractive. For Lord Fairfax himself had moved to the valley in 1749, asserted his ownership of all the land from Potomac River far south, and set up his land office and bachelor quarters at Greenway Court, twelve miles south of Winchester. Anyone who wanted land, in what are today Frederick, Clarke, Page, Shenandoah, and Warren Counties in Virginia or Berkeley, Hampshire, Hardy, Jefferson and Morgan Counties in West Virginia, now had to apply to Greenway Court.[46]

Lord Fairfax operated this vast and lovely tract as lord of a manor. This throw back to feudalism was not pleasing to Americans whose forebears crossed the Atlantic to get away from lords and manors. In addition to down-payments for his land, Fairfax required an annual quitrent of two shillings per 100 acres. This was roughly equivalent to the Virginia real estate tax, but on top of the quitrent he also expected certain "regalities" or feudal privileges. These privileges included "reversions" and "escheats" which entitled him to take back all abandoned and forfeited property, and the right to exact a "fine" from the tenant whenever a property changed hands.[47]

Many families, including some 150 Quaker families were living on the land claimed by Lord Fairfax before he moved to Greenway Court in 1749. Fairfax barraged these families with law suits even before 1749, seeking to have their deeds revoked--even though they had already paid Alexander Ross and Morgan Bryan or Robert McKay and Jost Hite for the land.[48] The suits were not successful, and nearly all the families kept their farms. Morgan Bryan, Jr., however, was disgusted by the legal harassment. He gave up his land when Fairfax began to sue and took his family south down the trace from Linville Creek in 1748. After three months the Bryans reached Yadkin County, North Carolina, and settled there.[49]

Two famous Quaker families tarried on Linville Creek about 1750--the families of Squire and Sarah Boone[50] and John and Rebecca Lincoln.[51] Both came from Exeter Friends Meeting near Reading, Pennsylvania. They were related by marriage.[52] The Boones' son Daniel, 16-years-old in 1750, became America's fabled frontiersman. The Lincolns' great grandson Abraham became America's president.

Boones and Lincolns evidently worshiped at the Linville Creek (later Smith's Creek) Meeting, just on the edge of Lord Fairfax's great tract. The Boones stayed only a year and then followed the Bryans south to Yadkin. The Lincolns stayed on Linville Creek for two or three generations.[53]

Other families, including many Quaker families, followed the Bryans and Boones south as the Wagon Road widened and lengthened--through Staunton, Lexington, Big Lick (Roanoke), Rocky Mount, Martinsville, and on into North Carolina. The Quakers established New Garden and Cane Creek Meetings in wilderness Guilford County and Alamance County, North Carolina.

Some Quakers from Pennsylvania were content to settle in northwest Virginia in spite of Lord Fairfax's dampening feudal influence. The six Friends' meetings there grew a little, and two *new* meetings appeared after 1750 and before 1755 when the Indian troubles stopped migration:
- Ridge Meeting began in or near Joseph and Mary Lupton's cabin. Their neighborhood came to be called "Apple Pie Ridge" after the mouth-watering pies brought to meeting for "pot luck" meals by the Quaker wives.[54]
- Howard's Lick Meeting began on the west bank of Potomac River's South Branch near present-day Petersburg, West Virginia. It was sited just outside the Fairfax tract, probably because the families of William Zane and widow Sarah Howard,

who founded the meeting, wanted nothing to do with Lord Fairfax. Wyandot Indians over-ran Howard's Lick in 1753. They captured little Isaac Zane, 9, and took him to Ohio. He married a chief's daughter and remained all his life with the tribe, known as "Wyandot Isaac." The U.S. Congress awarded him 10,000 Ohio acres where Zanesville stands today for his help in negotiating peace treaties.[55]

When hostilities ended in 1758, new settlers poured into Virginia's back country by the Wagon Road,[56] including a number of Friends. Three more new meetings appeared in northwest Virginia, all under the care of Hopewell Meeting: Back Creek west of Hopewell, Mill Creek and Middle Creek to the north.

East of the Blue Ridge between 1750 and 1763, eleven new meetings sprang up and three old ones were laid down:

- Two of the 11 new meetings were in Loudoun County: Gap Meeting near Hillsboro and South Fork near Unison.
- Five started up in "old" Virginia: Black Creek in Southampton County (not to be confused with Black Creek, New Kent County), Johnson's in Isle of Wight, Langley's near Petersburg, Stanton's in Sussex, and Swamp in Hanover. The three meetings laid down: Hunnicutt's, Surry, and Sugar Loaf Mountain Meeting in Albemarle County.
- Three more started around what is now Lynchburg when the Friends of Sugar Loaf Mountain moved all together to the new country south of James River. The three, South River, Goose Creek in Bedford County (not to be confused with Goose Creek Meeting, Loudoun County), and Kirby's Meeting in Halifax County.
- The eleventh new meeting was Ladd's in Mecklenburg County, founded in frontier country by a pioneering family from Lower Virginia.

So now in Virginia in 1763 there were forty-nine meetings of the Friends of God, where there had been forty-two in 1750.

The oldest house in Winchester was once a Quaker home. This is Abram's Folly, home of Hollingsworth family, built 1754. Edward Stabler the Elder and his family lived in the Petersburg house (below) from 1758 to 1785 when Edward for many of those years was clerk of Virginia Yearly Meeting. It is probably Petersburg's oldest house.

# VIII

# FAREWELL BRITANNIA
## 1763-1775

*Any Established Church is an established crime...an enemy to human liberty.*
*--Mark Twain*

For twelve years beginning in 1763 a great tide of change swept Virginia. The tide rearranged her old church-going ways and style of government.

The place of the established Church in Virginia began to change when the Parsons' Cause was tried in 1763. All Anglican ministers then were paid 16,000 pounds of tobacco a year by law. In 1758 the tobacco crop was poor, and the price of tobacco went sky high. Much public grumbling arose over the rich pickings in store for the parsons.

In response to public feelings the Virginia Assembly passed a law--the Two Penny Act--allowing Virginians to pay their church taxes in cash at the rate of two pennies per pound of tobacco, instead of tobacco itself which the parsons could sell at six pennies per pound. The King vetoed this Act; whereupon several Virginia parsons filed suit to force their parishes to pay them in tobacco--a difference of four pence or £266. The Reverend Mr. James Maury, respected minister of Fredericksville Parish in Albemarle County, sued the tax collectors of his parish for this sum. The trial was held in Hanover County Court, December 1763.

Patrick Henry, 27, of the Hanover bar represented the tax collectors. He called the parsons "rapacious harpies." The Two Penny Act is a *good* law, he said, because it helps our planters. He fiddled with his papers and cleared his throat. Then he said loudly that the King was acting like a *tyrant* when he abolished the Two Penny Act. When a king behaves like a tyrant, he thundered on, then the king no longer deserves to be *obeyed*!

Lawyer Henry was flirting with serious trouble here, daring to say what had never been said in a Virginia court before. Nevertheless the Hanover jury agreed with him. It awarded Mr. Maury only one penny for damages instead of £266. In effect the jury vetoed the King's veto. The parsons lost their cause, Lawyer Henry won fame, and the King's authority over Virginians was clearly fractured.[1]

\* \* \*

In Virginia the Presbyterian Church grew fast beginning in the 1750s, and the Baptists grew faster beginning in the 1760s. While the Dissenting churches grew, attendance in the Established churches thinned. By 1774, Thomas Jefferson estimated that dissenters--Baptists, Presbyterians, Quakers, and the valley Germans--made up two-thirds of Virginia's church-goers.[2]

One reason for such fast change was the appeal of the evangelical worship style introduced by George Whitefield. Another was the worldliness and snobbery that afflicted the established Church. It had become more a social than a spiritual institution. Wealthy planters dominated the parish vestries and many of the parsons catered to them. Short and comfortable sermons, read with elegance from high pulpits by men in snowy surplices, made the congregations feel comfortable in Zion. Uncomfortable prickles of conscience were avoided. Some parsons were earnest and godly, but, as Bishop Meade noted:

> ...It is a melancholy fact that some of them had been addicted to the race field, the card table, the ball room, the theatre--nay more to the drunken revel.
>
> One of them [was] president of a jockey club. Another preached...against the four sins of atheism, gambling, horse racing and swearing...while he practiced all the vices himself. When he died in the midst of his ravings he was heard hallowing the hounds to the chase.
>
> Another...wished something done and convened [his vestry] for the purpose. A quarrel ensued. From words they came to blows and the minister was victorious. On the following Sabbath the minister justified what he had done in a sermon from a passage of Nehemiah--'And I contended with them, and cursed them, and smote certain of them, and plucked off their hair.'[3]

Until the Baptists came to ally with them, Virginia's Friends had been standing alone a hundred years for the principle of religious liberty. In all that time they refused to pay church taxes, steadily losing crops, farm animals, hay, tools, hats, saddles, beds, and frying pans, all confiscated by the county sheriffs in lieu of the unpaid church taxes.

The Presbyterians in Virginia settled for religious *toleration*. They did not combat the colony's right to collect church taxes or to license ministers. In 1765, however, the Baptists came to stand with the Friends, declaring that "there can be no compulsion in religion."[4] Baptist ministers generally refused to be licensed. For ten years, from 1765 to 1775, Baptists joined forces with Friends.

In January 1765 Elder Samuel Harriss, a convert of Shubael Stearns and a leader in the new Dan River Baptist Church of Pittsylvania County, came up to Culpeper to spread the Baptist word:

> He preached the first day without interruption and appointed for the next. He then next day began to preach but opposers immediately raised violent opposition, appearing with whips, sticks, clubs, etc., so as to hinder his labors; in consequence of which he went that night over to Orange County and preached with much effect. He continued many days preaching from place to place, attended by great crowds....[5]

Elder Harriss's meetings continued three years, from 1765 into 1768. In that time he seeded the Baptist church all through central Virginia. His converts attracted more converts and everywhere the Establishment violently opposed them. Some converts refused to stop their unlicensed preaching and exhorting in spite of stern warnings from the county courts. Finally, in June 1768, five Baptist preachers including James Chiles of Spotsylvania were jailed in Fredericksburg. Patrick Henry rode to Fredericksburg after the five had been jailed forty-three days and succeeded in getting them released--thus adding to his fame as a champion of dissenters.[6]

Virginia's county courts continued to jail Baptist preachers; yet the number of such preachers and their converts kept climbing. The names of Joseph Anthony and six more preachers, jailed in Chesterfield between 1770 and 1774, are chiseled on a monument at Chesterfield Court House. The monument cites the seven men as "apostles of religious liberty" and bears a Bible passage dear to dissenters:

> Whether it be right in the sight of God to
> hearken unto you more than unto God,
> judge ye; for we cannot but speak the
> things we have seen and heard
> --Acts IV.19-20[7]

Virginia Friends increased modestly in the 1760s and 1770s. It was clear, however, that the evangelical and outward style of the Presbyterians and Baptists had much more popular appeal than the silent inward Quaker way of worship. In spite of the difference in styles, however, Friends and Baptists appreciated each other as allies in the cause of spiritual liberty:

- In 1768 John Burruss, who became minister of the Baptist church in Caroline County now called Carmel Church, married 19-year-old Rachel Terrell. She was a member of Caroline Friends' Meeting, and John Burruss remained on good terms with the Caroline Quakers all his life. He and his Baptist friend James Gatewood jointly gave an acre of ground to the Caroline Friends for their burying ground in 1779.[8]
- On a First Day in March 1771, Samuel Neale, 42, a Quaker traveler from Ireland, encountered "five justices, and a Baptist preacher lately enlarged from jail" who were worshipping with the Friends of Cedar Creek Meeting. Neale noted "great Divine Power in this meeting."[9]
- During the summer heat of 1773, Robert Pleasants, Quaker of Curles Meeting wrote to Justice Archibald Cary of Chesterfield County on behalf of Baptist preachers then locked up in Chesterfield Jail. Robert Pleasants urged Justice Cary to "direct the Gaoler to allow them more air by opening the inward door in the day time."[10]

The Baptist way appealed to a few Quakers so much that they joined the Baptists. Joseph Anthony, 21, of the Louisa County Quaker Anthonys, was imprisoned three months as a Baptist exhorter in Chesterfield County. Anthony's cousin, Christopher (Kit) Clark was a Baptist preacher for a time too, but both these young men later rejoined Friends.[11]

In the winter of 1769, while he was still a Baptist, Kit Clark came with James Chiles to South River Meeting, where many members were Kit's relatives, to preach there. Rachel Wilson, 49, a spirited Friends minister from Kendal, England, happened to arrive at South River that First Day. She wrote in her journal:

> On First Day got up pretty early and crossed James River and got to the Meeting in good time, 12 miles. To our surprise, found that Friends had given way for two Baptists to preach there that day, which at first affected my mind pretty much. It was evident there was a divine hand in bringing us there that day, and the testimony of Truth was exalted over the heads of gain-sayers.

One of those called Baptists came to me and said he was glad I was sent to visit the people, and it was in his mind that day whilst I was on my visit to give me a little money, as Providence had blessed him with plenty. I told him He had done so to me too and that I hoped I should ever keep my hands clear of taking bribes. He used some argument to engage me to take it but all to no purpose. After this they drew the people into the Meeting house, it being very cold, the snow upon the ground, and many of them had come many miles to hear 'em.

I got on my horse but could not with ease go forward, so alighted and went [in] to the Meeting house where the same man that offered the money was upon his knees with a good deal of zeal or fire--to me it seemed to be of his own raising--his name was James Chiles.

The other, Christopher Clark, immediately stood up with his Testament in his hand, taking his text that of "you search the Scriptures, in them you think to have eternal life, but you will not come unto Me that you may have life." which he drew into three heads or parts and went on a pretty while. The other spoke directly, pretty much in praise of what they had heard that day, and that he thought he should not have opened his mouth that day, but now he believed [it was] his place, and was just going to open his Testament.

As my mind was full, I craved a little time which was granted, in which I had to point the necessity of silence before we could learn Christ Jesus aright, and how inconsistent it was to take the expressions of David in their mouths when they had no knowledge of his experience, it appeared to me [the makings] of a lie.

I then found myself easy, and came away exceeding thankful....[12]

\* \* \*

The scent of freedom had entered Virginia's air by 1763. Many Virginians were pulling away from the Church of England, and they were also becoming unhappy with the way England was governing them. The impulses toward religious freedom and political freedom are close-related.

Friends were seriously involved in the tide of change from 1763 (when the French and Indian War ended) to 1775 (when the Revolutionary War began). In those years they added a new dimension to their peace testimony. Before the French and Indian War, Friends were concerned only to keep *themselves* guiltless of bloodshed and violence. Now as more war threatened they were led to be active peace-makers concerned for *humankind*. Along with Jesus' teaching to turn the other cheek, now Friends paid new attention to His declaration, "blessed are the peace-makers."

Soon after Patrick Henry defeated the Parsons' Cause in Virginia, Parliament in London began to debate ways to have the American Colonies pay their own way. A stamp tax was devised but the Americans to be taxed were never consulted. Protests--"Taxation without Representation is Tyranny!"--broke out in Virginia and all up and down America.

Friends were among the protest leaders. In 1764, two Friends--one in America, the other in London--wrote against the stamp tax. Stephen Hopkins, 57, the Quaker governor of Rhode Island, put out a pamphlet, *The Rights of the Colonies Examined*, rejecting Parliament's right to tax Americans. In London Dr. John Fothergill, Jr., stood up for the Americans. He wrote *Considerations Relative to the North American Colonies*, declaring that foregoing the stamp tax would convince Americans of the King's friendship and insure their loyalty. Lord Dartmouth, president of the Lords Commissioners of Trade and Plantations, received both pamphlets and presumably read them.[13]

Nevertheless, Parliament passed the Stamp Act in spring 1765, with the tax to become effective November 1. That May Patrick Henry, a member of Virginia's House of Burgesses only nine days, spoke out so strongly against the tax that the Speaker warned him "You have spoke treason."[14] Stamp distributors were appointed, one for each colony, and these men instantly became as unpopular as the tax collectors of the New Testament. The Sons of Liberty formed a secret society which threatened to tar and feather the stamp distributors. A mob visited George Mercer, the Virginia distributor, in Williamsburg and made him promise he would not distribute the stamps. Mobs trashed and smashed the homes of Massachusetts's and Maryland's distributors. This violence stalled the Stamp Act.[15]

America's Quakers were concerned lest their young men become involved in the violence. Philadelphia Yearly Meeting wrote to Virginia Yearly Meeting in 1765 that "many of these Provinces seem filled with rumors, noises and confusion from without, on account of human policy and affairs of government...may we be watchful to keep out of these things." And Friends generally did keep out of the violence. When the protest broadened, however, to include a boycott of English goods, many Friends felt free to join the nonviolent boycott. On 6 November 1765, over eighty Quaker merchants of Philadelphia signed an agreement not to import from England. The American merchants then asked their trading partners in London to help in getting the Stamp Act repealed.[16]

The London merchants accordingly formed a committee which included as leaders Quakers Capel Hanbury (successor to John Hanbury in Hanbury and Co.), Daniel Mildred, and David Barclay (Robert's great-grandson). Capel Hanbury enlisted his Quaker cousin, William Neave, who was master of the Merchants Venturers of Bristol (which controlled two seats in Parliament); Neave and the three London Friends vigorously lobbied Parliament. They testified before the bar of the House of Commons--Hanbury was questioned for two hours and David Barclay for a shorter time--after which Dr. Fothergill wrote to James Pemberton in Philadelphia that "all came off with reputation." When it became clear that the Commons would repeal the Stamp Act, Fothergill wrote again to Pemberton, urging him to do everything possible to keep the Americans from crowing over their triumph. And Pemberton led in persuading the Pennsylvania Assembly to send addresses of thanks to the King and Parliament.[17]

\* \* \*

All was tranquil for a while, but Parliament still needed money to finance the expenses of empire. In fall 1767, Charles Townshend, Chancellor of the Exchequer, promoted bills to impose duties on such English goods as paper, glass, paint, lead and tea, the duties to be collected on the goods' arrival at Norfolk and other American ports. Immediately, violence flared again in America. Virginia's House of Burgesses declared again that Parliament had no right to tax the colonies. When Governor Norborne Berkeley dissolved the House for this impertinency, the burgesses walked down Duke of Gloucester Street in a body and met as private citizens in Raleigh Tavern. There they agreed to join other colonies in boycotting English goods.[18]

Dr. Fothergill resumed his support of the colonies in London. Avoid all violent conduct, he counseled in letters to American Quakers:

> Soft language, conduct not servile--patience repeated--prudent application will make [you] friends, and will enable those who would serve you from just principle to do it effectively.[19]

John Dickinson, 36, emerged in 1768 as an American leader. A lawyer trained in London, he was born a Quaker, a great grandson of Dickinsons who fled from Corotoman Meeting, Lancaster County, Virginia, in 1659. It is uncertain whether John Dickinson worshiped with Friends in 1768, but his wife and children did; he himself used Friends' speech patterns, and he attended Friends' Meeting in Wilmington, Delaware, at his life's end.[20] Dickinson published the first of his *Farmer's Letters* in December 1768. These letters, appearing as a series of newspaper columns, stated America's case passionately. They made John Dickinson better known in England for a time than any other American. In the Quaker spirit he counselled neighborliness on both sides. In a less Quakerly spirit, he wrote that a resort to arms *would* be justified if the King tampered with American liberty.[21]

In April 1770, Parliament repealed all the Townshend Acts except the tax on tea. Repeal came after England's trade with the colonies dropped 97 percent.[22] Parliament had been persuaded to repeal the Stamp Act in a few months, but now, ominously, that body kept the Townshend Acts in force for two and a half years and insisted on retaining the tea tax as a symbol of the Crown's right to tax its colonies. This sort of repeal did not mollify the Americans, and they kept up their boycott of tea. Feelings were hardening on both sides. Mention of arming "as a last resort" was heard more and more often around American dinner tables. That worried the Quaker peacemakers.

In London Patience Wright, a Quaker woman, spent nearly two hours with King George, urging him to be kind to the Americans. London Yearly Meeting wrote to American Friends thus: "Let us...watch carefully the times, and...be made the instruments of averting the calamities which...overtake those who are harried...into hurtful excesses." And Philadelphia Yearly Meeting issued a warning against "joining with the measures publicly proposed for the support of civil liberties." Do not, the letter urged, "contend for liberty by any methods or agreements contrary to the peaceable spirit and temper of the Gospel."[23]

But now, with the dogs of war growling louder, it was hard for Friends to know what methods were peaceable and what were not. All Friends were clear that the tar-and-feather methods of the Sons of Liberty were unacceptable, but now some began to wonder whether the continuing boycott of English tea might be encouraging violence.

Furthermore, there was a growing suspicion that the attitudes of some leading Philadelphia Friends were affected by considerations concerning money. Israel Pemberton (1715-1779) and his brothers, James (1724-1809) and John (1727-1794), were leaders in Philadelphia Yearly Meeting in those years about 1770. Their grandfather and father before them had been clerks of the Yearly Meeting, members of Pennsylvania's Assembly, and wealthy merchants. John Pemberton, the youngest brother, devoted himself entirely to serving the Society of Friends. Israel and James, however, along with their Quakerly activities were active as politicians and they also worked assiduously in their counting house to increase their already imposing fortunes.[24] Most of their profits came through dealings with London and Bristol merchants. Along with peacemaking, they were evidently interested in preserving the American trade connection with Britain.[25]

* * *

In May 1773, Parliament gave the East India Company a monopoly on the tea trade with America, hoping to break the tea boycott. At this news the Virginia House wrote to the King declaring, "No Power on earth has a right to impose taxes upon the People...without their consent." Some members drafted a proposal envisioning an inter-colonial network of Committees of Correspondence. They mailed copies to the legislatures of the other twelve colonies, inviting them to form such committees.

That autumn in 1773, ships leased by the East India Company were loaded with temptingly low-priced tea. They sailed from England for four American ports: Boston, Philadelphia, Annapolis, and Charleston. In Philadelphia two Quaker firms--James and Drinker, and Thomas and Isaac Wharton--at first agreed to act as the Company's tea agents; but both resigned when it became clear that unloading the tea would result in violence. The tea ships for Boston were owned by Quakers--the *Dartmouth* by Francis Rotch of New Bedford and the *Beaver* by William Rotch of Nantucket Meeting. Francis Rotch was in Boston when the tea ships arrived. Seeing the crowd called out by the Sons of Liberty, he did his best that afternoon to obtain clearances for the ships to turn around without unloading. But the royal governor, Hutchinson, refused; after which, the crowd held the celebrated Boston Tea Party and dumped the tea in the harbor.[26]

Parliament, furious, then passed the Coercive Acts, ordering the port of Boston closed until the tea was paid for. General Thomas Gage with four regiments was sent to place all Massachusetts under military law, effective 1 June 1774.[27]

In Virginia that May, the House designated June 1 as an infamous day, calling for fasting and prayer. Virginia's Governor John Murray, Earl of Dunmore, then dissolved the House; after which the burgesses again walked out from the State House to Raleigh Tavern, and resolved there to support the defiant Bostonians.[28]

Two of the burgesses who walked had recently been disowned by the Society of Friends:

- Charles Lynch, 38, was a burgess from Bedford County. He married a Quaker girl when he was 19, was a founding member of South River Meeting near Lynchburg and the clerk of that meeting until he was disowned for taking the oath of office as a burgess in 1769. Charles's black sheep brother John reformed his way of life about the time Charles was disowned. John joined South River, was a Quaker leader for forty years and founded the city of Lynchburg.
- Isaac Zane, 31, was elected to the House from Frederick County and was newly disowned by Philadelphia Friends. He was a cousin of Wyandot Isaac Zane and the son of a devout Philadelphia Friend. Isaac the burgess operated Marlboro Forge, an iron works on Cedar Creek in Frederick County. He was educated in Anthony Benezet's school and raised with many advantages. Yet he turned away from Friends and went into the world wearing a full-bottomed flaxen wig and calling himself "a Quaker for the times."[29]

Virginia's burgesses sent their resolution in support of the Bostonians to all the colonial Committees of Correspondence. All thirteen colonies then agreed to send delegates to meet in Philadelphia on September 5. In this way the foundation footing of the American Union was poured.

\* \* \*

That steamy August of 1774 the burgesses met informally in Williamsburg and chose seven of their number to go to Philadelphia: Peyton Randolph,

Richard Bland, Patrick Henry and Richard Henry Lee, Edmund Pendleton, Benjamin Harrison, and George Washington. The seven Virginians then rode north to Philadelphia, a sunburning eight-to-ten day journey by roads deep with dust. They did not know then, that they were on their way to be Founding Fathers. All of them were landed aristocrats, slaveholders, attenders of the Church of England, and all were acquainted one way or another with Virginia Friends. Indeed, four of the seven were related to Friends by blood or marriage:

- Peyton Randolph's people, the Randolphs of Henrico, were inter-married with Quaker Pleasantses, Woodsons, and Flemings. Peyton had two Quaker-born aunts and several Quaker-born cousins.[30]
- Richard Bland was named for his great grandfather Richard Bennett, the old governor who was convinced into becoming a Quaker by Elizabeth Harris. Bland was an ally of the Virginia Quakers in their efforts to help the slaves. He received this memo from Friend Robert Pleasants on 15 March 1770:

> To Col Richard Bland--Thou wert pleased to say thou would make a motion to the next Assembly to repeal the law which prevents a man from rewarding faithfulness with freedom for his servants...[31]

- Patrick Henry through his mother Sarah Winston was related to the Hanover County Quaker Winstons.[32] He sympathized with Friends' views about slavery and war, and he befriended the Friends from the beginning of his public career. Rachel Wilson wrote in the journal of her Virginia visit:

> 3-31-1769--Called by the way [she was travelling with Rachel Janney and Edward Stabler to Fork Creek Meeting] to see one of the Assembly men who was a man of great moderation and had appeared in Frs' favor, his name Patrick Henry. He received us with great civility....[33]

When Rachel Wilson came by in 1769, Henry was living on Roundabout Creek in Louisa County, but he moved soon afterward to the plantation called Scotchtown near Cedar Creek Meeting, Hanover County. He wrote a remarkable letter to Robert Pleasants from Scotchtown:

Hanover January 18th 1773--Dear Sir--I take this opportunity to acknowledge the receipt of Anthony Benezet's book against the slave trade. I thank you for it...

It is not a little surprising that Christianity whose chief excellence consists in softening the human heart...should encourage [slavery] a practice totally repugnant to the first impressions of right and wrong.... Every thinking man rejects it in speculation, how few in practice...!

The world in general has deny'd your people [Quakers] a share of its honors...a people whose system imitates the example of Him whose life was perfect...believe me, I shall honor the Quakers for their noble effort to abolish slavery.

Would any one believe that I am master of slaves of my own purchase! I am drawn along by the general inconvenience of living without them. I will not, I cannot justify it....

Silent meetings (the scoff of reverend doctors) have done that which learned and elaborate preaching could not effect. I exhort you to persevere....

Your humble servant<br>Patrick Henry Junior[34]

Patrick Henry and Robert Pleasants established a friendship in 1773 and 1774. Friend Pleasants called at Scotchtown when he went to Friends' Meeting in Cedar Creek Meeting house nearby. On 7 October 1774, Roger Atkinson, the Pleasants' non-Quaker brother-in-law, wrote a family letter to Robert Pleasants' brother Samuel in Philadelphia. He included some information about the seven Virginia delegates to the Continental Congress then going on in Philadelphia, including the following:

The 4th a real half Quaker, Patrick Henry, your brother's man. Moderate and mild and in religious matters a saint, but the very devil in politics--a son of thunder.[35]

- Benjamin Harrison was connected with Friends through his kinsman, William Harrison IV (1740-1819) of Skimino. This William was an active member of Skimino Meeting in York County from the day in 1768 when he married blonde Margaret Jordan after the manner of Friends.[36]

As for the other three of Virginia's seven delegates:
- Edmund Pendleton, 53, was a lawyer and justice of Caroline County.[37] Many Friends of Caroline Meeting had been tried in his court for failing to show up on militia day, or refusing to come to St. Margaret's Church on Sundays. He knew well the Quakers and their ways.
- Richard Henry Lee, 42, was an aristocrat of the Virginia aristocrats, yet he was an ally of the Friends in their efforts to check the growth of slavery from the time he became a burgess in 1758. His brother, Arthur Lee, also opposed slavery in the House.[38]
- George Washington, 42, and his family had Quaker connections even before George was born. George's Uncle John Washington, living on Mattock's Creek in Westmoreland County in 1721, held a Friends' meeting in his home which was attended by Dr. John Fothergill's father, then travelling through Virginia as a Quaker minister.[39] In 1727, George's father, Augustine, went partners with two Friends--William Chetwynd, an English Quaker, and John England, an ironmaster from Maryland--in the Principio Iron Works. They operated an iron mine and a smelter on Accotink Creek in Fairfax County until the mine played out in 1753.[40]

George himself had Quaker friends from 15 years of age when he tramped the May-time valley of Virginia to survey Lord Fairfax's land there. John Vestal and Robert Worthington, young valley Quakers, were his companion surveyors. They spent a memorable night with a Quaker bachelor named Isaac Pennington near present day Berryville. George wrote, "I had for my bed a little straw matted together, with one threadbare blanket with double its weight of lice and fleas."[41]

At 19, George and his brother Lawrence holidayed in Barbados. When both of them caught the smallpox, Quaker Doctor William Hillary was their physician.[42] At 24, as previously noted, George was the military commander in war-torn Winchester where he tried vainly to get the "Cedar Creek Seven" to soldier. A few years later he made a trip to Philadelphia where "Reese

Meredith, a [Quaker] merchant of Philadelphia, seeing Washington in a Coffee-House, was so pleased with his personal demeanor as a genteel stranger, that he invited him home to dine on fresh venison. He formed a lasting friendship...." Washington, when he became the nation's first president, appointed Reese Meredith's son to be the first treasurer.[43]

Beside all these connections, George and his family associated with the Hanburys. Their company handled the Washingtons' tobacco sales in London. Augustine and Laurence Washington and John Hanbury were three of the twelve organizers of the Ohio Company, formed to develop 500,000 acres of western land in 1748.[44] Lawrence Washington wrote urgently to Hanbury in 1753, asking him to lobby Parliament for a tax break on these lands.[45]

Some of the seven Virginians carried letters of introduction with them to various Philadelphia Friends, all written by Robert Pleasants. He and Edward Stabler of Petersburg were Virginia Yearly Meeting's principal lobbyists. They visited Williamsburg often when the House was in session "to speak Truth to power," as Quakers say. As good lobbyists they came to be on friendly terms with the politicians they called on.

Robert Pleasants was 51 years old in 1774. He was not a typical Virginia Quaker for most of them were farmers while he was a man of business, a merchant banker. Instead of homespun, he wore broadcloth. Nevertheless, this Robert was a Quaker through and through. His great grandfather, the first John Pleasants of Curles, was a leader among the Quakers of the upper James and so were his grandfather John Jr., and his father John III. All of them paid dearly in property confiscations or imprisonments for their faith. Robert's mother, Margaret, was a Jordan from Chuckatuck, and Robert was her first-born. Just after his birth in 1723, the Henrico sheriff, for fines the family refused to pay, took away the feather bed where Robert had been born and where Margaret was recovering.[46]

Robert went to Philadelphia in his teens to learn the trade of merchant in the Pembertons' great counting house. When he returned home in his early twenties Friends chose him at once to be clerk of Curles Monthly Meeting. At 30, he succeeded his father as clerk of Virginia Yearly Meeting and served as its clerk for many of the years thereafter. A level-headed, trim, middlesized, articulate, likeable man, he was known in his family as "Bob." He managed not to allow the family's wealth to corrupt him. Most of his sisters, brothers, and Pleasants cousins--and all his beloved children--

turned away from Friends and became worldly, but he did not. When the Quaker movement turned toward service in the world, he joined in wholeheartedly. Having inherited many slaves, he was among the first Quakers to free them.

He must have been there in Williamsburg that August day in 1774 when the First Virginia Convention chose their seven delegates for Philadelphia. He dated the letters of introduction he wrote for them just about the time the Convention closed. Here is one of the letters:

> Virginia 8 mo. 20th 1774--Dear Friend--This is intended by the Commissioners from this Colony appointed to meet in General Congress at Philadelphia on American affairs, and to recommend them to thy particular notice as men of influence and capacity viz. Peyton Randolph, Rd. Bland, Patrick Henry, R.H. Lee, E. Pendleton, B. Harrison, G. Washington, who have deserved well for their attachment to the interests of their country, and most if not all of them for their favourable sentiments and services to Friends, as well in a legislative as private capacity, particularly our friend Patrick Henry to whose character and sentiments thou art not altogether a stranger.
>
> I doubt not thou will be well pleased with an acquaintance with several of them, and believe any marks of friendship or favours thou may confer on them (which no doubt will be agreeable to every man in a strange country) will not be unworthily bestowed, may tend to promote the good opinion they generally entertain of Friends, and will lay an additional obligation on me.
>
> And am with very kind respects to self and yours
>
> Thy affect. Friend
>
> Anthony Benizette                    Robert Pleasants[47]

\* \* \*

Philadelphia in September 1774 was a red brick city of 24,000, sycamores shading the sidewalks, the largest city in America. The seven Virginians evidently used Robert Pleasants's letters to get Quaker help in finding lodgings. Patrick Henry called on Anthony Benezet,[48] and George

Washington dined with the Pembertons[49] and with Robert Pleasants's brother Samuel[50].

The First Continental Congress--fifty-five men representing all the colonies except Georgia--convened after breakfast on the sunny morning of 6 September 1774. Peyton Randolph, with long experience as Speaker of Virginia's House, agreed to chair the gathering. They met in the hall of the Carpenter's Company near the corner of Fourth and Chestnut Streets. A Friends' meeting house and school (now William Penn Charter School) stood on the corner. The delegates could hear the Quaker schoolboys' chatter on their way to school.

Six of the fifty-five delegates were dressed more or less in plain Quaker gray, being Quaker born--although some had lost their Quaker status because of worldly involvement in politics. They were: John Dickinson, Joseph Galloway, Charles Humphreys, Thomas Mifflin and Samuel Rhoads of Pennsylvania and Stephen Hopkins of Rhode Island. Some of the six kept their hats on through all the sessions, after the accustomed Quaker style. For some unknown reason, Patrick Henry also dressed in Quaker gray while in Philadelphia.

Peyton Randolph banged the gavel, and the delegates got right down to business. A split soon developed between those who favored a nonviolent solution to the struggle with the Crown and those who favored armed resistance with no more shilly-shally. Five of the six-man Quakerly group were for nonviolence along with three of the Virginians: Peyton Randolph, Benjamin Harrison and Edmund Pendleton.[51]

Certain articulate members of Philadelphia Yearly Meeting--Israel Pemberton, Anthony Benezet and Samuel Allinson, a Quaker lawyer of New Jersey among them---found opportunities to speak with various delegates. These Friends urged moderation and cool thinking. "Use every lenient measure by way of petition from the United Colonies, enforced by a respectable embassage, before other means of an offensive nature are pursued" was their advice.\*

Friend Anthony Benezet, 61, and Patrick Henry had been writing back and forth for several years. Benezet was French-born, of a Huguenot family that fled to London when he was small. His father had been the London business agent of Voltaire. Anthony joined Friends at 14 and became a schoolmaster in Philadelphia. John Woolman's report on slavery in the

---

\* Robert Pleasants wrote Israel Pemberton on 27 August 1774 to suggest this approach. *William and Mary Quarterly*, series 2, vol. 1, page 176.

South aroused Benezet's pity, and Benezet wrote in 1766 a little book called *A Caution and Warning...on the Calamitous State of the Enslaved Negroes*. It impressed Patrick Henry and many others.[52] So Benezet got along very well with Henry while they discussed the need to do away with slavery. They did not agree, however, when Benezet got around to urging "lenient measures by way of petition" in dealing with England. Patrick Henry shrewdly remarked that one or two Quakerly members of Congress favored war-like measures; and Benezet could only reply (with a Gallic shrug?) that they were only luke-warm Quakers.[53] He failed to change Henry's well-known "Liberty or Death" mind-set.

Benezet got along well as a lobbyist but Israel Pemberton did not. By 1774 Israel had become known in Philadelphia's coffee houses as "the Quaker Pope" or "King of the Quakers." His imperious and terribly blunt manner did not sit well with the Congressmen--particularly with John Adams of Massachusetts who came to dislike Israel actively.[54]

The First Continental Congress held from 6 September to 26 October, 1774, while Philadelphia's sycamore trees turned bright autumn colors. The two sides, peacekeepers versus firebrands, were in balance until about October first. After that the firebrands took control, led by Patrick Henry and the Massachusetts cousins, Samuel and John Adams.[55] In its seven weeks, the Congress sent a petition to George III titled "A Declaration of Rights and Grievances," asking him to restore harmony. At the same time, however, the Congress called for a new boycott of British goods--referred to as "the Association"-- and also approved the use of force in resisting British taxes. It was agreed that a second Congress would meet in Philadelphia on 10 May 1775.

\* \* \*

Philadelphia Friends Meeting for Sufferings, James Pemberton the clerk, pushed through a "Testimony of the People Called Quakers" in January 1775. "Our religious principles discountenance disaffection to the King," the Testimony stated. "We disapprove of the recent addresses and writings whose spirit and temper was...destructive of...peace and harmony." The best way to win civil rights is to address the Crown respectfully.[56]

This Testimony did not represent the unanimous sense of the Philadelphia Friends. One member, possibly Samuel Wetherill, entreated the others not "to mix politics and religion." Many felt that their peace testimony was cheapened by the political position implied in the Testimony.[57]

The Philadelphia Testimony troubled English Friends who felt generally that the Americans' bid for independence was right and just. For the first time in history the Friends of Philadelphia and of London quarreled; and the irony of it was that the Londoners supported the Americans' cause while the Philadelphians upheld the King's. David Barclay wrote from London to James Pemberton that the Testimony was

> a handle...to the disadvantage of the [Quaker] community--the language of the Court being that they have the Quakers' approbation.

Dr. Fothergill was equally dismayed. He wrote James Pemberton

> We have seen the Testimony given out by Friends and [all England] hath seen it. If America relaxes both you and we are undone. I wish Friends would studiously avoid everything adverse either to the administration here on one side--or the Congress on the other.[58]

The Virginia *Gazette* published dispatches from London about the English Friends' support:

> From the *Gazette* for August 4, 1 774--"London, May 4. The ministry have been greatly alarmed at the conduct of the Quakers, fearing the firmness of that most honorable body, who are the only people which virtually maintain the upright principles of the Oliverian firmness. Alarmed at their standing forth to support their American brethren, they have left no stone unturned to warp their virtue and to bribe their leaders."

> September 29, 1774--"London, July 16. Though the Quakers do not choose to demonstrate their dissatisfaction in the noisy manner...it is said they profess themselves ready to concur in every measure which promises to preserve the national rights of the Americans."

The Friends of Virginia Yearly Meeting followed a neutral course. When Virginia's Upper Quarterly Meeting met in November 1774, the members decided not to sign any resolutions or associations which "may be inconsistent with the peaceable principles we profess" and to "avoid as much as possible engaging in unnecessary conversation regarding these disputes."[59]

Upper Quarterly Meeting met next in February 1775. According to the minutes, "Report was made that the Committees in some counties require Friends to sign the Association or give reasons for their refusal; and in order that Friends may comply with the latter, this Meeting hath drawn up the following answer, viz.

> It is well known that we have always been a peaceable people, and firmly believe all war (as to us) unlawful, wherefore we cannot sign the Association or act in any manner in matters which may have a tendency to the shedding of blood. We nevertheless believe that both religious and civil liberty are the natural right of every man, and think it our duty to comply with the laws and regulations of Government under which we live, in all cases not interfering with tender scruples of conscience.[60]

Some Philadelphia Quakers chose to ignore the new boycott on English goods, but Robert Pleasants complied with it at considerable expense to his business. Early in January 1775, Pleasants's ship, the *Peggy*, brought an English cargo to his warehouse at Curles, including 3,596 bushels of salt. Pleasants turned the whole cargo over to the Henrico Committee of Safety to be sold at public auction.[61]

Ironically, King George III used a Quaker letter to justify a military solution of his problems with the rebellious Americans. Some Philadelphia Friends wrote this letter in September of 1774--no doubt the same Philadelphia Friends who wanted to keep the Colonies loyal to the Crown. George III was a plump, imperious man, somewhat stubborn, somewhat neurotic. After reading the letter he advised his Prime Minister, Lord Frederick North, that the Quaker writers showed

> ...that coolness which is a very strong characteristic of that body of people....I was in hopes it would have contained some declaration of their submission to the Mother Country [but] they seem to wish for England giving, in some degree, way to the opinions of North America. The die is now cast, the Colonies must either submit or

triumph. I do not wish to come to severer measures, but we must not retreat....˙ [62]

A month or two after the Quakers' cool letter, George III received the Continental Congress's petition, asking him to correct the injustices that were angering Americans. True to his word, George rejected the petition, saying he would deal only with his separate colonies. The die indeed was cast.

\* \* \*

In those days of great change in Virginia, while the Revolutionary War loomed, Virginia's Friends kept changing too. For one thing their ideas about peacemaking changed. Also, their abhorrence of slavery took root, and became a central concern:

- In 1764: Yearly Meeting advised "Friends who are possessed of Negroes...impartially to consider their situation...instruct...them in the principles of the Christian religion...make a diligent inspection into their usage, clothing and feeding...earnestly desiring that their state and station may more and more become the particular care and concern of each individual.[63]
- 1766: Yearly Meeting decided to witness publicly against slavery--a historic decision, for *it was the first time Virginia Friends as a corporate body entered the lists on behalf of a cause and a people outside their own ranks*. They purchased four dozen copies of *A Treatise on Slavery* by Anthony Benezet to "put in the hands of those in power for their perusal."[64] Robert Pleasants, Edward Stabler, and other Friends then began to lobby vigorously in Williamsburg.
- 1768: It was made a rule of discipline that "none of our members for the time to come shall be permitted to purchase a negro or other slave."[65]
- 1771: Anthony Benezet wrote joyfully to his friend Benjamin Franklin that Virginia Yearly Meeting planned to petition the

---

˙ This comes from the King's memo to Lord North, given in *The Correspondence of King George the Third* John Fortescue ed. London, 1967, volume 3, pages 129-31. The Quakers' letter, if it still exists, has not been published. Its authors are unknown.

Virginia House for a law forbidding any more importation of slaves.[66]

- 1772: the Virginia House passed that law. Edward Stabler, clerk of Virginia Yearly Meeting, then wrote to Friends in London asking them to urge the King to approve the law. Unhappily, the King vetoed it, but London Yearly Meeting in its annual letter to the American yearly meetings praised Virginia's effort. When Maryland Friends read in this letter from London about the Virginia Friends' effort, they presented copies to their own legislature. So it reverberated, back and forth across the ocean and across the American colonies.[67]

\* \* \*

The twelve years of change in Quaker emphasis, 1763 to 1775, was also a time of spiritual revival. Friends in Virginia and everywhere set out to rid their meetings of worldly "spots" acquired over the years since "our first rise as a people." Speakers in the meetings warned worshipers that "the Spirit whispers--the World shouts." Friends who neglected to walk the walk and talk the talk were disowned from membership till they mended their ways. Other Friends who had come to enjoy worldly pleasures too well simply stopped coming to meeting and "ran out from Truth" or "went into the world"--which in Virginia often meant that they joined the Church of England. One out of every five Pennsylvania Friends was disowned in those years,[68] and a comparable number were disowned in Virginia.

Many young Friends were disowned because they "married out" to "one of the world's people." Such marriages often involved a Quaker girl, bewitching in cap and kerchief, who caught the ardent attention of a non-Quaker youth in her neighborhood. Others were disowned even though they married Friends, because the marriages were "contrary to Discipline." This usually meant that the young couple, having fallen in love, were unwilling to wait out the lengthy Friends' nuptial procedure. This required them to "pass meeting"--appear before a clearness committee and before two successive monthly meetings--in order for their marriage to be allowed. The Discipline was singularly powerless in face of young love, and it was proved over and over that

> Creeds and kin are things apart
> When weighed against a maiden's heart.

A good many of those disowned for their marriages later "condemned" their misconduct in letters to the Meetings and were restored--after which the husband or wife of the restored person frequently joined Friends. The following letter to South River Meeting is typical:

> Dear Friends--I once had a right amongst you and knew not the worth of it, and by taking undue liberty and suffering myself to be married by a hireling minister, caused me to lose my right, which I found to be a great loss when it pleased the Lord to open my eyes and show me where abouts I was. Therefore, like a returning prodigal, I make request to come under your care again.
> --Judith Brown[69]

Other disownments were occasioned by alcoholism, adultery, "using ill words," fighting, adopting "vain fashions and ways of the world," "frequenting places of sport and gaming," and "spreading a report to the injury of his neighbor."[70]

About this time there was much looking backward to the good old days--a sign of spiritual revival. William Stanley, 29, of Cedar Creek Meeting--one of the seven who, when marched to Winchester in 1756 refused to fight there--wrote a letter in 1758 to "the Elders of the People Called Quakers in Virginia" decrying the decline of Virginia's Quakers in purity and zeal.[71] In 1764, John Smith, an old Friend of London Grove Meeting in Chester County, Pennsylvania., looked back sixty years to the Society as it was in 1704:

> Friends were a plain lowly-minded people...there was much tenderness and contrition...20 years from that date, the Society increasing in wealth and in some degree conforming to the fashions of the world, true humility was less apparent...meetings in general were not so lively and edifying...at the end of 40 years many of them were grown very rich...so the powerful overshadowings of the Holy Ghost were less manifest in the Society...the weakness that has now overspread the Society and the barrenness manifest among us is a matter of much sorrow.[72]

Virginia Yearly Meeting published a new Discipline in 1770. It is enlightening to compare this Discipline of 1770 with the Yearly Meeting's first Discipline, issued in 1702:[73]

Ten items in the new Discipline were unchanged over the sixty-eight years since 1702:
- *Widows, Orphans and Poor Friends*--The Meetings are to support them "in all such things as they stand in need."
- *Differences between Friends*--Settle these by mediation within the Meeting. "Go to law" only as an extreme last resort.
- *Disorderly Walkers*--Disown them "if they will not be reclaimed."
- *Oaths*--Friends' testimony against taking oaths is implied in the 1702 Discipline and explicit in 1770.
- *Marrying a Non-Friend*--"Marriage to one of the world's people" is forbidden.
- *Friends' Children*--Raise them "in the fear of God, in modest apparel and in the plain language."
- *Friends in Business*--Keep out of business dealings beyond your capacity. Bankruptcy is scandalous.
- *Wills*--Make your will "while in health."
- *Word and Promises*--Keep your "word and promises and perform them punctually."
- *Tobacco and Strong Drink*--The 1702 Discipline enjoins Friends to "keep out of excessive smoking of tobacco" and "take heed of being overcome by strong drink". In 1770 the query is "Are Friends careful to avoid...unnecessary frequenting of taverns, excess in drinking and intemperance of every kind?"

One item was changed in the interest of simplicity:
- *Meeting Records*--In 1702 Monthly Meetings were advised to keep written minutes of their meetings for business and also five more kinds of records--of Friends sufferings at the hands of the government; of "eminent judgments against persecutors"; and of births, deaths and wills. By 1770 the only record-keeping requirement beside business minutes is "a regular record of births and deaths."

And six new items appear in the 1770 Discipline:

- *Love and Unity*--The 1770 Discipline asks "Are love and unity maintained amongst you and do you discourage tale-bearing and detraction?"
- *Defrauding the King*--"Do none defraud the King of his just dues?" This refers to smuggling, which was widespread in America in 1770. The Discipline here upheld the concept that Christians are "to render unto Caesar the things that are Caesar's."
- *Priests' Wages*--"Are Friends careful to maintain a faithful testimony against the payment of priests' wages or...church rates?" Clearly such taxes were not considered to be rightfully Caesar's.
- *Slaves*--"Are Friends clear of importing or buying negroes or other slaves; and do they use well those they are possessed of...?" This addition indicates that John Woolman's protest to Virginia Yearly Meeting in 1757, finally had its effect.
- *Lotteries*--Are disapproved of in the 1770 Discipline.
- *Certificates of Removal for Friends Moving from One Meeting to Another, Regular Reading of the Discipline, None but Friends to Attend Meetings for Business*--Those formal requirements appeared in the 1770 Discipline, all designed to improve "the good order of Truth practiced among us."[74]

The wording of the 1770 Discipline indicates that Virginia's Friends were developing a concern for the well-being of disadvantaged people outside their own membership. The increase in disownments indicates that Friends now were intent on ridding their membership of half-hearted men and women and returning their Society to its first purity and zeal. In those years, Friends deliberately turned away from the goal of becoming a mainstream denomination. Instead, after 1763, they tightened their discipline, disowned half-hearted members, adopted a new and unpopular witness--against slavery--and put fresh emphasis on distinctive dress and speech.

\* \* \*

As the Revolution approached, Virginia's Quakers came to be treated more kindly by the authorities.

In winter 1767, William Jolliffe, the clerk of Hopewell Meeting, rode south to Curles to meet with Friends of Virginia Yearly Meeting. There they prepared a petition to the House of Burgesses requesting relief from militia fines. Friends handed in the petition 28 March 1767, and a sub-committee headed by Patrick Henry brought in a bill which promptly passed, exempting Friends from military services or fines "except in cases of invasion." Each of Virginia's monthly meetings gave the militia commander of its county a list of its male members between 18 and 60, and those men were exempted.[75]

So for a time, Virginia's Friends were freed from the militia penalties they had been paying year by year for over a hundred years. Only the fines for failure to pay church taxes remained.[76] *

In 1768 Norborne Berkeley, Lord Botetourt, arrived in Virginia to be governor. He had a Quaker business partner back in Gloucestershire, namely William Champion, the metallurgist who discovered zinc. Berkeley and Champion jointly owned the Wormley Copper Works.[77] Virginia's Friends evidently knew about this connection for the Yearly Meeting sent a message of welcome to Berkeley on his arrival:

...the humble address of the people called Quakers: May it please the governor, we beg leave, in an honest simplicity, to congratulate thee on thy safe arrival in this government. Permit us...to assert our loyalty and firm attachment....

The Virginia *Gazette* printed this somewhat fulsome welcome on 24 November 1768, together with a cordial reply by Norborne Berkeley. Thereafter for several years the *Gazette* reported on various Friends' activities in quite a complimentary way.

No doubt the fury of Virginia's leaders toward the upstart Baptists had something to do with diverting public attention and putting the Quakers in a better light. The support of England's Quakers for the American cause must have helped, too, and also the continuing reputation of Quakers for friendliness and reliability. Micajah Crew, who kept a general store near Negro Foot in Hanover County, typifies the reason for this reputation. All the neighborhood sent their children and servants to him with notes, confident he would treat them fairly:

---

* Only one instance is known when Friends were excused from fines for church taxes. That was in 1765 when the Reverend Mr. William Davis of Charles City County requested sheriff Billy Christian not to collect taxes for his support from the Friends of Weyanoke Meeting--*VMHB*, vol. 59, pp. 359-61.

Sir-Be Pleased to send by the Bearer Billy one Lofe of Sugar and Oblige

To Mr. Crue's
                                   Yours and c
                                   Mary Goodall

The bearer comes for a Bottle of Rum out of what my Brother bespoke of Micajah Crew yesterday Sunday morning
                                   George Dabney

Friend Crew please to let Thomas Webb take the value of six shillings in thy store and oblige thy friend
                                   Thomas Stanley[78]

\* \* \*

All through the 1760s, the Great Wagon Road in the valley of Virginia was busy with wagons and pack-trains of families moving south into the back country of the Carolinas and Georgia. In the summer of 1768, however, a newly married Quaker couple, impossibly daring, decided to try their fortune to the *west* over the Alleghenies. A sprinkling of mountain men, trappers, hunters and fur traders were the only white men living over the mountains then, and the number of white women probably could be counted on one's fingers.

This daring Quaker couple was Henry Beeson, 24, and his bride Mary Martin, 22. They grew up on neighboring farms along Tuscarora Creek where Martinsville, West Virginia, stands today. Providence Meeting house was built on the Beesons' farm before Henry was born, and that most likely was where Henry and Mary married. They headed west, Henry leading a packhorse or two and Mary riding side saddle.

After Fort Cumberland they followed the trail hacked out by Braddock's army. Having come some hundred miles they reached Redstone Creek near the Monogahela River. They took up 255 acres along the creek, where Henry built their cabin and Mary swapped her saddle for a cow. One evening when Henry was away, Indians appeared in the dooryard. Mary, expecting her first baby, was frightened; but an old brave explained to his fellows with gestures that Mary's man was a "broad brim" (Quaker), and the Indians did no harm.[79]

William Zane, 56, the Quaker of Howard's Lick Meeting who lost a son to the Wyandots, arrived on Redstone Creek with three sons and three daughters the same summer of 1768 as the Beesons. The Zanes stayed at Redstone only a year, and then pushed on fifty miles further to the Ohio River shore. They were the founding family of Wheeling, West Virginia.[80]

Henry Beeson stayed on Redstone Creek, built a mill, acquired more land, laid the land off in lots and founded Beeson Town, now Uniontown in Fayette County, Pennsylvania. Some Friends from Virginia and Pennsylvania bought lots, and Redstone Friends Meeting started up in Beeson Town early in the 1770s. Redstone was the first Friends Meeting and surely one of the first Christian gatherings, west of the Alleghenies.[81]

\* \* \*

His excellency John Murray, fourth Earl of Dunmore, Viscount Fincastle, Baron of Blair, Moulin, and Tillymont came to govern Virginia in 1771 after a time as governor of New York. He was a Scot, stockily built with a lofty manner. Upon arriving in Virginia he secured the title to an immense acreage around Beeson Town, Wheeling and Fort Pitt. Both Virginia and Pennsylvania claimed this land.

Dunmore did not call the Virginia House into session at all in 1771 and 1772. After the session of 1773, he wrote his superior in England that "There are some Resolves which show a little ill humor in the House of Burgesses but I thought them so insignificant that I took no notice of them."[82] He showed thereby an appalling lack of awareness, for those Resolves called for the organization of Committees of Correspondence in the thirteen Colonies to make decisions without the Royal Governors' interference!

Governor Dunmore dissolved the House in May 1774, after the Burgesses had the gall to protest the closing of the Port of Boston. Then, confident that the colonials could make no more trouble in Williamsburg, he set off westward at the head of a militia force. He had sent ahead two agents, Michael Gresap and John Connelley, with instructions to stir up trouble with the Indians, and they had done a gruesome job of it. The purported purpose of Dunmore's militia force was to put down the ensuing Indian uprising; the real purpose was to occupy the land claimed both by Virginia and Pennsylvania, to get the land under Virginia's control and to protect Dunmore's investment there.[83]

Michael Cresap and a few heavily armed men came to the Zane's cabin on the Ohio River bank. They invited William Zane's son Ebenezer Zane, 27, to join them in waylaying Indians on the river. "This measure," Ebenezer reported years later, "I opposed with much violence, alleging that the killing of those Indians might involve the country in a war." Nevertheless Cresap and his party canoed up the Ohio and "in a short time the party returned...I examined the canoe and saw much blood and bullet holes in the canoe. This fully convinced me that the party had killed the two Indians and thrown them into the river." That same afternoon Cresap and his men canoed down river to a Shawnee village and returned to Zane's next day with "a fresh scalp and a quantity of property which they called Indian plunder...the transactions which I have related happened in the latter end of April 1774; and there can be scarcely any doubt that they were the cause of...Dunmore's War."[84]

Governor Dunmore's plan worked well. The outraged Shawnees took the warpath under Cornstalk their chief, and Dunmore's militia mowed them down at Point Pleasant on the Ohio River, 6 October 1774. Dunmore established Virginia's claim to the disputed area and returned to Williamsburg with some Shawnee prisoners in his train.[85]

In Williamsburg the governor found things much out of hand. The colonials had become quite insubordinate, daring to call a convention in St. John's Church near the hamlet of Richmond in March 1775, without permission. Patrick Henry, soaring to new heights of oratory, persuaded the St. John's convention to organize militia, two regiments to be controlled by the Virginia Committee of Correspondence and not at all by the Governor.[86]

On 18 April 1775, a column of British regulars up in Massachusetts marched out of Boston to confiscate arms cached by the colonials in Concord. Next morning the British killed some American militiamen, and on the way back to Boston the column was riddled by American rifle fire coming from barns and houses, stone walls and trees along the way. So war began in New England.

In Virginia, on the very next night, April 20, Governor Dunmore sent a detachment of royal marines to remove the gunpowder stored in Williamsburg magazine. The marines were discovered in the act, and Williamsburg erupted--bell of Bruton Church ringing, militia called out and the citizens in an uproar. The governor panicked and took his family aboard HMS *Fowey*, a man-of-war at anchor in York River. Things quieted down three weeks later and Dunmore returned to Williamsburg. But the burgesses turned down his proposal of conciliation. Then Lord Dunmore, his family and all, fled again to the *Fowey* in the middle of a dark June night. And that was the end of royal government in Virginia.[87]

The cottage of Christopher and Betty Moorman Johnson, Quakers of South River Meeting, is Lynchburg's oldest house built about 1767. Christopher made 14 horseback trips to Georgia and South Carolina from this house to win freedom for black people unjustly sold into slavery.

## IX

## THE FRIENDLY VIRGINIANS
## AND THE AMERICAN REVOLUTION
## 1775-1781

[We humans are] tormented atoms in a bed of mud
Devoured by death, a mockery of fate;

But thinking atoms, whose far-seeing eyes,
Guided by thoughts, have measured the faint stars.
Our being mingles with the infinite...

-- Voltaire

Lord Dunmore in the *Fowey* stood on and off the Virginia Capes all that summer and fall of 1775. Slowly he collected a flotilla--three sloops-of-war, three armed merchantmen, and some smaller craft. Several red-coated companies of His Majesty's 14th Foot came to him from Florida. With this force in November 1775, his lordship occupied Norfolk, the largest town in Virginia with 6,000 inhabitants. But Virginia and North Carolina militia arrived in December, won a battle at Great Bridge, and drove the British back to their ships.

In revenge Dunmore ordered Norfolk flattened. On New Year's Day of 1776 in the early afternoon, the English flotilla ranged offshore in Elizabeth River and opened up with all guns. Shore parties set fires along the water front. When the cannon fire stopped the next day, 914 houses were destroyed. Many citizens were left desperate for shelter and food. Smallpox broke out. When the Virginia militia departed the area in February, they burned down the remaining 416 houses to deny them to Dunmore's force. The desolation was complete--except for St. Paul's Church which stands yet today with a cannonball imbedded in its wall.[1]

Virginia's Quakers organized a relief fund for Norfolk's people. Norfolk had no Quaker meeting--the relief was intended for non-Quakers. It was an early instance of the Society of Friends' developing emphasis on caring for all God's children of whatever condition: Indians, slaves, and now, victims of war.

That February Robert Pleasants and Edward Stabler visited Lord Dunmore's ship, still at anchor in Elizabeth River. Robert wrote that the former governor "treated us kindly" and invited the Friends to send "as much provisions as we pleased."[2] Accordingly, when Upper Quarterly Meeting met in Henrico on February 24: "The necessitous situation of many of the late inhabitants of the town of Norfolk was represented...," whereupon a hat was passed and thirty-five Friends gave £26 in sums from five shillings to £5. Then ten men were appointed to receive further contributions from Friends of their monthly meetings at home.[3]

Money and supplies were given generously but they never reached Norfolk. The American General Charles Lee, an eccentric English-born soldier of fortune, arrived in Williamsburg on March 29 to head up military operations in Virginia. General Lee disliked Quakers, as he wrote to Robert Morris in November 1775:

> ...Did ever impudence and cant match that of the Quakers, to enjoy all the blessings of liberty without contributing a single mite? [That] is a degree of iniquity which none but the disciples of Jesuitism can arrive at.[4]

He refused to allow the supplies to enter Norfolk. As reported in the Virginia *Gazette* for 13 April 1776:

> The Quakers and several others have collected provisions for the poor inhabitants of Norfolk whose town has been destroyed, but find it disagreeable to Gen'l Lee to distribute them. Those poor persons who need them apply to: Joseph Scott, Nansemond; Anselm Bailey, Surry; John Crew, Charles City; Robert Pleasants, Henrico; Reverend William Harrison and Edward Stabler in Petersburg.

So Virginia's Quakers embarked on war relief. As far as known, no other body made such an effort to help Norfolk's people. Five of the six men named by the *Gazette* were Quakers. The sixth, Reverend William Harrison, was probably the rector of Petersburg's Blandford Church and a friend of Edward Stabler.

Lord Dunmore and his flotilla hung around Norfolk long after the town burned down. He occupied Portsmouth for a while, disrupting the shipping in Hampton Roads until Americans under General Lee drove him away in May of 1776. Dunmore then tried to establish a base on Gwynn's island but was dislodged there in July. Finally he sailed back down Chesapeake Bay with all his ships, out of the Capes and out of history. Then the fighting in Virginia stopped. For three years, Virginia's only Revolutionary activities were to furnish soldiers and supplies for the American army. The fighting was all to the north, around Boston, New York and Philadelphia.[5]

\* \* \*

After Lord Dunmore left off being governor in June 1775, Virginia was governed *ad hoc* for two months. In mid-August the members of the old House of Burgesses, meeting as the "Virginia Convention," elected an executive authority to replace the governor--an eleven-man Committee of Safety. Edmund Pendleton chaired both the Convention and the Committee of Safety. On May 15, 1776, the Convention set out to frame a constitution for Virginia. On June 12 it unanimously adopted the Constitution's preamble--a Bill of Rights written chiefly by George Mason, a black-eyed, blue-jowled planter of Fairfax County. Late that June the convention approved the entire Constitution.[6]

The Virginia Bill of Rights is a noble document in sixteen sections, based on William and Mary's Bill of Rights of 1689. It opens with a statement that all people are equally entitled to freedom. It affirms the sovereignty of the people and the rule of the majority; separates the legislative power from the executive and judicial; confirms trial by jury and the freedom of the press; and decrees that the military is subordinate to the civil power. The most important section for Virginia's Quakers was the sixteenth and last. It provides for religious freedom thus:

> Religion, or the duty we owe our Creator, and the manner of discharging it, can be directed only by reason and conviction, not by force or violence; and therefore all men are equally entitled to the free exercise of religion according to the dictates of conscience; and...it is the duty of all to practice Christian forbearance, love and charity towards each other.

Section 16 was apparently drafted by "that real half Quaker" Patrick Henry.[7] Twenty-five-year-old James Madison, a convention member from Orange County, then edited it. Madison changed Henry's words prescribing *toleration* for all manner of worship to words declaring that *free exercise* of religion is a natural and absolute right. The difference is profound. As Tom Paine explained, "Toleration is not the opposite of intolerance, but is the counterfeit of it. The one assumes to itself the right of granting liberty of conscience, the other of withholding it."[8]

James Madison tried to get the convention to put teeth in Section 16 and to end all the privileges of the established church.[9] His proposal was voted down, but the convention--when it reassembled in the fall of 1776 as the Commonwealth of Virginia's first General Assembly--did order the Anglican clergymen removed from the public payroll, and did exempt dissenters from paying taxes to support the established church.[10]

Thus ended triumphantly Friends' testimony against "paying the priest" which they had been upholding against heavy odds since 1660.

So the established church was essentially disestablished. Since it still kept some tenuous privileges, the separation of church and state was not complete. Nevertheless June 1776 was a red letter month:

- In Williamsburg that month the Bill of Rights was passed, its Section 16 virtually a victory for the cause of religious independence that the Friendly Virginians had been upholding 116 years.
- In Philadelphia Thomas Jefferson, a Virginia delegate to the Second Continental Congress, wrote America's Declaration of Independence.
- In London the King and his ministers mobilized the largest English task force ever sent overseas, to crush the insolent, ungrateful Americans.

\* \* \*

Peace makers may influence events in peace time, but they become handcuffed when war fever sweeps the public. Friends began to counsel together in 1775 how best to meet the brooding evil at hand. Their first concern was for the young men of the Society. The Society had closed ranks, and Friends were better prepared to witness for peace than twenty years before during the French and Indian War. But it is a hard thing in any age to be faithful when the drums begin to roll, the fifes to whistle, and every other young buck in the neighborhood goes off to sign up with the recruiting sergeant.

Community pressure builds and the whittlers on the porch of the general store taunt "Slacker!" and "Yellow belly!" No one cares or understands that a follower of the Prince of Peace cannot soldier. Nor ponders what a stupid thing it is for the nations to settle their differences by bidding young men to kill and maim one another. It takes more raw courage to declare oneself a noncombatant when war is coming on than to sign up as a soldier. So, in spite of all the Quaker elders could say in the meeting house and Quaker mothers could say at home, a few young men slipped away from their meetings to join the colors.

The Virginia *Gazette* carried a story on 16 June 1775 which threw cold water on the Quaker peace witness:

> Williamsburg, June 16--Last Wednesday morning Col. Richard Bland arrived in town from the [Second Continental] Congress at Philadelphia. The City of Philadelphia has raised 28 companies of 100 men each...; four of them wholly composed of the people called Quakers, one company light horse and another consists of expert rifle-men who wear hunting shirts.
>
> In short, the most martial spirit has diffused itself over the whole province of Pennsylvania, as well as the other colonies; so that...there is little doubt of America's being able to resist, with success, every vile attempt to deprive her sons of their rights and liberties.

Richard Bland's report and others like it were spread deliberately through the colonies to discredit the troublesome Quaker witness that peace is the way and war is evil. Bland's story disturbed Friends in Virginia. Edward Stabler wrote to Israel Pemberton in Philadelphia on June 19 that Richard Bland was trying to make Virginians believe "a large majority of the Friends in Philada had taken up arms."[11] Robert Pleasants wrote to his brother Samuel on September 16, asking "How many Friends in Philadelphia *have* taken up arms?" Robert added:

> I believe the reports here are greatly exaggerated. As for Virginia, four Friends have been chosen [county] committee men and five young men have enlisted in the independent companies--viz, our kinsman John Pleasants, three sons of Charles Woodson (our nephews) and a son of Charles Keesee. Our brother, Jonathan, also has occasionally acted.[12]

The story of Quaker enlistments in Philadelphia, though exaggerated, did have some substance. The "Quaker Blues" was organized by John Cadwalader, a wealthy Quaker who was soon disowned, and the "Silk

Stocking Company" by Joseph Copperthwaite who had been disowned earlier. These companies enlisted some sons of wealthy Quaker families, and others joined the company of light horse now known as the First City Troop. However, only sixty-six Friends in Philadelphia were "dealt with" for military activities during 1775; and of those sixty-six it appears that less than thirty were disowned by Friends for refusal to discontinue their warlike activities.[13]

Friends' witness for peace also requires refusing to pay war taxes. "I'd as soon go into the war as pay the tax" was the sentiment expressed by many Friends as the Revolution came nearer. Yet it was foreseen that the government would severely punish tax refusers. So, on 22 December 1775, fifteen elders of Virginia Yearly Meeting met at John Harris' house west of now Ashland along with Mahlon and Joseph Janney, John Hough and Samuel Canby. The last four Friends came from Fairfax Monthly Meeting in northern Virginia (under Philadelphia Yearly Meeting.) They had ridden south two days from Waterford to Ashland to discuss the perplexing war tax problem. From the minutes of this gathering--as they sat around John Harris' fire:

> After a time of solid waiting in silence, in which the calming influence of our heavenly Father's love was measurably witnessed amongst us, we took under our weighty consideration the following matters respecting the Society--
>
> 1st. Concerning Friends receiving or paying the paper bills of credit that are or may be issued for the purposes of carrying on War...
>
> 2ly. Respecting the propriety of Friends voluntarily paying or refusing to pay the taxes that may be laid for sinking or redeeming the above paper bills of credit...

The Friends calmly agreed as to the first matter that they should "adopt and recommend to the notice of Friends the advice given by the last Yearly Meeting in Philada" (meaning, refusal to use Continental paper dollars). They did not reach an agreement on the second matter, about war taxes.[14]

In fall 1776 Philadelphia Yearly Meeting invited the other five American Yearly Meetings to send representatives to Philadelphia in order to consider "the conduct that ought to be observed by our Society throughout the Continent in these times of probation and difficulties."[15] This gathering was the first time ever that Friends all up and down the line of American states came to counsel together. New England, Philadelphia, Maryland, Virginia and North Carolina Yearly Meetings were represented. Friends from New York Yearly Meeting were kept from coming by the war activities in their State. Robert Pleasants and Edward Stabler came for Virginia along with James and Amos Ladd of Weyanoke Meeting, Thomas Draper of Black Creek in Southampton County, Samuel Parsons of White Oak Swamp, and Samuel Hargrave, the clerk of Caroline Meeting.[16]

The Friends in Philadelphia hammered out a paper that defined four aspects of their peace testimony in the circumstances of the Revolution. The paper enjoined all American Friends to

- Perform no military service and pay no fine in lieu of military service.
- Avoid any trade or business likely to promote the war.
- Help all war victims, Quaker or non Quaker.
- Withdraw from political activity, even voting in elections, since government for the time being "was founded and supported in the spirit of wars and fighting."[17]

The matter of paying taxes was not defined and was left to the consciences of individual Friends.

\* \* \*

Even while they braced themselves to suffer for their faith in war time, Friends continued to care about Indians and slaves:

The Indians had been pretty well pushed west across the Appalachians by 1775 and Thomas Beals, 56, was among the first Friends to visit them there. As a youth of Hopewell Meeting this Thomas knew the dignified and quiet hunters who camped near Hopewell then. Now in 1775 he was a minister of Westfield Meeting in Surry County, N.C., just south of the Virginia line. He crossed southwest Virginia with three other Quaker men to call on the Senecas, but an encampment of Virginia militia stopped them near Cumberland Gap. The camp's commander could not understand why the Quakers wanted to risk their lives among savages. He kept them under arrest until Thomas Beals preached to the soldiers on why Indians deserve friendship. Beverly Milner, a 19-year-old soldier, was moved by the sermon to join Friends.[18]

Thomas Beals crossed the mountains often after 1775 to comfort Senecas, Mingoes and Delawares dispossessed from their ancestral homes. He moved to Ohio in 1799, a patriarch of 80 with his wife, two sons and grandchildren; died there in 1801 and was buried in the Ross County forest, with a butternut log hollowed out for his coffin. A stone nearby in the yard of the Friends Meeting House at Londonderry is scribed "In memory of Thomas Beals, 1719-1801, First Quaker Missionary to the Indians of the Northwest Territory."[19]

Hopewell Meeting's Friends remained conscience-stricken that they had not paid the Indians when the first Hopewell Friends moved into the valley in 1730s. Long after the tribes all were gone, the Meeting still was uneasy, even though no tribe ever had claimed the land around Hopewell as their own.[20] Eighty-four Hopewell families contributed £665 for the Indians in 1777, but still found none to pay it to.[21]

Such Quaker tenderness for Indians was despised by the back country Scotch-Irish who opined that the Friends were only kind to the Indians in order to make money from them. A Parson Barton of Lancaster, Pa, probably wrote the poem titled *Cloven Foot Discovered*. One stanza reads:

> In many things change but the name
> >  Quakers and Indians are the same...
> Those who the Indians' cause maintain
> >  Would take the part of bloody Cain
> And sell their very souls for gain.[22]

While the Friends of frontier Virginia were concerned for Indians, the Friends of "old" Virginia focussed on the plight of slaves. Virginia's Bill of Rights largely written by George Mason, and America's Declaration of Independence by Thomas Jefferson, both were published in June 1776. Both set forth the right to freedom of all people, and both were terribly flawed. For both writers owned gangs of enslaved people, not free at all, planting and harvesting at Mason's Gunston Hall and at Jefferson's Monticello. Quakers were quick to see the hypocrisy here.

Robert Pleasants touched on this matter early, on January 16, 1775. He wrote a reply that day to Robert Bolling, Esq., of Buckingham County who was suggesting that the Quakers, since they would not fight, should be "sequestered" during the coming war. Pleasants defended the Quaker peace position, and then suggested that Americans ought to free their slaves while they freed themselves from the English yoke:

> It would be consistent with our interests as well as our duty, while we are contending with the mother country...to [free] our dependents. This I believe would speak louder for the cause...than cannon.... The justice I speak of is [not] only due to dissenters...or to our Society [of Friends]; I wish it were extended to the poor slaves who have an equal right to freedom with ourselves.[23]

Pleasants developed this idea further when he wrote his Quaker brother-in-law, John Thomas of Maryland, four months later:

> But while we are condemning the mother country for endeavoring to deprive us of [liberty] let us consider our own conduct...'Cast out the beam that is in thy own eye', said our blessed Saviour, and 'Do unto others as we would they should do unto us.' But alas! our actions don't keep pace.... I believe the work [Quaker witness against slavery] will go forward...so that slavery will cease among a people so sensible of the value of liberty and so tenacious of their right to enjoy it.[24]

Patrick Henry was elected the first governor of the *State* of Virginia, a Colony and a Dominion no longer, in June 1776. He turned over Scotchtown, his plantation in Hanover County, to his Quaker cousins, John and Mary Payne, and then moved into the Governor's Palace in Williamsburg. He soon began to receive letters and visits from Quakers. In the spring of 1777 Robert Pleasants and Edward Stabler called on him. Robert then wrote to Israel Pemberton that Governor Henry "received us very kindly; and gave us to understand that he expected the next session [ of the Virginia Assembly] would be likely to allow liberty to all [slaveholders] to act as they may see cause in [freeing slaves]." When the two Friends mentioned that they had already started to free their *own* slaves, the Governor went on to say that "the code of laws now forming (in which George Wythe has a principal hand) allows the manumission of slaves [and also] abolishes the pay and power of the clergy."

Along with this good news, Robert wrote to Israel, "I apprehend trials ahead for Friends." No doubt he had already had some words with neighbors who did not take kindly to the Quakers' radical nonsense about freedom for slaves, and the evil of fighting with guns and cannon.

\* \* \*

George Wythe (1726-1806), as Governor Henry mentioned, was a member of the new General Assembly's three-man Committee of Revisors which was preparing a new code of laws for the new State. The other members were Thomas Jefferson, suddenly famous as the author of America's Declaration of Independence, and Edmund Pendleton.

He was named, George Wythe was, for his grandfather, Quaker George Walker and his great grandfather George Keith, the man who was a world class Quaker before he broke away in the 1690s. Margaret Walker Wythe, George's widowed mother, was herself raised a Quaker, and she had the independence of Quaker women and their attitude of intellectual equality. She taught little George at home in Hampton, Latin and Greek, logic and mathematics--George held the Greek Testament by his mother's knee while she read to him from the English version. As an adult he said that the Quaker principles taught by his mother were ingrained in him.

George Wythe stood for these things as a public man: decent treatment for Indians, negroes and the insane (they all have human rights, he said); co-equal education for men and women; applied sciences in college education; the separation of church and state; freedom of thought and speech.[25]

Wythe at William and Mary College was America's first professor of law. He taught law to Thomas Jefferson, and Jefferson called George Wythe "my earliest and best friend...to him I am indebted for first impressions which have had the most salutary influence on the course of my life."[26] And it is evident from the course of Jefferson's life that those first impressions were colored with George Wythe's Quaker-based principles concerning the rights of all humankind.

The Committee of Revisors, Wythe, Jefferson and Pendleton, labored for two and a half years. In 1778, at the Revisors' suggestion, the Assembly passed a bill forbidding further imports of slaves[27]--the same law Quakers had lobbied for in Williamsburg and London and that King George vetoed in 1772.[28]

In June 1779 the Revisors finished drafts of 126 bills--a proposed code of laws for the new State.[29] The Assembly adopted many of the 126 at once, while the more controversial were tabled. One proposal adopted was to move the State Capital from Williamsburg to Richmond, which was thought to be less vulnerable to attack by the British army. This move was made in the spring of 1780.

Two proposals tabled in 1779:

- A proposed Act for Religious Freedom mainly written by Thomas Jefferson. It was intended to implement completely Section 16, the Religious Freedom section of Virginia's Bill of Rights. Virginia's Baptists had handed in a petition for full religious freedom in 1776 signed by 10,000 persons. Hanover Presbytery also had sent a series of similar petitions, thus stiffening the Presbyterians' earlier quest for mere toleration. Still, the Assembly tabled the proposed Act for Religious Freedom.[30]
- A proposal to repeal a 56 year old law forbidding slaveholders to free their slaves. This "Manumission Act" had been suggested by Quaker lobbyists as early as 1770.

\* \* \*

At first, the new State government treated Friends kindly. For one reason Governor Henry admired them. For another, the Quakers in England were continuing to befriend the American cause. The following item appeared in the Virginia *Gazette*:

> July 7, 1775 (from a letter from London, April 10, 1775)--The Quakers in England have petitioned the King themselves as a people...; all join in one voice against the Ministry and all are faithful to the people in America. The Quakers are most hearty in the cause and see the dreadful consequences of a civil war.

And ten days later, on July 17, the Virginia Convention published its decision to continue its eight-year-old exemption of the Quakers from military duty:

> At a Convention of Delegates for the Counties and Corporations in the Colony of Virginia, held July 17, 1775--Chapter I - An Ordinance for Raising and Embodying a Sufficient Force for the Defence and Protection of This Colony...all Quakers and the people called menonists, shall be exempted from serving in the militia.[31]

This is the first time that "Menonists" were mentioned in Virginia statutes. They were the German-, Swiss- and Dutch-born Mennonites, now settled in considerable numbers in the Valley of Virginia and now firmly allied with the Quakers in witnessing against war. A few German-speaking and peace-witnessing members of the Church of the Brethren commonly known as Tunkers or Dunkers (from their practice of baptizing by triple immersion) also lived in the Valley by 1775.³² They doubtless were counted as "menonists" under this ordinance.

By the spring of 1776, however, war clouds were gathering. The need for able-bodied men suddenly became urgent. That year nine regiments organized in Virginia to fight in the Continental Army to the north;³³ and now the exemption was revoked:

> At a General Convention of Delegates and Representatives from the Several Counties and Corporations of Virginia, May 6, 1776...Chapter XII--An Ordinance for Raising and Embodying a Sufficient Force etc--All quakers and menonists in Virginia shall be enlisted into the militia and be subject to the same rules and regulations...as the rest of the militia...but the said quakers and menonists shall not be obliged to attend general or private musters.³⁴

This last ordinance proved to be unenforceable. The recruiters simply could not wheedle many Quaker, Mennonite or Brethren men into taking up muskets. Then in October 1777 someone in Williamsburg hit on a bright idea--to excuse any "quaker or menonist" who refused to serve, but at the same time to collect from him a sum sufficient to hire a substitute to soldier for 18 months--calculated to be £14 sterling. This plan worked. Quakers and Mennonites generally refused to pay the substitute sums, but the county sheriffs knew from long experience how to collect "by distress."³⁵

Along with the substitute sums, there came another requirement that Friends could not obey--the Test Oath. In 1776, the British commander Sir William Howe, announced from his New York City headquarters that he would pardon and protect any American who swore allegiance to King George. The Continental Congress countered by requiring all men who were not obviously American patriots to swear loyalty to the United States or be regarded as enemies. This was the Test Oath law. In Virginia, refusal "to take the Test"--and the Friends' meetings disowned any Friend who did take it--³⁶disqualified the "non-juror" from buying land or suing for debts, and resulted in confiscation of his hunting gun, powder and shot.³⁷ In October 1777, it was also enacted that every one who failed to take the Test Oath would be required to pay *double* taxes.³⁸

Suddenly Friends' fell into new disfavor, for their peace witness detracted from the hate-the-enemy atmosphere that every war needs. The First Day gatherings in 1776 in Virginia's 53 Friends Meeting Houses became more quietly centered, the silences took on new depth and nuance. Once again speakers stood in the silence to remind Friends of Jesus' clear and present teachings--"Blessed are the peacemakers" and "Blessed are ye when men shall revile you and persecute you, and shall say all manner of evil against you falsely, for my sake."

This time the Friends were more faithful than 20 years earlier, back in the French and Indian War time. About four thousand Friends lived in Virginia during the Revolution including 880 men of military age. Of these, the Meetings dealt with 104 for shortcomings concerning the War and 69 were disowned, cast out of meeting when they failed to correct their conduct.[39] This means that about 11 of 12 able bodied men Friends were faithful, while one of 12 caught the war fever, and was disowned.

\* \* \*

A Friend who became a famous military man was Nathanael Greene (1741-1786) of Warwick, Rhode Island. He left Friends when he joined the Rhode Island legislature in 1770, and went on to become the ranking general in the Continental Army next to George Washington. His mother, having failed to keep him from joining the army, saw him off saying "Nathan if thee gets shot I hope thee'll not be shot in the back."[40] His cousin, Patience Greene Brayton (1733-1794), was a Friends' minister who came down from New England to visit the Southern meetings in 1771.[41]

Others disowned for going to war were Thomas Mifflin (1744-1800), a Philadelphian who became Washington's first Quartermaster General; and John Lacey (1755-1814) of Buckingham Meeting in Bucks County, Pa., made a general of Continental troops at age 22. The names of Greene and Mifflin are memorialized in Virginia: Greene County is named for the one, and Mifflin Hall, the main building at Fort Lee, the army post near Petersburg, for the other.

The two ex-Quakers in the Virginia legislature, Charles Lynch and Isaac Zane, also became famous in the public's eyes and infamous in Quaker eyes, during the Revolution:

Charles Lynch (1736-1796) found a bed of saltpetre near his Alta Vista home and began to manufacture gunpowder in the spring of 1775.[42] Then he re-opened the Fort Chiswell lead mine (near the New River east of Wytheville) which he managed with his friend James Callaway and his cousin Robert Adams. This mine became an important source of bullets for the Continental army.[43]

Managing this mine was not easy. Some or all of the miners were reluctant convicts, including slaves who had been armed by Lord Dunmore to defend Norfolk and then captured by the American force.[44] Tories lived near the mine who tried to sabotage mine operations. Charles Lynch used savage methods to overcome those hindrances--methods which gave rise to the dark terms "lynching" and "lynch law."[45] He and his associates also practiced a kind of lynching of the Tories around Alta Vista, hanging them up by their hands or thumbs to a tree until they "repented." Some tavern minstrel composed a song about it:

> Hurrah for Colonel Lynch
> Captain Bob [Adams] and Callaway
> They never turned a Tory loose
> Until he shouted 'Liberty'[46]

Lynch was rewarded for his services, being made a colonel of militia and elected a state senator after the war. The legislature then passed an Act to Indemnify Certain Persons in Suppressing a Conspiracy against This State, which reads:

> Whereas divers ill-disposed persons in the year 1780 formed a conspiracy and did actually attempt to levy war against the Commonwealth: and...William Preston, Robert Adams, Jr., James Callaway and Charles Lynch and others did...suppress such conspiracy; and whereas the measures taken for that purpose may not be strictly warranted by law, although justifiable from the imminence of the danger...they are indemnified and exonerated.[47]

As for Isaac Zane (1743-1795) of Frederick County, he turned his Marlboro Iron Furnace into an armory. Instead of making stoves and fireplace liners, he converted to "cannon, roundshot, double-headed shot, sliding shot and chain shot of weights from four to 24 pounds." One shipment took 65 wagons to haul it to Fredericksburg.[48] He was made a brigadier-general for his war efforts.

In those times and in these, peace makers are not nearly as well known as war makers. One Virginia-born Friend, however, gained international fame as a peace maker and reconciler: Warner Mifflin (1745-1798).

Warner Mifflin's fame relates to the fact that Quakers and Quakerism were topics of keen interest to French writers from George Fox's day on. According to Guy Miege writing early in the 1700s:

> The Quakers or Trembleurs...reject all kinds of ministers and orders, they mock at premeditated preaching. Even the Holy Scriptures are not a rule to them, only the inspiration and light which they claim to have, guides them.... Men and even women who feel themselves seized by the Spirit and illumined by the Light, preach...whatever comes into their minds, be it good or bad. They have no sacraments and consequently are only half-Christians. One of their principles is that all [people] are equal.... They affect great simplicity.... They have a reputation for being frank and honest in their dealings. The relations I have had with some of them make me think so too, but some think they are crafty and deceitful.[49]

Voltaire wrote about "les Amis" too. In the article on Christianity in his *Dictionnaire Philosophique* published in 1764, he describes Quakers as a deeply religious people despite the fact that they have no sacraments, or dogmas--"A Socratic people...as yet they are without temples, without altars, as the first Christians were for 150 years. They work like them, they serve each other as they did, like them they hate war."[50] Thus "Quaker" was fixed in the French mind as a word typifying a virtuous person.

Two French writers produced books about America soon after the Revolution--Hector St. John de Crevecoeur, whose book is *Letters of an American Farmer*; and Jacques-Pierre Brissot de Warville, *New Travels in the United States of America*. They both met Warner Mifflin in America, and both saw in him the good things that Voltaire had written about Quakers.

Actually Warner was a mild-mannered, pipe-smoking Friend with intense convictions. De Crevecoeur describes him as "a man who wore a flat-brimmed hat, a gray suit without buttons, who wore no powder in his hair and whose shoes were tied with laces."[51] He was raised at Pharsalia, a Virginia plantation overlooking the Chesapeake near Chincoteague Island. His parents kept up a little Friends' meeting there. They had slaves at Pharsalia and Warner, when he was 14, had a talk with one of the field hands who asked him, in effect, How is it that you're free and I'm not? Warner could find no answer and, as he said, began to feel that the slave system was wrong. When he was 30 he freed his slaves being among the first Quakers to do so. About the same time, he moved north to settle near Duck Creek Meeting at Smyrna in Kent County, Delaware.

In October 1777 the British army occupied Philadelphia and the Continentals tried to dislodge them, attacking through the Germantown suburb. At this point Warner, leading five other Friends right across the battlefield, visited General George Washington and gave him a printed Testimony about the foolishness of war, along with some appropriate remarks. The Friends then walked through the lines into Philadelphia and gave the British general Lord Howe a copy of the Testimony.[52]

Brissot rhapsodized over all this in *New Travels*:

> I was sick. Warner Mifflin came to see me. You know Warner Mifflin, having read the touching tribute to him in the *Letters from an American Farmer*. It was he who first freed all his slaves. It was he who, without a passport, passed through the British lines and spoke to General Howe so firmly and with so much dignity [and] went to General Washington.... This angel of peace and charity came to see me. 'I am Warner Mifflin', he said. '...I have read [thy] book.... I learned thee was here and I have come to see thee.' What humanity! What charity![53]

So the fame of Warner Mifflin spread across Europe. He became the very incarnation of the good Quaker. He was the hero of *The Quaker*, August von Kotzebue's 11-scene play in German (although the playwright calls him "Walter" Mifflin). The play has to do with the conversion of General Howe, a purely military man, to a man of compassion. It ends thus:

> Gen.: Strong man, give me your hand.
> Mifflin: Here is my hand.
> Gen.: Could you but give me your strong faith with this hand's pressure!
> Mifflin: Would to God it were so, my brother! Then shouldst thou stand fast in sorrow or joy. Fare thee well! And if thou comest into the County Kent, see Walter Mifflin.
> Gen.: God guide you.
> Mifflin: I hope he will. Come, Marie. (Exit)
> Gen.: Ha! What a people! Could I conquer this half the world, should I be as happy as Walter Mifflin?
>
> Curtain[54]

\* \* \*

In the beginning years of the Revolution, 1775 and 1776, hundreds of Virginians of British sympathies--Tories--were driven from the Commonwealth. Some left plantations and property and fled, fearing tar-and-feathers or worse. Others put "I-intend-for-England" notices in the Virginia *Gazette*, and tried to collect their accounts receivable before taking ship. The property they left behind was auctioned off by escheators appointed by the State. Remarkably, only one Quaker, Joseph Elam of Petersburg, was among those Tory refugees. It seems that Virginia's Quakers had made their position clear--that they would not fight for either side.

There were very few Tories among the *Pennsylvania* Quakers either, but the efforts of Israel Pemberton and his friends to preserve the connection with England created considerable suspicion in Philadelphia. Richard Henry Lee wrote from Philadelphia to Governor Patrick Henry in Williamsburg on September 8, 1777 that this suspicion had resulted in the imprisonment of "old Pemberton and several others, to prevent their mischievous intervention in favor of the enemy."[55] On September 15 then, when Governor Henry met with his Council it was resolved:

> ...that the governor be advised to write to the first or any other magistrate of the Counties of Henrico, Nansemond, Hanover, Loudoun and any other County where meetings of Quakers are held, to inform them of the grounds of suspicion and requesting them to seize the meetings' records and arrest any Quaker found guilty of treason.[56]

The Meeting's records were seized at Cedar Creek in Hanover County and perhaps elsewhere. Cedar Creek's records were kept a month or two and then returned to John Payne of Scotchtown, the Meeting's clerk. No treason was discovered.

\* \* \*

As Richard Henry Lee reported, Israel Pemberton and other Philadelphia Quakers were arrested on the morning of September 2, 1777. Philadelphia was then in a feverish state. Ten days earlier General Howe with 16,000 British and Hessian troops, had come by sea from New York City, through the Virginia Capes, up Chesapeake Bay, and landed at Elkton, Md. Now the task force was moving ponderously toward Philadelphia. The Continental Army under General Washington was racing from New Jersey to get between Howe's force and Philadelphia.[57] The Continental Congress was packing to leave town for York, Pa., and Pennsylvania's Revolutionary Council was preparing to move to Lancaster, Pa.

Amidst all this alarm, the case of the Spanktown Papers came before the Congress. On August 24, General John Sullivan in East New Jersey wrote to Congressman John Hancock that he had come across some traitorous papers. The papers, Sullivan said, gave the strength and locations of the American Army and they were intended for British use. They came, he said, from the "Spanktown [Rahway] Yearly Meeting of Friends." Sullivan then denounced Quakers as a class, calling them "the most dangerous enemies America knows."[58]

No such Meeting of Friends existed. The papers were a hoax. Nevertheless, Congress named a three-man committee to investigate the charge: John Adams, chairman, Virginia's Richard Henry Lee and William Duer of New York. This committee convened immediately to review the Spanktown Papers and the various Testimonies issued by Philadelphia Yearly Meeting over the past two years. Evidently no Quaker witnesses were called; but the committee concluded that the Quakers were a menace and that eleven leading Philadelphia Quakers "maintain a correspondence and connection that is highly prejudicial to the public safety."[59]

Congress approved the Adams Committee's report with lightning speed. It called on the thirteen state governments to "apprehend and secure all persons, as well among the Quakers as others" who evidence "a disposition inimical to the cause of America." It specifically requested the Pennsylvania Council to take into custody the eleven Philadelphia Quakers named by the committee. The name of Israel Pemberton headed this list. He was widely known in Philadelphia as "King of the Quakers." John Adams disliked him for his bluntness, and Tom Paine, the great pamphleteer of the American cause, had just rushed into print a pamphlet titled *The Crisis* which castigated the Philadelphia Friends for refusing to join the war effort. Paine was himself the son of an English Quaker. At times in his life, he was a friend of the Friends. In 1777, however, he called them in *The Crisis* a "fallen, cringing, priest-and-Pemberton-ridden people," adding "a religious quaker is a valuable character [but] a political quaker is a real Jesuit."[60]

So the Council sent three armed men who rounded up Israel Pemberton and some forty other Philadelphia suspects. The arrested men were required to sign a pledge not to aid the English. Those who complied were freed, but not all complied. Some strong-minded suspects insisted they had a right to know the charges and face their accusers.[61] Among them were Israel Pemberton and his brothers--James Pemberton, who was clerk of Philadelphia Yearly Meeting; and John, clerk of Philadelphia's Meeting for Sufferings; Samuel Pleasants, the Pembertons' Virginia-born brother-in-law; Henry Drinker of the mercantile firm of James and Drinker, who was clerk of Philadelphia Monthly Meeting for the Northern District; and John Hunt and Thomas Gilpin, prominent merchants. Quaker Elijah Brown, who also insisted on his innocence, had a six year-old son at home named Charles-- Charles Brockden Brown (1771-1818), who wrote America's first novel (*Wieland*) in 1798 and was probably the first American professional writer.[62]

Congress debated this demand for a hearing for five hours, then decided to exile the stubborn suspects to Staunton, Virginia without a hearing.[63] A shabby decision, but the English army was coming, and hysteria shrilled in Philadelphia's air.

It was probably Richard Henry Lee who suggested Staunton, that back country village of thirty houses, to be the place of exile. Twenty men, eighteen of them Quakers, were told they were to be sent there. On September 5, the Pennsylvania Council received a petition for a hearing of the case signed by 105 Philadelphia Friends. Council refused, saying that Congress must decide; and Congress declared on September 8 that *it* shouldn't decide because the prisoners all were Pennsylvania citizens.[64] The prisoners then published *An Address to the Inhabitants of Pennsylvania*, a broadside to protest this cat-and-mouse game; and the Council countered by releasing the phony Spanktown Papers to the newspapers, thus besmearing the Quaker prisoners and the whole Society of Friends.[65]

The twenty prisoners were sent off for Staunton on the morning of September 11 without any hearing. Some were dragged into the vehicles by force. The mutter of cannon was heard in the city from Brandywine Creek twenty-five miles away where General Washington was trying to stop the ponderous British advance.[66] The prisoners were detoured north up the Schuylkill to stay clear of the battle. They rode in a raggle-taggle procession: two carriages, two one-horse shays, eight on horseback, a couple of baggage wagons, and a few troopers of the First City Troop to guard them.[67] Some people along the streets jeered at them as they left Philadelphia.

At Reading, the guards received a writ of habeas corpus granted by Chief Justice McKean of the new Pennsylvania Supreme Court. The writ was canceled, however, by an *ex post facto* act rushed through the Pennsylvania Assembly to deny habeas corpus to the twenty.

Stones were thrown at the twenty in Reading, but the two Isaac Zanes, senior and junior, met them there; and Isaac, Jr., disowned Quaker though he was, comforted the group. He promised he would arrange for them to be held in Winchester instead of Staunton--Winchester, a town where Quakers lived and where they would see friendly faces.

The twenty exiles arrived at Winchester on September 20, tired and mud-splashed. Sure enough, Isaac Zane, Jr., who represented Frederick County in the Virginia Assembly, had pulled political strings. Three rooms were waiting for them in Winchester's Bush's Tavern. They had to sleep two to a bed and three or four beds to a room, but it was a relief to settle in there.[68]

Winchester was considerably excited. Three hundred Hessian prisoners-of-war encamped outside of town the same day the exiles arrived. Isaac Zane, Jr., had arranged for the Hessians' arrival too--no doubt to provide hands for his cannon factory on Cedar Creek. For a little time the exiles were jostled and hooted in Winchester's streets, and guards were posted around the tavern. Militia officers tried to press a young Winchester Quaker, Isaac England, into this guard duty on October 3, and Isaac was roughly handled when he refused.[69]

The hooting and the guards lasted only a week or two. John Smith, Frederick County's Lieutenant and leading citizen and Isaac Zane, Jr.'s friend, came to join the exiles in meetings for worship. Israel Pleasants wrote to Robert Pleasants and Edward Stabler, asking them to intercede in Williamsburg for the exiles.[70] Pleasants and Stabler visited Governor Patrick Henry, who responded by calling an all-day meeting of his six-man Council on October 15. From the Council minutes:

> His Excellency [Governor Henry] having communicated to the Board sundry letters and other papers relating to the Quakers and others who have been apprehended in Pennsylvania by order of the Executive Council of that State as enemies to the independence of America and [sent to Winchester in Frederick County] and the Lieutenant of that County informing the Governor that he wanted His Excellency's sanction for confirming them as prisoners of war...the Board advised His Excellency...to write to the said County Lieutenant...directing him...to afford humane treatment to the said prisoners [and] to permit them to walk in the day time in any part of the town for the benefit of their health.[71]

After this a great many distinguished Virginians came to visit the exiles in Winchester. John Augustus Washington, General George's brother, came down from Berkeley County. Colonel Francis Peyton, Loudoun's leading citizen, visited with Loudoun Quaker John Hough. Colonel George Gilpin, brother of the exile Thomas Gilpin and a Fairfax County justice, spent four weeks with the exiles.[72] The exiles now were trusted to go where they wished around Winchester. They went to worship at Hopewell Meeting six miles north of town and at Centre Meeting held at the Widow Hollingsworth's (in the stately house now called "Abram's Folly") just south of town. They encouraged the Hopewell Friends to continue their collection for repaying the Indians, and they helped the Hollingsworths, Parkinses, and Luptons to build Centre's first meeting house.[73] They held meetings for worship in the Dutch (Lutheran) and Calvinist (Presbyterian) meeting houses in Winchester.

Presently they moved out of Bush's Tavern to board in threes and fours in Quaker farm houses outside of town.[74] They were unhappy when the two non-Quakers among them, a physician and a dancing-master, betrayed their captors' trust and escaped from Winchester.[75]

All this time, the exiles' friends kept up a steady drumfire of protests:

- In October 1777, Philadelphia Yearly Meeting gathered. The assembled Friends were anxious about the exiles and the smear on the Society's reputation. They issued a Testimony stating that Friends were not enemies of the American cause, but rather were "led out of all wars and fightings by the principle of Grace and Truth." There is no "Spanktown Yearly Meeting" this Testimony declared, and the Spanktown Papers are false.[76]
- January 1778: five Friends headed by Isaac Zane, Sr., and Joseph Janney of Fairfax Meeting in Virginia, went to York to present the exiles' case to the Continental Congress. Congress then resolved to set the exiles free *if* they would affirm allegiance to their State, but the exiles refused this condition.[77]
- February 1778: a delegation headed by Warner Mifflin visited the Pennsylvania Council in Lancaster. Mifflin said the treatment of the Virginia exiles violated the Declaration of Rights of the state's new constitution. Test oaths and loyalty affirmations infringe on freedom of conscience. Friends could not make such oaths or affirmations. They could not take sides, he said.[78] But no action was taken on his appeal.

February then and now is a sickly, slushy month. The Virginia exiles became somewhat discouraged in February of 1778, not knowing when or whether they ever would see their homes. Many of them caught the flu or flux that February. John Hunt, 66, their brightest preacher, cheered them through the month, "express[ing] the beauty and excellency of our being in such a state of mind that we may be content with every allotment of divine Providence."[79] But Thomas Gilpin took sick, died on March 2 and was laid to rest in Hopewell's burying ground. Soon after, John Hunt's infected left leg became gangrenous and was amputated on March 22. The surgeon was Adam Stephen,[80] who had been an American army general, sent home by Washington for drunkenness at the Battle of Germantown five months earlier. It can be guessed that he did crude surgery. At any rate John Hunt died too on the last day of March. The remaining sixteen exiles were disconsolate.

In all these seven months, the exiles' wives had been gallantly coping at home, raising children, writing upbeat letters to absent husbands, and fending off the British soldiery roaming Philadelphia's streets. Among the gallantest were Mary Pleasants, 36 and Samuel's wife, and Elizabeth Drinker, 38, who kept a sprightly journal. Quaker women are traditionally strong-minded and these wives were of that tradition. That lugubrious March of 1778 they held all-women counsels in their various parlors. Mary Pleasants drew up a paper to the politicians:

> We...request you...to take off the bonds of those innocent and oppressed Friends...who have evidenced their strong attachment to their native country, and a benevolent disposition to mankind in general.... One of [Christ's] excellent precepts was 'Whatsoever ye would that men should do to you, do ye even so to them.'[81]

Eighteen women signed Mary Pleasants' paper.

Then on April 5 Mary, Elizabeth Drinker, Susanna Jones, and Hannah Pemberton set out in the Pleasants' coach with four horses and two coachmen to bring the husbands home. They sailed smartly west on the Lancaster Road under budding trees; talked their way past the British sentry posted on that road; passed Merion and Haverford Meeting houses; then turned north until they encountered the outer picket of the American camp at Valley Forge. They informed the astonished sergeant of the guard that they were come to see the commanding general. George Washington had dined twice at Mary Pleasants' table, and she had found him an approachable, persuadable man.[82]

After quite a delay at the picket post, word came that the general would see the ladies. Their coach rattled on past log huts and gawking soldiers to Washington's headquarters in the fieldstone home requisitioned from Quaker widow Deborah Hewes. Martha Washington, up from Mt. Vernon for a little stay with her husband, met them at the door. The women liked one another, and the visitors stayed for supper and then the night. George Washington was reached by the Quaker women. After supper he wrote a note for them to take to the president of Pennsylvania's Council, Thomas Wharton at Lancaster. The next morning after breakfast he wrote a second, warmer, note to Wharton which closed:

...As they [the four Quaker women] seem much distressed--humanity pleads strongly in their behalf.

> I have the honor to be, sir,
> Your most obedient servant,
> G Washington

This note did the trick. The four women went on to Lancaster, handed in Washington's letter to Wharton, and presto! the Virginia exiles were ordered freed on April 10.[83] The exiles never did receive a hearing, but instead were given American passports for return to Philadelphia--while Philadelphia was still occupied by the British--indication enough that the charges against them had been dropped and the Society of Friends' good name cleared.[84]

\* \* \*

For three years after Dunmore's departure there was no major fighting in Virginia, but there were vigorous preparations to fight nevertheless. Winchester looked like this to a visitor in 1776:

Here every presence is warlike, every sound is martial! Drums beating, pipes and bagpipes playing...every man has a hunting-shirt, which is the uniform of each company--almost all have a cockade and bucks tail in their hats, to represent that they are hardy, resolute and invincible natives of America.[85]

Daniel Morgan (1736-1802) recruited the Eleventh Virginia Regiment, better known as Morgan's Rifles, in Winchester in 1777. He was born a Quaker, this Daniel Morgan, whose parents worshiped in Crooked Run

Meeting north of Front Royal.[86] At 20 he ran off to be a wagoner in General Braddock's supply train; struck a British officer whose orders did not suit him; and acquired a hate for all things British after he was "introduced to the gunner's daughter"--that is, tied across a cannon barrel and whipped. A few Quaker boys, lured by the fifes and drums, were among Morgan's Rifles when they marched north late in 1777.

But only a few--most were faithful to the Friends' witness for peace. On September 23 of that year 1777, fourteen Quaker men of the valley meetings were hustled into Winchester and into the ranks of a battalion of militia. Officers "with drawn swords pushed the Friends into rank, threatening they would have their blood if they did not comply." When they refused to take rifles, the rifles were tied to them and the battalion headed up the Wagon Road toward Philadelphia.

The Quakers were prodded and shoved along. Half of them dropped exhausted on the way and were left to return home as best they could. The other half arrived at Washington's camp on the Skippack Pike above Philadelphia half-starved. Clement Biddle, a colonel and a Philadelphia ex-Quaker, saw them there, and he got Washington's permission to send them home on October 18. That day "they went to most of the officers who had taken them to camp, who seemed generally pleased with their release and took their leave of them in a friendly manner, wishing them well and safely home."[87]

Another group of Quaker men from Loudoun County's meetings--Fairfax, Goose Creek, Gap and South Fork--were forced to march north, too.[88] Several southside Virginia Friends, taken by force during the mobilization of 1777, were freed by Governor Henry when they reached Williamsburg. Stephen Peebles, 26, of Burleigh Meeting in Prince George County was not so fortunate. He was marched clear to Valley Forge before he was released and allowed to hike home.[89]

The farther the Revolutionary War progressed, the less popular Quakers became. The Virginia *Gazette* for 25 April 1777, published the last in its series of stories about the English Quakers' support of the American cause:

> Philadelphia, April 9--We have the best authority to assure our readers that Dr. John Fothergill of London (of the Society of Friends)...still continues to act the part of a firm friend of America, upon her just and necessary claims of independence.

Seven months later, however, the *Gazette* ran a false story that Quakers were aiding the British army of occupation in Philadelphia:

> Philadelphia, November 14, 1777--the Quakers made Friend Howe a free gift of £6,000 on his entrance into Philadelphia and on the 25th ult, by his positive command, they were to pay 20,000 more.

This rapid shift in the public's attitude came from the Friends' refusal to aid the war effort: refusing not only to soldier, but also to honor the authority of the new Revolutionary government. For a time many Friends refused to use Continental paper dollars. Their reasoning: Christians, true enough, are called to render unto Caesar the things that are Caesar's and unto God the things that are God's; but now it was not clear who "Caesar" was, whether the King or the new government.[90] As late as 1780, the Frederick County court fined sixty-five families of Hopewell Meeting for refusing to co-operate even in an assessment of the value of their farms.[91]

In a similar court case the judge was puzzled by Quaker intransigence. He asked the Quaker defendant, "Your principle is passive obedience and non-resistance?" The defendant's answer, "On the contrary, our principle is active obedience [to God] and passive suffering."[92]

By 1779, efforts to break down the Friends' peace position had become harsher. This is the account of William Davis, 24, married to Mary Gosney three years earlier and a Friend of South River Meeting near Lynchburg:

> I was warned to appear the 2nd [of Sixth Month 1779] at a certain place in order to join a company of militia who were to march to the barracks at Charlottesville to guard a number of British prisoners, which I refused, believing it to be wrong for me to be active in any way assisting in warlike measures.
>
> Upon which I was taken and carried to the place afore appointed and had various offers which I refused and was then put under guard, a sergeant and four men. After marching about 20 miles the captain offered me his horse to ride which I accepted. He offered me a gun which [he] himself had carried to ease an elderly man of his company. I immediately felt an uneasiness and refused, letting him know I acknowledged his kindness in offering his horse, but had rather walk than meddle with arms, which displeased the officer much, but was permitted to ride without carrying the gun. This

small trial was followed with peace of mind and afforded encouragement.

The next request was to answer to my name when called on the list, which I could not be free to do because it was answering the place of a soldier.... I was then carried before the Colonel by the guard, who informed him I refused to obey orders. He asked my reasons. I told him our Saviour was styled the prince of peace and they that followed must follow him in peace.

'Then I suppose you are a Quaker,' said he. I said I was called so, and after some other ensnaring questions which I made little answer to, he ordered me to be carried to the guard house where I was kept for a few days and then had before a court-martial under the accusation of disobeying orders and asked if I was guilty or not. I said I had refused to bear arms....

And after eight days' close confinement, I was carried to a place where was a ring of soldiers and officers and I being carried to the middle there the sentence of the court martial was read (which was kept from me til then) which was 39 lashes to be well laid on my bare back.

I was then ordered to strip myself which I did not do, but the officer who had the management of this business ordered me to be stripped.[I] was then tied by my hands...at which time I endeavored to make the people sensible of the cause of my refusing to obey...to which much attention was given by the people, but the Colonel who had the command showed himself to be very [rude?]...saying there was no time for preaching now. I believe he thought it would [take] with the people (many of the [Albemarle] County people were present) and make the conduct of the officers appear less honorable.

The execution was performed by three men who laid on by turns...with what is called a cat of nine tails... In the time of execution I had to express these words viz 'Blessed are the merciful for they shall obtain mercy.' I believe the Colonel was a little touched by these words and ordered the whippers to strike light.

After being loosed...I was ordered to go to my duty, meaning that of a soldier. I answered publicly 'I am of the same principle now as I was before I suffered, and the God I profess to serve is the same yesterday, today and forever', and then the men were marched off.

The Colonel and myself were left alone. He discoursed with me until dark and in some measure excused himself for their cruelty, adding the law obliged him to do as he had, and the consequence would be the like punishment as had been if I refused to comply. I signified I should not.

...I stayed until I was discharged...was often threatened and endeavors used to get me to wait on the sick.... I let them know I could not supply the place of a soldier even to wait on the sick.[93]

Mary Davis waited at home with her two small sons. When the news came about her man's ordeal, she said that she grieved for Will's bloodied back, but was so proud he stood by the peace principle.[94]

\* \* \*

Friends from Virginia Yearly Meeting conferred regularly during the war years with delegations from America's five other Yearly Meetings. They met each fall in Philadelphia in the Friends' meeting house close by Independence Hall where the Continental Congress held its sessions. One body planning for peace, the other for war.

A main concern of the Friends' wartime conferences was What taxes should Friends pay to the new Revolutionary governments? Clearly, taxes levied for war purposes should not be paid, but the trouble was that war taxes were mixed in with taxes for peaceable purposes. There was no way to know which was which. Any Friend who refused to pay *all* taxes would probably lose his or her farm and all worldly possessions. In the fall of 1776, the conference could only agree that Friends should take "care to avoid complying with the injunctions and requisitions made for the purpose of carrying on war."[95] The mixed taxes issue was left up to the consciences of individual Friends.

Virginia Yearly Meeting when it gathered in Curles Meeting house in May 1779 discussed the issue for a long time. Finally the assembled Friends decided "to leave all hope of help as to the outward" and to advise all members not to pay "the single tax"--that is, any tax where it is impossible to disentangle war purposes from peaceful purposes.[96]

Just how many Virginia Friends took this hard step is not clear. It is clear that those who did become tax refusers were honored by their meetings. That December Robert Pleasants wrote to Thomas Nicholson, the patriarch of Perquimans Quarterly Meeting in North Carolina. "We have heard the Friends of your Quarter have decided to pay the single tax," Robert wrote. He then urged Perquimans Friends to reconsider, saying, "Friends, consistent with their principles, can no more pay the Tax than take the Test."[97]

Remarkably, this decision to refuse the single tax was taken at a time when Virginia's Friends were under heavy pressure. There were men in the Virginia Assembly who wanted to crush the Quakers and their stubborn, embarrassing witness against the War. Virginia's double tax, levied in 1777 against all persons refusing to take the Test Oath, was raised to a *triple* tax late in 1778 and a bill to banish tax refusers from Virginia nearly passed in the Assembly. In 1779 the triple tax law was rescinded. Nevertheless, the drain on Virginia Friends' worldly resources continued.

In the years before the Revolution, 1750 to 1767, the county sheriffs seized goods from the families of Virginia Yearly Meeting worth about £85 every year for muster and church fines. From 1768 to 1776 the seizures were negligible. During the war years 1777 to 1783, however, they leaped astronomically, to more than £860 a year. The wartime seizures from the Valley, and Loudoun Friends (who were associated with Philadelphia, not Virginia Yearly Meeting) were nearly as heavy. The total sum of Quaker sufferings in Virginia, 1777 to 1783, exceeded £11,221.[98]

\* \* \*

War came to Virginia in 1779 when the British altered their grand strategy. By this time the British army had abandoned Philadelphia and returned to New York City. Lordly planners in London studying great maps over cups of tea now decided that the Americans' soft underbelly was to the South. Hold New York City and take Virginia and the Carolinas, that was the decision. So, on 9 May 1779, Admiral Sir George Collier sailed his flotilla in to Hampton Roads, occupied Portsmouth and Suffolk, and burned many buildings and supplies. Another English force under General Leslie occupied the Hampton Roads area in October 1780.

Early in 1781 Benedict Arnold, the American traitor become a British general, led 1,600 redcoats up the James. Arnold's force landed at Westover and marched to the new State Capital of Richmond. Virginia's government--now headed by Thomas Jefferson, the state's second governor, succeeding Patrick Henry--fled to Charlottesville.

The British bivouacked around Curles Meeting House at Varina on their way to Richmond and again on their return down river a few days later.[99] They ransacked the plantations of Robert Pleasants and Frederick Woodson. Robert Pleasants lost his favorite horse and most of his daughter Margaret's clothes were stolen. When Robert went to the British colonel quartered at Woodson's, to inquire for his horse, he was arrested and held there all night.[100]

The British invasion caused wild excitement--too much for some young Quakers, smarting under the taunts of non-Quaker neighbors. As Arnold's task force came up the James, eight Quaker men, mostly from Curles Meeting, made it known that they would be willing to abandon their place as peacemakers in order "to serve our Country as cavalry." They demanded that the state supply "the necessary accoutrements and pay"[101]--a rather unusual requirement, for most of Virginia's cavalry troopers provided their own horses and equipment in order to avoid service as foot soldiers. Nevertheless, Governor Jefferson agreed. No doubt he hoped more Quakers of military age would follow, and so eliminate the witness against the wisdom of war that Quakers were keeping up all across his state.

Robert Pleasants had only one son, Robert, Jr., who had friends and cousins among the eight who joined the cavalry. Robert, Jr., was tempted to join them. He did not join them in the end, but he did give his father some days of exquisite anxiety. Robert, Sr., wrote to his brother Samuel that the ruin of his plantation by British soldiers was upsetting, "but nothing gives me so much pain of mind as a fear lest my son should...take up arms."[102]

Robert Jr., reconsidered and stayed faithful to Friends' peace witness, but five of the eight young men who did abandon Friends were Pleasantses--John, Samuel, Matthew, Isaac and Philip. Two were Woodsons--Samuel and Isham. The other was John Cheadle of Caroline Meeting.[103] The Friends made every effort to salvage the eight. Robert Pleasants wrote to his young relative Matthew Pleasants:

> Report having been made to our monthly meeting that thee had so far deviated from thy education and practice of Friends as to attend at muster and act as a military man, Amos Ladd and myself

were appointed to visit and endeavor to convince thee of the impropriety of such conduct....

If the report should be true and if thou should have seen the inconsistency of such practices so as with sincerity to condemn them...lose no time in communicating that desirable intelligence, whereby thou may be restored to the unity of thy Friends, who are concerned for thy welfare and happiness....

Solidly consider the matter, and if thou can not justify war from the doctrines and example of our Saviour, His apostles and the primitive Christians, would it not be a dangerous innovation to set up thy own judgment in opposition to the highest authorities? Wherein should thou be mistaken after having been favored with a different education, the greater will be thy condemnation.[104]

On 29 April 1781 another English fleet with 2,600 soldiers under Major General William Phillips, anchored in the James abreast of Robert Pleasants' house. By this time, everybody in the Varina neighborhood excepting Robert, two of his clerks, and neighbor Ryland Randolph, had fled. Robert was fired at from a gunboat, then arrested and interrogated. He was grieved to learn that another of the gunboats was commanded by Joseph Shoemaker of Philadelphia, once a Friend. The invaders went on up river, plundering and burning. They plundered the Pleasants' plantation in Goochland County. On their return down river in May, they torched the Pleasants' two tobacco warehouses at the mouth of Four Mile Creek.[105]

As the British were ravaging the neighborhood outside, the Virginia Yearly Meeting of May 1781 was held in Curles Meetinghouse. Although some Friends wanted to cancel the Meeting, they resolved to gather with their clerk, John Crew.[106] Joshua Brown, a visiting minister, wrote that Friends had the evil of slavery on their minds. Evidently they spent as much time on the plight of slaves as on their own plight in the midst of a war zone. Joshua Brown noted that one Friend present decided then and there to free his forty-three slaves.[107]

As for Robert Pleasants, he accepted his losses--warehouses and all--with stoic grace. After the close of Yearly Meeting, he wrote to General Phillips, then in Petersburg, asking him to look out for twenty-one blacks who had gone off the Pleasants place with the British soldiers. The blacks had all been freed or were scheduled to be freed, Robert explained. He asked the general to insure they would not be re-enslaved. He also mentioned his "horse...his gentle good qualities to a person of my years was very valuable." He wrote that he would "be glad to reclaim" the horse.[108]

\* \* \*

All through the summer of 1781 Virginia along the James, from Scottsville to Hampton Roads, was a field of war. In the days of the French and Indian War twenty-five years before, Virginia west of the Blue Ridge had been the battlefield; but now old Virginia suffered while frontier Virginia was hardly touched. English raiding parties under Generals Arnold, Phillips, and Cornwallis burned and looted. Smaller American forces generalled by Lafayette, Mad Anthony Wayne (whose mother was a Pennsylvania Friend), and Baron von Steuben opposed them. Anthony Wayne for a time used Robert Pleasants' house as his headquarters.

Charles Lord Cornwallis, the senior British general in Virginia, decided that summer to move the British base from Portsmouth to Yorktown. While Cornwallis was fortifying Yorktown, the Continental army outside of New York City was re-enforced by 7,000 French soldiers and a French fleet.

Benjamin Franklin, America's wartime envoy to Paris had convinced the French to support the American cause. He was no Quaker, Benjamin Franklin, but in Paris he dressed Quaker style.[109] The French thought of him as a Quaker and lionized him as another Warner Mifflin--the very prototype of "the good Quaker" so much written about by French writers in those days.

Late in August 1781, General Washington, the Continental army and the 7,000 French soldiers marched down from New York to Elkton, Maryland, and embarked on French ships for Virginia. There they besieged the British holed up in Yorktown. After three weeks, while the French fleet held off British reenforcements and the cannon of both sides battered away and blew soldiers into pulp, Cornwallis suddenly surrendered. On October 19, 1781 the British army band played an old tune titled "The World Turned Upside Down" during the surrender ceremony. The Revolutionary War after six and a half weary years was almost over.

Skimino Friends Meeting house lay about 18 miles from Yorktown. Antoine Jay, a French writer, told a story concerning Skimino in his novel, *Le Quaker*, which he certified to be true: a Skimino Friends family took in a French officer wounded at Yorktown. The family's daughter nursed him. The Frenchman seduced her and then ran away; but his conscience bothered him and he returned months later. He found the young woman, their baby in her arms and her weeping father standing in the Meeting among the Friends. The father was telling the story of the betrayal. The Frenchman confessed before the Meeting and married the young woman. Later they moved to Newport, Rhode Island, where he became a Quaker minister.[110]

\* \* \*

The surrender at Yorktown did not entirely end the War. The last shot fired by a British soldier occurred outside the home of the Zanes on the Ohio River bank where Wheeling stands today. It happened in September of 1782, eleven months after Yorktown. Ebenezer Zane and his sister Betty, the children of Quaker William Zane, were the battle's heroes.

Ebenezer and Betty were Friends themselves, or at least they thought of themselves as Friends. Ebenezer used the plain language in letters, and Friends meetings were held in his home[111]; and Betty was just returned from Friends' school in Philadelphia. Nevertheless, Ebenezer was called "Colonel Zane," and he was in charge of Fort Patrick Henry--a stockade built sixty yards away from his house. On the afternoon of September 11, forty British soldiers and 260 Indian warriors surrounded Fort Henry and Zane's home. The defenders stood off attacks all that day and night, but the fort was in trouble the next morning because most of the remaining gun powder was located in Zane's house. In this emergency, young Betty volunteered to run for the house and try to bring back powder. As the story goes:

> Her services were accepted. Divesting herself of some of her garments...she stood prepared...and when the gate was opened she bounded forth.... Wrapt in amazement the Indians beheld her spring forward, and only exclaiming 'a squaw, a squaw,' no attempt was made to interrupt her progress.
>
> Inside the house, Betty's brother Silas tied a table cloth around her waist and emptied a keg of powder into it. Betty then ran back to the fort powder and all, dodging bullets as she went and made the gate safely. That night the attackers left. Of Fort Henry's defenders none were killed and two wounded.[112]

\* \* \*

After Yorktown, Virginians known to have been British sympathizers were tried and punished.[113] None of Virginia's Quakers were tried although some resented them for having not helped the American fighters. Robert Pleasants wrote to his brother-in-law John Thomas, rejoicing at the war's end, hoping it had done *some* good:

> It clearly appears to me that the dispute between Great Britain and America has been a means of opening the eyes of princes as well as people...to show the inconsistency of sacrificing the lives of thousands to gratify the ambition of the few.

Then, pondering the situation of the slaves:

> How careful ought we [Americans] now to be to act consistent with our own arguments and allow to others what we have demanded as a right.

Virginia's old Capitol at Richmond's 14th and Cary Streets saw some persuasive Quaker lobbying right after the Revolutionary War.

## X

## AFTER SO MANY AGES
## 1782-1800

> The Virginia act for religious freedom has been received with infinite approbation...after so many ages during which the human mind has been held in vassalage.
> -- Thomas Jefferson to James Madison, 1786

Virginia's State Capitol was housed in Cuninghame's Warehouse on the muddy corner of 14th and Cary Streets, Richmond, from 1780 to 1788. The building was splintery and drafty, abandoned by its Tory owner. It stood empty from May to October 1781, while the British army threatened the town and the General Assembly tried to conduct the state's business in Charlottesville, then in Staunton. But two acts of the Assembly--upon the delegates' triumphant return to the warehouse just after the Yorktown victory--were enlightened and historic and both were inspired largely by the Friendly Virginians.

One, passed in 1782, was an act of compassion for black Virginians. The other capped the long struggle for religious freedom in Virginia. It passed in 1785.

The Friends had begun pleading for the black Virginians long before 1782. Sometimes they sought outright abolition of slavery, sometimes limited steps toward abolition. Friend Robert Pleasants had prodded legislator Richard Bland on 15 March 1770, to "make a motion in the next Assembly to repeal the law [of 1723] which prevents a man from rewarding faithfulness with freedom for his servants." In 1771, Friends petitioned the Assembly for a law forbidding the importing of more slaves into the state, and in 1772 the House passed that law--although the King vetoed it."[1] But in 1778, when the King no longer had a say in Virginia's affairs, the Assembly again passed the law, no doubt with renewed Quaker persuasion.

---

* Thomas Jefferson cited this veto in his first draft of America's Declaration of Independence, as a reason why America should separate from Great Britain. But the passage was struck out when the Declaration was adopted "in compliance to South Carolina and Georgia."

In 1777 Robert Pleasants wrote a three page letter to Governor Patrick Henry urging freedom for the *children* of Virginia's slaves.[2] This would have resulted in the gradual disappearance of slavery in the State. The Committee of Revisors, Wythe, Jefferson, and Pendleton, seriously considered Pleasants' proposal when they were writing Virginia's first Code of Laws, then chickened out and dropped the idea.[3] Instead they re-introduced the earlier Quaker suggestion, to repeal the law of 1723 which made it a crime for slaveholders to emancipate their slaves. But the Assembly tabled this repeal bill titled "A Manumission Act" in 1779.

Virginia Quakers worked hard for three more years at persuading the Assembly to pass the Manumission Act. Early in February 1781 Robert Pleasants wrote to Anthony Benezet that "We failed to get a bill passed in the Virginia Assembly at their last session to confirm manumissions of slaves; but I hope the time will come."[4] In the summer of 1782 Robert Pleasants and Edward Stabler invited Delaware Friends Warner Mifflin and John Parrish to Richmond. The four worked non-stop for nearly three weeks at and around 14th and Cary Streets to persuade the Assemblymen how right it is to allow slaveholders to reward faithful slaves with freedom.[5] On July 4, 1782, Robert Pleasants wrote the victorious result to his brother-in-law, John Thomas:

> Our Assembly I expect rises today. They have, in consequence of a memorial from Friends, passed an act allowing general liberty under certain circumstances to emancipate slaves.[6]

The passage of these Quaker-inspired laws in Virginia--first forbidding imports of slaves after 1778 and then allowing slaveholders to free their slaves as of 1782--*had a major impact all across the English-speaking world*:

- In 1779, Anthony Benezet and other Philadelphia Friends visited the new Pennsylvania state legislature. They spoke to every legislator on behalf of a bill to forbid importation of more slaves to Pennsylvania and also to give freedom to the children of slaves. No doubt Benezet and his Quaker co-workers cited the example set by the Virginia Assembly in 1778. Their bill passed in 1780. So slavery ended in Pennsylvania.[7]
- Maryland, New York, and New Jersey soon followed Virginia with laws forbidding import of more slaves. In 1784 Connecticut and Rhode Island passed gradual abolition laws similar to Pennsylvania's. In 1786, North Carolina imposed a £5 tax on every

slave imported. Thereafter only two of the thirteen States had no law to prevent or restrict slave importing--South Carolina and Georgia.[8]
- Philadelphia Yearly Meeting wrote to London Yearly Meeting in August 1782, relating that Virginia's Friends had succeeded in getting the great Manumission Act of 1782 passed. But "the [slave] trade to the African coast is still supported by authority on your side," the letter noted. "Whilst this continues, you cannot be clear of pollution.... We therefore beseech you, brethren...to embrace all opportunities of promoting the discouragement of it."[9] And in June 1783 London Friends did hand in a petition signed by 273 of them urging abolition of the slave trade. It was the first such petition ever presented to Parliament,[10] the first step in a campaign that lasted 24 years, until Parliament did abolish the business of trading in human beings.

No doubt Virginia's Friends were aware of the far reach of their efforts for the slaves. They also knew they had failed to get slavery abolished in Virginia. They kept urging the Assembly on toward that goal:
- In 1783, the Assembly voted in two more laws favoring slaves. One decreed that any slave who had substituted for a free person in the Revolutionary army was to be freed. The other defined "citizen" to include freed blacks.[11]
- 1785. It was voted that slaves brought into the State and remaining twelve months should be freed.[12]
- 1788. An act passed making the enslaving of any child of free blacks a crime.[13]
- 1792. Virginia Yearly Meeting petitioned for stiffer penalties against slave dealers who kidnapped free blacks in order to sell them back into slavery.[14]
- 1795. It was enacted that any black person who claimed to be free must be allowed to sue and be heard in court.

Robert Pleasants and other Friends wrote letters to influential Virginians to promote abolition in the 1780s and 90s.[15] Pleasants wrote to John Michie, urging him to consider the Golden Rule (a favorite *Bible* text among Friends) and disagreeing with him that slave-holding is one of life's necessities. He fired off anti-slavery letters to the editors of the *Gazette*, the Virginia *Independent Chronicle* and the Richmond and Manchester *Advertiser*, signing himself "Humanity" or "A Virginian." He sent anti-slavery pamphlets to Charles Carter of Shirley even though "thou once told me thou did not wish to be further informed in respect of the principles of slavery"; and to Robert Carter of Nomini Hall (the wealthiest man in Virginia) "I rejoice that thee's freed so many slaves."[16]

Warner Mifflin wrote to the war hero and ex-Quaker Nathanael Greene at Mulberry Grove on the Savannah River (a plantation given to Greene by the state of Georgia in recognition of his war services). Warner addressed the general as "Respected Friend Nath'l Green" and then invited him to repent of his worldliness and war activities and to come out in favor of freedom for the slaves.[17] Robert Pleasants sent a somewhat similar letter to George Washington in 1785, enclosing an anti-slavery pamphlet "said to be wrote by John Dickinson," and urging him to free his slaves. "O remember, I beseech thee, that 'God will not be mocked' and is still requiring from each us to 'do justly, love mercy and walk humbly before him'," Pleasants wrote.[18] George Washington never answered this letter, but he did confide to Marquis de Lafayette the next year that abolition "assuredly ought to be effected."[19]

\* \* \*

Virginia Yearly Meeting was itself not quite done with slaveholding in those years. It was the last of the six American Yearly Meetings to decide to *disown* members who refused to free their slaves. The three northern-most yearly meetings--where few Friends held slaves--were the first to decide: New England Yearly Meeting in 1772, Philadelphia in 1774 and New York in 1776. The three southern yearly meetings followed: Maryland in 1778, North Carolina in 1783 and finally Virginia in 1784.[20]

In Virginia and everywhere, slavery posed a difficult decision for families who were torn between the creature comfort that slaves provided and the spiritual comfort of a clear conscience. The American Quakers--virtually alone among all the new nation's Christian denominations--came down corporately on the side of conscience.

In 1782, after Virginia's Assembly passed the Manumission Act, the number of slaves freed by Friends swelled. Robert Pleasants freed seventy-eight. He resettled the freed families, deeding them plots of land on his Henrico plantations at Varina and Gravel Hill. The whole business cost him most of his fortune--about £3,000 sterling. William Binford, also of Curles Meeting, freed eighteen slaves, Samuel Parsons nine. John Lynch of Lynchburg freed sixteen, and his neighbors William, James and Christopher Johnson freed twenty-two among them.[21]

Those who could not bear to part with their slaves were not disowned all at once. Friends labored patiently with hesitant members. Ministers in the meeting houses stood in the silence to speak to the condition of Friends still holding slaves, often mentioning the Golden Rule. Committees from the meetings and traveling ministers visited them in their homes. One series of visits was recorded by Norris Jones, who travelled through Virginia with Sarah Harrison, 40, a Philadelphia minister, in the summer of 1788:

> 6th mo 22, 1788--We went with a committee of the monthly meeting of Black-water appointed to visit slave-holders. We visited four, one of whom manumitted one slave after hard laborious work.
>
> Next day we...visited a man and his wife who held seven slaves--a searching time it was! Sarah Harrison prayed that the key which opened the heart of Lydia might be permitted to open the heart of the woman Friend present; which was granted and she united with her husband in setting their slaves at liberty. I said in my heart, miracles have not ceased....
>
> In the afternoon, we had a hard laborious opportunity with I.W. which lasted several hours. A manumission was written for his slaves, but he would not sign it; although he was fully convinced, yet the power of darkness kept him bound. We took our leave of him and went to J. Bailey's to lodge.
>
> 24th. This morning the above Friend, I.W., came on foot to our lodgings, having no rest. He brought the manumission and signed it, liberating four slaves. The power of Truth over-shadowed us. Sarah Harrison appeared in supplication and we parted with feelings of mutual joy.
>
> Then we went to N.J.'s. The most hardened spirit appeared in him that we have met with. Sarah and myself labored with him but...he declared he would not sign the manumission. So we left him and rode to M. Bailey's, 15 miles, where we lodged.
>
> Next morning he [M. Bailey] set 22 free.
>
> We then went back to N.J.'s to try him once more, but on our first seeing him he appeared as determined against it as before....

> We said a good deal to him as we sat in the wagon, and his wife desired he would set his slaves free. At length the power of the Highest softened his hard heart. He came and gave me his hand, and was broken even to weeping. He asked us into the house...then got the manumission and signed it...the devil was cast out and he...shed many tears, as did most or all present.
>
> 26th. We called to see a young woman who holds slaves, it being the second visit to her. But she would not give them up....
>
> Next day we had a full opportunity with a widow who held slaves. She desired I would write a manumission but did not choose to sign it till her son saw it.
>
> We also had an opportunity with a man who holds about 20. He said he hoped he should see the evil of the practice.
>
> So, after being honest with them, we left them and went toward Burleigh [Friends Meeting in Prince George County]....

For ten years after 1784 the Friends in Virginia labored with members who could not quite bring themselves to give up their slaves. Late in the 1780s, Cedar Creek Meeting reluctantly disowned thirteen families as slaveholders.[22] In 1792, a committee of Gravelly Run Meeting visited Robert Langley who lived on Appomattox River near Petersburg, because he did not "show a disposition to do much if anything for [his sixty slaves'] enlargement and education." Langley told the committee that he would free his slaves after the harvest; however, he died that September, and the slaves were not freed.[23]

By 1794, Virginia's Quaker families were substantially clear of slaveholding, either through disownment of the slaveholders or manumission of the slaves. The only exceptions were a few families where slaves were owned by non-Quaker wives, or the like.

As the numbers of freed blacks increased, slaveholders became concerned over the discontent that such freed people caused among the slaves. It was well known that the Friends were a principal cause of the increase, and they were criticized accordingly. Thomas Jefferson, while he was U.S. ambassador to France, wrote from Paris to Edward Bancroft in London, January 1788: "To give liberty to slaves is like abandoning children,"

Jefferson opined. "Many Quakers in Virginia have seated their [former] slaves on their land as tenants." He had heard that this arrangement was not working out well, "but am going back to Virginia in the fall and will inform myself about it."[24]

The Friends opposed Mr. Jefferson's view that giving liberty to slaves is like abandoning children. They were perplexed by Jefferson's position as champion of the rights of man on one hand and master of many slaves on the other. Robert Pleasants wrote to St. George Tucker of Williamsburg in 1797, "I conclude from Thomas Jefferson's letter to Benjamin Banneker [a black man accomplished in mathematics, surveying and astronomy, and befriended by the Quaker Ellicotts of Ellicott City, Maryland] that he has changed his opinion" about the inferiority of blacks.[25]

Thomas Scattergood, a Philadelphia Friends' minister, made several visits to Virginia's Friends. He stayed with Clark and Rachel Moorman while visiting Cedar Creek Meeting, and wrote in his journal for 30 March 1793: "After dinner the black [freed tenants'] children came in with their books to read their lessons and I was comforted in beholding such care and attention towards them." Some days later Thomas Scattergood came to Richmond where Friends bravely arranged for him to speak to a gathering of "the black people." Robert Mitchell the mayor came to this unprecedented event. He told Thomas that some citizens had wanted him to stop the meeting; but, Thomas wrote, "the mayor confessed that the doctrine was suitable to [blacks] and whites also."[26]

Virginia's Friends were especially concerned for certain blacks freed under the wills of their Quaker owners, but then re-enslaved and never given freedom by the wills' executors. The slaves of Samuel Hargrave, Glaister Hunnicutt, and Charles Moorman all were cheated this way.[27] The Moorman slaves were sold south to keep Friends from rescuing them; but Christopher Johnson of Lynchburg made fourteen journeys to South Carolina and Georgia between 1788 and 1797 to argue their cases in court. He succeeded in getting many freed.[28]

* * *

Quakers' saddle horses were often hitched outside the 14th and Cary Street State House in the 1780s, switching flies and patiently waiting. Inside, the Quaker lobbyists spoke earnestly with the Assemblymen. Sometimes they urged compassion for black Virginians, sometimes religious freedom for all Virginians.

The Assembly was debating two opposing bills on religion in those days:

- One was titled "A Bill for Establishing a Provision for the Teachers of the Christian Religion," introduced by friends of the old established church. It proposed that *all* Christian denominations be supported by tax monies collected by the state.[29] The proposal had an obvious appeal, but also would have put the churches under the state's thumb for all time to come.
- The opposing bill was an "Act for Religious Freedom" written by Thomas Jefferson and tabled by the Assembly in 1779.

The delegates debated these opposed concepts long and hotly on the floor of the warehouse at 14th and Cary. George Washington, Richard Henry Lee, John Marshall, and other Episcopalians spoke for the Christian Teachers Bill, and Patrick Henry--who had become during his term as Virginia's first governor vastly more conservative than the flaming liberal he once was--was floor leader for that bill. But James Madison, George Wythe, Charles Lynch, and Isaac Zane supported religious freedom.[30]

Orators for the Christian Teachers Bill claimed that public morals had declined as a result of Section 16 of Virginia's Bill of Rights. Financing religion by passing the plate, they said, is

> ...Very inadequate...men of genius and learning will be discouraged from engaging in the ministerial office...the State deprived of one of the best means of promoting its virtue, peace and prosperity.

> Any layman or mechanic...may leap from the anvil or the plough and in a few minutes go forth a preacher of the word of GOD.

Ministers, rather, should be "men of real merit...men of family and education." Only such learned men are fit to lead "in public and stated expressions of...veneration." These clergymen should be supported "in a liberal and plentiful manner." They should not have to wait hat in hand "to be compensated by the capricious will of a multitude."[31]

As for the backers of the Act for Religious Freedom--they rejected the notion "that Christian knowledge and liberal arts and sciences are...connected":
- They recalled that the first apostles of Christianity were simple, unlearned men who yet were able to advance the Gospel "against all the powers of the Earth." Wealth and learning, they

said, are the marks of those worldly powers that have always opposed spiritual advancement.
- Religion is "the duty which we owe to our Creator" and so "the religion of every man must be left to the conviction and conscience of every man." The State has no business meddling with religious matters.
- The Christian Teachers Bill would infringe on the rights just won from England. "It is proper to take alarm."[32]

Virginia's Quakers and Baptists united in opposing the Christian Teachers Bill while the Presbyterians and the German denominations took no position about it until 1784. That fall, Hanover Presbytery finally announced that it favored the bill. A vigorous effort then began to have it passed into law. Eleven petitions for its passage reached the General Assembly. But eighty protests against it also came, including a protest sent jointly by Virginia Yearly Meeting and Hopewell Monthly Meeting. The "yes" signatures totalled 1,020, the "noes" about 11,000. The Christian Teachers Bill was voted down decisively in the Assembly. Then James Madison re-introduced the Act for Religious Freedom and it was voted into law on 17 December 1785. It reads:

> We, the General Assembly of Virginia, do enact that no man shall be compelled to frequent or support any religious worship, place or ministry whatsoever, nor shall be [made to] suffer on account of his religious opinions or belief; but that all men shall be free to profess, and by argument to maintain, their opinions in matters of religion.[33]

So Virginia declared for the clean-cut separation of church and state--a principle of law new to the Atlantic world. It was copied by the federal government through the First Amendment to the U.S. Constitution and eventually by every state in the Union.

Thomas Jefferson was so proud of his part in establishing that historic principle that he had it carved on his gravestone:

> Here lies the body of Thomas Jefferson
> Author of the Declaration of Independence
> Of the Statute of Virginia for Religious Freedom
> And the Father of the University of Virginia.

But the Friendly Virginians played a prouder part. George Wilson, John Hale, and Henry Vaux, Quakers all, died martyrs for the cause of religious freedom in Virginia. Levin and Mary Denwood and their friends of Nassawaddox Meeting possibly, and Thomas and Margaret Jordan and their friends of Chuckatuck Meeting surely, they were the first to hold out successfully in Virginia for the right to worship God their way. Then, for four generations thereafter from the 1660s to 1785, the Friends kept up the struggle, and kept bright the principle.

\* \* \*

Three new persuasions--Catholic, Jewish and Methodist--appeared in Virginia during the last years of the struggle for religious freedom:

A few Virginians made it known by 1785 that they were Catholics, members of Christendom's mother church. (The first Catholic service held openly anywhere in the British Colonies occurred in November 1733 in Philadelphia, even though Catholic services were forbidden by English law under penalty of life in prison.)[34] Father John Carroll, Prefect Apostolic of the Church in America, wrote from Baltimore to Rome in 1785 that "there are no more than 200 [Catholics] in Virginia."[35] Most of them lived around Alexandria where a priest from Maryland visited them four or five times a year. Abbe Jean Dubois, a refugee from the French Revolution, was the first priest to celebrate the Holy Sacrifice of the Mass in Norfolk and then in Richmond. Virginia's first Catholic church was built in Alexandria in 1796.[36]

Judaism, even older than Catholicism, came to Virginia at this same time. A Torah scroll was brought to Richmond during the 1780s, and by 1789 Beth Shalome, a Jewish congregation, was celebrating the Simchat Torah (Rejoicing in the Law) there.[37]

Catholics and Jews, followers of those two most ancient creeds, were vastly out-numbered, however, by Christians attracted to the evangelistic "New Light" or "New Side" approach to God, introduced to Virginia by George Whitefield in 1739. The Baptists--who adopted evangelical methods fervently--became Virginia's largest denomination in the 1780s. The Methodists, when they split off from the old Established Church in 1784, immediately became the second largest.

Methodism was founded by John Wesley (1703-1791), the same John Wesley who was a member of the Holy Club at Oxford University along with George Whitefield. After Oxford, Wesley and Whitefield wrought a religious revolution in England and America, preaching the doctrine of salvation from eternal hellfire through belief in Christ and Him crucified. Wesley began to organize Methodist societies in England in the 1740s. He considered himself to be reforming the Church of England from within and remained a minister of that church until his death. Nevertheless the Methodist Episcopal Church was clearly a separate church by 1784.

The Methodist way *per se* was introduced to southside Virginia in 1763 by Devereaux Jarratt, the 30-year-old rector of three Anglican churches in Dinwiddie County. He had heard Wesley and Whitefield preach in London. Robert Strawbridge, an immigrant from Ireland to Frederick County, Maryland, introduced Methodism to northern Virginia soon afterward and established Virginia's first out-and-out Methodist congregation in Leesburg. The Leesburg congregation built the first Methodist church building in America, about 1768.[38] The number of Virginia Methodists climbed from 0 in 1763 to 17,605 in 1793--including about 4,000 black members.[39]

So then at the close of the 1700s, *Catholics*, *Jewish* and *Methodist* congregations arose and prospered in Virginia. The *Baptists* grew mightily, the German churches, *Mennonite*, *Brethren* and *Lutheran*, and the *Society of Friends* grew modestly; and the *Presbyterians* held their own.

From all this one would think that the spiritual state of Virginians was on the rise. But that was not so, for the collapse of the established church in Virginia--re-named the *Protestant Episcopal* Church in 1785--caused many families to stop going to any church. At the Revolution's beginning, Virginia had 95 established parishes with 164 churches and chapels and 91 clergymen. At its close only 28 clergymen were left.[40] Most Anglican churches stood empty.[41] In 1796, Isaac Weld, an English traveler commented that he "scarcely observed one that was not in a ruinous condition with the windows broken and doors dropping off the hinges."

Some Virginians became followers of the Enlightenment movement of the time. They turned to reason and common sense, believing that humans can rely on their brains to discover truths. In America, Tom Paine and Ben Franklin were exponents of the Enlightenment, and also Thomas Jefferson and certain William and Mary professors in Virginia.[42] They were Deists who down-played the trust of Catholics in church tradition and dogma; of Protestants in the *Bible* (Jefferson advised his nephew to read the *Bible* just as critically as the writings of Livy or Tacitus); and of Friends in the guidance of the Inward Teacher.

But even while the Enlightenment was taking hold in Virginia, a great thinker in Europe was baring its weakness. Immanuel Kant (1724-1804) finished writing his *Critique of Pure Reason* in 1781. He held that human beings have an intuitive side, a hidden aspect superior to our limited power of reasoning, some stimulus or connection that, transcending time and material things, can teach us more than our five senses.[43]

\* \* \*

Of the nine other denominations in Virginia after religious freedom became state law, not one joined Friends wholeheartedly in their witness against slavery. The Methodists helped for a time, but not wholeheartedly at all.

John Wesley the founder of Methodism, began to oppose slavery in 1772 upon reading Quaker Anthony Benezet's book against slavery, *Some Historical Account of Guinea*.... Benezet was a close acquaintance of Wesley's evangelical ally, George Whitefield. Whitefield often stayed with the Benezets in Philadelphia. They argued about slavery for thirty years at night before bedtime. Whitefield argued that the *Bible* justifies slavery, Benezet that all people are God's children and none should be enslaved. Whitefield remarked one night just before he died in 1770 that God must have meant the South with its hot climate to be a place for slaves to labor under benevolent Christian masters.[44] So he died, in Benezet's view, unrepentant.

Therefore, it was a pleasing surprise for Benezet to open John Wesley's letter from England saying that he, Wesley, had been converted to Benezet's view by Benezet's book.[45] Anthony the master Quaker and John the master Evangelical wrote back and forth thereafter. In one letter Benezet described Virginia's slave laws as "savage" and quoted an ad in the Virginia *Gazette*:

> Run away [from] Prince George [County] on the 10th instant a lusty negro named Bob [describing him]. The said fellow is out-lawed and I will give 10 pounds reward for his head severed from his body or 40 shillings if brought home alive.[46]

Wesley wrote his own anti-slavery tract before he sent Dr. Thomas Coke and Bishop Francis Asbury to organize Methodism in America. Coke and Asbury both worked to rally American Methodists to the anti-slavery cause. Bishop Asbury chaired a Methodist conference in Petersburg in 1783 where "all agreed to the spirit of African liberty." In April of 1785, however, when Dr. Coke preached against slavery in a Virginia barn, a number of his listeners stamped out. When the Doctor was leaving the barn, they threatened to horsewhip him. Thereafter he toned down the subject of slavery when preaching to whites and finally dropped the subject altogether.

When preaching to slaves he stressed obedience to masters as a Christian duty.

Coke did join Bishop Asbury in circulating a 1785 Methodist petition praying Virginia's Assembly to pass an abolition law. When the two men called on General Washington at Mt. Vernon for his signature, the General received them courteously, but refused to sign. The Assembly angrily turned down this petition, ending official Methodist efforts against slavery in Virginia--although some thirty Virginia Methodist preachers meeting in Emporia in 1794 agreed not to hold slaves themselves.[47]

The time after the Revolution is said to be Virginia's Golden Age, when it was led by the founding fathers of the Republic--George Washington and Patrick Henry, then Thomas Jefferson and James Madison. The Friends tried to enlist all these men in the cause of freedom for slaves, but in every case (excepting only George Wythe who freed his slaves in 1782)[48] they only half-succeeded. The great men were willing to support certain measures to better the slaves' condition. When push came to shove, though, they were unwilling to free their own slaves. Here were men who risked everything for the right to live free and were at the same time slaveholders. Their shining ideals were smudged over with the pale cast of thought--thoughts of creature comfort, political advancement and social standing.

By and large then, the Friends continued to stand distinct and apart in testifying against slavery.

\* \* \*

The United States scarcely had time to unite before Friends began to witness at the national level against the slave trade. The Continental Congress was sitting in Princeton's Nassau Hall on 6 October 1783, when Friends Warner Mifflin, Anthony Benezet, James Pemberton and George Dillwyn arrived with a petition.

Congress was only a shadow of a governing body then, under the Articles of Confederation. These Articles were a weak plan of union, drafted during the War by a committee chaired by John Dickinson. Too weak--all the power was left in the hands of the thirteen states. Nevertheless, the Friends came to ask this Congress for freedom for America's slaves.

The petition was signed by 535 Quaker men, including 20 or more Virginians --Edward Stabler of Petersburg, Daniel Mifflin of Chincoteague, and the rest from northern Virginia meetings--Hopewell, Centre and Crooked Run Meetings in the valley, Gap, Fairfax and Goose Creek in Loudoun County; and Alexandria. Warner Mifflin read the petition on

October 8 at noon, having been introduced to the Congress by its president, Elias Boudinot. Warner stood before the members in Quaker gray, his broad brim set square on his head, his voice measured. He reminded the members of their "solemn declarations often repeated in favor of universal liberty" during the War years, and ended "We therefore earnestly solicit your Christian interposition to discourage and prevent so obvious an evil."[49]

President Boudinot bundled the petition with other papers and took it to Annapolis where Congress met the next month. There he referred it to a congressional committee of three--Thomas Jefferson, Jeremiah T. Chase of Maryland, and David Howell of Rhode Island. Early in 1784, the committee brought back its recommendation to Congress, that all the states that had not already outlawed the slave trade should be urged to do so.

The recommendation was not acted on by Congress. However, the Quaker petition had a historic effect. For Jefferson and his committee, while they were studying the petition in early 1784, were at the same time drafting "A Plan for a Temporary Government of the Western Territory." They wrote a paragraph into this Plan obviously inspired by the Quaker petition. It begins: "That after the year 1800 there shall be neither slavery nor involuntary servitude in any of the said [Western Territory]."[50]

The "Western Territory" was the wilderness north and west of the Ohio River--now the states of Ohio, Indiana, Michigan, Illinois and Wisconsin and some of Minnesota. Virginia ceded all this land to the United States on 1 March 1784, and Jefferson and his committee submitted the "Plan for a Temporary Government" to Congress the same day. Congress voted down the Temporary Plan's anti-slavery paragraph by one vote, but when the permanent plan--"An Ordinance for the Government of the Territory of the United States Northwest of the River Ohio"--passed in 1787, the anti-slavery paragraph passed too.

The 1787 agreement to ban slavery from the Northwest, Quaker-inspired though it was, gave tacit assent to slavery's future existence in other sections of the United States. But it did set the precedent for prohibiting slavery in defined areas of the nation--that is to say, for the "Free Soil Movement."

\* \* \*

The Northwest Ordinance was Congress's one great success while operating under the Articles of Confederation. Beginning 14 May 1787, fifty-five men chosen by twelve of the thirteen state legislatures (all except Rhode Island) came to Philadelphia to replace the Articles with a new Constitution. The fifty-five met for four months behind closed doors in Independence Hall. They kept no record of their proceedings except notes made by delegate James Madison for his own use. In the four months they figured out a complex, balanced, workable system of government, put down in a document that has become the world's oldest written Constitution.

Only John Dickinson was a Friend or close to being a Friend among the fifty-five, and Friends' influence on the Constitution is hard to assess.* Yet there was some such influence, for Article VI Section 3 decrees that national and state officials are to be bound by oath *or affirmation* to support the Constitution. It is known that Benjamin Franklin described to the delegates how Quakers settled their differences through clearness committees without going to court and endorsed that method. He also advocated that the nation's executives and legislators should serve without pay. "A respectable Society [has] made the experiment and practiced it with success for over a hundred years --I mean the Quakers," Franklin said. "...They are supported by a sense of duty and the respect paid to usefulness.... And indeed in all cases of public service, the less the profit the greater the honor."[51]

Pennsylvania's Abolition Society, consisting largely of Quakers, prepared a petition against the slave trade to be read by Ben Franklin to the delegates, but he never read it for fear of angering the South Carolina and Georgia delegates. John Dickinson did assert that "every principle of honor and safety demands the exclusion of slaves"; but the men from the deep South insisted that their states would never stand for that.[52]

Friends were dismayed that the new Constitution countenanced slavery. It provided that slave importing could not be interfered with by Congress until 1808, except to the extent of a 10-dollar-per-head import duty. As one New England Quaker, William Rotch, wrote to another, Moses Brown, "Whatever high encomiums are given to [the Constitution] it is evident to me that it is founded on *Slavery* and that is on *Blood*."[53]

Nevertheless, Friends were pleased with other aspects. The Constitution begins "We, the People of the United States, in order to form a more perfect Union...," thus declaring that the Nation is governed by and for its *people*. This harmonizes with the Quaker ethos, that *individuals* as the children of God are sacred and come first.

---

* Madison made this note of John Dickinson's Quakerly advice to the delegates on August 13: *"Experience* must be our only guide. *Reason* may mislead us."

But many of America's great men, the once-liberal-now-conservative Patrick Henry among them, considered "We, the people" to be wildly radical. Henry argued that the words should be "We, the States...."[54]

\* \* \*

Once the Constitution was ratified and George Washington installed as president in April 1789, Friends supported the new government cheerfully. Philadelphia Yearly Meeting sent a goodwill message to Washington upon his election. The President replied:

> I receive with pleasure your affectionate address and thank you.... Your principles and conduct are well known to me, and it is doing the people called Quakers no more than justice to say that (except for declining to share with others the burden of the common defense) there is no denomination among us who are more exemplary and useful citizens.[55]

On the other hand, Friends lost little time in urging the new U.S. Congress to act against the slave trade. The First Congress first met from March through September 1789 in New York City and re-assembled there in January 1790. Then a delegation of Philadelphia and New York Friends arrived to petition for a "remedy against the gross national iniquity of trafficking in the persons of fellow men."[56]

The Friends' petition caused the first bitter floor fight of the U.S. House of Representatives. On February 11 Representative Thomas Hartley of Pennsylvania introduced their petition and moved to refer it to a committee. William L. Smith of South Carolina objected and the fight was on:

- James Jackson of Georgia--a Savannah resident born in England --rose to point out that the *Bible* sanctions slavery from Genesis to Revelations. Why should Quakers set themselves up as a superior authority? "Is the whole morality of the United States confined to Quakers?" he asked. "Are they the only people whose feelings are to be consulted...? Is it to them we owe our present happiness? ...Did they, by their arms or contributions, establish our independence?"
- Michael Jenifer Stone of Maryland followed Jackson. I fear, he said, that any action of Congress against slavery will reduce the value of slaves and hurt Southern slaveholders.

- Theodore Sedgwick of Massachusetts derided Stone's fear. Until the year 1808 the Constitution allows only a $10-duty on slaves, he pointed out. As for Quakers, Sedgwick defended them saying "they conform their moral conduct to their religious tenets as much as any people in the whole community."[57]
- The Friends' petition was tabled on February 11, only to be revived the next day by a similar petition from the Pennsylvania Abolition Society, signed by its president Benjamin Franklin. It was probably the same petition that Franklin decided not to read to the makers of the Constitution in 1787, for fear of angering South Carolina and Georgia.
- Jackson of Georgia raged again, saying that Franklin should know better. And Franklin--then the most revered man in America after George Washington--replied by writing a letter to the *Federal Gazette*'s editor, a parody on Jackson's aspersions against him and the Quakers. In it the Divan of Algiers defends the advantages of keeping white Christians in slavery and derides the anti-slavery petition of a "sect called Erika or Purists." The letter was Benjamin Franklin's last public writing before his death at 84.
- Thomas Scott of Pennsylvania replied to Jackson that the slave trade is "one of the most abominable things upon earth." If I were a judge hearing a slavery case, he said, I would go as far as I could toward emancipation.
- Jackson assured Scott in return that such a judgment would not hold in Georgia--the judge might find himself in danger.
- Smith of South Carolina then described the petition as an attack upon the "palladium of the property of our country." He complained that a South Carolina gentleman could hardly bring his servants north without having them induced to run away by Quakers. He accused Quakers of sexual laxity and officiousness.
- James Madison of Virginia ended the day by moving to refer the petition to a committee, and the House finally approved, 43 to 14. Four Virginia Congressmen--Madison, Josiah Parker, John Page, and Alexander White (a Frederick County lawyer who was the nephew of Virginia Quaker William Hoge)--voted for the motion and two against.

The seven-man committee brought in its recommendation one month later. It favored the Friends' request. The bitter debate then resumed. Terrible charges against Quakers and defenses of them filled the air. Finally the committee's report came to a vote and was adopted 29 to 25 in the form of a statement as to what Congress could and could not do in regard to slavery until the year 1808.

James Madison wrote to Dr. Benjamin Rush on March 20, noting "The petitions on the subject of slavery have employed more than a week.... The gentlemen from S. Carolina and Georgia are intemperate beyond all example and even all decorum. They are not content with palliating slavery...but lavish the most virulent language on the [Quaker] authors."[58]

President Washington was not as sympathetic. He wrote his friend David Stuart of Virginia on March 28 that "the memorial of the Quakers (and a very mal-apropos one it was) has at length been put to sleep and will scarcely awake before the year 1808."[59]

Adam Stephen, ex-Revolutionary general and surgeon who amputated John Hunt's leg in Virginia, was entirely unsympathetic. He wrote to Madison from Martinsburg on April 25: "The Senate have met with great applause for not taking notice of the Quakers' Memorial, and people find much fault with your House for wasting so much time in a frivolous manner."[60]

* * *

After their petition to the First Congress, Friends kept on "speaking Truth to power." Nine anti-slave-trade petitions were sent in to the Second Congress by various Quaker-inspired state abolition societies in December 1791[61]. Warner Mifflin followed in 1792 with his own petition to limit the slave trade, and more petitions came from Quakers and state abolition societies in 1794 and 1797.[62]

These state abolition societies mark a new turn in Quaker progress. They were associations to meet an urgent human need which Quakers first led in organizing and then invited other humanitarians to join. Such invitations departed from the earlier Friends' tendency to keep clear of "the world's people." They were a natural extension of Friends' turn in the 1750s toward humanitarian service.

The first of the abolition societies formed on the evening of 14 April 1775 at a gathering in Philadelphia's Sun Tavern. Anthony Benezet was the organizer. This Society met only four times in 1775 and held no more meetings during the Revolution, until February 1784. In 1787 Ben Franklin, 81, became president with Quaker James Pemberton, vice president, doing most of the actual work. Similar societies appeared in New York (1785),

Rhode Island (1786), Delaware (1788) and Maryland (1789), in London (1787) and Paris (1788). This last was the Societe des Amis des Noirs, founded by Jacques-Pierre Brissot de Warville, the Quakers' great admirer.[65]

James Pemberton in Philadelphia wrote to Robert Pleasants in Virginia 14 Eighth Month 1788 enclosing "a few copies of a new edition of the Constitution of our Abolition Society in this city." He wrote to Pleasants again on 16 Eleventh Month 1789 and this time he enclosed "the last report lately received from London of the Society for the Abolition of the Slave Trade, which will give thee a view of the state of that important business." He mentioned that "A society is lately instituted at Baltimore and the number of members has in a small time increased beyond expectations.... If an association was practicable to be formed in your state similar to that here," Pemberton added, "considerable benefits might be obtained for the oppressed blacks."

Pemberton wrote a third letter to Pleasants 28 Second Month 1790. By this time Robert Pleasants had taken the bait, for Pemberton states "I herewith send thee a dozen copies of the Constitution of the Society here...with a view of their reaching thee in time for the proposed meeting at Richmond".[66] Robert Pleasants and six other Friends did organize the proposed meeting and did establish the Virginia Abolition Society in 1790.

Starting this Society required courage. George Washington suggested as much when he discussed Virginia-style slavery with Jacques-Pierre Brissot at Mt. Vernon in 1788. "It would be dangerous to make a frontal attack..." Washington said. "Nearly all Virginians are convinced that the general emancipation of Negroes cannot occur in the near future and for this reason they do not wish to organize a society which might give their slaves dangerous ideas."[67]

Nevertheless, Robert Pleasants and friends advertised the projected Society openly. Robert wrote his old friend Patrick Henry--now living in Prince Edward County--on 25 Fifth Month 1790, inviting him to join the Society.[68] "I expect thee will have seen [our notices] in the papers directed to the friends of liberty," Robert wrote.

Patrick Henry refused the invitation. So did other prestigious Virginians, such as Charles Carter of Shirley and Robert Carter of Nomini Hall. But a number of Methodists joined and the first officers of the Society were: Quakers, Robert Pleasants, president, and James Ladd, treasurer; Methodists, John Finney, vice-president, and James Smith, secretary. The executive committee consisted of five Quakers, John and Micajah Crew, Thomas Pleasants, James Harris and John Hunnicutt; and four Methodists,

Gressey Davis of Petersburg, Henry Featherstone, Richard Graves, and George Jones.[69]

Since this coalition of Friends with people of another faith was a new departure, some Friends disapproved. Robert Pleasants wrote to Samuel Bailey of Blackwater Meeting that he had "been told that divers Friends, especially on the south side of the [James] River and thou in particular disapprove of Friends being concerned in the...institution for promoting the abolition of slavery." He went on to defend the necessity for Friends to ally with others on behalf of the slaves and also defended his assumption of the title of president, which sounded pompous to Samuel Bailey.[70]

President Pleasants pressed on in spite of such objections:

- He wrote to James Pemberton Sixth month 1790 that Bishop Asbury approved Methodist participation in the new Society; and related with relief that "our Methodist friends" have agreed not to enroll slaveholders in the Society. Methodists make up a majority of members, he reported, but Friends are doing most of the work.[71]
- In Seventh month he wrote Dr. George Cheesman of York County that the Society then had about 100 members--but no Baptists "which I have a little admired [wondered] at, seeing they profess to be a reformed church, and a few of their members (and thou in particular) are said to have emancipated their slaves." He then urged Dr. Cheesman to join in.[72]

A letter came from James Pemberton to Pleasants in the third month of 1791, requesting two things: for the Virginia Abolition Society to join the Pennsylvania Society in petitioning Congress against the slave trade; and for Virginia Yearly Meeting to join with other Quaker yearly meetings in petitioning Congress to make allowance for conscientious objectors against war, in the Uniform Militia Bill then being debated. Pleasants immediately saw to it that both petitions were prepared as requested.[73]

In 1791 James Madison, that 40-year-old, short, slight bachelor of Orange County, was the star of the U.S. House of Representatives. He was famous as Father of the Constitution. Though he owned many slaves on his Montpelier plantation, he "philosophically" opposed slavery. Furthermore he had proposed (unsuccessfully) a clause of the Constitution's Bill of Rights that "no one religiously scrupulous of bearing arms shall be compelled to render military service."[74] Accordingly, Robert Pleasants decided to ask Madison to introduce both Virginia petitions in Congress.

The Congress had just returned to Philadelphia after meeting in New York City for five years. So Robert sent the petitions to Philadelphia along with a letter asking Madison to introduce them.[75] He also wrote in the letter "I wish to have thy judgment on the propriety of a petition to our [Virginia] Assembly for a law declaring the children of slaves" to be free upon reaching maturity.

Madison wrote his reply by candle light in his Philadelphia boarding house on October 30. He agreed to introduce the petition for conscientious objectors, but refused to have anything to do with the anti-slavetrade petition. "Those from whom I derive my public station are...greatly interested in that species of property," he wrote, and "I might be chargeable at least with want of candor if not of fidelity were I to [give] a public wound, as they would deem it, to an interest on which they place so great a value." As for the petition to the Virginia Assembly, Madison cautioned "Such an application as that to our own Assembly on which you ask my opinion is...likely to do harm rather than good. It may...produce successful attempts to withdraw the privilege...of giving freedom to slaves."[76]

Thus Madison, politician and realist, to Pleasants, Friend and idealist.


Virginia's Abolition Society proceeded vigorously during the early 1790s, circulating petitions, writing letters to the editor, urging the North Carolina Quakers to join in the battle,[77] and bringing lawsuits in behalf of free blacks taken as slaves. But unseen forces were at work against these efforts:
- New textile looms in England powered by steam engines used more and more cotton--a slave-labor crop.
- Eli Whitney patented the cotton gin in 1793 which extracted the seeds from the cotton, and made cotton-raising profitable.
- Louisiana turned to growing sugar cane--another slave-labor crop.
- Virginia's slave holders found a new profitable business in selling the children of their slaves South to the cotton, sugar, and rice plantations there. The slaveholders' new profits led them to muffle their sympathy for slaves and to contemn abolitionists as misguided do-gooders.


Dr. Elisha Dick, 33, a physician of Alexandria, visited a meeting of the Abolition Society's Alexandria chapter in 1795. He then petitioned the Assembly to outlaw such outrageous gatherings.[78] And the Assembly, composed largely of slaveholders, speedily passed the following Act:

> Whereas great and alarming mischiefs have arisen...by voluntary associations of individuals who, under cover of effecting justice towards persons unwarrantably held in slavery...have in many instances been the means of depriving masters of their property in slaves and in others occasioned them heavy expenses in tedious and unfounded lawsuits...[now therefore] any person who aids, abets or maintains any such person in prosecuting his suit shall pay the slave's owner $100.00 if the suit fails.[79]

The Assembly followed up with an Act passed January 1798 which disqualified "members of societies instituted for emancipating slaves" from sitting on juries to hear slaves' suits for freedom. All this official displeasure caused the Alexandria chapter of the Abolition Society to disband. The Virginia Abolition Society based in Richmond did not disband but its efforts to help the slaves were now handicapped.[80]

* * *

The Friendly Virginians in those days, along with their concerns for the social order and for peace, were concerned for their families and neighbors. The families were usually large and extended. All evidence indicates that a high proportion of Quaker marriages were warm, mutually valued, and lasting--though many were broken by the early death of one mate or the other, for medical knowledge then was scanty. Most Quaker farms stood distinct on the Virginia landscape, uncluttered and squared away, fence lines trim, with no sprawl of slave cabins. Young Friends typically met at Yearly Meeting time, fell in love, courted, married, raised *their* young, and tried to leave the world better than they found it.

As for falling in love, consider this springtime rhapsody written about 1790 by Billy Branson of Hopewell Meeting for young Jane Beeson who lived up toward Martinsburg:

"Altho I may be taxed with partiality," Billy scratched with his quill pen, "in the following description, by those who are not acquainted with the beloved object about which I am going to write--and by her own dear self with flattery--yet I sincerely declare that they are the candid effusions of an honest heart":

> In height she is a little above the middle size. But there is a peculiar gracefulness in her attitude and air. Her person and

features are extremely well-shaped. There is in her countenance something so interesting to humanity and innocence is so strongly depicted there that it is impossible to help loving her. She knows and makes use of the real essence of true politeness....

I have contemplated the opening charm of her well-informed mind with all the pleasure imaginable. Gentle are her manners. Her affections are the most ardent and sincere. Virtue not only plays around her heart but diffuses its sweets through every part of it. She spends not her time in large preparations for balls, tea parties and assemblies, but in the perusal of the most scientific writers. In her right hand she carries the morals of Socrates. In her left the beauties of [ink blot]--and in her heart the beauties of Mrs. Ratcliffe.

Not like most women proud and conceited, but simple in her dress.... Her smiles are the smiles of gentleness that enliven the common state of society. Her glowing eyeballs denote candor and purity of soul. She conforms not with the ways and fashions of the world. Her appearance is mild but majestic,--her voice like the sound of the divine harp.

The hair on her arms [is] like the down of a peach. Her snowy bosom represents the celestial globes. A soft satin covers her and let the audacious who shall dare to insult her be consumed with useless desires. Her hair floats on her shoulders like a ship on the sea when calm--her forehead like a cloud that covers part of the pale moon--her breath like the perfumed rose whose beauty charms the poet's eye. An inexpressible and beautiful vermilion colours her cheeks. Her hands small and delicate, and delicate nerves convey through all her senses the most rapid affections

...for you alone exists

W. Branson, Hopewell
for Jane Beeson, Mount Airy[81]

Acrostic poems were in favor in the 1790s. Patience Gawthrop of Ridge Meeting west of Winchester, wrote this for her six-year-old Hannah who was just starting school in 1796. The poem touches on the qualities Quaker parents tried to develop in their children then--

    H ave care, my child, while thou art in thy youth
    A nd learn thy book and mind to speak the Truth
    N o evil do, nor idle custom learn
    N o school tales tell; to schoolmate do no harm.
    A nd take good care thy books not to abuse
    H onor the Master, and obedience choose.

    G o straight to school and stay not by the way
    A nd learn thy lesson quick without delay.
    W hen noontime comes, beware of hurtful mirth
    T urn from the vanities which are on earth
    H ow lovely it is to see a youthful child
    R ejoice in virtue, and with aspect mild
    O vercome temptations which are in her way
    P erform the task assigned to her each day.[82]

Edward Stabler of Petersburg died suddenly in February 1785 leaving his sons William, 18, and Edward, Jr., 16, without mother or father. Will then apprenticed himself to a pharmacist in Leesburg and sent Edward, Jr., to live with Mary Hough, their 20-year-old married sister in Hillsboro, Loudoun County. Will wrote to Edward, Jr. soon after the brothers reached their strange new homes:

    Leesburg 3d month 14th 1785--Loving Brother,-- ...We are now in this transitory and visionary world without Father or Mother to direct our steps...Thee is settled with a good sister who will take care of thee...follow the dictates of Truth...We had an excellent example in our father who...always strove against the pride, fashions and vanity of this wicked world.... Oh my dear brother, I wish we may walk in his steps...by so doing after a short space of time it will become so familiar to thee that thee will not be ashamed of the [Quaker] profession...speak the plain language and act the same among other Societies as when with our own...try to set the young men of our Society an example of virtue and prudence.... Be not proud in thy own conceit...but thee must have pride enough...not [to] be slovenly. Fasten thy clothes tight and neat on thee--this thee may do without being counted proud; and if ever thee should be at a loss, ask the advice of thy elder Friends.[83]

Benjamin Shreve of the Alexandria Friends sent his son Isaac to Salem, N.J., to be a tanner's apprentice. The first letter Benjamin sent to son Isaac contains this advice:

> Alexandria, 29th, the 5th month, 1794--Dear Son Isaac:--Thee is now going...into the wide world...take good care how thee forms acquaintances. Let them be Friends if possible and steady sober lads, older then thyself and the fewer the better. A young man's happiness--both in this world and that which is to come--in a great measure depends on the connections he forms while young.
>
> Keep steady to Meeting and to plainness in apparel, and that God that made us will protect thee... Above all things, be true to thy trust, and defraud no man though the thing be small, but do unto other men as thee would that they should do unto thee....
>
> From thy loving father,
> Benj. Shreve[84]

\* \* \*

These last letters suggest that the wider world was pressing closer on the Friendly Virginians in the years after the Revolution. With religious freedom, it was no longer so necessary for Friends to stay apart from the world's people. And also Friends' divorcement from slavery increased their contacts with the outside world in an unforeseen way.

Most Friends in southern Virginia before the Revolution had made their livings from the land, mostly from tobacco, which is a labor-intensive crop. Without the slaves, however, Friends switched to corn and wheat, crops that demand less labor. Some foresook the land altogether and sent their sons away to learn a trade as Ben Shreve did. Some became millers and keepers of crossroads stores. Others turned to livestock. The Friends in the James River valley became famous for their home-grown hams and bacon.[85] Friends of Hopewell, Goose Creek, and Fairfax Meetings in northern Virginia raised turkeys and beef cattle; and Quaker men and boys herded them east through Leesburg to the river-port markets of Georgetown and Alexandria (the long hike was hard on the daintily-stepping turkeys, until it was learned that dipping their feet in tar shod them comfortably for the journey).[86] All these changes brought Friends a bit closer in touch with outsiders.

Tavern-keeping and distilling may have been considered as careers by some slave-less Friends, but in 1782 Virginia Yearly Meeting forbade its members to make their livings in those ways. Friends were not tee-totallers and the Yearly Meeting's advice from its beginning was for moderation. In 1701 Yearly Meeting had warned Friends against too much tobacco smoking[87] and in 1704 it had advised the members, "do keep out of unnecessary providing of strong drink and do keep in Christian moderation and at times of births, burials or marriages."[88] By 1782, alcoholism--which has shadowed all human history--had become a matter of increased concern for Friends. The minute of 1782 reads:

> As the distilling spirits from grain is believed to be wrong, Friends are therefore hereby prohibited using grain of any sort in that manner.... And as trading in spirituous liquors and frequent and unnecessary use thereof hath also appeared to have many bad effects, Friends are therefore advised against those practices.[89]

One Quaker couple whose life changed after freeing their slaves was John and Mary Payne of Scotchtown in Hanover County. John was 35 when he became Cedar Creek Meeting's clerk in 1775 and Mary 33 when she was named an elder of the Meeting the next year. They began to free their slaves early in the Revolution because, as John wrote, "I am persuaded that liberty is the natural condition of all mankind."[90] Then the Paynes discovered they could not make a go of the plantation without field hands. They sent their oldest son Walter to study medicine in Philadelphia, and in 1783 the whole family moved to Philadelphia, where John Payne became a manufacturer of starch.

The Paynes' oldest daughter Dolley, 15 in 1783, was a vivid beauty in gray Quaker dress, white cap and kerchief. In 1790 she married John Todd, a young Quaker lawyer. They went to housekeeping at Philadelphia's Fourth and Walnut Streets, two blocks from the nation's capitol, and had two sons. But Dolley was widowed when yellow fever swept the city in 1793. John Todd and a baby son died in the epidemic.[91] More later about Dolley.

\* \* \*

Closer contact with the world's people made Friends want better education for their children. Until the Revolution, education had been a subject of mixed feelings in the Society. On one hand, Friends placed their faith in the Inward Light for guidance and that made book learning seem a "creaturely" or "worldly" activity. On the other, George Fox himself had valued education. "See that schoolmasters and mistresses who are faithful Friends be placed and encouraged," he wrote, "...to forward their scholars in learning and in the frequent reading of the Scriptures and other good books...thus being seasoned with the Truth, sanctified to God and taught our holy self-denying way."[92]

Friends in England kept fifteen boarding schools for boys and four for girls at the time of the Revolution. But the only considerable Quaker schools in America were located about Philadelphia. The Friends of Virginia Yearly Meeting thought briefly about starting a school in 1759 but nothing came of that.[93] In 1780, however, the need for schools was vigorously voiced at Virginia Yearly Meeting.

Benjamin Russell, 44, a one-time sailor, was Virginia's only Quaker schoolmaster in 1780. His school was in Petersburg[94] and the Stabler boys were among his pupils. But soon after 1780, schools sponsored by local Friends Meetings sprang up all across Virginia:

- The first was near Lynchburg under the care of South River Meeting.[95]
- The Valley Meetings sponsored five schools--Hopewell (where some of the school books were printed in German for non-Quaker pupils from German-speaking families), Upper Ridge and Lower Ridge, Crooked Run and Mt. Pleasant.[96]
- Quakers James and Rebecca Dillon built a one-room log school in what is now Purcellville for their children and the neighbors',[97] and Goose Creek and Fairfax Meetings each started schools a few miles from Purcellville.
- Genito Meeting and Cedar Creek Meeting, seventeen miles apart, each started schools in 1791. Cedar Creek's was taught by Benjamin Bates, who had a way with children. Benjamin's son Micajah got into mischief one cold winter day when he was a pupil in his father's school. Accordingly, Benjamin said, "Micajah, sit in that chair and remain there until I tell thee to get out of it," and then left to go skating on a nearby pond. There he found Micajah skating along with his chair strapped to him. Teacher: "Micajah, did I not tell thee to stay in?" Micajah: "No. Thee told me not to get out of this chair."

Benjamin laughed and told the boy to unstrap the chair and enjoy himself.⁹⁸

- Susanna Davis was mistress of the school at tiny Hill's Creek Meeting. She had nine pupils. Joshua Evans, a traveling minister, visited the school in 1796. "From the great improvement the scholars were making," he wrote "I was convinced of the advantage of smaller schools, well managed."⁹⁹

The Philadelphia Friends began talk about the need for a boarding school in 1791. After John Dickinson of Continental Congress fame contributed a large sum, a 600 acre farm near Westtown, Chester County, Pennsylvania was purchased. A school house-meeting house with dormitories for girls and boys was built, bricks fired and lumber sawn on the place. When Westtown School opened in Fifth Month 1799, Israel Thompson of Fairfax Meeting was among the first twenty children to arrive. Some hundreds of Virginia Friends' children have attended Westtown since.¹⁰⁰

Some of the new Friends schools outside Virginia were "select"--that is, they enrolled only Quaker children. In Virginia, however, the new schools invited all the neighborhood children to enroll. Before the Revolution many of Virginia's old-field schools had been taught by Anglican ministers. Most of these ministers left during the War and their schools closed, so that the new schools' services were welcome. Furthermore the Quaker schools were appreciated for their special qualities. Along with teaching "all things useful in the creation"--which meant reading, writing and arithmetic--they instilled respect for truthfullness and introduced their pupils to the spiritual side of living.

The children of the Meeting schools attended Fifth Day (Thursday) meetings for worship. Some students fidgeted and whispered in these meetings. In their adult years, though, some remembered with pleasure the quiet meetings' tone and atmosphere.

No Friends' school for white children was started in Henrico County in the post-Revolution years. Instead Robert Pleasants and the Curles Meeting Friends started Gravel Hill School for children of freed black families in 1784.¹⁰¹ It was the first such school in Virginia.

No Friends' school started in Alexandria until 1815. But members of the meeting there were key figures in opening the first public library in Virginia in 1794. Friend William Hartshorne was a founding director of the Alexandria Library Company and Edward Stabler, Jr--now an Alexandria pharmacist--was the first librarian.¹⁰²

\* \* \*

Filippo Mazzei (1730-1816) was a man of the Enlightenment who came to Albemarle County from Florence, Italy, by way of France, in 1773. He lived in Virginia off and on until 1788, a friend and neighbor of Thomas Jefferson. In 1788 he wrote *Recherches Historiques et Politiques sur les Etats Unis* in which he lambasted Quakers, accusing them of "false humility, insidious politics, hypocrisy, love of gain and bad faith." His book affected Friends very little. The Enlightenment's "Bible" written by Thomas Paine, ex-Quaker, six years later, had a little more effect.

Paine's book, titled *The Age of Reason*, argued against Christianity and against atheism and in favor of deism. Part One of the book appeared in 1794 and Part Two in 1795. Robert Pleasants bought Part One as soon as it was published, then fired off a letter to the editor of the *Richmond and Manchester Advertiser*.[103] "*The Age of Reason* repels me as a work of great folly and impiety," he wrote. "I conceive it impossible to be truly wise and virtuous without religion." In March 1797, Elias Hicks, a Long Island Friends' minister visited Gap Meeting in Hillsboro, Loudoun County, and noted "There is a spirit of great infidelity and deism here. Thomas Paine's *Age of Reason* (falsely so-called) is much attended in these parts and some members of our Society, I was informed, were captivated by it."

This comment of Elias Hicks is the only hint that the Enlightenment movement exerted a pull on Quaker thinking.

There is evidence, though, that evangelicalism *was* influencing some Quakers in the 1780s and 1790s. A few of the ministers visiting Virginia then used religious language suspiciously like John Wesley's. Thomas Scattergood (1748-1814), who toured the Virginia meetings in 1793, is an example. He used traditional Quaker language most of the time, urging "unreserved obedience...to...the light of Christ Jesus in the soul,"[104] but at other times expressed himself in a somewhat unctuous way new to Quakerism: "Wait in patience, O my soul...to set up thy Ebenezer" and "[I] was favored...to water and be watered myself."[105] He corresponded with English Friends[106] who were quite concerned with the crucifixion and atonement of the historical Christ as the way to salvation (an aspect of Christianity which had until then played only a minor part in the thinking of traditional Friends), and with the absolute authority of the *Bible*.

Only a few Friends' ministers exhibited an evangelical tinge in those days and Job Scott (1751-1793) of Providence, Rhode Island, who visited Virginia in 1789, was not one of them. He preached the inward way to God in the classic Quaker manner:[107]

"Christ *within* was ever the alone hope of glory in all ages," Job declared. The sufferings of the *historical* Christ "could do no more toward reconciling a soul to God, than the blood of bulls and goats." As for the *Bible*, the gospel Truth neither began nor ended when the *Bible* was written. The Truth, Job Scott said, is "no upstart thing of only about 1,800 years standing."[108]

\* \* \*

Bishop Francis Asbury (1745-1816) was the great promoter of evangelicalism in America following George Whitefield. From 1775 until his death Asbury visited Virginia again and again, organizing Methodist churches and chapels everywhere. Robert Pleasants commented wryly about this when he wrote to Sarah Harrison in 1789:[109] "Many people, however, are anxious to hear preaching," he wrote. "Among the Methodists and Baptists there seems to be an emulation [rivalry] who shall make the most disciples [and] many are seeking the living among the dead.... O, may they be scattered and confounded."[110]

Bishop Asbury's message about the outward way to God was as foreign to most Quakers as the Quakers' devotion to the Inward Teacher was to Asbury:

Soon after arriving in America Asbury wrote "I visited the Quaker meeting (in Philadelphia); but wondered, to see so many sensible men come to hear two or three old women talk."

He "had some serious conversation with a Quaker" in Virginia's Valley "on the subject of the Holy Scriptures as the grand criterion of all inward and outward religion." When the Quaker objected, Asbury exclaimed:

> But to deny this is to oppose the present dictates of the Holy Ghost to its former dictates, which would be a most dangerous absurdity. How strange, how presumptuous to exalt the dignity of modern speakers beyond that of the prophets and apostles, who spoke as they were moved by the Holy Ghost....

Asbury and a companion pulled up in the yard of Barnaby Nixon, a Quaker minister of Prince George County, one freezing February day. They asked for feed for their horses, which Barnaby Nixon supplied. Then he invited the two strangers in for dinner. When Bishop Asbury offered to pray Methodist-style before dinner, however, Nixon objected and the Methodists left without eating. "We found the wind so cold and cutting as we made our way towards Petersburg, we could hardly bear up against it," Asbury wrote.

Nevertheless, Bishop Asbury felt some spiritual kinship for Friends, and the feeling was returned. He was invited to speak in a Quaker home in Westchester County, New York, and in Crosswicks Meeting house in New Jersey. The Quakers of Salem, New Jersey gave generously to help the Methodists build their church there.

Asbury admired the Quakers' stand against slavery and war, but he despaired of ending those evils--

- On slavery: Asbury tried hard to get Virginia's Methodists to oppose slavery as Friends did, but with indifferent results. "I spoke to some [Methodists in Dinwiddie County] about slavekeeping, but they could not bear it." In Brunswick County he wrote:

  My mind is much pained...I am brought to conclude that slavery will exist in Virginia perhaps for ages...Methodists, Baptists, Presbyterians in the highest flights of rapturous piety still maintain and defend it.

- On war:

  I called upon Joseph Perkins, the superintendent of the U.S. Armoury [at Harper's Ferry]. Here is a factory of stores of instruments of death, tastefully arranged, in several apartments. There may they remain forever! But will it be so? Alas! no.

He wrote from Stephens City, Virginia, to a Quaker, advising how the Society of Friends might be made to increase as vigorously as the Methodists. Mingle with others--read God's word--pray --hear others--have *speaking* in your meetings--do not think that George Fox and Robert Barclay are the only prophets--adopt rules. "I wish to lay before you these things," he ended, "although it is the general cry, 'You can do nothing with these people.'"[111]

\* \* \*

In spite of the Enlightenment and Evangelicalism, the Friendly Virginians prospered in the years after the Revolution. The gatherings of Virginia Yearly Meeting and of Fairfax Quarterly Meeting grew large after 1784.[112]

Visiting Friends from England and Pennsylvania often criticized Virginia's local meetings for worship but nearly always they praised the proceedings of the yearly and quarterly Meetings. Job Scott at the yearly meeting held in Weyanoke Meeting house, Charles City County 16-20 Fifth Month 1789, reported that it "concluded under a fresh sense of His divine goodness."[113] William Savery, visiting from Pennsylvania in 1795, found the Yearly Meeting "solid" and "refreshing."[114] And Samuel Smith at Fairfax Quarter in 1798 wrote "It proved a good time...uniting divers of us in near fellowship."[115]

The Society of Friends was definitely altruistic now; a Society with a settled intention to practice love and to oppose war and violence.[116] The Virginia Friends' anti-war witness was generally respected in the General Assembly where Isaac Zane, Jr., disowned Quaker though he was, spoke for them until his death in 1795--although there was always a strong opposing faction in the Assembly.

Quakers and "Menonists" were exempted from attending militia musters by a law passed in 1784. In 1791, the Assembly approved a petition (probably presented by Zane) on behalf of eighty-nine Friends of Hopewell and Crooked Run Meetings to repay them fines exacted for refusing to soldier during the Revolution.

By a law passed in 1793, however, Quakers and Menonists were exempt only if they furnished substitutes to serve in the militia; and in 1799 all exemptions were repealed. Thereafter Virginia's Friends, Mennonites and Brethren who refused to muster were once again harassed and fined.[117]

Friends also were concerned for the Indians, who were being pushed farther and farther west and away from their ancestral homes. Euro-Americans in general viewed the Native Americans as contemptible aliens. "May the Indians, enemies of America, be chastised by force of arms!", that was a Fourth of July toast of the time.[118]

The Quakers held a starkly opposed view. In 1792 the Philadelphia Friends asked President Washington and the Congress sitting in Philadelphia "to encourage the Indians to come forward with a full representation and statement of their grievances...that every just cause of uneasiness in their minds may be fully investigated and removed.... Nothing short of strict justice will ever be a basis of solid and lasting peace."[119]

President Washington certainly knew about the ancient friendship between Indians and Quakers. A plot of land in Philadelphia near Broad and Walnut Streets was the camping place for delegations of Indians visiting the Capital; and it was widely known that the Zanes, Drinkers and other

Philadelphia Friends regularly entertained Indian visitors.[120] Washington had tried twice to subdue the Ohio Indians forcibly and had failed twice when expeditionary forces were defeated in Ohio--General Harmar's column in 1790 and General St. Clair's in 1791. So the president decided to try friendship where force had failed. He approved of a Quaker embassage to the Cherokees in 1792[121]; and he approved again in 1793 when the Iroquois requested a Quaker presence at a conference between the tribes and the U.S. Government on Lake Erie's shore at Sandusky, Ohio.[122]

William Hartshorne, 51, a Quaker merchant of Alexandria, who had been on friendly terms with Washington for twenty years, was one of the six Friends who went to Sandusky. The six were away from home four summer months in 1793. Ten tribes were represented at Sandusky, of whom the Iroquois, Shawnees, Wyandots, and Delawares expressed pleasure at the Quakers' presence "as peaceable and just men." The six Friends listened quietly while Indian spokesmen addressed the U. S. commissioners, headed by Timothy Pickering, Washington's Postmaster General. Is the Great White Father willing to make the Ohio River the boundary line?, the Indians asked. Will he move the whites off our land west of the River? Timothy Pickering replied at length, saying in essence, No, it is not possible but the U. S. will pay well for the land.[123]

The Indians did not accept this reply, and another treaty talk was set for the summer of 1794 at Lake Canandaigua in New York State. The Iroquois asked for Quakers to be present again and William Savery and three more Philadelphia Friends attended. But this conference, too, ended inconclusively.

Then the U.,S. turned again to a mailed fist solution of the problem. In August 1794 Anthony Wayne commanding the Western Army crushed a force of 2,000 braves in Ohio's Miami River Valley. General Wayne then burned the surrounding Indian villages, and in 1795 he dictated the terms of the Treaty of Greenville. That opened the Ohio country for settlement and condemned the tribes to life on reservations.[124]

After Canandaigua, William Savery wrote to the clerk of Hopewell Meeting in Virginia[125] about the fact that Hopewell Friends had never paid the Indians for their land--a matter weighing on Friends' consciences for sixty years. Savery wrote that some chiefs of the Tuscarora nation had come to the four Friends at Canandaigua and "we were all of the opinion that the Tuscaroras were the people who formerly owned that country." He urged Hopewell Friends to honor the Tuscaroras' claim, adding "We do believe the testimony of Truth will suffer if compensation is not made them."

Now Hopewell Meeting still was holding the fund collected in 1777 to repay the Indians;[126] but there was considerable reason to doubt the Tuscaroras' claim after so many years. So it was decided in 1795 to use the fund for another purpose. Baltimore Yearly Meeting (to which Hopewell Monthly Meeting now was joined) formed an Indian committee after the news of the Indians' subjugation by General Wayne; and the fund was entrusted to this committee for the Indians' relief "and the encouragement of school education, husbandry and the mechanic arts amongst that people."[127]

Philadelphia Yearly Meeting formed an Indian committee at this same time. It was soon decided that Philadelphia Friends would help the Six Nations in upper New York, while Baltimore would befriend the Delawares, Shawnees and Wyandots in Ohio and westward. The Baltimore committee was made up of some twenty-seven Friends including many Virginians: Joseph Branson of Crooked Run Meeting, Joseph Bond and David Brown of Hopewell, John Butcher of Alexandria, Israel Janney of Goose Creek, Goldsmith Chandlee of Centre, James Mendenhall of Middle Creek. Others were Friends who had just moved from Virginia to Fayette County, Pennsylvania, and the Redstone and Westland Meetings there: Rees Cadwallader, Moses Dillon and James McGrew.

The Baltimore committee sent five men in 1796 (including Virginians Joseph Bond, Israel Janney and Jonathan Wright) to the Ohio Indians "to speak with you and get acquainted with your Nations." They took along a letter from Timothy Pickering (now U.S. Secretary of State) which gave President Washington's blessing to their trip; and they took a letter from the Baltimore committee which read:

> We have sent our beloved brothers...to shake hands with you in your tents and to ask you if you wish to be instructed how to raise corn and wheat for bread on your own land as we do; and to get meat at home without hunting, and to weave blankets and clothes...
>
> Also to enquire whether you wish to have your children taught to read and write, and to do such other things as will make you live comfortably under the shade of the great tree of peace.[128]

Notice now the tenor of this letter. It says nothing about converting the Indians to Quakerism. Evangelical churches had begun in 1792 to send out missionaries to the Indians[129] to win souls to Christ and to their various denominations' ways of worship. The Quakers, though, went only to befriend a distressed people in the spirit of Christ's teaching that "if you do it unto the least of these, my brethren, you do it unto me."

\* \* \*

Up until 1795 the Ohio country was a downright dangerous place. Three young men from Loudoun County, Virginia--Quaker Abel Janney, John Russell and Colman Wilks--dared to cross the Ohio River in the spring of 1782 to look the country over. Indians picked up their presence when they were only a half-mile west of the river, near Marietta. The Indians shot Russell and Wilks dead. They took Abel Janney prisoner and he did not get home for fifteen months.[130]

Marietta was settled by a few New England families in 1788 and Cincinnati in 1789, but the Indians menaced every white who dared to travel Ohio outside those two towns until General Wayne and the Western Army "pacified" them in 1795. Long before Ohio was safe, however, a trickle of Quaker families came to clear farms on the Ohio River's bank trusting, perhaps, that their broad-brims would keep them from harm. The clerk of Redstone Monthly Meeting minuted in 1793 that "a number of members of our Society are removed down Ohio River and more are likely to go which is a cause of uneasiness with us."[131] One stretch of the river bank across from what is now Huntington, West Virginia, came to be called "Quaker Bottom."[132]

In 1797 the Quaker Zane brothers of Wheeling contracted with the U.S. Government to clear a trail westward from Wheeling and Martin's Ferry. They ran it southwest across Ohio,[133] to present day Zanesville and Chillicothe, then on to the Ohio River at Aberdeen, Brown County. Zane's Trace became at once the route of many westbound migrants.

Virginia Quakers began to talk eagerly among themselves about the rich-soiled, slave-free Ohio country. Such talk unsettled the meetings. Joshua Evans, the traveling minister, having just visited some Virginia meetings in the spring of 1797 reported that he was

> ...concerned to caution Friends against a disposition that leads to unsettlement, and to ramble farther out into remote places, from whence the poor Indians have been driven, or their lands obtained by measures inconsistent with the holy principle of Truth.[134]

\* \* \*

Virginia in Revolutionary days was a vast and lovely landscape traversed by rutted roads and crossroads, snake rail fences, and roadside rows of blue-green locusts and cedars. General stores with hitching posts out front and gossips on their porches stood at the major crossroads, along with ordinaries (taverns) and blacksmith shops. The State had no towns worthy of the name excepting only Norfolk and Williamsburg.

After the state capital moved to Richmond in 1779, however, Richmond grew. In 1784 the General Assembly, cramped in Cuninghame's Warehouse, bought a hilltop seven blocks west and waited impatiently while a spacious new Capitol building went up there. The new capitol was built according to elegant plans sent home from France by Thomas Jefferson, now America's ambassador to Paris. Jefferson arranged for sculptor Jean-Antoine Houdon to execute a statue of George Washington for the new capitol's foyer. Benjamin West, the Quaker-born painter in London--with two brothers living in Virginia--suggested to Houdon the daring idea of doing the statue in modern dress instead of the robes of antiquity. Houdon was so taken with the idea that he even left off a button from Washington's waistcoat. The empty button hole has been pointed out to generations of sight-seers as an indication that Martha Washington was a less than perfect housewife.

By the time Virginia's government moved into the new building on 28 October 1788[135] Richmond was a boom town. It was home for some 3,800 inhabitants--2,300 white and 1,500 black.[136] The only church was St. John's on Church Hill. In 1780, fourteen Baptists began meeting in their homes and a Methodist group began meeting soon thereafter. The Protestant Episcopal Church organized at a gathering in the old Capitol in 1785, to supplant the Established Church. In 1789, twenty-six families established Richmond's first Jewish congregation.

But the first religious group to build a house of worship in Richmond (after St. John's) was the Friends. George Winston, a Quaker contractor, built Richmond Friends' brick meeting house at 19th and Cary Streets in 1797 and 1798. St. John's was 40 x 40 feet, the Friends' Meeting house 30 x 30. The Methodist meeting house was 30 x 25 feet when it went up in 1799.[137]

Alexandria became Virginia's second boom town after 1790, when Congress decided to meet in Philadelphia only for ten years and in that time to build a permanent capital on the Potomac River. A few Friends were already living in Alexandria in 1790, including William and Susanna Hartshorne and John and Ann Butcher, merchant families from New Jersey.

They started a meeting there about 1783, and put up a meetinghouse on St. Asaph Street[138] soon thereafter.

Ministers from outside and inside Virginia rode the long and terrible roads winters and summers to plead for purity in the Friends' meetings. Remarks in their journals about the state of the local meetings were often critical, particularly critical of the new meetings in Richmond and Alexandria where the boom atmosphere was hurtful. Friends there were not simple farmers, but often were merchants and speculators in real estate with their eyes on worldly wealth. This, as visiting ministers saw it, caused "enfeebling, numbing and stupefying effects," "a love of and conformity to the spirit and maxims of this world...", and "a declension from the life and virtue of Truth."

Thomas Scattergood in Richmond in 1793 wrote "O the wickedness and abominations of this little city! ...the mountebanks' sign which hung out in the street and their other wicked doings struck at my life." Elias Hicks who visited Alexandria Meeting in 1798 called it "a small weak meeting, very few manifesting any real concern."[139]

The Friends' urge to live up to their ancient testimonies made them cautious in the postwar years. Virginia Yearly Meeting in 1787 warned "of the snares and temptations Friends may be exposed to who accept of offices in governments,"[140] and Stanton's Meeting disowned Michael Bailey when he took the job of Sussex County's clerk.[141] The few new members who were admitted first underwent searching examinations by clearness committees.

Robert Pleasants enthusiastically supported the postwar revival movement. After the Revolution he cut back on business and focused his life on "advancing the Truth." To this end he wrote many letters, consoling or counseling Friends or "eldering" them:[142]

- "Thy son Exum," he wrote to John Crew, clerk of the Yearly Meeting, "says he's going to sea in an armed vessel with thy concurrence." He then urged John Crew not to concur.
- He advised Thomas Fleming Bates of Goochland County not to worry so much about money. "Loving Cousin," Robert wrote, "If the worst should happen, do not distrust blind Providence, but rather believe all will work together for good."
- He asked Barnaby Nixon, a minister of Burleigh Meeting, to change his style of speaking in meeting. "Do not ramble from one text to another," Robert bluntly advised.

Along with eldering, Robert Pleasants continued to represent the Yearly Meeting in promoting a range of Friends' testimonies, some new and some revived from the Quakers' early days. He rode the fourteen miles from his home to Richmond often in 1792 and 1793 with petitions from Virginia Yearly Meeting to the General Assembly. James Ladd, a minister of Weyanoke Meeting in Charles City County, John Hunnicutt of Burleigh and Pleasants Terrell of Caroline Meeting were his partners now that Edward Stabler had died. One petition urged the Assembly not to hire a chaplain--which, Friends feared, would be a step back toward control of religion by the state (rejected by the Assembly). A second petition asked for Friends to be allowed to wear their hats in court without having them forcibly removed by the bailiffs (approved after long lobbying).[143]

Thomas Harris of Cedar Creek Meeting, was 32-years-old in 1792 when he began to behave in a way that harked far back to the Quakers' earliest days. He was a respectable Hanover County farmer married to James Ladd's daughter, Chlotilda, with two small daughters. Then, as Thomas Harris said, "[I began to believe] it my duty in obedience to divine impression on my mind to undress...before a congregation as a prophetic sign."

This throw-back behavior greatly concerned Virginia's Friends. Robert Pleasants wrote to William Savery of Philadelphia about the matter saying

> It would be pleasing to receive a few lines [of advice] from thee.... [Thomas] has walked the most public street [in Richmond] six times stark naked and seems still to believe it his indispensable duty to continue to do so.... He has received some stripes, been jailed and was sent to the Hospital for Lunaticks in Williamsburg--but was returned on the stage the next day.... He says the...reason for his leading is completely hid from him.[144]

Not all Friends disapproved. Thomas Scattergood for one "expressed his approval of the singular and uncommon appearances of Thomas Harris who," as Scattergood observed, "like the prophet Isaiah had been concerned to go naked and barefoot through the city as a sign of impending judgments for the abominations practiced there."[145]

Thomas Harris never was disowned by Friends even though he continued to follow his extraordinary leading all his days. He was locked up in Richmond city jail on 18 September 1832 just before his death at 72. He wrote a codicil to his will in the jail with this preface: "I have been for some time past considered by many to be in a state of derangement and...I have had several trials before the magistrates of the City of Richmond and declared by them to be of sound mind except that of believing it my duty....to undress...as a prophetic sign."[146]

* * *

The number of Friends' Meetings in Virginia grew to a record high by 1800:
- The oldest Friends' communities, along James River, lost many families when Virginia Yearly Meeting banned slaveholding; so many that fourteen of the thirty-one meetings of the yearly meeting's lower and upper quarters closed their doors between 1763 and 1800. The fourteen losses included Chuckatuck, the oldest meeting in the state. The losses were partly offset by the appearance of six new meetings: Seacock and Vick's in Southampton County, Durham's and Ward's in frontier Mecklenburg and Brunswick Counties respectively, Gravelly Run (Dinwiddie County) and Richmond.
- There was talk in 1792 about transferring the meetings of eastern North Carolina, in Perquimans and Pasquotank Counties, from North Carolina's to Virginia Yearly Meeting's jurisdiction, but nothing came of it.
- Five new meetings started up in the neighborhood of Lynchburg: Banister (Halifax County), Upper Goose Creek and Ivy Creek in Bedford County, and Hill's Creek and Seneca in Campbell County. Those five meetings along with South River and Lower Goose Creek formed a new quarterly meeting, Western Quarter of Virginia Yearly Meeting, in 1797.
- Virginia Yearly Meeting put in a bid in 1787 to add northern Virginia's Fairfax Quarterly Meeting to it constituency. Fairfax Quarter was then part of Philadelphia Yearly Meeting's sprawling membership. But Philadelphia Yearly Meeting arranged instead to trade with Maryland Yearly Meeting, exchanging the meetings of Fairfax Quarter, and of Warrington Quarter in south central Pennsylvania in return for Maryland's meetings on the Eastern Shore of Maryland.
- The northern Virginia Friends grew vigorously, adding eight meetings to the eighteen they had in 1763. The eight new meetings: Alexandria; Culpeper, in what is now Washington, Virginia; Lower Ridge in Frederick County; and Berkeley, Dillon's Run, Richland, Sandy Creek and Wheeling, all located in present-day West Virginia.

- Seven more new meetings sprang up in the mountains of southwest Virginia: Mount Pleasant, Burk's Fork, and Fruit Hill (all in Grayson County); Road Creek and Ward's Gap (in Carroll County); Maple Spring (Scott County) and Reedy Island (Pittsylvania County). Most of the mountaineer Friends had moved to the area from North Carolina, and all seven meetings were part of Surry Quarter of North Carolina Yearly Meeting.

So then the Friendly Virginians had sixty-three meetings at the close of the 1700s, where there had been forty-nine in 1763.

Most smaller meeting houses of Virginia's Friends closed their doors after 1800 when so many members went west. Mill Creek Meeting House (above) in Berkeley County (now West Virginia) closed about 1805. Back Creek Meeting (below) near Gainesboro, Frederick County, (10 miles northwest of Winchester) kept on until 1829.

# XI

# TO THE WESTWARD WATERS
# 1800-1820

> Reader, would'st thou know what true peace
> and quiet mean; would'st thou find a refuge
> from the noises and clamours of the multitude;
> would'st thou possess the depth of thy own spirit
> in stillness....?--come with me into a
> Quakers' Meeting.
>
> -- Charles Lamb

New Year's Day of the Year of Our Lord 1800 dawned bright for the Friendly Virginians. Their sixty-three meetings, from Tuscarora high in northwest Virginia to Somerton in the southeast, formed a harmonious network. Their numbers were gently growing--an estimated 5,500 Virginia Friends as of New Year's Day 1800. Then with little warning, a jolting reverse.

"Ohio fever" caused the reverse. With the Indians subdued, all Virginia was buzzing with talk about the rich new country north and west of the Ohio River.

By 1800 thousands of Virginia families had already moved west, nearly all of them through Cumberland Gap by way of the Wilderness Road blazed by Daniel Boone in 1774. Those families were settlers of the Kentucky Country, the Dark and Bloody Ground *south*west of the Ohio. Few or no Quakers went to Kentucky; but when the Ohio country opened up to the *north*west it drew Quakers of Virginia, the Carolinas, and Georgia like iron to the magnet. The difference lay in this: that Kentucky was slave territory while Ohio was slave-free--declared so by the Quaker-inspired clause in the Northwest Ordinance of 1787.

Ohio fever among Southern Quakers was fed by the fervent vision of certain Friends from Meetings in western Pennsylvania who visited among the Southern meetings in 1799. As Borden Stanton of Contentnea Meeting west of New Bern, N.C. described it:

> For several years Friends had some distant view of moving out of that oppressive part of the land [the southern States], but did not know

where until the year 1799, when we had an acceptable visit from some travelling Friends of the western part of Pennsylvania. They thought proper to propose to Friends...whether it would not be agreeable to best wisdom for us unitedly to remove north-west of the Ohio river--to a place where there were no slaves held, being a free country.

This proposal made a deep impression on our minds: and it seemed as if they were messengers sent to call us out, as it were, from Egyptian darkness (for indeed it seemed as if the land groaned under oppression)

...It was at first very crossing to my natural inclination; being well settled as to the outward...at length I considered there was no prospect of our [Quaker] number being increased by convincement, on account of the oppression...I also thought I saw in the light that the minds of the [southern Quaker] people generally were too much outward...

Under a view of these things, I was made sensible beyond doubting that it was in the order of wisdom for us to remove....Friends generally feeling something of the same, there were three of them who went to view the country and one worthy public Friend. They travelled on till they came to this part of the western country [Mt. Pleasant, Ohio, a few miles west across the Ohio River from Wheeling, W. Va.] where they were stopped in their minds, believing it was the place for Friends to settle.

So they returned back, and informed us of the same in a solemn meeting; in which dear Joseph Dew, the public Friend, intimated that he saw the seed of God sown in abundance, which extended far to the northwestward....

The first of us moved west of the Ohio in the Ninth Month, 1800; and none of us had a house at our command to meet in to worship the Almighty Being. So we met in the woods until houses were built....[1]

This was the beginning of the great Quaker migration "to the Westward Waters." Trent River Meeting in Trenton, North Carolina moved in *a body* to Ohio in 1800.

Zachariah Dicks of New Garden Meeting, North Carolina became convinced that Friends must leave the South. In 1803, 71-years of age, he visited all the southernmost Friends meetings, those in South Carolina and Georgia. He dwelt on the massacre of French slave holders in Haiti where the blacks were revolting, and he prophesied a similar fate for American slave owners. He called Friends to get out of slave country, clear themselves of its taint. In Bush River Meeting, South Carolina, he stood in the silence and prophesied: "O Bush River! Bush River! How hath thy beauty faded. Gloom and darkness have eclipsed thy day!"

Zachariah's words, at Bush River and everywhere along his circuit, bit deep. The Quaker migration speeded up. South Carolina's Friends' meetings and Wrightsborough Meeting, the only Georgia meeting, were depopulated. The Friends sold their farms for whatever they would bring, loaded their furniture in wagons and started west.[2]

Not all Virginia Friends agreed it was right to pull up stakes and leave. Richard Mott and John Shoemaker, traveling ministers from Mamaroneck, New York State, and Abington Meeting near Philadelphia respectively, called at Hopewell Meeting in Tenth Month 1805. Shoemaker noted: "We found Friends much exercised about their members' moving away, which had stripped their meetings to such a degree as to induce a belief that they would be under the necessity of dropping some of their meetings."[3]

Nine years later, John Shoemaker visited Somerton Meeting in southeast Virginia. He was invited to stay at Jesse Copeland's where he found Jesse's wife looking after an exhausted black freedman. The freedman had been kidnapped and sold into Georgia by a North Carolina slave merchant, had escaped and returned on foot all the way from Georgia to Somerton. Jesse Copeland was gone to North Carolina to charge the slave merchant with his crime. Shoemaker wrote that night: "Friends are as a bulwark in this land, and I cannot see or feel that it would be right for them to remove from this country. They have already done much for this poor suffering branch of the human family and there appears to be much more to be done."[4]

Nevertheless Virginia's Friends did move West wholesale. By 1810, thirteen Virginia meetings had been "laid down"--their meeting houses swept and the grass of their burying grounds trimmed one last time with pathetic care. Among these thirteen were some old historic ones--Black Creek Meeting in New Kent County, Curles and White Oak Swamp in Henrico. From 1810 to 1820, seventeen more meetings disappeared. By 1820 there were thirty-three ongoing meetings plus two small new ones in Virginia, where there had been 63 flourishing in 1800.

The reason Friends moved so eagerly is suggested in certain memoirs written by Friends who grew up in Virginia and ended their days in the West. William B. Walthall (1818-1890), known to his schoolmates as "Botts" wrote:

...I was born the 25th day of 1st Month 1818, in Dinwiddie County, old Virginia.... My earliest home was situated on the public road leading from Richmond, Virginia, to Raleigh, North Carolina [three miles from Gravelly Run Friends Meeting House]. It [Virginia] being a slave-breeding state, I was early accustomed to seeing droves of slaves on their way to a southern market. The circumstances in my mind at that early age were frightful--noble men, manacled and handcuffed, driven to market like beasts....

My early schoolmates were children of slaveholders...It seemed natural to them...that the colored man had no rights that white children were bound to respect.... I claimed that the whole institution was wrong....

When I was about nine or ten years of age, a colored man living near our home was so anxious to learn his letters...that he offered to pay me if I would on Sabbath evenings help him. So we commenced the first Sabbath School in that part of old Virginia. It soon increased in numbers that they were beyond my control, as I was only a child [but] my dear parents would encourage me in the work so that it did continue for some time.... Word soon spread around that "Botts" was teaching a free "nigger" school, a term of contempt....

About the year 1828 my parents finding themselves left alone as members of Friends' church in a dense slave-holding community, and realizing the danger that would attend their effort to raise their children under such circumstances, resolved to move to Ohio.[5]

Three main roads led out of Virginia to the Ohio country:
- The northernmost was the National Road which followed the trace of General Braddock's old military road west of Cumberland, Maryland, to Beeson Town (now Uniontown, Pennsylvania) and on to the Ohio River at Wheeling.
- Then came the Kanawha or Magadee way, from Richmond west to Lexington, Va., and by White Sulphur Springs to the salt lick at Charleston on the Kanawha River, and down Kanawha Valley to the Ohio at Point Pleasant.

- Daniel Boone's Wilderness Road through the Cumberland Gap was used by families from southern Virginia and North Carolina, who then swung north through Kentucky to Ohio.[6]

In the early 1800s it took something like seven weeks for a family to remove to Ohio. Angelina Pearson wrote the saga of the Quaker Harvey family (who went to Ohio in 1806 from North Carolina just below the Virginia line) thus:

> Most families made the trip in a farm wagon drawn by two horses....The distance was called 700 miles or more. Every one of the family able to walk was expected to do so....
>
> Arriving at Cumberland Gap they were all tired out and all in the emigrant train pitched camp and rested here for two weeks. Cumberland Gap was considered all but impassable. No team could take a wagon down its steep slopes. There were two ways of descending. One was to unload the wagon, secure a strong rope to the tongue and wind it a time or two around a deeply rooted tree. Several men would then hold the rope, playing it out gradually and letting the wagon go down backwards.
>
> Grandfather [Isaac Harvey] chose the other way, that of unloading and taking the wagon to pieces, and carrying it piece by piece down the steep grade, as well as everything they had in the wagon. They were seven weeks on the road.[7]

After 1818, however, the travel time shortened to four weeks or so. Between 1811 and 1818 the National Road was made, with a roadbed 30 feet wide and 12 to 18 inches deep, the bed filled with stone broken by sledgehammers and rolled smooth, the trees axed down 18 feet on either side of the highway.[8] The teams made good time once they reached that modern engineering marvel.

Little Botts Walthall and his family traveled by the National Road:

> On the first day of the 10th month [1830], we left the old homestead, reached Petersburg late in the evening, stayed there over one day...a family of free colored people were our companions....

Crossing the Shenandoah River, entered Maryland, there meeting two slave merchants who took a fancy to two young colored men belonging to the family before mentioned, pleaded with Father to sell to them....

I well remember the scenery in nearing and crossing the Allegheny mountains. Their first appearance to us was that of a dark cloud rising. They were in sight some days before reaching them. When on the summit the view was grand beyond description. Our course was then towards Brownsville, Pa. We crossed the Ohio river at Wheeling and were glad to find ourselves on free soil.

At this time the waters were very low. We saw one ox team fording the Ohio river at Wheeling....

In Ohio we crossed the Muskingum and Scioto. This we crossed on a floating bridge. Our colored family left us for Columbus. Wilmington was our point. So our long journey terminated on the first day of 11th month in the year 1830 as we reached the comfortable home of old Uncle David Bailey in Clinton County, Ohio.[9]

\* \* \*

The Friends from Virginia settled in two definite Ohio locations: one in the southwest corner of the State along the Little Miami River; the other in eastern Ohio, across the Ohio River from Wheeling. The southwest Ohio Friends' settlements were spread over four Ohio counties: Warren, Clinton, Highland, and Greene. More than 1,800 Friends, 269 of them from Virginia, settled there by 1807.[10]

The first meetings for worship in southwest Ohio were held in the cabin of Rowland and Lydia Richards, located on the Little Miami's bank where Waynesville stands today. The Richardses came from Virginia's Crooked Run Meeting in 1801. Rowland was the first Friends' minister on the Little Miami and daughter Mary was the first Quaker bride.[11] Some 220 other Quaker meetings were to branch off from the Miami Monthly Meeting that began in their front room[12]--the first of them at Lee's Creek where Leesburg, Ohio, stands today. In 1806 Whitewater Valley of eastern Indiana opened up for settlement. A number of Miami Friends moved there. They formed the nucleus of a network of Friends' meetings along the Indiana frontier.

Indians still lived in the Little Miami country when the Friends arrived, frightened by the whites' coming on the land and resisting the proviso in the Greenville Treaty requiring them to leave Ohio. Indians murdered Catherine Harrod in spring 1803 and white men murdered Chief Wawillay in reprisal. The whites built a blockhouse then and fortified their cabins. The Friends of Lee's Creek lived close by the Indian camp but they fortified not at all. In this tense time Indians in war paint visited the Lee's Creek Friends.

Indians and Friends met under a great elm tree, the Friends' outdoor meeting place. Nathaniel Pope and Evan Evans, only recently arrived from Virginia, spoke for the Quakers. We will not harm you when we go to war against the whites, the Indian war chief told the Quakers, but you must give over half your possessions. Martha Pope, speaking for the Quaker wives, refused this demand with vehemence. Then the Indians stood young John Pope up against the elm and threw tomahawks into the tree trunk around him. Whereupon the Indians won out and received half the settlement's home-spun sheets, blankets and provisions. But no harm came to the Friends during the violence[13] that racked their neighborhood soon thereafter.

In *eastern* Ohio, the Friends settled in a five county area from Columbiana and Jefferson Counties south, through Harrison, Belmont and Guernsey Counties. The Quaker center of the area was Short Creek Meetinghouse, a few miles across the Ohio River from Wheeling. The town of Mount Pleasant largely inhabited by Quakers was laid out near Short Creek in 1804. Barnesville in Belmont County and Salem in Columbiana County were large Quaker communities to the south and north of Short Creek.

More than 800 Friends arrived in eastern Ohio by the close of 1800[14] and some 3,000 by 1810. Then Friends built a meeting house in Mt. Pleasant large enough for gatherings of Friends from all over the west--a great brick house, 62 by 90 feet to seat 2,000 people. Jacob Ong, a public Friend who came to Ohio from Middle Creek Meeting in Virginia, was the lead builder.[15] By 1813 when the meeting house was nearly finished, the largest Friends' place of worship ever built, Baltimore Yearly Meeting allowed the Ohio Friends to establish their own yearly meeting. Ohio's was the first new yearly meeting organized in over a hundred years, the seventh in the United States.

\* \* \*

Meanwhile back in Virginia the guard was changing. When 1800 arrived the state was mourning the deaths of Washington (1732-1799) and Patrick Henry (1736-1799), her two Revolutionary heroes. And now younger leaders emerged: Thomas Jefferson (1743-1826) and James Madison (1751-1836).

Washington and Henry had grown conservative as they grew grayer, as old heroes are prone to do. The new leaders represented a different emphasis--stressing democracy and the rights of the common man instead of stronger government. It was an ethos more in keeping with the Quakers' central conviction, that there is some thing of God in every man and woman.

Both Jefferson and Madison had Quaker ties. Jefferson's mother was a Randolph, the daughter of Isham and Jane Lilburne Randolph; and Jane, the grandmother of Thomas Jefferson, born in London about 1700, was related to John Lilburne the Leveller, a famous London Quaker of George Fox's day.[16] Further, the Randolph family in Henrico had intermarried with Quaker Flemings, Pleasants and Woodsons. Jefferson had Quaker cousins. As for James Madison, his wife Dolley, the love of his life, was Quaker born and bred.

Thomas Jefferson's life intersected with the Quakers at many points:

As a small boy, Thomas with his parents visited grandmother Jane Randolph at Dungeness, her plantation on the James upriver from Richmond. Isham the grandfather died there just before Thomas's birth, heavily in debt to John Hanbury, the Quaker tobacco merchant of London.[17] No doubt Jefferson at his grandmother's knee on Dungeness's veranda heard talk of Hanbury and Lilburne the Leveller. John Bartram, the Quaker botanist of Philadelphia, was Isham's friend and had stayed at Dungeness;[18] and grandmother Randolph may have reminisced about Bartram too.

Isham and Jane's daughter Dorothy, that is Thomas's Aunt Dorothy, married Quaker John Woodson; and Isham and Jane's daughter Anne, Aunt Anne, successively married Quakers Jonathan Pleasants and James Pleasants. So it is likely that Thomas Jefferson played with Quaker cousins on occasion under Dungeness's oaks.

Little Thomas probably heard stories about Quakers from his father too. For Peter Jefferson his father and Thomas his grandfather had both been county sheriffs and both had been obliged to confiscate the goods of Friends who refused to pay church taxes or turn out for militia drills.[19]

From age 14 to 17, Tom went to the Reverend Mr. James Maury's school some six miles north of his home at Shadwell. About halfway to school Tom rode his pony past an empty Friends' meeting house. The Friends of that meeting, called Sugar Loaf Mountain Meeting--Clarks, Lynches, Moormans, Terrells and others--had moved south in 1754 to the neighborhood where Lynchburg is now. Thirty years later Thomas Jefferson acquired the Poplar Forest plantation, 4,000 acres near Lynchburg. He employed Bowling Clark, a Friend who had grown up in Sugar Loaf Mountain Meeting, to manage Poplar Forest.[20]

Thomas went off to college at William and Mary in 1760. There he encountered George Wythe, America's first law professor and a man imbued with his mother's Quakerly outlook. George Wythe deeply influenced young Jefferson.

No sooner had he returned home to Shadwell from college than he, Thomas Jefferson, got into politics. In 1769 he was elected to represent Albemarle in Virginia's House of Burgesses. That same year Charles Lynch, Jr. (1736-1796), newly disowned by the Lynchburg Friends, was elected from Bedford County. And in 1773 Isaac Zane, Jr. (1743-1795), another Friend newly disowned, was sent up to the House from Frederick County. The three men, Jefferson, Lynch and Zane, were among the young liberals of the house. They voted together on many roll calls.

Thomas Jefferson was especially friendly with Isaac Zane, just his own age. Some of their letters exist still. The earliest was written by Jefferson from Monticello in February 1778. He ordered some salt pans and stoves from Zane's iron works; begged Isaac to sell him the spirit level that once had belonged to Lord Dunmore; and recognized Isaac's Quaker roots by closing the letter "I wish you every felicity and am, with more than religious form, Your assured friend."[21]

During February 1782, Isaac Zane sent a letter to Jefferson at Monticello in the hands of a Philadelphia Friend married to Robert Pleasants's youngest sister Molly.[22] The bearer is Charles Logan, Isaac wrote, on his way to his Virginia possessions by his wife. She is the heiress of the Pleasants family. Please show him civility and come to see me who has been ill.

This Charles Logan (1754-1794) was a grandson of James Logan, William Penn's right-hand man in the founding of Pennsylvania. Charles's brother George (1753-1821) was to be an associate of Jefferson's in the 1790s, when Jefferson was Vice President of the United States. George Logan is the U. S. Senator who infuriated President Washington by visiting Talleyrand in Paris in 1798 and averting war with France. The Logan Act, which makes it criminal for an unaccredited U. S. citizen to parley with foreign governments, is named for George Logan.[23]

In September of 1783, Thomas Jefferson detoured on his way from Monticello to join the Continental Congress in Philadelphia, going by way of Winchester in order to visit Isaac Zane. Isaac then gave Jefferson a letter to Isaac Zane, Sr, his handsome old Philadelphia Friend of a father. "Please render every civility to Colo. Thomas Jefferson (former Governor of Virginia)," the letter read. The next month Isaac quilled a longer letter to his sister Sarah Zane on behalf of Jefferson. "He is newly widowed and brings his little daughter to Philadelphia to be educated," he wrote, and "I would wish some of the most amiable and accomplished of thy acquaintance would be introduced to him."[24]

Thomas Jefferson became the Nation's third president, 1801 to 1809. During this peak-time of his career, the Quakerly influences of his earlier life were evident -- all the more evident by contrast with the Federalist administration of second president John Adams. President Adams disliked Quakers from the time of the First Continental Congress when he clashed with Israel Pemberton.

Jefferson expressed his Quaker bias in a letter to Elbridge Gerry, March 1801: "The mild and simple principles of the Christian philosophy," he wrote, "would produce too much calm, too much regularity of good, to extract from its disciples a support for a numerous priesthood, were they not to sophisticate it, ramify it, split it into hairs and twist its sense till they cover the divine morality of its author with mysteries, and require a priesthood to explain them. The Quakers seem to have discovered this. They have no priests, therefore no schisms. They judge of the text by the dictates of common sense and common morality."[25]

Note here that Thomas Jefferson was a little mistaken in judging just who Quakers are and what they stand for. Jefferson was a man of the Enlightenment. He trusted common sense and human reason as the means for humanity to find the way through. The Friends, however, trust in the intuitive kind of guidance that they seek in their silent meetings, and not primarily in common sense.

In the years of his presidency Jefferson dealt with several Friends on a footing of mutual respect.

He was friendly with Andrew Ellicott and Isaac Briggs, Quaker surveyors from Maryland, and their black assistant Benjamin Banneker. The three surveyors executed L'Enfant's spider-web street plan for the new city of Washington. After he negotiated the Louisiana Purchase in 1803, President Jefferson employed Isaac Briggs to lay out a 1,200 mile post road linking New Orleans and Washington. When this years-long job was completed,

Congress refused to pay Briggs because the president had neglected to get advance authorization for the work. Jefferson suggested some political stratagem to get the pay, but Isaac Briggs refused. "My Quaker faith," he said, "teaches me it is better to suffer than contend."[26]

President Jefferson had two mills built on the Rivanna River below Monticello. Then he asked Dr. William Thornton, his Commissioner of Patents, to find a first class miller to operate them. Dr. Thornton, a Quaker, consulted Quaker Jonathan Shoemaker, who had just moved to the raw new District of Columbia from Abington near Philadelphia and purchased the Columbia Mill on Rock Creek. Shoemaker offered to rent the president's mills, and send his son Isaac down to Monticello to run them. Dr. Thornton and Jonathan Shoemaker then called at the White House with this proposal; President Jefferson, who knew Shoemaker,[*][27] accepted. It was agreed that the rent would be $1,000 for the first year and $1,250 for each of four years thereafter.

Isaac Shoemaker arrived at Monticello late in 1806 and things went wrong right away. There was no place for him to stay. The mills were not quite ready to operate. Isaac was really no miller himself. He hired a miller who got the mill started, but the flour was only "middling." In 1807 while Isaac was struggling to right matters, an August thunderstorm swept away half the mill dam. By that time Martha Randolph, 36, Jefferson's daughter who lived two miles from Monticello at Edgehill, had come to dislike Isaac Shoemaker. She wrote to her father in Washington: "It would be better for you to get the mill back on any terms than to let him keep it. In the first place he is not a man of business...he has not one spark of honesty...nothing but necessity induces anyone to trust him with their grain.[28]

Isaac kept on trying but he never could pay Thomas Jefferson the rent. Finally, Jefferson began pressing Jonathan Shoemaker for payment. "It has been a sincere affliction for me to be so importunate with you on the subject of my rents," he wrote from Monticello, February 1810, "but my necessities

---

[*] Jefferson knew Shoemaker through his Secretary of State James Madison, and Dolley Madison. Jonathan Shoemaker's wife Elizabeth was a Philadelphia girlhood friend of Dolley's and they resumed their friendship in Washington. Elizabeth Shoemaker once sent one of her sons in to pick up Dolley at her F Street residence and bring her out to visit Elizabeth in a mill cart. Shoemaker's mill later was purchased by John Quincy Adams. it became known as "Adams Mill" and its site is marked by the place where Adams Mill Road crosses Rock Creek.

have forced it on me. I inclose for your perusal two letters received by the last mail which will show you how sorely I am pressed."[29] And Jonathan did pay the rent, although he nearly bankrupted himself in the process. He had to sell his mill and then his share of the stage line from Washington to Richmond which he owned with Quaker Nathaniel Ellicott.

On 10 February 1806, Dolley Madison arranged for Robert Sutcliff, a British Quaker, to visit President Jefferson in the White House. The President's informality amazed Sutcliff. "I was received by him with a shake of the hand, as though we had been long acquaintances," he reported. They had a friendly short chat and then "again taking me by the hand [the President] bade me farewell. From his disregard of all useless forms and ceremonies, not excepting those of religion, his enemies accuse him of being deficient both in religion and politeness. But...where true religion and true politeness most abound, there we see the least of forms and ceremonies."[30]

Eight days after Robert Sutcliff's visit, on February 18, President Jefferson wrote a letter to Thomas Cooper which suggests the effect of Quakerly thinking on Jefferson's outlook. From the beginning of his presidency he had worked to reduce the armed forces and to settle international differences by peaceful means, by embargoes and diplomacy. Now he wrote to Cooper that "something must be done to correct the impression in Europe that our government is based entirely on Quaker principles and will turn the other cheek when the right has been smitten."[31]

The Friends of Baltimore Yearly Meeting were so pleased with Jefferson's presidency that they wrote him a letter of congratulations during their annual gathering in 1807. They applauded him for three things: for "thy efforts to preserve our Country from the calamities and ravages of war..."; for "exertions...to ameliorate the condition of the Indian Natives"; and for "thy influence...to relieve our country from the complicated evils attendant upon this cruel and inhuman [slave] trade." The president answered:

> Friends and fellow citizens...I thank you for [your] approbation...it was not to be doubted that the Society of Friends, with whom [a conduct friendly to all] is a religious principle, would sanction it by their support.... In [efforts to help the Indians] I owe to your Society an acknowledgment that we have felt the benefit of [your] zealous cooperation.... And [as to slavery] I sincerely pray with you my friends, that all the members of the human family in the time

prescribed by the Father of us all, may find themselves securely established in the enjoyments of life, liberty and happiness.[32]

In spite of this exchange, Thomas Jefferson's view of the Society of Friends was not entirely approving. He had a notion that Friends were pro-British, possibly based on the efforts of the Pembertons to prevent the Revolutionary War. "Their attachment to England is stronger than their attachment to their principles or to their country. The Revolution[ary] War was a first proof of this."[33] So he wrote to James Madison in 1798. This opinion cropped up in his letters for years, until 1817 when he wrote to Marquis de Lafayette, "When war is proposed with England they have religious scruples, but when with France these are laid by."[34]

Jefferson was 70-years-old in 1813, in retirement at Monticello. That summer a letter came from William Canby, a Friend of Wilmington, Delaware, to "Esteemed Friend Thomas Jefferson." Canby wished for Jefferson that he should become a Christian and "turned to that Spirit which leadeth unto all Truth." Jefferson responded at once and at length:

> Sir An eloquent preacher of your religious society, Richard Mott*...is said to have exclaimed...that he did not believe there was a Quaker, Presbyterian, Methodist or Baptist in heaven.... He added that in heaven God knew no distinctions but considered all good men as his children and as brethren of the same family.
>
> I believe with the Quaker preacher that he who steadily observes those moral precepts in which all religious concur will never be questioned at the gates of heaven....
>
> Of all the systems of morality...none appear to me so pure as that of Jesus. He who follows this steadily need not, I think, be uneasy, although he cannot comprehend the subtleties and mysteries erected [in Jesus' name, such as] the demonstrations of St Athanasius that three are one, and one is three....

---

* Richard Mott was a public Friend of Mamaroneck, New York who visited the southern meetings in 1805. He did indeed preach in Maryland and Virginia that "there cannot be but one true church in the world and that, no doubt, is made up of the sincere-hearted of all religious denominations."

In all essential points, you and I are of the same religion; and I am too old to go into inquiries and changes as to the unessential.[35]

He was 83 when he died. In his sunset years, the Sage of Monticello, he wrote often and always favorably about Friends:

- To John Adams, 1 June 1822:

    I hope we shall prove how much happier for man the Quaker policy is, and that the life of the feeder is better than that of the fighter.[36]

- To Reverend Thomas Whittemore (a Unitarian minister) 5 June 1822:

    The religions of antiquity had no particular formulas of creed. Those of the modern world none, except those of the religionists calling themselves Christians. And even among these, the Quakers have none. And hence alone, the harmony, the quiet, the brotherly affection, the exemplary and unschismatizing Society of the Friends.... I hope the Unitarians will follow their happy example.[37]

- To Michael Megear, 29 May 1823:

    I thank you, sir, for the copy of the Letters of Paul and Amicus...and I shall learn from them with satisfaction the peculiar tenets of the Friends.... I think with them on many points.[38]

James Madison was Thomas Jefferson's Secretary of State. Then he became himself the nation's president, 1809-1817. As a young man living with his parents on their Montpelier plantation near Orange, he knew John Douglas and the Friends of Douglas' Meeting close by on Blue Run. When the Revolution was brewing in 1775 Madison wrote to a college friend, "The Quakers are the only people [in Orange County] who refuse to sign up with the Continental Association [but they] are too honest and simple to have any sinister or secret views."[39]

Madison likely was thinking of these "honest and simple" people in the 1780s when he worked for passage of Virginia's Statute of Religious Liberty; and in 1790 when he tried to insert a clause in the U. S. Constitution's Bill of Rights "for exempting [from military service] all persons conscientiously scrupulous of bearing arms."[40]

But Madison's close encounter with the Society of Friends began in 1794. He was a bachelor congressman then, 42-years-old, short, slight and bookish and living in a Philadelphia boarding house. He was famous for his work in forging the Constitution but, for all that, lonely of evenings. One spring day early in Congress' 1794 session, he chatted with Aaron Burr, the senator from New York state; and Burr spoke about a young Quaker widow for Madison to meet.

The young woman was Dolley Payne Todd, 25, shapely, brunette and trim in Quaker gray and white cap, with a lawn kerchief folded over her shoulders and pinned across her breasts. Dolley's Quaker lawyer husband, John Todd, and their newborn baby both died in the yellow fever epidemic that swept Philadelphia during the fall of 1793. Now she lived on at Fourth and Walnut Streets with Payne, her two-year-old son. Burr brought James Madison to call on Dolley on a May evening in 1794.

When Senator Burr informed Dolley of the impending call, she was a little flustered. She sent a note to Elizabeth Collins, who had attended her at her marriage to John Todd, saying "Dear Friend Thou must come to me--Aaron Burr says that the great little Madison has asked to be brought to see me this evening."[41] But when Madison came to be introduced she was collected, cool and lovely.

The candle-lit evening went well and Madison was enchanted. He learned that Dolley had grown up in Virginia, a cousin of Patrick Henry. Her sister Lucy had just married George Washington's nephew (over the objections of the sisters' mother, who did not want her children to marry out of meeting). Dolley's family had lived on the Scotchtown plantation in Hanover County, three miles from Cedar Creek Friends' Meeting and not fifty miles from the Madisons' Montpelier. Her father and mother, John and Mary Payne, both had been Cedar Creek's clerks. The Paynes moved to Philadelphia when Dolley was 15, having freed their slaves in Virginia ("I am persuaded that liberty is the natural condition of all mankind," John Payne wrote on the manumission papers) and then found it impossible to keep the plantation going.

On his next visit James Madison came a-courting. Within a month or two he asked Dolley to marry him. She said "no" at first, being not quite recovered from her husband's death; not wanting to disappoint her mother and the Friends of Pine Street Meeting by marrying one of the world's people. John Todd her husband and John Payne her father had been ardent members of the Pennsylvania Abolition Society, and Dolley may have been put off a bit when Madison told her he owned more than a hundred slaves.

But he was persistent and persuasive. That August Dolley and James Madison became engaged.

Dolley married James October 1794 at Harewood, the home of George Steptoe and Lucy Payne Washington, near Charlestown, Virginia (now West Virginia). It was an Episcopalian ceremony, the Reverend Mr. Balmain officiating; but Dolley married in her Quaker gray. She continued to wear Quaker dress for years thereafter although she had been automatically disowned by Pine Street Meeting upon her marriage. On one of their first holidays she and James rode from Montpelier to visit Cedar Creek.[42]

As Mrs. James Madison, Dolley turned out to be the perfect wife for a man in politics. She charmed people with directness and friendliness. The Quaker idea that everyone is a valuable being was implicit with her. In 1801, when newly elected President Jefferson called James Madison to Washington to be Secretary of State, Dolley charmed Jefferson. Jefferson, a widower, almost always called on Dolley to be the hostess at White House dinners. Mrs. Anthony Merry, wife of the British ambassador, criticized Dolley's state dinner arrangements as being like "harvest home suppers"; but few others objected to her style of hospitality.[43]

The Madisons lived at 1333 F Street Northwest while James was Secretary of State. Their home was quasi-Quaker, a compromise between James and Dolley's backgrounds. Dolley's mother, Mary Coles Payne who was a devout and sprightly Friend, lived with the Madisons in Washington.[44] Quaker Doctor William Thornton and his young wife Anna Maria were next-door neighbors. James and Dolley entertained such Quaker visitors as Robert Sutcliff from England. George Logan, the Quaker-born senator from Pennsylvania, met often with James Madison to counsel peaceful ways for dealing with Britain and France and to argue against the death penalty. George Logan had worshipped with the Payne family in Philadelphia Friends' meetings. He wrote home to his wife Deborah, "Dolley looks extremely well."[45]

Dolley wore Quaker attire at home in Washington--a dark graystuff dress with snowy cap and apron and modest kerchief.[46] In public, however, she wore increasingly stylish clothing--costumes of the Empire period, sky-blue, peach-bloom, chartreuse and white, with high waists, narrow skirts, hair bands, turbans, ringleted hair, heeled slippers, elaborate jewelry. After one White House occasion an eager miss wrote in from the country "Do tell me, cousin, what dress she wore." "Well, let me think," came the reply. "She had on her head a turban of white satin with three ostrich feathers hanging over her face very becoming indeed! Her dress, too, of white satin made high in the neck with long sleeves and large capes trimmed with swan's down was rich and beautiful...." At such times, too, Dolley carried an enamelled snuff box and cultivated the stylish snuff-sniffing habit. She took to playing loo, a ladies' card game.[47]

These worldly leanings concerned Dolley's mother and Dolley's old Quaker friends. When she visited Philadelphia in 1805 to see Dr. Physick about her ailing knee, two Quaker women called to remonstrate with Dolley. One was Nancy Mifflin, Warner Mifflin's widow and an exceedingly plain Friend who wore undyed clothing; the other, Sally Zane, the sister of Virginia's Isaac Zane, Jr. Their criticism, Dolley wrote, brought back "the times when our Society used to control me entirely and debar me from *so* many advantages and pleasures.... I really felt my ancient terror...revive."[48]

Nevertheless, when the Madisons moved in to the White House in 1809, Dolley continued to wear her graystuff dress and white kerchief at breakfast, with only her diamond engagement ring for jewelry. She no longer wore a Quaker cap but the rest of her Quaker garb remained.[49] That April she went to hear Stephen Grellet, a well-known Friends' traveler in the ministry. Stephen Grellet noted "At Washington City--my holy Helper strengthened me.... D. Madison, the President's wife, and her sister who were at meeting, appeared tender and invited me to go and see them. They were formerly members of our Society."[50] Quaker-like, Dolley was one of the founders of the Washington Orphans' Asylum.[51]

In June of 1812 she received a letter from a friend of her Philadelphia girlhood --Sally McKean D'Yrujo, now wife of a Spanish diplomat. "I am just as giddy and full of spirits as ever," Sally D'Yrujo wrote. "Indeed I am for the French principle, never to let anything trouble me much unless it is absolutely necessary."[52] That letter spoke to Dolley's worldly side.

To the other, Quakerly, side in 1813 came a visit from Rebecca Hubbs, a Friends' minister of Piles Grove, New Jersey. Rebecca was 41, Dolley 45 that year. As she set out from home to visit southern Friends, Rebecca felt "an apprehension that it was required of [me] to visit the President of the U.S." She and her companion Susan Scull visited some of the Virginia meetings. Then "way was made through the kindness of Micajah Crew of Cedar Creek Meeting," who had known Dolley's parents, for Rebecca and Sarah to visit the Madisons at Montpelier. There "the President and his wife received them very kindly and had a solid and satisfactory religious opportunity with them.... They parted with many tokens of affectionate regard. The President insisted on serving them with some refreshment and, following them to the carriage, placed in it some articles which he thought would be useful to them in their journey."[53]

Rebecca Hubbs wrote Dolley a thank-you note which suggests simultaneously that she had been caught by Dolley's famous friendliness and also dismayed by Montpelier's elaborate furnishings and its hundred slaves: "Dear friend...My soul's desire for thee is that thou may more and more come out of all that cumbers the earth...to war against vanity, pleasure, ambition and avarice, and to put from thee all the fading pleasures of this world.... Prize the crown immortal."[54]

As Secretary of State and then as President, James Madison behaved in ways that suggest his wife's Quakerly influence:

- He counseled the "peaceful coercion" foreign policy pursued during Jefferson's presidency, and he did his best in his own presidency to keep the United States at peace with France and Britain by diplomatic, non-violent means.
- In the Executive Office he received Paul Cuffey, a black sea captain and an elder of the Friends' meeting in New Bedford, Massachusetts. Captain Cuffey's ship was refused clearance out of Hampton Roads, whereupon he came overland to Washington and demanded to see the president. "James, I have been put to much trouble and have been abused," Cuffey said, even before Madison invited him to sit down. "I have come here for thy protection and have to ask thee to order thy collector for the port of Norfolk to clear me out for New Bedford." President Madison granted this request at once.[55]
- He also received Jesse Kersey, 46, a Friend of Chester County, Pennsylvania, who came to speak for the slaves. Madison, slave-holder though he was, talked with Friend Kersey seriously. Kersey asked the president what he thought about an idea being promoted by Paul Cuffey to send the slaves to Africa and help them establish colonies there. Madison said he thought that would be difficult. The only remedy he could see was to free them and spread them "among industrious and practical farmers."[56]

Ill feeling between Great Britain and the United States grew up despite Jefferson's and Madison's efforts for peace. The same kinds of incidents that cause all wars occurred: British war ships stopped American ships at sea and impressed American seamen--rumors circulated that British agents were stirring up the Indians--"War Hawks" in the U.S. Congress prophesied that a little military action would enable the United States to take over Canada. So the United States declared war in June of 1812.

When the District of Columbia's militia mobilized, an 18-year-old Quaker, Edward Stabler III of Alexandria Meeting, refused to join up. He was accordingly locked in the Alexandria jail. Young Edward's mother was Deborah Pleasants Stabler who had been a Quaker playmate of Dolley Payne Madison's in the old Virginia days. Deborah sent a note across the Potomac to Dolley in the White House about her boy's plight, whereupon Edward was soon released. When Deborah Stabler called at the White House later, Dolley told how the release had come about. "I tell thee, Debby, I gave Jimmy no rest until he ordered Edward's release!"[57]

In the summer of 1813 it was rumored that the British planned to sack Washington. Dolley wrote to her cousin Edward Coles:

> For the last week all the city and Georgetown (except the Cabinet) have expected a visit from the enemy...We are making a considerable effort for defense....[I} have always been an advocate for fighting when assailed, though a Quaker. I therefore keep the old Tunisian sabre within reach.[58]

In the heat of August 1814 the British suddenly appeared outside Washington to make good the threat. Dolley took charge of the White House while the President rode out with the defending U. S. troops to Bladensburg, Md. She stayed on while thuds of cannon fire ominously grew louder, loading state papers and valuables into a wagon. "Two gentlemen from New York," one of whom was Quaker Jacob Barker, helped her and urged her for pity's sake to hurry. At the last moment they cut the Stuart painting of George Washington out of its frame. Dolley entrusted that "precious portrait" to Friend Barker and his companion. Then she fled south down 14th Street her wagon trailing dust, over the Long Bridge and into Virginia. British soldiers set fire to the Capitol and the White House soon afterward.

President Madison spent two frantic days in the saddle while the British fought their way into Washington. He rode a tall gray mare, with a red-white-and-blue cockade on his hat. On the third day he and his Attorney General, Richard Rush, rode to Brookville--the Maryland Quakers' settlement north of Washington and near Sandy Spring Meeting House. They went to the home of Quaker miller Caleb Bentley and asked his daughter Henrietta for help. Henrietta is said to have replied "It's against our principles to have anything to do with war, but we receive and relieve all who come to us."⁵⁹ Madison and Rush stayed three days with the Bentleys until it was safe to return to Washington.*

The Madisons retired from the presidency to Montpelier in 1817. James, then 66, and Dolley lived happily with him at Montpelier till his death at 85. In 1837, the year following James's death she returned to Washington and lived on Lafayette Square.

Through all these years the tension in her life continued between elegant society lady and plain Quaker-born woman. After returning to Washington she attended a White House reception in an evening gown that bared her shoulders. Benjamin Hallowell, the Quaker schoolmaster of Alexandria, was there in Quaker gray but without his hat--which some Quaker men still wore, indoors and out, on public occasions. Dolley raised her wineglass to Benjamin and said gaily, "Here's to thy absent broad brim, Friend Hallowell." To which Benjamin replied with a stately twinkle, "And here's to thy absent kerchief, Friend Dorothy!"⁶⁰

When she was 77, Dolley joined St. John's Church on Lafayette Square; but to the end her friends spoke of the Quakerly touch in her bearing. Two who attended her funeral when she died at 81 were Quaker friends present at her marriage to John Todd sixty years before--Anthony Morris of Philadelphia, and the other Elizabeth Collins Lee who received Dolley's note that day in May 1794 when Dolley was about to meet James Madison: "Dear Friend--Thou must come to me...."

* * *

Jefferson and Madison were not Virginia's only capable leaders in the early 1800s. James Monroe, governor from 1799 to 1802, went on to be the Nation's president. John Tyler, Sr., who became governor in 1808, was an able man and father of a future president. Nevertheless, the state did not prosper. Northern Virginia around Alexandria did thrive after the Nation's capital moved right across the Potomac, and the hamlet of Charlottesville

---

* Historians never have explained how it was that the President took shelter with the Brookville Quakers. A clue: Dolley was friendly from girlhood with Elizabeth Brook of Brookville, who was cousin to Caleb Bentley's wife, nee Sarah Brook. President Madison and Dolley may have visited the Brooks of Brookville earlier and he may have come to share Dolley's friendly relationship with them.

leaped ahead when the University of Virginia materialized in 1819. But those were bright spots and exceptions.

Whittlers on the porches of Virginia's country stores advanced various reasons for the malaise of those years:
- Some said tobacco had worn out the land. This *was* part of the trouble, for countless "old fields" were to be seen, formerly tobacco land where now only sedge and cedars grew.
- Others blamed the departure of so many good neighbors, moved away to the south and west, and this surely was a drain.
- The Panic of 1819 hurt the whole nation. It was America's first great economic depression and store porch whittlers everywhere were mystified. Many turned to the supernatural for an explanation--God must be angry, they ruminated.[61]

The big reason for Virginia's static state, however, was the omnipresence of slavery. The slaves were a constant topic of conversation around the general stores and everywhere white Virginians congregated: church yards, courthouses, taverns. The story is told of a plantation house slave cook and her husband the butler, serving dinner on an evening when there were guests. "What are they talking about?" asked the cook in the kitchen as she helped her husband fill his tray with desserts. "Us! Talking about us!" he replied.

A dreaded thing had happened in 1800. That spring a slave in Hanover County instigated a rebellion. He was Gabriel, a mightily muscled 23-year-old blacksmith on Tom Prosser's plantation. The plantation lay on the road from Richmond to Louisa Courthouse (now Route 33) and not far from the Cedar Creek Friends' meeting house. Prosser had a reputation for brutality. Gabriel had lost two front teeth and was scarred about the head. But someone--probably Prosser's mother--taught Gabriel to read and write.

Gabriel mulled his plan while he swung the hammer at Prosser's anvil. Then he took counsel with his brother Solomon and with Ben, his neighbor in the slave quarters. The three men were allowed to make trips into Richmond. There in the town's back streets they recruited black men for "a society to fight white people for their freedom." From Richmond, membership in Gabriel's society spread to Petersburg, to Hanover Town and Charlottesville, and down the James River to Suffolk and Norfolk.

The rebellion was to begin Saturday night, August 30, on Prosser's plantation. They would kill Prosser first and then march on Richmond behind Gabriel. He would carry a flag lettered "Death or Liberty."[62]

All whites along the way were to be killed, except Quakers, Methodists, and French people. They were to be spared "because they believe in liberty."

Poor whites with no slaves would be spared too. They were expected to join the rebellion.

The plan did not work. A summer thunderstorm that Saturday dampened everything. Two of Mosby Sheppard's slaves reported the plan and Sheppard went straight to Governor James Monroe in Richmond. At first the Governor discounted the report; but reports kept reaching him on Sunday that Negroes were streaming *out* of Richmond contrary to their usual Sunday custom of coming *in* to town. Tuesday, September 2, Monroe met with the city council, called out the militia and ordered the arrest of all slaves acting suspiciously. Richmond city jail was jammed with suspects and the overflow was locked up in the new penitentiary. Some scythe blades honed by slaves as weapons were found.

The suspects were interrogated and forced to tell what they knew, and what they told was frightening. "It is clear" Governor Monroe reported to the Senate

> that a general insurrection was contemplated.... The plan of attack on the city was to commence by setting fire to the lower part where the houses are constructed of wood.... The slaves were well-organized with a commander [Gabriel] to whom they gave the title of 'General'.... While the attention of the people were attracted to the lower part of the town...they were to seize the magazine, the penitentiary, the Capitol, get possession of the arms and meet the unarmed citizens on their return.[63]

These disclosures triggered lightning action in the State's courts. Some twenty-seven conspirators were hanged, and others sold to the deep South. Gabriel nearly escaped by hurrying to Varina where someone smuggled him aboard the schooner *Mary* at anchor in Four Mile Creek where it enters the James.[64] Curles Meeting House stood nearby, and Quakers and former slaves freed by Quakers lived all around. What help they gave Gabriel will never be known. But Gabriel was recognized when the *Mary* reached Hampton Roads. He was arrested there and died among the twenty-seven.

Gabriel's Rebellion brutalized the attitude of white toward black Virginians. The argument of the Quakers and of democrats like Thomas Jefferson that blacks are humans too, lost much of its force. The Federalists, who were the conservatives of 1800, intimated that Gabriel and his rebels were egged on by hearing the democrats' rant about "Equality, Fraternity and

Human Rights." Indeed the editor of the *Virginia Herald* questioned the whole doctrine of human rights. He wrote on September 25:

> It has been most impudently propagated for several years, at our tables while our servants were standing behind our chairs. It has been preached from the pulpits, Methodists and Baptists alike without reserve. Democrats have talked it. What else could we expect except what has happened?

> There can be no compromise between liberty and slavery. The man who thinks so is a fool.... If we will keep a ferocious monster in our country, we must keep him in chains. No one would turn a lion or a tiger out in the streets.... Democracy, therefore, in Virginia is like virtue in Hell.[65]

So it was that the Assembly meeting in 1801 considered tough new laws affecting Virginia's 346,000 black residents. A law was passed to restrict their movements, and a public guard of sixty-eight men was established in Richmond to enforce the restrictions.[66] Another law was proposed to forbid the "common practice in many places" of allowing slaves to gather "at meetinghouses and places of public worship." A remarkable letter opposing this law appeared in the *Virginia Argus* signed by "A Friend to Religious Freedom."[67] The publisher of the twice-weekly *Argus* was Samuel Pleasants, an attender of Richmond Friends Meeting although not a very faithful one. Quite likely this letter was written by Samuel Pleasants or some Richmond Friend. Nevertheless, the proposal to keep slaves out of meeting houses and churches passed into law in 1804. It was amended in 1805 to permit slaveowners to bring their slaves "to any places whatever for religious worship" so long as that worship was conducted by "a regularly ordained or licensed white minister."

Still a third proposal brought up in 1801 was to repeal the Manumission Act engineered by Virginia's Friends in 1782. The Act of 1782 had resulted in a great increase in the number of freed blacks in Virginia--from less than 3,000 in 1782 to more than 20,000 in 1801. This repeal proposal, too, became law in 1806. No slaves thereafter freed were to be allowed to remain in Virginia. The legislatures of Kentucky, Maryland and Delaware promptly passed similar laws.[68]

The Rebellion also put an end to the Virginia Abolition Society. That society had been sending delegates regularly to the annual gatherings in Philadelphia of the American Convention of Abolition Societies. But John

Fairlamb who represented Virginia in 1801 reported that Gabriel's Rebellion "has reduced our Society to a languid and critical situation," and the Virginia society was not heard from thereafter.

All was not lost in those years, however. Many Friends in Virginia still contended stubbornly for the slaves. Virginia Yearly Meeting in 1801 urged Friends to speak of "black people" instead of "negroes," since "negro" has a slurring, de-humanizing connotation. In Henrico County, Friends kept the Gravelly Hill School for the children of freed blacks, and at Goose Creek Meeting in Loudoun County, black children attended the Meeting's school along with the white Quaker children--both schools being unique in Virginia and scandalous in the eyes of neighboring slave-owners.[69]

Andrew McKay of Crooked Run Meeting in Warren County left money "to aid in the emancipation of persons unlawfully held in bondage."[70] In other counties across the State, Friends brought law suits against slave dealers who meddled with freed black people or tried to enslave Indians.[71]

After the demise of Virginia's Abolition Society in 1801, the American Convention consisted of eleven abolition societies all sited in northern states. Quakers led in the activities of these societies. Senator George Logan of Pennsylvania--he was the first U. S. senator to affirm Quaker-style when it came time for him to be sworn as a new senator--read a petition from the American Convention on the Senate floor. It asked that importation of slaves into the new Louisiana Territory be prohibited by law. After bitter debate the Senate voted 21 to 7 to adopt the petition, thus strengthening the Free Soil Movement which began when slavery was prohibited outright in the Northwest Territory.[72] Quakers everywhere rejoiced.

John Taylor of Caroline, Virginia politician and slave holder who had Quaker neighbors, was bemused by such an attitude. "And yet an amiable and peaceable religious sect," he wrote in the *Arator*, "have been long laboring with some success to plunge three-fourths of a nation into a civil war...."[73]

\* \* \*

President Jefferson reminded Congress that the Constitution allowed for ending the African slave trade in 1808. Congress accordingly passed an act prohibiting imports of more slaves,[74] and this was greeted by Friends as a step toward abolishing slavery. In Virginia, however, the prohibition brought evil results.

At that time, 1808, there were some 1,190,000 slaves in the United States, of whom 390,000 or one-third lived in Virginia. Virginia was by far the largest slave state, followed by South Carolina with about 145,000 slaves.[75] So, with the flow of slaves from Africa cut off, the states to the south turned to Virginia as their main slave source.[76] This created a bonanza for Virginia's planters, and slaveselling became big business in Virginia. Slave merchants turned houses in Alexandria, south Richmond, and other Virginia towns into slave pens surrounded by high fences. Franklin and Armfield, slavedealers in Alexandria, shipped 1,000 to 1,200 slaves south each year, netting a princely income, about $33,000 a year.[77]

Now the sight of slaves herded south, the sight that revolted little Botts Walthall, became common. Often the slaves were driven in coffles, coupled two abreast, and locked to a long chain running between the couples. The clank of coffle chains was heard of nights along Virginia's roads south into the Carolinas. Knowledge of the coffles' fate heightened the dismal effect-- for slavery on the rice and cotton plantations of the deep South usually meant unremitting drudgery, short and mean lives under the lash.

Some Virginians quickly became calloused to the new development, others became uneasy, and others appalled:

- Baptists and Presbyterians, to judge by their official pronouncements, were unmoved.
- Virginia's Methodists became uneasy. They voted at their State Conference of 1813 that any member "guilty of carrying on...the trade of slave speculation...shall be expelled from the Church." In 1817 they voted "that the members of our Church shall not buy or sell any slave [except] for the express purpose of keeping husbands and wives, parents and children together, or from principles of humanity."[78]
- John Randolph of Roanoke (1773-1833) was visibly moved. This remarkable man, a spider-thin bachelor with a clear soprano voice, represented Virginia in the U. S. House of Representatives for most of 34 years. He spoke on the House floor soon after Gabriel's Rebellion to denounce any effort to abolish slavery. By 1811, however, Washington, D. C., and Alexandria had become headquarters for slave traders. Randolph then made another House speech, calling the new traffic "heinous and abominable, inhuman and illegal."[79]

Now Randolph of Roanoke was a major slaveholder, but in his youth, 1790 to 1794, he lived in Philadelphia where he came under some Quakerly influence (Philadelphia was then the Nation's Capital, and he lived there while studying law under cousin Edmond Randolph, the U. S. Attorney General.) Later he wrote that he had been "brought up among Quakers, an ardent *ami des noirs*." Sometime about 1811, he told Senator George Logan he had read Barclay's *Apology*, and confided to Jesse Kersey, a Friends minister who visited Washington in 1814, "I've been converted."[80] In 1822 he sought out Elizabeth Fry in London, introducing himself as "a friend of Jesse Kersey."[81] He died in Philadelphia, probably of tuberculosis, under the care of Dr. Joseph Parrish, a Quaker and an abolitionist. On his death bed, John Randolph again declared himself to be a friend of the blacks.[82] He owned 385 black slaves at his death and freed them by his will.

- Dr. Elisha Dick--the fashionable physician of Alexandria who petitioned the Virginia legislature in 1795 to outlaw Virginia's abolition societies--was appalled by the slave trade. In 1811 he resigned from Christ Church, Alexandria, joined Alexandria Friends' Meeting[83] and engaged in the work of ending slavery.

\* \* \*

For many years before 1808, various people had discussed "sending them back to Africa" as a solution to the slave problem. British Quakers and others established a colony in Sierra Leone on Africa's west coast in 1787 for that purpose; and among the first colonists were seventy from Tortola in the Virgin Islands. They were ex-slaves inherited and then freed by William Thornton (1761-1820) of Tortola Friends Meeting.

This is the same William Thornton who was to serve as Commissioner of Patents under Thomas Jefferson and who was James and Dolley Madison's neighbor on F Street in Washington. He was a medical doctor trained in Edinburgh. Soon after sending his slaves to Sierra Leone he came from Tortola to the United States where he began a colorful career which had little to do with medicine. In 1793 he won a competition for the best plan for the U. S. Capitol. The prize was $500 plus a building lot in the as-yet-unbuilt city of Washington. He and his bride Anna Maria had one of Washington's first houses built on the lot.[84]

In 1804 Dr. Thornton wrote a pamphlet proposing a colony in Africa for free blacks of the United States. The idea hung fire until 1810 or so when the up-springing of the brutal slave trade from Virginia south jogged many consciences. In 1813 the black Quaker sea captain Paul Cuffey sailed thirty-eight freed blacks from Boston to Sierra Leone aboard his brig *The*

*Traveller.*[85] In December 1816, Virginia's legislature requested Governor James Preston to write the President with a view to acquiring an asylum "for such persons of color as are now free [or] that may be hereafter emancipated in Virginia." Almost immediately a number of leading citizens met in the Hall of the U. S. House of Representatives to advance the idea. Henry Clay presided, and Daniel Webster, Francis Scott Key, Bushrod Washington of the Supreme Court, and Dr. Thornton were there. Virginians present included Bishop Meade, John Randolph of Roanoke, and John Taylor of Caroline. Out of this meeting came the American Colonization Society.

Many Friends at first supported the "ACS" and some kept on supporting it for many years. But the enthusiasm of most soon cooled. For one thing the Society's leaders, excepting Dr. Thornton, were slaveowners who showed no interest in abolishing slavery. The society did nothing at all to abate the selling of slaves to the South. The Baltimore Quaker editor Hezekiah Niles reported in *Niles' Register* in 1830:

> Dealing in slaves has become a large business. Establishments are made at several places in Maryland and Virginia at which they are sold like cattle. These places of deposit are strongly built, well-supplied with iron thumbscrews and gags and ornamented with cowskins and other whips often-times bloody.[86]

The American Colonization Society did send 1,420 freed black people back to Africa between 1817 and 1830[87] and did establish the Republic of Liberia there. One of Liberia's lieutenant-governors was a man named Richardson from Hanover County. He ascribed his freedom to the efforts of Nathaniel Crenshaw of Cedar Creek Friends' Meeting.[88]

* * *

In that eventful year of 1808 Benjamin Lundy, 19, arrived in Wheeling, to be a saddle-maker's apprentice. He was a slight and unassuming young Friend, raised in Rahway, New Jersey. He joined the little Friends' meeting begun by the Zanes, and he saw his first slave coffle in Wheeling. He wrote:

> This is the place, where my youthful eye first caught a view of the cursed whip and hellish manacle; where I first saw slaves in chains forced along like brutes to the Southern markets...droves of a dozen or 20 ragged men, chained together and driven through the streets bareheaded and barefooted in mud and snow.[89]

Benjamin completed his apprenticeship in 1814. He moved across the Ohio River to St. Clairsville and married young Esther Lewis, just come to Ohio with her parents from Hopewell Meeting in Virginia. Then he organized the Union Humane Society, dedicated to the abolition of slavery. Nearly five hundred people joined, including many Friends from Virginia recently moved to Ohio. Thereafter he, Benjamin Lundy, gave himself passionately to the anti-slavery cause.

He closed his saddle shop in 1817 and joined two other Friends just arrived in Ohio in a printing business in Mt. Pleasant: Elisha Bates, 36, an ex school master and former clerk of Virginia Yearly Meeting; and Charles Osborne, 42, a Friends' minister from Tennessee. The three men together got out a monthly paper called *The Philanthropist*, devoted the slave question. The three enjoyed working together, but differences developed. Osborne condemned the American Colonization Society as a clever device to quiet slaveholders' consciences, while Lundy hoped for some time that the society would be a force in destroying slavery. Osborne and Lundy supported the Free Produce Movement which meant abstaining from buying anything made with slave labor, while Bates couldn't see it.[90]

So after two years Charles Osborne moved on west to the new town of Richmond, Indiana; and Benjamin Lundy began to publish his own newspaper. Its masthead:

> The Genius of Universal Emancipation
> containing
> Original Essays and Selections
> on the subject of
> African Slavery
>
> Benjamin Lundy, Editor
>
> We hold these truths to be self-evident
> that all men are created equal.
> -- The Declaration of Independence

After a few issues in Mt. Pleasant Benjamin moved to Greeneville, Tennessee just south of the Virginia line. There he took over the press of Elihu Embree, a recently deceased Friend who had been publishing *The Emancipator* in Greeneville. But Tennessee was slave country and publishing an anti-slavery paper there was difficult. In the summer of 1824 Benjamin moved again, this time to Baltimore. He traveled on foot through North Carolina and across Virginia to Baltimore, stopping here and there to give talks in meeting houses and churches. He organized "12 or 14" anti-slavery societies in North Carolina. Then he "entered Virginia and travelled through the middle section of that state, holding numerous meetings and effecting the organization of several anti-slavery societies."[91]

These Lundy-inspired anti-slavery societies were the first in Virginia since 1801 when hostile laws snuffed out the Virginia Abolition Society. Considering the temper of the times, the success of Benjamin Lundy that summer--a sunburned hiker over Virginia's long dusty roads--is miraculous. Two of the societies he organized despite Virginia's laws were the Manumission and Emigration Society of Loudoun and the Alexandria Benevolent Society. Samuel McPherson Janney, a 23-year-old Alexandria Friend, was prominent in the Benevolent Society.[92]

Once in Baltimore, Friends helped Benjamin and Esther Lundy and their three children to find lodgings. Esther was worn out from trying to keep her husband's pace. She bore twins after arriving in Baltimore but died during their birth, at the age of 33.[93] Benjamin grieved for a time, then found a home for his children with relatives in Lowell, Illinois, and continued on. The circulation of the *Genius of Universal Emancipation* grew, and the paper became a weekly from a monthly in 1825. Benjamin announced proudly in the issue of 26 Eleventh Month 1826, that there were now one hundred anti-slavery societies in the United States, including seventy-three located in the slave states[94] (six of them in Virginia).

\* \* \*

The Friendly Virginians worked on into the 1830s for the black people around them. Virginia Yearly Meeting received $1,159.82 from London Friends to help with the education of blacks,[95] and the Friends' school at Gravelly Hill, Hanover County, for free black children continued strong-- although a Quaker man and wife were jailed for keeping a similar school in Richmond in 1820 which may have enrolled a few *slave* children.[96] When a Greenville County farmer freed his slaves without providing any way for them to get out of Virginia, the Yearly Meeting appointed three Friends who found new homes for them outside Virginia before they were "again reduced to slavery."[97]

James Pleasants (1769-1836), who was raised a Virginia Friend, was elected the state's governor, 1822 to 1825. He was an advocate of fair treatment for freed blacks.[98] Shortly before James Pleasants was elected,

Virginia Yearly Meeting petitioned the legislature to relax the law requiring freed blacks to leave the State. This petition was turned down cold. In 1828, however, the Friends of Hopewell Meeting petitioned again, and this time the "leave the State" law was relaxed.[99]

Such Friendly efforts benefited Virginia's freed blacks, but did nothing to help enslaved blacks. They now were being sold south from Virginia by the thousands. Nothing *legally* could be done for slaves, for Virginia's Assembly by the 1820s was firmly, callously committed to the institution of slavery. And now there appeared certain whiffs and whisperings, hints and clues that a few Virginia Friends were doing a few *illegal* things on behalf of a few slaves: namely and to wit, helping them to leave their owners and escape to the North.

Always before, Friends' disobedience to man-made law had been public and openly avowed, while this business of helping slaves to flee was in secret.[100] Here was a dilemma that caused Friends to wrestle with their consciences.

The first-known mention of this kind of activity comes in a letter from George Washington to Robert Morris, written April 1786, about some Philadelphia Quakers who were harboring slaves. This "society of Quakers in the city (formed for such purposes)" is illegal, Washington complained, "when slaves who are happy and contented with their present masters are tampered with and seduced to leave them."[101] The complaint was echoed by Senator William Loughton Smith of South Carolina in 1790. He complained on the Senate floor that a South Carolina gentleman could hardly bring servants to New York or Philadelphia without having them induced to run away by Quakers.[102]

One Philadelphia Quaker who succored slaves was Isaac T. Hopper (1771-1852), a plain Friend in knee-breeches who resembled the Emperor Napoleon. From 1797 on Isaac Hopper received, hid and passed on to the North escaping slaves. One Virginia slave trader who came to Philadelphia after an escaped slave woman upbraided Isaac Hopper for helping her to get away. "I hope I may live to see you south of the Potomac some day," the trader said. "Thou'd better go home and repent of sins already committed, instead of meditating the commission of more," Isaac replied.[103]

The first suggestion of activity *in the South* to help escaping slaves came in 1805. That year Sally Bell of Virginia's Richmond Meeting, the wife of Nathan, inherited seventy-five to one hundred slaves. She freed them legally, and then sent them north in wagons to settle near the Quaker settlement of Wright's Ferry, Pennsylvania, on the Susquehanna River. Soon after it was rumored that slaves were escaping out of Virginia to Wright's Ferry. The rumor was true, and William Wright was a leader among the Quakers there helping the incoming slaves.[104]

In 1819 Vestal Coffin and his sons Levi and Addison, Quakers of Greensboro, North Carolina began to escort groups of escaping slaves from North Carolina to Ohio, taking them right across southwest Virginia: Across Dan River near Stuart into Virginia, then west to Hillsville where Vestal's brother-in-law Seth Stanley had a farm. On over Clinch Mountain, follow New River and the Kanawha through grand mountain scenery clear to the Ohio River. Cross to free soil at Gallipolis.[105]

\* \* \*

From the remote shadows of history up to forever, in Virginia and everywhere, humankind has tried to figure out the mysterious universe. What does it mean and how does it work? Obviously there is a plan, seemingly imperfect but a plan: The stars wheel in their courses, there are exactly twenty-four hours every day, lovers fall in love and attractive babies appear on cue. What Power plans such marvels? What place have *I* in the plan?

Most people past and present look for the answers from a priest, preacher, pastor or shaman; some wiser expert who interprets and mediates for the rest, standing on a platform or in a pulpit poised between the congregation of men and women below and heaven above. This mode can be called the *outward* way to worship.

In various times and places, however, there have been a few people who seek the answers and find their way themselves, meeting themselves together, waiting for guidance from the still small voice within, with no professional leader. Such people trust that all have some inborn power to find the way without a middle man, some guiding faculty along with one's five rational senses. Such people are the seekers who follow the *inward* way.

In Virginia about the only people worshiping by the inward way were-- and are --the Friends or Quakers.

Only one person in a thousand or two or three or four thousand is attracted to the inward way as the Friendly Virginians followed and follow it. Quakers exclude ritual and pomp, stained glass and robes, prayer books and hymnals, all *theater* from their gatherings. Their meeting rooms are deliberately plain and simple. Nothing in them distracts the gathered worshipers from inward guidance. Most new visitors find the waiting silence- -"Be still and know that I am God"--meaningless or even unendurable. Even if one can cope with the silence, it is unsettling to find one's way with no guru for a guide.

The outward way to find God received a mighty push forward through the preaching of George Whitefield and John Wesley in America and in England. These two eloquent men gave definition and appeal to "Evangelical Christianity." Before their coming "Evangelism" usually meant preaching based on the *Bible*. But Whitefield and Wesley gave a new focus to the word. They made *Evangelical* mean a kind of Christianity founded on the *historical person* of Jesus Christ. Eternal life can be gained through a publicly expressed *belief* in Jesus Christ as Lord and Savior. To be "Evangelical," they also declared, one must see oneself as depraved, a sinner. A person can be saved by acknowledging Jesus' sacrifice on The Cross. The *Bible*, they asserted, is the Word of God, miraculously transmitted to humanity. Supplying all truth about spiritual matters that anyone needs or ever will need. And furthermore, all that ever can be procured.

Evangelicals, then, hold to the outward way, Friends to the inward. The two approaches differ in certain interesting details:

- Christian theologians conceive that God has three aspects--God as the Father (in Heaven), God as the Son (Jesus Christ), and God as the Holy Ghost or Holy Spirit. Evangelical Christians put emphasis on the Father and Son aspects, while Friends emphasize the Holy Spirit aspect of God's being.
- Instead of seeing people as born sinners, Friends optimistically view all as children of God, each born with some thing of God within. The great object is to live by the guidance of God's Light, not turning from the Light to darkness.
- Instead of seeing the *Bible* as the final word in spiritual matters, Friends hold that the Holy Spirit is still available, speaking to us by the still small voice, within.
- The great *Bible* verse for Evangelicals is John 3:16, which emphasizes <u>believing</u> in Jesus Christ; while the "Quaker verse" is John 15:14, which puts emphasis on <u>doing</u> God's will.

Whitefield and Wesley gave Evangelical Christianity a terrific new emotional appeal. Revival meetings and altar calls were part of their evangelical plan. Denominations that fully adopted revival methods grew to be giants after 1800. The Methodists and Baptists leaped ahead in Virginia. Presbyterians gained, too, but "old side" resistance to emotional revivals inhibited the Presbyterians and they fell behind in comparative membership.

Even the Episcopalians went evangelical. The Diocese of Virginia was almost dead by 1811 when William Meade (1789-1862) was ordained. Each Episcopal church in Virginia before the Revolutionary War had a "glebe," that is to say a dwelling house and 250 acres of land more or less, where the minister lived. All these glebes were sold by the Commonwealth after the Act for Religious Freedom became law. The proceeds went to support the poor--some to build poorhouses, and most to establish a "Literary Fund" which supported schools for poor children.

With government support gone, many of the Diocese of Virginia's churches were abandoned and others became sparsely attended. William Meade and his colleagues then revived the Diocese by introducing--in Meade's words--"methods of action...entirely different...from those by which the disgrace and downfall of the Church had been wrought." The new methods involved preaching on the theme of "Jesus Christ and Him Crucified." The depravity of human nature, the yawning pit of hell, the sacrifice of the Crucifixion, Christ as the only means of salvation, rebirth through belief in the historical Christ, the perfection of the Holy Scriptures-- all these became theological bases for rebuilding Virginia's mother church. The Episcopalian leadership stopped short of methods designed to produce hysterical excitement. Yet under the new evangelical preaching, the pews of Virginia's Episcopal churches gradually refilled.[107]

A few worshipers swam against the evangelical wave. They included the Unitarians whose movement developed in New England as an off-shoot of the Enlightenment and as a protest against the Puritan point-of-view. God's greatest gift is reason, the Unitarian ministers proclaimed. Reason and common sense will see us through. The congregation of King's Chapel in Boston was the first in America to adopt the Unitarian view in 1796. Unitarian churches appeared in Philadelphia in 1813; Baltimore and Charleston, 1817; and Washington, 1820. John Quincy Adams, the U. S. Secretary of State, and John C. Calhoun, Secretary of War, were charter members of Washington's Unitarian church. In Virginia Thomas Jefferson was the great friend of Unitarianism.

But in Virginia by 1820 most church-goers viewed evangelicalism as the only true form of Christianity.

\* \* \*

John Greenleaf Whittier wrote in his poem about George Whitefield, that "The Quaker kept the way of his own--A non-conductor among the wires, with coat of asbestos proof to fires." Meaning that Friends were not swayed by Whitefield and Wesley and evangelicalism. This judgment appears true, nearly up to 1800. But not thereafter.

In Seventh Month 1798, Hannah Jenkins Barnard, 44, a Friends' minister of Hudson Monthly Meeting, New York, traveled to Ireland. Hannah encountered a few Irish Friends who were disturbed over Old Testament stories where God commands the Hebrews to wipe out the Canaanites with the sword, to smite them hip and thigh. The Irish Friends were saying that such stories could not be true, in the *Bible* or not. And Hannah agreed that God would not order people to do things in one age which in another age God's son forbade. God is love. God never could order any nation to start a bloody war. She and her traveling companion, Elizabeth Coggeshall of Rhode Island, left Ireland for London in Fifth Month 1800. The Yearly Meeting of Ministers and Elders for the nation of Ireland endorsed their travel certificate, with thanks for Hannah's services.

In London, however, the two women encountered Friends who had come to agree with John Wesley's evangelical view that the *Bible* is not to be questioned. These London Friends, having heard that Hannah questioned Deuteronomy, were incensed. Hannah declared that she had unbounded confidence in the guidance of the Inward Light even though she had doubts about certain *Bible* stories. This did not sway London Friends. Hannah was officially advised to "desist from preaching and return home." The complaint against her was reported to her home meeting from London, and in Sixth Month 1802, Hannah was disowned by Hudson Monthly Meeting for "deviations."[108]

Hannah Barnard's fate is proof enough that evangelical views had influenced Friends. This influence spread rapidly. In 1806, both Philadelphia and Baltimore Yearly Meetings made it a disownable offense to deny "the authenticity of the Scriptures" or "Christ's divinity." This is the first time in Quaker history that any of the yearly meetings so directly prescribed what a Friend must believe.

* * *

Stephen Grellet and John Hall came down from Philadelphia in the first days of 1800--the first-known Quaker ministers ever to visit the Virginia meetings in a wagon instead of horseback. They rode in a "Jersey Wagon," four-wheeled behind a pair of horses,[109] their luggage joggling behind them in the wagon-bed. Virginia's roads still were rutted, with yawning pot holes and many unbridged creeks to be cautiously forded; but now in 1800, with winter frost in the ground, it was possible to travel off the main roads by wagon.

There were other improvements in Virginia travel about 1800: Richmond, population 5,700, had just acquired stagecoach services connecting with Alexandria, Williamsburg and Petersburg. The mail stage with places for some eight passengers left Alexandria at 4:45 a.m. and rumbled into Fredericksburg about 9 p.m.[110]; in Alexandria citizens were raising funds for Virginia's first toll-road, west from Duke Street in Alexandria to Aldie; and in Loudoun County some farmers were planning a second turnpike from Snicker's Gap in the Blue Ridge to Leesburg and on to Georgetown, D.C.

In 1802 the Potomac Canal opened, linking the Potomac River with the Youghiogheny, which flows into the Ohio and on to the Mississippi River. The "Canal" was really the Potomac River itself, made navigable from Cumberland, Maryland, to Georgetown by five mini-canals which detoured around falls and rapids. It was all planned by the board of directors of the Patowmack Company headed by George Washington. Washington was also president of the James River Company to make the James navigable from Lynchburg to Richmond; and of the Dismal Swamp Canal Company from Hampton Roads to the south.

For twenty-six years the Potomac Canal carried flour, whiskey and pig iron to Georgetown. But the Potomac was too shallow. The company's boats with four-man crews to pole them along could make it clear to Georgetown only a few weeks in most years. And so the Patowmack Company went bankrupt in 1828.[111] It was succeeded by the Chesapeake and Ohio Canal Company which dug a true canal sixty feet wide and six feet deep paralleling the Potomac's Maryland bank. Mules hauled the C & O boats, plodding the canal's towpath. The mule power made possible much heavier payloads and also permitted the C & O boats to carry loads upriver.

All these travel innovations presaged a great outburst of ingenuity, in Virginia and everywhere, to improve humankind's living conditions--The Industrial Revolution. The Revolution proper came about largely through the invention of steam boilers and steam power. A magical power to relieve humans and their beasts of burden of age-old moving and lifting kinds of drudgery. An immensely strong genie, hardly imagined before 1800.

In 1807, the *Clermont*, a boat driven by steam and built by Robert Fulton puffed up the Hudson River from New York City. A steamboat built by James Rumsey had run on the Potomac off Shepherdstown, Virginia, twenty years earlier; but Fulton's *Clermont* was the first to achieve practical success. Steam-powered boats immediately became the talk of the nation.

Marvel followed marvel. In September 1825 the world's first railroad opened in County Durham, England, with a steam locomotive having the power of fifty horses![112] The railroad idea leaped across the Atlantic. The Baltimore and Ohio Railroad Company was chartered in 1827. It laid rails from Baltimore west to Ellicott's Upper Mills in Maryland, and operated with horses until 1830 when a steam locomotive christened the *Tom Thumb* was built. The *Tom Thumb* lost a humiliating race to a horse and wagon, and was replaced by *The York*.

Now here is a curious fact. All the advances mentioned here, from stage coaches to railroads, involved some *Quaker's* enterprise!

- *Stage coach lines*: Jonathan Shoemaker, the miller on Rock Creek in the District of Columbia, and Nathaniel Ellicott, founder of the town of Occoquan, launched the Alexandria-to-Richmond stage service. Both were Quakers. (They were forced to sell the stage line in 1810 in order for Shoemaker to pay his debt to Thomas Jefferson.)
- *Toll roads*: William Hartshorne (1742-1816) and Phineas Janney (1778-1852), Quaker merchants of Alexandria, were the main promoters of the Little River Turnpike. After Phineas took over management of the Turnpike Company in 1802, it was observed that his reports to his board of directors were invariably "full of thees and thous and common sense."[113] Phineas's father, Israel Janney (1752-1823), Quaker farmer, store-keeper, and miller of Goose Creek, was a leading light for building the Leesburg-Georgetown Turnpike.[114]
- *Canals*: George Washington was the principal promoter of all three of Virginia's first canals: Patowmack, James River, and Dismal Swamp. However, Quaker William Hartshorne of Alexandria was the business manager-treasurer both of the Patowmack and Dismal Swamp companies;[115] and John Lynch of Lynchburg was a driving force in starting up the James River Company. Many northern Virginia Quakers were directors or first subscribers of the Patowmack Company, including Benjamin Shreve of Alexandria, and Joseph Janney, John Hough, Israel Thompson, William Brown, and Joseph Holmes of Loudoun. The C & O Canal Company had Phineas Janney as its first president.
- *Steam boats*: Israel Gregg was the captain of the *Clermont* on her famous Hudson River voyage. He grew up a Quaker boy in

Loudoun County's Goose Creek Meeting, a nephew and namesake of Israel Janney. His boyhood home was less than twenty miles from the Potomac River at Shepherdstown. It is a fair guess that he acquired his enthusiasm for steamboating from James Rumsey who built the earlier boat at Shepherdstown.

- *Railroads*: Quaker Edward Pease of Darlington, England, led in establishing the world's first railroad in County Durham. It was sometimes called "the Quaker Line." The clerk of Baltimore Yearly Meeting in 1825 was Philip E. Thomas, who also was president of Baltimore's Merchants' Bank. Philip as soon as he heard about the Quaker Line sent his brother Evan to England to check it out. Evan came back to Baltimore enthusiastic; and Philip immediately organized the Baltimore and Ohio Railroad. it was the first interstate railroad of the United States, and Philip E. Thomas, Quaker, was its first president. The B & O's first effective steam locomotive, *The York*, was designed by Phineas Davis, a Quaker of York, Pennsylvania. John Elgar, a Quaker from the same town, invented rail switches, turntables, chill bearings, and plate wheels.[116] The B & O's chief engineer was Quaker Jonathan Knight who saw to the bridging of rivers and tunneling through mountains as the road lengthened westward.[117]

The Quakers' calling emphasizes the spiritual and humane aspects of life, not business, technology and materialism--the things of God rather than things of Caesar. How is it then that Quakers in Virginia and elsewhere had so much to do with the coming of the Industrial Revolution?

Answering this question involves all the assumptions that follow on Friends' one central tenet: *There is that of God in everyone*. Working out the answer gives understanding that the Friends' faith is a simple one easily stated, but with a simplicity that lies on the other side of complexity.

The answer was suggested by George Fox when he set up the first Friends' school. Its purpose, as he wrote, was "to instruct [boys and] young lasses and maidens in whatsoever things are civil and useful in the Creation."[118] The implication is that the material world of daily toil is a world created by God where men and women are called to do God's work.

Fox's insight was amplified by William Penn's: "True godliness don't turn men out of the world but enables them to live better in it, and excites their endeavors to mend it."[119] A convinced Friend developed the insight still further, describing the manner of his convincement:

> I came to feel in my heart
> the unity of the transcendent and the worldly.
> I had always thought myself a human body and mind
> with a touch of soul around me somewhere
> and suffered mightily in the duality of that split.
> Now I came to see myself and all other life around me
> as Spirit embodied
>
> --human embodies, animal embodies, plant embodies,
> rock embodies.
> All sentient beings, embodiments of the Spirit.
>
> It *is* possible to live at two levels all the time:
> detached and transcendent and
> passionate and concrete.

As Robert Barclay, the Friendly Apologist, put it: "We do not hereby affirm as if Man had received his reason to no purpose.... We look upon reason as fit to order and rule Man in things natural." Though reason cannot by itself lead men to Truth, absolute and eternal, it can certainly guide man to understand truths, relative truths, about this perishing world of time and space.[120]

Furthermore, Friends have a method which seems to nurture their curiosity. Where George Fox describes his great insight, that "There is one, even Christ Jesus, that can speak to thy condition" he ends with "And this I knew *experimentally*." The Quaker reliance on direct experience instead of authority and tradition encourages trying new ways.

The Industrial Revolution soon progressed beyond locomotion and Quakers continued to play leading roles:

- Moses Brown (1738-1836), a Friend of Providence, Rhode Island (Brown University and Moses Brown School are named for his family and for him respectively) built a cotton-spinning mill on the West River at Pawtucket with Samuel Slater. Slater was an English immigrant of the Baptist persuasion who brought the secrets of English textile spinning to America. The Brown-Slater mill at Pawtucket was powered first by a waterwheel and then in 1828 by steam power. It became the first large-scale American factory.

- The indefatigable Quaker Janneys built Virginia's first cotton mill in 1828. It stood where the Alexandria-Richmond road crosses Occoquan Creek, four stories high and humming with a thousand spindles. Elisha Janney had once owned a little flour mill on the site. The great cotton mill was started up by Richard, Nathaniel and Samuel Hopkins Janney, and Samuel McPherson Janney.

All kinds of new-fangled wonders came along at the Industrial Revolution's onset. Husbands put up clothes posts and clothes lines for their grateful wives who had dried the wash on bushes and on the grass time out of mind. Cooking stoves first appeared about 1818. John Janney put one of the new slate roofs on his Alexandria warehouse instead of customary wood shingles. Men started to wear long pantaloons instead of knee breeches which had been the vogue for five hundred years. Friends took to all these new things (except, possibly, the long pantaloons. They were frowned on for a time as sign of the wearer's vanity.)

The Industrial Revolution represented a great forward leap in humankind's *material* condition. It was not matched, however, by a corresponding leap in *moral* and *spiritual* conditions. [121] Capitalism was on the rise and workplace relations were becoming less personal. Thoughts of machines, money, and worldly success were weaning people's minds, men's especially, from spiritual thoughts. Church attendance dropped a bit.

Friends, in the advance guard of the Industrial Revolution, were affected too. According to one observer, some Friends

> ...were becoming involved in making money...and it consumed them. It veiled, except in certain individuals, the pressing insights that were waiting to be recognized within their meetings for worship.... From being the shock troops of the Spirit, they were becoming the shock troops of commerce.[122]

Quaker minister Elias Hicks wrote to Philip E. Thomas in 1829 when Philip was simultaneously clerk of Baltimore Yearly Meeting and president of the new B & O Railroad. Elias minced no words. He questioned whether Philip should spend so much time "with roadbeds, bridges, tunnels, ties and railroad carriages." Preoccupation with business, Elias warned, stifles one's spirit. Railroading, he wrote, "belongs principally to men of this world, but not to the children of the Light whose kingdom is *not* of this world." In 1836 Philip resigned the presidency and the B & O Board passed a resolution praising him as "the father of the railroad system in the United

States."[123] He then transferred his energy to Quakerly efforts on behalf of the Indians.

\* \* \*

After 1800 the Friendly Virginians were affected: mainly by the departure of many families over the mountains West; somewhat by the pull of Evangelical Christianity; and slightly by the onset of the Industrial Revolution. Thirty of the sixty-three Friends meetings in Virginia closed their doors in the years from 1800 to 1820, after their families moved west, while two new meetings started up. The thirty-five kept serenely on First Day after First Day.

John Jay Janney (1812-1907) was born in Loudoun County in the Quaker neighborhood of Goose Creek Meeting. When his father died, John and his mother moved in with her parents, Mahlon and Mary Taylor. In his late 80s, living now in Cincinnati, he bought a red leather record book and wrote down his boyhood memories. Asa Moore Janney and Werner Janney, his "second cousins twice removed" edited John's memoirs and got them published in 1978. The book affords a window on the life lived by Friends in one Virginia community in the early 1800s.

John and his grandparents dwelt on a 263 acre farm called Rural Felicity. It bordered on the highway from Leesburg to Berryville (now Route 7) about a mile from Goose Creek Friends' Meeting house. No other house of worship lay within four miles of the meeting house which was the hub of a self-contained Quaker community with its own general store, blacksmith and cabinetmaker, hatter, shoemaker, and its own Friends'school. The families--Browns, Taylors, Greggs, Hirsts, Janneys, Nichols', Wilsons and others--were related and interrelated by marriage. In some respects the community was an extended family.

Farming set the pattern for the daily round. All year long cows were milked; pigs slopped; chickens, turkeys, and geese fed; and eggs found. The farm horses were tenderly cared for, two kinds being popular: the Royalty, a dark iron gray, and the Chester Ball, a light sorrel. Women carried milk, water, and foodstuffs from springhouse and root cellar to kitchen; made soap, made yeast, churned butter and made cheese, fed the kitchen fire with four-foot logs, blew the dinner horn at meal times; baked on Seventh Day, washed clothes on Second Day; ran the spinning wheel, or knit or darned after supper. As for the children, they went to Friends' school all the year round, Christmas day and all, except for two weeks during harvest. The children had chores morning and evening. Everyone went early to bed.

Beside these year round chores there were seasonal requirements, starting in early springtime with fence repairs and whitewashing. The flock of sheep was washed in the creek and sheared. Plowing and harrowing was followed by planting corn as soon as the leaves on hickory trees grew big as squirrel's ears. All through the summer the corn was cultivated and weeded.

At harvest time, the corn was shucked and cribbed. A hay crop was cut, scythes flashing steadily across each meadow. The fields were plowed again and fertilized. And seeded, with winter wheat seed broadcast by hand. Then the men went into the woods to cut thirty or forty cords of wood per family. About Christmas time, hogs were slaughtered and dressed. After which it was time to tread out the wheat, horses plodding round and around the threshing floor. The wheat went to a neighboring mill to be ground into flour. It was a proud thing to hear from the miller that one's wheat was clean, no white caps or cheat or cockleburs in it.

According to John Jay Janney, the Goose Creek Friends throve on all this work. "If you could look into the faces...," he wrote, "you would see a lot of handsome, bright, cheerful faces." He remembered with pleasure the winter evenings in his grandparents' kitchen:

> In the evening, after the dishes were washed and cleared off and the table set back, the candle stand would be moved out...and the whole family gathered around it; some of the men reading a newspaper or a book and the women sewing or knitting, or spinning flax or tow. If there was not room around the stand for all, one or more would hang a candle on the back of a chair...common splint bottoms with slat backs....
>
> The fireplace, always lighted, occupied nearly the whole west side of the room. Popcorn would be popped and sometimes there was beer.

The farmhouse at Rural Felicity was a two story, six room stone house with a log kitchen wing 18 by 23 feet--the log wing having been the Taylor's earlier home. The family had silver spoons and china cups for visitors and a limited amount of nice furniture: "The best was made of wild cherry and polished with beeswax." A cherry table, a mirror and desk-bookcase in the parlor; a dozen windsor chairs throughout the house; no rugs on the wide boarded floors; a cross-stitch sampler and a black-on-white silhouette or two on the walls.

The women and girls of the neighborhood came to quilting parties in such Goose Creek homes. After quilting and chatting around the quilting frame, they had supper together. Then certain young men would drop by, and the evening would be spent in playing parlor games. As John Jay Janney recalled it the games all involved singing. He remembered three lines of one song:

> Oats, peas, beans and barley grows
> but you nor I nor no one knows
> How oats, peas, beans and barley grows.

Most of the games had penalties which required kissing. One penalty called for a girl to kiss a boy "pigeon fashion," each taking an end of a string in their mouths and working it in their mouths until their lips thrillingly met. Another was for the "it" person to go around the parlor kissing one and missing one, and telling why each was kissed.

Children at Goose Creek Friends' school had their own good times. The boys played Town Ball (from which the game of Baseball developed. They used a softer ball and hit it with their hands instead of a bat, but the bases were the same). They played Antony Over, Corner Ball, Trap, Prisoners' Base, and Fox and Hounds. The little boys shot marbles while the girls jumped rope and scooped jacks. Their toys included goose quill "popguns," bows and arrows, willow whistles, kites, cornstalk fiddles, dolls, hoops, sleds.

The men of Goose Creek went off on coon and possum hunts of nights. The whole settlement came together for corn huskings and barn raisings. On Seventh Day afternoons the Goose Creek store drew a knot of farmers who bought a few staples and discussed the news. The younger men shot at a mark with their squirrel rifles, pitched pennies, had jumping contests, foot races and wrestling matches.

Goose Creek in 1820 was clearly in transition. It still was a largely self-sustaining settlement, each family growing most of its food and making most of its possessions right on the farm. Nevertheless, it was not so remote and hardscrabble as in pioneer days. By 1820 the turnpike to Georgetown and Alexandria was close by. The trip to those market towns took three days now instead of seven. Instead of herding live cows and turkeys into market, it was now more profitable to haul in wagon loads of flour and hams.

Much more of each farm's crop was grown for cash now, rather than for feeding the family. Four or six horses pulling covered wagons were nearly always seen on the road to Georgetown and Alexandria. The wagons bedded twelve barrels each holding 196 pounds of flour. Goose Creek farmers came home with dollars in their wallets, with a supply of salt and sugar and a few delicacies for the family--salt shad, say, or four or five bushels of oysters. Some time in the 1820s, Grandfather Taylor brought back one of the new cooking stoves for Rural Felicity's kitchen. The stove pleased his women folks.

The settlement's transition had not yet much affected Goose Creek Friends' Meeting. Some of the Meeting's families had gone west and a few had moved to Alexandria and Georgetown to seek their fortunes. But these departures were not much felt, for the Meeting, composed of about a hundred families,[124] opened a fine, new, two story brick meeting house in 1817. The members met there steadily on First Day mornings and again on Fifth Day afternoons. They waited for God's guidance there, in the silence, after the peculiar manner of Friends.

They were "peculiar" in more ways than worship. A visitor to Goose Creek could recognize the Quakers by a certain demeanor and dress. On workdays Quaker men wore Kentucky jeans and cowhide boots, but on First Days white linen shirts, waistcoats, dark coats with stand-up collars and a "shad-belly" cut, and broad-brimmed hats. The older men wore knee breeches and home knit woolen stockings, or boots; while some of the younger came in pantaloons. Women, who wore calico or linsey-woolsey dresses, and sun bonnets at home, came to meeting in white cap under a full bonnet, kerchief and Quaker gray dress over several petticoats.

Plainness was the rule. Rings and jewelry were never worn by men and seldom by women. The men's shirts had no ruffles, although young women contrived a ruffle here and there and sometimes let a carefully careless curl appear. Quite a few young women had a neat slim-waisted appearance aided by corset stays.

Life was not idyllic in the Quaker settlement. A few alcoholics got pitifully drunk. Will Schooley (1794-1860) who grew up near Goose Creek meeting house recalled getting tipsy at harvest time, and a cornhusking bee where "my most intimate friends had become intoxicated and committed many excesses."[125] An unconscionable number of the meeting's young men and women engaged in "indiscretions" before marrying, some to the point where babies arrived less than nine months after marriage.[126] This may be a reason why Thomas Scattergood, a Quaker minister visiting from Philadelphia, referred to Goose Creek as "this licentious little village" where he was obliged "to labor honestly for the good of the members, particularly the airy youth."[127]

Be that as it may, Goose Creek with its lot of handsome, cheerful faces was a remarkable community. It was surrounded by slaveholders, but no slaves were held by Friends. A few Friends had free black families living on their farms, and free black children went to the Friends' school where "they were taught and treated just as the other children were"--surely a rare thing in 1820s Virginia. As John Jay Janney noted, "Among the slaveholders and those living in their vicinity, every thing that could be was kept locked up. The mistress of the household would have a bunch of keys at her side." By contrast "The [Goose Creek] neighborhood was an orderly one.... I have no recollection of a theft or crime of any kind."

\* \* \*

Right into the 1820s Friends all across Virginia, dwindling in numbers though they were, held to their accustomed ways of meeting for business and of carrying out their traditional "concerns."

The meetings for business always opened with silence and ended with silence. They were spiritual occasions marked by the same expectancy of God's guidance as were the meetings for worship. No vote was ever taken, no parliamentary form pursued. The clerks who sat at the heads of the meetings did not preside in any autocratic sense. They were there only to introduce each item of business "according to good order" and to gather up and report "the sense of the meeting."

The settled custom was that nothing should be done that could not be done in unity, with the solid body of the meeting in favor of it. The concept was for each Friend to speak his or her mind according to his or her measure of inward light. The idea was to combine insights--many candles together making a greater illumination--the better to discover God's will. Each meeting was seen as an adventure into the mind of God.

After all the facets of a problem had been discussed, someone would suggest a solution and a sense of harmony typically would emerge. Then followed a chorus of voices: "I approve," "I unite with that," "the Friend speaks my mind," and the like; and the clerk would write a minute to record the decision. It was and is a method quite unique in Christendom.

In those days shutters still divided Friends' meeting rooms down the middle. The shutters were raised during meetings for worship and lowered during meetings for business separating men on one side from the women on the other. There were, however, many points of contact in the business being transacted, and the men and women often conferred. This was done through messengers. If it was a messenger from the women's meeting she would open the door of the mens' meeting and sail purposefully toward the clerk's table. Instantly there would be a hush--if anyone was speaking, he stopped. The messenger, having delivered the message, either left at once or sat waiting for an answer. Messengers from the men's meeting followed a similar procedure.

Items of business included arrangements for weddings and funerals, assistance for Friends in distress; and such mundane matters as repairing a leak in the meeting house roof. Individual Friends presented concerns or leadings that they felt called to act on, and asked the meetings' advice or support. Applications for membership were considered, and what was to be done about wayward members.

Much of the meeting's work was based on the recommendations of committees. Committees labored with members who planned to marry out of the meeting or who failed to come to worship regularly. Such committees often recommended that a member who failed to correct erring ways should be disowned. Then a paper of disownment would be prepared:

> Whereas Deborah Crew, daughter of Micajah and Margaret Crew, having so far deviated from the known rules of Friends as to join in marriage with a man not of our religious society, we therefore disown her from being any longer a member of the same until she make satisfaction. Signed in and on behalf of a monthly meeting held at Cedar Creek the 14th of 8 month, 1819.
>
> Lemuel Crew
> Rebecca Harris
> Clerks[129]

Business matters too extensive for the monthly meetings to decide were referred on, to quarterly meeting. Virginia Yearly Meeting had three "Quarters" until 1817--Lower, Upper, and Western Quarterly Meetings. By 1817, however, Western Quarter (South River Monthly Meeting in Lynchburg and nearby meetings in Bedford, Campbell and Halifax Counties) had lost so many members that it was "laid down." All the northern Virginia monthly meetings belonged to Fairfax Quarter of Baltimore Yearly Meeting. The few small meetings in Carroll County and adjacent counties of southwest Virginia belonged to Surry Quarter of North Carolina Yearly Meeting. So then Lower and, Upper (Virginia Yearly Meeting), Fairfax (Baltimore Yearly Meeting) and Surry (North Carolina Yearly Meeting)--these were the four quarterly meetings of 1820s Virginia.

The quarterly meetings were largely social events lasting two days where old friends renewed their friendships. Hearty meals were served, and Friends' ministers were present who spoke with power. But Virginia Yearly Meeting was the great annual week-long gathering. It took place in Fifth Month (May) as it had nearly every year since the first gathering in 1696. Yearly meeting was held in odd-numbered years in an Upper Quarter meeting house north of James River and even-numbered years in the Lower Quarter south of the James. After 1781 the "Upper" gathering place was Weyanoke Meeting house near Charles City. The "Lower" place was Blackwater Meeting house near Wakefield in Surry County. By 1805, however, only a few Friends remained at Blackwater and the yearly meeting's "Lower" place moved to Gravelly Run Meeting house west of Petersburg.

Robert Pleasants of Curles, the grand old man of Virginia Yearly Meeting, died in 1801, but able Friends were on hand to take his place. Micajah Crew, the storekeeper-miller of Cedar Creek; Thomas Pretlow of Blackwater Meeting; Benjamin Bates and then Elijah Bates, brothers and schoolmasters, and then Fleming Bates; and Robert Crew of Weyanoke: these were the yearly meeting's clerks from 1800 into the 1820s. Sarah Parsons of Richmond and then Margaret Crew of Cedar Creek were clerks of the Women's Yearly Meeting in those years.

These Friends served with dignity and good humor at the clerk's table even while the number of yearly meeting attenders fell year by year due to the great migration West. Shrinking though it was, the yearly meeting made historic decisions bearing on Friends' peace testimony, on their concern for oppressed blacks and Indians, and on the spread of schools. After 1800 the yearly meeting developed a new concern, the care of prisoners in Virginia's penal system.

A rare book in the New York City Public Library is titled *Laurie Todd's Notes on Virginia*. It describes yet another important aspect of Virginia's Yearly Meetings:

> ...I have a word to say about the Quakers. Their Yearly Meetings are held in Virginia [beginning] on the third Seventh Day in Fifth Month.... I have seen in all their public assemblies the young men seated on the west and the young women on the east gallery of the meeting houses.

Thus placed in contra-distinction they face one another...a very convenient opportunity here presents itself for the young folks, if undecided, to pick and choose. Here it is, in the house of God, that arises in the breasts of young men and maidens that attachment that often ripens into love.

Laurie Todd also meditates on the appearance of Quaker maidens-- evidently those attending Virginia Yearly Meeting:

Did you ever stand, on a mild Sabbath morning, inside the gate beside the walk leading to the meeting house door? If so, you have seen a group, say six in number, of plain Quaker maidens dressed in white muslin, both neat and clean, with fair transparent skin, a modest blush on the cheek, a mild and reverential feeling of devotion in their dove-like eyes. They are crossing the threshold of the sanctuary. Saw you ever anything more lovely?[130]

\* \* \*

Of all their concerns, the Friendly Virginians of the early 1800s put peace-making first. The county sheriffs set out with fresh determination to make Quakers into soldiers after 1799, when the state's General Assembly decreed yet again that there would be no more nonsense--no more exemptions from militia duty for the young men of the peace churches. From Alexandria in the north to Grayson County deep in southwestern Virginia, the sheriffs once again confiscated horses, wagons, watches, cows, and cash from Quaker, Mennonite and Brethren families because their men refused to report on militia days.[131]

The Friends of Mt. Pleasant Monthly Meeting in Grayson County petitioned the Assembly in 1804 for relief from militia duty "in obedience to the divine injunction of our Lord and Savior Jesus Christ operating on our consciences." They stated their conviction that war does not "promote happiness, prosperity, welfare or safety of any people." Five elders signed the petition.

The Assembly rejected Mt. Pleasant Meeting's petition. In Eleventh month of 1810 the Meeting for Sufferings (Executive Committee) of Virginia Yearly Meeting tried again. The committee hammered out an eleven-paragraph Memorial and Petition and sent it to Richmond in the hands of a committee which included Benjamin Bates, the yearly meeting's clerk.

The Friends' Memorial was read before the General Assembly, after which the Assembly adjourned for dinner. The Friends returned to the Capitol's lobby early to await an answer and were soon followed by George Hay, an eminent delegate and lawyer. Hay politely addressed one of the Friends, saying, "Don't you think, sir, that your request to be relieved from bearing your part in common with your fellow citizens...is a little unreasonable?" Benjamin Bates, standing nearby responded, and a conversation between Hay and Bates began. Delegates returning from dinner stopped to listen.

After a while, Hay heard mutterings from the circle around him: "The Quaker is too many for Mr. Hay"--"I never knew Mr. Hay beat till now"--and the like. He finally said, "Mr. Bates, some of your arguments are quite new to me; and that I may have an opportunity to consider them more at leisure, I will thank you to throw them on paper." And Bates did write a letter amplifying the Friends' Memorial, and forwarded it to Hay.

Hay was rooming in a Richmond hotel with William Wirt, the delegate from Madison County who later became U. S. Attorney General. He showed the letter to Wirt, who read it thoughtfully and then asked Hay what he intended to do with it. Hay answered, "I have not yet made up my mind...what would you do with it?" Wirt replied, "Pocket it--for it is unanswerable." Hay evidently took the advice, for Bates never received a reply.[132]

Virginia's General Assembly rejected the 1810 Memorial too; but it was cited by Friends for fifty years thereafter, as long as the state militia systems lasted, to explain Friends' refusal to join the militia.[133] The 1810 Memorial was a declaration of independence for conscientious objectors from the demand of the state that everyone must take part in blood-letting. It asked permission, as many Quaker petitions had done before, to practice peace according to Christ's teaching. And then, what was new, it proclaimed "the unalienable rights of conscience,", declaring that the Bill of Rights of the U.S. Constitution recognizes those rights. *Niles' Register* reprinted the Memorial, saying that "it perhaps forms a body of the ablest arguments that have ever appeared in defense of certain principles held by this people [Quakers]."[134]

The war clouds looming up in 1810 no doubt influenced the Assembly in its refusal. Virginia's newspapers were full of scare stories about the arrogant English and their dreadful deeds. When the War of 1812 actually began, Virginia's Friends were squarely confronted for the third time in their 157-year-long history with the choice: loyalty to the state or loyalty to Friends' peace testimony?

For the third time Friends received a mixed mark on the test. Some were disciplined by their meetings for taking part in war activities. Many more were disciplined by the state--their property confiscated when they refused to pay war taxes, or jailed, or marched off against their will to military camps.

Virginia's Governor James Barbour received these dispatches from two of his militia commanders:

- Brigadier General Robert Barraud Taylor, Norfolk, March 1813:

> Three Quakers [Will Copeland of Somerton Meeting and two others] have been sent down in the requisition from Nansemond. They have refused to do duty, to furnish substitutes or receive rations and have been put under guard.... I am at a loss to know what to do with them. Quakers are not included in the list of exemptions from military duty. I cannot bring myself to punish any men for a scruple of conscience, and yet fear to discharge them, lest Quakerism should become a predominant religion in our ranks. Will you direct what is to be done?[135]

- Captain Thomas Gregg*, 56th Virginia Militia, Leesburg, May 1813:

> Many Quakers here in Loudoun County refused to join the army and march to Richmond as ordered. They have been fined the enormous sum of $192.00 [apiece] by a court-martial, or to be imprisoned one month for every $5. Many are not worth half the sum! I hope you will not fail to relieve these sufferers....[136]

A British force entered Hampton Roads in June 1813. It was repelled from Norfolk by General Taylor's militia but succeeded in taking Hampton. The British troops raped, murdered, and pillaged in Hampton.[137] The next summer, 1814, the British attacked up the Potomac. All the Virginia troops were north of the river to defend Washington, and there was no military defense of Alexandria at all when two British men-of-war anchored at the foot of King Street. Alexandria's citizens, knowing what had happened in Hampton, panicked. Dr. Elisha Dick, Quaker of Alexandria Meeting by

---

* Thomas Gregg was a Quaker disowned by Goose Creek Meeting; a grandson of Jacob and Hannah Janney, the founders of that meeting.

convincement, and three other leading citizens were rowed out to the British flagship, where Admiral Cockburn and General Ross,[138] splendid in dress uniforms, received them.

No one knows just what was said aboard the flagship, but the results were happy for Alexandria. Edward Stabler, Jr., of Alexandria Meeting wrote what happened:

> [Thanks be to God for] the preservation of our city from outrage.... No personal insult nor even indecorum was offered to the inhabitants--their dwellings were not visited, nor their household property molested. They [the British] took flour, tobacco, cotton, groceries and shipping, to an amount it is supposed of less than 200,000 dollars; which is a loss so very inconsiderable compared to what we might have suffered....
>
> The previous attack on Washington had called away from Alexandria all our military men and military apparatus; so that when the English squadrons arrived before the town there was nothing in the power of the remaining citizens but to meet them in a spirit of unresisting negotiation. By this course, all irritation on both parts was prevented...[139]

Stabler was reasonably pleased with the behavior of Alexandria's Friends, but John Janney (also of Alexandria Meeting) was not so pleased. He wrote Micajah Janney Ninth Month 28 that

> The property plundered was taken from warehouses near the wharves.... Among the sufferers were a few Friends, perhaps not more than three or four.... Many Friends (as well as others) took flight to the country...a real loss...a want of confidence in [God].[140]

\* \* \*

Justice for the Indians also continued to concern Friends:

Baltimore Yearly Meeting's Indian Committee sent out delegations, always including northern Virginia Quakers, to the Ohio wild country in 1796 and again in 1797 to get a handle on ways to help the Indians. The 1797 delegation met with chiefs resentful and bewildered by their defeat at the hands of Anthony Wayne's army in 1795. For two years the chiefs made no response to Friends' offer of help. Then in spring 1799 a belt of wampum and a letter came to the Indian Committee from Tarkie (The Crane), chief of the Wyandot Nation in Ohio. "Brethren Quakers," Tarkie began:

> Brethren Quakers--You remember that we once...formed a chain of friendship...not a chain of iron; but...a chain of silver that would never get rusty.... Brethren, listen...we love you...because of the goodness of your hearts which has been talked of amongst our Nation long since...we would be very happy to see you...when you do come to see us...I will...conduct you safely to the grand council fire of the Sasteretsy, where all good things are transacted and nothing bad is permitted [and we will] talk of those things that were done between our Good Grandfathers, when they first met...upon our lands...upon this great island!

A few Friends rode out at once to Upper Sandusky where The Crane received them kindly in Sixth Month 1799. The Friends returned east disappointed, however. In every Indian town they saw sodden drunkenness. According to the Friends' report:

> They [are] being supplied with [whisky]...by Canadian traders residing among them...unless these traders can be restrained from furnishing them with this destructive article in exchange for their skins and furs, they will not...turn their minds toward agriculture and the useful arts.... We have no doubt but these unprincipled men will...keep [the Indians] in their present way of living.... Notwithstanding which [we] wish Friends may...keep under the weight of the concern, and...be prepared to proceed...whenever the way may open.

Way did open three years later, in 1802. That summer Little Turtle and Five Medals, chiefs of the Miami and Pottawattomie Nations, came east from Ohio. The Baltimore Indian Committee spoke to them about the whisky problem. Little Turtle replied:

> My brothers and friends.... You see the very evil which destroys your red brethren...it is an evil placed amongst us by the white people....

> [It] destroys our lives. There are more of us dead since the Treaty of Greenville [1795] than we lost by six years' war before. It is all owing to...liquor. When our young men have been out hunting and are returning home loaded with skins and furs; on their way, it happens that

they come along where some of this whisky is deposited, the white man who sells it tells them to take a little drink. Some of them will say 'No I do not want it.' They go on to another house where they find more of the same kind of drink. It is there offered again. They refuse. But finally, the fourth or fifth time, one accepts of it...[then] he wants another and then a third and fourth till his senses have left him.

After his reason comes back...he asks for his peltry. The answer is 'You have drunk them.' Where is my gun? 'It is gone.' Where is my blanket? 'It is gone.' Where is my shirt? 'You have sold it for whisky.'

The Indian Committee printed Little Turtle's speech and sent it to Washington together with a memorial asking Congress to prevent the whisky evil. James Mendenhall of Middle Creek Meeting in northern Virginia--he was then clerk of Baltimore Yearly Meeting--presented the request convincingly; and Congress passed a law in 1802 requiring President Jefferson to prevent liquor selling among the Indian tribes and to appoint agents to reside among the tribes. This was a first step leading to establishment of the Bureau of Indian Affairs (now a part of the Department of the Interior, but at first under the War Department).

Henry Dearborn, the Secretary of War, wrote to James Mendenhall soon after this law passed. He wrote that he had posted an Indian agent at Fort Wayne (now Indiana), and he invited Friends to recruit persons "qualified for different departments, such as blacksmiths, carpenters, and superintendents" to serve at Fort Wayne. This letter to James Mendenhall was followed by another in summer 1803 from Agent Wells at Fort Wayne. "[The] suppression of spirituous liquors in this country is the most beneficial thing which has ever been done for [Indians] by the United States," Wells wrote, "There has not been one Indian killed in this neighborhood for a year. In no preceding year since the Treaty of Greenville has there been less than ten and in some cases as many as thirty killed."

These letters encouraged Friends. Early in 1804 the committee sent a shipment of ploughs and harnesses, mattocks, mauls and wedges for splitting fence rails, axes and hoes, along with a Quaker farmer, Philip Dennis of Ellicott Mills, Maryland, to show the Indians at Fort Wayne how to farm. Friend Dennis brought a letter from the committee to the Indians which urged that young men, not women, should work on the land. Let the women keep house and raise the children, the Quakers' letter urged.

Philip Dennis did his level best from seedtime to harvest. He moved in with an Indian family at Boat Yard on the Wabash River, thirty-two miles southwest of Fort Wayne; fenced a piece of virgin Indiana land with some Indian assistance; and then called the Indian men to come and learn how to make a crop. But Dennis was trying to change the life patterns of a thousand years in one summer. Only one or two red men showed any interest in working the land for they were hunters and wood-roamers bred in the bone. Young women came out, offering to prepare the ground and tend the corn. But from this, Philip wrote, "I dissuaded them."

The men ceremoniously took seats on the fence each morning, watching Philip plough and hoe, with apparent interest but with no offer to help. Almost single-handed he raised 400 bushels of corn; turnips, potatoes, cucumbers, watermelons, pumpkins, beans and parsnips; a litter of hogs. He built a corncrib to store the crop and then went home to Ellicott Mills, his wife and five children.

Baltimore Yearly Meeting sent other Friends to continue Philip Dennis's work--among them William Kirk who had worshipped with the Goose Creek Friends of Virginia. But about 1805 a Shawnee chief named Tecumseh (The Shooting Star) began rallying the tribes in the vicinity of Fort Wayne to resist the advance of white settlers--a development which diverted the Indian braves' tenuous interest in agriculture entirely. Peace did not come to the West for ten years.

After peace came again, in 1815 the committee wrote to the U.S. agent for the Shawnees, now based at Wapakoneta in Auglaize County, Ohio, some 50 miles southeast of Fort Wayne. The Friends asked "whether the Indians...are desirous of renewing their connection with Friends." A reply signed by seven Shawnee elders came from Wapakoneta, dated July 8--

> Dear Friends--A few days ago your letter to our friend John Johnson was handed to us and explained to us by an interpreter...we were all glad.... Just as we were becoming able to receive and feel your goodness the war swept away everything from us...all the Shawanese rejoice in thinking that there is a prospect of the same help we received from our friends the Quakers before the war. With great regard and esteem....
>
> Black Hoof         Walker
> Butter             Yellow Feathers or Little Chief
> Big Snake          John Perry
> The Doctor

Ohio Yearly Meeting of Friends, set off from Baltimore Yearly Meeting in 1813, had formed its own Indian Committee by 1815 and the two committees now joined forces. English, Irish and American Quakers supplied new funds to help the Indians. Jacob Taylor, a Quaker who grew up in Virginia's Hopewell Meeting, moved with his family to Wapakoneta. Jacob's daughter learned Shawanese and opened a school for the Indian children. That was in 1819. Thereafter, Quakers focused on educating the Indian children. They bought 214 acres next to the Wapakoneta reservation, built a school house on it, and settled Isaac Harvey (son of a Hopewell Quaker) and his family there to be the Shawnees' advisers and teachers.

In 1819 four Baltimore Yearly Meeting men presented another memorial to Congress asking decent treatment for the Indians--Virginians Asa Moore of Fairfax Meeting and Edward Stabler, Jr., of Alexandria, along with Philip E. Thomas and Thomas Ellicott. They testified before Senate and House committees, both having members who held it impossible "to carry civilization among the aborigines." The four Friends, in the face of much skepticism and hostile questioning, held otherwise: "We should win to our confidence a race of men capable of the highest attainments...whose extinction would inflict upon our national character a stain that could not be effaced from...history," they declared.

Congress did authorize a measly $10,000 for "civilizing" the Indians. But that was not enough to save the Shawnees in Ohio. As land values climbed, the Indians living on their "guaranteed" Ohio land came under increasing pressure to leave. Congress passed act after act to allow division of the tribes' lands into sections for white farmers. In 1825 Captain Lewis, the chief of a Shawnee band living near Wapakoneta, informed the Harveys that his band must move west to a reservation in Kansas. In 1832 the Shawnees of Wapakoneta were forced to move too. On September 20 they departed on foot, nearly 800 strong, to walk the 800 miles to Kansas--men, women and children, including a 105-year old woman. They arrived about Christmas time of 1832 after much suffering.

Congress refused money to see the tribe through until they could raise a crop in Kansas, but the Quaker Indian committees of Baltimore, Ohio, and Indiana Yearly Meetings jointly sent wagonloads of bacon and flour; and the Harveys' son Henry and his family went to live with the Shawnees on the Kansas reservation.[141]

Meanwhile back in Virginia only a few pitiful remnants of the tribes remained. The Friends of Virginia Yearly Meeting had little contact with any Indians. In 1813, however, a member of Burleigh Meeting in Prince George County spoke at Virginia Yearly Meeting about a wretched band of Indians "reduced to a state of slavery" in Prince George. The county court had appointed this Friend to be "agent" for the band. Yearly Meeting promptly came under the weight of this concern, and worked over thirty years on behalf of the Prince George Indians. More than 200 of them were freed by the court over those years.[142]

Two things are remarkable about the Quakers' long relationship with Indians:

On one hand, Friends were always intent, from William Penn's day on, on nurturing the Indians *in terms of the white race's culture*. Teaching Indians to use whites' tools, read and write English, settle down in one place and farm, with men doing the farm work instead of women--these were the Quakers' aims. It seems never to have occurred to them to help the Indians live better in terms of the *Indians'* accustomed way.

On the other hand, Friends never seriously tried to change the Indians' religious beliefs. Certain other religious denominations sent out missionaries, whose principal aim was to bring the aborigines to Christ and to the missionaries' own denominations. The Friends sent counselors who were guided only by the Golden Rule--Do to others as you would be done by.[143]

It may be that the Indians' approach to the Great Spirit was so congenial to Friends that they saw no need for changing the Indians' way.

\* \* \*

Most of the schools begun by Virginia's Quaker meetings in the 1790s disappeared in the early 1800s when Friends caught the Ohio fever. As the meetings' schools died for lack of Friends' children, a new kind of school, Lancastrian schools developed by an English Quaker, appeared in the state.

Joseph Lancaster (1778-1838) was a short, stout, energetic man who understood children. He grew up poor on the streets of Southwark, London, where there were no schools for the cockney children. Being attracted by Friends' interest in education, he became a Quaker while a teen-ager. Before turning 21 he opened a school in one large room in Southwark's Borough Road, offering to educate all children who wished to come--for free if they were too poor to pay or else for a small fee.

Not having money to pay assistants, Joseph Lancaster hit upon the idea of having older pupils teach the young ones. The system of pupil "monitors," backed by Lancaster's gift for winning children over, was successful. In a few years he had 800 boys and 200 girls in his "Lancastrian" school.

Lancaster invented "merit tickets," awarded to successful students who could exchange them for toys; and "leather medals," worn with pride by honor students. His school room had kites, balls and hoops. He took the children for walks around London, once taking along 500 who kept "perfect order and peace." He introduced slates and chalk (to save paper) and "sand desks" where the children traced their alphabets and numbers. He had forty to sixty youngsters in for tea Sunday afternoons, the youngsters furnishing their own bread and butter and he the tea and sugar.

Soon he was invited to lecture on education, and he published pamphlets. King George III summoned him for an audience and personally subscribed toward the school's support. "How can you keep them in order?" George asked. "Please, thy majesty," Joseph Lancaster replied, "by the same principle thy majesty's army is kept in order--by the word of command." The old King then gave Lancaster a royal edict: "It is my wish that every poor child in my dominions should be taught to read the *Bible*."

Even with help from the King, Lancaster still failed financially. He was a terrible business man, fell £5,000 in debt, and was threatened with debtors' prison. London Friends and others formed "The Royal Lancasterian Society for Promoting the Education of Children of the Poor," paid Lancaster's bills, and tried to keep him solvent. In this they failed for Joseph Lancaster, penny wise but pound foolish, went from one financial crisis to the next. At the same time ninety-five Lancastrian schools started up in England, Ireland, Canada and America. By the time he was 33, some 30,000 children were learning by his system and he was famous.

He and his wife moved to the United States in 1818. By then Lancastrian schools were operating in Georgetown (at 3126 O Street with more than five hundred children and with Quaker Margaret Judge as a teacher), Washington, Alexandria, Richmond and Norfolk. In Caroline County, 115 citizens asked the Virginia Assembly for permission to sell the ornaments and plate from closed-down St. Margaret's Church in order to start a Lancastrian school. Joseph Lancaster in Quaker garb was welcomed to America by a reception on the floor of the U.S. House of Representatives. Congressman Burwell Bassett of Virginia lauded him there as "a man whose life has been devoted to the amelioration of the state of man."[144]

Some Lancastrian schools in Virginia, certainly those in Richmond and Norfolk, functioned successfully until the public school system emerged after the Civil War.[145] In England, the schools increased literacy nation-wide.

This increase was a factor in the rise of popular pressure for parliamentary reform and the abolition of slavery--which resulted in England's Reform Bill of 1832, and slavery abolition in 1833.[146]

The Lancastrian schools were designed for younger children. Some Virginia Friends opened schools for older students in the early 1800s. James Hargrave kept a school for day students in Dinwiddie County; while Benjamin Franklin Taylor of Hughesville in Loudoun County, and John R. Pierpont (1798-1880) in Alexandria kept boarding schools. Taylor kept Flint Hill Academy for boys. He gained a reputation as "the smartest man in Loudoun."[147] Pierpont gained a reputation for severity. He whipped students daily and was known as "Old Six Eyes" because he had four glasses in his spectacles.[148]

Of the Quaker educators then in Virginia, Benjamin Hallowell (1799-1877) was foremost. In 1824, after three years of teaching at Westtown School, he launched the Alexandria Boarding School at 609 Oronoco Street, Alexandria. For a generation thereafter his school served over a hundred boys and a few girls, 11 months every year. Courses included Mathematics, Chemistry, Astronomy, Geology; French, Latin and Greek; Drawing; English and History. The students gathered before breakfast for "collection," where Benjamin read from the Bible. They spent a little time in Quakerly silence at the opening and close of each day's classes. Many students, the children of wealthy slave-holders, experienced culture shock when they entered Hallowell's school, where plain living and high thinking were the rule.[149]

Ironically, these Quaker schoolmasters educated Winfield Scott and Robert E. Lee, who went on to be famous military men:

Winfield Scott, who became the U. S. Army's top general, was James Hargrave's pupil. General Scott recalled being present "when Mr Hargrave, who surveyed as well as taught for a living...[was accused by]...a stout bully with running a line wrong.... Just as the rowdy was about to strike the inoffensive Quaker [I leaped in and struck the rowdy down].... This punishment [I] repeated when the rowdy rose from the ground to strike a second time. 'Friend Winfield,' said the tutor afterward with great placidness, 'I always told thee not to fight, but as thou wouldst fight, I am glad thou wert not beaten.'"[150]

Robert E. Lee was one of Benjamin Hallowell's first pupils. The Lees lived in the house adjoining Hallowell's to the school on Oronoco Street, and Hallowell prepared Robert Lee well enough for him to graduate second in his class of '46 at West Point. Lee was not the only one of Hallowell's students to go on to West Point* and this troubled Benjamin. He wrote:

> On one occasion Senator Bagby of Alabama brought his son Arthur to enter my school and said he wished me to prepare him to enter West Point. I told him I did not do that. I was a Friend and disapproved of war. What they were learning in our school was practical knowledge of scientific principles that would be useful in any calling in life, and if the students made any other than a good use of it afterwards the fault was not mine.[151]

\* \* \*

On 21 March 1800, the Virginia Gaol and Penitentiary opened for business-- a horseshoe-shaped, brick-and-stone, three-story building on Gamble's Hill, sharp on the horizon to the west of Richmond. The new building represented a new response to the state's crime problem. Always before the state had exacted *vengeance* on offenders. They had been whipped, pilloried, burned on the hand or forehead, or hung. Now the state had a place called a penitentiary designed to induce offenders to *repent* of their evil ways and then to sin no more. Its cornerstone read:

> The Commonwealth of Virginia
> Having abolished the ancient sanguinary criminal code
>
> The first stone of an Edifice
> The monument of that Wisdom
> Which would reform while it punishes the Criminal
> Was laid on the 7th day of August
> In the year 1797, and of American Independence the 22nd[152]

---

\* Robert E. Lee, a professional soldier, had ambivalent feelings about Friend Benjamin Hallowell. Lee wrote from Mexico in 1848 to his wife Mary in Arlington; saying that he didn't want their son in Hallowell's school: "Benjamin at one time was an excellent teacher [but I hope that Custis] will not become like Hallowell's boys.... I would rather be pierced by a hundred Mexican bullets than to see him so."[153] Nevertheless Custis was enrolled in the Alexandria Boarding School and did become one of Hallowell's boys!

The penitentiary idea originated in England. It came over the ocean to America largely through Quaker efforts. Friend Richard Wistar (1727-1781) lived near the Philadelphia City Gaol at Third and High Streets. It was a debauched place, men and women, sane and insane, living in filth. The guards sold food and liquor, and prisoners with no money went hungry. They hung bags from the gaol's barred windows, imploring alms from passers-by and roundly cursing those who did not give. Friend Wistar started taking soup in to the prisoners. In 1776 he was an organizer of the Philadelphia Society for Assisting Distressed Prisoners, the world's first prison reform society. This society met only a few times, for the British Army soon entered Philadelphia and took over the gaol for its own purposes.

However the society revived after the Revolution. Caleb Lownes, a Quaker iron merchant, called a meeting on 8 May 1787 at the German School House on Cherry Street. It was now titled the Philadelphia Society for Alleviating the Miseries of Public Prisons, and most of the members were Friends.[153]

John Howard (1726-1790) of England began a series of horrified observations of British prisons in 1773. He published his book on *The State of Prisons in England and Wales* in 1777. Howard, who was no Quaker, wrote his book with the advice and support of Dr. John Fothergill, Quaker of London[154] (the same John Fothergill who was befriending the American cause in those revolutionary years). The Philadelphia Society corresponded with Howard and Fothergill, adapted their views to the situation in Pennsylvania, and began to lobby the Pennsylvania legislature for these eight principles:

- The State should have a Penitentiary.
- The Penitentiary's purpose: to reclaim and reform prisoners.
- Let it be in or near a large town or city, easily accessible to inspectors.
- Let inspecting and directing be assumed solely from a sense of duty and love of humankind, and not for any mercenary motive (a peculiarly Quaker idea).
- Use steady, lenient and persuasive measures in the penitentiary, rather than harsh repression.
- Separate young offenders from hardened offenders.
- Put hardened offenders in solitary confinement, on coarse diet, but seldom more than twenty or thirty days at a time.[155]

Lownes and his colleagues were persuasive. In 1790 the Pennsylvania legislature provided funds to remodel a jail in Walnut Street, Philadelphia, as a state penitentiary. The remodelling provided a series of "night rooms" about 18x20 feet for first offenders along with workshops and exercise yards. There were also sixteen six-by-eight-foot cells where the "hardened" offenders were to be locked in, solitary and without labor or exercise. The government of the place was vested in a board of twelve Inspectors appointed by the mayor and aldermen of Philadelphia. This board employed a full-time keeper, a paid officer responsible to the board; but one or more unpaid inspectors were to visit Walnut Street every day.

Most of the twelve inspectors were Quakers. They decided at once to provide spiritual nourishment for the prisoners. Religious services were held weekly and the Bible and other uplifting books read. The prisoners were offered "tough love." Those who showed they had truly repented were recommended to the governor for a pardon; but if convicted again, they could expect solitary confinement.

The new law of 1790 was so different from earlier penal laws that a time limit of five years was set to try it out. By 1794 the results were so remarkable that Pennsylvania's lawmakers went still further. They eliminated capital punishment except for the crime of murder. Caleb Lownes wrote in 1797 of the new system's results in Philadelphia:

> Our streets meet with no interruption from those characters
> who formerly rendered it dangerous to walk out of an evening.
> Our roads in the vicinity of the city, so constantly infested
> with robbers, are seldom disturbed....
>
> Out of near 200 persons pardoned by the governor, only four
> have been recommitted.[156]

Philadelphia in the 1790s was still the nation's capital city. The penitentiary's results were observed close up by congressmen from every state. News of the penitentiary idea's success spread across the nation. The governor of New York appointed a commission in 1794 to prepare a similar system for New York. Virginia soon followed suit, along with New Jersey, Kentucky, and Massachusetts, and later Vermont, New Hampshire, Maryland, Georgia and Ohio.[157]

In Virginia two men promoted the penitentiary idea:

One was George Keith Taylor (1769-1815) of Petersburg--lawyer and delegate to the Assembly, cousin of George Wythe and great-great-grandson of George Keith, the Quaker turned Anglican rector. He pushed a bill through Virginia's Assembly in 1796, practically identical with the Pennsylvania Penitentiary Bill of 1790. It was complete with a provision "that no crime whatsoever committed by any free person shall be punished with death except murder in the first degree."[158]

James Lownes was the second man. He was a founding member of Richmond Friends Meeting whose meeting house was just then being built at 19th and Cary Streets; and he was also a brother of Caleb Lownes, the Quaker mainspring of the penitentiary movement in Philadelphia. James Lownes, described as "a fine type of Quaker...with his broad brimmed hat, drab suit--the coat of plainest cut without a superfluous button, waistcoat in the same style, knee breeches, gray stockings and silver knee-and-shoe-buckles."[159] He was owner of The Falling Gardens on the Richmond hillside just east of the State Capitol--a place which attracted Richmonders among other reasons for its public baths.[160]

The building of Virginia's Gaol and Penitentiary began in August 1797. Thereafter enthusiasm for the new criminal code ran high. In 1799 Virginia abolished the death penalty *altogether*, except for slaves. The penalty for murder was changed from hanging to a sentence of one to ten years in the penitentiary, "fearing that some unfortunate victim may be deprived of life, contrary to those [humanitarian] principles."*[161]

Twenty one prisoners entered the penitentiary on 21 March 1800. Of the twelve-man Board of Inspectors appointed by Richmond's Hustings Court, three were Quakers, members of the tiny five-year-old Richmond Meeting: James Lownes, Thomas Ladd and Samuel Parsons.

Why were the Richmond Friends so involved? For one possible reason, their new meeting house lay close to the Henrico Gaol. This was a kind of cage open to the weather. For another, Lownes, Ladd, and Parsons all three came from Quaker families that had suffered at the hands of the law. Hugh Lownes, James and Caleb's forefather, having been imprisoned in Cheshire, England, for his Quaker faith, was so weakened by jail fever that he died before his wife and children came to America.[162] The Ladds and Parsons, both Quaker families in Virginia since the 1600s, had been harassed repeatedly by county sheriffs.[163]

Quaker Thomas Eddy was the principal planner and first keeper of New York State's first Penitentiary, called Newgate and sited on four acres in

---

* In 1802 the death penalty was reinstated for treason.

Greenwich Village. Virginia's Governor James Wood consulted Thomas Eddy on building Virginia's Penitentiary and Eddy's advice was generally followed, although he recommended an appropriation of $200,000 which the Virginia Assembly reduced to $30,000.[164] Hopes were high when the first 21 prisoners entered the Penitentiary on Gamble's Hill.

What actually happened, though, was disappointing. For one thing, responsibility for running the Penitentiary was divided, with the Keeper appointed by the Governor, and the 12-man Board of Inspectors appointed by Richmond's Hustings Court. For another, the building itself, a semi-circular architectural gem outside, was poorly planned inside. It was unheated in winter, breezeless in summer, and perpetually damp with a smelly sewage system. The cell doors were solid wood and oversight of the cells' occupants was impossible.

The cells were good-sized, 6-1/2 x 12 feet with high arched ceilings, intended one cell to one prisoner with room for the prisoner to work and exercise. By 1805, however, the courts had consigned so many prisoners to the Penitentiary that three or four were crowded into each cell. Legislators began to criticize the Penitentiary's increasing cost. Both the Keeper and the Board of Inspectors were upbraided and informed they must make the place pay its own way. The original benevolent purpose of reforming prisoners was lost in the shuffle.[165]

This loss of purpose was shared in the penitentiaries of all the states. All soon became overcrowded. Politics and patronage appeared. Many keepers resigned in despair--including Thomas Eddy who resigned as keeper of New York's Newgate in 1803.

In Virginia the governor (later the General Assembly) appointed and reappointed the Penitentiary's keeper year by year. From 1800 to 1816 there were three keepers. In 1816 a 33-year-old Friend of Richmond Meeting applied for the job and got it--Samuel Pleasants Parsons, son of the Samuel Parsons who served on the original Board of Inspectors.

Now Samuel Parsons the younger was the first Virginia Friend to hold a state job since 1663, when John Porter, Jr., was expelled from the House of Burgesses for being a Friend. Parsons set out in 1816 with two evident purposes in mind: to restore the humane purpose of the penitentiary and to be a good public servant--to serve God and to serve the state simultaneously.

An apartment for the keeper was built into the straight wall of the penitentiary that connected the open ends of the horseshoe building, but Samuel and his wife Elizabeth Ladd Parsons decided not to live there.

Instead they built a spacious house (still standing) at 601 Spring Street diagonally across from the penitentiary. While it was building Samuel plunged into his new work.

One terribly cruel aspect of the penitentiary's routine when Samuel took over was the solitary confinement rule. The law of 1796 required each prisoner to pass the first six months in a solitary cell, in silence and darkness.[166] This requirement it seems was included in the law as a sop to conservative legislators who were reluctant to give up the death penalty. But this solitary punishment was too much. Some prisoners went mad and the health of others was broken.

So Keeper Parsons' first recommendation was to change the solitary requirement. His recommendation was denied. It may have caused Parsons to be suspected as "soft" in the halls of the Capitol. Or he may already have been suspect, for his name appeared regularly on the masthead of Benjamin Lundy's *Genius of Universal Emancipation*, as the subscription agent in Richmond for that outspoken anti-slavery paper.[167]

To counter such a suspicion perhaps he wrote in a stern law-and-order vein October 30, 1820:

> Crimes continue to increase with a greater ratio than the increase in population. This lamentable circumstance will require a more rigid and certain course of punishment or the evil will continue to grow. The more the community becomes acquainted with this humane and benevolent mode of punishment, the less effect it has on society. It loses its terror, the only barrier (with wicked men) against the commission of crimes.[168]

If Parsons thought to turn aside suspicions that he was being humane to his prisoners, however, he failed. He kept sending recommendations to the governor for pardons of prisoners who had, in his opinion, repented and reformed. In 1823, the legislature took away the power to pardon from the Governor, and Samuel Parsons lost his place as keeper. His replacement was Edmund Pendleton, selected for his toughness, who promptly installed a treadmill to improve the penitentiary's discipline.[169] But Pendleton went too far, a maddened prisoner set fire to the place, and Parsons was rehired as keeper in 1824. Parsons' cousin James Pleasants, the Quaker turned politician who was governor of Virginia 1822-25, may have had a hand in the rehiring.

Once back in office Samuel Parsons supervised rebuilding, adding new buildings for workshops and a hospital, and a 20-foot wall around the penitentiary's two acres. He also began determined efforts to get back the right to pardon reformed prisoners and to lighten the solitary cell requirement. He wrote in 1825:

> There has not been a single instance [of] a convict whose sentence was for life that ever recovered from indisposition; having lost all hope under any circumstances of reprieve...they soon begin to pine and linger until the vital parts become extinct...nothing [is] more destructive to the health and constitution of convicts than the six months' close and uninterrupted confinement upon their first reception.... The scurvy and dropsy are the diseases most prevalent.[170]

In 1826 the Assembly did grudgingly reduce the initial period of solitary confinement to three months; but added a three month period at the end of each term as a final crack of the whip to warn the prisoner never to offend again. Parsons then expressed himself as pleased with this half-measure and wrote another hard-boiled report, probably to counter the suspicion that he sympathized with his prisoners. Convicts should not be encouraged to believe that they deserve pity. Too much sympathy is practiced in prisons, he wrote.[171]

He continued alternately to plead for better conditions for his prisoners and to declare that he had the no-nonsense view favored by Assembly conservatives. He was continually conscience-stricken by the high and rising number of deaths among the prisoners and continually bedeviled by demands to make the penitentiary pay its own way, which was impossible. In September 1832 cholera broke out and twenty-eight prisoners died. Most of the penitentiary's prisoners were sick that October, but the General Assembly refused to pay for medicines. Soon afterward, after sixteen struggling years on the job, Samuel Parsons resigned, exhausted. At the time he resigned, the Assembly finally changed the law, so as to require no more than one-twelfth of a sentence to be served in solitary.[172]

Tocqueville on his famous tour of the United States visited the Virginia Penitentiary just before Samuel Parsons left. "The superintendent of the Richmond prison receives annually $2,000," Tocqueville wrote, "yet he is the director of one of the bad prisons in the United States."[173] Here is one indicator that the pioneering effort of Samuel Pleasants Parsons, the first of the Friendly Virginians to try to serve God and the State together, did not work out well. A second indicator: When Charles Morgan took over Parsons's place he declared it was unclear "whether the [penitentiary] be viewed as a mere engine of torture for offenses committed, or whether of terror to prevent crime, or whether it be viewed as a school to reform felons, or as a manufacturing establishment to extract from the vicious the means to defray the expenses of their own punishment."[174]

Morgan kept the keeper's job for twenty-seven years but the penitentiary's purpose was no clearer at the end of his tenure than at the beginning. It is still unclear today.

The opposing views of Stephen Grellet (left) and Elias Hicks (right) tore apart the Society of Friends in Virginia and all across America.

## XII

## THE BLOOD OF CHRIST
## 1820-1833

> The blood of Christ--the blood of Christ--why,
> my friends, the actual blood of Christ in itself
> was no more effectual than the blood of bulls and goats.
> -- Elias Hicks, 1824

Every year anywhere from two to ten ministers from distant parts--public Friends --toured the Virginia meetings. Their arrivals were well advertised and large numbers of non-Quakers--"the world's people"--came to hear them. Not many of the world's people were sufficiently motivated to join the Society of Friends. The crowds that turned out, however, indicate that the traveling Friends often inspired their hearers.

Up until 1820 or so, the messages of these Quaker travelers were somewhat linked. Christ *within*, your hope of glory; the inward Christ as a guide for living; love and truth, justice and mercy, simplicity and the calling to live unstained by the world; do to others as you would be done by--these were usual themes. *Bible* passages were quoted, but only to support the insights that came to the speakers in their spiritual journeying.

After 1820 a good many of the traveling ministers continued to speak in this traditional way. But others came with an approach new to Friends that more and more resembled the style of George Whitefield and John Wesley. These ministers often *began* with a *Bible* text and then preached a sermon tailored to the text.

Nathan Hunt (1758-1853) of New Garden, North Carolina was the public Friend who visited the Friendly Virginians most often in the early 1800s-- eight extended visits by 1820. He wore an enormous beaver broad-brim and he did not mince words. "I would as soon hear an ass bray as a slave-owner preach the Gospel," he once declared.[1]

A certain class of public Friends were reputed to possess prophetic powers--such Friends were characterized by a rhythmic sing song way of speaking in meeting. Nathan Hunt was one of these. At the Virginia Yearly Meeting held in Fifth Month 1802 in Blackwater Meeting House, Nathan rose from the facing bench, laid aside his great hat and prophesied that "Death is near." A few weeks later, he noted in his journal, three young men of the wealthiest family in the neighborhood died. "These were all present at the meeting, I well knew, as I had lodged during my visit at the yearly meeting at their father's house," he wrote. Then he quoted Jeremiah 17:11 to support his insight why the tragedy occurred: "As a partridge sitteth on eggs and hatcheth them not; so he that getteth riches and not by right, shall leave them in the midst of his days, and at his end shall be a fool."[2]

Next after Nathan Hunt, the public Friends who visited Virginia most often were two from Long Island: Elias Hicks visited six times, 1798 to 1828; and Stephen Grellet came five times, 1800 to 1828. These two associated in a friendly way at first, but gradually became bitter opponents. The tension between them had terrible consequences, for the Friendly Virginians and for Friends across the United States.

Elias Hicks (1748-1830) was a tall Long Island farmer with a hawk's profile, the fourth-generation son of a Quaker family. He was recorded as a minister by Westbury Meeting in 1778.

Walt Whitman's parents took 10-year-old Walt to hear Elias one fall night in 1829. Here is Walt's recollection of the evening:

> It was thus...in Brooklyn city I saw and heard him.... Though it is 60 years ago since--and I a little boy at the time in Brooklyn, New York--I can remember my father coming home toward sunset from his day's work as carpenter, and saying briefly, as he throws down his armful of kindling--blocks with a bounce on the kitchen floor, 'Come, mother, Elias preaches tonight.' Then my mother, hastening the supper and the table-cleaning afterward....

> We start for the meeting.... Elias preaches anywhere--no respect to buildings --private or public houses, school-rooms, barns, even theatres.... This time it is in a handsome ball-room...of Morrison's Hotel-- a large, cheerful, gay-color'd room with glass chandeliers bearing myriads of sparkling pendants.... Before long the divan and all the settees and chairs are fill'd [with] all the principal dignitaries of the town...some richly dressed women...a group of uniform'd officers.... On a slightly elevated platform at the head of the room, facing the audience, sit a dozen or more Friends, most of them elderly, grim, and with their broad brimm'd hats on their heads. Three or four women, too, in their characteristic Quaker costumes and bonnets. All still as the grave.

> At length after a pause and stillness becoming almost painful, Elias rises and stands for a moment or two without a word. A tall, straight

figure, neither stout nor very thin, dress'd in drab cloth, clean-shaved face, forehead of great expanse, and large and clear black eyes, long or middling-long white hair; he was at this time between 80 and 81 years of age, his head still wearing the broad-brim. A moment looking around the audience with those piercing eyes, amid the perfect silence.... Then the words come from his lips, very emphatically and slowly pronounc'd, in a resonant, grave melodious voice, 'What is the chief end of man? I was told in my early youth, it was to glorify God and seek and enjoy him forever.'

I cannot follow the discourse. It presently becomes very fervid, and in the midst of its fervor he takes the broad-brim hat from his head, and almost dashing it down with violence on the seat behind, continues with uninterrupted earnestness. But, I say, I cannot repeat, hardly suggest his sermon. Though the differences and disputes of the formal division of the Society of Friends was even then under way, he did not allude to them at all. A pleading, tender, nearly agonizing conviction, and magnetic stream of natural eloquence.... Many, very many, were in tears.... While he goes on he falls into the nasality and sing-song tone sometimes heard in meetings; but in a moment or two more, as if recollecting himself, he breaks off, stops and resumes in a natural tone. This occurs three or four times during the talk of the evening, till all concludes.[3]

Stephen Grellet (1773-1846)--the same who drove his jersey wagon into Virginia in 1800--was born Etienne de Grellet du Mabillier of a wealthy and pious French Catholic family. His father manufactured Limoges porcelain, dinnerware so much admired by Louis XVI that he bestowed a title of nobility on the de Grellets. Stephen was educated at the College of the Oratorians in Lyons. Two of his sisters took the nuns' veil. When the Revolution came and Louis XVI beheaded, Stephen and his brother Joseph escaped to Long Island in America. Stephen heard the English Friend Deborah Darby speak there and became a convinced Friend in 1796. An eloquent and sincere young man with an engaging French way of rolling his r's, he was recorded as a Friend's minister in 1798 at the age of 25.

Elias Hicks spoke traditional Quaker language. His ministry focused on the Light of Christ, inwardly known. Stephen Grellet expressed himself quite differently, in a way that would have pleased John Wesley. "I unfolded this great Gospel treasure," he wrote. "Salvation through faith in Christ Jesus the Lord; what he had done for us, without us, through the blood of his Cross."

He preached the inerrancy of the *Bible* and the depravity of humankind in consequence of Eve's fall. These are evangelical usages.[4]

Friends were divided about Stephen Grellet's messages. The Friends of New York Yearly Meeting hesitated in 1805 when Stephen requested a travel minute. "A trying time for poor Stephen," Elias wrote to Hugh Judge, "he has much to bear... but I believe way will be made for him."[5]

Three years later in 1808, New York Yearly Meeting named Elias, then 60, and Stephen, 35, to a committee of six Friends who were to visit all of New York's local meetings. The committee was on the road nine weeks and attended forty meetings for worship. Elias was pleased with the trip, calling it "a season of renewed visitation."[6] But Stephen had a different view. "I became introduced," he wrote, "into very painful trials; for Elias Hicks, one of our committee, frequently advanced sentiments repugnant to the Christian faith, tending to lessen the authority of the Holy Scriptures, to undervalue the sacred offices of our holy and blessed redeemer.... My distress was great."[7]

During their Virginia visits both Elias and Stephen spoke *closely* to the Friendly Virginians, pointing out their shortcomings in dress and address. Both were critical of the Friends of Alexandria in their neat little meeting house at Wolfe and St Asaph Streets. Alexandria was a boom town then, growing fast because it was just across the river from the nation's new capital. "A small weak meeting," Elias wrote. "They [are] gathered there from different parts of the country, mostly for the advancement of their temporal interest.... O that we as a people were more weaned from the world and its fading enjoyments."[8] And Stephen wrote "At Alexandria [I was] greatly oppressed by a spirit of infidelity."[9]

At the Gap Meeting in Hillsboro, Loudoun County, Elias ran across some Friends who praised Tom Paine's *Age of Reason*. Their "spirit of great infidelity and deism"[10] upset him. Stephen was equally upset at Somerton Meeting by a wedding he witnessed there followed by a picnic supper outside the meetinghouse attended by 150 persons. "I have a great objection to such large and promiscuous companies, which frequently open the door for much dissipation," he wrote.[11] Whenever slaveholding Virginians were present, which was often, both denounced the evil of slaveholding.[12]

But here the resemblance stops. Elias the farmer usually traveled horseback in Virginia, while Stephen who had an independent income traveled in a wagon or carriage. Elias's stays in Virginia were never more than two weeks long. He visited only the "Baltimore" Friends' meetings in northern Virginia, never getting further south than Alexandria, Fairfax, Goose Creek and Hopewell. Stephen visited these meetings also and then traveled south, visiting the member meetings of Virginia Yearly Meeting often. His visits to Virginia lasted several months.

The greatest difference was in their respective messages: Elias' favorite message was supported by the *Bible* text "There is a Spirit in man and the inspiration of the Almighty giveth them understanding"; while Stephen made such entries in his journal after speaking in meeting as "The offer of salvation through Jesus Christ was made to them."[13]

Up until 1820 the disagreement between traditional Friends and those espousing Wesleyan doctrines was not very noticeable. Large areas of agreement remained. Of the out-of-state ministers visiting Virginia, most were traditional: including Mary Newhall of Salem, Massachusetts; Elizabeth Coggeshall, the Rhode Island Friend who accompanied Hannah Barnard on her ill-fated trip to Ireland; Mary Naftel from Cornwall in England; Rachel Price, the Westtown School matron; Jesse Kersey of Chester County, Pennsylvania; and Elias Hicks' friend, Hugh Judge, who once said, "Alas, Friends are becoming an outward people."[14] Among those whose messages were tinged with evangelicalism were Richard Mott, admired by Thomas Jefferson; John Shoemaker of Abington Meeting near Philadelphia; and Joseph Hoag of Vermont, a prophetic sing-song type of minister who foretold the coming of the Civil War forty years beforehand.

About 1820, however, the disagreement escalated. In Philadelphia Yearly Meeting--and in all the eight other yearly meetings* more or less-- Quaker leadership was in the hands of Friends who lived in cities. These weighty city Friends tended to be merchants and business people, whereas the country Friends were farmers. The Quaker leaders in Philadelphia had relatives who had left Friends as the families became affluent to worship at Christ Church Episcopal or the various Methodist churches around the city. Through their relatives and their business associates, Philadelphia's leading Friends had become influenced by "outward" religious practices. By 1820 these elders were pretty much on the new evangelical side of the Society of Friends.

---

* The nine yearly meetings in 1820: London and Ireland Yearly Meetings, and in the United States--New England, New York, Philadelphia, Baltimore, Virginia, North Carolina and Ohio. Indiana, a tenth yearly meeting, began in 1821.

The first serious set-to between traditional and evangelical Friends happened in the tenth month of 1819. The protagonists: Elias Hicks versus Jonathan Evans. Jonathan, 60, was a lumber merchant, successor to the Pemberton brothers as "king" of the Philadelphia Quakers. He had been clerk of Philadelphia Yearly Meeting for sixteen years.[15]

Elias was returning from a visit to Friends' meetings in Ohio. On his way home to Long Island he spent a week in Philadelphia, attending the city's five meetings. At Pine Street Meeting's monthly meeting for business Elias spoke "pretty close doctrine to some who stood as rulers or elders among the people."[16] Pine Street was Jonathan Evans's home meeting. Elias's "close" words stung him.

Elias said that "the rulers or leaders...were going round and round, as it were, like the children of Israel and not advancing forward." He then "expressed a concern" to visit the women's meeting on the other side of the shutters separating the men's meeting from the women's. Permission was granted with some muted expressions of disapproval; but while Elias was speaking with the women, Jonathan Evans adjourned the men's meeting. When Elias returned he found the men's side empty[17]--an unprecedented discourtesy. Elias shrugged off the incident, saying "It was kind of them to leave my coat behind when they went."[18] But the incident left a frost in the formerly Friendly air.

When Friends are at their best, loving-kindness predominates. At their worst, their focus on truth and forthrightness predominates, untempered by kindness, tact or courtesy. After Tenth Month 1819, the worst emerged.

Elias Hicks and his friends began to make blunt declarations, certain to ruffle any evangelical in earshot. Quakers after George Fox's day had generally refrained from criticizing "outward" religious practices, but now Elias led in attacking them.

The writings of Confucius may be as divinely inspired as the *Bible*, Elias suggested.[19] And

> A man may keep the Sabbath, may belong to a church and attend all the observances, have regular family prayers, keep a well-bound copy of the Hebrew Scriptures in a conspicuous place, and still not be a religious person at all.[20]

He asked Jonathan Evans' wife Hannah point blank: "Hast *thou* ever been sensible of any advantage that thou has derived from the crucifixion of Jesus Christ?"[21]

The fullness of the Godhead rests in every human and in every blade of grass."[22]

Stephen Grellet, Jonathan Evans and their side reciprocated. They made Elias out to be an atheist or deist:

"Elias Hicks...seeks to invalidate the Holy Scriptures and sets up man's reason as his only guide, openly denying the divinity of Christ."[23]

Elias is "an innovator upon religious principles and inclined to Unitarianism."[24]

Elias and his admirers practice "a loose, hollow kind of morality of that sly specious kind which just clears them from the laws."[25]

...They will generally practice any kind of dissimulation and misrepresentation to carry their points and promote their own selfish interests.[26]

Soon the exchange of words escalated to bitterness--bitterness that resembled the difference between George Keith and the Philadelphia elders four generations earlier. Then the elders were defending traditional Quakerism against Keith and orthodox Christianity. Now they were on the other side, standing for orthodoxy while Elias Hicks defended traditional Quakerism.

Beginning in Fifth Month of 1821, a series of newspaper columns written alternately by "Paul" and "Amicus" fueled the conflict. The newspaper was the *Christian Repository*, published in Wilmington, Delaware. Paul was the Reverend Eliphalet W. Gilbert, 28, a graduate of Princeton Theological Seminary and minister of Wilmington's Presbyterian church. Amicus was Benjamin Ferris, 41, a member of the Friends Meeting at Fourth and West Streets in Wilmington and grandson of Wilmington's first settlers.[27]

The series began with several columns that Paul addressed "To the Society of Friends." From Friends' style of dress to their view of Biblical

---

* This concept of Elias Hicks may have inspired Walt Whitman's *Leaves of Grass*: "I believe a leaf of grass is no less than the journeywork of the stars... I hear and behold God in every object."

authority, Paul castigated them. Presently he attacked Elias Hicks by name. At that point Elias's friends in Wilmington decided to answer and Benjamin Ferris agreed to write the Amicus answers.

Paul's targets were "the characteristic notions and conduct of your society"--that is, the things that make Friends Friends and not Presbyterians. Terms like *atheist*, *heretic* and *infidel* flowed from his pen. He attacked the "internal light" as a radical error. We Christians, Paul wrote, have "the letter of scripture," the only way to "know whether a way which seems right is right." He pilloried Quakers for their views on baptism, the Trinity, the historic Christ and atonement. Incidentally, he coined the term *Hicksite*.[28]

Amicus wrote with great respect for the *Bible*. He pointed out, however, that Paul claimed God spoke only through the *Bible* and so denied knowledge of the Divinity to three-fourths of the world's population. As for Paul's claim that the doctrine of the Trinity is "vitally essential," Amicus responded that it is "an impossibility," an invented relic of the apostasy into which the early church fell, never mentioned in the *Bible*. Dig down "through the vile rubbish of human tradition, accumulated by Priestcraft" he advised the *Repository*'s readers, in order to reach Christ the true cornerstone.[29]

The Paul and Amicus series ran for twenty-one months. Copies of the *Christian Repository* sold so fast that the publisher advertised he would buy back recent copies at six times their original price.[30] The series was published in book form--the book that Michael Megear sent to Thomas Jefferson.

The conflict took on new overtones in Twelfth Month 1822 when Elias visited Philadelphia again on the way home from Baltimore. Two "weighty" Philadelphia Friends called on him, said that reports were circulating about his unsound views, and invited him to meet with some of the Philadelphia elders. After some sparring Elias agreed to the meeting and seven elders assembled on Fifth Day afternoon, the Twelfth of Twelfth Month in Green Street Meeting house. They were surprised, however, when some twenty-one of Elias's friends came in with him. Thomas Wistar, who was clerking the session, objected that the elders expected "an opportunity with Elias Hicks and his companion" alone. One elder exclaimed that they "should take it for granted that the charges are true" if they could not meet privately with Elias. Elias replied that he preferred to hear any charges with witnesses present. Whereupon the elders stood up and left.[31]

Elias visited Philadelphia again in Twelfth Month 1824, again on the way home from Baltimore. He attended Pine Street Meeting on First Day the Fourteenth; and there he declared himself openly, bluntly and finally. Walt

Whitman wrote that "One who was present has since described to me" what happened:

> In the course of his utterance or argument [Elias] made use of these words: 'The blood of Christ--the blood of Christ--why, my friends, the actual blood of Christ in itself was no more effectual than the blood of bulls and goats--not a bit more--not a bit.' At these words, after a momentary hush, commenced a great tumult. Hundreds rose to their feet.... Canes were thumped on the floor. From all parts of the house angry mutterings. Some left the place, but more remain'd, with exclamations, flush'd faces and eyes.[32]

After the rise of meeting, Elias walked along the facing benches shaking hands. When he came to Jonathan Evans, the "king" absolutely refused his hand. As Walt Whitman wrote:

> "This was the definite utterance, the overt act which led to the separation. Families diverg'd--even husbands and wives, parents and children were separated."[33]

Significantly, Elias Hicks's "definite utterance" did not originate with him. He was paraphrasing Job Scott of Rhode Island, who preached acceptably to Philadelphia and Virginia Quakers alike in 1789. Job's words were "The sufferings of [Christ] could do no more toward reconciling a soul to God than the blood of bulls and goats toward the washing away of sin."[34]

The tumult, the cane thumps and angry mutterings, are a measure of the effect of Whitehead, Wesley and Evangelicalism on Quaker ways, 1789 to 1824.

\* \* \*

The separation mentioned by Walt Whitman came three years later--a sad three years for American Friends. Now Friends in their meetings could foretell which side a speaker leaned to after the first words. Traditionalists spoke pointedly of "the Inward Light" or "the Christ within" or "the Kingdom of God in *you*." Evangelicals emphasized "the Cross of Calvary," "Blood of the Redeemer," "Sinners saved by Grace." Friends asked one another anxiously "Is thee Hicksite?" or "Is thee Orthodox?"

The separation came in Fourth Month of 1827 at the 146th annual gathering of Philadelphia Yearly Meeting in Arch Street Meeting house. The proceedings were rancorous, with shouting and red faces. By Sixth Month Philadelphia's traditional (Hicksite) Friends and the evangelical (Orthodox) body had formally separated.

For several years before the separation a succession of evangelical Friends from England, most of them moneyed and patrician, arrived to put matters right among American Friends. Of these, three women--all of them supporters of Stephen Grellet --had leading roles in the events leading to the separation: Anna Braithwaite (1788-1859) of Kendal came three times, 1823, 1825 and 1827, along with her retiring husband Isaac; Elizabeth Robson (born 1771), wife of a Yorkshire textile manufacturer, arrived in 1824 and stayed in America five years; and Ann Jones (born 1774) with husband George was here 1826 to 1830.

The Braithwaites visited the American meetings in a carriage with a servant girl seated beside the whip. Anna Braithwaite was a forceful woman with a majestic air. She ministered at length in practically every meeting she attended. Ignoring the convention that one should speak only once in any given meeting for worship, she spoke seventeen times in one three-hour-long meeting.[35] Elizabeth Robson and Ann Jones were equally vocal. All were determined to put down Elias Hicks and his "blasphemous preaching."

All three were present in Fourth Month of 1827 at Philadelphia Yearly Meeting. All preached at length there, dwelling on the unsound beliefs they had encountered, warning Friends against those who did not believe in the Devil and praying that "this dividing spirit may manifest itself fully."[36]

The three Englishwomen then traveled on to other Friends' gatherings, intent on separating the evangelical wheat from the chaff represented by traditional Quakers. Thomas Shillitoe, 73, of London, soon joined them. He referred to Hicksite Friends as "seceders," encouraging the Orthodox to have nothing to do with the seceders.[37] These English bulldogs of evangelicalism had their wish. By the close of 1828, not only Philadelphia but New York, Ohio, Baltimore, and the new Indiana Yearly Meeting divided.

The split-up of Ohio Yearly Meeting in 1828 was the most violent of all. Many Friends born in Virginia but now settled in Ohio were among the 1,500 present in the great brick meeting house built in Mt Pleasant by Jacob Ong. Elisha Bates (1781-1861), a former clerk of Virginia Yearly Meeting, was there. Jonathan Taylor (1768-1834), the incumbent clerk of Ohio Yearly Meeting, had come to Ohio from Crooked Run Meeting near Front Royal, Virginia; Benjamin W. Ladd (1783-1851), who served as Ohio's clerk just before Jonathan Taylor, came from Virginia's Weyanoke Meeting; Mildred

Ratcliff, a doughty Ohio minister, once of South River Meeting, Lynchburg; the Updegraffs, formerly of Centre Meeting, Winchester all were there.

After Elias Hicks spoke on the first day, Elisha Bates rose to declare that Elias was no longer a recognized minister, that he did not even believe in the Devil or in a heaven or hell except in some kind of spiritualized sense. From there on, the tone of the Yearly Meeting descended low and lower, with jostlings and yells. Jonathan Taylor at the clerk's table resisted the efforts of several Hicksites to yank the table away from him. The walnut table broke to pieces. Jonathan fell out of a doorway, sprawled on the ground with his spectacles knocked off. In the melee, it was said, Benjamin Ladd bit a Hicksite on the shoulder.[38]

Thus the Quakers' reputation for brotherly love--noted by Thomas Jefferson in 1822 when he praised "the exemplary and unschismatizing Society of the Friends"--was destroyed. And the grand Quaker vision of a world at peace, clouded.

The divided yearly meetings of Philadelphia, New York and Baltimore were predominantly Hicksite as of New Year's Day, 1829. Philadelphia divided approximately 17,000 Hicksite Friends to 9,000 Orthodox. New York, 13,000 Hicksite to 6,000 Orthodox. Baltimore, 2,000 Hicksite to 500 Orthodox. Ohio Yearly Meeting, about 8,000 strong, divided nearly equally. But Indiana Yearly Meeting's Friends became mostly Orthodox, about 12,500 from a membership of 14,000. And in the Virginia, North Carolina and New England Yearly Meetings there was no division at all--they became Orthodox bodies.[39]

\* \* \*

Virginia Yearly Meeting made its decision in Fifth Month 1828. The annual gathering was held at Gravelly Run Meeting house west of Petersburg among flowering fields. Lemuel Crew of Cedar Creek--Micajah's son--and Priscilla Cook were the clerks. They were concerned by the low attendance--so many families had gone west. Joseph Butler and Thomas Hunnicutt, both ministers of Gravelly Run, were on hand but only one or two other ministers of the yearly meeting were there. Huldah Sears had died within the year, worn out from her efforts to strengthen the local meetings, driving from meeting to meeting with a horse and buggy purchased for her by the yearly meeting. Old William Porter of Somerton had just died too; and *so* many others had gone to the west.

There were, however, two visiting ministers present. Elias Hicks had planned to come, but he was 80 years old in 1828 and tired by his lengthy travels ("I...found my mind released without going into the yearly meeting of Virginia," he wrote in his journal). The two who *did* come were Stephen Grellet with Anna Braithwaite.[40]

Yearly meeting opened with a welcome to the visiting Friends and a reading of their travel minutes. Then epistles from other yearly meetings were read. But there were *two* epistles from Philadelphia, the Orthodox Epistle signed "Samuel Bettle, clerk" and the Hicksite, "Benjamin Ferris, clerk." All epistles were "received and read to satisfaction" except the Philadelphia Hicksite epistle. Lemuel Crew started to read it, but then someone objected--most likely Anna Braithwaite--and Lemuel referred it to a committee to be studied. The committee heard a recital of Elias Hicks's errors as orthodox Friends saw them and then reported that the Hicksite epistle "was a communication from a Meeting of the Separatists in Philadelphia and that...it ought not to be received or read in this Meeting." This recommendation was approved and Lemuel Crew was "directed to return it to the person signing it." So no separation took place in Virginia Yearly Meeting.[41]

Even so, the Orthodox-Hicksite struggle troubled Virginia's Friends. Four of Virginia's eleven monthly meetings extant in 1828, the four northernmost ones, were connected with Baltimore Yearly Meeting and not at all with Virginia Yearly Meeting. Many northern Virginia Friends were present in Baltimore's Lombard Street Meeting house for yearly meeting in Tenth Month 1828--some staying in tents pitched near the Meeting House, their horses grazing in the meeting's pasture lot.[42]

Ann and George Jones were the English Evangelicals present. When the Philadelphia Hicksite Epistle was introduced they objected. Hicks's supporters objected back, led by Edward Stabler, Jr. and Thomas Wetherald. After much debate Philip E. Thomas, the clerk, announced he would read the disputed epistle. Ann and George then left their seats and invited all present to join them in a walkout. A few--forty-six Friends according to a Hicksite count--did so. They went to a nearby schoolhouse to form what Hicksites called "the British Y.M."[43]

Most Friends of northern Virginia joined the Hicksite side. Alexandria and Fairfax Meetings remained undivided and Hicksite. Eight families or parts of Goose Creek's hundred odd families left Goose Creek Meeting to worship in the Orthodox manner in James and Hannah Hoge's home. As for Hopewell Meeting, about 260 members went with the Hicksites, about 65 Orthodox. Thereafter the Hicksites worshipped in Hopewell Meeting House on First Day mornings, Orthodox in the afternoons.[44]

\* \* \*

The separation hurt American Quakers nationwide. Right on its heels followed a second sad set of circumstances, hurtful for the slaves of the southern states and for their champions, the Southern Quakers.

General Andrew Jackson became seventh President of the United States in 1829, succeeding John Quincy Adams. Andrew Jackson was a slaveholder, military hero and Indian fighter with a world view opposed to Quakers'; whereas Adams was as friendly to Quakers as his father, the second president, had been unfriendly. J.Q. Adams knelt by his bed every night and prayed "Now I lay me down to sleep" as his mother had taught him. "I say it out loud always," he remarked, "and I don't mumble either."[46]

Numerous Friends, including Benjamin Lundy, Elizabeth Robson and Thomas Shillitoe, visited J.Q. Adams in the White House.[47] Washington Friends' Meeting house--a branch of Alexandria Meeting--stood on Eye Street near 18th, and President Adams frequently attended meetings there, as did Henry Clay, his Secretary of State. They admired the messages of Thomas Wetherald (1791-1832) who often spoke in that house.

Thomas Wetherald--English by birth, a butcher by trade and eloquent by nature, was a supporter of Elias Hicks. "We need not look for this [power of God] at a great distance and beyond the grave," he declared, "...It is in us a teacher." In 1829 after the Jackson administration came in, the Wetheralds moved to a farm near York, Pennsylvania, fearing that the Capital's new atmosphere would affect their five children.[48]

The incoming Jackson administration certainly did affect the attitude of slaveholders. Those who previously had been apologetic, now began to defend slavery as a positive good. During February 1830 the Virginia House passed a law prohibiting schools for blacks, slave *or* free. So the Friends' Gravelly Hill School was forced to close its doors.[49]

Gravelly Hill School was located three miles east of Curles Meeting house on 350 acres given by Robert Pleasants by his will in 1801. It operated under the care of Virginia Yearly Meeting

> to promote the spiritual and temporal interest of that unfortunate part of our fellow creatures, informing their minds in the principles of virtue and religion, and in common or useful literature, writing, ciphering and mechanic arts.[50]

The teachers during most of Gravelly Hill's existence were young Quaker men of the Crew family--Benjamin, Henry, James, Chappell, Terrell, David and Jacob."[51]

Up until 1830, Friends continued to lead the movement for abolishing slavery, in America and in Virginia:

- In America, Friend Benjamin Lundy's *Genius of Universal Emancipation*, was the strongest voice against slavery.[52]
- In Virginia, Friends led the anti-slavery societies inspired by Lundy. The first Virginia-wide Convention of these societies met August 1827 in the school house of Goose Creek Meeting with twenty-one delegates from seven local societies. Fourteen of the twenty-one delegates were Friends.[53] President of the Alexandria society that year was Samuel M. Janney, a newly married Friend trying to start up a drugstore in Alexandria. Just before the August convention he wrote and persuaded the Alexandria *Gazette* to publish a series of eleven essays urging gradual emancipation of the slaves.[54]
- That same year of 1827 Nathaniel Crenshaw, 36, of Cedar Creek Friends' Meeting, arranged freedom for sixty-five Hanover County slaves. He took them north into Pennsylvania to lead free lives.[55]

During Eleventh month 1829, Benjamin Lundy left Baltimore to visit some of the anti-slavery societies. He entrusted the issue of the *Genius* for Eleventh Month 20 to his enthusiastic, new, non-Quaker assistant, William Lloyd Garrison, 24. Garrison had been arguing with Lundy about the somewhat calm tone of the *Genius* arguing for a more aggressive tone, for attacking slavery head on, for calling for *immediate* emancipation of the slaves.

When Benjamin returned, he found the *Genius* shut down and Garrison in jail --charged with libel for a story headlined "Black List--Horrible News...The Ship *Francis*." The story reported that the *Francis* had sailed

---

* Dr. William Anderson, Jr., is an African-American psychologist assigned to the University of Virginia's Counseling Center. His grandparents live just across Long Bridge Road from Gravelly Hill School (now known as Gravel Hill School), which is today a Henrico County public school. Dr. Anderson's forebears were among those freed by Robert Pleasants and have lived in the Gravelly Hill area since Revolutionary war days. They used Quaker *thees* and *thys* within the family for generations.

from Newburyport, Massachusetts (Garrison's home town) with a cargo of slaves for the New Orleans market. The *Francis*'s owner and her captain were personally and unfavorably known to Garrison, who wrote in his story that they "should be sentenced to solitary confinement. They are the enemies of their own species--highway robbers and murderers; and their final doom will be...to occupy the lowest depths of perdition."[56]

Benjamin Lundy worked seven weeks to get Garrison out of the Baltimore jail. During that time Lundy was set upon in the street, beaten up and bloodied. He finally got money from Arthur Tappan of New York City to bail Garrison out; whereupon Garrison, unrepentant, announced he'd had enough of Lundy's gradual emancipation methods, and left for Boston to start his own *immediate* emancipation newspaper. Benjamin managed to raise money to re-start the *Genius*, but the paper never was a success again.[57]

William Lloyd Garrison put out the first issue of his *Liberator* in Boston, 2 January 1831--dedicated to a slam-bang, no-holds-barred attack on slavery and slaveholders. It was successful in the northern states, creating a wave of anti-slavery sentiment and a whole new network of anti-slavery societies there. But the *Liberator* was so harsh and denunciatory as to make Southerners furious. The southern papers quoted Garrison's vitriolic criticisms faithfully. He attacked the institution of slavery, as did Lundy, but then went on to attack the slaveholders and the whole culture of the South. As his notoriety increased in the South, grand juries indicted him in absentia, rewards were offered for his arrest dead or alive, and Southern governors demanded that the governor of Massachusetts suppress him.

\* \* \*

Southampton County, Virginia, has a neighborhood known as "The Cross Keys." It lies fifteen miles south of the county seat, named Jerusalem in 1831 but now renamed Courtland because of an awful event in 1831. A slave named Nat Turner lived in the Cross Keys neighborhood then, a preacher, the son of an African-born father who had escaped to the North. Nat Turner was 31, born in the year of Gabriel's rebellion. Like Gabriel he could read and write and like Gabriel he was noticeably scarred in such a way as to suggest maltreatment--scars on his forehead and the back of his neck and a lump on his right wrist. He was not a big man like Gabriel, being about five feet seven inches tall and 155 pounds. Gabriel and his followers had not actually killed any white people, but Nat Turner led a rebellion that killed sixty-three.[58]

Nat and nearly a hundred more slaves met in the woods near Cabin Pond, where no one went because of superstition--a slave had been burned to death there for murdering his master. They ate roast pig and drank apple brandy and set off on the road to Jerusalem--"marching to Jerusalem"--near midnight of Sunday, August 22. At houses along the road they broke in and butchered the sleeping families.

Armed citizens and militia converged on Nat Turner's rebels and slaughtered and scattered them all by Tuesday morning. But by then the thing white southerners had been dreading was done. It was the bloodiest slave insurrection in American history.[59]

The insurrection terrified Virginia and the South--with a notable exception. As John Jay Janney of Goose Creek recalled it:

> At the time of the Southampton or Nat Turner's insurrection, such dread overspread the country that in a neighborhood adjoining ours, as in all other slaveholding neighborhoods, patrols were organized, which patrolled the country every night for some time afterwards. In one case a calf had been killed and left hanging all night to cool. Seeing it, the patrol challenged, and the calf not answering they riddled it with bullets and buckshot.
>
> ...A woman living but a few miles from us...said she never went to bed without the fear that they would all be murdered before morning and their property burned; and that was 200 miles from the scene of the disturbance.
>
> In our neighborhood, among the Friends, there was no fear nor uneasiness. The patrols sent out were really more dangerous than the slaves.[60]

Right after Nat Turner's insurrection a flood of petitions came into Virginia's Assembly. Petitions came from Frederick County, Halifax, Amelia, Powhatan, Isle of Wight, Nansemond, York and Northumberland praying for the removal of all free blacks out of state. Loudoun, Fauquier, Prince William, Nelson, Washington, Hanover, and King William citizens petitioned for the state to purchase the slaves so that they too might be removed. Rockbridge, Caroline, and Charles City Counties and the Virginia Convention of Anti-Slavery Societies asked for gradual emancipation. There were petitions to prevent blacks from owning dogs or hogs; petitions to prohibit anyone from teaching any black to learn any trade; petitions against employment of blacks as millers.[61]

Of all these, the only petition the Assembly chose for consideration was sent in Eleventh Month 1831 by Virginia Yearly Meeting signed by Fleming Bates, clerk.*[62] The Friends asked for gradual abolition of slavery. The evil of slavery can now be seen in all its consequences, they wrote. God's law requires the abolition of slavery in Virginia. Let the inalienable rights of humankind be restored to the African race.[63]

William H. Roane of Hanover County presented the Yearly Meeting's petition on December 24, 1831. Then followed a month-long debate:

- Samuel M. D. Moore of Rockbridge led off, saying that the free Negro population was a nuisance and slavery a greater nuisance. He thought it time for some remedy to be considered.
- General William Broadnax of Dinwiddie was not ready for emancipation, but--he was unwilling to have the nation believe that Virginians refused even to think about delivery from "the greatest curse that God in His wrath ever inflicted upon a people." He said, "When men are forced to lock their doors at night, and open them in the morning to receive their servants to light their fires, with pistols in their hands, surely some measure of restoring confidence and security are necessary."
- Richard A. Bolling of Buckingham favored the Quaker petition. He was sure that slavery was causing the depression in Virginia.
- John A. Chandler of Norfolk was for the removal of free Negroes and for a plan to remove slavery from Virginia "at some future time."
- William C. Rives of Campbell County opposed any plan of emancipation. Its agitation just then would be injudicious.
- At this William O. Goode of Mecklenburg moved to reject the Quakers' petition. His motion lost by more than three to one, and Roane's motion to refer the petition to a committee prevailed.

---

* Virginia Yearly Meeting sent in this petition shortly after it had turned down an invitation from Indiana Yearly Meeting to join in petitioning the U. S. government on behalf of blacks. Due to "recent events in the South," the Virginia Friends wrote, their participation in a petition to the federal authorities would only hinder the cause of abolition.

On January 11, Thomas Jefferson Randolph of Albemarle (the grandson of Thomas Jefferson) got down to brass tacks. He proposed a law whereby slave children born after 4 July 1840 should become the state's property, males at the age of 21, females at 18. They were then to be hired out until they accumulated sufficient wages to leave the state.

Slaveowners took alarm at this practicable idea and began to lobby in earnest. Charles James Faulkner of Berkeley County and James McIlhany of Loudoun, both delegates with Quaker forebears, championed Randolph's proposal. But the slave interest prevailed. Slaves are *property*, it was argued, and property rights are sacred. On January 25 the Quakers' petition and Randolph's proposal were voted down, 65 to 58.[64]

Sarah Emlen, a Friends' minister from Delaware County, Pennsylvania was in Richmond during the great debate, she and her two companions staying with James and Ann Winston on Church Hill. The Friends of Richmond Meeting arranged a public meeting for Sarah to testify against slavery. Afterward, Sarah indignantly wrote home to her husband:

> The public meeting...was more designed for the men of the House than others but [they] were too much engrossed to give us their company and Oh alas! for the gross darkness of the people--'if Friends are very careful in what they say; in not touching upon the present agitated subject, they will not object to attending their meeting; and c."[65]

The 65-58 vote is a watershed in Virginia's history. It was the last time the Assembly seriously considered an end to slavery. When that was voted down, the only alternative was to subjugate the blacks altogether. So, a stern new black code was passed--laws forbidding blacks to assemble without a white person present, restricting black preachers, and reiterating the ban on teaching blacks to read or write.[66]

That same month, January 1832, W. L. Garrison organized the New England Anti-Slavery Society in Boston. The new society adopted the fiery approach of the *Liberator*. Where the earlier Quaker-backed societies had striven for reform through an appeal to the masters, the new northern society aimed at revolution through an appeal to the slaves.[67]

After this, "abolitionist" became a terrible thing to call a person in Virginia. By the end of 1832 all the Quaker-backed anti-slavery societies in Virginia and the South were wiped out, crushed underground. The Virginia

Convention of Anti-Slavery Societies disappeared in 1832 as completely as the Virginia Abolition Society disappeared in 1798.[68]

Professor Thomas R. Dew, 30, of William and Mary College wrote a defense of slavery in the June 1832 issue of the *American Quarterly Review*. Professor Dew pronounced slavery "perhaps the principal means for impelling forward the civilization of mankind." He scoffed at the idea of abolition--impractical and interfering with property rights, he wrote. The article was quoted by pro-slavery orators throughout the south, and Professor Dew was promoted to the presidency of William and Mary. Jesse Burton Harrison, 26, of Lynchburg (a nephew of the Quaker Harrisons of Skimino Meeting, though not himself a practicing Quaker) wrote a rebuttal of Dew's article for the December 1832 *American Quarterly Review*. The local response to Harrison's article was so angry that he had to move out of the state.[69]

From Nat Turner's Rebellion on, Virginia's Friends came under new whips and scorns, their reputation as "nigger lovers" fully revived. Benjamin W. Ladd in Smithfield, Ohio, wrote his daughter Isabella at Westtown School: "The bloody scene which has recently occurred in Va...that land of darkness and oppression will no doubt contribute materially to hasten...Friends' migration from thence."[70]

His forecast was correct. For Sarah Emlen wrote from Virginia to her husband soon after that "Friends are greatly to be felt for in this country. He [Joseph Terrell of Caroline Meeting] informed us that many would go in the spring...only waiting for the winter to be over."[71]

Edward Hicks painted many versions of Isaiah's vision of the Peaceable Kingdom. One early version known to art connoisseurs as "The Peaceable Kingdom of the Branch," includes Virginia's Natural Bridge in its background. Note also the grouping of tiny figures representing Indians and Quakers conducting Penn's Treaty with the Indians.

# XIII

# ON LAYING DOWN VIRGINIA YEARLY MEETING
# 1833-1850

> No pulpit
> All sit side by side there on the bench
> Among the rest in silence.
> Stillness spreads until it all but bursts with promise
> While the humming world is still
> Still
>
> -- Brotherly Love
> by Daniel Hoffman

The great migration of the Friendly Virginians swelled in the 1830s. By now the National Road stretched from Cumberland, Maryland, clear to Vandalia, Illinois and most migrants traveled West that way. After years of heavy use the road was in bad condition. According to Addison Coffin migrating from North Carolina, "The National Road was so bad that I avoided it by going aside and travelling...parallel roads. Twenty miles was a hard day's travel over pole bridges, log causeways and bottomless mud."[1]

Bad road or not, the Quakers' wagons rolled on West. Some families turned off to settle in the eastern Ohio Friends' settlements around Mt Pleasant and Barnesville; some in western Ohio around Miami and Wilmington; some in Richmond, Indiana, and further west in Indiana. Others kept on following the road toward the sunsets to the raw new Illinois country. And beyond. The most westerly Friends' meeting in America then was Vermilion Grove Meeting in Illinois, established in 1823 just west of the Indiana line. Some Virginia Friends' families stopped there. A few of the boldest kept on going toward the Mississippi River--not due west toward Missouri which was slave country, but north by west toward the Iowa region which was not.

Isaac Pidgeon was raised as a boy in the South River and Hopewell Meetings of Virginia. In 1835 he crossed the Mississippi with his family. They built the first Quaker cabin west of that river, where the village of Salem, Iowa, stands today.[2] When Ruth Pidgeon married Stephen Hockett at Salem in 1839, they were the first to marry after the manner of Friends in the immense new country west of the Mississippi.[3]

The Friends' meetings of Virginia dwindled and dwindled. There were twenty-seven in the State in 1830, twenty-one by 1840; and some of those remaining were tottery, including South River Meeting at Lynchburg.

William Davis, Jr., 70, wrote from Lynchburg in Eighth Month 1840 to his friend Nathaniel Crenshaw:

> From death and removals our number [of South River Friends] is very small and the situation of the female part is such, but one monthly meeting has been held by them this year, and it is doubtful whether another will be held.[4]

After this letter the only South River Friends left were Will Davis and three more old men--Daniel Candler, Gerard Johnson, and Robin Johnson. They gravely assembled at the meeting house First Day after First Day, worshiped together for an hour, then lingered to talk over old times and old ways. Of the four, Will Davis died first. One First Day in 1845 only Daniel Candler and Gerard Johnson appeared along with 15-year-old John Jay Terrell. Robin Johnson was sick in bed. That day Quakers met for the last time in South River Meeting house. Until Robin's death the Friends held their meetings at his bedside.[5]

Virginia Yearly Meeting saw handwriting on the wall even before Nat Turner's Rebellion. The membership was down two-thirds by the summer of the Rebellion, and thereafter the exodus of Quakers to the West accelerated. But no yearly meeting in all Quaker history had ever died, and the Friendly Virginians stubbornly resisted the thought of laying down Virginia's.

So they kept on gathering year after year while the number of Quaker attenders diminished. They conducted their week long annual gatherings with dignity while the Friend at the clerk's table presided serenely as though all was well. Friends gathered in Fifth Month according to long custom--at Gravelly Run Meeting near Petersburg (in years with even numbers) and at Weyanoke Meeting close to Williamsburg (odd-numbered years). But nearly all the members of those two meetings were gone from Virginia by 1832. Thereafter the yearly meeting gathered alternately at Cedar Creek Meeting north of Richmond and Somerton Meeting near Portsmouth.

Curiously, the numbers of non-Quakers who attended these gatherings increased, as the Quakers decreased. *The Friend* (an Orthodox Quaker periodical published in Philadelphia) reported the 1833 gathering at Cedar Creek thus:

It was large, attended by many not of our Society. Many had to stand outside.... The promptitude and energy with which [Virginia Friends] have for many years stepped forward on behalf of people of color...must induce regret that Friends will soon be removed from that country. Notwithstanding the contrariety of opinion between Friends and the slaveholder yet...many [slaveholders] express much reluctance at parting with them. The respectful manner in which their last remonstrance [ of 1831] was received by the legislature of Virginia...evidences...the esteem entertained for them.[6]

Lemuel Crew (1778-1853) of Cedar Creek was a pillar of the yearly meeting. He and his father Micajah before him often served as yearly meeting's clerk and Lemuel was clerk in 1840, 1841 and 1842. But after the 1842 gathering Lemuel announced that he and wife Anna and six of their grown children would be moving west. The Crews' departure more or less took the heart out of the struggle to keep up Virginia Yearly Meeting.

So Friends discussed for a long time at the 1843 gathering what to do when their beloved yearly meeting should be no more. The Baltimore, North Carolina and Philadelphia Orthodox Yearly Meetings all were willing to take them in.

The 1844 gathering was held at Somerton with Nathaniel Crenshaw as clerk. John Pease, a visiting English Friend--the son of Edward Pease who invented railroads--spoke eloquently in the meetings for worship, and the business meetings were well led by Clerk Crenshaw. Finally Friends agreed to lay down Virginia Yearly Meeting. Its two quarterly meetings, Upper and Lower, with about 300 members remaining between them,[7] were combined to be a half year's meeting joined to Baltimore Yearly Meeting Orthodox. The half year's meeting would meet alternately at Black Creek near Franklin, Virginia, and in Richmond. A Committee to Defend the Freedom of Colored Persons was formed within the half years' meeting to continue the work on behalf of Virginia's blacks.[8]

So ends the grand 148-year record of Virginia Yearly Meeting, 1696 to 1844.

Of the twenty-one Friends' meetings left in Virginia after 1844, nine in southside Virginia and two in northern Virginia--Hopewell Orthodox and Goose Creek Orthodox--belonged to Baltimore Yearly Meeting *Orthodox*; and nine more, all in the north belonged to Baltimore Yearly Meeting *Hicksite*. The twenty-first was Sandy Creek Meeting of Monongalia County in extreme western Virginia--it was part of Ohio Yearly Meeting. The northerly meetings did not lose quite as many families as the southern ones, but the losses still were severe. It was a disheartening time for Friends.

Benjamin W. Ladd, who left Virginia in 1814, was anxious for his fellow Quakers to follow him to Ohio. He wrote to his nephew Joseph J. Pleasants back in Virginia:

> If any of you with growing families are to escape...the evils of slavery, you must come away while the children are young. It is by far more probable that the Society of Friends in those parts will be melted down and run into the general mass than that slavery will be abolished soon.[9]

\* \* \*

Just at this low time, an energetic new Quaker meeting magically appeared in Virginia. In First Month 1846 two members of the Moorestown, New Jersey, Meeting --Lucas Gillingham and Thomas Wright--came to Virginia to look for land.[10] The men represented a group of New Jersey Friends with a vision. They intended to found a community in slave country where they would demonstrate that farms and enterprises employing free workers are more profitable and more soul-satisfying than those with slaves. It was a spirit opposed to Ben Ladd's judgment that slavery was too strong an institution to be overcome by the Society of Friends.

Some of these New Jersey Friends--Gillinghams, Troths, Garwoods, Wrights--were associates in business with William Cramp, the Delaware River ship-builder.[11] They knew the demand for white oak timber for ships and railroad ties, and they wanted to find a supply of oak somewhere in the South where they could establish a lumber business and so maintain the community they envisioned.

Friends Gillingham and Wright explored Tidewater Virginia, then reported: "We were pleased with a part of the Mt. Vernon property belonging to Lawrence Lewis, a grand nephew of G. Washington, in Fairfax County, Va., fourteen miles from Washington and seven from Alexandria, containing 2,000 acres of beautiful valley land and a large mansion built of brick and completely furnished, and including 1,000 acres of timber, mostly oak."[12]

This 2,000 acres was the Woodlawn estate, given by George Washington to his nephew Lawrence Lewis after Lawrence married Nellie Custis (Martha Washington's daughter) in 1799. Quaker Dr. William Thornton was the architect of Woodlawn's mansion. The New Jersey Friends bought the place for $12.50 an acre, plus an adjoining 1,000 acres. By Christmas day of 1846, Lucas and Elizabeth Gillingham with Thomas and Sarah Wright and their families moved into the mansion.[13] Friends began to meet for worship in Woodlawn's drawing room and soon formed an indulged meeting under the care of Alexandria Meeting.

More Friends' families moved to Woodlawn from Pennsylvania, New Jersey and New York--Buckmans, Stiles, Hunters, Tysons, Greens, Dorlands, Browns, Collins', Haights, Haines', Wills, Ridgeways, Roberts, Suttons, Waltons, Ballingers, Gibbs'--and settled on 80 to 200 acre farms.[14] The meeting, having overflowed Woodlawn's drawing room, moved to the miller's cottage at Washington's old mill on Dogue Creek. Friends started a school there. In 1853 Woodlawn Meeting house was built, and the school removed to Accotink. Accotink became the business center of the Friends' settlement with a store, flour mill, and saw mill. Schooners came right up Accotink Creek to lade flour and lumber.

Fairfax County in George Washington's day had been a plantation country with slave gangs tending great tobacco fields. But by the 1840s much of the land lay exhausted. Weedy old fields alternated with stretches of woods. The plantation houses were dilapidated, some empty--the Lewises had abandoned Woodlawn seven years before selling the place to the Friends. Pohick Church stood empty, door ajar and roof caving in. And this decay was clearly the result of the slave system.[15]

John A. Washington--another of George's grand-nephews--owned Mt. Vernon when the Quakers came to be his neighbors at Woodlawn. He wrote to Jane his wife:

> [If the Woodlawn Quakers] are successful in their undertaking of which there is little doubt, they will produce quite a revolution in the neighborhood.... We shall eventually be obliged to send off our slaves and have recourse to white labor...and this change...will benefit us beyond any present calculation.... I am fully persuaded that, in less than ten years, our lands will double in value.[16]

* * *

Even after reinforcement by the Woodlawn Friends, Virginia's Quakers were in a weak condition. But as the saying goes, God tempers the wind for shorn lambs, and two leaders emerged to keep the Friendly Virginians on course: Nathaniel Chapman Crenshaw (1791-1866) of Cedar Creek Meeting near

Ashland; and Samuel McPherson Janney (1801-1880) of Goose Creek, a hundred miles to the north.

Crenshaw--known all across Hanover County by the nickname of "Granger"--began life as an Episcopalian boy. He was a soldier in the War of 1812 and then became a pioneer in scientific farming methods. In 1819 he married Deborah Crew, the delicate sister of Lemuel Crew. She was disowned for marrying out of meeting, then died in childbirth a year later. Nathaniel, heart-broken, joined Friends soon after, along with his infant son John Bacon Crenshaw. He became a Quaker with all his heart. He built his house called Shrubbery Hill near Cedar Creek's meeting house in 1826[17]-- was fined for refusing to muster with the Hanover militia--and soon was chosen by Cedar Creek Friends to be the clerk of their meeting.

As for Samuel Janney, he was a birthright Friend, the great-grandson of Jacob and Hannah Janney who founded Goose Creek Meeting nearly sixty years before his birth. He grew up in the friendly environs of Goose Creek until he was about 14-years-old. Then his family moved to bustling Alexandria where his father, Abijah, and uncle Phineas Janney became major merchants. Samuel set out to be a business man in his father's footsteps, first starting an Alexandria drug store and then moving to Occoquan in 1828 to be a manager of the great Janney-owned cotton mill there. But his heart was not in business. After ten uneasy years in the mill, at age 37, he moved back to Goose Creek with wife Elizabeth and their three children. There he started Springdale Boarding School for girls and spent the rest of his life as a schoolmaster, writer, and devoted Quaker.[18]

Their lives were linked, for Crenshaw (as his fourth wife) and Janney took wives who were cousins--both named Elizabeth and both named for the same grandmother. The grandmother was Elizabeth Hopkins of the famous Maryland Quaker Hopkinses (Johns Hopkins--1795-1873--was a brother of the Elizabeth who married Crenshaw.) But this link is superficial compared with the thing Granger Crenshaw and Samuel Janney passionately shared. They were alike in dedication to the Quakers' guiding principle that every person has worth and dignity. As such they detested slavery, stood against it and suffered for their stands. Both of them went into action against the slave interest in the 1820s.

Nathaniel Crenshaw owned five slaves in 1825 when he joined Cedar Creek Meeting. His venerable uncle Charles Crenshaw, who sometimes attended Friends' meetings,[19] owned sixty more. Nathaniel immediately began planning to free his slaves and Uncle Charles put a clause in his will freeing his slaves too. Slaves could not be freed in Virginia then unless they left the state at once. So Nathaniel offered the sixty-five slaves to the American Colonization Society for emigration to Liberia.[20] This plan did not work out, probably for lack of funds, but Nathaniel persisted. On July 4 1827, Benjamin Lundy announced in his *Genius* newspaper "the arrival at York, Pa., of Nathaniel Crenshaw of Hanover County, Va., with 65 emancipated slaves."[21]

Samuel Janney was 26 and just married in 1827. One spring evening he attended a gathering in Alexandria Friends Meeting house where Benjamin Lundy was the speaker. Lundy persuaded the audience to organize an anti-slavery society which was duly titled the Alexandria Benevolent Society. Samuel Janney and his father were among its founding members, and Samuel immediately became its penman. He wrote a petition to Congress in favor of abolishing slavery in the District of Columbia (which then included the city of Alexandria); and also a series of eleven articles in the Alexandria *Gazette*, published from 30 April to 21 July 1827, in support of the petition. Members of the Society persuaded all the District's judges,\* nearly all the ministers and over 1,500 voters of the District to sign the petition--but Congress turned it down.[22]

As we shall see, Granger Crenshaw and Samuel Janney worked together in their later lives in behalf of Virginia's slaves. Nevertheless they varied somewhat, both in their approaches to the slave question and in their understandings of Quaker principles. As for the slave question they did not see eye to eye on the role of the American Colonization Society. As for Quakerism, Crenshaw chose to become an Orthodox Friend while Janney chose the Hicksites at the time of the Separation of 1828.

Most Friends supported the American Colonization Society when it first was organized, but the enthusiasm of nearly all of them cooled after a few years. The trouble was that ACS agents in the North held up their program as an anti-slavery measure; while in the South it was touted as a safeguard for slavery, a means of ridding the country of free blacks and so making the slaves more docile. Samuel Janney joined the ACS, then resigned when he

---

\*The judges were probably persuaded to sign by Francis Scott Key (1779-1843), the Washington lawyer who, then and now, was famous as author of the *Star-Spangled Banner*. He liked to say that no one opposed slavery more than he did and worked actively with the Alexandria Benevolent Society. He grew up near Pipe Creek Friends Meeting in Carroll County, Maryland, and sent his daughters to the Quaker boarding school, Fair Hill School in Sandy Spring, Maryland.

"became convinced that the tendency of the scheme of colonization was to quiet the conscience of the people, lead to a false security, and put off to a distant day the work of emancipation."[23] But Granger Crenshaw never resigned and was never disillusioned. He was an active ACS member lifelong, raising funds and sending freed blacks off to Liberia as late as 1858.[24]

Janney's and Crenshaw's dissimilar understanding of Friends' principles reflects that Janney was a Friend of northern Virginia (where most Friends joined the Hicksites) and Crenshaw of southern Virginia (where most became Orthodox Friends.) Geography was not the main determinant though. Samuel Janney, who was 26 when the Separation came about, made his decision thoughtfully. His younger brother Richard (1806-1874) disagreed with him and "went Orthodox."

Richard Janney was named for Richard Mott, the public Friend admired by Thomas Jefferson. Mott stayed with the Janneys in their Goose Creek home in 1805, just before Richard Janney's birth, when Samuel was a four-year-old toddler. When the Separation came in 1828, Richard Mott joined the Orthodox branch of Friends, and twenty-six years after that Samuel Janney and Richard Mott, now 85, met again in New York City. They had a conversation then about their Hicksite-Orthodox differences.

As reported by Janney, he indicated that his main objection to Orthodoxy was the "doctrine of Vicarious Satisfaction" whereby a person needs only to believe in the divinity of Christ to atone for his or her sins. Richard Mott kindly replied that "this is not an essential doctrine," and then remarked that "Hicksites do not now hold the views of Elias Hicks who in [my] opinion had imbibed some of Priestley's [Unitarian] views." To which Samuel Janney answered "We [do] not profess to be followers of Elias Hicks.... If we must take the name of any man we should choose to be called Foxites, but we profess to be followers of Christ."[25]

Nathaniel Crenshaw left no memoirs and just what were his religious views is conjectural. However, the traveling Friends who stayed with the Crenshaws at Shrubbery Hill all had distinctly Orthodox views; and one can assume that Nathaniel's agreed with his guests'. The guests included William Evans, son of Jonathan Evans, the old "king" of Philadelphia Yearly Meeting, and Jonathan Taylor and Benjamin Ladd, both of Ohio Yearly Meeting Orthodox. Daniel Wheeler (1771-1840) of London, Czar Alexander of Russia's friend and spiritual advisor, was the Crenshaws's guest in 1839. A year earlier Joseph John Gurney of Norwich, England, stayed at Shrubbery Hill. "He is a great minister," Nathaniel noted.[26]

\* \* \*

The numbers of traveling Friends who visited Virginia in the 1830s and 1840s may have dropped a little by comparison with earlier years. The numbers who visited any one Virginia meeting certainly dropped, since the Orthodox ministers now visited only the Orthodox meetings and the Hicksite ministers only the northern Virginia Hicksite meetings. The messages of many of these ministers were predictable, with the Orthodox dwelling on "Christ and Him crucified" and the Hicksites on "the Inward Christ." The message of Edward Hicks (1780-1849), however, was unique.

This Edward Hicks was Elias Hicks' cousin and admirer, a minister of Newtown Friends Meeting in Bucks County, Pennsylvania. He was a painter of coaches and signboards. In an age when Friends frowned on the arts, he turned out scores of paintings without being censored--probably because his paintings dwelt on themes that Friends approved. More than sixty of them were based on Isaiah's vision of the world at peace: "The wolf also shall dwell with the lamb, and the leopard shall lie down with the kid; and the calf and the young lion and the fatling together; and a little child shall lead them." The paintings are famous today. They sell at auctions for bids in six figures.

Edward Hicks drove his gig down to Virginia in First Month 1837. He stayed with the Janneys when he reached Goose Creek. On the first First Day of Second Month he stood in the silence of Goose Creek Meeting and spoke at length. A listener wrote down the message, which was printed, 100 pages, as *A Little Present for Friends...by a Poor Illiterate*. The little book is a key to the meaning of Edward Hicks's Peaceable Kingdom paintings.

The paintings, Edward explained, describe the nature of good and evil, of humans' virtues and failings. The ox, lamb, kid and cow stand for the good in people, the wolf, leopard, bear and lion for the evil side:

- The wolf, he said, is the emblem for usurers, seekers after wealth, the vain-glorious, the suicidal.
- The leopard, "the most beautiful of all the carnivorous animals of the cat kind," represents those who rob "innocent females of their virtue," who tear their friends to pieces. The words of Thomas Paine, he said, are like the leopard's screaming.
- The bear is "cold, unfeeling, dull, inert" until it becomes hungry. Then it is ferocious and will devour anything--like a bill collector (Edward Hicks was in debt most of his life.)
- The lion represents pride and arrogance. Edward thought that he himself, Saint Paul, Napoleon and Jonathan Evans partook of

the nature of lions. Jonathan Evans, who had opposed Edward's cousin Elias so totally ten years before, was too often "malignant and bitter"; and I, Edward confessed, have the same failing.

As for the good animals, Edward saw the ox, powerful and docile, as submissive to the will of God. Edward did not doubt that there was yet time for Jonathan Evans, old as he was, to change his ways and "eat straw like the ox." The lamb, kid and cow are innocent, liberal and patient. They will win out over "devouring, tearing, oppressing and killing," and will bring in the Peaceable Kingdom.

Along with his Biblical figures, he often placed in a corner of his paintings a grouping of Indians and Quakers representing Penn's Treaty with the Indians. This event he saw as a harbinger of the Peaceable Kingdom. One version includes the Natural Bridge of Virginia in the background along with Penn and the Indians. The Natural Bridge symbolized to Edward "the beckoning of the divine continuum into a place of peace."[27]

\* \* \*

Traditional Quaker worship is simplicity itself. Friends consult the Inward Light for guidance in the living of their lives with no theological framework or professional guidance. Traditional Friends are, as John Greenleaf Whittier wrote, "Vague of creed and barren of rite/But holding, as in his Master's sight/Act and thought to the Inner Light." The emphasis is on doing God's will, rather than studying about God.

One consequence of this inward style of worship is a comparative absence of theological debating among the worshippers. From George Fox's day in the 1670s until the 1820s--for some 150 years--there were no serious schisms to divide the society. Thomas Jefferson noted it in 1822 "...alone the harmony, the quiet, the brotherly affections, the exemplary and unschismatizing Society of Friends."

After the Separation of 1827-1828, those Friends who kept up the traditional Quaker way continued to meet together in comparative harmony. Orthodox Friends, having imbibed some of the theology of Whitefield and Wesley, however, were soon troubled with disputes and more separations.

In 1826 the Society of Friends was one united body. By 1846 the society in America had divided into four separate tendencies or branches--one Hicksite and three Orthodox.

The first of the Orthodox disputes began in Hardshaw East Meeting of Manchester, England. Isaac Crewdson (1780-1840), the leading minister of this meeting, adopted extremely evangelical views sometime about 1830. A succession of anti-Hicks Quakers came to Hardshaw East to hear Isaac Crewdson. Elizabeth Robson came often and she agreed with Crewdson completely. So did Isaac and Anna Braithwaite and so did Elisha Bates, the American Friend from Ohio.[28]

But John Wilbur (1774-1858) took another view. He was another American Friend visiting England in those years, a farmer-school teacher from Hopkinton, Rhode Island. The state of the Society of the Friends in England--of which Isaac Crewdson and his friends were an extreme faction--dismayed him. He wrote a series of letters in 1832 to express his dismay. The letters were published in a little book titled *Letters to a Friend, on Some of the Primitive Doctrines of Christianity*.[29]

Three years later Isaac Crewdson published his own book, *A Beacon to the Society of Friends*. He attacked Elias Hicks in it. The Inward Light idea is an error, he wrote. The only place to find religious truth is in the *Bible*.[30]

The *Beacon* caused controversy. London Yearly Meeting appointed a committee of thirteen to visit Hardshaw East and deal with Isaac Crewdson. The committee recommended that Isaac should henceforth refrain from speaking as a Friends' minister. Whereupon Isaac and some followers resigned from London Yearly Meeting. They formed a separate body that they styled "Evangelical Friends" and which grew to about 300 members. Many of them eventually left Friends to join the Plymouth Brethren, a sect based on literal interpretation of the *Bible*.[31]

Elisha Bates, having returned home to Mt. Pleasant, Ohio, remained committed to Isaac Crewdson's evangelicalism. He wrote and argued for Crewdson's views. When it was put to him that these views opposed George Fox's, he answered that Fox sometimes mistook imagination for revelation.[32]

This Elisha Bates was Virginia-born, raised on a farm six miles from Williamsburg, a birthright member of Skimino Meeting, a handsome, well-spoken man. He married Sarah Harrison in Skimino Meeting house when he was 22-years-old. At 24 he was master of the Skimino Friends' school. At 32 he was chosen to be Virginia Yearly Meeting's clerk, 1813-1816.\* The

---

\*Benjamin Bates was Virginia Yearly Meeting's clerk from 1807 until his death in 1812. His younger brother Elisha was clerk 1813-1816; and his youngest brother Dr. Fleming Bates was clerk eight of the fifteen years from 1817 to 1831. Then Micajah Bates, Benjamin's son, took over and was clerk

following year, 1817, he moved with his family to Ohio and became a printer and magazine publisher in Mt. Pleasant. He also became the leading Quaker of Ohio. He was clerk of Ohio Yearly Meeting six of the years between 1819 and 1831.

Sarah, his wife, died in 1828. She was Elisha's balance wheel and he became something of an extremist after he lost her. He had a leading part that year in the shouting match in Ohio Yearly Meeting's house which resulted in the split-up of that yearly meeting. In 1833 he traveled to England, visited Hardshaw East and allied himself with Isaac Crewdson and his "Beaconite" Friends. In 1836 he returned to England and out-did even the Beaconites in evangelicalism by having himself baptized by a Protestant minister. When Ohio Friends heard of this last departure from Quaker ways the Orthodox Yearly Meeting there forced him to resign from Friends--at just about the same time Isaac Crewdson and friends left London Yearly Meeting.[33]

Some Ohio Orthodox Friends supported Elisha Bates to the end. Chief among them were David and Rebecca Updegraff of Mt. Pleasant, a Virginia-born couple. They thought of themselves as evangelical Quakers and they raised their eight children in that concept.

One of the committee of thirteen appointed by London Yearly Meeting to settle the Isaac Crewdson affair was Joseph John Gurney (1788-1847). He agreed with Crewdson in most respects. In fact he had written to Crewdson that certain passages of the *Beacon* are "in accordance with the sentiments of every sound and enlightened Christian." But Gurney appreciated, as Crewdson no longer did, Friends' silent and unpremeditated way of worship.[34] Crewdson and Gurney--they saw almost but not quite eye to eye.

Joseph John Gurney, of Earlham Hall and Goat's Lane Meeting in Norwich, is a remarkable figure on the Quaker horizon. His great-great grandfather, John Gurney, was a founder of Goat's Lane, who spent most of the four years 1682-86 in jail for his Quaker faith. His mother was a great-great granddaughter of Robert Barclay the Apologist. By Joseph John's day the Gurneys had become a banking family tremendously wealthy. The only bank larger than Gurney's was the Bank of England. The Judge in Gilbert and Sullivan's *Trial by Jury* celebrates the Gurneys' wealth when he sings basso "At length I became as rich as the Gu-urn-eys."

---

1832-1834, 1838, 1839, and 1843.

Wealth had its effect on the Gurneys. Joseph John was one of ten brothers and sisters, raised as "wet" (nominal) Quakers amid luxurious surroundings. Half of the ten children turned Anglican and half remained Quakers. Joseph John's sister Elizabeth Gurney Fry decided to become a plain Friend when he was ten years old. Fourteen years later, in 1812, Joseph John followed Elizabeth's example and began to wear Quaker gray. His uncle John Gurney and Stephen Grellet encouraged him to make the decision.[35]

But even after that decision Joseph John Gurney associated more with Episcopalians and Methodists than with Friends. Evangelical views predominated over Friends' views in his thinking. His Episcopalian friends chided him for rejecting the church's outward rites, baptism and communion (Gurney called them "ritual shadows"). Quakers chided him for valuing the authority of the *Bible* over the authority of the Inward Light.[36]

By the 1830s Gurney was a leader--although a controversial leader--among English Friends. He was a hero among Friends influenced by the evangelical winds sweeping England, and was opposed by traditional Friends. John Wilbur grieved after he went to Norwich to visit Gurney. "A superficial, busy spirit...seems to prevail" in Norfolk, Wilbur wrote, "with the shunning of the cross of Christ..., a love for the friendship of the world.... Unsound doctrines have crept in."[37]

Gurney felt a leading in 1835 to visit Friends in America. The Friends of Goat Lane approved, but objections were voiced in London Yearly Meeting's Committee of Ministers and Elders. Sarah Grubb, 62, led the objectors. She was a traditional Friend who prayed for the inward coming of Christ in every man and woman and deplored worship of the historical Christ as "head knowledge."[38] The committee held three meetings over ten days to discuss Gurney's proposed trip, the last meeting lasting nearly five hours. Finally William Allen, the clerk and Gurney's friend, signed his travel certificate with no agreement reached by the Ministers and Elders. Gurney sailed on the packet *Monongahela* 8 July 1837. He arrived in Philadelphia after nearly seven weeks at sea, in late August.

He expected some resistance in Philadelphia, knowing that certain Friends had written ahead, describing him as "an Episcopalian in disguise." When he spoke in Philadelphia's Orthodox Meeting house at Fourth and Arch Streets, the house and its galleries were jam-packed, but the prevailing mood was not friendly. Gurney tried to deflect his critics by preaching in praise of William Penn and early Friends: "The memory of the just is blessed" was his theme. Some Friends were won over, but the majority, led by "King" Jonathan Evans, now 79, were not. Evans opposed Joseph John

Gurney as vigorously as he had opposed Elias Hicks ten years earlier.[39] The reason is suggested in a letter Evans wrote to Mildred Ratcliff three years before Gurney arrived in Philadelphia:

> Philadelphia, Seventh Month 22d, 1834--Beloved Friend Mildred Ratcliff:-- ...By letters and other accounts received from England, things are verging to a very sad pass among the members of our Society. Many of them in the foremost stations are shaping their course toward the Episcopal Church.... Some of those in the station of ministers in our Society say that the faith in the outward is sufficient for salvation, and very much set at naught the necessity of deep inward crucifixion to the spirit of the world.... They strive to exalt the Scriptures so much as to make them a primary means of salvation. And many other departures from our ancient testimony.... Hicksism is only one among the many engines that the enemy is making use of to lay waste...our Society....--With much sympathy and love, I remain thy friend--Jonathan Evans[40]

After three days in Philadelphia, Gurney went right to Ohio where he visited eighteen Friends' meetings and the annual gathering of Ohio Orthodox Friends. He encountered some opposition in Ohio, but not as much as in Philadelphia. Then he traveled on to Richmond, Indiana, to attend Indiana Yearly Meeting Orthodox. There he was cordially received: "A finer Yearly Meeting I never attended...such an extensive mark of *true* Christianity," he wrote.[41]

From Indiana, he set off in a spring-wagon for the 600-mile trip to North Carolina and Virginia. After seven weeks in North Carolina he spent his first night in Virginia, Twelfth Month 30, 1837, in John and Edna Hare's home hard by Somerton Meetinghouse.[43]

If Joseph John Gurney met with opposition from any Virginia Quaker during his subsequent tour of Virginia there seems no record of it. Dr. Fleming Bates, the Virginia brother of Elisha Bates, met Joseph John at the Hares' with his buggy and escorted him through the south side of the state. They held appointed meetings with the shrinking groups of Friends left in Virginia Yearly Meeting. Gurney noted:

> Resident as the Friends of North Carolina and Virginia are, in the midst of slaves and slaveholders, they are often placed in trying and

difficult circumstances...to this condition of things it is chiefly owing that so large a number of them have migrated to the Western states. In the meantime, they are bearing as a Christian body a conspicuous, though quiet and inoffensive testimony to the eternal principles of justice in reference to [slaves].[44]

Gurney and Fleming Bates criss-crossed James River on their way to Richmond. From Somerton (south of the James) they held meetings at Weyanoke (north) and Gravelly Run (south of the river). In Richmond they met with Friends three times in the meeting house at 19th and Cary. They held another meeting in the penitentiary and two large public meetings--one in the Capitol, the second in the Methodist church. Joseph John made some remarks about the evil of slavery in these public meetings and there he did meet opposition. Of Richmond he wrote, "It is a hotbed of slavery."[45]

Before leaving Richmond, Gurney visited Governor of Virginia David Campbell and spoke to him about the good effect of Great Britain's emancipation of slaves in the West Indies. The governor agreed, but hastened to complain how the northern abolitionists had set back the anti-slavery cause.[46]

Gurney and Bates then continued on their buggy journey. They held a meeting in Genito Meeting House and wound up at Nathaniel Crenshaw's Shrubbery Hill where Gurney noted "There is much of a generous and gentlemanlike demeanor attaching to the character of the people of Virginia...marked politeness and hospitality."[47] He spoke in the Cedar Creek and Caroline Meetings then boarded a steamer at Aquia Creek and went on up the Potomac to Washington.

Joseph John visited certain Hicksite meetings of Maryland and Virginia in the fall of 1838 but those visits were not so pleasant. When he applied to the Hicksite Friends of Baltimore for leave to lecture in their Lombard Street meeting house, they turned him down, though they invited him to come to Lombard Street's First Day meeting to speak as he felt led. He refused this invitation and then published a pamphlet to explain why he refused.

Elias Hicks, Gurney charged, held that Jesus "was only a human prophet--endued, indeed, with a large measure of the Spirit of God --but a mere man like ourselves." Since you Hicksites continue to hold this view, "you deny [Jesus'] propitiatory death and sacrifice on the Cross." Therefore you are no Christians and so I will not worship with you.

Gurney then quoted George Fox's letter to the Governor of Barbados in order to prove that Gurney's views agreed with Fox's.[48] This is the first-known use of the Barbados letter by an Orthodox Friend to make this point without reference to the *un*-Orthodox views set forth in Fox's *Journal*.

From Baltimore Joseph John went to Fairfax, Goose Creek and Hopewell, Hicksite meetings in northern Virginia, to persuade Friends there of the error of their ways.[49] His receptions were friendly enough, but he evidently did not change any minds.

When he reached Washington it became apparent that this gray-clad Friend, fresh from traveling America's back roads, had tremendous stature in the larger world. Gurney was the managing partner of England's largest private bank. As such he had the reputation of a latter-day J. Pierpont Morgan. In Washington he was received by Daniel Webster, Henry Clay, John Quincy Adams and President Martin Van Buren.

Speaker of the House James K. Polk invited him to preach in the Hall of the House on Sunday morning, 28 January 1839, and the president, cabinet members and senators came. The meeting began and ended with Quaker silence. Joseph John spoke on this text: "I am the Way, the Truth and the Life."[50]

From Washington he traveled on to visit Quakers in New York, and New England. In New England he encountered the familiar if unsympathetic face of John Wilbur--Wilbur, the Yankee farmer-school teacher who had visited Gurney in Norwich six years earlier--who had turned most Philadelphia Friends and many Ohio Friends against Gurney.

John Wilbur had a long, unsatisfactory talk with Gurney when the two met in Newport, Rhode Island.[51] Wilbur then traveled through New England, New York and Philadelphia Yearly Meetings, circulating extracts from Gurney's writings which he labeled "departures from the Truth."

Wilbur was certainly opposed to Hicksism, too, but his position was closer to Elias Hicks's than was Gurney's. Wilbur put the Inward Light just *ahead* of the *Bible* as a source of truth[52], and he deplored Gurney's greater emphasis on the *Bible* and the outward Jesus. He had theological differences with Gurney about "justification," "sanctification" and "imputed righteousness." He objected to Gurney calling First Day "The Christian Sabbath" and he objected especially to Gurney's "love of the friendship of the world."[53]

He was so vehement against Gurney that New England Yearly Meeting disowned John Wilbur in 1845. About 500 of that Meeting's 6,500 members separated and formed a new "Wilburite" Yearly Meeting. The tension between "Gurneyites" and "Wilburites" then spread to the Orthodox yearly meetings of Philadelphia and Ohio. Most Friends in both those yearly meetings sided with the Wilburites.[54]

Mildred Ratcliff (1773-1847) was a leader among the Wilburite Quakers of Ohio. She was a Virginia-born woman, "tall and slender, having a keen and penetrating eye...a prophetess and discerner of spirits...frail and delicate [yet] grave and dignified." Born Mildred Morris and raised as a Baptist near Williamsburg, she married Quaker Harrison Ratcliff when she was 15. When she was 20, according to her memoirs, "I picked up John Woolman's *Journal* and said in my heart 'I will look in this book to see if there is sense in anything a Quaker can write.' But before I had read many pages...I was blinded with tears.... I saw the beauty of holiness shine in his remarks." Reading Woolman led her to join South River Meeting of Friends near her Lynchburg home. She became a minister there before she and her husband moved on to Ohio.[55]

One story about Mildred's prophetic power concerns a dream she had that led her to stop smoking her corncob pipe.[56] Others, told by her bosom friend Ann Branson, have to do with her decision to oppose Evangelical and Gurneyite Friends, and to join the Wilburites:

> When [Virginia] Friends were about to recommend Elisha Bates as a minister, Mildred thought she saw the Absalom spirit in him, and uttered this impressive warning, 'It will be well with him if he is not yet hung by the hair of his head.' The subsequent course pursued by E. Bates, his grievous apostasy and the trouble and distress he brought upon Friends showed that her [vision] was correct.
>
> She appears to have been the first individual in Ohio Yearly Meeting who saw the approach of the enemy under the specious garb of Gurneyism. [She said] to a friend...'When God showed me what was coming upon us, my trouble and distress were almost greater than I knew how to bear.'

Mildred once visited the New England meetings. Of that visit she related

> 'I one day saw a carriage on the same road I was going, some distance before the one in which I was riding. Presently I saw a stream of light extending from my carriage to the one before us. Then I felt near unity and fellowship with some one in that carriage,

but knew not who was in it. When the carriage stopped, John Wilbur got out of it, and the unity and fellowship were with him.'[57]

So it was that the Society of Friends in America, one united body in 1826, divided into four separate tendencies or branches. The four branches represent a continuum: Evangelical Quakers putting their faith entirely in the *Bible*; Gurneyites holding with the *Bible* and placing the authority of the Inward Light a distant second; Wilburites holding Inward Light and *Bible*, inward and outward authority, nearly on a par but with the Inward Light foremost; and Hicksites, holding to Friends' traditional faith in the guidance of the Inward Light with the *Bible* as a steadying secondary guide.

At one end of the rainbow spectrum, Children of the Book--at the other end, Children of the Light.

As for Virginia's Friends, they divided south and north. The Friends of southern Virginia, most of them Gurneyite; of northern Virginia, mostly Hicksite.

\* \* \*

Thus far in this history, Virginia's Friends have been observed as innovators and adventurers, forerunners in certain grand areas of the social order. They have been seen making a difference in terms of religious liberty; relations with Indians; peace and nonviolence; the place of women; and the treatment of slaves. They have tried also to improve the treatment of prisoners, but that with ambiguous results.

Now at this point in time, many Friends mixed into their spiritual view of things a dollop of orthodox Christianity, of the kind made popular by George Whitefield and John Wesley. Some Friends held fast to the traditional, inward way to guide their lives. Others blended in aspects of the outward way. The question arises: what difference does that make?

In 1846 the Friends' branching was still new. All Friends in Virginia and elsewhere still wore the plain clothing and spoke the plain thee and thou speech that distinguished them from their neighbors. Yet even in 1846 some differences are observable in the usages of Friends of the various branches.

Generally speaking, the Hicksites continued Friends' traditional testimonies, trying to live by the Golden Rule; while the people of the new Orthodox branches leaned more toward evangelizing the world, that is, toward missionary work, persuading the unpersuaded to adopt Orthodox Christianity. The differences are subtle but significant. They are typified by the outlooks of three leaders identified with the new Orthodox tendencies: Elisha Bates for Evangelical Friends; Joseph John Gurney for the Gurneyites; and John Wilbur for Wilburites.

Elisha Bates was a strong anti-slavery Friend during his early years in Virginia. Charles Osborne, traveling in Truth's service in 1816 stayed overnight at Skimino in Elisha's home. Elisha, then 35, was clerk of Virginia Yearly Meeting, and Osborne described him as "a dear Friend, a man of good education, much interested in the cause of the suffering African race, endeavoring to form an abolition society."[58] The next year, 1817, just before moving from Virginia to Mt. Pleasant, Ohio, Elisha published a book titled *Moral and Political Observations, Addressed to the Enlightened Citizens of Virginia*. In it he urged Virginians to organize against slavery.[59]

Upon settling in Ohio, Elisha joined Charles Osborne and Ben Lundy in getting out their monthly anti-slavery journal, *The Philanthropist*, and he joined the anti-slavery Union Humane Society.[60] But sometime between 1817 and 1819 some thing cooled his interest in the anti-slavery cause.

In those years, members of the Union Humane Society organized a Free Produce Store in Mt. Pleasant. Since nothing produced by slave labor was to be sold in the store, its patrons could strike a blow against the slave interest. Osborne and Lundy promoted the store whole-heartedly, whereas Bates decided not to be a patron and spoke against the idea at the annual gathering of Ohio Yearly Meeting in 1819. He then left *The Philanthropist* and launched his own *Moral Advocate--a Monthly Publication on War, Duelling, Capital Punishment and Prison Reform*.[61]

At first the *Moral Advocate* was a reform journal in the approved Quaker tradition. Elisha wrote the first editorials against the death penalty ever published in Ohio. But he wrote less and less about slavery and other blemishes of the social order. After four years he suspended *The Moral Advocate*, then wrote and printed on his press (in 1825) his second book, titled *The Doctrines of Friends*.

The contrast between Elisha's first and second books is startling. By 1825 his focus had shifted from the cause of the slaves to the cause of blending Quaker and Evangelical brands of Christianity. Benjamin Lundy, Elisha's quondam partner, wrote an unfavorable review:

> Elisha Bates of Mt. Pleasant, Ohio, has lately published...a full and complete Quaker creed...the author is a zealous advocate of the new-fangled system of Quaker Orthodoxy...he would be pleased to see his notion of religion...made a standard.[62]

Elisha's neighbor in Mt. Pleasant was the Reverend David McMasters, a Methodist minister from Virginia. He built the first house in the village in 1810.[63] It is a fair guess that McMasters influenced Elisha, for *The Doctrines of Friends* has 320 pages and 16 chapters of intricately reasoned theology. The first half of the book deals with such evangelical matters as the Original and Present (Fallen) State of Man, Rewards and Punishments, Sanctification and Justification. The last half has a more Quakerly tone, advocating silent worship, a free unsalaried ministry, and inward baptism by the Holy Spirit instead of the outward rite of baptism by water.

As it turns out *The Doctrines of Friends* marked only the first phase of Elisha's glide toward the evangelicals. As previously noted, he visited England in 1833 and allied himself with the extremist Beaconites. In 1836 he had himself baptized by water, left Friends, and joined the Methodists.

By that time the passion of Elisha in his Quaker youth for a just social order was dimmed to zero, supplanted by a passion for theological thinking.

Joseph John Gurney developed a concern for the slaves soon after he became a plain Friend in 1812, although he never actually saw slaves until he visited Virginia twenty-five years later.[64] His anti-slavery concern, unlike Elisha Bates', lasted life long. He joined with his non-Quaker brother-in-law Fowell Buxton, member of Parliament, in a great campaign to abolish slavery in the British colonies. This campaign resulted in the 1838 Act of Parliament which freed some 750,000 black people. In America that same year, 1838, Gurney spoke to the governor of Virginia, to President Van Buren, to Clay, Webster, and Calhoun, urging them to follow Great Britain's lead.[65]

He gave money to purchase land which considerably enlarged Liberia as a refugee for freed blacks.[66] He also supported his sister Elizabeth Fry in her work of helping prisoners, and he gave money to help American Indians. He worked to purify English elections and was interested in the growth of public schools, especially Lancastrian schools. Work for temperance, for abolishing the death penalty and for helping poor people--all these Quakerly concerns were his.[67]

There are certain jarring and *un*Quakerly aspects, however, of Joseph John Gurney's view of the social order. For one thing he was a class-conscious man who certainly did not believe all men and women to be equally children of God. He disliked in America "the universal determination among the people to do what you please; or in other words *ultra-radicalism*. The tendency of democracy [contributes] to this dangerous condition of society."[68] Universal suffrage for whites, practiced in

Pennsylvania and New York, "without any respect whatever to the distinctions of property or education" repelled him.[69]

Joseph John especially lacked sympathy for Quaker belief in the equality of women. He was aghast at "the practice...becoming prevalent in America of the public lecturing by females in the anti-slavery and other philanthropic causes...connected with the new-fangled notion that women have in all respects equal civil and political rights with the stronger sex...this notion, so dangerous to the best refinements and comforts of society, has been pointedly discouraged in this country [England] and there is reason to hope that in America it is gradually but surely fading away."[70]

As for John Wilbur, he had practically no interest in righting worldly wrongs. He knew Friends' history well and he upheld such Quakerly practices as "our ancient testimony of simplicity and plainness" and keeping apart from the world ("I am not able to discover any more safety in our mingling with other people than there was for the Israelites under the law"). But in all the 400-odd pages of his Journal he entered only one reference to the social order. There he deprecated "the laws of the Carolinas [that] tolerate the kidnapping of a free person of color and authorize the kidnapper to sell him as a slave."[71]

\* \* \*

Did Joseph John Gurney know that the main fomenters of the new fangled notion he despised--women have equal rights with the stronger sex, indeed!--were Quaker women? Ring-leaders were the sisters Sarah and Angelina Grimke, and Lucretia Mott.

Sarah and Angelina grew up in Charleston, South Carolina, the daughters of wealthy Judge John Faucheraud Grimke. The city had a House of Correction where constables dragged in unruly slaves. Muffled sounds came from that grisly house which induced the sisters to rebel against slavery and their own aristocratic life style. When Sarah brought her ailing father north for his health in 1819 she encountered Quakers. Soon after, she induced Angelina to come to Philadelphia and to join Friends with her.

In 1835 Angelina wrote a 36-page *Appeal to the Christian Women of the South*: "The women of the South can overthrow this horrible system of oppression and cruelty," she wrote of slavery. The sisters then embarked on a series of anti-slavery lectures, speaking in New England where public speaking by women was not done. An association of Congregational ministers, scandalized, issued three Pastoral Letters denouncing women-lecturers and women-reformers;[72] and Sarah Grimke fired back with her *Letters on the Equality of the Sexes and the Condition of Women* (1838). She indicted the controls exercised over women in the name of protection. "The page of history teems with women's wrongs...it is wet with woman's tears," she declared.[73] This generated much newspaper publicity.

Lucretia Mott (1793-1880) encouraged the Grimke sisters. Lucretia was a petite and cheerful minister among Philadelphia Friends, a mother of five children, who dared to appear in public as a speaker even before the Grimkes--Lucretia spoke at the convention in 1833 where the American Anti-Slavery Society was organized. When that society decided not to admit women, Lucretia formed a separate Philadelphia Female Anti-Slavery Society with sixty black and white women members including the Grimkes.[74]

Lucretia Mott was a firmly traditional Hicksite Friend. She often quoted William Penn's "Men are to be judged by their *likeness* to Christ rather than their *notions* of Christ"[75] And "Truth for Authority, not Authority for Truth" was another insight she valued. In 1848 she attended the Genesee Friends' Yearly Meeting in upstate New York, and took tea there with three other Quaker women--Jane Hunt, Mary Anne McClintock and Lucretia's sister Martha Wright--and with Elizabeth Cady Stanton, who was Lucretia's non-Quaker friend. Over the tea cups the five women planned a Woman's Rights Convention. The Convention took place July 19 and 20 of 1848--the first the world had ever known--with marvelous consequences.[76]

\* \* \*

The ferment over women's rights must have reached Virginia's Quaker women. Some must have read Angelina Grimke's *Appeal to the Christian Women of the South*. The women of the northern Virginia meetings surely heard Lucretia Mott on the subject, for she visited those meetings twice: once in 1818 with Sarah Zane, and again in the fall of 1842 when she spoke in seventeen meetings in eighteen days.[77] The Woman's Rights Convention in 1848 received extensive news coverage, mostly from enraged editors who predicted that equal rights would degrade women.[78]

Nevertheless, no Virginia Quakers spoke out on the subject at that time. They did speak out vigorously, though, on other subjects of Quakerly concern: peace-keeping, education, the Indians, and the evil of slavery....

Friends in Virginia and everywhere opposed the propaganda build-up for the war with Mexico (1846-1848). A newspaper cartoon of 1844 shows a broad-brimmed Quaker saying Nay to politicians James K. Polk and Henry

Clay.⁷⁹ But Clay thundered on the floor of Congress that Texas in the hands of Mexico was "subject to the vile domination of the Inquisition and superstition"; and Polk won the presidency on a platform of Manifest Destiny, implying that the United States had a God-given right to extend west to the Pacific. So the war was fought and by it the U. S. acquired Texas, along with California, Nevada, Utah, Arizona and New Mexico, and parts of Colorado and Wyoming--that is, over half of Mexico.

Virginia's Quakers refused to join the war effort. The sheriffs of Nansemond, Isle of Wight, and Southampton Counties continued as their predecessors had for six generations, seizing the possessions of Quakers who refused to show up for militia musters. Zachariah Doyle and William Harris lost "carts and wheels," Oliver Binford a gun, Jeremiah Chappell, Robert and Joseph Pretlow, Robert and William Hare, cash, and so on.⁸⁰

Then suddenly the seizures ended, in 1849. That year the United States abandoned the militia muster system in favor of conscription. Henceforward the state would punish persons who refuse to join the military by jailing instead of fining them.

Education was another Quaker interest. In southside Virginia the meetings had become so small by the 1830s that none of them kept schools; but in northern Virginia a number of new Friends' schools started up. In Fairfax Quarter, where six schools operated under Friends' care in 1808, there were nineteen in 1852. The nineteen schools enrolled 700 children, of whom 112 were Quakers.⁸¹

All these schools evidently used one or the other of two grammar books written by Quaker educators. Both were intended to hammer home good morals as well as good grammar. Lindley Murray's grammar features such examples of proper sentence structure as "Dissimulation in youth is the forerunner of perfidy in old age. Its first appearance is a token of growing depravity and future shame."⁸² John Comly's grammar inculcates good habits even in its examples of *im*proper sentences: "By observing of truth, thou wilt command esteem, as well as secure peace," and "Patience and diligence overcomes difficulties."⁸³

An increasing proportion of these schools' teachers were young women, who controlled the children with character and spirit instead of spanking. The pupils remembered them with affection:

- Martha Ann Wilson who taught Goose Creek Friends' School about 1835 reportedly scolded a recalcitrant Quaker pupil thus-- "Thee little *you*, thee!" On another day, Martha Ann had this interchange with a beginner boy who stumbled over the word "bed": Martha Ann--"What does thee sleep on?" Boy --"Oh! B-E-D, that spells 'Sheepskin'."[84]

- Hannah Gifford taught Pleasant Valley Seminary near Hamilton, Virginia, a school for the children of Orthodox Friends. She was a New Englander from Cape Cod, raised in the Sandwich Friends Meeting there. Her year-end report to Elmina Holmes's parents suggests the manner of her teaching:

> Elmina R. Holmes has made good progress in all her studies this past year, has committed verses of Scripture and by her good behavior generally has merited the affection of her schoolmates as well as the love and regard of her
>
> well-wishing Teacher
> Hannah Gifford[85]

A variety of boarding schools were available for Virginia Friends' children if no local schools would do: Fair Hill School in Sandy Spring, Maryland operated on and off from 1815 to 1850 under the care of Baltimore Yearly Meeting. Then there was Westtown School under Philadelphia Yearly Meeting's care. Right in Virginia were Benjamin Hallowell's Alexandria Boarding School, Flint Hill Academy and John Pierpont's School, all boarding schools for boys.

At this time also the first Quaker schools for higher education, which later developed into accredited colleges, started up. Haverford School in Pennsylvania (now Haverford College) opened its doors in 1833; Friends' Boarding School (Guilford College), near Greensboro, North Carolina in 1837; and Friends' Boarding School in Richmond, Indiana (Earlham College) in 1847.[86] Orthodox Friends of Joseph John Gurney's bent launched these three "higher" schools, and Earlham was named for the Gurneys' estate in Norwich. Virginia-born Benjamin Ladd was one of the founders for whom Haverford's Founders' Hall is named, and Nathaniel Crenshaw enrolled his son John Bacon Crenshaw in one of Haverford's first classes.

In 1839 Samuel Janney started the Springdale School for girls, close by Goose Creek Meeting. It was somewhat unique among Virginia's female academies. Courses offered most Virginia girls tended to be ornamental-- music, drawing, painting and French. Some did cover such subjects as Latin and arithmetic, but antebellum girls were not commonly supposed to be interested in such profundities. Springdale's curriculum offered drawing, needlework and the French language also, but included bookkeeping, rhetoric and composition, chemistry and algebra.[87] It enrolled twenty-five to thirty lively teen-agers--some boys as well as girls in the school's later years--and was an immediate success.

Beside managing Springdale School, Samuel Janney served on the Goose Creek School Committee. He also promoted public education, which was non-existent in Virginia excepting schools for poor white children financed by the Literary Fund. When Governor James McDowell called a State Educational Convention in Richmond in 1845, fifty-one counties and cities sent delegates--114 delegates in all. Janney was a delegate from Loudoun.

He was appointed to a committee on Common School Education, chaired by Thomas Jefferson Randolph. Soon after the committee convened, Mr. Plumer, a Richmond clergyman, said in substance "I assume we all want to continue the schools for poor children and none of us wants any change." The committee agreed, except Janney and a member of the General Assembly from Wheeling. Janney then stood up and objected to "the pauper system." He proposed a system of free schools like New York State's and bolstered his position with statistics. The committee then voted thirteen for "no change" and two (Janney and the man from Wheeling) for free schools.

The committee reported its majority and minority views to the convention which debated them for a day and a half. Samuel Janney spoke so convincingly for free schools that his minority report carried the Convention by a vote of three-fourths. The next agenda item was a proposition for funding a second military school in addition to Virginia Military Institute, which Janney helped to defeat in a close vote.

The General Assembly debated both of the Common School Committee's reports and then passed a law permitting Free Schools, but only in those counties where the people should vote two-thirds for them. Only six counties did vote Yes, and Samuel Janney was disappointed that Loudoun voted No. Slaveholders in Loudoun and everywhere generally opposed free schools, foreseeing that they would encourage the abolition of slavery.

Nevertheless, the idea of education for every Virginian received a powerful push in 1845, and Samuel Janney deserves much credit for that.[88]

Andrew Jackson, the old Indian fighter, persuaded Congress to designate an Indian Territory far to the west soon after he became president. He then proceeded to force the Indian tribes to move west yet again. All through his presidency and thereafter U. S. army troops pushed the tribes west, goading them on with bayonets when they would not move quietly.

When white people first came to North America, it is estimated that forty tribes with about 190,000 Indian people lived east of the Mississippi. By 1850 about 12,000 were left there. Half of the tribes were extinct, the rest decimated and scattered across the West.[89] All the American Quakers' years of befriending the Native Americans had availed very little.

But the Quakers had not quit. Henry and Ann Harvey and their six children stayed on for nine years with the Shawnees in Kansas who walked there from Wapakoneta in 1832. Baltimore, Ohio and Indiana Yearly Meetings supplied supporting funds. In 1841 two more Friends' families replaced the Harveys.

The next year John Lang and Samuel Taylor came from New England Yearly Meeting for a visit. The Shawnees in Kansas had increased from 800 to 1,200 by 1842. The two New England Friends admired the Shawnee Tract, beautiful land a hundred miles long by twenty-five broad; and the farms and the school where twenty-three boys and fourteen girls learned English (while they spoke Shawanese at home). A 74-year-old Shawnee woman told them she'd lived near the Quaker settlement at Evesham, New Jersey, in her girlhood (so rapidly had her people been pushed West). She remembered Jonathan Evans "the Friend with the long beard...I thought him the best man in the world...and I always loved the Quakers," she said.

Friends Lang and Taylor did *not* admire the drunkenness and despair they saw. The Shawnee chief was drunk at the time he appointed to meet them. A sub-chief greeted them, then told them gravely that the people lived in fear the government would uproot them yet again:

> A long time ago your [Quaker] old men talked to us about your religion and they told us that though your religion was different from our religion, yet if the heart was right we could travel together through this world...tell our friends the Quakers all about what you have seen...that many of us have good farms...and many of us do not drink whisky.... Brothers, that is all I have to say.[90]

Beginning in 1839 the Indian Committee of Baltimore Hicksite Yearly Meeting made common cause with the Genesee, Philadelphia and New York Indian Committees. The cause: to keep the U. S. government from driving the peoples of the Six Nations in western New York away from their native lands. Benjamin Franklin Taylor of Goose Creek was a Baltimore committee member with Philip E. Thomas the committee's clerk. The members visited Presidents Van Buren, Tyler, and Polk and various governors of New York.

After years of visits the committee negotiated a title for the Indians to 52,000 acres. The Indians had first called Philip Thomas *Sagoah* (The Benevolent). Now they changed his title to *Haiwanoh* (Ambassador.)[91]

But of all their concerns, the plight of the slaves was foremost for the dwindling body of Friends left in the southern states.

In December 1833 William Lloyd Garrison and sixty others (twenty-one of them Quakers) organized the American Anti-Slavery Society in Philadelphia. The new society immediately created a commotion, North and South, fueled by Garrison's provocative writing in *The Liberator*. Within four years over a thousand local AA-SS branches formed in the North with over 100,000 members. But Garrison's slashing style also angered millions of whites, and massive opposition to the new society developed.

Many violent things happened in the North and many of them involved Quakers. Prudence Crandall, a Friend of Black Hill Meeting in Connecticut, opened her school to black children after which her neighbors wrecked the schoolhouse. Achilles Pugh in Cincinnati set out to publish a journal for the Ohio Anti-Slavery Society, whereupon thirty or forty men broke into his printing shop and wrecked the press. Numerous Quakers were present at the Anti-Slavery Society's meeting in Philadelphia's Pennsylvania Hall on the night when a mob descended on them and burned down the Hall.[92]

In Virginia, the situation was even more tense: The General Assembly passed a resolution in February 1836, asking all the non-slaveholding states to suppress societies "purporting to be or having the character of abolition societies". Henry Ruffner, the president of Washington College in Lexington, was fired from his job when he advocated a plan for gradually freeing slaves. And all Christian denominations in the state, all, that is, except the Religious Society of Friends, disavowed any interest in freedom for slaves. The Southern Methodists, Baptists and Presbyterians severed relations with the northern churches of their denominations over the issue.[93]

Virginia Yearly Meeting in its epistle for 1836 declared that "the extreme attitudes being voiced in the North have closed the doors of usefulness to us in behalf of the slave...we must now warn all friends against the Abolitionists" (Baltimore and North Carolina Yearly Meetings issued similar warnings at the same time).[94] In the following year two Orthodox Quakers--Gilbert Congdon of Providence, Rhode Island, and James Kite of Philadelphia--exchanged letters touching on this position of the Virginia Friends.

Gilbert Congdon, 26, was an ardent Abolitionist. He opened the correspondence by congratulating James Kite on James's recent marriage and wishing that he, Gilbert, might marry one day. Gilbert then relayed the latest news about New England Yearly Meeting; touched on his interest in Animal Magnetism; and wrote passionately about the need to abolish slavery ("Oh, that I could feel deeper than I do for the 2-1/2 millions of my fellow heirs of immortality who are unrighteously held in cruel bondage. Oh, Americans, my fellow countrymen, how long in this land of boasted liberty shall the iron hand of wicked oppression chain and fetter our fellow creatures[?]").

James Kite replied four days later. He quoted an unnamed Virginia Friend who said that Abolitionists were hurting the efforts of Friends in Virginia to help the slaves; and declared that he, James, was bound to agree with the Virginian. Congdon fired back seven heated pages:

> My friend James I do not see that thou gains anything by the testimony of the Virginia Friend.... Do I understand that because the South believes or professes to that the Abolitionists are wrong, therefore [Virginia's] Friends ought not to injure their good *name* by identifying themselves [with Abolitionists]?.... Oh spare me from the situation of him who fails to...'relieve the oppressed, judge the fatherless and plead for the widow' because he might thereby lose some of the *respect* of our ungodly generation.[95]

Gilbert Congdon must have changed his mind about Virginia's Friends, however, for he was to marry one of them.

The next year, 1840, Virginia Yearly Meeting in its epistle wrote, "We are still continuing our efforts on behalf of the...African race amongst us illegally held in bondage. The subject of petitioning our Legislature for an amelioration of the laws...relative to that much-injured people [has been referred to] our Meeting for Sufferings."[96] And four years later, right after Virginia's Yearly Meeting had been laid down, a group of southside Virginia Friends did petition for repeal of the state law whereby free blacks were jailed for failing to carry their "free papers" with them at all times.[97] In 1848 the Friends of Fairfax Quarter sent Samuel Janney and Benjamin Hallowell to Richmond with still another petition--this one requesting repeal of the law forbidding schools for black children. It reads:

> The Memorial of the Society of Friends commonly called Quakers, comprising Fairfax Quarterly Meeting and residing in the counties of Berkeley, Jefferson, Frederick, Loudoun, Fairfax and

Alexandria...respectfully represents...that our Yearly Meeting at its last session...urged upon all its members to be faithful in imparting the blessing of education to...the free colored children in our respective neighborhoods.... but being citizens of the State of Virginia we find ourselves straitened...in consequence of a law of the State in opposition thereto...we respectfully ask such a modification of the law...as will admit our compliance with...the injunction of the blessed Jesus, 'As you would that men should do to you, do ye even so to them.'[98]

\* \* \*

Nathaniel Crenshaw and Samuel Janney led Friends in southern and in northern Virginia respectively in efforts to aid their black neighbors:

In 1837 Nathaniel attended the Orthodox Friends' Yearly Meeting in Philadelphia. He brought home a thousand copies of a Quaker tract on the evils of slavery. On distributing some of them he was indicted, jailed, brought before Hanover County's grand jury and warned.[99]

In spite of the warning, Nathaniel kept trying to help blacks. His sister-in-law, Margaret Crew, who lived with Nathaniel and looked after Nathaniel's little son, kept an illegal school for black children at Shrubbery Hill.[100] Nathaniel himself went into court again and again to sue for the freedom of blacks held as slaves who had a claim to freedom. He succeeded in winning freedom for hundreds and helped them to re-settle in Ohio, Canada, Pennsylvania and Liberia. Some slaveholders he sued were the children of Quakers who refused to liberate blacks as decreed by their Quaker parents' wills.[101] One black who credited Nathaniel for his freedom, a man named Richardson, became lieutenant-governor of Liberia.[102]

During the winter of 1841-1842 Nathaniel wrote three letters to Gerrit Smith, a wealthy Presbyterian philanthropist living near Syracuse, New York. Nathaniel began his first letter by stressing that "*it must be confidential*, and if thou art willing to aid me, it must be after the injunction of our *Divine Master* of not letting the left hand know what the right hand doeth." He then asked Gerrit Smith for money to purchase certain slaves in order to save them from the negro traders. "I have been instrumental in relieving more than 200 persons from slavery myself, besides acting with a committee of our Yearly Meeting who have relieved many more," he wrote. Gerrit Smith replied by offering moral support but no funds. Toward the end of the correspondence, Nathaniel stressed again the need for secrecy:

> My anxiety on this subject does not arise from any fear of being known here as an abolitionist, for that I publicly profess to be...but it is the connection with the northern abolition societies and all intercourse with them, and I must say to thee that whilst I give [them] credit for good intentions I fear they have done many things...prejudicial to the interest of the poor slave and exceedingly embarrassing to us.[103]

Samuel Janney worked as vigorously for the poor slave, but in a different way: The cotton mill at Occoquan absorbed his time, 1828-1838; but soon after establishing Springdale School, Janney returned to the struggle against slavery. He toured Virginia in 1841, speaking out bravely at public meetings in Warrenton, Culpeper, Madison, Orange and Charlottesville, and then north up the valley--in Waynesboro, Staunton, Port Republic, Weyer's Cave, Harrisonburg, Columbia Iron Works, Winchester. This speaking trip made him unpopular with Loudoun's slave-owners.[104]

Beginning in 1843, he prodded certain newspaper editors in Baltimore, Alexandria and Richmond until they took the risky step of publishing series of Janney-written feature articles in favor of emancipation for slaves. Of his series in the Baltimore *Saturday Visitor*, Samuel wrote to a Quaker friend: "My articles to start the abolition discussion in the Baltimore *Visitor* have lost some subscribers but gained a good many."[105] The Alexandria *Gazette* published an equally controversial series by Janney that ran from April to December 1844.[106] A third series, just as controversial, appeared in the Richmond *Whig* late in 1845.

The *Whig*'s editor was John Hampden Pleasants (1797-1846). He was Governor James Pleasants's son, who shared the anti-slavery sentiments of his many Quaker cousins, and was therefore vulnerable to Samuel Janney's friendly persuasion. Actually it was Samuel's brother, Asa Moore Janney (1802-1877), then living in Richmond, who persuaded John Hampden Pleasants to publish the articles. Samuel wrote in Second Month 1844, "The Richmond *Whig* has come out boldly in defence of free blacks. I believe the Divine Spirit is moving!"[107]; and on 7 Seventh Month 1845 he wrote John Hampden Pleasants, saying

> J. H. Pleasants Respected Friend,--My brother Asa having informed me that thou art now ready to publish my series of essays on slavery--and that the copy sent thee cannot be found: I have prepared another copy which I herewith send...I hope much from thy vigorous and independent spirit...the present is a most propitious

time.... May we then stand up and dare to acknowledge the glorious principle of liberty proclaimed by our fathers....

I have not put my name to the essays...as I expect to continue writing on the subject for some years it would seem too much like courting notoriety. If thou shouldst be likely to suffer in any way from their publication thou canst then give my name and throw the responsibility on me. I have counted the cost and made up my mind to do and to suffer what duty may require, but I do not apprehend any danger whatever.[108]

There *was* danger, though, and John Hampden Pleasants bore the brunt bravely. The *Whig*'s competitor was the Richmond *Enquirer*, a conservative paper that advocated slavery. Thomas Ritchie, Jr., its editor, furiously attacked the *Whig*'s anti-slavery series and smeared Pleasants's character in the process. Pleasants never involved Samuel Janney, but instead challenged Ritchie to duel. They met with pistols on the south bank of the James and Pleasants was mortally wounded.[109]

Some cautious Friends including Samuel Janney's uncle Phineas warned him that his school would suffer if he kept on against slavery. Samuel answered, "My school may suffer and perhaps has suffered by my open opposition to slavery but, when duty calls, interest must not stand in the way."

Janney found two courageous editors of Leesburg newspapers who sided with him--C. C. McIntyre of the *Washingtonian* and Thomas C. Connolly of the *Loudoun Whig*--and his unpopularity among slaveholders grew as his hard-hitting articles appeared in those papers. "It is a painful fact," Benjamin Franklin Taylor wrote to a friend, "that he [Samuel Janney] manages some [way] or other to excite a degree of public odium against himself which is unparalleled in our community, and which his goodness of heart and truly Christian character does not merit."[110]

In 1849 Samuel and Connolly were on the verge of moving to Richmond to start an antislavery paper there. That summer, however, the Reverend William A. Smith made a proslavery speech in Leesburg. He was president of Randolph-Macon College and a leading Methodist apologist for slavery. The speech made Samuel Janney grit his teeth. He responded with three strongly worded articles, two of them published in *The Washingtonian*.[111]

Those articles caused the Commonwealth's attorney for Loudoun to indict Janney for writings "calculated to incite persons of color to make an insurrection." Janney pleaded his own case before a grand jury in Leesburg's courthouse and was let off with a warning against "meddling with the delicate question of slavery." But thereafter Samuel Janney was a marked man.[112]

\* \* \*

Meanwhile Virginia's slave merchants kept right on selling Virginia-born slaves down south. The voices of Virginians calling justice for the black people were drowned by the voices of slave auctioneers. Prices climbed all through the 1830s and 1840s. The average auction price for a slave jumped to $600 in 1836. Twenty years later the Omohundro brothers, slave merchants of Richmond, were paying plantation owners $1,500 for field hands and still averaging a clear $100 profit. At Robert Lumpkin's slave jail in Richmond (known as the Devil's Half Acre and located on the present-day campus of Virginia Union University), a prime hand went for $2,000-- whereupon someone in the auction crowd exclaimed, "Dammit. How slaves has riz!"[113]

T. Jefferson Randolph spoke about it on the floor of the General Assembly: "Human flesh is now the great staple of Virginia," he said. Our state has "been converted into one grand menagerie where men are reared for the market like oxen for the shambles."[114] But such protests had no effect at all.

Virginia's blacks understood well enough the existence waiting for them in the deep South's cotton and rice fields. Increasing numbers, desperate, decided to try to escape North. Some whites were sympathetic enough and foolhardy enough to help them get North.

One August night in 1839, a Washington, D. C. patrolman came by the east entrance of the Capitol A 17-year-old black fellow stood by the steps in shadows, listening as for a signal. Questioned, he refused to say what he waited for or where he came from, only that his name was Jim Jones. He was jailed overnight and taken to a blacksmith's the next morning. There his thumbs were forced into the smith's vice and as the screw was turned:

"Now you black son of a bitch why were you at the Capitol last night?"
"Massa, a white man told me."
"What did he want of you?"
"Fo to go North"
"And so you were going?"
"Yes, Massa-I-was-for-to-go"
"How?"
"On a railroad-under-the-ground."

A Washington morning paper reported the incident saying in part "They gave the screw another turn when he said, 'The railroad goes underground all the way to Boston.' Our citizens are losing some of their best servants.

Some secret Yankee arrangement has been contrived."[115] And that is how, as it seems, the term "Underground Railroad" (UGRR) came to be.

"Underground Railroad," a catch phrase. It caught on at once, both South and North:

- In the South, the blacks murmured and chuckled it to one another in their secret meetings in the midnight woods. There was new hope in the night meetings. Presently the slaves began to sing some new songs half spirituals and half escape songs: "Go down, Moses, way down in Egypt la-and/ Te-ell old Pha-a-aroh/ Let my people GO!" and "Steal away/ steal away/ steal away to Jesus" and "Follow the drinkin' gourd/ Follow the drinkin' gourd/ For the old man is a-waitin' for to carry you to FREEDOM/ Follow the drinkin' gourd."
- To the North, above the Potomac and Ohio Rivers, certain whites and a few freed blacks formed "Underground Railroad lines" to help escaping slaves--a web of nighttime paths, stream fordings, wagon, train and boat routes. All haunted by the specter of recapture. The "stations" were the houses, barns and corn-cribs of the Roads' "station-keepers"--men and women who refused to believe that slavery and decency can exist together.[116]

All or nearly all the railroaders were religious people, Christians of one kind or another, with members of the Society of Friends predominating. All were united by certain concepts found in the depths of conscience and in the sense of some *Bible* passages: "Thou shalt not deliver unto his master the servant which is escaped"; "Woe to him that...uses his neighbor's service without wages"; "Hide the outcasts, betray not him that wandereth"; "Is not this [a better way to serve God than by fasting] to let the oppressed go free, and [to] break every yoke?"--"Neither be called masters [for] whosoever shall exalt himself shall be abased."*

And they were equally united in denying the favorite *Bible* texts of slaveholders: "Cursed be Canaan; a servant of servants shall he be"--"Both thy bondmen and thy bondmaid's...shall be of the heathen...of them shall ye buy bondmen and bondmaids"; and "Servants be obedient to them that are your masters...."**

It was not really an *organization*, the Underground Railroad; it was more like a volunteer *movement*. Anyone caught working on this railroad was punished sorely, and so the workers' identities were secret. No one knew all

---

*Deut 23:15, Jer 22:13, Isa 16:3 and 6, Matt 23:10-12

**Gen 9:25, Lev 25:44 and Eph 6:5

the names, although the Railroad had a president or rather two presidents, and it was in fact two railroads overlapping instead of one:

President of the western Underground was Levi Coffin (1798-1877). He was one of the Quaker Coffins of Greensboro, North Carolina, who began to escort escaping slaves across Virginia to Ohio in 1819. Levi and his wife Catherine White, "Aunt Kate," moved to Fountain City, north of Richmond, Indiana, in 1826 and then to Cincinnati in 1846.[117] Their home with Levi's store was a kind of Union Station for slaves fleeing north out of Kentucky and Tennessee.

Daniel Neall, a Philadelphia Quaker, first headed up the eastern UGRR.[118] He was presiding at the Anti-Slavery Society's meeting in Philadelphia's Pennsylvania Hall that night in 1838 when the mob burned down the hall. The eastern Road mainly served slaves fleeing north from Delaware, Maryland, Virginia, and North Carolina. As for slaves in the deeper South, South Carolina and southward, it was a rare thing for them to get away to freedom.

After the Civil War a few books were published about the UGRR, describing its routes and naming its workers *in the North*. But any Virginian known to have helped slaves to escape would have incurred the community's wrath for years after the war. So it is that the story of UGRR activities in the South has never been written. Yet the slaves certainly must have had some help in coming up through Virginia. Tradition says they traveled by night following the North Star and the Dipper ("Follow the drinkin' gourd" is a veiled reference to the Little Dipper). But they must have had some earthly guidance too, along with the heavenly.

What ways did fleeing slaves follow up through Virginia? And who helped them in their flight? One clue lies in the observation that four of the UGRR's trunk lines to Canada had stations on or near Virginia's northern border. The northern border of 1840s Virginia stretched in a great jagged 550-mile, west-to-east arc--from Huntington on the Ohio River, bordering the free states of Ohio and Pennsylvania for some 350 miles arc-wise, then bordering the slave state of Maryland all the way east to the Atlantic Ocean above Chincoteague Island. The lift of the Appalachian Mountains running south to north divides the arc roughly in half, like an arrow fitted to the bow.

Of the four UGRR stations on or near Virginia's border, one lay west of the Appalachians and three east. The west station was on the *Ohio bank* of the Ohio River. To the east were stations in the *Great Valley* which extends up from the valley of Virginia; in *Washington*, D. C.; and in the region of *Hampton Roads*.

So then, four Freedom roads led North out of Virginia--four leaks for Virginia's slaveholders to seal off. Let us consider the four Roads one by one:

*To the Ohio Bank*--This Road in Virginia ran across the Blue Ridge and the Appalachians through the Kanawha River Valley, right by Charleston, Virginia, on to the Ohio.[119] The Coffin brothers of Greensboro, North Carolina guided North Carolina slave groups this way from 1819 on. In Richmond, Virginia Quaker Henry Crew evidently helped Virginia slaves to escape this way too.

Henry Crew in his youth taught the black children of Gravelly Hill School. Now he was the eastern manager of Benjamin Ladd's enterprises--Ladd, the Friend from Virginia who went to Smithfield, Ohio, and became wealthy as a pork packer. Ladd and Company's covered wagons, each pulled by five or six belled horses, hauled bacon and hams eastward to Richmond. Henry Crew loaded the wagons with dry goods and groceries for the return trip to Ohio, and he must have loaded fugitive slaves too. For, as is now known, Ben Ladd--respected businessman, clerk of Ohio Yearly Meeting Orthodox and a founder of Haverford College--was also an Ohio station master on the Underground Railroad.

Houses and barns dotted the Ohio bank, where fugitives could hide once they got across the river. The vicinity of Wheeling, Virginia was a favored crossing place. Fugitives who crossed there sheltered in Quaker-run stations on the Ohio side:

- Widow Sarah Bundy's barn at Powhatan Point was one of these. Sarah's son William guided "passengers" inland to the farms of Joshua Hoge and Eli Nichols (all three of these Quaker families, Bundys, Hoges and Nichols' being recent emigrants from Virginia).
- Other passengers crossed three miles above Wheeling and went to Joshua Cope's mill at the mouth of Glenn's Run, close by the Quaker settlement at Mt. Pleasant. Joshua, raised as a boy in Virginia's Hopewell Meeting, said many runaways hid behind the spray of his mill-wheel while he chatted with planters and U.S. marshals in pursuit of them.[120]

Fugitives in Ohio stole northward at night from station to station, a hundred miles or more, until they reached a Lake Erie port--Ashtabula, Cleveland or Sandusky. Way stations were located on Ben Ladd's farm in Smithfield and in the Quaker settlement at Salem, Ohio. Hubbard and Co., commission agents, received the slaves in Ashtabula and the merchant Joseph Garretson in Cleveland. Some were smuggled across the lake aboard the *Arrow*, an "abolition boat" that landed them in Malden, Canada. Others crossed in scows, sailboats and sharpies.[121]

A few stayed on in Ohio. Ben Ladd bought fifty acres near Sandusky and tried to settle four hundred blacks there in 1821. The blacks were driven away, and Ladd then arranged for a permanent black community called Hayti, near his home.[122]

*Up the Valley*--As for the UGRR line running up the valley of Virginia, across the narrow neck of Western Maryland and on into Pennsylvania, the chief clue comes from Frederick Law Olmsted (1821-1903). He was no Quaker, but a landscape architect, the man who designed Central Park in New York City. Olmsted struck up a conversation with Uncle Tom, a 61-year-old slave, deep in southern Louisiana in 1853. Uncle Tom, born in Virginia and sold south during his young manhood, led off:

> "Does you live in Tennessee, mass'r?"
> "No--in New York."
> "There's heaps of Quakers in New York, ain't there, mass'r?"
> "No--not many."
> "I've always heard there was."
> "In Philadelphia there are a good many."
> "Oh yes! In Philadelphia and in Winchester and New Jersey. I know-ho! ho! I've been in those countries and I've seen 'em. I was raised right by Winchester, and I've been all about there. Used to iron wagons and shoe horses in that country. There's a road from Winchester to Philadelphia--right straight. Quakers all along. Right good people, them Quakers. Ho! Ho! I know."

Olmsted wrote that this conversation was "evidently an allusion to the Underground Railroad which is generally supposed to be managed mainly by Quakers."[123]

Joseph N. Jolliffe (1813-1894) was an Orthodox Quaker of Hopewell Meeting who lived at Swarthmore Farm about six miles north of Winchester on the Philadelphia Road. He and his family were most likely among the good Quakers Uncle Tom remembered.[124] Jolliffe's relative was John J. Jolliffe (1804-1868) who emigrated to Cincinnati. As a trial lawyer there he defended many fugitive slaves pro bono.[125]

Goose Creek Meeting twenty miles east of Hopewell was also rumored to be a UGRR center. Samuel Janney never admitted being a UGRR station master but Asa and Werner Janney found a section of wainscoting in their Uncle Samuel's Springdale schoolhouse that came out when pressed right. Behind is a space just big enough to hold a man. And Yardley Taylor (1794-1869) of Goose Creek was actually arrested and tried for helping a slave to escape.[126] From Hopewell and Goose Creek the slaves passed on north to Pennsylvania.

*Via Washington, D.C.*--The Road that led right into Washington, D. C. was risky. It came up from southside Virginia, along present-day U. S. Routes 1 and 95, right by the slave pens of Petersburg, Richmond, Fredericksburg, and Alexandria. This was slave country and plantation country, unlike western Virginia. Night patrols watched the roads and the sheriffs kept bloodhounds to track down black strangers. The hoarse bays of those hounds coursing the night woods alarmed the neighborhood like a firebell.

Nevertheless, slaves followed this "Washington Line" to freedom, from deep in North Carolina and all along the way through Virginia. Stations were kept up every twenty to thirty miles along the way. The station masters answered light uncertain taps at all night hours, opening the door to find briar-scratched, famished fugitives there, some so scared they could not tell even their names or whence they came, some whispering a sort of password-- "Is you for the North Star, Missus?"

The Washington Line north of Richmond was marked by nails in trees and in fence rails at forks in the roads. If the right hand road was to be taken the nail was driven in the right hand side of the tree trunk, belt-high. If no tree but only a fence corner, the nail was to be found in the second rail from the top, on the inside, to the right or left of the corner post. Conductors marked the way and changed it when necessary. They showed the fugitives how to cross the rivers--Appomattox, James, Pamunkey, Mat, Ta, Po, Ni, Rappahannock, Occoquan, at last the Potomac (tie together four to six fencerails for a raft; cut the rails apart after crossing and let them float on down river to destroy the trace of your crossing). The stationkeepers rarely kept their stations more than ten years, for the strain was great.[127]

None of the Washington Line's stationkeepers are certainly known, although strong indicators point to free black and Quaker families. A black with the alias "Hamm and Eggs" was a conductor in and around Richmond.[128] Among the Quakers, Nathaniel Crenshaw and his son John B. are suspect. The Crenshaws had a farm called Rocouncy six miles north from Richmond along the stretch where nails guided the refugees along. Furthermore they exchanged warm letters with Richard and George Mendenhall, brothers of Jamestown, North Carolina, who certainly put slaves on their way North via the UGRR.[129] Henry Hallowell (1829-1899) is another suspect Quaker conductor. He was Benjamin Hallowell's oldest son, known as an ardent abolitionist in Alexandria before and after he attended Yale University in the early 1850s.[130]

Five Quaker meeting houses stood close by the route of the Washington Line --Richmond, Cedar Creek, Caroline, Woodlawn, Alexandria. The Friends of Caroline were nearly all gone West by the 1830s, but Woodlawn was a thriving Friends' center. Jacob Troth, whose clapboard farmhouse faces the highway to Alexandria, probably was Woodlawn Meeting's leading UGRR stationkeeper.[131] In any case Quaker homes were easy for fugitives to find. Lydia Maria Child wrote in 1848, "A traveller recently told me that the farms cultivated by Quakers, who employ no slaves, form such a striking contrast to other portions of Virginia that they seem like oases in the desert."[132] And James Curry, who escaped from a plantation near Roxbury, North Carolina, related that

> I knew the way to Petersburg, Virginia, having been several times sent there by my master with a team. Near Petersburg we passed a neat farm house with everything around it in perfect order, which had been shown me by a slave as I was driving my master's team to the city. 'That' said he, 'belongs to a Friend, they never hold slaves.' I was strongly tempted, but dared not stop there. So, not knowing the North Star, we took the lower arm of the Great Bear for our guide and went on.... Near Philadelphia I fell in with members of the Society of Friends, whom I never feared to trust.[133]

The slaves who reached Washington sheltered in a station managed at first by Charles Torrey (1813-1846) a Congregational minister and Yale graduate. He helped nearly 400 slaves to get North before he was detected and died in prison. Then Joshua Bigelow took over--a mysterious bachelor who lived at 7th and E Streets NW, listed himself in the Washington city directory as a General Agent and used the alias William Penn.[134] He passed the fugitives along to Elisha Tyson, a Baltimore Quaker, who sent them on to Thomas Garrett, the Quaker hardware store proprietor of Shipley Street, Wilmington, Delaware.

*Sea Way*--The Atlantic Ocean served as the fourth way for slaves to flee North. Slaves from tidewater North Carolina and Virginia fled this way, stealing to one of the four Hampton Roads port cities, Portsmouth, Norfolk, Newport News or Hampton, where they stowed away in ships headed north.

Lazarus Pearson and wife, of Contentnea Friends Meeting, kept a station on their farm near Goldsboro, North Carolina--the southmost depot of the

UGRR as far as is known. The Pearsons sent some of their passengers forty miles east to New Bern to be smuggled aboard ocean-going vessels. Others they routed north to Friends of the North Carolina meetings just below the Virginia state line--Rich Square, Cedar Grove and Piney River.[135]

These North Carolina Friends were in danger. The people in their neighborhoods dealt violently with "man stealers." Both North Carolina Yearly Meeting and Rich Square Monthly Meeting issued denials in 1843 of the meetings' involvement in UGRR activities. "One or two [of our] members have suffered themselves [to] give shelter improperly to one or more slaves and thus occasioned several of their fellow members to be accused," Rich Square's statement read, and "we have therefore thought it due to ourselves and to the people at large of the country in which we live to make known our...disapproval of such interference.... At the same time we do not in the least degree relinquish our testimony to the injustice of slavery."[136] In spite of this disavowal, however, the members who were giving such shelter continued giving it, and they were more than one or two.

Henry and Dolly Copeland of Rich Square were leading station-keepers. Their house had an L with a separate attic entered through an upstairs bedroom. Seven runaways or more could hide there and a chest pushed up against the wall concealed the entry.[137] Other "keepers" were John and Edna Hare of Somerton Meeting in Virginia and later of Rich Square. Isaac and Jane Parker of Rich Square sheltered "passengers" in their barn, and sometimes disguised the women in Quaker bonnets and shawls.[138]

Still others, names unknown, lived on in the memory of the Reverend C.W.B. Gordon, the son of a slave. Interviewed when he was an old man, Reverend Gordon said

> My father was educated by Quakers in Hertford County, N.C...the Underground Railroad had only one office in the South and that was in Hertford County at Winton.... Anybody who wanted to go...free...went from Winton by the hands of Quakers.[139]

Winton is about fifteen miles south of the Virginia state line, twenty miles south of Somerton Meeting and forty miles south of Portsmouth. It is a fair guess that slaves setting out for freedom from Winton went up to Portsmouth by way of the settlement of Quakers at Somerton. Jane Pyatt who was a slave in Portsmouth recalled in 1937 that

> On North Street [in Portsmouth] there was an old brick building. The cellar of the building led into an underground railroad. This passageway extended to the ferry of the Elizabeth River. Boats stayed there all the time, making it possible for many slaves to escape.[140]

\* \* \*

The Industrial Revolution in the United States picked up speed while Andrew Jackson occupied the White House, 1829-1837, and thereafter. An acceleration of changes, a rite of passage, a quickened American tempo, the Jacksonian Age:

"Our age is wholly of a different character from the past," Daniel Webster orated. "Society is full of excitement."

"The whole continent presents a scene of scrambling and roars with greedy hurry," a visiting Englishman dourly observed. "'Go ahead!' is the order of the day."[141]

"Go ahead!"--what on earth did that mean? In America it meant a drive to make money, to acquire "the conveniences." These conveniences were becoming plentiful as invention followed ingenious invention: canned food, ice boxes, indoor plumbing, matches. Anesthesia was discovered by Dr. Morton the dentist in 1842; Samuel F. B. Morse's telegraph in 1844; Elias Howe's sewing machine in 1846.

Of all the southern states, Virginia changed most in the Age of Jackson. The changes were not as obvious as in the North but they were there: Richmond became the world's tobacco capital. Virginia's chewing tobacco, pipe tobacco, snuff and cigar factories produced more tobacco products than all the other states combined. Great flour mills appeared on the river banks of Alexandria, Richmond, and Petersburg. Farmers began to by-pass their neighborhood grist mills because the big new mills paid better money. The Gallego Mill in Richmond turned out nearly a thousand barrels of flour a day, exported around the world. Virginians contributed to the list of inventions, the most famous being the Virginia reaper patented by Cyrus McCormick of Rockbridge County in 1834. It could harvest wheat four or five times faster then a man with a scythe.[142]

Not all Virginians took a part in all this "Go ahead." Most stayed on the farm, their life patterns not much disturbed. Most of the Friendly Virginians stayed on the farm, but some joined in the scramble:

- At least one young Friend went out to California in the Gold Rush of 1849, struck it rich and came back home to Virginia. He was John Purcell, 22, of Hopewell Meeting who found gold in a California creek.[143]

- Sarah Janney Michener of the Fairfax Meeting Janneys managed the Gallego Mill in Richmond until 1829. She started the Gallego brand of flour on the way to world fame.[144]
- Lewis and Joel Lupton of Hopewell Meeting were business partners and inventors: Lewis inventing a road scraper, Joel an adding machine and a reaper that rivalled McCormick's.[145]
- John Griffith (1778-1870), another Hopewell Friend, became an authentic big businessman. He established a profitable textile mill, the Friendly Grove Factory of Winchester, with Asa Hoge, his brother-in-law (Griffith and Hoge); he was the major partner in mills in Wilmington, Delaware (Griffith, Dupont and Co.) and Philadelphia (Griffith, Hance and Co.).[146]
- Two Friends of Alexandria Meeting, Phineas Janney and Robert H. Miller, planned the Orange and Alexandria Railroad which laid track from Alexandria southward late in the 1840s.[147]
- But the Friend who made the greatest contribution to Virginia's economic well-being was Matthew Harris (1801-1882). He was a Sussex County farmer, a Friend of Black Creek Meeting who married Nancy Babb under care of that meeting. One summer Seventh Day in 1842 Matthew visited the Norfolk docks. He chanced upon a West Indian trader there who sold him a bushel of peanuts --exotic legumes unknown in Virginia. He took the curious things home, planted them and produced the first commercial crop of peanuts in the United States. The crop was a godsend for southside Virginia where tobacco had worn out so much of the land.[148]

Whether these Friends were affected in a spiritual sense by the "Go ahead" drive of the times, that is uncertain. A traveling Friend who visited the homesteads of John and Rachel Griffith and of Matthew and Nancy Harris commented on the Quakerly simplicity and well-brought-up children he found in both homes.[149] On the other hand, the numbers of Friends' ministers who visited the Virginia meetings after 1840 gradually decreased. Perhaps the speeded-up times were making it more difficult to get away from one's workplace in order to travel in Truth's service.

\* \* \*

In May of 1827, a tall 24-year-old Unitarian minister fresh out of Harvard Divinity School boarded a north-bound boat in Alexandria, Virginia. His name, Ralph Waldo Emerson. He had been south for his health and now was on his way home to Boston. Aboard the boat he met Edward Stabler, Jr., 58, Friends' minister of Alexandria Meeting, ally of Elias Hicks and proprietor of the drugstore on Alexandria's Fairfax Street. The two men fell into a conversation, after which Emerson noted in his journal

> It was said of Jesus that 'he taught as one having authority....' There are a few men in every age, I suppose, who teach thus. Stabler the Quaker, whom I saw on board the boat in Delaware Bay, was one.

Later on he wrote of Edward Stabler as one who "ministered to my highest wants." He quoted Stabler as saying "If a man sacrifices his impurity, purity should be the price with which it should be paid; if a man gives up his hatred, he should be rewarded with love."[150]

Five years later Emerson resigned as minister of Boston's Second Church (Unitarian), declaring he no longer regarded the Lord's Supper as a sacrament, and could not continue to administer it. He moved to nearby Concord where a group of friends began to meet in his parlor to discuss philosophy and literature. Presently the group became known as the Transcendental Club. It included such remarkable members as Henry David Thoreau, Bronson Alcott, Nathaniel Hawthorne and Margaret Fuller. All were appalled by the preoccupation of the nation with economic matters and concerned that spiritual progress was not keeping pace.

The Transcendentalists led by Emerson worked out a philosophy of their own. It was based on Quakerism, on Eastern mysticism, on German philosophy, on Wordsworth and Coleridge the English romantic poets, on all the thinking of the time that celebrated humankind's essential goodness. They rejected evangelical doctrines, original sin and the like, as "pale negations." "To know what is right," a Transcendentalist said, "I need not ask what is the current practice, what say the Revised Statutes, what said holy men of old, but what says conscience? what, God?"[151]

Emerson became a lecturer and writer, spreading Transcendentalism far and wide. He lectured on humans' unbroken connection with God, on the Oversoul, on self-reliance. In February 1835 he lectured in Boston on the life of George Fox. In his travels he met such Quakers as Lucretia Mott and Mary Rotch of New Bedford, Massachusetts. Late in life he wrote, "The Quakers in their best representatives appear to me to have come closer to the sublime history and genius of Christ than any other of the sects."[152]

Emerson was the first distinctively American thinker to influence European thinkers. He influenced Friedrich Nietszche, Maurice Maeterlinck and the French philosopher Henri Bergson. The philosophy he espoused is said to represent "the flowering of New England." But this flowering was not rooted entirely in New England. One root grew out of the life and thought of the Virginia Friend Edward Stabler, Jr.

\* \* \*

Now it is 1850 in Virginia, the moon and stars having followed the sun in a steady round to that year. That spring, just as in the springtimes of these present years, the Virginia woods were all changing, shifting colors. The spring came on and the trees budded, oaks and chestnuts, tulip trees and locusts. The colors changed from winter gray, mauve and dusted purple to tender pink and many greens. Here and there redbuds and dogwoods flowered and flared.

Some 1,400,000 people lived in the state that spring. Nine out of ten Virginians lived out in the country, but now some towns were sizeable-- Richmond the largest with a population near 30,000, Norfolk second with 16,000. Railroads laced together many of the towns and their whistles echoed through the springtime woods.

After seventy years of almost continuous depression, Virginia's economy was swinging up.[153] Many farmers had turned from growing tobacco to wheat. The economy was better balanced. The price of farmland was increasing. Before the 1850s ended Richmond was the nation's third most affluent city with (white) citizens worth an average $1,593.42. But this impressive worth was not typical of the whole state.[154]

Virginians in 1850 lived by a three-tiered caste arrangement, planters and professional men at the top, slaves at the bottom:

Some men of the ruling caste were addressed as Judge or Doctor, though more went by Colonel or Major, titles which had no relationship to military rank but were status symbols.[155] They went to the Springs in the warm months--Warm Springs, the Hot, the White Sulphur, the Sweet, the Salt Sulphur or the Red Sulphur. The hospitality of their homes was legendary. Until 1850 the state's government was in their hands.

The more ordinary Virginians vastly out-numbered the colonel-and-major caste. By 1850, more white Virginians lived west than east of the Blue Ridge, and few of the western Virginians were aristocrats. That year, after long agitating, the western Virginians finally got the state to adopt a more democratic constitution. The Constitution of 1850 provided for universal (white) manhood suffrage and election of the governor by the people instead of the legislators.[156]

For every two free people there was one slave.

The caste arrangement was roughly reflected in Virginia's churches: the ruling class in high hats and cravats, crinolines and silk dresses went to the high-spired Episcopalian churches. The Episcopal Church in Virginia was reverting from a period of low church, evangelical practice to its original emphasis on liturgy, the *Book of Common Prayer* and artistry in church music, church interiors, and church ceremony[157] --the ordinary people continued to attend the Methodist, Baptist and Presbyterian congregations which were thriving[158] in Virginia in spite of the separation of all three denominations into southern and northern branches. As for black Virginians, they had been occupying the galleries of the main line churches segregated from the whites for generations. Most blacks preferred the fervent evangelicalism of the Baptist churches.

In the 1840s the Baptists began to allow black members to have their own separate churches with white ministers and committees of black deacons in charge. The Afro-Baptist churches soon took on a distinctive style. The congregation would listen patiently until the white minister's sermon ended, then would respond passionately to black exhorters or deacons who led them in lengthy prayer. After the white minister left the church, most of the congregation would stay on for a time of more exhorting, with hand shakes of fellowship and rhythmic, spontaneous, deeply felt singing. At last black Virginians had places they could call their own.[159]

Beside the steeples of the four main line churches--Episcopal, Methodist, Baptist and Presbyterian--many others appeared along Virginia's skyline by 1850. These included St. Peter's in Richmond, the cathedral church of the Catholic Diocese of Virginia (established 1820); churches of the Disciples of Christ, a denomination divided off from the Presbyterians and Baptists early in the 1800s; and Universalists and Unitarians. There were three Jewish synagogues in Richmond, and five denominations in Virginia where the services were in German--Lutheran, Reformed, United Brethren, and (strong in the valley of Virginia) the Church of the Brethren (Dunkers), and Mennonites.[160]

Of all these, Virginia's Friends were closest to the Brethren and the Mennonites, who built their first church buildings in Virginia in Rockingham and Augusta Counties in the 1820s.[161] All three, Brethren, Mennonite, and Quaker, stood against war. They were known collectively as the Peace Churches.

The Friends, however, differed from all others, being the only worshipers who waited for God's guidance against a backdrop of silence, without professional preachers, priests or rabbis.

Virginia's drawback in 1850 was the institution of slavery. Slavery is an impossible anomaly in a nation dedicated to life, liberty and the pursuit of happiness. Virginia and all the southern states were on the defensive, absorbed in justifying the contradiction to which they clung. Yankee-bashing by Virginia's newspaper editors was on the upswing, animosity toward Northerners increasing.

Samuel McPherson Janney (1801-1880) (left) of Goose Creek was an inspiring leader of northern Virginia's Hicksite Friends in his day. John Bacon Crenshaw (1820-1889) (right) like his father before him led the Orthodox Friends of Southside Virginia.

## XIV

## O, VIRGINIA! VIRGINIA!
## 1850-1865

> O, Virginia! Virginia! the land of my nativity, how has my spirit secretly mourned over thee.
> -- Mildred Ratcliff

Growing bitterness over slavery flavored the nation's headlines in 1850. Of the thirty States, fifteen were slave states and fifteen free. When California applied for statehood as a free state, fire-breathing Southern congressmen threatened to lead their states out of the Union if California got in. A second sore point was the continuing escapes of slaves north via the Underground Railroad. *Secession* and *Interposition*, terrible words meaning "Let us keep the slave system or we'll break up the United States" re-entered the language.

Virginia was not much involved in the secession struggle. The state's new Constitution which gave the vote to all white men was just then being passed and Virginia's fire-breathers blamed the state's lack of involvement on this development. Beverly Tucker, a William and Mary College professor, deplored that Virginia is "sunk in the slough of democracy, which has no sense of honor."[1] Somehow Southern slaveholders had intertwined the concept of Southern Honor with the Institution of Slavery.

The struggle over slavery as waged on the floor of the U. S. Senate resulted in the Compromise of 1850. On January 29 Senator Henry Clay of Kentucky introduced eight resolutions, designed to resolve the struggle and save the Union. Congress debated them thunderously through February. On March 7 Daniel Webster of Massachusetts made a famous speech in favor of the eight resolutions, and the Senate eventually voted them into laws. California was admitted as a free state (a concession to the North); a tough new Fugitive Slave Law passed (a concession to the South); and it was tacitly agreed that the interstate slave trade--the shipment of Virginia and Maryland-born slaves south--could continue (another concession to the South). Both sides made other minor concessions.[2]

Senator James Mason of Virginia (George Mason's grandson) wrote the new Fugitive Slave Law. It was the part of the Compromise that led to its undoing, for it offended too many consciences, including Quaker consciences North and South. John Greenleaf Whittier wrote a poem titled *Ichabod* as "the outcome of the surprise and grief and forecast of evil consequences which I felt on reading the Seventh of March speech of Daniel Webster."

"From those great eyes/The soul has fled:/When faith is lost, when honor dies,/The man is dead!" So reads *Ichabod*.

Under this Fugitive Slave Law, a man capturing fleeing blacks needed only to swear they were his slaves. The blacks could not testify or have a trial by jury. Citizens were forbidden to help fugitives. It was widely said that the law made everyone a "slave-catcher." Many citizens north of the Potomac River resisted and ignored it.

Blood first flowed over this law in September of 1851. The place was Quaker Levi Pownall's farm near Christiana in Lancaster County, Pa. Slaves of Edward Gorsuch, an Anne Arundel County, Md. planter, had fled there via the Underground Railroad. (Edward Gorsuch was a discendant of the Quaker Gorsuches who removed from Corotoman in Virginia to the site of Baltimore in the 1650's; but the family long since had departed from Friends.)

He arrived at Pownall's farm with his son Dickinson Gorsuch and an armed party at daybreak on September 11. When they approached the tenant house where the slaves were hidden, someone blew a horn from an upstairs windows, and some seventy black men came running with clubs, corn cutters, and guns. Quaker Elijah Lewis and another white neighbor, Castner Hanway, came too.

Elijah Lewis and Hanway warned the blacks against violence and advised Edward Gorsuch to leave. But Gorsuch declared he would "get his property or breakfast in hell." Whereupon shots rang out, Edward and Dickinson were wounded, and the slaves escaped. They carried the Gorsuches to Pownall's farmhouse, where Edward died.

The Christiana Riot excited the nation. President Fillmore sent forty-five marines to Christiana. They arrested thirty-five blacks, Elijah Lewis and Hanway, and Joseph Scarlett--another Quaker who had arrived during the shooting. All were indicted for treason, murder, and riot; defended before a federal judge in Philadelphia by Pennsylvania Congressman Thaddeus Stevens; and found "not guilty."[3]

Even while Virginia's newspapers were indignantly reporting the Christiana affair, Harriet Beecher Stowe's novel, *Uncle Tom's Cabin*, appeared in print. She was a Cincinnati minister's wife who admired the Underground Railroad activities of Levi and Catherine Coffin in Cincinnati. Her book paints a dark picture of slavery. The Coffins appear in it as kindly Quakers Simeon and Rachel Holliday, who befriend Eliza Harris and her child escaping from slavery over the Ohio River ice. The book sold millions of copies and aroused fever-pitch feeling South and North.

\* \* \*

All this excitement had profound political effects. The major American political parties as of 1850 were Whigs and Democrats. As early as 1839, however, the Whigs began to split over the slavery question with Cotton Whigs (proslavery) opposed to Conscience Whigs (antislavery). A succession of new antislavery parties then developed--first the Liberty Party, succeeded by the Free Soil Party, with the Free Soilers in turn succeeded by the Republican Party. The Whigs disappeared by 1854.

Up until this time, Virginia's Friends had engaged very little in politics. None had served in an elected office since 1663 when the General Assembly ousted John Porter for being a Quaker. For one reason, Friends had shunned political activity as worldly; for another, the requirement of an oath to qualify for political office was a bar. But the emergence of the antislavery parties induced Virginia's Friends to take more interest.\*

When Samuel Janney toured Virginia in 1841 to speak against slavery, he certainly did not speak as a politician. During that tour, however, he seems to have enrolled two men in the antislavery cause who were to be Virginia's first Republican politicians--George Rye, the saddlemaker of Woodstock, and John C. Underwood of Clarke County.

Janney wrote in 1844 that "We [Quakers] should look well to our steps before we become active members of any political party, for I apprehend none of them are conducted on our principles."[4] In 1848 he refused to be a candidate on the Free Soil ticket, saying that "it is not expedient for ministers of the Gospel to take any [political] office."[5] But he probably was present at the historic political meeting in Goose Creek Friends' Meeting house on 15 March 1856, when the Republican Party organized in Virginia.

The *Democratic Mirror* reported the meeting under the headline "BLACK REPUBLICAN MEETING IN LOUDOUN." According to the *Mirror*, this meeting was "more disgraceful in its character than anything of a similar nature that has ever been enacted upon Southern territory...proclaiming boldly and impudently the vilest Black Republican doctrines." The *Mirror* castigated George Rye and a number of Goose Creek

---

\* Perhaps they were influenced also by the first venture of English Friends in politics. The Reform Bill of 1832 enabled Friends to serve in Parliament without taking an oath. The next year Joseph Pease, the Quaker son of Edward Pease the inventor of railroads, was elected to Parliament where he served nine years. John Bright, a Friend of Rochdale in Lancashire, was elected in 1843. He served forty-six years, for the rest of his life, and was a cabinet minister.

Friends who were present--including Jesse Brown, Jesse Hoge and Yardley Taylor--for speaking against the Fugitive Slave Law and the like.[6]

\* \* \*

The Friendly Virginians were still shrinking in their numbers--only eighteen meetings in the State as of 1850--and only fifteen as of 1860 after Caroline, Johnson's in Isle of Wight County, and Mt Pleasant in the south end of Frederick County closed their doors. Friends were still moving west, and very few non-Quakers in Virginia were interested in joining a people so peculiar in their views on slavery and such.

In 1855, several families of Hopewell, Goose Creek, and Fairfax--Russells, Schooleys and others--took the steam cars across the Mississippi to Salem in Cedar County, Iowa. They formed a Hicksite meeting there called Prairie Grove as a monthly meeting of Virginia's Fairfax Quarter. For ten years committees of Virginia Friends made sooty train trips to visit the new meeting. Then it became part of a newly formed Prairie Grove Quarterly Meeting.[7] Eighteen fifty-five also appears to be the year when Friends first held meetings on the Pacific Coast. That year Abel Bond, who is thought to be the grandson of Virginia (Hopewell) Friends, traveled by foot along the California coast in Truth's service.[8]

In just 200 years in North America, 1655-1855, Friends traversed the continent, coast to coast, Virginia to California, Elizabeth Harris to Abel Bond.

Since the Friendly Virginians were fewer in the 1850s, fewer Friends' ministers came to visit. Among the notable visitors was Elizabeth Newport, of Abington Meeting near Philadelphia and of the Hicksite persuasion. Arriving in Washington, D. C., in early March of 1852, Elizabeth invited both houses of Congress to meet with her to discuss the slavery question--"but," wrote Tacy Pancoast who was Elizabeth Newport's young traveling companion, "owing to its being on the same evening as the President's last levee there was but few came."

Elizabeth and Tacy then spent a month in northern Virginia visiting Quaker meetings. They also called on slaveholders along the way and Elizabeth spoke earnestly with them. Tacy wrote about one such call:

> 20th [of Third Month 1852 in Loudoun County, Va.]--rode 2-1/2 miles over terrible roads to Isaac Piggott's [a Quaker family], stopped a while and then went on to William Benton 's, a

slaveholder [who] owned 900 acres but really not many comforts from appearances. Elizabeth had a very plain, open opportunity with them and he acknowledged every word to be true to his case. Here we had to stay and take dinner with them which was something of a trial to me.

Five days later Elizabeth spoke in Centre Meeting house near Winchester to Friends and slaveholders both. Tacy wrote

> Elizabeth was constrained to speak in a plain manner on the evils of slavery...that a day of awful retribution awaited those that were guilty...except they repent, which she called on some in a very impressive manner that they should do. The meeting was quiet....[9]

William Forster, 69, an evangelical London Friend, visited Virginia with his brother Joseph, the year after Elizabeth Newport. On an earlier visit to America William Forster saw a party of fourteen escaping slaves sheltered in the Coffins's Underground Railroad station in Cincinnati;[10] and he came to America in 1853 on behalf of the slaves. He intended to deliver an antislavery message to the president and to the governor of every American state.

The brothers visited President Franklin Pierce in the White House and then Virginia's Governor Joseph Johnson in Richmond. Both the president and governor received the Forsters courteously. They went on to Ohio, Kentucky, Indiana, Illinois, and Wisconsin, then south through the slave states, Louisiana, Mississippi, Alabama, Georgia and South Carolina. But in Tennessee near Knoxville William Forster died, worn out by his year of travel. Friends buried him near their meeting house at Friendsville, Tennessee.[11]

* * *

Records of the Virginia Friends' meetings for the 1850s betray nothing about members' activities on behalf of slaves. Nevertheless, three clues remain:
- Peter Petty was one of twenty-one Norfolk slaves hidden away in Captain Fountain's coasting schooner in Norfolk and delivered to Thomas Garrett, the Underground Railroad station master at Wilmington, Delaware, in 1855. Peter was the slave of Joseph Boukley, a hard master although he took Peter to Methodist church on Sundays. Peter said that the preaching he heard there was always "Servants, obey your masters--good servants make good masters--when your mistress speaks to you,

don't pout out your mouths." He declared he never heard but *one* preacher speak against slavery--a Quaker lady whose words "caused an uproar in the church."[12]

- Loudoun County's slave-holders suspected Yardley Taylor of Goose Creek Meeting of slavehelping activities. One of them published a handbill to accuse Yardley. Yardley evidently had stated publicly that the Fugitive Slave Law violates the higher law, for the handbill declared in rebuttal,

> The principle of moral and positive laws is the same and the same obligation rests upon us to obey one as the other. The good man makes no distinction...he must obey the law. The *Bible*, morality and patriotism all alike unite in enjoining it as a solemn duty.[13]

- Gilbert Congdon and Elizabeth Crenshaw stood together in Cedar Creek Friends' Meeting house on 14 Second Month 1856, to say their wedding promises. This is the self-same Gilbert Congdon, abolitionist of Providence, Rhode Island who wrote so passionately that he hated slavery, in 1837. The bride was Nathaniel Crenshaw's 25-year-old daughter.

Quaker custom is for all present to sign the wedding certificate, and certain ones of the forty-eight signatures on Elizabeth and Gilbert's certificate are thought-provoking. Five are the names of Quakers now known to be committed fully to freedom for slaves: *Gilbert* the bridegroom; *Nathaniel* the bride's father; *John Crenshaw* her brother; *Margaret Crew*, her aunt; and *Samuel Janney*, whose presence as a Hicksite minister at an orthodox Quaker wedding a hundred miles from his home is wildly unusual. Robert W. Biglow was also there, which suggests some connection with *Joshua Bigelow*, the Underground Railroad station master of Washington, D.C.[14]

Suspicion hangs heavy that certain anti-slavery or Underground Railroad plans were laid, along with the celebration of that winter wedding at Cedar Creek.

\* \* \*

Harper's Ferry, Virginia (now West Virginia) lay ten to twelve miles north of the Fairfax and Goose Creek Meetings of Friends in Loudoun County.

On a Sunday night, 16 October 1859, gunfire awakened Harper's Ferry. Armed strangers were in the streets.

At daybreak the townspeople spotted men wrapped in blankets and cradling Sharpe's rifles along Shenandoah Street. Some white, some black. More strangers held the gate to the U. S. Armory, the rifle works on Potomac Street. A B&O east-bound train stood empty in the station. Presently men with rifles herded the train's passengers and crew out of the hotel and back to the train which then pulled out toward Washington. The towns people stayed in their houses all the morning.

By 12:30 p.m. a hundred militiamen, the Jefferson Guards, arrived from Charles Town. Five of the strangers took shelter in the little brick firehouse of the rifle works. Militia men killed or captured nine more. Four or five escaped west over the Blue Ridge. Militia and townspeople hemmed in the firehouse. Then ninety U. S. marines under Lt Colonel Robert E. Lee arrived from Washington. Early Tuesday morning marines rushed the firehouse door with a ladder for a battering ram. They brought four men bloody but alive out of the firehouse and laid them on the grass.

That morning the nation's newspapers picked up the story: "FEARFUL AND EXCITING INTELLIGENCE! NEGRO INSURRECTION AT HARPER'S FERRY! EXTENSIVE NEGRO CONSPIRACY IN VIRGINIA AND MARYLAND! SEIZURE OF THE UNITED STATES ARSENAL BY THE INSURRECTIONISTS! SEVERAL PERSONS KILLED! TELEGRAPH WIRES CUT! TROOPS DISPATCHED...FROM WASHINGTON AND BALTIMORE!" Those were the headlines.

One of the four bloodied men was tall and bearded with a crest of gray hair. Someone in the crowd standing around called out

"Are you Captain Brown of Kansas?"
"I am sometimes called so."
"Are you Osawotamie Brown?"
"I tried to do my duty there."[15]

This was amazing news for John Brown, "Old Brown of Osawatomie" (1800-1859) was a famous abolitionist, notorious in the South! The second man lying there was Edwin Coppock, a Quaker from Iowa! The third was Shields Green, a black man; the fourth, Watson Brown, John's son, wounded so badly he died the next day.

John Brown became famous in 1856. He and five of his sons went to Kansas Territory where antislavery and proslavery forces were struggling for control. Proslavery marauders from Missouri had gunned down a number of antislavery men at Lawrence, Kansas. Brown and his sons took vengeance by slaughtering five proslavery men on 24 May 1856. This act and Brown's success in withstanding several hundred attacking Missourians at Osawatomie, Kansas, in August was widely publicized.

Brown had come to Harper's Ferry with a plan to free all slaves. As he explained it, "Nat Turner with 50 men held Virginia five weeks...20 men in the Alleghanies could break Slavery to pieces in two years...when the bondmen stand like men, the Nation will respect them." His plan was to spark a slave rebellion at Harper's Ferry, arming the slaves with weapons from the armory as they came in to join him. Rumor was that he was financed by Gerrit Smith of New York state and by certain New Englanders allied with the Transcendentalists.

When reporters heard *this* news, their papers had a field day. The Richmond *Enquirer* declared that the raid "has advanced the cause of Disunion more than any other event." Virginia Senator James Mason called for a Senate investigation. It was carried out in an atmosphere so hostile that most senators took to carrying derringers. Senator Henry Wilson of Massachusetts eulogized Brown, saying "by his bearing, his courage, his words, his acts, he has excited the deepest sympathy." But Senator Jefferson Davis of Mississippi called the raid "the first...of those violent proceedings which can only be called civil war." And Senator Mason saw it as "the first tap of the drum in the villages," the first act in a plot against the South.[16]

Osawotamie in Kansas lay just south of the Shawnee Tract with its Friends' school; and some Quaker families had farms in the Osawatomie neighborhood. John Brown and Richard Mendenhall, a Quaker of Osawatomie, became acquainted there and Richard Mendenhall spoke to Brown about the Quakers of Springdale Meeting in Cedar County, Iowa, where the Mendenhalls had recently lived.

In 1858 Brown and his sons stole a dozen slaves in Missouri and carried them north to Springdale. The Springdale Quakers sheltered the Browns and the slaves, but were repelled when John Brown told his plan to start a violent slave rebellion. However two Quaker brothers did join Brown's band and were with him at Harper's Ferry. They are the Coppock brothers, Edwin and Barclay.[17]

John Brown and Edwin Coppock were tried for treason and murder with the three other members of their band captured alive at Harper's Ferry (Barclay Coppock was among the band's members who escaped West). The Virginia Court sentenced all five captives to death by hanging and Governor Wise rejected all appeals to change the sentence. All through November of 1859 the five waited in the Charles Town jail, vilified in the South, lionized in the North, receiving many letters. One letter came to from Quaker Elizabeth Buffum of Providence, Rhode Island. She assured John Brown:

> Very many Friends love thee with all their hearts for thy brave efforts on behalf of the poor oppressed; and though we...believe it better to reform by moral and not by carnal weapons...yet...we openly approve thy intentions, though many Friends would not think it right to take up arms.

Brown replied at once:

> "May the Lord reward you a thousand times for the kind feeling you express toward me.... I always loved my Quaker friends, and I commend to their kind regard my poor, bereaved, widowed wife.[18]

Rebecca Buffum Spring, who was Elizabeth Buffum's sister, took the cars with her son to visit John Brown in jail. In the Baltimore railroad station she met Thomas Stabler, who helped her with her bag and advised her to look up David Howell in Harper's Ferry (the Quaker brother-in-law of Samuel Janney). But David Howell, fearing the wrath of his neighbors, refused to help at all, and Rebecca was not allowed to see John Brown[19]. (He learned of Rebecca's effort to see him, however, and he sent his last letter to his wife to Rebecca, asking Rebecca to deliver it.)

Mary Lippincott, a Quaker grandmother of Moorestown, New Jersey, wrote to her grandson the day before John Brown's hanging:

> A Friend just returned from Virginia says that in Loudoun County some [Friends] think they will be ordered to leave the State. The measures of the Governor of Virginia seem like a challenge for a civil war.... I mourn over our country.

Mary Lippincott visited Virginia relatives two months later and wrote again to her grandson:

> The Quarterly Meeting [held in Fairfax Meeting House] was unusually large; perhaps the excited people wanted to hear whether or not Friends would have anything to say about John Brown. They heard no allusion to him or to politics. We desire nothing but to persuade men to be Christians.[20]

Fanny Berry was an ancient ex-slave living in Petersburg in 1937. "Yes, I remember something about him [John Brown] too," she told an interviewer. "I know my master came home and said that on his way to the gallows old John stopped and kissed a little nigger child." Fanny also remembered: "This is the song I heard my master sing:

Old John Brown came to Harper's Ferry town
Purpose to raise an insurrection.
Old Governor Wise put the spec's upon his eyes
An' showed him the happy land of Canaan.[21]

Elsewhere another song was sung:

John Brown's body lies a-mould'ring in the grave
But his soul goes marching on....

* * *

During the affair at Harper's Ferry, a national election campaign was underway to determine who would succeed President James Buchanan. The Republican Party, barely six years old, fielded Abraham Lincoln (1809-1865), a lanky, craggy Illinois lawyer. He had represented Illinois in Congress as a Conscience Whig during the 1840s, but his opposition to the Mexican War ruined his chances for a second term.

Early in the presidential campaign Lincoln made a speech touching on slavery, saying "I do not expect the Union to be dissolved--I do not expect the house to fall, but I do expect it will cease to be divided; it will become one thing or the other." That speech made Lincoln suspect in the South, and his name was left off the ballots in ten Southern states. At election time in Virginia, November of 1860, Lincoln received less than two thousand write-in votes. He won out, though, in Loudoun County's two Quaker-dominated precincts surrounding Goose Creek and Fairfax Friends' Meetings.[22]

Lincoln won the national election against three other candidates with some two million out of four and a half million votes cast. At that, seven states in the deep South led by South Carolina seceded from the Union, between 20 December 1860, and 1 February 1861. The seven states formed a Confederacy, choosing Jefferson Davis for its president, in Montgomery, Alabama, on February 9.

Virginia's General Assembly split on whether to leave the Union. Governor Letcher called a state convention to decide the issue. It convened in Richmond on February 13. Loudoun County sent John Janney, 62, of Leesburg as a delegate.

John was Samuel Janney's cousin. Their fathers had been partners in the great Occoquan cotton mill, and they had been boys together in Alexandria Friends' Meeting. Both returned to Loudoun, the Janneys' ancestral home county, later in their lives. John read law in Leesburg and lost his membership in the Society of Friends when he "married out" to

Alcinda Marmaduke, a relative of the Lees. (Alcinda took pride in her FFV background, but John twitted that her family couldn't compare to his for antiquity. The Janneys, he said, dated back to *Bible* times--St Paul stating in 2 Timothy 3:8 that the Jannes and Jambres withstood Moses!)[23]

He entered politics as a Conscience Whig, won fame as a lawyer, and in 1839 Henry Clay supported him for the U. S. vice-presidency. "He is the first man in Virginia and has no superior in the U. S.," Clay declared. John Janney lost the Whig nomination by a single vote (because he refused to vote for himself) to John Tyler.[24] Tyler became vice-president and then president when William Henry Harrison died after a month in office.

Though disowned, John Janney stayed close to the Friends. When out-of-state Friends visited Leesburg, he invited them to stay in his home on Cornwall Street.[25] And even though he opposed secession and slavery, the state convention in Richmond elected him to preside over its proceedings.

The convention met over two months, out of the winter and into the spring of 1861. On March 4 Abraham Lincoln was inaugurated. On April 12 the new Confederate army fired on the U. S. army's Fort Sumter in Charleston harbor. Lincoln then called on the nation for 75,000 volunteer soldiers and on Virginia for three regiments. Whereupon the convention voted 85 to 55 for Virginia to secede. That night Richmonders lit bonfires and marched by torchlight through the city while bands played "Dixie."

The governor nominated Colonel Robert E. Lee to command Virginia's armed forces. On the morning of April 23 Lee entered the hall of the House of Delegates escorted by Marmaduke Johnson, his Richmond relative. John Janney, presiding, met the pair halfway up the center aisle as the delegates cheered. He said:

> Major General Lee in the name of the people of our native State here represented I bid you a cordial and heartfelt welcome to this hall, in which we may yet almost hear the echo of the voices of the statesmen and soldiers and sages of bygone days who have borne your name...you are at this time among the living citizens of Virginia, 'first in war'.... Yesterday your mother, Virginia, placed the sword in your hand...draw it only in defense...fall with it in your hand rather than...fail.[26]

In this manner John Janney, Quaker bred and Quaker principled, came to have a leading part in launching the Civil War. Later that year he resigned and never again took part in politics.[27]

\* \* \*

At first the slave state of Maryland separated Virginia from the northern free states. But Maryland opted to stay with the Union and so Virginia became the northernmost of the eleven Confederate states. An orthodox Quaker of Baltimore had much to do with keeping Maryland from seceding. He was Francis T. King, the same Francis who traveled through Virginia with Joseph John Gurney in 1837.

It was a close call in Maryland. On April 17, five days after the firing on Fort Sumter, the Sixth Massachusetts Regiment marched through Baltimore from one rail depot to another, hurrying to protect Washington, D. C. Southern sympathizers fired on these troops and men on both sides fell dead--the first lives lost in the war. That day Francis King returned from a business trip to New York.

King went first to Baltimore's city hall, close by the Friends' meeting house on Courtland Street. He told the mayor and city council about the massive war preparations he had seen in the North. Then he hurried to Annapolis where Maryland's Governor Hicks met him at midnight. King impressed on the governor that the North was ready to fight to keep Maryland from seceding. The governor, who was preparing to submit the question of secession to his legislature, then decided not to summon the legislators. So Maryland stayed with the Union.[28]

Virginia became even more exposed when fifty-five of her counties, those west of the Appalachian ridge, refused to go along with secession. These counties organized as a separate state, West Virginia, a Union state. Now Virginia was bounded north and west by hostile governments. Her Quaker meetings--only fourteen of them left after Blackwater Meeting in Surry County closed its doors in 1860--now constituted fourteen little islands, anti-slavery and anti-war, in a surrounding sea of secessionist citizenry.

Right after Abraham Lincoln's election a delegation from Goose Creek went to Washington to solicit a post office for their community. Since their precinct had just voted Republican the new administration granted their request, and the name Lincoln was agreed on. Rodney Taylor, the Friend who ran a sawmill, a woodworking shop, undertaker parlor, and a shoemaker shop on the grounds of Goose Creek Meeting, was to be Lincoln's postmaster. When Virginia seceded, however, the post office plan was shelved for the duration.[29]

At this secession time, Friends of Woodlawn in Fairfax County noticed strangers in uniforms, and campfires dotting their neighborhood in the spring nights. Southern militia units were moving quietly into Fairfax County, purposing to capture Washington before the North could protect it. After meeting for morning worship on First Day, 21 Fourth Month 1861, Woodlawn Friends met again that afternoon in David and Jemima Ann

Walton's home. After silent waiting they decided "to take our families north of Washington out of the way until things assume a different appearance here." They wanted to keep their young men from being forced into the army and to keep their young women out of the way of the army.

Next morning Chalkley and Keziah Gillingham, both 54, headed north in their market wagon with several young women. The rest of the families followed a day later--about eight carriage and wagon loads. They drove forty miles north to Nathan Haines's farm near Pipe Creek Meeting in Union Bridge, Maryland, where Nathan put them up in his house and barn. Many of the Woodlawn families traveled on to shelter with relatives in New Jersey, but the Gillinghams stayed with the Haineses for a few weeks, helped with Nathan's spring planting, then drove home to Woodlawn. They found some possessions gone and all their cattle driven off. Chalkley set his jaw and rescued the cattle after two trips to the Confederate army post at Fairfax Courthouse.[30]

* * *

The Confederacy chose Richmond for its capital city. By mid-July the Union army felt strong enough. "Forward to Richmond" blared the Northern headlines. The army in blue, 40,000 strong, moved south from Washington. The Confederates massed behind a creek called Bull Run, a line of gray-clad soldiers nine miles long astride the road to Richmond and thirty miles below Washington. The Union army attacked, the Confederates flank-attacked, the Union front wavered and broke. Soon the whole Union army was routed, straggling back to Washington in the rain.

The U. S. Congress, sobered by the debacle, appropriated $500,000,000 to mobilize 500,000 men. Then as Chalkley Gillingham wrote in his journal:

> Troops are constantly coming from the North at the rate of about 1,000 per day, and everything and every place for 10 miles around Washington is covered with troops and wherever they are devastation follows...everything like flowers and crops are destroyed and also in many places the dwellings.[31]

From Washington to Richmond the road wends a hundred miles, through Virginia all the way. Plainly now a tremendous struggle was coming, with Virginia the main theater. The Friendly Virginians braced, foreseeing an ordeal. Right after the battle of Bull Run, Goose Creek Friends led by Samuel Janney wrote a declaration of Friends' principles adapted to the scary situation. At the same time Virginia Half Years' Meeting wrote its own declaration with Nathaniel Crenshaw and his 41-year-old son John B. the main authors.

Goose Creek Friends presented their declaration to the quarterly meeting held in Fairfax Meeting house in the Ninth Month of 1861. Quarterly meeting approved it and appointed Samuel Janney to carry it to yearly meeting (Baltimore, Hicksite). It made two points:

> We deem it our religious duty to take no part in [this war]; and to abstain from every act that would give aid in its prosecution,

and

> Our solemn duty [is] to comply with the laws of the land [*but* if any laws should be passed contrary to] the religion we profess and, as we conceive, the true spirit of Christianity [then we must] remain entirely passive under them, suffering all penalties.

The southside Friends of Virginia Half Years Meeting issued their statement after a long discussion on 7 Tenth Month in the meeting house at 19th and Cary Streets, Richmond. Since they were unable to stay in touch with Baltimore Yearly Meeting Orthodox, Friends forwarded their statement on to North Carolina's Yearly Meeting. The southside statement compares with the northern Virginia Friends' declaration in an interesting way. Its main points:

> [We will be] careful to abstain from war and everything connected with war.

> [We will not] pay any fines...for non-performance of military duty, but rather quietly submit to have the value of the same distrained....

> Yet [we will] pay all taxes imposed on us as citizens, remembering the injunction 'Tribute to whom tribute is due...' believing that upon the Government rests the responsibility of how they expend this tribute.[32]

Samuel Janney did carry the declaration to Baltimore for yearly meeting, but getting there and back was a risky thing. As he tells it:

> When the battle of Ball's Bluff was fought [21 Tenth Month 1861]...the Confederate pickets were then for a few days withdrawn

from the line of the Potomac.... I was then under appointment from our Quarterly Meeting to attend the Yearly Meeting in Baltimore. I felt it my duty to go if possible.

A young friend accompanied me as far as the river; we met with no interruption.... [In Baltimore] only three other Friends from Virginia were in attendance, namely William Holmes and Yardley Taylor from our Monthly Meeting and Job Throckmorton from Hopewell....

After the rise of Yearly Meeting I...obtained from the Provost Marshal a passport that I supposed would enable me to return through the Federal lines, but on reaching the Potomac I was informed by the officer in command of the guard that he could not permit me to pass. [Later] a young Virginian connected with the Federal army called on me and stated that my friend William Holmes had been taken over the river by him, and he was willing to convey me across that night in a boat.

...I accepted his offer and was safely conveyed to the Virginia shore. There I found a citizen whom I knew to be a Union man and accepted his invitation to go with him to his house about a mile distant. When we approached the house sometime after dark he said to me 'Stand behind this tree while I go in and see if any secessionists are there.' He soon returned and reported that some of his secession neighbors were in the house. He then conducted me to a door and told me to take off my boots, walk softly up stairs and go to bed. Next morning...my kind host furnished me a horse, with a boy to bring it back.

Taking an unfrequented road we avoided the Confederate pickets and when I came within two miles of my house, I...proceeded afoot. My family were well and we rejoiced together.... But...on the following day...the soldiers came for me and conducted me to Leesburg, nine miles distant, where General Evans of the Southern army had his headquarters. I was taken before him...

Gen Evans: When did you come from Maryland?
SJ: Yesterday.
Gen: What did you go for?
SJ: To attend Friends' Yearly Meeting.
Gen: Don't you know that your first duty is to your country?

SJ: No. My first duty is to God.

Gen (after a pause): Yes, but your second duty is to your country.

SJ: I do not know that I have violated any law of my country.

Gen: If you haven't violated any law of your country, you have transgressed a military order. Why did you not apply for a permit to pass our lines?

SJ: Because I was pretty sure I could not obtain one.

General Evans (Nathan "Shanks" Evans, 37, a West Pointer with fierce black mustachios) then ordered Samuel Janney to stay in Leesburg until further notice. When he learned that Janney had recently brought a load of bread and vegetables contributed by Goose Creek Friends to a soldiers' hospital in Leesburg his attitude softened. After four days he allowed Janney to go home.[33]

\* \* \*

Travel restrictions were only one difficulty:
- Many of the Quaker meeting houses in Virginia were taken over for army uses.
- Troops bivouacked on Quakers' farms, destroying cattle, crops and fences.
- Soldiers trashed the meeting houses in Alexandria, Winchester and Richmond so badly that Friends could never use them again.
- Soldiers overturned the benches in Hopewell's meetinghouse to make troughs for bread dough; and carried away the stones of the burying-ground wall for their fire places.
- During Tenth Month of 1861 the Union army's picket line moved south to Woodlawn, 14 miles below Washington. Thereafter Woodlawn meeting house was right on the fighting front with skirmishes and firefights all around. The meeting house served as a headquarters and barracks of Union border guards.
- A troop of Southern cavalry commandeered Fairfax Meeting house in Waterford. Samuel Janney wrote about the cavalrymen:

When they first came to Waterford they seemed to entertain a strong prejudice and animosity against Friends [as] Union Men and abolitionists; but on becoming better acquainted, some of the soldiers acknowledged that the store-keepers who were Friends dealt with them more fairly than any they had met with on their march from the South, and their prejudices were removed.[34]

Many Friends' families early in the war were ruined financially:
- Robert and Ruth Ann Roberts of Alexandria Meeting had eight children, a mill and a neat 100-acre farm on Cameron Run just west of town. Their place became a Union army camp and was wrecked.
- Aaron Griffith of Winchester was jailed for writing in a letter "We are getting on very well except for the [Confederate] hangers-on, who annoy us very much." His horses and much property disappeared while he was in jail, his textile mill robbed of its machinery and $20,000 worth of cloth. The machinery wound up in the mill of a Southern-sympathizing neighbor.
- Six or seven thousand horses and a thousand wagons were taken out of Loudoun by Confederate soldiers before the war was four months' old. Very few Loudoun Friends had transport thereafter.
- Edward and Elizabeth Gibbs of Woodlawn lived at Hollin Hall, once George Mason's home. After the battle of Bull Run, a gang of fifty deserters from both armies plundered the place. The Gibbses and their four daughters providentially escaped.
- Hillman Troth and Walter Walton of Woodlawn were carried off as "Union men" to Manassas, held two days and released. They were arrested a second time and held for several weeks.[35]

Soldiers encamped near the Virginia Friends' meeting houses often came to worship on First Days. On First Day, 12 First Month 1862 Chalkley Gillingham of Woodlawn Meeting wrote:

> At our Meeting today there were an unusual number of [Confederate] soldiers.... I had considerable to say in regard to practical religion and in contrast with the speculative, formal religion (if religion it might be called) wherein men can make all the demonstration of religion and go to church as they call it, and at the same time plot treason against the government and be active in this rebellion, causing blood to flow like water....
>
> I did not know while I was speaking that the chaplain of the regiment was in the meeting. After I sat down he arose...to make a few remarks, which he did to good satisfaction.... The Meeting was exceedingly quiet and orderly.[36]

At Fairfax Meeting on or about that same First Day, Miriam Gover, 70, a tiny quavery Friend in a plain bonnet, was led to minister. The cavalry captain and a good many troopers then occupying the meeting house were present. Someone there described the occasion:

In one corner of the room the Stars and Bars were unfurled. In an opposite one was a large fireplace with a blazing fire over which was roasting a large turkey, also some hominy cooking. Overcoats were hung up all about, knapsacks and saddles were strewn around.... And when she [Miriam Gover] knelt to invoke a blessing on the little band assembled there she also prayed the wings of peace might ere long be spread over our once happy and prosperous land, and for the strangers that day gathered in their midst. Until loud sobs broke from [the seated soldiers].[37]

\* \* \*

After the Confederate victory at Bull Run, both sides began a massive buildup of armies. At first the various states did the recruiting, using posters, propaganda and martial music. As volunteers grew fewer, the states resorted to conscription laws, drafting men into the military willy nilly.

Then on 3 March 1862 the U. S. Congress voted in a sweeping *national* conscription law, "An Act for Enrolling and Calling Out the National Forces." It decreed the drafting of able-bodied men between ages 20 and 45, exempting only men who furnished substitutes or paid "commutation money of $300.00." Six weeks later the Confederate Congress passed *its* conscription law, "An Act to Further Provide for the Public Defense." This law allowed substitutes, but it made no allowance for conscientious objectors.[38]

Neither law satisfied Quakers, South or North. They wanted their position respected as a people who can not resort to killing. So Quakers appeared again in Richmond and Washington to plead their case to the governments. South and North the Society of Friends was only a tiniest minority. Yet their plea was listened to, they did succeed in reaching the president of each government, and they did succeed in altering both conscription laws.

Southern Friends began trying to change the Confederate conscription act on April 18, two days after it became a law. That night four Friends visited President Jefferson Davis in Richmond's White House of the Confederacy. Jefferson Davis (1808-1891) was a West Point graduate who had been U. S. Secretary of War, a Mississippi cotton planter with many slaves, a Baptist who joined St. Paul's Episcopal Church after coming to Richmond. The four Friends who visited this President were Nathaniel Crenshaw and his son John B. with Dr. William Nicholson and Joseph Elliott both of North Carolina. According to John Crenshaw's journal:

> On the 18th father and I went [with Friends Nicholson and Elliott] to see the President. After waiting for hours we were informed that we could not see him before 9 p.m., at his residence, whither we repaired at that hour. We were politely received, but he positively refused to...send a message to Congress recommending that Friends be released from military duty.... He said...that it would be special legislation and open the door against us for further persecution on a future day."[39]

The Friends kept plugging away, however. Four months after President Davis turned them down, on Eighth Month 27, 1862, they petitioned the Confederate Congress directly, placing a copy of their petition on the desk of each congressman. The petition was referred immediately to the House Military Affairs Committee, and John Crenshaw arranged with Chairman William P. Miles of South Carolina for a meeting the next evening. John came with four North Carolina Friends led by Dr. Nereus Mendenhall, who was John's classmate at Haverford College in the class of 1839. As Crenshaw recalled,

> It being a warm summer night [we met] out on the Capitol grounds. [We felt] that Nereus Mendenhall was preeminently the man to present our case.... Chairman Miles said 'Gentlemen, the Committee is ready. Please state your case.' A dead silence followed.
>
> In a few minutes, fearing the committee would not understand...a silent Quaker meeting...I reached over and gently touched Nereus. He arose slowly, and when fully aroused and warmed to the subject I thought I never heard such an exposition of the doctrines of Friends on the subject of war.

The same five Friends went on to visit Jefferson Davis again, who again received them courteously and again refused to help them. On this second visit President Davis pointedly expressed regret that there was a body of people in his Confederacy unwilling to fight for it.[40]

Despite the president's refusal, Friends received some help. On 11 October 1862 the Congress of the Confederacy enacted a law exempting Friends, Dunkards (members of the Church of the Brethren), Mennonists, and Nazarenes from service in the Confederate army upon payment of $500 or upon performing certain noncombat duties.

John Crenshaw credited Nereus Mendenhall's "exposition" with the passage of this law. Credit is due too to Church of the Brethren leaders who sent in two petitions during the summer of '62. The law of October 11 satisfied Virginia's Brethren and Mennonites even though payment of the exemption money would be hard for them. The Brethren appointed 1 January 1863, a day of thanksgiving for the law's passage.

But Quakers were not satisfied. They were no more willing to pay the $500 tax than enlist in the army. Nathaniel and John Crenshaw wrote a protest which Virginia Half Year's Meeting enthusiastically approved. The meeting printed copies for all the congressmen, and John Crenshaw argued the Quakers' case late one November night before Chairman Miles and his Military Affairs Committee. "They treated me respectfully but declined to do anything for Friends," John Crenshaw reported.[41]

\* \* \*

Both the Confederate States and the United States had presidents with Quaker ancestors:

Jefferson Davis descended from Quakers Morgan ap David (c. 1622 - 1694) and Catherine his wife, who came from Glamorgan, Wales, to Pennsylvania in 1684. They made 410 acres of virgin woods into a farm (now the campus of Haverford College) and Morgan left a bequest to Haverford Friends Meeting in his will. Jefferson's grandfather Evan Davis moved south to Georgia and then to Todd County, Kentucky, where Jefferson was born.[42]

Abraham Lincoln's Quaker forebears were "Virginia John" Lincoln (1716-1788) and his wife Rebecca (1720-1806). They came down from Exeter Friends Meeting near Reading, Pennsylvania into the valley of Virginia north of present-day Harrisonburg where they reared their children.

Jefferson Davis may not have known his family's Quaker past, but Lincoln did know something about his. He is quoted as claiming that he inherited two Quaker traits -- honesty and long silences. It is said that he once prayed this Quakerly prayer:

> Oh Lord if it is all the same to thee
> Give us a little more light
> And a little less noise.[43]

Four key officers of Abraham Lincoln's administration also had Quaker ties--three of them *Virginia* Quaker ties:

- Edward Bates (1793-1869), Lincoln's attorney-general, was born in Goochland County, Virginia and educated in the Quaker school taught by his kinsman, Benjamin Bates.[44]
- Isaac Newton (1800-1867), the first U. S. secretary of agriculture, joined the Eye Street Meeting in Washington late in his life.[45]
- Noah Haines Swayne (1804-1884), appointed to the Supreme Court by Lincoln in 1862, came from a Southland Friends Meeting family with a farm near Culpeper. He once was a pupil in Fairfax Meeting's one room school.[46]
- Edwin M. Stanton (1814-1869), secretary of war, came from a Quaker home in Steubenville, Ohio; his mother, Lucy Norman, was raised in Virginia's Southland Meeting.[47]

Throughout the war, northern Friends visited President Lincoln and Secretary Stanton. Many of them came to plead for young men of the northern meetings who, having refused to pay the $300 in exemption money, were dragged into the Union army and maltreated. In such cases Lincoln and Stanton consistently showed a friendly attitude. One or the other of them ordered the young men sent home "until called for."

At least once, *southern* Friends came to Washington for help from Lincoln and Stanton. In early September of 1863 Union soldiers arrested Ball and Belt, two Loudoun County men accused of helping Southern guerrillas ("Lige White's Comanches"). At dusk on the day of the arrest, some Comanches rode into the Quaker settlement of Waterford to retaliate. They abducted two leading Quakers, "Union men," from their Waterford homes and sent them south as hostages to Castle Thunder, the Confederate military prison in Richmond. The hostages: William Williams, 46, clerk of Fairfax Friends Meeting, and Robert Isaac Hollingsworth, 49, teacher of the Fairfax Friends' school. The Comanches also tried to snatch a third Friend, Asa Moore Bond, but were driven off by Asa's wife Sarah Alice and her sister who counter-attacked with rolling-pin and broom.

Mary Elizabeth, the wife of William Williams, immediately went to Samuel Janney in her distress, and Janney wrote a petition to Secretary Stanton. Since prisoner exchanges were common during the war, Janney asked Stanton to release Ball and Belt from the prison camp near Wilmington, Delaware in order to obtain freedom for hostages Williams and Hollingsworth. Janney then set out for Washington with the petition, taking along Mary Elizabeth Williams and her brother.

They called first on Frederick Cochran, a member of Hopewell Meeting who held some post in Lincoln's administration. Cochran gave them a note of introduction to President Lincoln. Then they went to John Underwood, the Clarke County Republican, now a federal judge in Washington.

Underwood put on his hat and set out for the White House with the three Friends.

Abraham Lincoln received the party in the White House. Janney wrote home to his wife that

> He recd us very kindly & heard our statement of the case which was very brief. He requested Judge U. to go with us to Genl Hitchcock who attends to exchange of prisoners and he handed the Judge a card to take to the General.

What happened then is a cat-and-mouse story, well known to anyone who deals with bureaucracy. General Hitchcock said there was "a peculiarity in the case which made it necessary to have an order for the release of Ball and Belt, either from the Secty of War or the Prest." The Friends hurried back to the White House but found it closed for the day. They then met with an acquaintance "who introduced us to an officer [believed to be Isaac Newton] who is on intimate terms with the Secty of War, & that officer agreed to take our petition...to the Secretary. We expect to hear from him tomorrow." But when tomorrow came, Secretary Stanton refused to knuckle under to hostage-taking.

Samuel Janney went for help to every Republican he knew in the government --to John Jolliffe, to his cousin Henry Janney, to Judge Underwood, Henry Gover, Fred Cochran--he went home to look after his family, came back to Washington and made the rounds again--with no success. Things looked bad for the two Quaker hostages in Castle Thunder.

The two were sitting out in the prison yard one warm fall day, when a strange man at the gate called "Are there any Quakers in here?" William Williams walked over to the man, who turned out to be John Crenshaw. As the story goes, Crenshaw went to "people in authority" (he had made a friend of John A. Campbell, who was the Confederacy's assistant secretary of war, an Alabaman and a former justice of the U. S. Supreme Court) and got the two Quakers released. Crenshaw took them to Rocouncy, his farm north of Richmond. William Williams had a bout with smallpox which he caught in Castle Thunder, after which the two got home to Waterford on Christmas Day, 1863.

Once they were home, Friends of Fairfax Meeting wrote to Washington, telling of the release and requesting the Federal authorities to reciprocate by releasing Ball and Belt. "We were all exceedingly gratified," William Williams wrote, "that the request was granted."[48]

\* \* \*

Along with visits on behalf of young Quakers caught in the draft, President Lincoln also received other Friendly visits and letters:
- In Twelfth Month 1861 he received a letter from Friends of London Yearly Meeting to say that English Friends would do all they could to keep Great Britain from "active cooperation with the South and Slavery against the North and Freedom." Lincoln replied "I...gratefully appreciate your...suggestions in the interest of peace and humanity."[49]
- 9 First Month 1862: The clerk of Western Yearly Meeting (in western Indiana) sent him a letter of support.
- 8 Second Month: New England Friends wrote, praying for peace. To this Lincoln answered "Engaged as I am in a great war, I fear it will be difficult to understand how fully I appreciate the principles of peace inculcated by...the Society of Friends...I look forward to an early end of war and return of peace."[50]
- 20 Sixth Month: Thomas Garrett, the erstwhile Underground Railroad station master of Wilmington, Delaware and five other Progressive Friends called on Lincoln in the White House. They came to urge immediate emancipation for the slaves. The president agreed that slavery is wrong but the puzzle is, he said, how to get rid of it. As far as he could see, a proclamation of freedom "could not be enforced in that part of the country [the South] now." The Friends said they hoped God would guide him. Then Lincoln thoughtfully said

I have sometime thought that perhaps I might be an instrument in God's hands.... It will be my earnest endeavor, with a firm reliance upon the Divine arm and seeking light from above, to do my duty.[51]

- 11 Eighth Month: William Ladd in Ohio, a son of Benjamin Ladd, wrote to President Lincoln and Secretary Seward "to assure you of the sympathy and prayers of Friends."[52]
- Ninth Month on a rainy First Day morning: Eliza Kirkbride Gurney (1817-1881) came to the White House with John Whitall and a few other orthodox Philadelphia Friends. She was a Westtown School graduate who met Joseph John Gurney when he visited America, he 52 years of age, she 23. She married him as his second wife in 1841. Eliza charmed Lincoln as she had charmed Gurney. Of the meeting in the White House, John Whitall wrote

I cannot possibly describe the scene: the solemnity of the silence and the impressive address of our Friend [Eliza Gurney], during which tears ran down the cheeks of our honored President...as we arose to go, he retained the hand of Eliza P. Gurney and made a most beautiful response. [He] began and ended with the words, 'I am glad of this interview.'[53]

- 19 Ninth Month: Isaac and Sarah Harvey came from Ohio to see the president. Salmon P. Chase, once governor of Ohio and now Secretary of the Treasury, got them in to him. "Will thee pardon me if I do not remove my hat?" Isaac Harvey asked, to which Lincoln smiled and said "Certainly, I understand it all." He put his chair between theirs and listened while they urged him to proclaim freedom for the slaves. They spent a half hour together and Lincoln penned a note for them to take home. "I take pleasure in asserting that I have had profitable intercourse with Isaac Harvey and his good wife Sarah Harvey," Lincoln wrote. "May the Lord comfort them as they have sustained me."

The next day after the Harveys' visit Lincoln wrote his first draft of the Emancipation Proclamation. Two days later he officially announced it. Until that time, the only stated reason for waging civil war was "to save the Union," but now a declared purpose was to wipe out slavery. Abraham Lincoln called the Emancipation Proclamation "the central act of my administration."[54]

\* \* \*

The Civil War went pretty well for the Confederacy in its first two years, not counting the best and brightest of her young men killed and maimed. Five times blue armies set out to reach Richmond, five times were turned back after bloody battling: once at Bull Run, a second time within sight of Richmond's church spires, again at Bull Run, and the fourth and fifth times at Fredericksburg and Chancellorsville, both fifty-five miles short of Richmond. All five times the Northern armies lost more men than the South; but the South had a smaller populace to draw on. After each campaign, recruiters combed the countryside for able-bodied men.

After the Confederate victory at the second Battle of Bull Run, General Lee set out to invade the North. His regiments crossed the Potomac (Lee stopping briefly enroute in Leesburg to pay his respects to John and Alcinda Janney). The army was stopped a few miles into Maryland at Antietam, losing 10,000 men. After the Chancellorsville victory, Lee invaded the North once more. In the first days of July 1863 his army met the blue armies massed in the farm country near Gettysburg, Pa. This time some 36,000 of Lee's soldiers and 23,000 Union soldiers died or were mutilated. The Confederacy's need for manpower changed from urgent to desperate.

The Civil War forced young Quaker men to make tough choices. Their Society opposed both fighting and slavery, and the only practical way to oppose slavery now was to fight on the side of the North. So Quakers of draft age South and North, having consulted their consciences, made one of five choices: 1) to become a soldier; 2) perform non-combat duties in the army, like hospital service; 3) pay the exemption tax and become a conscientious objector within the law; 4) leave home and hide; 5) refuse to have anything to do with the war and take the consequences.

These are the choices made by Virginia's Quaker young men:

*None* became soldiers for the South (and indeed only one Friend living anywhere in the Southern states did so. Isaac Harvey of New Garden Meeting, North Carolina withstood the officers' orders to take up a gun for some weeks after being drafted, then became discouraged and gave in. He died in battle soon afterward.)[55] *Six* entered the Northern armies, as far as known--David and Henry Hough of Fairfax Meeting, John Marshall Taylor of Goose Creek, and David and John Howell of Hopewell (the Howell brothers lived at Harpers Ferry, sons of the David Howell who refused to help Rebecca Spring when she came to visit John Brown). The sixth was James Throckmorton of Hopewell. He enlisted in rage and grief after his father died of maltreatment as a Southern prisoner.[56] David and Henry Hough and Jimmy Throckmorton were cavalry soldiers who saw combat. Whether Taylor and the Howell brothers chose combat or noncombat duty, that is unknown.

Many Quakers paid the exemption tax of $500 after the Confederate Congress refused to exempt men of the peace churches from that tax. Of the 107 Virginians who paid the tax[57] nearly all were Quakers, Brethren or Mennonites.

As many or more than those who paid the exemption tax, escaped through flight. According to Hopewell Meeting's minute book,

> The first summer of the war a few of our young men were forced out in the militia and placed to work on fortifications, but through the favor of a kind Providence were soon enabled to [escape] as refugees into the loyal states.[58]

Thereafter many escaped by camping up in the Appalachians or going to relatives in the North. The Friends who opted to keep out of the army by escape were those living in northern Virginia generally speaking, while those who chose to pay the $500 tax were southside Friends. Samuel Janney chose to send his only living son Phineas off to stay with relatives in Waynesville, Ohio. John Crenshaw chose to pay the tax for his only grown son Natty.

None of the choices described above squares absolutely with the Friendly declarations made at the war's beginning to "suffer all penalties" and "quietly submit." By 1863, however, the Southern meetings had receded from their original positions, making it known that their young men were to feel free to pay the exemption tax "under protest" or to evade the enlisting officers if their consciences allowed it. Nereus Mendenhall, John Crenshaw and other Southern Friends' leaders agonized, but in the end they relaxed the positions they had declared in 1861.[59]

There were, however, certain Friends who made the fifth choice, who did refuse to have anything to do with the fighting and who did take the consequences.... It is fitting now to record the names and fates of those who "took the consequences." They were the fools for Christ, the followers in the footsteps of Christ, the Quakers' truest heroes, the friendliest of all Friends. They suffered in order to witness that war is evil, a curse from hell:

- *Edward Harris* (son of the Matthew Harris who raised the first American peanut crop) was drafted on 29 March 1862, along with his cousins James, Tilman, and William Harris, and Oswin White. They were taken from home in Southampton County to "the entrenched camp below Norfolk." After twelve days of refusing to drill, they were lodged in a dungeon. John Pretlow of their meeting (Black Creek Meeting), and another unidentified person, paid their exemption taxes after nine days in the dungeon. Then they were allowed to return home. But Edward Harris took sick in the dungeon and died seven days after release.[60]
- Job Throckmortona (1805-1862) was a miller on Mill Creek near Darkeville in Berkeley County. (An earlier Job Throckmorton wrote a famous satire on the Anglican Church, "The Martin Marprelate Tracts," in 1589.) Job with wife Leah and their five children joined Hopewell Meeting in 1854. One First Day in the spring of 1862 Job rode the twelve miles down the valley to attend Hopewell's monthly meeting. Two and a half miles from the meeting house he encountered a Confederate picket post. There he was arrested--probably because he refused to swear allegiance to the Confederacy. Then he was hurried to

Winchester and herded south on foot with twenty other Union men, along the Valley Pike and in the van of the retreating Confederate army. Many of the twenty escaped but Job said "I came in at the door and don't propose to go out anywhere else"--meaning that he intended to get a hearing and defend his peace position. In Harrisonburg, sixty-eight miles south of Winchester, wet, limping and half-starved, he died of pneumonia.[61] *He and Edward Harris were the first Quaker martyrs to die in Virginia in 200 years, the first since George Wilson died in Jamestown Jail.*

- *Joseph Jackson* (1808-1896), and *Amos Wright*, the clerk of Hopewell Meeting, were arrested and herded south with Job Throckmorton. Their Confederate captors abandoned them in Harrisonburg, whence they hiked home to Winchester "looking when they got there more like dead men than living ones."[62]

- *Jesse Osborne*, the son of Matthew Osborne of Spring Meeting in Alamance County, North Carolina was drafted early in 1862. He marched to Richmond with a North Carolina regiment and, refusing to wear a uniform or take a rifle, was treated so roughly that he died in Richmond the first day of Eighth Month 1862.[63]

- *John and Stephen Hobson*, brothers and Friends of Chatham County, North Carolina tried to escape by wagon to Indiana along with their families in the fall of 1862. However, the Chatham County sheriff and a posse overtook them. John and Stephen were then forced to march with army units into Virginia. Stephen wound up in the Confederate camp at Drury's Bluff on the James near Richmond. He endured months of abuse before being released with a broken arm and leg. John died after similar trials and was buried near Orange Court House sometime in 1863. John Crenshaw noted in his diary for 1 Tenth Month 1863 "Found the grave of John Hobson. His father much distressed."[64]

- *William Hockett* (1828-1880) belonged to Center Meeting in Guilford County, North Carolina. He was the great-grandson of an earlier William Hockett who came from Virginia to found Center Meeting in 1750. He was drafted Ninth Month 1862, furloughed and allowed to go home three times. Nine months later, however, on 8 Sixth Month 1863 the recruiters came for him and assigned him to the 21st North Carolina Infantry Regiment which marched at once to Richmond and joined Lee's army enroute to Gettysburg. William Hockett steadily refused to cooperate. Somewhere around Winchester the regimental colonel in person undertook to straighten him out. As William described it:

> I told him that I would not take a gun or march in the drill so he said 'Which will you choose, to be shot evening or morning?' I told him I should choose neither but if [God] permitted him to take my life I should submit to it.

He was then taken before a firing squad. "Their guns were pointed directly at my breast," he wrote. "I raised my arms and prayed....Not a gun was fired. They lowered them without orders and some of the men were heard to say they 'could not shoot such a man.'" All the rest of the way to Gettysburg efforts were made to force him to soldier. His captain clubbed him with a rifle butt, starved him, had him pricked with a bayonet, and finally urged him to run away which he refused to do. He lived unharmed through Gettysburg, then was captured by Union cavalry and shipped to Fort Delaware, a prisoner of war.[65]

- *J. Harvey*, evidently a North Carolina Quaker, was released from the Confederate camp at Drury's Bluff after refusing to soldier. All we know of him is this entry in John Crenshaw's journal: "Twelfth Month 10.1862. General Daniel tells us that an order has been issued for the release of J. Harvey."[66]

- *Thomas Hinshaw*, 32, was clerk of Holly Spring Meeting near Asheboro, North Carolina in 1862. Late that year the home guard rounded him up along with his brother Amos, 24, and Cyrus and Nathan Barker, 23 and 20, also brothers and Holly Spring Friends. All four were assigned to the 52d North Carolina Infantry at Camp French near Blackwater, Virginia. For eight months they marched to and fro with that regiment, treated kindly by some officers and bullied by others. The regiment fought at Gettysburg on the first day of battle. The colonel, lieutenant-colonel, major, sergeant-major and all the captains of the regiment died or were wounded and a lieutenant was left in command. The four Friends, however, got through unscathed. They found their way to the farm of Friends of nearby Menallen Meeting. Union soldiers discovered them there and sent them as prisoners to Delaware where they met William Hockett.[67]

Up until the battle at Gettysburg then, four Southern Quakers died martyrs in the Civil War and ten suffered within Virginia's borders, to witness that war is evil and peace is the way.

\* \* \*

After Gettysburg, Lee led his riddled army back toward Richmond. That same day, 4 July 1863, a Union force under Ulysses S. Grant defeated a Confederate army at Vicksburg, Mississippi. The Confederate commander was one John C. Pemberton (1814-1881)--a great grandson of Israel Pemberton, "King" of the Philadelphia Quakers in Revolutionary days!

The reappearance of this Quaker family in the person of a Confederate general has the flavor of a morality play. Israel Pemberton amassed a fortune in his lifetime, even though Anthony Benezet and others eldered him, saying that the pursuit of material wealth is unworthy of a Friend; and that he, Israel, would harm his children and childrens' children by leaving them vast wealth.

Sure enough, what Benezet predicted happened. Israel's only son, Joseph Pemberton, and Joseph's wife Ann, left off wearing Quaker dress in favor of the mode of the day. Their son John got into politics, supported Andrew Jackson and was appointed naval officer of Philadelphia's port by Jackson. When the opportunity came for John to get a West Point appointment for *his* son (John C. Pemberton), he took it even though he still claimed to be a Friend. After West Point, John C. Pemberton married Patty Thompson of Norfolk, Virginia, who persuaded her husband to join the Confederate side when the war came on.

The defeat at Gettysburg scarcely affected Robert E. Lee's popularity, but the Vicksburg defeat ruined John C. Pemberton. Prejudice in the South against northern-born Confederates was strong. Pemberton resigned his generalship in disgrace, offered to serve in the ranks as a private soldier and wound up the war as a lieutenant-colonel in Richmond. He lived out his days after the war in Warrenton. Just before his death he said to Patty and their children "Except for leaving you--I am not sorry that my time has come."[68]

\* \* \*

After Gettysburg and Vicksburg, the war got uglier. In April 1864, 120,000 Union soldiers started south from Washington to make a sixth try at capturing Richmond. Ulysses Grant, the hero of Vicksburg, was the commander. Lee and 60,000 Confederate soldiers set themselves to stop Grant's army....

The attitude of Virginians toward the Friends in their midst always had blended affection with a find of puzzlement or suspicion. In the days after Gettysburg and Vicksburg both these feelings intensified:

Affection came from some Friends' settled intention to be good neighbors:

- *Jesse and Lydia Wright* and their seven children lived near Hopewell Meeting House in a countryside that changed hands, from Confederates to Union and back again, seventy-six times. Both armies shot over and through the Wrights' farmhouse and Johnny Wright their oldest son went to the mountains to keep from being conscripted. Through all this the Wrights comforted a variety of people--deserters, wounded, refugees rendered homeless by the war. They fed strangers whenever they had food. When a neighbor died, Jesse prepared the body for burial. One hectic night the Wrights sheltered twenty wanderers of various descriptions.[69]
- *Will Hough* and *James C. Janney*, Friends of Fairfax Meeting, were known Union men. Both of them often visited Union army camps in Loudoun County at the request of Southern-sympathizing neighbors, to beg for the return of the neighbors' confiscated horses and wagons.[70]
- *John Crenshaw* was a source of consolation in the convulsed countryside just north of Richmond. From his diary for 4.5.1865, "Went to see some of my neighbors," and for 4.8, "A number of the neighbors called to ask advice. The fright and harassment from robbers continues. At the request of neighbors I drew up a statement...to General Wirtzel. The general promised...to repress the disorders."[71]

Suspicion of the Friendly Virginians came largely from the fact that nearly all of them were Union supporters who openly, obviously hoped for an end to slavery:

- *Joseph Jolliffe* of Hopewell Meeting was brought before the Confederate general Jubal Early in 1864, charged with being a Union man. The general required Jolliffe to show him the local roads. "Now, friend Early, you know the roads...as well as I do, and you know I wouldn't show them to you anyway," Jolliffe replied. The general then instructed Jolliffe to swear allegiance to the Confederate government. He replied "When you get it established and not before." An officer standing by said, "Mr

Jolliffe, you're the first Quaker I ever saw who says *you* instead of *thee*." The general said, "That makes no difference. He has the principles," and released Joseph Jolliffe with a mild admonition to pray for the Confederacy."[72]

* *John Griffith*, also of Hopewell, was 83 when the war began. He bore the loss of crops, horses and cattle bravely, but mourned his gold-rimmed spectacles which two Confederate soldiers swiped from his parlor.[73]

* Six Confederate riders kidnapped *Levi Stiles*, a Woodlawn Friend, in the snowy dawn of 12 First Month 1864. Four Woodlawn men and four Union cavalrymen tracked the raiders south in the snow, caught them at Pohick Creek after a six mile chase and liberated Levi.[74] The Richmond *Examiner* early in the war had published two stories charging that Levi guided Union troops through the Confederate lines; and Richmond Friends Meeting had purchased a full page ad to refute the charge.[75]

* *Jonah and Lydia Lupton* lived close by the little meeting house on Apple Pie Ridge near Winchester. For months their farm was hazy with cannon smoke, and cannon fire jolted the meeting house. The Lupton's wheat crop was taken and passing soldiers appropriated much property. Their sons hid for much of 1863 and 1864 in the mountains west of their farm. Meanwhile Lydia fed passing soldiers of both sides. "Yesterday three [Confederate] soldiers called and wanted their breakfasts. They were sick," Lydia wrote. "Poor dirty fellows...one of them could not eat, but lay on the grass and groaned.... I made a cup of tea for him, he drank it, said it tasted good.... I thought of my own poor boys, perhaps they were somewhere sick."[76]

The troubles of Quakers at home was as nothing compared to the trials of the young Quaker objectors to war drafted into the armies: In the North, the friendliness of Abraham Lincoln and his administration kept most Quaker objectors clear of the army. But not all the northern c.o.'s escaped.

Right after Gettysburg, in July of 1863, the draft took three young Vermont Quakers--Cyrus Pringle, Lindley Macomber and Peter Dakin. All three refused to pay the exemption tax and were sent as recruits down into Virginia. They were forced into Union uniforms, refusing to carry rifles until the rifles were tied to them. Cyrus Pringle kept a record:

> We were urged forward through the streets of Alexandria; and...upon a long train...started for Culpeper. We came over...desolated and deserted country...once...happy with a thousand homes, now laid with the ground.

Four miles from Culpeper

...We were taken to the 4th Vermont Regiment...required immediately after to be present at inspection of arms. We declined...were ordered by the colonel to be tied and if we made outcry to be gagged also.... After two or three hours we were relieved and left under guard...soon fell asleep from exhaustion.

Next morning [9.25.1863] the officers told us we must yield.... We were threatened with great severities and even death.

9.26--Yesterday...doubts and fears and forebodings seized me...I was alone...as if God had forsaken me...the Tempter whispered that afterall I might be only the victim of a delusion...but this morning I enjoy peace and feel as though I could face anything.... I am as a lamb in the shambles yet I do cry 'Thy will be done.'

On the evening of the twenty-sixth, the Colonel came to Cyrus and his companions, urging them to accept noncombat duty in the regiment's hospital and saying that "if we persisted in our course death would probably follow." At first they accepted the offer. "A great load seemed rolled away from us; we rejoiced in the prospect of life again. But soon there prevailed a feeling of condemnation as though we had sold our Master." They worked a day in the field hospital near Culpeper, then went to the colonel "with an explanation of our distress of mind, requesting him to proceed with court-martial."

The colonel was enraged. He shouted "that a man who would not fight for his country did not deserve to live," and ordered punishment. Two sergeants "tied cords to [Cyrus's] wrists and ankles and these to four stakes driven in the ground somewhat in the form of an X." Spread-eagled under the September sun, Cyrus "wept, not so much for my own suffering as from sorrow that such things should be in our own country, where Justice and Freedom and Liberty of Conscience have been the annual boast of Fourth of July orators."

When spread-eagling failed, the colonel shipped the three Friends back to Washington where they arrived 3 Tenth Month. There they met Edward Holway of Sandwich, Massachusetts and Charles Austin of Nantucket, two Friends who had refused to soldier in the ranks of the 22d Massachusetts Infantry. Isaac Newton took all five Friends in hand and persuaded them to work in Washington's Douglas army hospital until President Lincoln could parole them home. Isaac Newton explained that "Friends in the Army and refusing service had attracted public attention so that it was not expedient to parole us at present." He promised that work at Douglas Hospital would be "quite free from objection...we would release none from active service in the field, as the nurses were hired civilians."

Cyrus Pringle took sick with something like pneumonia after a week or two of hospital duty. When Isaac Newton reported Cyrus's condition to the president, Lincoln exclaimed "I want you to go and tell Stanton, it is my wish all these young men be sent home at once." So on 7 Eleventh Month, the five Friends started for New England. Cyrus Pringle was running a high fever and he became delirious on reaching New York City. He recovered after many weeks, "through the mercy and favor of Him," Cyrus wrote, "who in all this trial has been our guide."[77]

During the same week that he freed the five New England Friends, Edwin Stanton made a proposition to two Friends of Baltimore Yearly Meeting Orthodox who came to visit him. As the pair reported:

> The Secretary set forth with much feeling and stress the embarrassment caused...himself personally in his efforts to grant us exemption unconditionally, for which he had no law. He spoke of a large draft which will soon be enforced, and the necessity of some definite settled course for him to pursue.
>
> He wished Friends to have a general conference...to consider a proposition...which he believes would satisfy them...and the Government.... He proposes to create a Special Fund for...Freedmen and to exempt Friends from military service upon the payment of $300 into this fund.... Friends can have the disbursement of it through their own agents.

Baltimore Friends called a gathering of Friends representing all the northern Orthodox yearly meetings to discuss this proposal. They met on the 7 Twelfth Month 1863, the first and only time during the war that Friends from a number of American yearly meetings gathered to discuss their conscientious position. They decided to reject the proposal, since accepting it would be "a compromise of vital principle." But at the same time they expressed "sympathy with those now in authority" and appreciation for "the kindness evidenced at all times by the President and Secretary of War."

Instead of being rebuffed, Edwin Stanton risked his political future to protect the Quakers' "vital principle." He ordered, the army's Provost Marshal General to parole *all* conscientious objectors "until called for," law or no law.[78]

Quaker boys in the South had friends in high places too. John Crenshaw received hundreds of letters from young Friends asking for help to escape the Confederate armies' clutches. Most came from North Carolina Friends, a few from Virginia and a few more from Tennessee (these three states being the only Confederate states where Friends resided.) Here is one example:

The Eleventh Month 13th 1864--Richmond, Va.--Dear Friend Crenshaw--We the undersigned have bin arrested and brought hear under arrest for service and assigned to the Sixth N.C. Regt. We the undersigned friends wants thee to do something for us as soon as theye can if thee can soon. Hear we will give thee over names and meeting. We belong to
                    Back Creeke [North Carolina]
                    Henry Stuart
                    William F Bell
           Molboro [Marlboro, N.C.]
                    Clark Milliken
                    John R. Beckerdite[79]

John Crenshaw spent most of his waking hours responding to these letters. He succeeded in getting many Friends discharged through his friendly relationship with the Confederacy's assistant secretary of war, John A. Campbell. Some six hundred men and their families joined various southern Friends' meetings *after* the war started and Campbell was dubious about the sincerity of these "War Quakers"[80]; Crenshaw, however, even succeeded in persuading the authorities to free many War Quakers from the military.

But the South after Gettysburg was hungry for manpower and Crenshaw could not save all. After Gettysburg three more young Friends gave up their lives for conscience' sake in Virginia. All three were North Carolinians and all were War Quakers:

- *Isaiah Macon* joined Holly Spring Meeting where his father and mother were members, after the war began. The home guard rounded him up and he was shipped to a North Carolina regiment in the valley of Virginia. One of the many battles for Winchester was about to begin, and the hasty order was, "If Macon will not fight, put him in the front to stop bullets for those who will." So Isaiah went to the front in the thick of the firefight, a plain country man in farmer's jeans with no gun. When the bugle blew "Retreat," he sat down on the ground.

Then Union troops "captured" him and sent him to Point Lookout prison. He died in the prison a few days later.[81]

- *Ahijah Macon* was Isaiah's brother. He was conscripted right after the war began, served out the term of his enlistment, and then went home repelled by military life. He joined his parents in the Holly Spring Meeting, but then was rounded up and sent again to the army, his discharge papers disregarded. He was put in a Richmond prison when he refused to fight and received only cane-seed meal to eat. Becoming sick, he went from his cell to Winder Hospital in Richmond where he died.[82]

- *Seth Laughlin*, 27, and his wife Sarah joined Marlboro Meeting near Asheboro in the Second Month, 1864. Soon after, Seth was taken for the army and sent to the trenches east of Petersburg, Virginia. Refusing to take up a gun there, he was first kept without sleep for thirty-six hours, a soldier standing by to jab him with a bayonet whenever he closed his eyes. Then he was "bucked down" for three hours for several days and hung by his thumbs for an hour and a half. As he still refused the rifle, a court-martial sentenced Seth to die. The regiment turned out to witness Seth's execution. He was marched out before a twelve-man firing squad, six handed loaded rifles and six unloaded. He asked time for prayer, then prayed not for himself but for the firing squad, "Father, forgive them for they know not what they do"--whereupon the squad refused to raise their rifles at the command. Seth's death sentence was revoked, and he was imprisoned in Richmond. But he caught jail fever there and died in Winder Hospital about the same time as Ahijah Macon.[83]

That brings to seven the number of Quaker men who died in Virginia in the days of the Civil War, to witness that war is evil and peace is the way.

\* \* \*

General Ulysses Grant's army, 120,000 men headed for Richmond, met General Lee's 60,000 in the Wilderness west of Fredericksburg on 5 and 6 May 1864. Fifty-five miles from Richmond, bloody fighting and wholesale death. The Union columns tried to detour the Confederates and got twelve miles farther toward Richmond, to Spotsylvania Court House. There the Confederates blocked the way again, the mayhem as terrible as at Gettysburg, whole regiments of young men dead and disabled. Grant, implacable, shifted his columns again around the Confederate trenches and reached Cold Harbor on White Oak Swamp, just a few miles north and west of Richmond. The Confederates blocked again there and 9,000 men died. Now the Union army spread south across the James and began a siege of Richmond and Petersburg.

That May and June of 1864, Grant squandered 55,000 men. Lee lost a smaller number yet that loss was more serious because the young manhood of the Confederacy was about used up. Now they were pressing old men and boys into the Confederate army.

The besieging Union army, large as it was, could not surround Richmond and Petersburg completely. The besiegers encamped in a half-moon thirty-five miles long to the east of the two cities. The west lay open and food supplies came in to the cities' defenders from the valley of Virginia. So, early in August Grant ordered General Philip Sheridan to take an army into the valley, overcome General Jubal Early's force of some 20,000 men there, and then destroy the Valley's crops.

In pursuance of these orders, Sheridan encountered three Friends-- Samuel Janney, Rebecca Wright and Elizabeth Comstock:

Samuel Janney visited Sheridan late that August after a troop of Sheridan's cavalry swept through the Goose Creek neighborhood capturing able-bodied men, Quaker and non-Quaker. Samuel caught up with the troop in a patch of woods near Purcellville where they had spent the night. He learned that the prisoners were being taken to Carroll Prison near Washington so that the Confederacy could not use them for soldiers. He persuaded the major in command to release "those I would vouch for as Union men." Then he headed for Washington to plead for the rest of his captive neighbors. He talked his way into the office of C. A. Dana, the assistant secretary of war. But Secretary Dana said Samuel would have to see General Sheridan, who then was at Harper's Ferry fifty miles away.

Taking a B&O train, Samuel rode to Harper's Ferry. He found General Sheridan in a tent with his army camped for miles around him. Sheridan was courteous but answered Samuel's plea by saying "We must all bear the burdens imposed by this war. I and my soldiers have to bear our burden...and you people of Loudoun must not complain." When Samuel kept on pleading, Sheridan bent a little, agreeing to release the old men and two doctors among the prisoners. As to the rest he promised to telegraph the War Department in Washington about them.

So Samuel took the cars back to Washington and the War Department. Sheridan's promised telegram had not arrived. Samuel was advised to write to General Grant. He did that and finally succeeded in getting all the Loudoun men released to go home, on their promise "to do nothing to the injury of the United States government."[84]

Amos Wright, quondam clerk of Hopewell Meeting, lived in Winchester. Rebecca and Hannah were the two pretty daughters of his family. Rebecca had taught in the Goose Creek Friends' School and now in 1864 had a little school of her own in Winchester. Since her father had been abused nearly to death by Stonewall Jackson's soldiers in 1862, Rebecca was an outspoken upholder of the Union. Sister Hannah, however, had Confederate soldier beaux who called to chat with the sisters in their parlor.

Rebecca Wright was alone in her classroom at the noon recess on 16 Ninth Month, when a black man entered. He asked Rebecca if she was "Miss Wright the Unionist." Rebecca assented. The man muttered "I have a letter for you from General Sheridan," took a moist ball of silver foil out of his mouth and slipped it to her. When Rebecca began to tear off the foil, he said "Don't do that--you'll need it to wrap your reply in."

The letter read:

Sept 15, 1864--I learn from Major General Crook that you are a loyal lady and still love the old Flag. Can you inform me of the position of Early's forces...an his probable or reported intentions? Have any more troops arrived from Richmond?... I am Very respectfully your Most Obedient Servant,

        P.H. Sheridan, Major General Commanding
        You can trust the bearer.

Since Friends were enjoined not to help either side in the war, Rebecca must have hesitated; but she did write an answer, including some information she picked up from the Confederate soldiers who called on Hannah and her. The old man wrapped her answer in his silver foil, put it in his cheek, and carried it off to General Sheridan now headquartered at Millwood. Rebecca wrote that Kershaw's division of infantry and Cutshaw's artillery had just left Winchester to rejoin Lee in Richmond. Accordingly, on the nineteenth before daybreak Union cannon began to roar on Winchester's outskirts and Sheridan's soldiers captured the city that day.

Aaron Griffith's daughter Hatty, 26, who was Rebecca Wright's chum and fellow Unionist greeted Generals Sheridan and Crook when they rode in to town. Hatty guided the two generals to Rebecca in her schoolroom, and Sheridan, at Rebecca's desk, wrote his dispatch to annouce the victory.

Sheridan and his soldiers remained in the Valley six months. After taking Winchester they systematically worked southward, wrecking the countryside from Winchester to Staunton, ninety-two miles. Sheridan to Grant from Woodstock on 7 October:

I have destroyed over 2,000 barns filled with wheat, hay and farming implements; over 70 mills filled with flour and wheat; have driven in front of the army over 4,000 head of stock and have killed and issued to the troops not less than 3,000 sheep.... A large number of horses have been obtained.[85]

Three years later Philip Sheridan sent Rebecca Wright a gold watch inscribed to commemorate her part in his victory at Winchester. That victory was the making of Sheridan. He received congratulations from A. Lincoln, followed by two rapid promotions in rank. It did not work out as well for Rebecca Wright. The people of Winchester were furious when they found out about Rebecca's gold watch. The family had to move to Philadelphia. Rebecca, who married William Bonsall in 1871, worked in the Treasury Department in Washington until her death in 1914.[86]

Elizabeth Comstock (1815-1891), an English-born Friend, a widow, was a station keeper in Michigan on the Underground Railroad. When war broke out, she toured the Union army hospitals, nursing the soldier patients. In Washington she visited Agriculture Secretary Isaac Newton, Attorney General Edward Bates, War Secretary Edwin Stanton and President Lincoln. After she prayed with Lincoln in the White House 30 Tenth Month 1864, he held her hand so as to have her stay longer, and gave her a flower from the table. Elizabeth gave a public talk that night attended by Edward Bates with Mary Lincoln, the president's wife. A newspaper reporter described "her firm clear silvery voice." Edward Bates called Elizabeth, "as true an ambassador of Christ as I ever saw."

Isaac Newton got Elizabeth a pass to visit the war front in the valley of Virginia. She came from Washington with two other Quaker women on a military train. Where guerrillas had burned a railroad bridge the women held their skirts, then clambered down into a creek valley and up to where another train was waiting. This train also was stopped five miles from Winchester. Elizabeth and her companions arrived in Winchester in the back of an army wagon with the houses dark, no street lights and the streets deep in mud. They found their way to Aaron Griffith's bullet-scarred house where the Griffith's greeted them warmly enough but the house was icy cold. Winchester's trees were gone and there was no firewood.

Next morning Aaron Griffith took his visitors to General Sheridan for his permission to visit his army's hospitals. The sight of the women in their Quaker bonnets made the general nervous. He took Aaron Griffith aside and asked "What do these women want? Have they come here to lecture me?" When Aaron explained matters, Sheridan reportedly said, "Well, I am relieved. They frightened me more than all the enemy in front for I knew what to do about them. But this army of Quaker women. I didn't know...."[87]

Hit-and-run guerillas harassed Sheridan's supply line: John S. Mosby's company, Lee White's Comanches, the bands of Gilmore and McNeil. Mosby's men killed Sheridan's quartermaster and his medical director. Loudoun County was the base of operations for Mosby and White. On November 28 therefore Sheridan ordered the First Cavalry Division under General Wesley Merritt to clear Loudoun of forage and foodstuffs so as to deny the guerrillas their refuge there.

Loudoun County was already pretty well flattened--five times armies had crossed the county and despoiled it. But the operations of Merritt's men in December of 1864 were the *coup de grace*. They did not burn the Loudoun Friends' houses, but their mills, barns, and corn cribs went up in fire along with wagons, plows, buggies and harness. They drove off horses and cows, slaughtered pigs and sheep. On 2 December burning barns and haystacks lit up the night all around Goose Creek and Waterford. Friends lost over $100,000 worth of worldly goods.[88]

\* \* \*

All through the summer and fall of 1864 and the following winter, Grant's blue army lay east of Richmond and Petersburg, digging trenches, attacking and cannonading, trying to break through the stretched-out line of defenders.

Early in the siege Lt. Colonel Henry Pleasants, an engineer officer of the 48th Pennsylvania regiment, had a compelling idea. Pleasants was a great grandson of Robert Pleasants's brother Samuel, the Quaker brother who left Virginia for Philadelphia and married Molly Pemberton there. Colonel Pleasants's idea--to dig a tunnel from the Union to the Confederate line, lay explosives in it and explode a hole right through the Confederate defenses.

When General Grant assented, Pleasants took charge of digging the tunnel, 510 feet long, done in six weeks. At 4:44 a.m. on 28 July, four tons of gunpowder exploded under the Confederate trenches east of Petersburg. A mass of dirt, rocks, men and cannon rose into the air, 278 men killed or hurt, a crater thirty feet deep and sixty wide torn in the ground.

It happened that the Crater was blown under a sector commanded by Confederate Major General Bushrod Rust Johnson--born a Quaker in a family from Loudoun County, Virginia that migrated to Ohio twelve years before Bushrod's birth. Bushrod's brother Nathan was a Quaker physician in Ohio, a conductor of escaping slaves in the time of the Underground

Railroad. Bushrod's men succeeded in stopping the Union soldiers before they got through the crater gap. So it was that two men with Quaker roots played leading parts in a macabre and futile incident of the siege.[89]

The Friends of Richmond Meeting met faithfully on First Days all through the siege, the silence of their worship continually punctuated by gunfire. Their 19th and Cary Streets meeting house was taken over early in the war for an army hospital. Now they met in Friends' homes--usually in Jane Whitlock's parlor at 2316 East Broad Street. John Crenshaw was the meeting's only recorded minister.

Johnny Crenshaw, five years of age, died in Eleventh Month 1863 and Willie, two years, and Mary, ten months, the Crenshaws' youngest children, died the following summer, the summer of the siege. They died of some fever, no doubt caught from the soldiers camped around Rocouncy. Their loss took the heart out of their parents. John Crenshaw kept no journal for a while. But in the Tenth Month, 1864, he reemerged as publisher of *The Southern Friend*, "a Religious, Literary and Agricultural Journal." It was designed to fill the void left for southern readers of *Friends Review*, published in Philadelphia and no longer deliverable in the South.

Richmond was in a desperate pass by the last day of March 1865. Some citizens were starving. That day a travelling Friends' minister came to Richmond, the first in years. He was Joseph James Neave, 29, from Suffolk, England. While attending the London Yearly Meeting in 1864, he said, "It was clearly laid upon me to go to America to support and comfort Friends in their time of suffering."

He met for First Day worship with Richmond Friends in Jane Whitlock's parlor on 2 Fourth Month. Jefferson Davis, worshiping that same hour in St. Paul's some blocks away, was called out in mid-service by a messenger who whispered that the Union troops had broken through.

John Crenshaw's wife took Joseph James home to Rocouncy, four miles north by buggy, after the rise of Friends' meeting. She thought it queer that the soldier at the toll bar on Brook Road was gone--he had been there when she came in the morning. John Crenshaw and 16-year-old daughter Deborah Anne, who attended Cedar Creek Meeting with John's father that day, joined them at home in the evening.

Joseph James wrote in his diary:

> About four o'clock next morning (3 Fourth Month) we were aroused and the doors and windows shaken by a very loud explosion.... John B. Crenshaw felt pretty sure the end of the siege had come. His son started as usual about six o'clock with milk for the city, but soon returned saying the Federal troops were in

Richmond and the roads were full of Confederate soldiers who were fleeing from it.

After breakfast J. B. Crenshaw...asked me to go with him to the city. We saw many negroes going in who looked very bright and cheerful; we saw many Southerners hastening away.... At the toll bar was a Confederate officer...saying he would not fall into the hands of Yanks--he would not go to a Yankee prison, etc.

...A large part of the city was in flames.... Before the Confederate troops left the city, they had set fire to tobacco warehouses and inflammable buildings and cut the hose belonging to the Fire Brigades; their last act being to blow up the powder magazine, which was the cause of the noise we heard in the early morning....

The state of things in the city that night had been truly awful...the mob broke into the liquor stores and scores...drunk, perished in the fire....

We made several calls and those we called on were much reassured and comforted.[90]

General Lee and 30,000 men of his army retreated west. The Federals pursued, surrounded and stopped them seventy miles west of Richmond at Appomattox Court House on 9 April 1865. And to all practical purposes that ended the Civil War and ended the institution of slavery in Virginia.

* * *

How unexpected, that the history of the Friendly Virginians, a tiny religious minority, should have to do so largely with the winning of freedom. From the 1650s to 1782, say 125 years, this account had to do with attaining *religious* liberty; from the 1760s to 1865, another hundred years, with liberty *for the slaves*....

Liberty for the slaves came in a horrific, sad, regrettable way, through Civil War, wholesale hate and violence. Friends' peace testimony lost ground, yet not entirely. The seven Friends who died in Virginia to witness that peace is precious, they gave something shining and true to humankind: Edward Harris, Job Throckmorton, Jesse Osborn, John Hobson, Isaiah Macon, Ahijah Macon, Seth Laughlin.

This photo of a winsome Quaker comes from Janney Wilson's home in Purcellville, Virginia, lived in by six generations of the Wilsons of Goose Creek Meeting since 1780.

# XV

# THEY LEAP THE HEDGE
## 1865-1900

> In '61 the war begun
> In '62 twas half way through
> In '63 the slave was free
> In '64 twas almost o'er
>
> In '65 they ceased to strive

The end of the Civil War was joyous news for the Friendly Virginians. Moses Watson, not a Friend, who owned slaves and a mill near Goose Creek, recorded the somewhat scandalous behavior of his Goose Creek neighbors. Many that he names here were Friends:

> Thursday, Aprile 13th 1865 their is great Rejoicing with the Union People in regard to Fall of Richmond and the Surrender of General Lee.
>
> It is said that Saml M Janney Had the Old Gobbler killed and Invited Many of his Union Friends to Eat and be Merry. William Tate Shut him Self up in a room and Laughed his Fill. Joseph Nichols has been riding hunting hands to go to his house to drink Cider get drunk and be Merry. Bill Lemmon and Lot Tavenner is gone Fishing to day: they Say the Work is done. Thornton Whitacre Says the Backbone of the Confederacy is Broken and the war is about Over. It is the prevailing Opinion that the South Can Fight No longer.
>
> Buck Bolon has a heap of Fun a bout My Negroes. He asked Me if I did not think them very Valuable. If I would Not like to Sell them and What I Asked For Negroes Now. Henry S. Taylor says the Secesh aught Never to be allowed to vote again and aught to be made to Eate With a Iron Spoon the balance of their life and Not to be alowed to hold any office of any kind.[1]

The joy was soon tempered, for word came that Abraham Lincoln was dead, murdered Friday evening, April 14th. Samuel Janney noted the news in his journal:

I felt for him an affection and reverence that I never felt for any other statesman, and having had some acquaintance with him, I mourn his death as the loss of a personal friend. Many of the secessionists who four years ago reviled his character, having lately become convinced of his benevolent disposition and remarkable lenity toward his enemies, now regret his removal by the hand of the fiendish assassin, and look forward with dread to the rigid measures anticipated from his successor.[2]

Lincoln's assassin was John Wilkes Booth, 27, an actor of a theatrical family raised on his family's country retreat north of Baltimore. Wilkes as a small boy went to the school under the care of Gunpowder Friends Meeting near Cockeysville, Maryland, but the experience did not take. He referred to his Quaker teachers as "thee-and-thous" and finished his education at St Timothy's Hall in Catonsville. He was a violent partisan of the South in the war.[3]

Eli and Sibyl Jones, Quakers from China, Maine, were in Washington that April, staying with Isaac Newton. They were come to see what New England Friends could do for the freed black people who were flocking in to Washington in droves and to visit the long wards of mangled soldiers in Washington's military hospitals--Seminary Hospital, Camp Fry, Douglas, Stanton, Emery, Harwood, Finley.

At the news of Abraham Lincoln's murder, Sibyl Jones walked to the White House to visit Mary his wife. Mary Lincoln was in bed "all crushed and broken under the heavy stroke. I spoke to her of the Heavenly Chastener's love and care," Sibyl wrote, "and said that He could bind up the broken heart and give peace." She and Eli then went on south to visit Richmond's Friends; but Sibyl Jones received word there that Mary Lincoln, still grieving (and referring to Sibyl as "that holy woman") wanted Sibyl to come to her. So Sibyl returned to Washington and "after a season of feeling prayer" parted tenderly with Mary Lincoln.[4]

The war impoverished Virginia's Friends, their farms ruined and livestock gone. The Friends of Goose Creek lost over $80,000 worth of their worldly goods and Fairfax Meeting's Friends over $23,000. Aaron Griffith of Winchester alone lost over $23,000, mostly from the ruination of his textile mill.[5] John Crenshaw in Richmond lost so much that he had to sell Rocouncy, his beloved farm.

They were no worse off than most other Virginians, for the whole Virginia landscape, its ethos and outlook, was a wreck in 1865. Indeed Friends may have been a little better off than others, for the northern meetings took up subscriptions of money to help the southern Friends get back on their feet. This enabled the Richmond and Winchester Centre meetings to replace their ruined meeting houses and helped Asa Moore Janney to replace his burned-out mill near Goose Creek.[6] Then too Samuel Janney went to Washington, patiently pressing Congress to repay the wartime losses of Loudoun County's Union families. After seven years, in 1872, Congress did appropriate $61,821.10 to pay for stock driven off by Union troops; but property burned and destroyed (a much larger loss) never was paid.[7]

One northern Friend provided funds that went a long way toward salvaging the whole town of Charlottesville. He was C. A. Furbush of Furbush and Gage, textile machinery manufacturers in Philadelphia. In the fall of 1867, Henry Clay Marchant, 29, a wounded Confederate veteran, visited Furbush and Gage's offices. He had inherited the ruins of a woolen mill on the Rivanna River in Charlottesville--burned down by Union troops under General George Custer--and was trying to find capital to rebuild.

Furbush's English partner, D. T. Gage, wanted no truck with penniless rebels, but Furbush heard out Henry Marchant, felt for him, loaned him $5,950 and provided him with machinery. The Charlottesville Woolen Mills, rebuilt, became one of the few means for bringing dollars into the community, and Furbush and Henry Marchant became lifelong friends.[8]

* * *

Samuel Janney wrote a meditation about Virginia's future, soon after the war's end: "The conditions now required for the prosperity and happiness of the Old Dominion," he wrote, "are the restoration of the national authority and civil law, peace, free labor and free schools."[9] Samuel knew, even as he meditated, about efforts under way toward those four conditions.

The war had hardly begun when delegates from Virginia's western counties and a few to the east met in Wheeling; condemned the secession of Virginia from the Union; and set up "the Restored Government of Virginia," independent of the administration in Richmond. Francis Pierpont, 47, a Fairmont lawyer, was elected the governor.

Francis's grandfather John Pierpont (1742-1796) grew up as a boy in Fairfax Friends Meeting. John Pierpont left Friends before enlisting in the Revolutionary army, and moved west after the Revolution. Francis was born on his grandfather John's mountain farm near Morgantown. Some of Francis Pierpont's relatives were faithful Fairfax Friends even while Francis served as the "Restored" governor.

When West Virginia split off to become a separate state, Pierpont declined to be the first governor of West Virginia, preferring to continue as governor of Restored Virginia. He and a few staff people moved from Wheeling to Alexandria in spring 1863. As governor there he controlled only the Virginia areas held by Union troops--Alexandria and Fairfax and Prince William Counties on the Potomac River, the two Eastern Shore counties, and the James River Valley from Norfolk to City Point.

Once settled in Alexandria, Pierpont received the enthusiastic support of three Fairfax County Quakers--*the first Quakers in Virginia since John Porter in 1663 to engage out and out in politics*. These were the Hauxhurst brothers, John and Job, and Jonathan Roberts:

The Hauxhursts came in 1846 from Westbury Meeting, Long Island, to settle in Fairfax County--the sons of a Quaker minister who toured Virginia's meetings twice while John and Job were growing up. The brothers ran a flour mill on Difficult Run. Both of them were elected delegates to the Restored legislature in May 1863. It consisted of six state senators and 11 delegates to the lower house.

Jonathan Roberts with wife Abigail and three children came from Moorestown, New Jersey in 1849 to live in Accotink near Woodlawn Friends Meeting house. Jonathan served as a Fairfax County election commissioner along with John Hauxhurst in 1862 and the Fairfax voters elected him their county sheriff that May. Evidently the Woodlawn Friends approved, for they met to worship in Jonathan and Abigail's Accotink parlor in the summer months after his election, when Union soldiery occupied the meeting house.

After the Gettysburg battle in July 1863 it became more and more clear that the South could not win the war. Then the great question in Washington came to be, what should be done with the South after the war is over and done? Three schools of thought developed:

- The "Moderate" or "True" Republicans led by Abraham Lincoln held that the eleven Confederate states, their leaders and all, should be welcomed back into the Union kindly, "with malice toward none, with charity for all." The slaves should be empowered to become full citizens through education, and opportunity for upward mobility. Edwin Stanton and Isaac Newton in Lincoln's cabinet supported this position.
- "Radical" Republicans made up the party's other wing. They agreed that the slaves should be helped all right, but they disagreed violently with the Moderates about treatment of the white Confederates. We should treat them as *criminals*, the Radicals insisted, and must not re-admit them or their states to the Union until they have apologized and recanted their evil ways. Congressman Thaddeus Stevens of Pennsylvania and Massachusetts Senator Charles Sumner led the Radicals.

- The Democrats, often called "Conservatives," agreed with the Moderate Republicans about welcoming the Confederates back into the Union kindly and quickly. The Democrats were cool, though, about spending a lot of money on the slaves. They were unsure that the Emancipation Proclamation was a good idea, suspected that blacks were suited only for peonage, and sympathized with slaveholders plunged into poverty by the loss of their slaves. Andrew Johnson, who was Lincoln's vice-president and a former governor of Tennessee, privately thought as the Democrats did.

As for Francis Pierpont, the Hauxhurst brothers, and Jonathan Roberts, they all favored Abraham Lincoln and the Moderate Republicans. The Restored government held a constitutional convention which met from 22 January to 7 April in Alexandria's city council room. John Hauxhurst as a delegate to this convention proposed immediate and uncompensated emancipation for slaves, and all except one of his fellow delegates voted with him there. He proposed a system of free public schools and the convention approved that too. But John made other proposals that were just too extreme: permit blacks to testify in court (only two others voted with John there); permit black men to vote; submit the new constitution to all Virginia voters for their approval (which implied no harsh treatment for Virginia's whites after the war's end); and free education for black children as well as white. None of these last proposals was incorporated in the Restored Constitution of 1864.[10]

In May 1865, the month after the South surrendered at Appomattox, Governor Pierpont moved his offices from Alexandria to Richmond and became governor of all Virginia with the blessing of the federal government. He immediately invoked the Constitution of 1864 as Virginia's basic law and called a session of the Restored legislature in Richmond. Then he persuaded the legislature to repeal that article in the 1864 Constitution which denied the vote to Virginians who had held offices in the Confederate government or military forces. Pierpont intended this as a gesture of forgiveness, a way of welcoming Virginia's war-time leaders back into the Union. But his olive branch was slapped aside. In the election that followed the electorate voted out the Hauxhursts and other Moderate Republicans in favor of Conservatives who represented Virginia's old-line, prewar thinking.

Before 1865 ended, the new conservative Assembly passed a Vagrant Law which provided that blacks without means could be hired out as laborers. Any who tried to run away could be worked "with ball and chain" or "confined in jail on bread and water." The law savored of slavery. It practically canceled emancipation, for just about all the black people of Virginia were "without means" in 1865. Edwin Stanton, Secretary of War, ordered the law negated, and the northern newspapers indignantly attacked it and similar laws of other Southern states, calling them "Black Codes."

Those Black Codes stirred the U.S. Congress to form a Reconstruction Committee, fifteen senators and representatives headed by Thaddeus Stevens. They called forty-nine witnesses to Washington--including Robert E. Lee and Quakers John Hauxhurst and Jonathan Roberts from Virginia--cross-examined them sternly, and then concluded that the Southern states still were impenitent and unfit to rejoin the Union. The Congress accordingly denied seats to Virginia's elected representatives.[11]

Congress's actions were contrary to the wishes of Andrew Johnson, Lincoln's successor in the White House. In February 1866 Congress passed a bill to undo the Black Codes. It also extended the life of the Freedmens' Bureau, a federal agency created in 1865 to coordinate the services of various voluntary agencies in behalf of southern blacks--feeding and sheltering them, finding them work, providing schooling and medical aid, and defending them from white terrorists. President Johnson vetoed this bill.

Two months later he vetoed a Civil Rights Act to give blacks the same rights under law as whites and also vetoed a second Freedmens' Bureau Act. But Congress over-rode these last two vetoes and then initiated the 14th Amendment to the Constitution, thus confirming the provisions of the vetoed Civil Rights Act.

When Virginia's Assembly met in December, Governor Pierpont urged softening the Vagrant Act and ratifying the 14th Amendment. But the Assembly balked, and this prompted the U.S. Congress to pass a drastic Reconstruction Act in March 1867. President Johnson vetoed it too, but Congress quickly re-passed it.

Under this Reconstruction Act the South was to be dealt with as a conquered province, divided into five military districts (of which the state of Virginia was Military District Number One.) Military rule was to continue in Virginia and in every Southern state until that state ratified the 14th Amendment, adopted a state constitution that entitled blacks to vote, and barred former officials of the Confederacy from voting.

Accordingly, another constitutional convention gathered in Richmond in December 1867, to hammer out a new constitution for Virginia according to the requirements of the Reconstruction Act. It was a revolutionary gathering, for the Act decreed that the convention's delegates must be chosen by the votes of *all* Virginians black and white, and black delegates mingled with whites on the floor of that convention for the first time in Virginia's history. Twenty-four of the 105 delegates were black. By party, 72 of the 105 were Republicans (some Moderate and some Radical) and 33 were Conservatives who represented the old planter class.[12]

The convention elected Judge John Underwood to preside and George Rye to be secretary. John Hauxhurst was the only Quaker delegate, although a second Quaker offered as a delegate. This was John Crenshaw, hesitantly entering politics. Burwell Toler, an illiterate black preacher, defeated Crenshaw in Hanover County.[13]

The delegates wrangled in Richmond over four months, Republicans offering one innovation after another, Conservatives battling to hang on to Virginia's old ways. John Hauxhurst again proposed many far-out innovations, as many as he had during the fashioning of the Restored Constitution of 1864. The public schools which he advocated in 1864 was approved again; and his proposal to allow blacks to testify in court (voted down in 1864) was this time approved, with the added provision that blacks could also serve on juries. Hauxhurst also led in pushing through the proposal to obtain most of the state's revenue through property and income taxes instead of the poll tax, thus making Virginia's taxing system a progressive one.

When the convention came to debate the matter of extending the vote to black people, John Hauxhurst tried to have suffrage declared a natural right, "inherent and God-given." Conservatives fought this extreme idea, declaring that it implied the equality of all men, to which no conscientious Conservative could subscribe; but in the end the convention ratified impartial suffrage for white and black alike. Furthermore, it decided that voting would be by secret ballot in order to prevent intimidation at the polls--a precaution previously unknown in Virginia.

The Conservatives objected strenuously to the clause that denied ex-Confederates the right to vote. But the Radical Republican delegates, including all the convention's black delegates, insisted on "making treason odious" and the clause was retained in the draft constitution when it was completed 17 April 1868.

On account of this controversial clause the "Underwood Constitution" was not submitted to Virginia's voters for more than a year. The Conservatives, insisting that no constitution was acceptable that barred the state's leading men from politics, sent a committee of nine men to Washington to offer this compromise--the Conservatives would agree to voting rights for black men if the clause in the constitution barring voting rights for ex-Confederates could be voted on separately from the rest of that document. Congress agreed to the offer and the referendum on the Underwood Constitution took place across Virginia on 6 July 1869. The Constitution was voted in, the bar against voting rights for ex-Confederates was voted out, and Virginia was practically back in the Union after four years of civil war and four more years of reconstruction.

That same July 6, 1869, Virginians elected a new governor and a new General Assembly. The new constitution represented a triumph for Moderate Republicans since it recognized both black ex-slaves and white ex-Confederates as full citizens, with malice toward neither and with charity for both. The new governor was Gilbert C. Walker, a Moderate, and many Moderates won General Assembly seats. Among these winners were three Quakers:

- Thomas E. Taylor (1832-1892) lived in 1869 on Coolbrook Farm, his birthplace near Goose Creek Meeting house. He went to the Senate after serving as clerk of Loudoun's circuit court, to represent Loudoun, Fairfax, and Prince William Counties and Alexandria city.
- John Hauxhurst was elected to the House from Alexandria.
- John Crenshaw was sent to the House by Henrico County and Richmond voters, having first been assured that he would be excused from the Assembly to attend the Richmond Friends' mid-week meetings for worship. Before Gilbert Walker's inauguration, John Crenshaw explained to him the virtue of *affirming* the truth rather than *swearing* to it; and Crenshaw, as Gilbert Walker's good friend and as a Quaker minister, stood up with the new governor on inauguration day and "affirmed him in" to office.[14]

Crenshaw was 49 in 1869, a handsome and vital man. He lost his first wife in 1858, three of his young children died during the Civil War and he encountered financial reverses, yet he kept a cheerful disposition. "If there is a man in the State who has a right to speak as a true friend of the colored man," he declared, "I claim to be that man."[15] Right after the war's end he raised money from Friends in the north, to build both a Friends' Asylum for Colored Orphans in Richmond (on land donated by the city)[16] and also a substantial new Friends' meeting house at 7 East Clay Street, Richmond.[17] In the Virginia House he served on the Committee of Asylums and Prisons and introduced a bill which resulted in Central State Hospital (of which more later). He also opposed the death penalty; and was nominated to be Speaker of the House, but declined that honor.

\* \* \*

As far back as 1862, a few northern people began to discuss the future for blacks in the war-torn South. The word *Contrabands* crept into the language, meaning slaves abandoned by their masters, left to wander the southern roads. As the war wore on the Contrabands' numbers swelled from thousands to hundreds of thousands.

Quakers were certainly not the only ones who cared, but they were among the first "to come under the weight of the concern." By April 1862, women Friends around Philadelphia organized a "Womens' Aid" to sew clothes for the Contrabands. At the same time a National Freedmen's Relief Association formed in New York City with Hannibal Hamlin, vice-president of the U.S., its president. When Hamlin invited the Womens' Aid to distribute its clothing through the new association, the Quaker women accepted at once.[18] This acceptance marks a new Quaker willingness to work with "the world's people," another breaking through the hedge which Friends had long cultivated to keep themselves clear of worldliness.

About this time the northern yearly meetings began plans to send Quaker task forces south in aid of the Contrabands. Two Friends, however, members of Pleasant Street Meeting in Worcester, Massachusetts, could not wait: Lucy Chase, 39, and her sister Sarah, 25. Right after Union troops got control of the area around Norfolk, in December 1862, Lucy and Sarah appeared there in their Quaker bonnets. They came as emissaries of the Boston Education Commission, a group organized by the governor of Massachusetts. General Ben Butler, military governor of Norfolk, assigned the sisters to work with 2,000 ragged and bewildered Contrabands, quartered in the former Confederate army camp on Craney's Island six miles from Norfolk--the same camp where Edward Harris earlier that year sickened to his death as a war refuser.

Craney Island's muddy crudeness shocked the sisters. They marvelled at the quirks of their black charges. Late into the nights they heard swelling spirituals sung, the chant-and-response sermons of black preachers. They survived severe home-sickness. Army regulations frustrated them. They scrounged for supplies, acted as teachers, nurses, mediators, counsellors, comforters. When a delegation of New York Friends came to build them a school house, they were glad.

The blacks' desperate, confused feelings pulled the sisters this way and that. One woman told them sobbing how her old master "took me to Richmond prison and sold me there." Another woman came to Lucy leading a girl of 18: "See my daughter," she cried. "They sold her away from me when she was just old enough to rock [in] the cradle and see how they've done her bad, see how they've cut her up. From her head to her feet she is scarred."

In the circumstances it took a while for Lucy and Sarah to get their bearings. But Doctor Joseph Parrish (Hicksite) and Marmaduke and Regina Cope (Orthodox) made friendly visits, then went home to Philadelphia to organize support for the sisters. Soon they began to receive crates of clothing from Philadelphia and New York Friends, "all things wanted, and all things right." Presently Sarah Smiley from Maine, "a lovely Quakeress of much executive ability" came to them with plans for an industrial school in Norfolk.

By early 1864 the Union armies had pushed up the James from Norfolk half-way to Richmond. A company of eight or nine Friends came then to set up a Contraband center in the newly won area. The newly formed Friends Freedmen's Association of Philadelphia sent them and Edward Holway of Massachusetts (one of the five young Friends released from the military by President Lincoln in November 1863) led them. By this time Sarah and Lucy were seasoned refugee workers, and Holway turned to the sisters for their advice.[19]

It happens that Isaac Wistar, 36, was commanding general of the newly-conquered Military District of Eastern Virginia. He was a one-time Philadelphia Friend and Haverford College student.[20] General Wistar prepared the way for Holway and company by developing Slabtown, near to Yorktown. It was a village for 400 refugee families, one-room cabins built along regularly laid-out streets. Homeless blacks from up and down the Tidewater flocked there.[21]

The Quaker company doled out army-supplied rations, and clothing sent from Philadelphia. Dr. James Rhoads set up a medical dispensary. Their goal was to have "the shiftless, slovenly, lazy habits contracted in slave life give place to cleanliness, industry and self-respect." They organized parties of black men to build a community center, a warehouse, schoolhouses. Other work parties tended truck gardens for Slabtown's food supply.[22]

Eunice Congdon from New England headed up the teachers at Slabtown. When she brought Lucy and Sarah Chase out from Norfolk to visit Slabtown in mid-June 1864, the sisters were impressed. Lucy wrote home, "The Friends have already done a great work here. They have nearly 300 pupils in their day school and a large night school of adults. [They] have accomplished wonders in cultivating the morality of the community."

The Chase sisters were delighted that the Slabtown Friends "design putting colored teachers in their schoolhouses." During their visit a mass wedding of contraband couples took place in a schoolhouse--forty couples whose marriages were never recognized when they were slaves--followed by lemonade and wedding cake. "Old men and women hand in hand coming up to their 'bridal'," Lucy wrote.[23] And James Rhoads wrote home to his wife Margaret in Philadelphia about the remarkable morale of Slabtown's young women teachers: "Our ladies...teach and keep house through the day and crowd three or four or five in a room chiefly in beds on the floor at night. Yet they seem the happiest of people."[24]

On March 3, 1865, when Grant's blue forces were close to capturing Richmond, the U. S. Congress passed the Freedmen's Bureau Act with Abraham Lincoln's blessing. This law established a Bureau of Refugees, Freedmen and Abandoned Lands, to be organized by Secretary of War Stanton. When the war ended that April, Stanton named Oliver O. Howard, a one-armed general, to head up the new bureau.

After Lincoln died the bureau met stiff opposition. Andrew Johnson tried to kill it. But Edwin Stanton and the Republican Congress kept it alive. And under the umbrella of the Freedmen's Bureau there arose a host of volunteer agencies to help the South's ex-slaves--now "freedmen" and no longer "contrabands".

There were at least seventy-nine volunteer agencies, most of them short-lived, merging and separating, frequently changing their officers and their names. Many of them had an evangelical bent and engaged in proselytizing the freedmen for their churches.

As for the Quakers, every one of the northern yearly meetings formed freedmen's associations or committees. The Philadelphia, Maryland, New York, and New England yearly meetings, both Orthodox and Hicksite, operated along non-sectarian lines, encouraging the freed people to develop their own richly emotional way of worship, not trying to influence their religious styles. The Western yearly meetings, however, were divided. Levi Coffin helped to organize the nonsectarian Contraband Relief Commission based in Cincinnati, but then withdrew to join the Western Freedmens' Aid Commission which sent out missionaries as well as teachers.[25]

Colonel Orlando Brown of Connecticut headed up the Freedmen's Bureau in Virginia, where about thirty agencies were active during the reconstruction years, 1865-1870. Elsewhere the American Missionary Association was largest, but in Virginia the leading agencies were those of the two Philadelphia Friends' yearly meetings, Orthodox and Hicksite. The agencies had unwieldy names: The Friends Association of Philadelphia and Its Vicinity for the Relief of the Colored Freedmen (Orthodox) and Friends Association for the Aid and Elevation of the Freedmen (Hicksite). Both yearly meetings chose Virginia as their main field no doubt because of Friends' wartime work with the Contrabands at Slabtown. New York Yearly Meeting's Committee on Colored Refugees and New England Yearly Meeting's Committee to Relieve Those Freed from Bondage also were active in Virginia.

The northern Friends focused their help for Virginia's freedmen on educating them:

Lucy and Sarah Chase came up from Norfolk to Richmond within a week of Richmond's surrender. On 20 Fourth Month 1865, they visited the battlefield east of the city, still strewn with caps and bayonets, with the feet and hands of some hastily buried soldiers protruding from the ground. By the month's end they had a school underway in Richmond's First African Church, soon enrolling a thousand black children and seventy-five adults.[26]

Sarah Smiley joined the Chase sisters in Richmond to start her industrial school for adults there. She brought nine young Quaker teachers from the north to Richmond. She established a "Teachers' Home" in Richmond,[27] and very likely she was the person who established the shelter for abandoned black children that John Crenshaw and Richmond Meeting later made the Friends Asylum for Colored Children. Sarah Smiley joined Richmond Meeting in First Month 1866 and the meeting recorded her as a minister that Tenth Month.[28]

At Slabtown, James Rhoads succeeded Edward Holway as head of the Freedmens' Center. James Van Blarcom, a teacher from Friend's Oak Grove Seminary in Vassalboro, Maine, succeeded Rhoads.[29] The three men in their turn looked after four Freedmens' schools: at Slabtown with 324 pupils; Williamsburg, 92 pupils; Williams District, 47 pupils taught by a black man; and at Fort Magruder near Williamsburg, 136 pupils. A board member of the Orthodox Friends Freedmen's Association visited the schools in 1867. Concerning Fort Magruder he commented: "In strange contrast with the late occupancy of this fort by soldiers armed to the teeth in defence of...slavery, do we see two young Quaker girls [Martha Haines and Maggie Thorpe] apparently defended only by their weakness and innocence, housing alone in a building inside the fort and conducting a large school for freedmen just outside the walls."[30]

James Van Blarcom died of a fever at Slabtown in 1868, and Alfred Jones of China, Maine, succeeded him. Jones, however, moved the Friends' operations base from Slabtown, 150 miles south and west to Danville, Virginia.[31] An energetic Westtown School teacher named Yardley Warner (1815-1885) had been raising money from Philadelphia Friends to start one-room schools in western North Carolina, Tennessee and southwest Virginia-- an area centering on Danville. By 1868 these schools enrolled some 2,100 black children and adults. In Virginia they included schools at Danville, Bristol, Wytheville, Salem and Lynchburg; at Hillsville in Carroll County; Draper's Valley, Dublin, and Newbern (all in Pulaski County); Christiansburg and Alleghany Springs (Montgomery County); and Clarksville (Washington County).[32]

Charles Schaeffer started the school at Christiansburg. He had been a Union army captain, was a Baptist and it is believed, a boyhood friend of

Yardley Warner in Germantown, Pennsylvania. At any rate, Schaeffer worked with Warner to organize the schools in Pulaski and Montgomery Counties. In May 1866 he moved to Christiansburg to teach in the log cabin school just north of town. He started out with twelve black pupils and helped their parents form an African Baptist Church in the schoolhouse. Both school and church grew rapidly with funds provided by the Friends Freedmen's Association. The school became Christiansburg Institute, training blacks to be teachers, printers, farmers, barbers, cooks, seamstresses, carpenters, wheelwrights. The board that guided it consisted of Philadelphia Friends, many of them Haverford College alumni--Elliston Perot Morris, Morris Leeds, Henry Scattergood, Joshua Baily, Henry Comfort.*[33]

Anna Gardner, 49 and peppery, came to Charlottesville from Nantucket Island in 1865. She was a sixth generation Quaker whose family sheltered slaves escaped from Virginia in their home during Anna's girlhood. Anna in Charlottesville established a primary school at "Mudwall" (a building at 7th and Main Streets used as an army hospital and later as a black Baptist church). Then she started a second primary school, an intermediate school (Lincoln School), and finally in 1869 a teacher training school (Jefferson School). She wrote a poem to celebrate Jefferson School's opening:

> ...Six years ago--and on this ground
>     We dedicate today
> Hundreds of human souls were bound
>     In abject slavery...
> Then Knowledge, Education rolled
>     The heavy stone away
> From buried mind--whose untold wealth
>     Folded in darkness lay...

Anna asked James Southall, editor of the Charlottesville *Chronicle*, to provide diplomas for a graduating class. Editor Southall answered that he wanted to see the Negro educated. However, "the idea prevails," he wrote, "that you instruct them in politics and sociology...that you communicate to the colored people ideas of social equality with the whites." To this Anna

---

   * These Friends turned over the institute in 1934 to Montgomery County's school board to be a regional high school for the black youths of southwest Virginia's nineteen counties. In 1966, just a hundred years after its founding and with the integration of Virginia's black-white schools well begun, Christiansburg Institute closed its doors. The spire of Schaeffer Memorial Baptist Church and a street called Scattergood Lane mark its site.

replied "I teach...the fundamental principles of 'Politics' and 'sociology' viz: 'Whatsoever that men should do to you, do you even so to them.' Yours in behalf of truth and justice."[34]

Emily Howland, 30, came from the Poplar Ridge Meeting of Aurora, New York to Washington in 1857. Petite with direct, dark eyes, she taught in Myrtilla Miner's school for blacks at 20th and N Streets. When war came she taught and nursed the contrabands flocking to Washington. In 1866 her father helped her to buy 317 acres near Heathsville on Virginia's Northern Neck. She set up Arcadia there, a community of homesteads for freed families complete with a school. Emily's friends, Carrie Putnam and Sallie Holley, started another school at Lottsburg four miles away--the Holley Graded School. For some sixty years the women supported these schools, until the Northumberland County school board took them over in the 1920s. Emily died at 102, in 1929. On her gravestone: "I strove to realize myself and to serve."[35]

The Friends Freedmen's Association created freedmen's schools across northern Virginia-- at Camp Rucker, eight miles from Alexandria; in Fairfax Court House, Vienna, Lewinsville, Great Falls, Greenfield, Herndon, Leesburg. But not all of these schools were created by out-of-state Friends. During Sixth Month 1865, Samuel and Elizabeth Janney with brother Asa convened a school for children of the two black churches near Goose Creek Meeting. "This is the first Negro School I ever herd of being in Virginia," Moses Watson noted. And the freedmen's school in Waterford was taught by Sarah Steer of Waterford's Fairfax Meeting.[36]

\* \* \*

The end of the war profoundly disturbed Virginia's white people. It wrecked their value system, pecking order, world outlook.

On New Year's Day of 1866, a crowd of 15,000 freedmen thronged in front of the State Capitol. A black Richmond preacher read Deuteronomy 8 (And thou shalt remember all the way which the Lord thy God led thee 40 years in the wilderness), there were emotional speeches and the crowd cheered great swelling cheers. The whites, still stunned by events, stayed home. There was shooting from a hotel window and someone burned down two black churches.[37]

Again on 4 July 1866, Richmond's black people came out to jubilee. Blacks adorned the statues in Capitol Square with green wreaths and placed American flags in the hands of Thomas Jefferson and George Mason.[38] Such a turnabout in the order of things generated terrible anger in the white community. Before that summer ended, whites murdered eighteen black Virginians.[39] Thereafter such murders escalated.

Whites vented some of their rage on the Friendly Virginians, the traditional protectors of slaves in the state. Right after the war ended two Nansemond County men armed and in military dress came to the home of William Henry Hare, 49, an elder of Somerton Meeting. They demanded $500, which William Henry gave them. Then as he turned away one shot him in the back of his head. The bullet fractured his skull and lodged behind his ear, but he eventually recovered.[40]

In the next year, persons unknown burned down Somerton Meeting house and its schoolhouse, where freedmen were being taught[41]

As for the volunteers from the North, Virginia's newspapers soon pilloried them as carpet-baggers and fortune-hunters. The editor of the Richmond *Times* led off January 16, 1866, thus:

> White cravatted gentlemen from Andover with a nasal twang and pretty Yankee girls with the smallest of hands and feet have flocked to the South as missionary ground, and are communicating a healthy moral tone to the 'colored folks', besides instructing them in chemistry, botany and natural philosophy, teaching them to speak French, sing Italian and walk Spanish, so that in time we are bound to have intelligent and, probably, intellectual labor.[42]

When Julia Shearman, a young Quaker teacher, arrived in Lexington from Brooklyn, New York, late in 1865, college students there followed her into a store. "Come take a look at the Yankee at 25 cents a look," they called. Men on the street greeted her as "damn Yankee bitch of a nigger teacher." Storekeepers refused to sell her food. After she attended the Presbyterian church, the sexton brought her a message from the owners of the pew she had sat on instructing her never to sit there again.    Other northern teachers and their schoolhouses encountered physical violence in Winchester, Lynchburg, Warrenton, and Stanardsville, in Petersburg and Richmond and at Fort Monroe. Arsonists burned down eight freedmen's schoolhouses in Virginia by the end of 1866.[43]

The teachers also met hostility from some black preachers who feared that education might cause them to lose control of their congregations.[44] After 1868 white hostility intensified when the Ku Klux Klan appeared in Virginia, an organization of men "who go about at midnight committing outrages."[45]

Despite all that, the teachers gave a great lift to the black people. In the five years from June 1865 until June 1870 (when the Freedmen's Bureau closed down in Virginia) the teachers brought over 50,000 black people out of illiteracy; and 38,000 more were enrolled in the schools as of mid-1870."[46]

\* \* \*

The Friends in Virginia kept on shrinking in their numbers through the 1860s. Where there were fourteen meetings in 1861, only eleven were alive in 1870. Alexandria, Goose Creek (Orthodox), and Sandy Creek (the only Friends Meeting remaining in West Virginia) all closed their doors during the decade. In 1871, Cedar Creek Meeting closed after 150 years, and then there were ten.

In southside Virginia, Richmond, Black Creek, and Somerton Meeting founded by Fox, remained--all three of them Orthodox meetings. To the north Winchester Centre, Ridge (very small), Hopewell Hicksite and Hopewell Orthodox (which met in opposite ends of the same meeting house), Goose Creek, Fairfax and Woodlawn--all of them Hicksite except Hopewell Orthodox. In all, about 165 members in four Orthodox meetings and about 800 in the six Hicksite meetings.

The diminished membership was no accident, for the minutes of the monthly meetings, 1860 to 1880, suggest a loss of vision, a dulling of the Quaker dream. Friends in their business meetings dealt more with material matters, leaks in the meeting house roof, cushions for the benches; less with bringing the kingdom of God to their earthly neighborhoods. Fewer ministers were inspired to speak from the silence with insights on truth and love, justice, mercy and compassion. Young Friends continued to marry out of meeting and the meetings continued to disown most of those who married out. Their parents, recovering from the war years, attained material prosperity which often causes spiritual poverty.[47]

Quaker plain dress and plain speech had taken on a kind of stylized, formalized, predictable, smug, tribal, ingrown, institutional aspect. It was time for a change, in Virginia and everywhere in the Quaker world.[48]

This is not to say that the Friendly Virginians lost *all* saltiness and savor. Here and there the drive of the dream kept on:

---

\* In those five years and in round figures, freedmen's schools in Virginia cost $725,000. Of this, $300,000 came from the U.S. Government, $50,000 from the freedmen themselves, and $375,000 came from freedmen's aid associations. More than half of that $375,000 came from the Friends Freedmen's Association (Philadelphia Orthodox) alone.

- In 1868 Richmond's Friends led by John Crenshaw raised the funds to keep up the shelter for homeless black children started in Richmond by northern Quaker women. Crenshaw persuaded the city council to donate a corner lot at St. Paul and Charity Streets, and the Friends built their Asylum for Colored Children there, complete with school-rooms. In 1871 they turned the place over to a board made up of Richmond's black ministers and a few Friends.*[49]
- In 1870, John Crenshaw as a member of Virginia's House of Delegates, introduced a bill which resulted in Central State Hospital. It was the first hospital *in the world* for humane treatment of mentally disturbed black people. Central State (now located in Petersburg) had its genesis in a seventy-two-bed ward for the insane which had been part of a Freedmen's Bureau hospital, Howard's Grove Hospital near Richmond. Before the Bureau went out of business in March 1870, Crenshaw persuaded the General Assembly to take over Howard's Grove and to keep its "lunatic" ward in operation.[50]
- After the long military occupation there was a corps of prostitutes and unwed mothers in Richmond. The women of Richmond Meeting started the Magdalene Association, a shelter for such "fallen women," in 1872. It was located on Spring Street near the penitentiary.[51]
- Chalkley Gillingham of Woodlawn Meeting was named to the federal grand jury meeting in Norfolk to decide the fate of Jefferson Davis, the late Confederacy's president. That was in May 1866. John Underwood, the presiding judge, appointed Chalkley to be the jury's foreman, over Chalkley's strong objection. "My business is to promote 'Peace on earth Goodwill to men/ Not judge or jury Man to condemn,'" he protested. Most of the jury voted to indict Jefferson Davis for treason, but Chalkley voted "Nay." "I held up the testimony of Truth before the people and got no blame," he wrote in his journal.[52] Per Chalkley's journal for 14 First Month 1871:

I have been very busy the past two weeks...to help [inaugurate] public free schools according to a recent act of the State Legislature. Have started two colored schools one on each side of my place, at Woodlawn and Gum Spring, and of which I have had the charge so

---

* It continues today as a day care center and provider of counseling and adoption services, now called the Friends' Association for Children.

far.... We also expect to start a white school on 2nd day next in our Mg House.... The three schools all free. Friends of Philada. furnish 10 dols per mo. for each col. school and the State 15 dols making 25 dols each. The white school at the Mg House has 15 dols per mo from the State and 15 per mo. from Friends Fairhill School Fund.[53]

\* \* \*

Virginia's history after the reconstruction years fluctuated up and down: On the upside were the accomplishments of Governor Gilbert Walker and the Moderate Republican Assembly, 1869-1874. Of these accomplishments, the foremost was the launching of free public education in 1871--the same year incidentally that Parliament introduced free education for British children.[54] On the downside, the obsessive and successful effort of governors and general assemblies from 1874 on to deprive black Virginians of rights. All the governors of Virginia from 1874 to 1902 were Confederate army veterans. In 1871 the 181-member General Assembly (43 senators and 138 delegates) included 27 black members, but their number declined steadily until the last black member was voted out in 1891. A year later when Joseph Holmes, a black man of Charlotte County ran for the Assembly, a white in the audience he was addressing shot him dead.

As for Quaker legislators, John Hauxhurst and John Crenshaw served only one term, 1869 to 1871, while Senator Thomas E. Taylor served to 1875. Then there were none.

The General Assembly enacted Virginia's public school law while all three Quaker legislators were in office. Within a year 130,000 Virginia children were enrolled in 2,900 elementary schools.[55] The schoolhouses were plain one or two room buildings for white children and even plainer ones for black children. The state paid for them to be open five months in the year, and later seven months; in some counties they operated an additional two months with money from private sources. Many of the black schools had been started by the various freedmen's aid associations and were taken over lock and stock, teacher and pupils by the new school boards.

The schools for white children in five Virginia counties were offshoots of schools started under Quaker auspices: one of *Frederick County's* public schools was a continuation of the Quaker school held in Ridge Meeting house, and Friends paid for two months of this school's operations; in *Loudoun*, Friends gave over both their one-room schoolhouses (adjacent to Goose Creek and Fairfax Meetings) for public school use; in *Fairfax* the public school in Woodlawn Meeting house was probably that county's first. As for southside Virginia, Holmes School near Somerton Meeting in

*Nansemond County* had Quaker teachers and so did the Black Creek and Ivor public schools in *Southampton*. Black Creek's Friends built a new schoolhouse for their neighborhood in 1889. It housed a nine-month school, supported seven months of the school year by state funds and two months by money from Baltimore Yearly Meeting and Black Creek's members.[56]

The law forbade state-supported high schools. Accordingly, Friends started several schools to bridge the gap between grade school and college. Jonathan K. Taylor, 31, founded Loudoun Valley Academy in Hamilton in 1869. The students mainly were Quakers, mostly day students. Many of them became teachers in Virginia's new public schools. Soon after, Oakdale School started up under the care of Goose Creek Meeting, and Corinth Boarding School under Corinth Meeting.[57] Some Quaker students from Virginia attended Sidwell Friends School in Washington, D.C., opened in 1883, and George School, which Hicksite Friends founded in Bucks County, Pennsylvania in 1893.[58]

Friends founded no colleges or universities in Virginia, but they did found them south and north of the state. In the south Dr. J. D. Garner started Friends' Normal School for whites and Yardley Warner a normal school for black students, both in Marysville, Tennessee. In the north, a group of Hicksite Friends including Lucretia Mott and Benjamin Hallowell opened Swarthmore College in 1869. Ezra Cornell (1807-1884) founded Cornell University, New York in 1868 (he intended it for men only until Emily Howland persuaded him to allow women students too). Johns Hopkins (1795-1873) endowed the university named for him in Baltimore, 1873, and Joseph Taylor (1810-1880) endowed Bryn Mawr College for women in 1885, near the men's college at Haverford.[59] Dr. James Rhoads, who headed the Friends Freedmen's Center at Slabtown in Civil War times, was Bryn Mawr's first president.

Young Virginia Friends left home to attend some of these schools of higher learning, as well as Guilford, Haverford, and Earlham. There they absorbed fresh new concepts and thereby Friends took another step out, made another break through the hedge that long guarded the society from the world.

\* \* \*

They leaped the hedge entirely in the 1870s. Friends in Virginia and everywhere gave up many of the practices that had marked them so long as a separate people. They seem to have done it deliberately, yet the minutes of the meetings have little to say about it. As it seems, an unconscious groundswell swept the Quaker world--a silent agreement, time for a change.

What other people noticed most was the clothing. Friends generally stopped wearing their broad-brims and shad-belly coats, their dove-gray dresses, lawn kerchiefs and caps. Once the plain garb had marked Friends' desire to avoid everything that smacked of worldliness, vainglory, sophistication, a sign of commitment to the will of God. But now after seven generations the Quakers' uniform had come to be a formality and so a burden.

Back in 1700, that early in Quaker history, Margaret Fox opposed the uniform wearing of Quaker gray. "A poor silly gospel," she called it. The gray stood for a creeping emphasis on outward uniformity and formal rules, so Margaret thought. And now in the 1870s it was as though Quakers everywhere had come to agree with Margaret.

Along with the change in Quaker dress came other changes, all of which can be seen as a discarding of outward uniformity and formal rules: the plain speech (thee and thy, First Month and First Day) was heard less; men and women began to sit *together* in meetings for worship (although Friends on the facing benches often continued to sit women on the left, men right-- and the shutter no longer descended to separate men from women in business meetings. The meetings ceased the historic sternness of disowning members who married non-Friends (a practice that had cost the Society of Friends countless thousands of its members). Significantly, the title of the book published periodically by each yearly meeting for members' guidance changed from "Rules of Discipline" to just plain "Discipline" and in some yearly meetings to "Faith and Practice."

Perhaps the most positive change had to do with Friends' acceptance of the creative arts, plays and novels, music and paintings. At last they came to acknowledge Keats's insight: "Beauty is truth, truth beauty."

A Lyceum Hall was built next door to Goose Creek Meeting in 1874 and many Friends came for the Hall's grand opening entertainment--a production of "Ten Nights in a Barroom." The climax of this drama comes when Little Mary enters the bar to get her drunken father. She pipes "Father, dear Father, come home with me now!," is hit over the head with a beer bottle and dies from the blow. When the Quakers in the audience applauded and wept as the curtain fell, that marked the beginning of a new dispensation.[60]

The new dispensation did not come in a twinkling. On into the 1900s, some aged Quaker men kept on their hats in meeting for worship, only removing them when they were moved to speak or in time of prayer; and a few old ladies in Quaker bonnets still sat on the left side of the meeting across the center aisle from their menfolks. The last-known woman in Virginia to wear the traditional Quaker costume was Lydia Janney Brown of Lincoln. A daughter of Asa Moore Janney, she wore it until her death at 81, in 1925.⁶¹ When Elizabeth Comstock, then 76 years of age, re-visited Richmond Friends Meeting in 1891, she was both pleased and dismayed at the new order of things. "There is a nice little meeting of Friends in this city, 50 members including children," she wrote to her sister. "Not much *appearance* of Friends in costume, and very little regard for the Scriptural and grammatical thee and thou."⁶²

\* \* \*

Well, what were they now, the Friendly Virginians--hedge gone, shrinking in numbers, branched out in loyalty between Hicksite and Orthodox, old time dress and address abandoned?

Some members missed the old conventions and mourned the old ways. But religion cannot be saved if it tries to save itself. A religious people must adventure beyond their old safe frontier. Otherwise they desiccate, become dry bones in a spiritual desert.⁶³ In the 1870s the rules Friends as a society had used so long to control the members were loosed. Now it was left more to the conscience and the light within, to guide members in the living of their lives. The change may have weakened Friends as a society, may have strengthened them as individual wayfarers.

There were certain signs of new strength and spirit:

For one, Friends kept up their traditional concerns in new contexts suited to the new times. Beginning in 1869, some Virginia Friends played leading parts in aiding the Indians (of which more presently); in 1873, Goose Creek Friends sent a memorial to the General Assembly urging abolition of the death penalty; and in 1887 Richmond Friends petitioned Governor Fitzhugh Lee for the same purpose⁶⁴--in the Ninth Month of 1892, right after the Spanish-American War's end, five Friends from Virginia or with Virginia backgrounds (Jonathan K. and Emma Taylor, Edward Stabler III and O. Edward and Anne Janney) visited President McKinley in the White House. Make the United States a power for peace among the nations, they urged. McKinley's thoughtful reaction (according to the Baltimore *Sun*) was "I sometimes think that a large naval armament conduces toward peace in that it compels peace; but on the other hand, a nation so equipped is like a man who walks around with a chip on his shoulder."⁶⁵

For another sign, large and larger crowds turned out for the Virginia Friends' quarterly meetings. The "May Meetings" at Black Creek lasted three days. They attracted so many people that the Norfolk and Western Railroad ran a special train to Sedley every morning. In 1899, 4,000 came for the May Meeting at Hopewell.⁶⁶

A new kind of spiritual poise and a lively comic spirit appeared among Friends in the 1870s--fun based on Friends' own practices. Such stories were told as the one about the hen who enters the meeting house during monthly meeting for business and clucks down the center aisle to the clerk's table. "What has thee to lay before us?" the clerk asks the hen. Now the meetings held ice cream parties[67] and there was a general lightening-up, that was still far from frivolity.

Teen-age Quakers acquired blank books for their friends' autographs. The book of Lizzie B. Smith who attended Lincoln Academy in 1881 contains such entries as:

> In ourselves our failure lies
> Life is what we make it.
> -- Thy friend and schoolmate
> Emma

and

> Our lives are albums written through
> With good or ill, with false or true
> -- Thy friend and schoolmate
> D. Walton Ballinger.[68]

\* \* \*

As soon as the Civil War wound down, American Friends renewed their concern for the Indians. The government had moved most of the tribes westward again and again, cheating and debasing them at every move. Now railroads were building right through the Indians' hunting grounds and white hunters were killing off the buffalo herds.

The tribes on the high western plains were making a violent, hopeless stand. Western newspapers responded to the tribes' resistance with terrible editorials. Kearney (Nebraska)'s *Herald* in July 1866 referred to "the Indian savage" as "these heartless creatures...having no respect for word or honor...this barbarian monster...in all of his original desperation. The best and only way to reconcile the blood-washed animal will be to impose upon him a worse schooling then has ever befallen the inferior races." The editor of the Kansas *Daily Tribune* was more explicit that same month: "There can be no permanent lasting peace on our frontiers till these devils are exterminated."[69]

By 1867 both Hicksite and Orthodox Friends organized for the Indians. Representatives of six Hicksite Yearly Meetings met in Baltimore and sent a plea to the president and Congress for humane treatment for the Indians.

Seven Orthodox Yearly Meetings formed the Associated Executive Committee on Indian Affairs, which sent a similar plea through Senator James Harlan of Iowa, a politician with Quaker roots.

President Andrew Johnson's administration ignored both Quaker pleas--although the Washington *Weekly Chronicle* published a supportive editorial:

> The treaties made by William Penn were always respected...and the peaceful sect of [Quakers] have been traditional friends of the aborigines...if the Society of Friends who so successfully colonized and civilized the Senecas in western New York...could be induced to take charge of...the Indian territory and instructing the Indians, they might prepare them for the inevitable future.[70]

The voters on 4 November 1868 elected Ulysses S. Grant to be president. Friends did not expect much from this cigar-smoking whisky-drinking military hero, especially after he said publicly in Chicago just before election day that the western settlers must be protected even if it meant the extermination of every Indian tribe.[71]

It happened, however, that Grant had an advisor named Ely Samuel Parker (1828-1895), a full-blooded Seneca from Genesee County, New York, with one foot in the white man's world and one in the red man's. As Lieutenant-Colonel Parker he had been Grant's aide de camp who drew up the surrender agreement at Appomattox. As The Wolf--the translation of his Indian name--he was a sachem of the Senecas of western New York with the title Donehogawa (Keeper of the Western Door of the Long House). Evidently he shared the Senecas' gratitude for Quaker friendship. And evidently he prevailed on President-elect Grant to give the Quakers a hearing.

Grant and Parker met with a committee of Orthodox Friends on 25 January 1869, and with a Hicksite committee the next day.[72] On 15 February, Parker wrote identical letters to the clerk of each committee. "Sir:" Parker wrote, "General Grant, the President elect, desirous of some policy to protect the Indians...and appreciating fully the friendship and interest which your Society has ever maintained in their behalf, directs me to request that you will send him a list of names, members of your Society...as suitable persons for Indian Agents."[73]

In his first message to Congress upon becoming president, Grant announced a new Indian policy, saying

> I have attempted a new policy towards these wards of the nation...The Society of Friends is well known as having succeeded in living in peace with the Indians.... They are also known for their

opposition to...war, and...for their strict integrity and fair dealings. These considerations induced me to give the management of a few reservations of Indians to them.[74]

The press reported the new policy extensively. It became known as the Peace Policy or Quaker Policy.[75] The Eastern newspapers that had backed Grant for president praised it: the Boston *Daily Advertiser* predicting that Friends "will deserve the lasting gratitude of the country," the New York *Times* finding "We have never before had such a favorable state of things for maintenance of pacific relations with the Indians."

But most Democratic and Western papers were critical. The Baltimore *Evening Commercial* protested that "these appointments [of Quakers] are the first in the history of this Government made solely upon religious profession. Never before has an office been conferred based upon the denominational connection of the individual. Religion has been kept separated from the State.... But Gen. Grant, by selecting only Quakers for the Indian business, has impliedly asserted that no other denomination was fit to be entrusted with such appointments.... There are certainly many honest and upright Quakers, but there are just as many dishonest men in that Church as in any other."[76]

Grant appointed Ely Parker to be his Commissioner of Indian Affairs, and Parker promptly assigned fourteen Indian agencies to the Quakers' care. Five of the fourteen were located in the two-year-old state of Nebraska. The remaining nine lay south of Nebraska, in Kansas and the Indian Territory (now Oklahoma). Fourteen huge pieces of the wild West scattered six hundred miles north to south. Peopled by the remnants of tribes once proud and self-sufficient, now reduced to rags and bewildered, burning resentment.

The Quaker committees, Hicksite and Orthodox, arranged between themselves for the Hicksites to take charge of the six northern-most Agencies which they called "The Northern Superintendency." All six lay in Nebraska, except one 48,000-acre reservation just below the Nebraska line in Kansas. The Hicksite committee persuaded Samuel Janney, now 68 years of age, to leave his quiet home in Lincoln and head up the Northern Superintendency, to be based in Omaha. Benjamin Hallowell, 70, and living now in Sandy Spring, Maryland, became clerk of the Hicksite committee.[77] He was to remain in Sandy Spring and keep in touch with Ely Parker in Washington. As for the Orthodox committee, they took over the other eight agencies, organized as "The Central Superintendency" with headquarters in Lawrence, Kansas, near the Friends' Shawnee School.

Samuel Janney arrived in Omaha in a pouring rain, the streets very muddy, on 26 Fifth Month 1869. Travelers crowded the town, en route to see the driving of the famous golden spike at Promontory Point, Utah--the spike that would complete the nation's first transcontinental rail line. Three of Janney's six Quaker agents came with him: his beloved brother Asa Moore Janney with wife and two daughters; Edward Painter and wife of Little Falls Meeting near Baltimore (they owned the general store in Fallston); and Albert Green, 29, a Philadelphia Friend. The other three agents arrived a few days later: Jacob Troth and family, formerly the Underground Railroad station keepers of Virginia's Woodlawn Meeting, and Howard White, and Thomas Lightfoot and family, Philadelphia Friends.[78]

Omaha city lies on the Missouri River's west bank. Three Northern Superintendency agencies lay upriver from Omaha, two downriver and one 120 miles west along the new Union Pacific railroad:

- Northernmost, 200 miles up from Omaha, was the reservation of the *Santee Sioux* which Samuel Janney assigned to the care of his brother Asa.
- The *Winnebago* and the *Omaha* tribes' reservations lay cheek to jowl, midway between the Santee reservation and Omaha city. Howard White became agent of the 1,300 Winnebagoes and Edward Painter of the Omahas.
- Downriver seventy miles from Omaha City was the *Otoes' and Missouria's* reservation, 160,000 acres where Albert Green became agent; and another eighty miles further down, in Kansas, the *Great Nemaha* Agency assigned to Thomas and Mary Lightfoot.
- The *Pawnee* Reservation, 120 miles west of Omaha, was assigned to Jacob Troth. It was the most populous of the six reservations with some 2,400 Indians.[79]

The Native Americans were shrinking in their members in 1869, and the reason was easy for the Friends in Nebraska to see. All the tribes under Quaker care were uprooted peoples. "These wards of the Government," a committee of Quaker visitors reported, "were found in a very depressed and degraded condition, as a general thing, poor, hungry, idle from want of means and inducements to labor; destitute of suitable clothing; complaining of unfulfilled treaty stipulations; living in lodges with several families in a single apartment...the lodges dark, unventilated, often filthy...sickness extensively abounding, especially among the children--scrofulous gatherings and ulcers, sore eyes, debility and consumption [tuberculosis]."[80]

The only course that the Quakers in 1869 seriously considered for saving the tribes was "to educate them for citizenship"--which meant teaching them to live as white people do. A hundred years earlier John Woolman wanted "to spend some time with the Indians, that I might feel and understand their life...or that they might in any degree be helped forward.[81] But in 1869, the

Friends came to Nebraska not so much to understand the Indians' life as to teach them white ways. Woolman's concept that the tribes could best be saved by nurturing them as unique societies within the framework of the national culture, that did not re-occur for another sixty years, when the nation had acquired a Quaker president and a Quaker Commissioner of Indian Affairs.

For the first year in Nebraska Samuel Janney and his six Quaker agents made considerable progress. Samuel sent an upbeat report to the Hicksite Friends who met in Philadelphia on the Indian Concern in Fifth Month 1870. He reported the reservation lands being surveyed for 80-acre-farms; saw mills and flour mills being built; 400 acre fields of wheat and corn ploughed and seeded; timber cut and sawed to build houses; fences built, wagons, ploughs and harness purchased; some Indian ponies broken to pull the wagons and ploughs; some Indian men willing to do the farm work traditionally done by their women; medical help obtained for the many sick Indians. "But our chief reliance is on the education of the young," he wrote, mentioning the establishment of grammar schools teaching English on all six reservations; and of one industrial school for seventy-five older boys and girls "who are boarded, clothed and taught the most useful branches of an English education. The boys are taught to work on the farm and the girls instructed in household work."*[82]

Along with the kinds of activities reported by Samuel Janney in 1870, many Americans believed that converting the Indians to Christianity must be part of the civilizing process.[83] It is interesting therefore that Samuel Janney reported no missionary activities. "No teaching of religious truth will be of much avail without a pure and consistent example on the part of the Agents, employers and traders" he wrote in 1870; and in 1871, "Religious instruction should be given adapted to their condition, and the practical part of Christianity illustrated by example."[84]

While Samuel Janney and his six Hicksite agents labored in and near Nebraska, Superintendent Enoch Hoag and eight Orthodox Quaker agents held forth to the south, in Kansas and the Indian Territory. Where the Northern Superintendency cared for some 6,600 Indians, the Central Superintendency oversaw 17,700. The largest Central reservation was located near Fort Sill, where bearded Laurie Tatum was agent for 6,100 Kiowas and Comanches. Nearly all the Central agents came from Iowa.

---

* Asa Moore Janney's daughter Cosmelia organized that industrial school. It was located on the Pawnee reservation near Genoa, Nebraska.

Hicksites' and Orthodox efforts to help the Indians were quite similar, except that the Orthodox laid more stress on Christianizing their charges. Laurie Tatum reported a meeting of Central agents in Lawrence in Twelfth Month 1870 thus: "Our difficulties and trials, failures and successes were discussed. The agents were encouraged to use every effort to Christianize and civilize the Indians...."[85]

All the Quaker workers encountered trials and temptations emanating from "the Indian Ring", from Washington, and from the Indians themselves....

The Indian Ring was composed of speculators and suppliers who made money one way or another from the reservations. When Albert Green arrived at the Otoe reservation, the man he was to succeed as Agent closed the office door for a confidential chat. He explained that he had recently escorted the Otoes' chiefs to Washington where they had signed a treaty selling the entire reservation, 160,000 acres, at $1.50 an acre. The treaty was awaiting Senate ratification. The retiring Agent was to receive a choice 640 acre section upon its ratification. He begged Albert to go along with the deal. Later a silk-hatted delegation called on Albert to say that they wanted to give him, too, 640-acres out of gratitude for his support of the treaty. Albert, however, called a council of the chiefs. They said they had only agreed to the treaty after being promised they could obtain land nearer the buffalo. Albert then reported the matter to Benjamin Hallowell through Samuel Janney--and Hallowell in Washington scotched the swindle.[86]

Washington and its bureaucracy presented more problems: On 14 March 1870, Benjamin Hallowell and his committee asked the Congress to appropriate $140,000 for "wagons, teams, tools, agricultural implements, livestock, seeds, etc, and to erect suitable houses." Although President Grant endorsed the request, Congress appropriated only a disappointing $30,000. It developed then that many Western senators and congressmen, including the entire Nebraska delegation, opposed the Quaker Policy, chiefly because it took away their patronage power.[87]

And the Indians themselves generated multiple problems. In the beginning the red men tried to intimidate the newly-arrived, unarmed and peaceful-seeming Quaker agents. Brinton Darlington, an elderly Quaker from Muscatine, Iowa, was assigned to the Cheyenne and Arapaho tribes of the Upper Arkansas agency. When a party of Cheyenne braves rode down on their new agent brandishing weapons, Brinton removed his set of false teeth, held them out toward the braves and clicked them rapidly. The braves wheeled about and rode off in terror. Thereafter the Cheyenne sign for "Agent" was a gesture of taking something out of the mouth.[88]

The Pawnees of Jacob Troth's agency were traditional enemies of the Sioux who frequently stole the Pawnees' horses and took their scalps.

Samuel Janney interviewed the Sioux chief Red Cloud saying to him in effect "I want thee to make peace." But Red Cloud haughtily refused, replying in effect "The Pawnees were once our friends and brothers, but then they joined the whites against us and killed some of our men. Now we consider them no better than the whites."[89]

Albert Green, however, had better luck in settling the immemorial war between the Otoes of his agency and the Osages, whose Quaker agent was Isaac Gibson in Kansas. Albert arranged with Isaac for forty Osage chiefs to meet with forty Otoes. The chiefs, wearing hereditary bear-claw necklaces, eagle feathers, earbobs and painted faces assembled around a council fire. They passed a peace pipe and their Quaker agents gently prodded them into making a peace treaty. That treaty, Albert Green proudly noted sixty years later, was never broken.[90]

Before its first year was out the public rated President Grant's Quaker policy a success. Baltimore's *Sunday Morning Chronicle* for 23 January 1870 concluded its editorial on "The Quaker Indian Agent System" with "The views of these philanthropic Friends are entitled to the gravest consideration...their humane plan, if it has not been found entirely perfect, is the nearest approach yet made to the solution of the problem."[91]

Two months later Grant ordered Commissioner Parker to invite other religious denominations, both Protestant and Catholic, to join in. With this step, the Quaker Policy ceased to be an experiment and the government became fully committed to it. By 1872 the Grant administration had entrusted thirteen separate denominations with seventy-three agencies where nearly 240,000 Indians lived.[92]

The success cost the Quakers who accomplished it considerable wear and tear. Benjamin Hallowell retired in 1871, quite ill. Samuel Janney followed him that same year, worn down by the work. He, his wife Elizabeth, and daughter Cornelia left Omaha on 1 Tenth Month 1871, but had to stop over for two weeks in West Liberty, Iowa, staying with Friends who had once been their Loudoun County neighbors, while Samuel recovered from the ague. Asa Moore Janney followed Samuel home with his wife and daughters-- Cosmelia (who organized the Northern Superintendency's industrial school) and Thamsin (she took charge of the Santee Agency's dispensary, studied medicine after she returned home to Lincoln, and became the first woman doctor known to practice in Virginia). Jacob and Anne Troth and Samuel and Ella Walton and their children went home to Woodlawn in 1873.

So ended the foray of Virginia Friends on behalf of the Western Indians. One mark of that time is a dot on the map of Knox County, Nebraska, marked "Bazille Mills." Here Asa Moore Janney built a flour mill and a saw mill on Bazille Creek for the Santee Sioux.[93]

President Grant kept up the Quaker Policy all of his eight years in the White House, even though the Indian Ring criticized it continually. Ely Parker's support of the policy made him powerful enemies. Tried by a committee of the House of Representatives late in 1871 for "defrauding the Government," he was cleared of the charges and then resigned heart-broken.[94] In the summer of 1876 the Sioux surprised Lt. Colonel George Custer on the Little Big Horn River in Montana Territory, killing Custer and 264 cavalrymen. The public reacted to this news with a loud call for vengeance. The Quaker Policy was sneered at as "false philanthropic sentiment"[95]; and in 1878 Rutherford P. Hayes, who succeeded Grant as president, abandoned it.

\* \* \*

When the Friendly Virginians leapt the hedge in the 1870s they landed in a speeded-up Virginia. Fifty years earlier there had been no telegraph lines or railroads. Now indoor bathrooms replaced some privies; oil lamps, candles; windmills and hand pumps, well sweeps. Bicycles came along in the 1880s. The city of Richmond acquired the nation's first electric trolley cars in 1887. Richmonders had a telephone system and gas street lamps. A few homeowners installed the new electric lights. A few typewriters clattered in business offices. In 1893, the Duryea brothers built the first gasoline-powered auto.

But Virginia by and large was still a farming state. Virginians sitting out in the July evenings still spoke of "hearing the corn growing." Their porch-rocker conversations still included church and meeting matters, but the spectacular technological advances of the time took up an ever-larger share of attention.

These years were the first when Americans could safely admit in polite society that they were skeptics or atheists or agnostics. The influence of the churches on the people had lessened to that extent. On the other hand, membership in the mainline churches, Catholic, Methodist and Baptist, increased tremendously. The 815,000 Baptist church members of 1850 multiplied to five million in 1900.[96] Catholic congregations increased through immigration from Catholic countries. The Protestant churches competed for new members through revivals and door-to-door canvasses. Many of the new recruits proved to be only lightly committed. An increasing member of husbands showed up for church only at Easter and Christmas.

Dwight L. Moody (1837-1899) emerged as America's leading revivalist in the 1870s. He was an impressive figure of 280 pounds with a clarion voice, who preached much the same evangelical message as George Whitefield in the century before him. He set out with Ira D. Sankey, his equally robust singer, "to evangelize the world in this generation." Like Whitefield, he attracted crowds, in Philadelphia in 1875, in Baltimore in 1878-1879, in Richmond in 1885 and again in 1894.

Significantly, Moody and Sankey in Philadelphia were sponsored by a committee of Gurneyite Quakers. This committee arranged a revival meeting that packed Wanamaker's Depot.[97] In Baltimore Dr. James Carey Thomas of Baltimore's Orthodox Friends' Meeting chaired the Moody and Sankey Committee of Management.[98] In Richmond too Friends helped to arrange Moody and Sankey revivals.[99]

\* \* \*

Moody and Sankey's successes inspired Baltimore Yearly Meeting Orthodox to enter the competition for new members. It appointed a Pastoral Committee in 1877 "to develop the individual meetings, the spiritual life of our members, and to bring the unconverted to Christ." In eight years the Pastoral Committee raised funds, visited distant communities, and saw the yearly meeting increase from 550 to 825 Orthodox members. Most of the new members were Virginians and four new or revived Orthodox Quaker meetings came into being in Virginia:

- *Bethel* and *Corinth* Meetings both started in Southampton County in 1880, as off-shoots of Black Creek Meeting. Bethel's Friends met on John D. Pretlow's farm five miles south of Black Creek. They met at first in a brush arbor, then built a meeting house in 1885, 24 by 50 feet. Members of the Raiford family with Bradshaws, Hedgepeths and Stephensons started Corinth Meeting near Ivor, some four miles north of Black Creek. They put up their meetinghouse, 24 by 36 feet, in time to drive to it for worship on the First Day of Sixth Month 1882. While they were worshiping that day a hailstorm came up; marble-sized hail stones rained down; and Anne Elizabeth Bradshaw, the oldest Friend present, cried out "O Lord, pity the poor horses!"[100]
- *Lincoln* and then *Silcott Springs* Meetings began in Loudoun County. Lincoln Meeting was a renewal of Goose Creek Meeting Orthodox, which had been suspended during the Civil War. Five Orthodox Friends led by Isaac C. Hoge began in 1882 to meet again for worship, in the Lyceum Hall next door

to Goose Creek Meeting house, on First Day afternoons. Baltimore's Pastoral Committee helped them to organize a *Bible* class and prayer meetings for the neighborhood, and, in 1886 (with substantial funds contributed by English Friends), to build a fine brick meeting house. More than 800 people came to the first meeting for worship in the new house, and Moody-style revival meetings were held for nine days, when "many hearts were reached by the message of the Gospel of our Lord and Savior Jesus Christ and covenants were entered into by many."[101] Silcott Springs Meeting originated in 1885 with a series of prayer meetings in Purcellville led by Dr. Richard H. and Mary Snowden Thomas of the Pastoral Committee. A meeting house was built in 1894.

Another new meeting, also Orthodox, appeared near Ararat in Patrick County about 1885. It was a part of Blue Ridge Friends' Mission--an enterprise of North Carolina Friends inspired by David Sampson (1845 - 1916). He came from England to North Carolina in 1875 and soon joined New Garden Friends' Meeting. Then he moved to "Buffalo Mountain"--the wild and backward area encompassed by Patrick and Carroll Counties, Virginia, and Stokes and Surry Counties, North Carolina--to Christianize the mountaineers and to battle the bootleggers.[102]

Baltimore's Pastoral Committee adopted some of Moody and Sankey's methods, but also held on to some of the old Friendly ways. Like Moody and Sankey the committee used revival methods to bring in new members, putting the emphasis on converting the world to Quakerism instead of Friends' traditional effort to relieve sufferings and promote peace in the world. Unlike Moody and Sankey, the committee went about its work through the unpaid efforts of many workers instead of professional religious experts. In 1896 Dr. Thomas, of Baltimore, a Pastoral Committee leader from its beginning, summed up twenty years of the committee's work thus:

> In the prosecution of [our] work [we] have had no evangelists who have devoted their whole time to work in the field, nor deputed anyone to reside in a neighborhood...for the building up of the meetings...the plan of work has been to hold short series of meetings...without prearrangement or human leadership...what are known as general revival methods have not been used.... Where there has been singing, it has been entirely spontaneous and...kept in proper check. The importance of its being done only under the

immediate impulse of the Holy Spirit...has been much dwelt upon."[103]

So those of Virginia's Friends who were attached to Baltimore Yearly Meeting Orthodox held on in some degree to the inward way of seeking God's will--under the immediate impulse of the Holy Spirit."

Two Friends groupings in Virginia did, however, became fully evangelical in their style of worship. These two came to be called "Friends Churches" rather than "Friends Meetings." They began as missions of Ohio Yearly Meeting Damascus. The first Friends Church appeared at Portsmouth in 1886, the second at New Point (a Chesapeake watermen's community in Mathews County) in 1894. Frank Hill was Portsmouth's first full-time paid pastor, and Charles Diggs was New Point's. Thus paid professionals appeared among Virginia's Quakers after 221 years of unpaid ministry.

\* \* \*

These two Friends Churches were the only Quaker-related bodies in the State to adopt general revival methods before 1900. But orthodox and evangelical Friends west of the Alleghenies *did* adopt such methods beginning soon after the Civil War. Frances Trollope, a high church English woman, described a typical Western revival that she attended one summer night before the war in Cincinnati's principal Presbyterian church. After an opening hymn and hearing a minute description of hell's torments, a number of terrified penitents came forward to the anxious benches. The preacher

> proclaimed 'the tidings of salvation,' and from every corner of the building arose in reply short sharp cries of 'Amen!' 'glory!' 'Amen!' While the prostrate penitents continued to receive whispered comfortings.[104]

Night meetings in this revival style started up in many Western Friends' meeting houses. The first occurred at Bear Creek Meeting in Dallas County, Iowa, early in 1867. They featured tearful praying, shouted testimonies, singing from hymn books and people prostrate on anxious benches.[105] Soon these innovations appeared in First Day morning meetings for worship. Traveling evangelists, Methodists and others, were invited in to preach and

---

"This summary appeared in *The Interchange*, the newsletter that Baltimore Yearly Meeting Orthodox began in 1884.

some younger Friends themselves began to preach after the highly wrought style of the evangelists.

Presently a kind of podium or pulpit appeared in certain meetings, occupied First Day after First Day by the same preachers who delivered prepared sermons. Members gave money to pay the pulpit preachers. That is how, in those meetings, Friends' testimony against "hireling priests" was abandoned and paid Friends' ministers came to be.

Only the two "Damascus" Friends Churches employed paid preachers in Virginia. All the Orthodox meetings in the state, however, put new emphasis on converting the world to Christianity:

- In northern Virginia, *Hopewell's* Orthodox Friends started a mission station at Millbrook six miles from Hopewell Meeting house and a chapel at Rocky Glen where they held Sunday afternoon *Bible* classes and revivals for non-Quakers. *Lincoln* Meeting joined other churches to hold Union Bible Schools at Ketoctin and Purcellville; and members of Lincoln Meeting were the principal organizers of an annual Bush Meeting in Purcellville. Revivalists and temperance speakers --including William Jennings Bryan and Billy Sunday--held forth to crowds of two and three thousand people at the Bush Meetings, held for three days every August.[106]
- To the south, *Richmond* Friends rented a house in the city's Oregon Hill section where they held a *Bible* school and a Gospel meeting on Fifth Day evenings.[107] And Robert and Sarah Harris of *Black Creek* (the children of Matthew Harris of peanut fame) established a mission meeting for black people, called Berea. A wealthy English Friend, Mary Ann Marriage Allen, provided funds for a school to train black teachers at Berea.[108]
- Also, Lewis Neill Hoge and his wife Susanna of Hopewell built Neill Chapel at the mouth of Upper Machodoc Creek in King George County in the mid-1890s. It was a preaching point and Sabbath School for oystermen from the Eastern Shore who lived in that neighborhood in the winters. This chapel was partly supported by Baltimore's Pastoral Committee.[109]

\* \* \*

Many of the new paid preachers in western orthodox meetings came from non-Quaker backgrounds, but some were birthright Friends. Of these last, David Brainerd Updegraff (1830-1894) was one who departed far from Friends' traditions. He was born and died in Mt. Pleasant, Ohio, the home town of Elisha Bates, a son of the Updegraff family that supported Elisha Bates and kept alive the tradition of Evangelical Quakerism after Elisha's death.[110] David Updegraff attended Haverford College as a youth and was "born again" at a revival in Mt. Pleasant's Methodist church when he was 30.

The Mt. Pleasant Friends recognized him as a minister in 1872. The next year, when he happened to meet Samuel Janney on a railroad train crossing Ohio, David catechized Samuel about his religious beliefs. Reconstructed from Samuel's account, the exchange ran like this:

> David: Do you believe in the Bible as an infallible record of the truth of God?
> Samuel: I do not see how fallible men could write an infallible book. I believe that Jesus Christ was the only infallible person.
> David: I believe the *Bible is* an infallible record.
> David: Do you believe in the miraculous conception of Jesus?
> Samuel: I do believe in the Evangelists' account of that event, and in the miracles and the crucifixion and resurrection of Jesus. He came to bear witness for the truth and he suffered for the truth--but not as a substitute to pay the penalty of man's transgression.

"I told him," Samuel wrote, "I thought [Orthodox Friends] had departed in doctrine and worship from the early Friends, and he gave me to understand that he did not think it important to adhere to their example, but to take the Scriptures for a guide."[111]

After that exchange, David Updegraff more and more adopted a Wesleyan way. He was the first Quaker preacher to install the "anxious bench" (which he called "the altar of prayer") as a regular feature of revival meetings.[112] And he preached a "Holiness" or "Four Fold Gospel" system which stressed that "fallen man is a total ruin" who can only be saved by a plan of justification and sanctification.[113]

Then in 1878 David Updegraff publicly repudiated the concept of the Inward Light. It is unsound and unscriptural, he declared. He persuaded Ohio Yearly Meeting's Committee of Ministers and Elders to support this declaration, and thereby shocked the rest of the Quaker world. John Greenleaf Whittier called it "an entire abandonment of the one distinctive and root doctrine of our religious Society."[114]

Virginia's Friends lost four long-time leaders in the post-Civil War era: Miriam Gover died *during* the Civil War when Fairfax Meeting had 192 members and that meeting steadily lost strength thereafter; Samuel Janney died in 1880; and Chalkley Gillingham in 1881. John Crenshaw died, a white-bearded patriarch in 1889, just after his last appearance as a speaker in Richmond Meeting. "Friends, mind your calling in the Lord," was his farewell message.[115]

It signifies the confused and divided state of Friends' affairs following their leap over the hedge, that no outstanding leaders immediately appeared to fill the four Friends' places, and that the Friendly Virginians declined in numbers after they departed.

Virginia's six Hicksite meetings--Woodlawn, Fairfax, Goose Creek, Center, Hopewell and Ridge, east to west--kept to the old Friends' ways *sans* the old distinctive costumes. It was a time of readjustment, some puzzlement and uncertainty and some quiet despair, for the meetings were not growing and silverhaired oldsters made up a large proportion of First Day meetings for worship. The only place of Hicksite growth anywhere nearby was Washington, D.C. Friends there replaced their old meeting house at 1811 Eye Street with a fine new one, 40 by 80 feet, in 1880. All seven Hicksite yearly meetings contributed to build it, and Thomas Sidwell opened a flourishing school in the new house in 1883.[116]

About 1890 the orthodox meetings in southern Virginia also stopped growing, and now there were signs of reconciliation between the two Quaker groupings. Virginia's Orthodox Friends had never hired preachers, they still worshipped on the basis of silent waiting, and the Orthodox--Hicksite division was never as wide or as bitter in Virginia as in the Western states. Right after the Civil War, the two yearly meetings, Baltimore Orthodox and Baltimore Hicksite, had exchanged friendly letters. When they formed a joint committee to divide Quaker property according to the number of members of the two branches--one-fifth to the Orthodox and four-fifths to Hicksites--both sides experienced "kind and brotherly feelings."[117]

In northern Virginia, the meeting houses of the Lincoln (Orthodox) and Goose Creek (Hicksite) Friends were just along the street from one another, and many members of the two meetings were relatives. At Hopewell, the Orthodox Friends met on First Days in one end of the big old meeting house and Hicksite Friends in the other end. Sometime about 1890 each branch began to invite members of the other branch to join them whenever their quarterly meetings met at Hopewell.[118]

In 1881 Rufus Jones, 19, a young, red-headed fellow raised in the Orthodox Friends' Meeting of South China, Maine, entered Haverford College. He swept all before him, attaining a Phi Beta Kappa key, editorship of *The Haverfordian*, presidency of his class and election as Spoon Man (outstanding member of his class of 1885). He studied philosophy under

Pliny Earle Chase (an older brother of the Chase sisters who cared for Virginia's freed people during the Civil War), and Professor Chase assigned Ralph Waldo Emerson's essays among the course readings.

Certain Emersonian passages about mysticism and the Oversoul excited Rufus as did Emerson's appreciation of Quakerism (to which the Virginia Quaker Edward Stabler introduced Emerson). It dawned on Rufus then that the quiet Quaker meetings of his Maine boyhood were in fact *mystical* exercises, where the worshipers waited for inward guidance from God without relying on their five external senses. Professor Chase encouraged Rufus to write his graduation thesis on "Mysticism and Its Exponents"--wherein Rufus concluded that George Fox and John Tauler who lived three hundred years before Fox, represented the purest type of mystics. Rufus defined mysticism as "The type of religion which puts the emphasis on direct and intimate consciousness of the presence of God."[119]

For sixty years thereafter Rufus Jones, Haverford professor, philosopher, editor, and author of 54 books, wrote and lectured on Quakerism as a type of mystical religion. Thereby he made an invaluable gift to the Society of Friends. For Rufus, when he identified Quakers with mysticism, was commending the kind of Quakerism practiced by Hicksites. At the same time he was an Orthodox Friend and an engaging man who had the confidence of most members of that branch. He brought Orthodox Friends, or at least those Orthodox Friends who worshipped without paid pastors, and Hicksite Friends to a better understanding of one another.

\* \* \*

Although the rift between the eastern Quakers somewhat healed in the years before 1900, those among western Quakers widened. This last came about largely through David Updegraff's influence.

In the years after 1877 when David Updegraff repudiated the Inward Light--calling it dangerous and unsound--he moved toward an extreme evangelicalism. He adopted a hell-fire style of preaching, saying that terror is "the only effectual way."[120] He preached now that the world is steadily growing more wicked, trying to improve it is no use, the only bright spot is that Christ is coming soon to begin a reign of righteousness, sickness is due to sin, anyone who becomes sanctified will be delivered from disease, every word in the *Bible* is literally true, the idea of evolution (introduced by Charles Darwin in 1859) is anti-Christ.[121]

Presently David decided that water baptism is necessary for a real Christian. In 1884 he had himself baptized in the Berean Baptist Church in Philadelphia, following the example of Elisha Bates forty-eight years before.

But where Elisha was disowned by Friends for breaking with Quaker practice, David was not. David defended himself vigorously, quoting many *Bible* passages and declaring that "he felt it to be his duty to fulfill all righteousness." Ohio Yearly Meeting Orthodox considered deposing David as a recorded minister but decided even against that. Whereupon its members in large numbers proceeded to be water-baptized.[122]

Ohio Yearly Meeting's failure to discipline David Updegraff concerned Orthodox Friends everywhere. The acceptance of baptism by water clashed with the society's testimony against signs and symbols as substitutes for living a life committed to God. During 1886 nine Gurneyite yearly meetings, including Baltimore, ruled that none of their ministers or elders were "to participate in or teach the necessity of the outward rite of baptism or the supper."[123] And Indiana Yearly Meeting called a summit conference of all the Gurneyite groups for fall 1887, to resolve the issue.

Ninety five Friends representing twelve yearly meetings (eight Friends from Baltimore but none of them Virginians) met for five days in Richmond, Indiana's, Eighth Street Meeting house. The Conference appointed a committee of twelve to prepare a Declaration of Faith, and the twelve did turn out a sound declaration of Gurneyite principles. The declaration stated "our continued conviction that Our Lord appointed no outward rite or ceremony for observance in His church.... It is with the Spirit alone that any can thus be baptized."

But while its declaration thus denounced water baptism, the conference waffled and did not decide at all what should be done with recorded ministers who advocated water baptism--which was the main reason for the Conference in the first place. This omission can be attributed to masterful maneuvering by David Updegraff, who was one of Ohio Yearly Meeting's fourteen delegates. He spoke long and frequently, urging the conference to refrain from doing anything controversial or argumentative. When the delegates were about to go home with the matter of disciplining undecided, David was relieved. He was the conference's last speaker, saying "I appreciate, I think, very highly indeed, the spirit of brotherly love and condescension and desire upon the part of the committee to say something to which none of us would object."[124]

So it was that David Updegraff and Ohio Yearly Meeting's flight to full-blown evangelicalism went unchallenged. Ohio Yearly Meeting refused to adopt the Richmond Declaration of Faith despite David Updegraff's appreciation, thus signaling that it no longer saw eye to eye with other yearly meetings. Henceforward Ohio was to be a fully evangelical body, distinct and separate from Gurneyite Friends.

In this way the tendency toward evangelical Quakerism begun by Isaac Crewdson in England and imported to America by Elisha Bates came to full flower. Now there was a distinct, separate *fourth* Quaker branch. Along with the Hicksite or Traditional, the Wilburite or Conservative, and the Gurneyite or Orthodox branches, there came into being the Evangelistic branch of Friends.

At first the only evangelistic yearly meeting was the Ohio Yearly Meeting (Damascus), headquartered for a time in the hamlet of Damascus just west of Salem, Ohio. It acquired its own school--Friends' Bible Institute in Cleveland (which today is Malone College in Canton, Ohio.) Walter and Emma Malone founded the school to impart the kind of *Bible* teaching espoused by Dwight L. Moody. Emma Malone had been convinced of the evangelical way's rightness by Moody at a mass revival in Cleveland.[125]

Ohio Yearly Meeting Damascus soon established missions outside Ohio. Two such missions started up in Virginia before 1900--and one in Washington, D. C. Joseph Dempsey, once a Catholic priest, was in charge of the Washington mission until he broke away to start a short-lived "First Holiness Church of the Society of Friends" in Washington.[126]

Hicksite Friends held their counterpart conference of all places in Virginia's Goose Creek Meeting house on a sunny Fifth Month week in 1892. More than 300 Friends from the seven Hicksite yearly meetings arrived by buggy, carryall, and Washington and Old Dominion Railroad trains.

Several of these yearly meetings had been holding joint conferences ever since the Civil War: a few Friends met in West Chester, Pennsylvania in 1867, to discuss the operations of First Day Schools and thus began a conference held every two years to develop materials for religious education of children; in 1878, Illinois Yearly Meeting wrote to the other six Hicksite bodies suggesting a united effort "for the uplifting of our fellow beings...to influence legislative bodies, or in any way by united action promote the desired end"; and this brought into being the Friends' Union for Philanthropic Labor which held periodic meetings--the Young Friends Association formed and began to meet. The conferences and gatherings of these Hicksite groups overlapped. Presently Friends agreed it would be a good idea to hold them at the same time and place, and Goose Creek was chosen for the first meeting place.

John William Gregg, 21, of Goose Creek, in charge of housing and transportation arrangements, worked himself and his committee to a frazzle. Goose Creek's women cooked in apron-clad relays sleeves rolled high, preparing enormous platters of chicken, biscuits and other country fare for meals under a circus tent on the meeting grounds. Earnest circles discussed First Day School methods, the nurture of blacks and Indians and poor people, Young Friends' concerns, and the like. There was much camaraderie and some "spooning."[127]    John Gregg met Agnes Woodman from Wrightstown Meeting in Pennsylvania at the conference. They married a few years later, after John finished at Cornell University.

Anna Jeanes (on the left) provided the means and Virginia Randolph (right) pioneered a way to help the black people of the South help themselves.

# XVI

## THEE INTERESTS ME
## 1900-1950

> It is a bold and colossal claim that we put forward--
> that the whole of life is sacramental.
> -- Barratt Brown,
> an English Friend, 1932

History does flow along in ripples, waves, and tides. In the first years of the 1900s the tide of American affairs flowed out, receding far and farther from the Peaceable Kingdom visioned by Friends. The lineaments of a land at peace lost definition, blurred and faded.

The United States until 1900 or so was a farming nation. Farm homes were strongholds of traditional values. Until 1900 or so. But now comes a new Industrial Age. Business, finance and factories take first place. Malefactors of great wealth emerge. A city taste for power and money elbows ahead of country kindliness and neighborly ties. The kind of nation dreamed of by Thomas Jefferson eclipsed by Alexander Hamilton's.

By 1900 the nation was just over the Spanish-American War, when American troops invaded Cuba, took over that island, the Philippines and Puerto Rico from Spain and so made the United States a colonial power. Most Americans gloried in the new-found power. Teddy Roosevelt, the Rough Rider of San Juan Hill, was America's newest hero. His popularity propelled him to the presidency, 1901-1908.

In Virginia and all across the South the new rough-riding, power-loving order of things played itself out in a determination by whites to sink black people back to the bottom-of-the-heap place they had occupied before the Civil War.

Agitation to scrap the Underwood Constitution of 1869 and take the right to vote away from Virginia's blacks began in 1888. That year Virginians voted on the proposal for a new constitution and defeated it 63,125 votes to 3,698. Nine years later, 1897, they defeated it 84,435 to 38,326. But Carter Glass editor of the Lynchburg *News*, kept beating the drum for disfranchising blacks, and the editors of the Richmond *Times* and Richmond *Dispatch* joined in.

Taking away the blacks' vote will "simplify the race problem" wrote Carter Glass. And the *Dispatch* editor denounced the Underwood Constitution time and again, calling it "the miserable apology to organic law which was forced upon Virginians by carpet-baggers, scalawags and Negroes, supported by federal bayonets." So on 24 May 1900, the writing of a new state constitution was approved 77,362 to 63,375.[1]

In that year, 1900, the General Assembly introduced the "Jim Crow" era to Virginia, voting--by a one-vote margin--to segregate black passengers on railroad cars. The next year, segregation on streetcars and steamboats passed. In 1902, the convention called to work out the new constitution for Virginia, chaired by Carter Glass, effectively took away the vote from black citizens. The new constitution required would-be voters to qualify by giving "a reasonable explanation" of any section of the constitution, unless the applicant paid property taxes or was a Civil War veteran or the son of one. It also required payment of a poll tax in order to vote.[2]

Stealing the right to vote was only part of Jim Crow:
- Night-riders dressed in bed sheets spread terror. More than a hundred blacks every year from 1900 through 1910 died at the hands of Southern lynching parties.
- The one room schools for blacks went largely unfinanced by rural school boards, in spite of the U. S. Supreme Court's 1896 dictum that schools, where they were "separate" must be "equal." There was no good equipment and most black teachers had only scanty schooling. The resulting education was pathetic.

So then a small, shawled Quaker woman from Philadelphia did a decisive thing. Although they never knew her, she enriched the lives of hundreds of thousands of Southern black children.

Anna Jeanes (1822-1907) was the youngest and the last survivor of ten children, their father an enthusiastic member of the Pennsylvania Abolition Society, their mother dying when Anna was four. Anna wore the old time Quaker dress all her life. She also painted with talent, wrote a book of poems titled *Fancy's Flight*, read French with ease and studied the world's religions. By 1904, at 82 years of age, she had inherited the fortunes of her merchant brothers and was a wealthy woman indeed. She disliked publicity and employed stealth and anonymity in giving money to many causes. However, the president of Virginia's struggling Hampton Institute, Hollis Frissell, penetrated Anna's cover. He visited her in Philadelphia.

The Friend heard out Dr. Frissell in silence, straight-lipped and with folded hands. He finished his appeal for funds for Hampton and then she spoke clearly: "Yes," she said, "I know all about Hampton and I won't give money to *that*."

Dr. Frissell concealed unhappiness and Anna Jeanes continued: "I want to hear about the poor little Negro-cabin, one-teacher rural schools. Can thee tell me about these schools?"

Dr. Frissell, a Yale graduate and Presbyterian minister, complied with eloquence. When he had done, Anna remarked mildly "Thee interests me." She went to her bedroom and returned to Frissell with a check for $10,000. A few days later, she mailed a second $10,000 and then a third for $200,000. Finally in her will she bequeathed the sum of $1,000,000. It was to be devoted, she directed

> solely to the assistance of Rural Community or Country Schools for Southern Negroes...for the purpose of rudimentary education and to encourage moral and social refinement which shall promote peace in the land and goodwill among men.

The trustees of the Jeanes Fund--as it came to be known after Anna died--floundered a bit until May 1908. Then Jackson Davis, superintendent of Virginia's Henrico County schools suggested the idea of appointing one "Jeanes Teacher" to a county. The Jeanes Teacher's job would be to show the black schools' teachers how to teach "industrial" subjects, and also to link up school and community through Improvement Leagues and so arouse the black people to help themselves.

The trustees decided to try out the idea in Henrico County. Jackson Davis then named Virginia Estelle Randolph, 34, daughter of an ex-slave, a teacher in Henrico's Mountain Road School for sixteen years--to be the first Jeanes Teacher. Her pay, $40 a month, her responsibility twenty-two schools.

In her first report to Jackson Davis, Miss Randolph told how she viewed her new work:

> The destiny of our race depends, largely upon the training the children receive in the schoolroom and how careful we should be....

> 'Cleanliness is next to Godliness' and when this law of hygiene is obeyed, [the pupils] have conquered a great giant. they must also see that their schoolroom is neat and attractive with curtains at the windows, pictures on the walls, stoves kept neatly polished, and the grounds neat and clean, have a book on the 'Laws of Health' hung in the schoolroom and each child made to make himself familiar with it....

My first step was to organize School Improvement Leagues, the Constitution says, that...everything must be done to make an attractive school. Each scholar is expected to pay the sum of five cents per month and from time to time, give entertainments to strengthen the treasury but they must have a tendency to elevate the community morally and educationally.

Miss Randolph then listed the accomplishments of each of her twenty-two schools in the first year. For example:

Geter's School, Teacher, Mildred A. Cross: Enclosed the school with hedges, set out trees and flowers, taught sewing, making mats and carpentry. Much interest is being manifested in the school garden. Amount collected, $22.23. Expended, $6.63. Balance in treasury, $15.60.

She bought a buggy and an old horse and tried to visit two of the twenty-two schools every day, pushing the buggy out of mudholes and resting the horse on the uphill grades, leaving home at 6:30 am and returning at 9:00 p.m. In the twenty-two schools she ran into indolent teachers, jealous teachers, incompetent teachers. Somehow she coaxed, pleaded and cajoled her way to success.

What Miss Randolph did needs heroic words. She helped Henrico's downtrod black people to help themselves up--she taught that people should be proud of the work of their hands; she insisted, to a people in rags and shacks, that they must beautify their surroundings; she organized people addressed as "Auntie" and "Boy" and "You Black Bastard," for improvement and uplift. Don't wait till you reach the Golden Shore, the way the preacher says, Virginia Randolph in effect told her people. Do it here and now.

Four years later, in the 1912-1913 school year, 25 Virginia counties had Jeanes Teachers and 428 Improvement Leagues were operating in connection with the Jeanes schools. There were 198 Jeanes Teachers in Virginia and the South by 1917; 320 by 1932.[3]

Anna Jeanes would have been pleased.

\* \* \*

By the turn of the Twentieth Century, the new Industrial Age was accelerating. One effect of the era was to make life in America less local and more national, even global. Thus many strands of the Friendly

Virginians' history from this point on will be intertwined with the story of Quakerism outside Virginia's boundaries.

For example; among Europe's nation-states the new age expressed itself in a will to acquire new world power. The new German Empire threatened the old British Empire. Both built ever-larger armies and navies. In June 1914, inevitably, the world's first World War broke out. British and German armies and allies turned France and Belgium into bloody, muddy killing fields.

The Quakers of Great Britain reacted quickly. London Yearly Meeting immediately published a re-statement of the Society of Friends' stand for peace. Before the summer of 1914 was out, the Friends of Folkestone Meeting atop the White Cliffs of Dover were feeding streams of Belgian refugees. Some young men of the Society formed a Friends' Ambulance Unit. They entered the French war zone with forty-three men and eight ambulances, and grew to 600 men and hundreds of ambulances, with dressing stations at the front and hospitals to the rear. Older Friends established Friends' War Relief. By November 1914 an advance party of twenty-five men and women set up a base in Sermaize, a flattened town in the Marne Valley, to serve the valley's bombed-out families. They established three Friends' hospitals and a convalescent center in the area and removed hosts of Marne Valley children to foster homes.

Parliament passed a draft act in 1916. Then began a struggle for the souls of Britain's young Friends--whether they would give in to the draft law and the accompanying barrage of war propaganda about Huns and Boches and the way those monsters maimed unsuspecting Belgian tots by handing them live grenades, or whether they would stick to the Quaker peace position.

About one-third of draftable British Quaker youths gave in to the draft law and entered the armed forces. At the spectrum's other end, over 140 absolutely refused involvement in the war and witnessed for their faith in prisons. More than half did alternative work with the Ambulance Unit or War Relief Mission or the like. Friends overseas wore the Quaker Patch, a red and black six-pointed star. A relief corps of British Friends had worn this emblem during the Franco-Prussian War in 1871.[4]

America stayed clear of the World War for nearly three years. Woodrow Wilson was the nation's president then, a one-time Bryn Mawr College professor turned statesman, who won the White House largely on the strength of his promise to keep us out of war. "Peace is the healing and elevating influence of the world and strife is not," he declared. But in 1915 a German submarine torpedoed the liner *Lusitania* and 128 American passengers lost their lives. Teddy Roosevelt, the old Rough Rider, called for vengeance. The president and his supporters are "mollycoddlers and flapdoodle pacifists," he denounced.[5]

American Quakers were prominent among the mollycoddlers. Just about every yearly meeting and quarterly meeting in the country issued statements urging peace. Baltimore Yearly Meeting Hicksite declared in 1915 that

> Warfare...violates every principle [we hold dear], encouraging hatred in place of love, violence in place of gentleness, cruelty in place of brotherly kindness, horror in place of happiness, lust instead of purity, ambition instead of meekness, covetousness instead of justice.

And the Friendly Virginians of Fairfax Quarter added,

> Friends should impress upon the public mind that war is incompatible with Christianity.[6]

Then the American meetings began to send funds to support the British Friends' war work. Four young American Quakers, two recent graduates of Haverford and two of Earlham College, joined the English Friends' Ambulance Unit in France.

American Friends both Orthodox and Hicksite met at Winona Lake, Indiana in July 1915 to organize a National Peace Committee. Rufus Jones, the Haverford professor, soon emerged as a leader of the Friends' antiwar movement, and the national committee early in 1917 published this declaration in many U. S. newspapers and magazines:

> The alternative to war is not inactivity and cowardice. It is the irresistible and constructive power of goodwill.... The present intolerable situation among nations demands an unprecedented expression of organized national goodwill.

But the war party triumphed and America declared war on Germany 6 April 1917. On 30 April, fifteen Friends--nine Orthodox and six Hicksite--met at Haverford College to organize goodwill.

The Friends at Haverford formed "the American Friends Service Committee," with Rufus Jones the chairman. On June 1, the AFSC opened its office in Philadelphia; 23 June, nine young Friends, five men and four women, embarked for France as AFSC volunteers to serve with British Friends in the Marne Valley's mud and blood; early in July, six more young people, all women, took ship across the Pacific for Russia.[7]

Of those first fifteen AFSC emissaries, one was a Virginian: Nancy Babb, 33, member of Corinth Meeting and of the Babb family whose history stretches far back in the annals of the southern Virginia Friends.* She was a Westtown School graduate and one of the six women who went to Russia.

The six entered Russia by the back door, so to speak, for no women were allowed to pass through Europe's various war zones. They sailed from Vancouver to Japan, crossed the Sea of Japan to Vladivostok, then travelled eight days on the Trans-Siberian Railroad to the district of Buzuluk. This district, roughly the size of Maryland, lies on a flat and treeless steppe. Most of the villages that dot the steppe are one street lined with one-room huts.

Some 30,000 Polish refugees, driven from their homes when the German army pushed through Poland into the rim of Russia, were existing miserably in the villages, and a handful of British Quakers wearing the red-and-black star were there to serve them. The British Quakers were distributing food and clothing, running a school, an orphanage, and three hospitals to combat the cholera, typhus, malaria and trenchmouth endemic all across Buzuluk.

The three hospitals needed nurses. Nancy and her five companions were school teachers and social workers with no nursing experience. Nevertheless they donned nurses' pinafores with red-and-black stars sewn on, and went to work in the hospitals. There they handled non-stop lines of sick people speaking a babel of languages--Polish refugees, Russian peasants, Austrian prisoners-of-war, Tatars, Cossacks and Kirghese.

The work exhausted three of the six women. They left within a year, but Nancy Babb, Emilie Bradbury and Anna Haines stayed on into 1918. That October with the revolutionary Red Army, hostile to English and Americans, advancing from the west, Nancy, Emilie, and Anna boarded a freight car on the last eastbound train that got away before the Reds arrived.

At Omsk in Siberia, a thousand miles east of Buzuluk, they encountered 12,000 refugees living in dugouts, freight cars, and corridors of the City Hall. They stayed in Omsk to befriend these refugees all through a winter when the temperature hit -71°; and got back to Philadelphia July, 1919.[8]

The AFSC's main effort in those years, however, was in France rather than Russia. When the World War mercifully ended on 11 November 1918, 258 AFSC men and 40 women were waging goodwill in France. Of these, four were Friends from Virginia--Herbert and Howard Babb of Corinth Meeting (Nancy's cousins), Richard Ricks of Richmond and Henry Stabler of Alexandria.

---

* An earlier Nancy Babb married Matthew Harris of peanut fame in 1826.

Many more were scions of the Quaker families who migrated west out of Virginia in slavery days--with names such as Bates and Beals, Chandlee and Charles, Hare, Hinshaw, Hollowell, Holmes and Hunnicutt, Jay, McKay and McPherson, Moon, Newlin and Norton, Outland, Pike and Ratliff, Steere and Votaw, Way and Winston and Wright.[9]

After Armistice Day, AFSC's workers in France took on the job of restoring Verdun and the Argonne Forest areas, smashed and ruined by the bombardments of the war's last weeks. They put up *maisons demontables* (prefabricated houses) and distributed seed potatoes, rabbits and baby chicks to returning families. By 1 April 1920, they had succored in some form or degree 1,666 French villages and 46,000 families.[10]

On 1 April the AFSC closed its work in France, and so ended its first three-year chapter. The work was epoch-making. It engaged the loyalties of all four Quaker branches and it reunited and energized Friends. It provided a way for the Society's men who refused to fight as soldiers to demonstrate "the irresistible and constructive power of goodwill."

Not all American Quaker young men joined the AFSC. At least thirteen wound up in prisons, absolutely refusing to cooperate in the war. The draft boards and military services released 250 or more to do farm work, and an unknown number served with the Red Cross and YMCA. More than 600 served as noncombatants in the armed services as medical corpsmen or the like (Edward White of Virginia's Bethel Meeting was one of these). And two or three thousand entered the military all the way, hearkening to the government's claim that this war was the War to End Wars, the war to Make the World Safe for Democracy.[11]

\* \* \*

In 1913, while World War I loomed, women in the United States girded to war for their own self-respect. The women had been struggling ever since the Seneca Falls Convention of 1848, for sixty-five years, to win equality with men. Quaker woman Lucretia Mott led this struggle nearly until her death in 1880. Susan B. Anthony (Quaker) and Elizabeth Cady Stanton (non-Quaker) succeeded her.

They worked for woman suffrage state by state. The territory of Wyoming gave its women the right to vote (in territorial elections) in 1869. The new state of Colorado followed suit (1893), Utah and Idaho (1896), Washington (1910), California (1911), Kansas, Oregon and Arizona (1912)--all Western states.

The women also worked at the national level in Washington city. In 1878 Susan Anthony persuaded a congressman to introduce this amendment to the U. S. Constitution:

> The right of citizens of the United States to vote shall not be denied or abridged by the United States or any state on account of sex.

Each house of the Congress then appointed committees on women's suffrage which held annual hearings where members of the National American Woman Suffrage Association (NAWSA) testified vigorously. But Susan Anthony retired as the movement's leader in 1900 at age 80, and the annual hearings in Congress died away.[12]

Enter now Alice Paul, a slim young Quaker from Moorestown, New Jersey, and Swarthmore College's Class of 1905. She took a master's degree in sociology at the University of Pennsylvania in 1907, then went to Woodbrooke, the Quaker study center in Birmingham, England. There she joined the British suffragettes led by fiery Emmeline Pankhurst. Alice picketed Conservative political meetings and heckled such notables as Winston Churchill and Lloyd George. She endured jailings in England and Scotland, hunger strikes and forced feedings; and came home to Moorestown in 1910, determined to give all to get American women the right to vote.

Alice Paul and her red-headed friend Lucy Burns persuaded NAWSA's board to let them revive the drive for passage of Susan Anthony's Amendment--they promised to raise the necessary funds themselves. They opened an office in the basement at 1420 F Street in Washington on 2 January 1913, and immediately laid plans for a great Suffrage Parade, a purple, white and green extravaganza of women. The parade was to proceed up Pennsylvania Avenue. from the Capitol to the White House --on the day before President-elect Woodrow Wilson's Inauguration Parade and on the Inauguration Parade's exact same route.

Gargantuan difficulties immediately rose to oppose the Suffrage Parade:

- Police Chief Sylvester contemptuously refused a permit for the Parade--whereupon Alice Paul mobilized a committee headed by Mrs. Robert LaFollette (wife of Wisonsin's senator) and Mrs. William Kent (wife of a California congressman) which pried the permit loose.
- NAWSA's leadership objected to purple, white, and green as official parade colors. Those were the colors of England's militant suffragettes and it was feared that the colors would stamp NAWSA as radical and militant. Alice clung to the

purple-white-green motif but promised that she would no longer refer to them as *official* Parade colors.
- A contingent of black women applied to march in the parade, thus introducing a racial issue that would keep most white women from marching since strong racial prejudice existed in Washington. Alice solved this problem by welcoming the black marchers but persuading them to march scattered among the northern and Quaker parade sections.

So the Parade went off as scheduled on 3 March 1913. The Washington *Post* that morning predicted:

> It will be an impressive sight. Nothing like it has every been seen before. It will be a milestone in the progress of women.

A hundred thousand people, come to Washington for the Inauguration, turned out to see 5,000 women march. The Parade was a series of near riots. Hostile, shouting men overflowed Pennsylvania Avenue's sidewalks, leaving only a narrow lane for the marchers. By Sixth Street and Pennsylvania Avenue, police protection gave way altogether. Many marchers were in tears. Cavalry troopers from Fort Myer restored order then and most marchers managed to reach the reviewing stand at the White House.

Next day many newspapers carried editorials protesting the disorder and calling for a congressional investigation. The investigation was carried out and reported in news stories favorable to the women's cause.

The Parade split the suffrage movement. Thereafter NAWSA led by Carrie Chapman Catt concentrated on persuading the states, state by state, to give the vote to women; while the Paul group separated completely from NAWSA, forming a separate National Women's Party devoted to getting the Susan Anthony amendment passed. Both parties had many Quaker-connected members from Virginia and elsewhere:
- NAWSA's arm in Virginia was the Equal Suffrage League of Virginia, which had local chapters. Virginia Hirst of Goose Creek Meeting was president of the Purcellville League, and Mrs. George Hauxhurst, daughter-in-law of Job Hauxhurst, was president of the Arlington County League.[13] Mary Elizabeth Pidgeon, a Friend of Hopewell Meeting, was a NAWSA field secretary.
- Alice Paul's group included Mabel Vernon and Martha Moore, Swarthmore College graduates, and three sisters of Haverford

Meeting, Pennsylvania: Mary and Ellen Winsor and Ernestine Evans.
- Eliza Walker of Fairfax Meeting in Waterford, Va., worked for both parties. She was president of the Waterford League (NAWSA) and also made frequent trips in to Washington to help out Alice Paul.[14]

NAWSA's field secretaries worked with enthusiasm after the Great Suffrage Parade. They suffered many defeats and much ridicule from state legislators. But in 1914 the legislatures of Nevada and Montana made it legal for woman to vote.

Mary Elizabeth Pidgeon (1890-1977), the NAWSA field secretary, was the very prototype of a Friendly Virginian. She grew up on an Opequon Creek farm, of a family who were faithful Hopewell Meeting members. She graduated from George School and then from Swarthmore College; taught in the Media, Pennsylvania Friends School for a time; and then went to work with NAWSA. Carrie Catt assigned Mary Elizabeth to work out of Buffalo; and she played her part in 1917 in winning New York as the first Eastern state for womens' suffrage.

Right after that victory Mrs. Catt sent Mary Elizabeth to South Dakota where she labored through a sub-zero winter. She toured the county seats, pleading with scornful politicians, traveling the frozen countryside on the wartime trains, long, slow and rattly. She lived out of her suitcase, stood before heckling audiences, and preached "Suffrage!"[15]

Meanwhile in Washington, D.C., Alice Paul and party went to work to persuade new president Woodrow Wilson. Before he had been in the Oval Office two weeks, Alice Paul called with three other women. Wilson said suffrage was a new subject to him. He invited them to keep him posted.

Delegation after delegation of Alice Paul's colleagues called on President Wilson. For years he gave vaguely encouraging responses to the women, but actually did nothing. The second Mrs. Wilson opposed the suffrage crusaders, calling them "disgusting creatures." When Wilson addressed a NAWSA convention in 1916 his wife said it was "the only speech of my Precious One that I ever failed to enjoy."[16]

President Wilson held the women at bay for nearly three years with sweet talk. Then on 10 January 1917, Alice Paul posted women pickets at the White House gates. They stood there silently carrying lettered banners:

> Mr President, What Will You Do
> for Woman Suffrage?

> How Long Must Women
> Wait for Liberty?

All Governments Derive
Their Just Powers from the Consent
of the Governed.

That April the United States declared war on Germany. Government officials ordered Alice Paul to give up suffrage and get her women behind the war effort. She refused. The public's mood turned ugly then. On 21 June Washington's police chief telephoned Alice that he would arrest her pickets if they dared to come out again; and the police hustled the pickets away in a paddy wagon the next day.[17]

For eight months thereafter Alice Paul sent women out to picket. Two hundred and eighteen of them were arrested and ninety-seven sentenced either to pay fines or go to prison. Invariably they chose prison, in the D. C. Jail or the District's Workhouse at Occoquan, Va.[18] Alice Paul herself and Eliza Walker of Fairfax Meeting were among the Quaker women jailed. The women at Occoquan refused to work, went on hunger strikes, protested nonstop and were treated with increasing brutality by Occoquan's Superintendent Whittaker. He locked them in punishment cells and had the hunger-strikers force-fed with tubes through their noses. Occoquan's other women prisoners called the suffragists "Stra-a-ange ladies!"

News about the strange ladies of Occoquan and their travail hit the headlines and made the public sympathetic again. A blizzard of letters and petitions reached Washington. On January 10, 1918--just a year to the day after Alice Paul's pickets went on White House duty--the House of Representatives voted for the Susan B. Anthony amendment 274 yea and 136 nay. Five months later the Senate approved too.[19]

Then the field secretaries of NAWSA and Alice Paul's women united in a drive to persuade three-fourths of the forty-eight states' legislatures to ratify the amendment and so make it part of the U.S. Constitution. Within a week Wisconsin and Michigan ratified and so did six more northern states before June was out. On 28 June Texas ratified and Arkansas a month later. But these last were the only two of the eleven states of the old Confederacy that came even close to ratifying. The South's tradition, to put its women on pedestals and out of men's affairs, continued very strong.

Carrie Catt sent Mary Elizabeth Pidgeon to West Virginia, to Tennessee, to North Carolina and finally home to Virginia to lobby legislators. Virginia's legislators received Mary Elizabeth courteously and Virginia's Equal Suffrage League and its 30,000 members headed by Lila Meade Valentine worked well with her. But Senator Thomas Martin of Charlottesville, the boss of the state's courthouse machine, absolutely opposed women's suffrage and the amendment lost in Virginia.[20]

Nonetheless, states to the north and west steadily ratified and on 9 August 1920, Tennessee ratified, the 36th state. So the measure written by valiant Friend Susan B. Anthony became the 19th Amendment. It passed in time for America's women to vote in the 1920 presidential election.

The suffrage work in Virginia bore results in spite of Senator Martin. In 1919 the University of Virginia's graduate schools opened to women for the first time. The university employed Mary Elizabeth Pidgeon in its Extension Division to teach Citizenship and Virginia Government to the newly franchised women. These are believed the first such courses introduced by any university,[21] and Mary Elizabeth appears to be the university's first woman faculty member. She led in establishing pioneer chapters of the League of Women Voters and American Association of University Women in Charlottesville, early in the 1920s.[22]

As for Alice Paul she began work on an Equal Rights for Women Amendment in 1923 (she called it the Lucretia Mott Amendment). At 91 she was alive and still crusading. "Women are still voiceless," she told a reporter, and

> We have to work until complete equality becomes a reality. I grew up in a Quaker family, and Quakers believe in the equality of the sexes.... When you put your hand to the plow, you can't put it down until you reach the end of the row.[23]

\* \* \*

No sooner had the first chapter of the American Friends Service Committee's saga ended, than the second began. The American people after World War I felt a responsibility to restore the ruined European countrysides and peoples. President Wilson in 1919 called on one Herbert Hoover, 45, to be his Relief Administrator.

Hoover was a sixth-generation Quaker descended from the Haworths who helped to found Smith's Creek Meeting in Virginia in the 1730s. He was born into the West Branch, Iowa, Friends Meeting, son of the town's bearded blacksmith; orphaned when ten years old; and raised by Quaker relatives in Iowa and then Oregon. He took an engineering degree with Stanford University's first graduating class (1895); then managed mines in New Mexico, California, and Australia, and by 1900 was chief engineer of China's Bureau of Mines. In the Boxer Rebellion he helped to distribute relief to thousands of refugees. In 1901 he became partner in a London-based mining firm and presently became a multimillionaire. In London when World War I broke out he organized a committee that helped a hundred thousand Americans to get back home. Wilson made Hoover U. S. Food Administrator in 1917, and head of the American Relief Administration (ARA) in 1919.

Soon after this last appointment Herbert Hoover appeared in Philadelphia to meet with Rufus Jones. He told Rufus that very few American agencies were willing to help the hated Germans and then asked whether the Friends Service Committee would be willing to distribute food in Germany to succor starving German children. Rufus, surprised, passed along Hoover's request to AFSC's board, which agreed to take on the task.*

Nineteen Friends wearing the red and black star arrived in Germany on January 2, 1920, and served their first meal in Berlin on 26 February. The meals were for children and nursing mothers, who came to schools and community centers to eat them. Money for the meals came from Herbert Hoover's ARA and from private donations. Germany's government provided flour and sugar. Forty thousand Germans helped to prepare the meals in cities and towns across the nation. At the peak, in the third week of June 1921, 1,010,658 children and mothers received daily meals in 1,640 communities.[24] One memento of that time remains in Frankfurt-am-Main where the name of a downtown street is "Quaker-Platz."

Just what Virginia Friends served with AFSC in postwar Germany is unknown, but records remain of three who served with AFSC contingents in Yugoslavia and in Russia:

Fifteen AFSC workers went to the Serbian part of Yugoslavia including young Virginians Cecil Cloud of Corinth Meeting and Arthur Rawson, 23, of Goose Creek.[25] They built houses with the help of 200 Bulgarian prisoners of war and fifty mules, opened an orphanage and medical clinic at Leskovac and a hospital at Pec, and fed children and mothers.

Cecil Cloud, whose parents supervised Corinth Friends' Academy back in Virginia, was assigned to the supply wagons bringing food from the port at Dubrovnic. Armed bands of ex-soldiers infested the wooded mountains between Pec and the sea but Cecil refused armed guards for his convoys. "I came here to relieve the Serbians, not to shoot them," he said.

"You'll be way-laid," he was warned, and in fact brigands did way-lay him. He told them he was carrying food for starving children, and they let him through. Thereafter he came and went unmolested and unarmed. In appearance he was only a frail young man. He died soon after coming home to Ivor, Virginia, from Yugoslavia.[26]

---

*The Board included a Virginia-born Friend: T Janney Brown (1867-1956) raised in Goose Creek Meeting.

As for Russia, it happened that no rain fell in the Volga valley throughout the summer of 1921. The crops failed, starvation threatened the people for the coming winter and the Friends returned a relief party to Buzuluk. It is a wonder that they were allowed to do so, for the United States and Great Britain both were withholding shipments of goods to Russia in hopes of toppling the new Communist government, and hostile U.S. and British military forces were operating inside Russia.[27] Permitting the Friends to return to Buzuluk indicates the new government's desperation. Perhaps too it indicates the impression Nancy Babb and her companions made on that countryside during their wartime year there.

Virginian Nancy herself, along with two English Quaker men, brought in the first trainload of supplies to Buzuluk. That was in October 1921, just three years after she left the place by freight car. What she saw was frightening. Dead horses and cows cluttered the roads. Desperate men and women showed her pancakes made of powdered grass and gelatine from horses' hoofs, all they had to eat. Some people were eating mud to ease their hunger.[28]

Refugees from all around central Russia packed Buzuluk's rail center, fleeing famine. Among them was a group calling themselves Quakers (!) who were waiting to board a train for the Kuban region. Ten of them talked with Nancy and Tom Copeman in the train station. "We could not help being struck by their fine faces, especially the face of a matronly woman who sat silent with folded hands," Copeman wrote:

> They said they had always been called Quakers by other people, and according to tradition had been started '300 years ago by some one from England.' In all they considered that...they numbered one million, but as they had neither any form of organization nor, apparently, any test of membership, it was hard to say.

The Russian Quakers related their aversion to killing. They did not even kill lice but "put them somewhere else." In the Czar's time, six hundred refused to bear arms and most of them were imprisoned. But the Kerensky government released them and excused them from military service.

They said they did not believe in oaths but in brotherly words. They did register their marriages with the government but believed they were guided by the Spirit in marrying, and that registrations or oaths were unnecessary. They held Meetings for Marriage when "the brother declares to the sister they will be married." If matrimonial troubles arose an elderly Friend was called in.

In time of worship they sought to be moved by the Spirit and had no set forms....

After we had finished our questions we had a short period of silence and they sang a hymn. It was a most wonderful experience. And that, so far as I am aware [Copeman wrote] was the last contact between [American and] English Friends and Russian Quakers.[29]

That contact was the only "wonderful experience" for Nancy Babb and her friends on their arrival in Buzuluk. Nancy caught typhus and did not recover until December. Then she went to Totskoye--a steppe village of 1,100 people--with two other Friends, established a workroom and warehouse with red-and-black stars over the doors, and set out to do what could be done for the people of forty-three villages in an area of 3,000 square miles.

Starved corpses lay along the roadsides that December. One Friend came upon a crazed man eating his dead wife. Nancy and her companions were standing on a desolate frontier of death. Nancy visited her villages by sleigh, refusing a guard of soldiers, wolves following her sleigh. She established food centers marked by the Quaker star, and local food committees.

Some of the Tartar villages had mosques. The Muslim mullah headed the food committee of one such village. On Nancy's first visit the Mullah asked her, "How dare you come alone? What can all this generosity mean? Has God not forgotten us?" She recalled that the sun was setting gorgeously as they talked, over the vast white steppe. "One God and the brotherhood of man" was the best she could find for answer.[30]

May came in Buzuluk in 1922 with a warm sun and rains. All the dead bodies re-appeared as the snow melted, and squads of men set out to bury them. Food came from the outside world; roads, bridges, schools, and clinics were repaired. The Friends obtained tractors to plough the land for farmers who had eaten their horses. With the crisis past, the Soviet government refused to have anything more to do with Herbert Hoover's American Relief Administration out of resentment over the U.S. government's anti-Communist rhetoric.[31] Nevertheless, Hoover continued to furnish funds, food, and seed for Nancy Babb's AFSC unit.

Nancy re-opened a 125-bed childrens' sanatorium near Totskoye. She arranged for cultivation of 850 acres to raise food for the patients. In 1924 when the AFSC officially closed its work in Germany and Russia, Nancy and a few others stayed on. She oversaw sale of the sanatorium and its farmland to the government in 1925, then used the proceeds to build a 30-bed hospital in Totskoye. She and her co-workers made bricks on the premises, hauled lumber from the forest a hundred miles away. They dedicated the new hospital in 1928, on the tenth anniversary of the Russian Revolution.[32]

Then Nancy, the Friend from Ivor, returned to the United States. Of all the AFSC's pioneer volunteers, she may have stayed on the job the longest and accomplished the most.

* * *

Soon after 1900 the Society of Friends in America created some new agencies which somewhat changed the society's structure. The first two of these agencies sprang respectively from the Richmond Conference of 1887 and from the Hicksite Friends' gathering at Goose Creek in 1892.

In 1902, delegates from ten Gurneyite Yearly Meetings including Baltimore Yearly Meeting Orthodox met in Richmond, Indiana, to establish an umbrella organization. It was called at first the "Five Years Meeting," but now Friends United Meeting (FUM). The delegates adopted a standard Book of Discipline for the ten member yearly meetings; tacitly endorsed the practice of hiring ministers; formed sub-committees on Evangelistic and Church Extension, Education, Legislation, Negro Welfare, Foreign Missions, Indian Affairs, and Peace; and agreed to convene every five years (later, every three years). By 1912, Five Years Meeting had acquired *The American Friend* (later titled *Quaker Life*) as its official publication, and established an office in Richmond, Indiana.[33]

Also in 1902, members of five Hicksite Yearly Meetings including Baltimore Yearly Meeting Hicksite came together as "Friends General Conference (FGC)." This new body established a central committee of 100 Friends with subcommittees to promote First Day Schools, Philanthropic Labor, Education, and Advancement of Friends' Principles. FGC provided an opportunity every two years for Friends "to study, worship and discourse together"--usually by the seaside in Cape May, New Jersey. Its staff was sited in Philadelphia, and *The Friends Intelligencer* (now *Friends Journal*) was the publication that served and still serves its membership.[34]

In 1924 the American Friends Service Committee became a third nationwide and permanent Quaker organization. It had organized ad hoc in 1917 to meet the crisis of World War I, and continued on in 1919 at Herbert Hoover's request. By 1924 the crisis had abated. Over seven years of crisis the Service Committee had succored millions of suffering people, and added measurably to the reputation of the Society of Friends. In the Ninth Month of 1924 Rufus Jones, the chairman, called a meeting of concerned Friends to decide the Service Committee's future.

Rufus thought the committee should not go on "unless we have a vital mission to perform nor unless we can speak and act for the corporate membership of the Society of Friends." He then made it clear that he believed the committee should continue. He named the missions that seemed vital to him: to interpret "our Quaker spirit and way of life" at home and abroad with emphasis on the Quaker peace testimony--home relief for distressed Americans--promoting fair play for certain minorities in the U.S., particularly blacks, Japanese and Italians--and uniting the Society of Friends.

Those present approved Rufus's remarks. They decided to continue permanently, and the AFSC set off on its new tack. It re-organized, with an executive secretary and four sections: European, Interracial, Peace, and Home Service sections.[35]

The decision to continue permanently was controversial. On one hand, clearly, the AFSC could accomplish wonders to advance peace and justice in the world--especially those parts of the world where no Friends dwell. On the other hand, some Friends said, to have a permanent committee of this kind meant moving the Society of Friends away from its roots (that is to say, its Root). Now the volunteers who first energized AFSC's efforts were to be replaced by experts and professionals; unpaid workers motivated by concern, replaced by paid staff. Now, some said, the AFSC, at first a spontaneous movement, would become an institution, a bureaucracy, a hierarchy.[36] Hiring paid workers to stand in the front line would vitiate the Society of Friends and its testimonies--this was feared.

\* \* \*

The Friends' Meetings in Virginia in 1900 numbered seventeen: fourteen of these were traditional meetings, gathering in silence; and now three were programmed meetings with paid ministers who delivered prepared sermons. Two of the three were evangelical Friends churches in Portsmouth and in New Point, Matthews County, and the third was Blue Ridge Mission Meeting near Ararat in Patrick County. This last was under the care of North Carolina Yearly Meeting Orthodox.

As the 1900s wore on, more Friends' Meetings with professional leaders appeared in Virginia:
- 1901: An evangelical "Church of Friends" with a pastor opened in Achilles, a village of Chesapeake Bay watermen in Gloucester County.
- 1903: Baltimore Yearly Meeting Orthodox sent George and Katherine Wise to Ivor "to engage in religious work on a paid basis," and Corinth Friends provided a house for them there. George Wise served both as a teacher at Corinth Friends' Boarding Academy and as secretary or administrator for the meetings which then made up Virginia Half Years' Meeting--

Corinth, Bethel, Somerton, Black Creek and Richmond. He preached in all five meetings from time to time.[37]

- 1905: North Carolina Yearly Meeting Orthodox sent Samuel Pickett to pastor the new Center Valley Meeting, two miles from Galax. The next year James Bartlett with his sons Claude and Fred built Mountain View Meeting house nearby and James Bartlett was the first pastor there.[38] In 1928 a third pastoral meeting under North Carolina's care began right in Galax.
- 1906: Ohio Yearly Meeting (Damascus) opened an evangelical Friends Church with a pastor in Hampton. The same yearly meeting opened similar churches in Rescue, Isle of Wight County, in 1913; in Peniel, Matthews County, 1920; and in Newport News, 1927.
- 1923: Baltimore Yearly Meeting Orthodox did not favor the hiring of ministers since some of its English-born members opposed the practice.[39] Nevertheless, Lincoln Meeting did employ Ralph Boring as its minister in 1923. He came to Virginia from the Friendsville, Tennessee Monthly Meeting.

So, in the years from 1900 to the year of the great depression in 1929, the number of Virginia Friends' Meetings or Friends' Churches with programmed services and full time paid ministers increased from three to thirteen.

In those same years, 1900 to 1929, *no* new Friends Meetings of the traditional unprogrammed kind started. What is more, two traditional meetings closed their doors and two more reduced to vestiges of their former selves.

The meetings laid down were Fairfax, which closed in 1929, after 187 years; and the Ridge Meeting, laid down in 1920 after 165 years. The weakened ones were:

- Richmond: Friends there sold their meeting house at 7 East Clay Street in 1909, after average First Day attendance sank to six. Thereafter Richmond Friends met in a room of the city's Y.M.C.A.[40]
- Woodlawn: In 1917 the U.S. Army pre-empted thousands of acres around the Woodlawn Friends' meeting house, buying up the farms of Woodlawn's members by right of eminent domain. Friends kept their veranda'd gray meeting house and its burying ground (which remain today right in the center of the Fort Belvoir army post), but the membership was decimated. First Day meetings fell to one a month beginning in 1921.[41]

In 1929 then, the Friends' meetings in Virginia totalled twenty-four: eleven traditional and thirteen programmed with paid pastors. The increase in programmed meetings reflects the dominance that evangelical religion had then, when Billy Sunday and Aimee Semple McPherson were making headlines. And not only in Virginia was traditional Quakerism limping. The "unprogrammed" Friends of the Philadelphia yearly meetings, who numbered over 25,000 in 1827, were reduced to a few more than 15,000 by 1927.⁴²

Even so, there were stirrings of new vigor:

About 1915, college and university communities across the country mysteriously discovered the worth of unpremeditated Quaker worship. The first of these was Ithaca, New York, where teachers and students of Cornell University started a Friends meeting. William Wistar Comfort, a Philadelphia Friend who chaired Cornell's French faculty* may have been responsible for the start-up of Ithaca Meeting. But more such meetings soon appeared close by the Universities of Michigan, Wisconsin, and Northwestern, of Harvard and Yale, of North Carolina, Penn State and Rutgers.

A good deal of this new energy came out of the writings and speeches of Rufus Jones, who never lost his down East accent through all the years he taught philosophy at Haverford College. He grew up among Orthodox Friends and remained an Orthodox Friend life-long. But his study of mysticism and mystics and his discovery of the mystical spiritual outlook of the first Quaker, George Fox, moved him steadily toward advocacy of the inward way of worship and away from evangelicalism. "The *Bible* can no longer be read in an attitude of Bibiolatry," he wrote,

> The theory of its verbal infallibility is of course gone. The idea that it is a divinely 'dictated' book is untenable.... It is a library of books--the selected spiritual literature of a remarkable people covering more than a thousand years of history.... Writers draw on ideas and views that were current in Assyria, Babylonia, Egypt, Persia, Greece. What we have is a growing revelation.

---

*W.W. Comfort became president of Haverford College in 1917. He was known to a generation of Haverford students as Uncle Billy.

Instead of puzzling over the Resurrection and what became of Jesus' body, Rufus wrote, better pay attention to Christ's continuing invisible Spirit and guidance. There is a Sense beyond our five common senses.[43]

He expressed such views in fifty-four widely read books. Thus he led some seekers in the universities and elsewhere, to turn to the Quaker way as an alternative to popular religion.[44]

\* \* \*

The new energy touched Virginia's capital city late in the 1920s. The handful of Quakers in Richmond had met in the Y.M.C.A. since 1909, just barely surviving. The meeting was held together by Margaret Crenshaw (1849-1940) who was John Crenshaw's daughter. Margaret's nephews and niece--Hoge, Arnold and Katherine Ricks--presently joined her in the Meeting. Their father was Richard Arnold Ricks of Caroline County (descendant of Isaac and Katherine Ricks who led in the founding of Virginia Yearly Meeting in 1696), and their mother was Eliza Kate Crenshaw, Margaret's youngest sister. In 1926 a few more Richmonders joined the little Meeting. By 1929 the Meeting regained the strength to buy its own meeting house--a white-stuccoed church building at Park and Meadow Streets.[45]

Baltimore Yearly Meeting Orthodox held its 1928 gathering in Black Creek Meetinghouse at Sedley, Va. It was the first time for that Yearly Meeting to be held outside of Baltimore. The re-location signified that the bulk of the Yearly Meetings's membership now were Virginians. Black Creek Friends built a kitchen and dining room especially for the occasion, and the women of Somerton, Black Creek, Bethel and Corinth, some of them famous cooks, took turns at preparing the meals.[46]

Three men were there at the Yearly Meeting at Black Creek who led lives as light-filled as any in all the Friendly Virginians' history. Two came from Richmond Meeting and the other from Somerton:

James Hoge Ricks (1886-1958) was a Richmond lawyer who promoted merciful handling of children by Virginia's courts, and parole and probation for adult offenders. He was the first judge of Virginia's first Juvenile and Domestic Relations Court, and he wrote most of Virginia's first Childrens' Code. For 40 years, 1916 to 1956, he dealt kindly with Richmond children in trouble with the law. He directed witnesses in his courtroom to *affirm*, not swear, that their testimony would be true, and he induced 40 years' worth of troubled children to trust him.[47]

He was clerk of Richmond Meeting many years. At Black Creek in 1928, Friends appointed him clerk of the Yearly Meeting and he held that position for 20 years. Among Friends he was a quiet counselor. Friends' children, away at school, were often surprised to receive notes in his handwriting.[48]

Edward F. Raiford (1893-1953) was a birthright member of Corinth who moved to Somerton Meeting with his family in 1927. Through his mother he was related to Nancy Babb. This Edward was clerk of Virginia Quarter, 1924 to 1949. He made his living as a school teacher, a merchant and postmaster of Holland, Va. After Hoge Ricks left off as Yearly Meeting clerk, Edward Raiford took the post for four years, 1949 through 1952.

While Edward was its clerk, he wrote three pages on trends within the Yearly Meeting, 1925 to 1950:

> Perhaps the most significant trend during this period has been the increasing sense of unity within the two Yearly Meetings [Baltimore Orthodox and Hicksite]. Though actual union may be within the indefinite and unpredictable future, its eventual accomplishment would appear to be almost inevitable.... A Young Friends' Yearly Meeting has functioned during the entire period...it is probably correct to attribute the trend toward union...to these gatherings of Young Friends.

Referring to the Friends of Virginia Quarter he mentioned

> A definite trend toward 'discipline'...toward less dependence on a paid leadership, with more participation in meetings for worship.... Friends have re-discovered the vitality that may be had in non-programmed meetings; less dependence is placed on outward helps such as music and the prepared sermon.[49]

Emmet Frazer (1903-1962), Iowa-born, became a Friend while in college. He taught two years at Friends' Indian School, Quaker Bridge, New York. Then he came to Richmond, 25 and newly married, to join the faculty of Virginia Union University, a struggling school for black students. After seventeen years there, he became director of what is now the Chaplain Service of the Churches of Virginia--providing spiritual support for prisoners in Virginia's prisons and for patients in her tuberculosis sanitoria. Emmet himself acted as chaplain for the men in the ancient state penitentiary on Spring Street.

Of all the fifty states, Virginia's prison chaplains are the only ones not on the state's payroll, but rather supported by churches. This subtle distinction means that prisoners in Virginia can confide in their chaplain without fear that their confidences will become part of their records. Gaining the churches' financial support was Emmet's accomplishment.

Emmet succeeded Edward Raiford as yearly meeting clerk, 1953 to 1959. Richmond Friends prepared a memorial after his early death that read "Emmet Frazer gave every fiber of his being to the furtherance of the Kingdom of God on this earth."

\* \* \*

Herbert Hoover became president of the United States in 1929--the first Quaker to come anywhere close to that political pinnacle. After he wound up the affairs of the American Relief Administration he had received two job offers: President Warren Harding invited him to be Secretary of Commerce at $15,000, and Daniel Guggenheim invited him to run the Guggenheim brothers' mining dynasty at $500,000 a year. Herbert chose to become the Secretary of Commerce and kept the job through the presidencies of Warren G. Harding and Calvin Coolidge. He was nominated for president at the Republican convention of 1928 in spite of right-wingers who did not like him. The party's Wall Street element was offended by Herbert's efforts to slow the runaway boom that made many millionaires in the 1920s.[50]

The boom went bust in 1929 and a great Depression settled on America. President Hoover's popularity sank as a spate of speculators flung themselves from skyscraper windows. Nevertheless American Quakers kept right on supporting Hoover:

- Two Philadelphia Friends took charge of the Bureau of Indian Affairs at Hoover's request. They were Charles Rhoads (the son of Dr. James Rhoads who served the freedmen at Slabtown, Virginia in Civil War days) and Henry Scattergood.
- Hoover asked the AFSC to help out in the coal regions after the Depression closed down most coal mines. That was in 1931. Within five months Service Committee volunteers were serving meals in 563 communities of western Pennsylvania, West Virginia, Kentucky and Tennessee. One Quaker volunteer was young Werner Janney of Goose Creek Meeting who spent a summer helping the out-of-work miners of Republic, Pennsylvania to build homes. Another is Daniel Houghton who settled in Arlington, Virginia after he helped to start up the Mountain Craftsmens' Cooperative in West Virginia.[51]
- When Herbert and Lou Henry Hoover moved into the White House, the Friends of the two meetings in Washington, D.C.-- 1811 Eye Street (Hicksite) and 13th and Irving (Orthodox)--put aside their differences. They jointly raised money to build a

graystone meeting house on Florida Avenue, suitable for the Quaker president to attend. Mary Vaux Walcott, a Friend with Philadelphia roots, bought the land, and Lucy Wilbur of Rhode Island put up $75,000 for the building. Friends first met for worship there 4 January 1931. A Secret Service detail searched the place and then required all present to rise when the Hoovers arrived.[52]

Quite a few families in nearby northern Virginia joined "Florida Avenue," including Dan and Anne Houghton, David and Laurel Scull and Ed and Vernice Behre.

\* \* \*

One winter evening in 1938 two graduate students were at work in the basement of the University of Virginia's famous Rotunda, which then housed the university's library: Werner Janney, and Charles E. (Chic) Moran of Charlottesville. Chic was working on his Master's thesis in international relations. Werner was sorting a stack of three by five catalogue cards. When he accidentally elbowed the cards onto the floor he exclaimed "My, I'm glad I'm a Quaker!"

Werner's identification of himself as a Quaker caught Chic's immediate attention. Chic's mother reacted negatively to the brutality of World War I and she had conveyed that reaction to Chic. Getting to know Werner, the first live Quaker he had ever met, opened a new way of looking at the world for Chic.

Sometime in March 1938 the two young men began meeting for Quaker worship. Before the end of the semester one or two other students joined them. The worship group grew a little more the following school year and quite a bit more in 1939-1940 after Hitler's armies invaded Poland.[53]

This worship group in Charlottesville was the first new budding of traditional Quakerism in Virginia in fifty-eight years.

\* \* \*

World War I failed miserably to make the world safe for democracy. Germany was crushed and shamed. Adolf Hitler, a most articulate war veteran, used the Germans' shame to climb to power. He organized the National Socialist German Workers' (Nazi) party, and maneuvered his way to become dictator of a new German government called the Third Reich. Hitler declared Jews and pacifists enemies of the Third Reich. His Gestapo, the secret police, herded them into death camps--Buchenwald, Dachau,

Sachsenhausen, Ravensbruch--by the millions. German armies marched again, taking over the Rhineland, then Austria, then Czechoslovakia. When they invaded Poland, that triggered the second World War--within twenty years of the first.

Three Friends sailed on the *Queen Mary* for Berlin, soon after the invasion of Poland--Rufus Jones, now 75, Robert Yarnall of Philadelphia, and George Walton, the principal of George School. In Berlin after twelve days of trying, the three gained entrance to the Gestapo's headquarters.

The three met Regierungrat Dr. Lischka and Standartenfuhrer Dr. Erlinger in a fifth floor waiting room. They said that they wanted to help Jews to emigrate from Germany. The Gestapo men left to consult Heinrich Himmler, their dread chief. The three visitors settled in silent prayer after the manner of Friends--the only Quaker meeting ever held in the Gestapo. The room almost certainly was bugged but all the microphones picked up was quietness. Presently the Gestapo men returned. Lischka said

> I shall telegraph tonight to every police station in Germany that the Quakers are given full permission to investigate the sufferings of Jews and to bring such relief as they see necessary.[54]

AFSC workers, allied with English Friends and other relief workers, then set out to get proscribed people out of Germany before the Gestapo called for them. The Quakers evacuated many to the Gurs camp in southern France--a sea of barracks almost two miles long in the shadow of the Pyrenees. When the German army over-ran France in 1940, Gurs became another death camp.

One notable prisoner at Gurs was Herbert Jehle, 33, the pacifist son of German general Julius von Jehle. Herbert had become a Quaker while studying for his doctorate in physics at the University of Berlin. A Frenchwoman of the Gurs staff described Herbert as "Very tall, with an ample golden beard and a sparkle in his eyes." For clothing he wore a blanket cinched around his waist and another draped over his shoulders. Jeanne the Frenchwoman wrote

> In this strange costume he went for a walk with me one evening along the main road. Feeling very discouraged, I told him of my horror for these barracks, the odors, the suffering.
>
> He said to me 'Do not look at the camp. Raise your eyes and contemplate the magnificent heavens and the worlds that follow into infinity....' The starry sky...twinkled above us in that extremely cold evening. Then he began to talk to me of Einstein's theories. That

lesson coming from a man who had lost everything and who found in his faith and in his science the means to carry on, did me incomparable good.[55]

Herbert was one of a few who managed to leave Gurs for freedom. He came to the United States, became a Harvard instructor and wound up years later as a Friendly Virginian.

Congress began early to prepare America for World War II. On the day the Germans captured Paris, 20 June 1940, the House opened debate on the Burke-Wadsworth Bill, to draft Americans for military service. It was written in language that assumed most conscientious objectors would willingly serve the military in noncombat roles.

Friends General Conference at Cape May that July wrote a protest and sent Paul French to present it in Washington. French soon became coordinator of the Historic Peace Churches'--Friends', Mennonites' and Brethrens'--efforts to modify the bill. The churches requested six modifications. The Congress denied three and accepted three.

Denied were these requests: To exempt absolute objectors, (those whose conscience forbids *any* kind of service) completely; To exempt *all* C.O.s from combat duty whether they come to the C.O. position through "religious training or belief" or by any other means--to appoint a *civilian* bureau to deal with conscientious objectors. (Congress did place the draft process in the hands of a Selective Service Administration which ostensibly was to be composed of civilians; but General Lewis Hershey soon became the administration's director. He appointed military officers to be his principal assistants and Selective Service was in fact owned and operated by the military). But Congress accepted these requests by the churches:

- Provide a way for C.O.s to do work of national importance, under the direction of a commission appointed by the Historic Peace Churches. (When Congress accepted this request, that was the genesis of Civilian Public Service.)
- Set up a National Board of Appeals for men whose claims to be C.O.s were denied by local draft boards. (No such board was created, but instead the Attorney General was designated to handle appeals. There would be no military courts-martial for C.O. draftees as there were during World War I. Civilian courts would try their cases in the future.)
- Maintain an official register of Conscientious Objectors.

So the Burke-Wadsworth Bill which became the draft law for World War II improved on World War I's. It brought the government closer than ever before to admitting that citizens have a right to keep clear of war and its attendant horror.[56]

A total of 34,506,923 American men registered for the draft during World War II. Of these, 72,354 or about two-tenths of one percent applied for C.O. status. In round numbers, 6,000 of the 72,354 went to prison as absolute objectors; 26,000 accepted noncombat status in the military; and 28,000 failed the physical examination; and 11,996 chose Civilian Public Service. The religious preferences of the 11,996 "CPSers":

| | | | |
|---|---|---|---|
| 4,665 | Mennonite | 192 | Presbyterian |
| 1,353 | Brethren | 149 | Catholic |
| 951 | Quaker | 108 | Lutheran |
| 673 | Methodist | 88 | Episcopalian |
| 223 | Baptist | 44 | Unitarian |
| 209 | Congregational Christian | 3,341 | "Other" |

The CPS men went off to serve in camps built in the 1930s depression days by the Civilian Conservation Corps. While millions of America's young men waged bloody war overseas, these thousands waged the moral equivalent of war at home, creating instead of destroying. Their work included forest and soil conservation, forest fire fighting, dam building, care of mentally ill patients, hookworm control, being guinea pigs for medical experiments, food production. CPS camps were scattered from Maine to California. Sixty seven were under the care of Friends, and ten were located in Virginia.

At least seventeen Virginia Friends served in CPS: six from Bethel, five from Richmond, three from Corinth and one from Black Creek. Werner Janney and Chic Moran went off to CPS from the little worship group in Charlottesville. When they went in the summer of 1942, the worship group died away.

As always more Friends went off to war than those who witnessed for peace. Edward Raiford brooded on his situation. In Somerton at the height of the war in 1944, he wrote:

> Whose fault is it that so few of our young men are in Civilian Public Service camps, and so few have felt that no other way was open to them but to accept service in the army or navy...? We must somehow see to it that the next generation...shall not have to choose...because so many of their elders have not worked hard enough at...putting into practice the teachings of Christ.

The Quaker reputation for honesty originated in the seventeenth century and continues in the twentieth. Numerous firms include "Quaker" in their names and trademark to signify dependability.

## XVII

## I THINK OF THE GREAT WORK
## 1950-Present

> I think of the great work done by the Society of Friends. It gives all of us who struggle for justice new hope.
> -- Martin Luther King, Jr. 1957

Now we come to recent times, and this narrative of the Friendly Virginians must shift gears. Some say "modern history" is no history at all. Real history needs perspective, a knowledge of how hopeful beginnings worked themselves out, time enough to discover whether seedlings flourish or wither away. Without perspective how to tell the ripples from the waves, or waves from tides? Yet an historian can write more truly, in one sense, of days and things and people experienced and touched and talked with firsthand.

Virginians numbered 16,000 in 1650; 293,000 by 1750; 1,420,000 by 1850; and 3,319,000 by 1950 and growing fast. So many people made a heavy burden on some of the Commonwealth. Demographers called the eastern corridor of Virginia, from Alexandria south to Richmond and Norfolk, a megalopolis. There were traffic jams along Route 95. Ever-increasing real estate developments--with names like Brookmore Heights and Montfair Estates--girdled the courthouse towns. The Industrial Age was in full cry.

Still, Virginia's woods and meadows, streams and swamps--no matter how torn up, bridged, bulldozed, asphalted or built over--keep a certain elan. The descendants of old Virginians still walk here. Many landscapes are bucolic as ever. The springs come on lovely as ever in tender pinks, whites and greens, still followed by star shadowed summer nights and moody November days.

Many more Virginians nowadays spend Sunday mornings on the golf links, at the carwash, or behind the Sunday papers, more interested in sport, machines or politics than the spiritual side of things. Yet spires still rise along the skylines of every town and city, over churches where Virginians receive spiritual nourishment through ordained ministers; and Virginia's Friends as for 339 years still assemble to wait for the guidance of the Inward Light.

\* \* \*

Five new Friends' gatherings appeared in 1950s Virginia--two evangelical churches and three traditionally unprogrammed meetings. Church planters of Ohio Yearly Meeting Damascus launched the churches: Longview Evangelical Friends Church in Danville and Providence in Virginia Beach.[1] The three traditional meetings are:

- *Charlottesville*, where Chic Moran, come home from work with the AFSC in Europe, had married Fermine Colvin. The worship group of university students that Chic and Werner Janney started in 1938 was long gone. The Morans with Keith and Mary Wiley and their children began to meet monthly for worship in the fall of 1952. A few more Friends moved to town and the group, slowly growing, then gathered weekly. In 1959 Herbert Jehle, the Quaker who had been a prisoner in the camp at Gurs, with wife Dietlinde and two little sons, came to join the group. Herbert often read from the poetry of Rabindranath Tagore during worship. In 1962 Baltimore Yearly sent a clearness committee--it included Asa Moore Janney, Werner's brother--to visit the Charlottesville Friends. Soon thereafter the worship group became a regular monthly meeting of Baltimore Yearly Meeting.[2]
- *Virginia Beach* started up in 1954 led by Louise Brown Wilson and her husband Robert. It was the first Conservative or Wilburite Quaker meeting ever in Virginia, which may be attributed to the fact that Louise Wilson grew up in Cedar Grove Meeting, a Conservative North Carolina meeting. Virginia Beach Friends built a handsome brick meeting house on Laskin Road and built a school nearby in 1955. It was and is Virginia's only Friends' school, the first since Corinth Boarding Academy closed in the 1920s.
- *Langley Hill* opened in 1958 in an abandoned black Baptist church on Lawyers Road, Vienna. Most attenders belonged to Florida Avenue Meeting in Washington and the worship group in Vienna operated under Florida Avenue's care. After two or three years the group moved eight miles north, buying an old Methodist church building on Georgetown Pike. It grew rapidly thereafter.

\* \* \*

The 1950s mark a turn in two matters important to Virginia's Friends. One, the number of Friends' meetings in the state began to grow a little as just observed. Two, dawn lightened the long night of suppression of the state's black people.

The black people resumed their uphill struggle for recognition as human beings when the National Association for the Advancement of Colored People organized in 1909. By 1939 Eileen Black, a Norfolk teacher, screwed up the courage to sue for the same pay as white teachers: She not only lost her suit but was fired for being uppity. When Dr. Palmer, the principal of Norfolk's segregated Huntington High School, brought a similar suit he too lost and was fired. In those days, every judge, prosecutor, sheriff, mayor, lawmaker and voting registrar from Virginia southward was white.

Then in 1940 about Christmastime, David Scull (1914-1983) and his young wife Laurel moved to Annandale in Fairfax County. David, a member of Swarthmore College's class of 1936, joined the Friends' Meeting on Swarthmore's campus in his freshman year. He became a disciple of Swarthmore philosophy professor Jesse Holmes (whose forebears worshipped in Goose Creek Meeting). David worked for Jesse Holmes when Holmes ran for governor of Pennsylvania on the Socialist ticket.

In March 1934 David rode the ten miles from Swarthmore to Haverford College for a conference on race relations. Then he wrote to his parents,

> After having such problems as the race problem presented so really and brought convincingly home, I feel more and more that when I get out of college I want to be in some measure prepared to meet them.[3]

Once in Annandale, David became the first white member of the NAACP in Fairfax County and, quite possibly, in the whole state. The Sculls sent their children to Burgundy Farm School in Alexandria and, through their encouragement in 1950, Burgundy Farm became the only Virginia school attended by white and black children together.[4] Agnes Sailer (1904-1990), the Vassar graduate who was Burgundy Farm's principal, joined Friends soon thereafter.

In the hopeful days after the Civil War, in 1872 and 1873, Congress had passed laws outlawing segregation in the District of Columbia. These laws were dead letters by 1950, many years forgotten. Then local activists began to debate whether they could test the old laws in court and revive them.

So it came about that four respectably dressed people, three black and one white, walked into Thompson's Cafeteria on Washington's 14th Street, the afternoon of Friday, 27 January 1950. The four were: Dr. Mary Church Terrell, 85, a retired teacher; Geneva Brown, a union official; Reverend W. H. Jernagin, pastor of Washington's Mt. Carmel Baptist Church--and David

Scull, identified as a member of the Religious Society of Friends living in Virginia.

They picked up trays and got into the cafeteria line. The cafeteria's manager then required them to leave since Thompson's did not serve Negro customers. The four did leave, and then filed a complaint with D.C.'s corporation counsel under the 1870s laws. Thus began the Thompson's Restaurant case. It zig-zagged through the courts and ended three years later on 8 June 1953 when the U.S. Supreme Court ruled 8-0 for David and the other plaintiffs.[5]

The ruling represents a tremendous triumph for civil rights. When Judge Nathan Cayton died--he sat as a judge in the District of Columbia for twenty-nine years--his obituary chiefly noted that "he wrote the Thompson Restaurant case appellate decision...upheld by the Supreme Court."[6]

This Thompson Restaurant ruling went radically contrary to the tide of the times, for every one of the myriad white restaurants in Virginia and the south served blacks through a window or by the back door if they served them at all. David Scull and his three colleagues upset the established scheme of things.

Frederick Vinson ended his career as the Supreme Court's chief justice with the Thompson Restaurant decision. He retired the day after announcing the decision. Earl Warren succeeded him. While Vinson was still on the bench, however, and while the Court was deciding the Thompson Restaurant case, it took up *Brown v. the Board of Education of Topeka*.

*Brown* was actually a collection of five cases appealed from decisions made by courts of the District of Columbia and four states: Kansas, Delaware, South Carolina and Virginia. Each was slightly different but all asked the court to decide one basic question: Does segregation of children in public schools on the basis of race deprive the children of the minority race of equal education?

The Virginia case arose in Prince Edward County in 1951 when Moton High School's students walked out to protest the segregated school's shabbiness. Francis Griffin, black minister of the First Baptist Church of Farmville, "the Moses of Prince Edward County," led them.

On 17 May 1954 Chief Justice Warren announced for the protesters. Thus the Supreme Court threw out separate but equal, the legal fiction that had sheltered out-and-out injustice for fifty-eight years.[7]

The *Brown* decision brought joy and thanksgiving in Virginia's black churches and in the meetinghouses of their old champions, the Friendly Virginians. Elsewhere there were loud protests, howls of protest. Letters to the editor flooded Virginia's newspapers proposing "Death to race-mixers" and "Keep white schools white!" The Byrd Machine that now controlled the state government in Richmond took three increasingly defiant steps in the name of "massive resistance:"

- Governor Thomas Stanley appointed an all-white commission headed by state Senator Garland Gray of Sussex County. Gray was a segregationist and his commission's purpose was to figure out a way to get around the Supreme Court's ruling. After one public hearing in Richmond's Mosque and a year of closed hearings, the Gray Commission came up with this stratagem: to use state tax monies for "tuition grants." These grants would enable white students to attend private segregated schools instead of the public schools. On 9 January 1956 Virginians voted by referendum and by more than two to one in favor of the tuition grants.
- James J. Kilpatrick, editor of the Richmond *News Leader* resurrected the notions of "state's rights" and "interposition." Virginia, he editorialized, could ignore the hated *Brown* decision by imposing its sovereign authority between itself and the Federal government, as it had in Civil War days. In February 1956 Virginia's Senate passed an Interposition Resolution by thirty-six to two and the House followed eighty-eight to five. Four or five other southern state legislatures liked the idea so well that they passed similar resolutions.
- Then Governor Stanley that August persuaded the General Assembly to pass a law closing any public school under court order to integrate. He went out of office a few months later, proud that no black pupil had entered a white public school during his watch.[8]

Soon after the *Brown* decision, an organization of white segregationists formed in Virginia--the Defenders of State Sovereignty and Individual Liberties. J. Barry Wall, editor of the Farmville *Herald*, and Robert Crawford, who owned Farmville's laundry, were the organizers. Within two years the Defenders had sixty local chapters in Virginia with about 12,000 members--all white.[9]

At the same time the Virginia Council on Human Relations formed--an organization of black and white Virginians with purposes exactly opposed to the Defenders'. Of the Virginia Council's twenty-four chapters at least three had Quaker founding members: David Scull in Fairfax, Chic Moran in Charlottesville, and a Quaker family in Petersburg.

The council statewide was the largest of its kind in the southern states, yet it never exceeded 2,700 members--the reason for the small total suggested by the experience of Petersburg Council's founders. They received hate mail and hate telephone calls through the nights. Autos with grim-visaged strangers parked at their curb. Nearly all the city's white ministers *said* they favored the new organization, but only one retired minister came to meetings.

While Thomas Stanley still was governor, the General Assembly established a Committee on Law Reform and Racial Activities, chaired by Delegate James Thomson of Alexandria. Thomson was a white supremacist. His committee's massive resistance role was to stop the work of the NAACP and other pro-integration forces in Virginia. He predicted that the committee would "bust [the NAACP] wide open."

Thomson's committee travelled around the state for a year, holding closed door hearings. Some witnesses refused to testify, but the committee in such cases routinely obtained court orders, and the witnesses then complied. In September 1957, however, the committee came to Arlington County and called a witness who flatly refused to comply, court order or no-- to wit, David Scull.

The questions David refused to answer focused on his mailbox--P.O. Box 218, Annandale, Virginia. It was a return address for many of the pro-integration organizations that David had joined--the Fairfax County Parent-Teachers Association, American Friends Service Committee, Community Council for Social Progress, Southern Regional Council, Fairfax County Council on Human Relations, Fairfax County NAACP, B'nai B'rith and the like. Thomson and his committee were trying to establish that these organizations and David himself were Communist-inspired.

In refusing, David said, "It is for me a matter of conscience and my position is consistent, I believe, with the ancient testimony of the Religious Society of Friends upholding the rights of the individual against the tyranny of government." The Arlington County court then found him guilty of contempt, fined him $50 and sentenced him to ten days in jail. Virginia's Supreme Court refused to hear the case on appeal, and *Scull v. Virginia* then went up to the U.S. Supreme Court.

In May of 1959 the court under Chief Justice Warren unanimously threw out David's conviction. It did so on the ground that the Thomson Committee did not tell David clearly what it wanted when it questioned him. The justices did not rule whether David was within his rights in refusing to answer (although a footnote to the decision suggests that four of the nine justices believed he *was* within his right).

When Chairman Thomson heard the decision, he said "With the complexion of the Court the way it is--protecting subversives and people interested in integration--what other result could you expect?"[10]

While *Scull v. Virginia* was wending its way to a decision in the summer of 1958, some 2,800 Friends including a contingent of Virginians, gathered for a Friends General Conference in cool Cape May, New Jersey. Martin Luther King, 29, the minister of Dexter Avenue Baptist Church in Montgomery, Alabama, spoke to the assembled Friends on a pier built out over the Atlantic. Waves crashing against the pilings accented the measured cadence of his words.

Beginning in December 1955 this Reverend King had led Montgomery's black people in a year-long boycott of the city's buses. He and his followers had overturned the Jim Crow law requiring blacks to ride in the backs of the buses.

Early in his Cape May talk, King said, "I think of the great work done by the Society of Friends. It gives all of us who struggle for justice new hope." He thanked the Friends for the AFSC's support.

Then he described his plan to fight for the black people's rights. We are going to win equal justice with *love*, he said. "Our opposers can jail us, insult us, burn crosses and wear hoods to frighten us and we will love them, we will overcome them with love and goodwill." He called on the quiet assemblage to be *maladjusted* to segregation, to "conditions which take necessities from the masses to give luxuries to the classes...to the madness of militarism and...physical violence." Martin Luther King inspired the Quakers at Cape May.[11]

Massive resistance crumbled in Virginia in January 1959. Virginia's Supreme Court outlawed the closing of public schools then, ruling that "the state must support...public free schools...including those in which the pupils of both races are compelled to be enrolled and taught together, however unfortunate that situation may be." On 2 February, twenty-one black children entered the formerly white schools of Norfolk and Arlington. Virginia's other public schools then followed suit. There was resistance-- white students of Petersburg's high school mobbed their Quaker schoolmate when she undertook to welcome the first blacks; bumper stickers proclaiming NEVER were frequently seen; Confederate flags appeared here and there, and little cast iron horse-holder statuettes with black faces--but school integration kept steadily on.

One exception was Prince Edward County, where the supervisors refused integration. They appropriated no money for schools in 1959. Prince Edward's white children enrolled in a private academy and the black children were left school-less[12].

\* \* \*

In 1959 a delegation of some twenty Quakers came to the state capitol in Richmond "to speak truth to power"--the first such delegation since Civil War days. They came to ask the state to stop killing criminals in its electric chair. Their leader was Albert Turner of the newly-formed Virginia Beach Meeting. Dorothy McDiarmid, who represented Fairfax in the General Assembly--a Swarthmore graduate and the daughter of Daniel Shoemaker, once clerk of Florida Avenue Meeting--arranged for the group to testify before the Assembly's Courts of Justice Committee.

En route to the Capitol that rainy afternoon, Friends passed a picket line of black students demonstrating before two downtown Richmond department stores. The stores allowed black customers but had no black employees. Policemen in raincapes and holding police dogs in check stood glowering along the curbs. The effect was menacing.

The Courts of Justice Committee consisted of ten white male legislators convened in a basement room of the Capitol. One after another, the Friends testified before the committee. They spoke of the sanctity of human life, of that of God in every person. They pointed out that the murder rate in states that have no death chairs is lower than states that have them. They quoted the *Bible*: "Vengeance is mine saith the Lord." They observed that state-sanctioned killing mocks the Judaeo-Christian injunction, "Thou shalt not kill!"

At the long afternoon's end, the committee's chairman thanked the Friends courteously. His committee then voted nine to one to keep Virginia's death penalty on the statute books. With no change at all.

Though the delegation failed to change the death penalty, one positive thing came from it, in the form of an All-Virginia Friends' Conference. Some members of the delegation led by Evelyn Bradshaw of Virginia Beach decided it would be well for Friends of all four varieties in Virginia to come together periodically "for growth in the Spirit and to join in endeavors as we may be led." This conference met first in the Ninth Month of 1967 and has met generally twice a year since. It supports the work of the state's prison chaplains, the Virginia Council of Churches, Offender Aid and Restoration, and similar causes.

The meetings are attended almost entirely by Quakers from traditional unprogrammed meetings. Virginia's evangelically oriented meetings and churches have not joined in. The conference has met in many Virginia locations, but in recent years it has met most frequently at The Clearing in Amelia County. This is a 75-acre wooded retreat center donated by Louise Whittington to the Richmond Meeting in 1983.

\* \* \*

In 1960 another shooting war threatened. It was halfway across the world this war but yet the U.S. Government felt bound to get involved.

This war developed out of the struggle of the Vietnamese people for independence from France. Their rebellion began in 1946. It concerned Washington because Ho Chi Minh, the rebel leader, had the support of Russia and China--Reds! The U.S. first sent weapons to Ho's opponents in 1950 and kept on sending them after Ho ousted the French in 1954. The weapons then went to a U.S. backed government in Saigon in South Vietnam.

Quakers began vigorously to protest American involvement in Vietnam and in "cold war," in 1957 and 1958. In February 1958 a Quaker skipper and mate sailed the 30 foot ketch *Golden Rule* for the Marshall Islands to witness against the nuclear bomb tests there.

The voyage of the *Golden Rule* inspired Ed Behre, a Friend who lived in Alexandria, Virginia. In 1960 Ed organized a peace vigil to be held at the Pentagon Building. The Pentagon is headquarters for all U.S. military activities, located on the Virginia bank of the Potomac River. Ed and wife Vernice drove right by it on their weekly way to Florida Avenue Meeting.

On Sunday, 13 November 1960, a thousand Friends from all across the country worshiped solemnly at Florida Avenue and then walked the three miles to the Pentagon. Some held signs reading "Quaker Peace Witness, 1660-1960" to mark the 300th anniversary of the Quaker peace testimony. That originated in 1660 when Friends declared to King Charles II

> All bloody principles and practices we...do utterly deny.... All outward wars and strife and fighting with outward weapons, for any end or any pretence whatsoever.

Neither the voyage of the *Golden Rule* or the Pentagon Vigil deterred Washington's powers-that-be: The *Golden Rule*'s crew was jailed in

Honolulu before they could reach the Marshalls. On the Monday after the vigil, Quakers called at the White House to urge President Eisenhower to wage peace instead of war. They did not even get in to see the president. Their vigil had no apparent effect.[13]

\* \* \*

Back home in Virginia, in Prince Edward County, 1,700 black children had no schools to go to at summer's end in 1960. The public school buildings were padlocked. Some of the county's white churches had built additions on their buildings to provide classrooms for a new, private, all-white academy.

Early on, the American Friends Service Committee sent Helen Baker, a diminutive black social worker, to Prince Edward. Francis Griffin, Helen Baker and some local black women organized a series of neighborhood centers where most of the school-less black children came in lieu of school. But the women in charge of the centers had very little education themselves. The centers were morale boosters and stop-gaps, nothing more. The AFSC found foster families outside Virginia for sixty-seven high school age youngsters who wanted education badly enough to leave home and brave the unknown. The sixty-seven went to homes, Quaker and other, in Pennsylvania and seven other states. Many of the 67 were later to go on to college.

The AFSC presently interested Bobby Kennedy--the President's brother and also his attorney-general--in the plight of Prince Edward's black children. Kennedy and others raised a million dollars to open a Free School, which enrolled 1,500 black and six white children for the 1963-1964 school year. That year the U.S. Department of Justice won a Supreme Court decree ordering Prince Edward to re-open its schools.

The AFSC then set out to reconcile the county's embattled black and white citizens. All that summer of 1964, volunteer couples, Quakers and others, trudged the county roads knocking at the doors of whites' homes. "If the public schools re-open in September, will you send your children?" they asked. Most answers were equivocal or uncertain. When September came, only a dozen white Prince Edward children enrolled in the re-opened schools; but that number increased slowly each subsequent September.[14]

\* \* \*

Beginning December 1961, the U. S. sent combat troops to bolster the government in Saigon. More than 11,000 American soldiers were in Vietnam by the end of 1962. When a military coup overthrew President Diem in Saigon in 1963, the U.S. kept right on propping up the military dictators who followed Diem in and out of power--ten of them in eighteen months. The successive dictators kept up the war despite strong popular feelings. Seven Buddhist monks in and around Saigon set themselves afire and gave their lives in protest during 1963. The Saigon governments rounded up other dissidents wholesale, locking many in bamboo "tiger cages."

Antiwar feeling grew in the United States too, with Quakers playing a prominent antiwar part. Two years after the Pentagon Vigil, a thousand Quakers assembled again, this time around the Washington Monument, to hold a Witness for World Order.[15] Ed Behre again coordinated the gathering. Six Friends visited the President, appealing to him for support in strengthening the United Nations.

President John F. Kennedy occupied the White House, 1961-1963. Some hopeful things happened then, even while the war in Vietnam slowly escalated. Friends had established a Committee on National Legislation (FCNL) in Washington in 1943, and the Washington atmosphere during Kennedy's time was somewhat attuned to the FCNL's goals. The committee's Quaker lobbyists tipped the scales in Congress for passing the bill which established the U. S. Peace Corps in 1961. They also midwifed the birth of the U.S. Arms Control and Disarmament Agency. Marian Krebser, a Fairfax County Friend, interviewed seventy-two Representatives, six Senators and ten members of the White House staff in behalf of the bill that established the Disarmament Agency.[16]

A zealot in Texas murdered John Kennedy in 1963, and Vice President Lyndon B. Johnson took his presidential place. New President Johnson continued many of Kennedy's hopeful programs. He launched Kennedy's "War on Poverty," establishing community action agencies across the country "to wipe out poverty in our time." He engineered a bill attacking race discrimination. In the fall of 1964 when campaigning for re-election he promised to extricate the nation from Vietnam. The United States, he declared, "is not about to send American boys nine or ten thousand miles away from home to do what Asian boys ought to be doing to protect themselves."[17] This promise persuaded Quakers in Virginia and everywhere to vote for Johnson.

No sooner was he re-elected, though, than he changed from dove to hawk. He ordered American jets to begin bombing North Vietnam in February 1965, and the number of American boys in Vietnam climbed from 27,000 to near 200,000 during 1965, and 525,000 by 1967. Fifteen thousand Americans died in jungle fighting, 109,000 grievously wounded.

Johnson kept promising peace just ahead, but no peace came. The press reported Americans' use of napalm to incinerate peasant villages; of Agent Orange to defoliate the jungle; of the massacre of Mylai's villagers by Lt. Calley's platoon in order to "liberate" that village. When the North

Vietnamese, supposedly on the run, launched their bloody Tet offensive in February 1968, the credibility gap--the gulf between the president's promises and the truth--overstretched.*

LBJ's support dropped away. A poll in March 1968 showed that only 26 percent of Americans--compared with 83 percent in 1965--approved his conduct of the war. Multitudes joined the peace movement and President Johnson got the message. On Sunday evening, 30 March 1968 he announced on television that he would not run for another term as president.[18]

\* \* \*

Suddenly in the mid-'60s a kind of lightening smote American life. Then came the time of the Flower Children, of peace symbols and love beads, of young people in ragged blue jeans dancing in the streets. The Beatles, four engaging fellows from Liverpool with rather long hair, set the mood with their music. It was a rift in the Industrial Age, a wave in history when the spiritual side of things challenged business as usual, money, technology--materialism.

No one is quite sure what brought the New Age. Some say, a revolt against the horror of Vietnam. Others think the new freedom won by black Americans. Or the invention of the Pill. Or a loss of trust in the nation's leaders. Or, all of the above?

Whatever, the pattern of America's culture was shaken then and somewhat rearranged. Teach-ins, love-ins and be-ins happened everywhere. Young men burned their draft cards ceremoniously. Women young and old unceremoniously declared their liberation. Poets wrote poems with rude rhythms and artists applied their paints by dribble instead of brush. Communes started up from coast to coast where earnest groups set out to live their ideals.

The new pattern was not altogether beautiful. Explosive differences of viewpoints between the generations tore families wide apart. Marijuana and "upper" and "downer" drugs challenged alcohol as ruinous aids to Nirvana. Many lost the way while groping from old lifestyle to new. And members of the Establishment, upholders of the pre-1965 American way, gave full publicity to these blemishes.

---

*One young Quaker from Virginia witnessed the Tet battle at Qui Nhon. He was a conscientious objector serving with International Voluntary Services, building shelters and digging wells for Vietnam's homeless refugees.

The Flower Children harmonized in many ways with Quakers in their emphasis on equalness, on peace, community, kindliness, simplicity. The time of the Flower Children buoyed Friends considerably, at least those who worshiped in the traditional unpremeditated manner.

Until the 1870s, Friends wore distinctive Quaker gray clothing to meetings for worship. Thereafter and for nearly a century they wore their best clothes--"Sunday go to Meeting clothes"--women in dresses, hats and heels and white gloves; men in vests, neckties, shined shoes and white collars. Then in the mid 1960s, the mode of meeting dress changed yet again. Younger Friends began to worship in simpler, quite informal clothing, in T-shirts and jeans or shorts, sneakers or sandals or sometimes, indeed, barefoot.

As in the 1870s so in the 1960s, some older Friends resisted. When Frank Adams came to Richmond Meeting with his small son by bicycle, both in summer shorts, that caused something of a sensation. One old-line Quaker couple quit the meeting altogether. But not long after, the meeting in general adopted the new unpretentious dress.

In the 1960s too, most unprogrammed Friends rearranged their meetinghouses. They positioned the benches in concentric circles or squares, abandoning the raised benches traditionally reserved for recorded ministers. The raised benches had set the ministers apart and above the main body of worshiping Friends. Now Friends at worship face one another, see one another's faces instead of the backs of one another's necks.

* * *

Baltimore Yearly Meeting's Friends healed the division in their ranks in 1968. In 1828 they split into Baltimore Hicksite and Baltimore Orthodox Yearly Meetings. In 1968 they came together again. It was the fifth yearly meeting to heal its Hicksite/Orthodox difference: New England Yearly Meeting reunited in 1945, and Philadelphia, New York, and Canadian Yearly Meetings in 1955.

In 1923 the Baltimore Hicksites in their yearly meeting assembled sent "greetings" to the Orthodox body. Orthodox Friends responded with "a wish that the feeling might grow and find us closer together."

The feeling did grow. The two bodies named a joint committee in 1926 "to develop cooperation." The Young Friends of the two bodies merged as one group in 1931. The roof of Goose Creek's Hicksite meeting house blew off in a 1943 hurricane; the Orthodox Friends of Lincoln Meeting just up the road invited the Goose Creekers to worship with them, and thereafter the two groups worshiped together. In 1944 Washington's Florida Avenue

Friends declared themselves to be a *united* meeting and in 1949 Hopewell Meeting followed suit.

By 1960 the joint committee of the two yearly meetings was working purposefully. Virginia Friends on that committee during the 1960s included Hicksite Friends Herbert Brown (Langley Hill Meeting), Asa Moore Janney (Goose Creek), and Ed Behre (Florida Avenue); and Orthodox, Robert Clark (Richmond), Theodate Souder (Lincoln), and Lucy Wellons (Bethel).

In 1963 each yearly meeting requested the Committee "to study what in our religious experience justifies union--is there a religious basis on which we can unite?" The committee's members labored long over this question. They found much "in our religious experience which justifies union"; but replied, "no" to the question itself. They could not quite agree that worship based on the inward way, on the Light of Christ Within, correlates with the outward way to God, based on the authority of the *Bible*.

The spirit of the 1960s was such, however, that Baltimore Friends decided to unite willy nilly. They established a united Baltimore Yearly Meeting with Hicksite and Orthodox sections. All sessions of the reunited body were to be in common except for a session of each section at least once during each annual gathering. Each monthly meeting could then belong to either of the two sections or to both.[19]

All of Baltimore's monthly meetings agreed with this plan to unite except two. These were Corinth and Somerton, Orthodox meetings in southern Virginia. They and the Upriver and Piney Woods meetings in North Carolina, just below the Virginia line, were already loosely linked in an organization called Tidewater Friends Conference. In 1967 Corinth and Somerton decided to transfer from Baltimore to North Carolina Yearly Meeting Orthodox, with a paid minister to serve them. A few years later, Bethel Meeting which lies between Corinth and Somerton, also decided to transfer to North Carolina Orthodox.

So it was that Baltimore met as one yearly meeting in 1968. So ended the separation of 140 years.

\* \* \*

Ideal classic Quakerism since the 1750s has had two alternating elements:
- For one, Friends retreat into silence, waiting on the still small voice for guidance, and ministering to one another "to the refreshment of the Children of the Light."
- For the other, Friends leave the silence to serve the world, to bring God's kingdom closer to the workaday world.

In 1960s Virginia, Friends found new energy for serving the world. They worked for peace, for the equalness of all Virginians and for the succor of impoverished Virginians. In some ventures Virginia was the stage, in others Friendly Virginians were the actors....

On Tuesday noon, November 2, 1965 Norman and Anne Morrison, a Quaker couple ten years married, ate lunch in their North Baltimore kitchen. Norman was home from work with a cold. Norman over lunch told Anne the news story he'd just read about Father Currien, a French priest serving Vietnamese refugees. U.S. planes had napalmed the refugees' church and village. "I have seen my faithful burned up in napalm," Norman had read. "I have seen the bodies of women and children blown to bits. My God, it is not possible." Norman asked in some anguish "How long can this go on?"

Anne left home about three p.m. to get Ben, six, and Tina, five, from school. When she returned, Norman was gone along with Emily, the year old baby. He drove across the Potomac into Virginia; carried Emily into the great echoing mall of the Pentagon Building; settled her against a wall; sat down on the floor fifteen feet away; poured kerosene over himself, lit a match and gave his body to be burned in protest against the barbarity in Vietnam.

Two days later Anne received the note Norman mailed to her from Virginia just before he died. "Dearest Anne," she read

> For weeks even months I have been praying only that I be shown what I must do. This morning with no warning I was shown as clearly as I was shown that Friday night in August 1955, that you would be my wife. Know that I love thee but must act for the children of the priest's village.

Norman's act made front pages across the nation followed by a rain of letters to editors. Some deprecated what Norman had done, suggesting he was crazy, off his rocker. Others called it heroic, demanding a stop to the carnage in Vietnam. Hundreds of poets wrote threnodies for Norman.

Robert McNamara, U.S. Secretary of Defense, was in his Pentagon office that day. Years later he spoke of Norman's death as "a personal tragedy for me." Before November was out McNamara began to send memos to the White House, suggesting hidden doubts, urging a pause in the bombing. In North Vietnam "Norman Morrison" became a sainted name. The government there issued a postage stamp with Norman's picture on it.[21]

Friends held a memorial service for Norman in Florida Avenue Meeting house. One who spoke then was Norman's friend John Roemer. He said

For Norman reason was not the key to Quakerism...the central reality was the inner experience of God's presence.... Norman felt an ultimate claim was directing him in an inward way to witness against the unspeakable horrors of Vietnam.[22]

After 1965 the Friendly Virginians and Quakers everywhere, worked for peace in new ways:
- Richmond Friends Meeting lent its meeting house to be state headquarters for a Vietnam Summer when Quakers and students organized a summer-long series of anti-war protests.
- Friends in Washington purchased William Penn House near the national Capitol. A succession of Quakers stayed there overnight: to call on their Congressmen, to attend antiwar vigils, read the names of the war dead on the Capitol steps, to build a replica of a "tiger cage" by the Capitol's entrance.[23]
- Friends in Charlottesville held silent vigils on their post office's steps, evoking anger in some postal patrons and whispers of encouragement from others.[24] Baby Jane Pyron, a vigilante in a bassinet, displayed this sign above her downy head: "Life is Precious."

\* \* \*

The Virginia Council on Human Relations chose David Scull for its president in 1965. The next year the council employed Frank Adams, a young newspaperman and member of Virginia Beach Friends' Meeting, for its staff director (VCHR's office was in Richmond, and, yes, this is the same Frank Adams who daringly appeared in Richmond Meeting in summer shorts). No sooner did Frank come to Richmond than VCHR began to pulsate with initiatives to win equality for black Virginians. These included
- Investigating the state government's hiring practices. This revealed that the number of black employees in state agencies approached zero.
- Holding workshops to find ways of building low-cost housing for black families living in shacks.
- Training paramedics to provide health care in rural areas without doctors.
- Registering blacks to vote. In November 1967 Dr. William Ferguson Reid, a Richmond physician, won a seat in the House of Delegates, the first black in Virginia's General Assembly

since 1891. S. O. Sykes, a stonemason, won a place on the Board of Supervisors in Southampton County, the first black elected there since Reconstruction; and Charles City County's voters elected James Bradby, a black man, to be sheriff--unprecedented in Virginia's history![25]

Other Quakers worked in the state on behalf of black people and poor people in ways that would have delighted John Woolman and Robert Pleasants:

- Peggy Spangenthal of Richmond Meeting started Grace House in a blighted Richmond neighborhood--a nursery school, recreation for older children, family counseling, health tips, literacy training.[26]
- Charlottesville Friends moved their meeting place in spring 1967 from the University of Virginia's grounds to a slum house on Charlottesville's Sixth Street. They fixed the house up for use as a Hope House, a community center in the slum. Some neighboring houses had kitchens with dirt floors, and leaky roofs. The Friends came to a sense of the outrage and despair of their black neighbors at having to live on their rickety, segregated street.

Soon after the move to Sixth Street, a woman of the meeting brought together a group of women of the neighborhood. The Quaker woman suggested making necklaces and bracelets out of beans, cloves, and seeds for sale. The neighborhood women took up the idea. They named their handiwork "Hope Beads." For ten years "The Bead Ladies" sold the beads--ranging from gentle dawn colors to hot psychedelic dyes--to shops across the United States. The proceeds supplemented the Bead Ladies' incomes and gave them a sense of self respect and solidarity.

Sometime in June 1968 Victoria Cooley, the meeting's clerk, sent the first of a year-long series of letters to Charlottesville City Council, suggesting steps to improve slum conditions in the city. Council stonewalled the suggestions and did nothing. Finally the Friends nerved themselves to "speak Truth to power." They held a silent vigil on the steps of City Hall, 21 July 1969, then attended that evening's council meeting to press their suggestions. Councilman Joe Wright called Quakers "unAmerican" that sultry evening (referring to the voyage of the *Phoenix*, a vessel with a Quaker crew which had delivered a cargo of medicine to the North and South Vietnamese alike amid much newspaper publicity), and the council continued to do nothing. Of the five all-white councilmen, only Mitchell van Yahres supported the Friends' requests.

Charlottesville's Friends visited city council twice more, supported by a growing number of non-Quaker sympathizers. They requested a fair housing ordinance; an inter-racial committee for unity; an ombudsman for the city's black citizens; more black school board members; and a council of students to advise the school board. This caused Councilman Ken Davis to label the Quakers "anarchists," Council absolutely refused to act.

The Friends then announced a three-day fast for racial harmony in a city park. They invited the five city councilmen to break bread with them at 5:00 p.m. on 2 September 1969, the last day of the fast (council was to meet that evening), but only Mitchell van Yahres accepted the invitation.

That evening 200 black people joined Friends attending the council meeting in City Hall. Some black youths had painted portraits of their heroes on a long wall in the city's Carver Recreation Center--including Frederick Douglass, W. E. B. DuBois, Martin Luther King, Medgar Evers, Charlie Parker, Stokely Carmichael, Malcolm X. The city promptly had the portraits painted over and obliterated. The blacks came to council demanding "Give us back our Wall of Respect." But council refused and instead passed an ordinance outlawing such portraiture on city property, over the deafening objections of its audience. The audience was increasingly noisy at subsequent council meetings, and Mayor G. A. Vogt announced in October that council would hold its meetings in the afternoons (when most residents, having nine-to-five jobs, could not attend).

Councilman Davis added that residents who do not like council's decisions have an alternative: "the courts are always open...so is the ballot box." And when election time came in November, sure enough, all the incumbent councilmen were voted out of office, except Mitchell van Yahres. Charlottesville's first black council member, who later became the city's mayor, was one of the new incumbents.[27]

The Friends of Virginia Beach also acted for their black and poor neighbors. They created the Virginia Beach Friends Housing Corporation in 1969, obtained a Federal grant and built a community of 110 living units for low income families. They called the community Friendship Village and to this day they provide family counselling and similar support for the families.

Richard M. Nixon, a champion of the Establishment, followed Lyndon Johnson into the White House in 1968. He was a member of Whittier Friends Church in California and the son of Hannah Nixon, nee Milhous (a Quaker family for many generations). He was also an ambitious politician who won elections by "playing hardball" and crying "Communist."

As president he set out vigorously to squelch the New Age and restore America to business and politics as usual. His vice-president, Spiro Agnew, inveighed against "nattering nabobs of negativism" and his attorney-general, John Mitchell, demanded "law and order." They largely succeeded. After the colleges opened in September 1970, the campuses were quiet once again and the movement of the Flower Children largely dispersed. Largely but not entirely dispersed.

\* \* \*

Among the early casualties of the hopeful movements of the 1960s was the Virginia Council on Human Relations and its Quaker director. Virginia's black people grew progressively less dependent on their white friends as the sixties wore along. By 1969 suggestions were coming from the black community for "honkies" to step down from civil rights leadership roles in favor of blacks.

In 1969 the Ford Foundation granted funds to VCHR to train blacks for newspaper careers. Frank Adams, VCHR's Quaker honky director, and his friend Raymond Boone, editor of the Richmond *Afro-American*, designed the year-long program. They called it the Frederick Douglass Fellowships in Journalism program and enrolled fifteen fellows: fourteen black and one chicano, nine men and six women.

Frank launched the program in June with typical energy. All went well until the fall, when some of the students demanded payment of their stipends in advance and voiced other grievances. Presently they called for a black to lead the program instead of Frank, and Frank promptly resigned both as program director and as VCHR's director.

His resignation was a bittersweet happening. It symbolized the end of one kind of white participation in the rights struggle and also a coming of age of the blacks' own leaders. Frank accepted the situation with maximum grace. He said of his erstwhile students

> In terms of today's realities, they "got themselves together" and revolted against the establishment. This is in the best tradition of the growing self respect in the black community.[28]

Since VCHR's funds and membership declined thereafter, Richmond's Friends invited the council to move its offices into their meeting house, now at 4500 Kensington Avenue. This was in 1971. Racial discrimination was still high. The Richmond Zoning Board soon ordered the meeting to answer a complaint that it was allowing "business operations" in a residential area. A committee of Richmond Friends tried valiantly to overturn the complaint, but an ouster petition signed by 1,200 residents won out. The council ceased to operate a little later.

Before Frank Adams left, however, VCHR developed an interest in the plight of prisoners. A Quaker member wrote a proposal in aid of the army of people passing through Virginia's city and county jails. The proposal envisioned a corps of volunteers in each Virginia community to work in the jail, help the prisoners to find their way to self-respecting life styles.

Frank and the Quaker VCHR member visited the Virginia Council of Churches and the state's Chaplain's Service to obtain their sponsorship of the proposal. It was named the Offender Aid and Restoration (OAR) project, funds raised and operations begun in six Virginia locales in 1970, and still going and growing.

\* \* \*

A countersurge to the New Age of the 1960s swept Virginia and the nation in the 1970s and 1980s. Conservatism and fundamentalist Christianity went on a roll. The people elected Jimmy Carter, a born again Baptist, to the presidency. But Carter's constituency splintered when evangelical church people became dissatisfied with his views on moral and military matters. According to Richard Viguerie of Falls Church, a fund raiser for conservative causes, President Carter had "surrounded himself with many people who routinely rejected Biblical principles regarding sexual behavior, family responsibility, abortion and other key moral issues."[29]

Two leaders of this conservative wave were Virginia ministers who preached over television networks to millions of listeners: the Reverend Jerry Falwell who broadcast from Lynchburg via the Old Time Gospel Hour, and Reverend Pat Robertson whose Christian Broadcasting Network was based in Portsmouth.

Both men preached the style of Christianity introduced to Virginia by George Whitefield 250 years before. Both became so popular through their preaching as to grow powerful in politics. Jerry Falwell organized the Moral Majority, a coalition of conservatives that helped Ronald Reagan to out-vote Jimmy Carter for the presidency in 1980. In 1985 Pat Robertson began a serious bid for the presidency himself.

Reverend Robertson's young proteges were Jim and Tammy Bakker. They hosted a talk/variety show in Portsmouth, then left to found their own successful PTL (Praise The Lord) Network in Charlotte, North Carolina.

In those years the success of America's mainline churches was mixed:
- The two largest denominations--the Roman Catholic Church and the Southern Baptist Convention--grew rapidly. The Catholics

reported 46,246,175 American members in 1965 and 52,654,908 in 1985. The Southern Baptists reported 10,770,573 members in 1965 and 14,447,364 in 1985.
- Other major denominations declined--Methodists from 11,067,497 to 9,291,936 (a loss of 16 percent); Presbyterian Church U.S.A. from 3,984,460 to 3,048,235 (loss of 23 percent). The Lutheran churches and Episcopalians lost members too.
- Two Gallup polls, one conducted in 1978 and the second in 1988, found that 78 million adults or 44 percent of the U.S. population did not regularly attend a church or synagogue in 1988, compared with 41 percent ten years before. The main reason given for quitting church was that the churches were too concerned with money matters. Others said they did not respond well to a "hierarchy telling people what to do," and "too much pomp and circumstance and dogma."[30]

In 1987 Jim Bakker scandalized his followers by misusing moneys sent in for PTL purposes and by sexual misconduct. Jimmy Swaggart, a famous Texas television evangelist, caused another scandal in 1988. The resulting publicity certainly damaged the fundamentalists' cause. Just as the age of the Flower Children largely ended in 1970 so, as it seems, the counterwave of reaction to that age largely subsided in 1988.

\* \* \*

During all the ferment of the 1960s, 1970s, and 1980s the Friendly Virginians grew in their numbers. Eighteen new meetings, churches, and worship groups started up in Virginia while one--Black Creek Meeting in Southampton County--closed its doors in 1968, after 213 years.

Three of the eighteen new Friends' gatherings had pastors: *Hanover* Friends Church in Mechanicsville, *West End* Friends Church in Richmond, and *Kings Community* Church in Chesterfield. They were organized by church planters of Ohio Yearly Meeting Damascus, which now was re-named Evangelical Friends Church, Eastern Region.

Fifteen of the eighteen met to worship in unprogrammed quietness, in the following order of appearance:
- 1966: Twin worship groups formed in *Roanoke* and *Blacksburg*. The two held monthly meetings for business together and presently became Roanoke-Blacksburg Monthly Meeting.
- 1978-1979: Two more worship groups appeared in the vicinity of Harrisonburg. One became *Harrisonburg* Monthly Meeting affiliated with Baltimore Yearly Meeting; the other *Rockingham* Monthly Meeting, of Ohio Yearly Meeting Conservative.

- 1980-1982: Three worship groups assembled: one in *Washington*, Va., near the former site of Culpeper Meeting; one in the hamlet of *Lively*, Lancaster County, now known as the Northern Neck of Virginia Worship Group and sited close by the long-gone Corotoman Meeting; the third in *Reston*, a planned Fairfax County community.
- 1983: *Williamsburg* Friends Meeting came into existence.
- 1985: as did *Maury River* Meeting near Lexington.
- 1986: Richmond Meeting, overflowing with new attenders, established new worship groups at *Ashland* to the north and *Midlothian* southwest of Richmond.
- 1989-1990: Four more worship groups formed, in *Farmville*, *Fredericksburg*, *Woodstock* (Shenandoah Allowed Meeting), and *Norfolk* (where Elizabeth Harris first seeded Quakerism in Virginia in 1655.)

By the latest account:* Forty-four Friends' groups abide in Virginia: twenty-three unprogrammed, twenty-one with paid pastors.[31]

\* \* \*

In these yeasty latter years a flood of Quaker issues emerged. Three of them especially engaged the Friendly Virginians. They have to do with the world's oceans, gay people, and the longheld enmity between the world's two great powers, the United States and the Soviet Union.

Samuel and Miriam Levering are the Virginia Friends especially concerned for the oceans. Having met and married as Cornell University students, they own a famous apple orchard in mountainous Carroll County, close by the North Carolina line. Along with apple growing they have raised six children; helped to found United World Federalists; and pioneered world law and disarmament initiatives. They worship with the Friends of Mt. Airy Meeting in North Carolina.

Sam chaired the executive council of Friends' Committee on National Legislation for sixteen years. Then in 1972 he agreed to promote a law of the sea treaty, first called for by President Richard Nixon thus:

---

\* FWCC Friends Directory for 1992.

> The nations of the world are now facing decisions of momentous importance to man's use of the oceans...whether the oceans will be used...for the benefit of mankind or whether they will become an arena of unrestrained exploitation.

Accordingly, Sam launched the U.S. Committee for the Oceans, a lobbying project he directed while Miriam headed a separate Ocean Education project. Their aim: to persuade the United States and United Nations to ratify a modern International Law of the Sea. They worked at it in Virginia, Washington, New York and Geneva, lobbying Congress and the U.N., making speeches, writing articles.

The United Nations held Law of the Sea conferences generally twice a year for ten years and generally attended by one or both Leverings. The group finally hammered out a draft treaty in 1982. In 1984, however, President Reagan refused to commit the U.S. to the treaty fully. He decreed that the U.S. would view the treaty's provisions--controlling pollution, conserving fish life, sharing the oil and ore under the ocean bed--as customary law but not as binding *treaty* law.

As of 1991 forty-five of the United Nations had ratified the Law of the Sea Treaty. When sixty U.N. nations ratify, the treaty will have full international force. The nations then will lose a little in terms of sovereign power, but will gain a lot in terms of peaceful co-existence.[32]

Late in the 1960s, America's homosexual men and lesbian women came out of the closet. For thousands of years church and society had denounced them. Their decision to declare themselves, to defend their position, was historic.

The emergence of the gay people horrified conservative Americans. Anita Bryant, a one-time Miss America contestant, led the conservative reaction. She headed a 1977 campaign to repeal a Dade County, Florida, ordinance that forbade job and housing discrimination against gays. Then she and her husband founded Anita Bryant Ministries "to bring America back to God." Conservatives of many creeds backed Anita, including supporters of the Reverend Jerry Falwell, Catholic Archbishop Coleman Carroll, and the Miami Beach B'nai B'rith.[33]

Virginia's Friends divided in their counsels. Some saw every homosexual as a willful pervert who is perfectly capable of normal heterosexual behavior. Others thought that homosexuality represents a variation like left-handedness, an innate tendency, no sin in itself. They came to look on the gays' struggle for equal rights as a new opportunity for Friends, similar to the times when their Quaker forebears had stood up for their own religious rights and for the rights of minorities and women.

Gradually the "no sin in itself" Friends gained strength:
- In 1978 the Friends of Richmond Meeting welcomed the Metropolitan Community Church, a gay Christian congregation, to meet in their Friends' meeting house. Richmond Friends then supported MCC during anti-gay leafleting of their cars, protests from neighbors and a bomb threat.
- 1979: Pendle Hill, the Quaker study center near Philadelphia, published for its Pamphlet Number 226 *Homosexuality and the Bible--an Interpretation* by Walter Barnett.
- 1979 on: Virginia Friends' Meetings welcomed avowed gay people to their memberships, including two Presbyterian ministers whom their denomination refused to ordain.
- 1988: Baltimore Yearly Meeting's new *Faith and Practice* (which several Virginia Friends helped to edit) included this fresh advice:

Friends have a loving concern for the varieties of supportive relationships that exist...persons living alone, two-parent families, single parent families, married and unmarried couples, homosexual and heterosexual couples, single adults or extended families sharing a household, and larger communal groups. At present Friends are divided on the wisdom or rightness of some of those relationships. Nevertheless, we recognize that there are many kinds of domestic living situations in which...a caring, sharing, supportive relationship can grow.

Kent Larrabee, a Philadelphia Friend in his mid-sixties, visited many of the Virginia meetings in 1983. He was just returned from a walk across Russia where he passed out peace leaflets and photographed many attractive Russian faces.

In that year "Communist," "Russian" and "Red" were hate words, commonly used to connote all that good Americans should detest. Kent's message was that "Russians are people too." He related a midnight vision that came to him in his Moscow hotel room. The vision: a Quaker presence in Moscow, a Quaker meeting or center there to work for peace and friendship between the nations.

Janet Riley, then of Charlottesville Friends Meeting, came, as Friends say "under the weight of the concern." She was the main organizer of a group called The Quaker US/USSR Committee. She and other Friends traveled to Moscow. They met Tatiana Pavlova there, a historian who writes about early Quakers. Presently a little worship group began to meet in Tatiana's apartment to seek God's will after the manner of Friends.

The US/USSR Committee created *The Human Experience*, a first-of-its-kind book, published simultaneously in the United States and the Soviet Union. It brings together forty celebrated writers--half of them Americans (including Henry S. Taylor, the Pulitzer Poetry Prize-winner clerk of Goose Creek Meeting) and half Russians--who contributed stories and poems intended to convey the two countries' textures and nuances, how they differ, what they have in common.

Early in the book is a poem by Yevgeny Yevtushenko, *On Borders*. A few lines suggest the book's flavor:

> It was borders who invented police,
>     armies and border guards
> It was borders who invented
> customs-men, passports, and other shit.
> Thank God,
>     we have invisible threads and threadlets,
> born of the threads of blood
>     from the nails in the palms of Christ.
> These threads struggle through,
>     tearing apart the barbed wire.
> leading love to join love
>     and anguish to unite with anguish....
>
> While borders still stand
>     we are all in pre-history
> Real history will start
>     when all borders are gone.

Janet and the Quaker US/USSR Committee are continuing. In 1989 they brought the Russian contributors to *The Human Experience* to the United States for visits to schools and meetings in Virginia and elsewhere, and to join American contributors for three days of literary talk in Florida Avenue Meetinghouse. Four of the American writers paid a return visit to Moscow in 1990.

Now the committee has paired eight schools in the U.S. (including Clark and Johnson Schools in Charlottesville) and eight in Russia, where the boys and girls exchange letters, songs, stories, and dance techniques, and come to know one another as friends.

\* \* \*

The time is the present and still the bipolar tension continues, the dynamic tension between the Inward Light and Scripture, mysticism and orthodoxy that has characterized the Society of Friends since its rise.

Back in 1977 John Linton lectured in London on "Quakerism as Forerunner." The lecture inspired some Friends to form the Quaker Universalist Group in Britain, followed five years later by the Quaker Universalist Fellowship in America. Several Virginia Friends soon joined.

Linton joined the Society of Friends in the belief that Friends are "a group of sincere seekers who eschewed dogmas." But, he said, he soon found that most British Friends still tacitly accepted the orthodox Christian dogmas and assumed the superiority of the Christian religion over all others, whereas Truth is to be found in all religions--"Beyond all the different formulations of words, the Truth remains the same." He then argued that Quakers should abandon their allegiance to Christianity and adopt a universalist position.

John Linton went on to suggest that Quakers, as the mystical wing of Christianity, should realign with the mystical wings of the world's other great religions--Sufi Moslems, Zen Buddhists, Hasidic Hebrews and the like--to be "a worldwide religion, without any particular bias Christian or otherwise, but enshrining the supreme truths of all religions." Mystics of the world everywhere, join hands. Such a realignment would free Friends from the outward, the formal, the legal and the institutional, and focus attention on the Divine that is within.[34]

Early in 1991, leaders of Southwest Yearly Meeting in Whittier, California, made another quite different proposal, to the members of the eighteen yearly meetings that compose Friends United Meeting. The Southwest Friends urged that the "Christ centered *Bible* believer" components of FUM should merge with Evangelical Friends Church; that any others should go to Friends General Conference; and that FUM should be abolished.[35]

Both proposals have plusses and minuses: The Universalist Friends' proposal would preserve Friends' mystical emphasis all right, but it would also sever one of their historic roots, for traditional Friends have viewed the Christian *Bible* as a valuable guide from George Fox's day on. In order to transform the Society of Friends in this way, would not the transformers have to synthesize and braid many traditions? And would not the braiding process give rise to much negotiating, compromising, formalizing and institutionalizing?

The Southwest Friends' proposal certainly would make Evangelical Friends a more homogeneous and like-minded body. But it would also cut them off completely and finally from their historic roots, and leave them with little distinctive character among scores of minor Christian denominations.

The Universalist Friends quote Mahatma Gandhi when he spoke to a gathering of Christian missionaries in Calcutta:

> I do not know what you mean by the Living Christ. If you mean the historic Jesus then I do not feel his presence. But if you mean a spirit guiding me, a presence nearer than my hands and feet...then I do feel such a presence.... Call it Christ or Krishna: that does not matter to me.

But Gandhi also wrote:

> If I could call myself, say, a Christian, or a Mussulman, with my own interpretation of the *Bible* or the *Koran*, I should not hesitate to call myself either. For then Hindu, Christian and Mussulman would be synonymous terms.... During our earthly existence there will always be these labels. I therefore prefer to retain the label of my forefathers so long as it does not...debar me from assimilating all that is good anywhere else.[36]

As already mentioned, Baltimore Yearly Meeting (to which nearly half the local Friends groups in Virginia relate) published a new *Faith and Practice* in 1988. The new book is, in effect, the fifteenth edition published since Baltimore Yearly Meeting formed three centuries ago--the first edition to be fully approved by the members since the yearly meeting reunited in 1968. It is illuminating to see the 1988 edition, blue covered and loose leafed, next to a copy of the 1793 edition, brown and spotted, with its "s's" looking like "f's." The committees of dedicated Friends, both including numerous Virginia Friends, who wrote these editions took years painstakingly to distill and put down on paper the essence of the Quaker faith.

What can be learned by comparing these two statements by the same Quaker body--the one made 150 years after the Quakers' rise, the other 195 years still further along the Quaker way? What new insights have come to Friends since 1793? What had been discarded, what changed, and what remains constant and unchanged through all the years?

- New:  The 1988 book declares that "Art may carry spiritual force.... Friends may express their own creative spirit through whatever media or in whatever ways seem appropriate." This concept is altogether missing in the 1793 book. Indeed in the older book it is "seriously advised, that no Friends suffer

romances, play-books or other vain and idle pamphlets in their houses or families."
- Discarded: Friends in 1793 were instructed to practice meekness. "A Christian prudence and meek deportment will bear a becoming testimony," declared the discipline. Let "the restoring spirit of meekness and Christian love abound," it urges a few pages later. All Friends are advised to "use few words in their dealings lest they bring dishonor to the Truth of God through their forwardness."
- Changed: A pull exists always in any community of men and women between those who regard the well-being of the whole community as more important and those who believe that each individual must be free to work out his or her own destiny. This tension has always been strong in the Society of Friends, between the authority of the meeting on the one hand, and its mystically minded members on the other who feel themselves taught of God and jealous of any authority but that of the Light Within. It is clear from reading the two books that the authority of the meeting was more controlling in 1793 than it is today.

  The 1793 discipline states positively what Friends must or must not do, while the 1988 *Faith and Practice* has a much less authoritarian tone, rather a tone of shouldness or oughtness. The older book lists a long series of practices for which offending Friends are to "stand disowned, till they shall repent and give satisfaction," from "excess of drinking, swearing, cursing, lying" to "unseemly company-keeping with women" to "taking oaths" and "military service." The 1988 book contains none of these rules. Rather, it emphasizes the role of the meeting as a spiritual community and as a caring community. It calls for Friends to labor "lovingly and patiently in a spirit of reconciliation" with any member whose "conduct or publicly expressed views appear to deny Friends' beliefs" before "termination of membership for cause."
- Unchanged: After all the additions, discards and changes, there remains a profound kinship between the two books that bridges the six generations between their Quaker authors:

*Love* and *the Truth* are words written over and over in both books. They describe the Quaker concept of what God is like, and they also are used as the principal guideposts for Friends to follow in the living of their lives. "Love" appears eighteen times in the old book, twenty-nine times in the new. "Truth" appears thirty-one times in 1793 and seventeen times in the new edition.

Friends still value simple life-styles:

1793: Advised that Friends take care to keep to...plainness in language, habit, deportment and behavior, that the simplicity of truth not be lost.

1988: Sincerity, simplicity and moderation are vital to all the dealings of life.... Self indulgent habits and luxurious living dull our awareness.

The testimony for peace and against violence remains steady:

1793: ...Importance of being clear from the blood of all men.... In the peaceable spirit of Christ.... ...Such as do not maintain our ancient Christian testimonies against...military services...let them be speedily dealt with.

1988: Friends have a settled intention to practice love and to make peace. As peacemakers we hold that attitudes of justice and compassion are basic.

Both orthodox and universal-leaning Friends could take some comfort in this 1988 *Faith and Practice*:

- For the orthodox it is clear that Friends still respect the Judaeo-Christian tradition. There are twenty references to the *Bible* and seventeen references to Christ.
- For universalists, there are the 1988 book's opening words, the insight of Quaker elders gathered at Balby, Yorkshire in 1656:

Dearly beloved Friends, these things we do not lay upon you as a rule or form to walk by, but that all, with the measure of light which is pure and holy, may be guided,; and so in the Light walking and abiding, these things may be fulfilled in the Spirit, not from the letter, for the letter killeth while the Spirit giveth life.

\* \* \*

Now it is the summer season. The windows of Virginia's Quaker meeting houses open to soft air. Bird song punctuates the silence and the swish of passing cars. Worshippers rise in the silence to voice inmost thoughts. God, God, love and truth, compassion, peace, God. The words come quietly, passionately, comforting, meant. Presently the clerk turns gravely smiling and shakes a neighbor's hand. The Friends rise from their meeting then and return to the world. The meeting is over, the service has begun.

Who but God can say what is to happen next, this season, in the seasons waiting to come? Poised delicately in time, an avalanche of seasons.

END

# QUAKER MEETINGS IN VIRGINIA
## With Meetings Existing in 1993 Underlined
(numbers correspond with locations on endpaper map)

1. <u>Achilles Friends Church</u> begun 1922 in Chesapeake.
2. Alexandria (1783-1885) Alexandria Monthly Meeting has been based in Woodlawn's meeting house in recent years. See Woodlawn below.
3. Amelia (1721-1793) also known as Pattison's Meeting and Appomattox. In Amelia County.
4. <u>Ashland Indulged Meeting</u> begun 1986.
5. Back Creek (1759-1869) aka Jesse Pugh's Meeting. In Frederick County.
6. Banister (1758-1811) aka Halifax and Kirby's. Halifax Co.
7. Bear Garden (1767-1809) Hampshire Co., now WVa.
8. Beaver Dam (1755-1783) Hanover Co.
9. Bennett's Creek (1731-1821) Portsmouth.
10. Berkeley (1778-1832) Formerly Bullskin Meeting. Jefferson County, now WVa.
11. <u>Bethel Monthly Meeting</u> begun 1880. Southampton Co.
12. Binford's (1699-1721) and 1820-1826) aka Merchant's Hope. Prince George Co.
13. Black Creek (1691-1805) New Kent Co.
14. Black Creek (1760-1968) Sedley, Southampton Co.
15. <u>Blacksburg Monthly Meeting</u> begun 1966.
16. Blackwater (1721-1860), first known as Surry. Surry Co.
17. Blue Ridge Mission (1883-1916) Friend's Mission. Patrick Co.
18. Bluestone (1781-1783) Tazewell Co.
19. Bufkin's (1698-1780) aka Leven Bufkin's. Portsmouth.
20. Burk's Fork (1800-1812) Montgomery Co.
21. Burleigh (1696-1832) or Burley. Prince George Co.
22. Butler's (1698-1800) Dinwiddie Co.
23. Camp Creek (1747-1790) Louisa Co.
24. Caroline (1739-1844) at Golansville, Caroline Co.
25. Cedar Creek (1721-1860) Hanover Co.
26. <u>Center Valley - Mountain View Monthly Meeting</u> begun 1905. Galax.
27. <u>Centre Monthly Meeting</u> begun 1734. Winchester.
28. <u>Charlottesville Monthly Meeting</u> begun 1938 to 1942. Resumed 1952.
29. Chestnut Creek (1785-1841) Grayson Co.
30. Chuckatuck (1656-1768) Portsmouth.
31. <u>Corinth Monthly Meeting</u> begun 1880. Southampton Co.
32. Corrotoman (1656-1659, then revived a few years later and continued until about 1686) Lancaster Co.
33. Crooked Run (1756-1810) Warren Co.
34. Culpeper (1777-1797) Rappahannock Co.
35. Curles (1678-1805) Henrico Co.
36. <u>Danville-Longview Friends Church</u> begun 1952.
37. Dillon's Run (1795-1822) aka Great Cacapon. Hampshire Co., now WVa.
38. Douglas's (1748-1806) Orange Co.
39. Duff's (1699-1743) earlier Peter Skinner's. Westmoreland Co.
40. Durham's (1790-?) Mecklenburg Co.
41. Fairfax (1733-1929) Waterford, Loudoun Co.
42. Faith (1977-1984) Fairfax Co.
43. <u>Ferry Road Friends Church</u> begun 1947. Danville.
44. Fine Creek (1756-1775) Cumberland Co.
45. <u>First Friends Church of Hampton</u> begun 1906.
46. Fork Creek (1746-1778) Louisa Co.
47. <u>Fredericksburg Preparative Meeting</u> begun 1989.
48. Fruit Hill (1790-1814) Grayson Co.
49. <u>Galax Monthly Meeting</u> begun 1926.
50. Gap (1756-1810) Hillsboro, Loudoun Co.

51. Genito (1723-1833) first known as Dover. Goochland Co.
52. Goodspur (1790-1800) or Dugspur. Carroll Co.
53. Goose Creek (1757-1813) or Lower Goose Creek. Bedford Co.
54. Goose Creek (1788-1812) or Upper Goose Creek. Montvale, Bedford Co.
55. Goose Creek Monthly Meeting, begun 1744. Lincoln, Loudoun Co.
56. Gravelly Run (1767-1830) Dinwiddie Co.
57. Gravel Springs (1700s) Frederick Co.
58. Guilford Creek (1677-1729) or Muddy Creek. Accomack Co.
59. Harrisonburg Monthly Meeting begun 1983.
60. Hill's Creek (1778-1803) Campbell Co.
61. Hopewell Monthly Meeting begun 1732, aka Opequon. Frederick Co.
62. Hopewell (Orthodox) (1829-1935) Frederick Co.
63. Howard's Lick (1750-1767) or North Fork. Petersburg, now WVa.
64. Hunnicutt's (1718-1762) Prince George Co.
65. Ivy Creek (1795-1812) Bedford Co.
66. Johnson's (1761-1845) Southampton Co.
67. King's Community Church begun 1987. Chesterfield Co.
68. Ladd's (1790-1808) or Taylor's Creek. Mecklenburg Co.
69. Langley Hill Monthly Meeting begun 1958, formerly Vienna Meeting. McLean, Fairfax Co.
70. Langley's (1755-1767) or Whippanock. Dinwiddie Co.
71. Lawnes Creek (1699-1710) Surry County.
72. Leesburg (1787-1807)
73. Lincoln (1837-1948) Loudoun Co.
74. Little Cacapon (1748-1755) Hampshire Co., now WVa.
75. Magothy Bay (1705-1732) Northampton Co.
76. Maple Spring (1807-1813) Scott Co.
77. Maury River Monthly Meeting begun 1985 nr Lexington.
78. Middle Creek (1762-1828) Darkesville, Berkeley Co. now WVa.
79. Midlothian Preparative Meeting begun 1986. Chesterfield Co.
80. Mill Creek (1759-1800) Arden, Berkeley Co., now WVA.
81. Mount Pleasant (1771-1809) aka Fawsett's or Cedar Creek. Frederick Co.
82. Mount Pleasant (1790-1825, and revived briefly during the 1980s) Grayson Co.
83. Murdaugh's (1710-1766) aka Marshy Creek. Suffolk
84. Nansemond (1677-1730) aka Southern Branch. Nansemond Co.
85. Nassawaddox (1656-1716) nr Franktown, Northampton Co.
86. Neill Chapel (1894-1901) Westmoreland Co.
87. New Hope Friends Church begun 1987. Chesterfield Co.
88. New Point Friends Church begun 1911. Mathews Co.
89. Newport News-Colony Friends Church, begun 1927. Formerly Deep Creek.
90. Norfolk Worship Group (1656-1663 and resumed 1990)
91. Northumberland (1650s and 1660s) Northumberland Co.
92. Onancock or Occahannock (1678-1699) Northampton Co.
93. Pagan Creek (1673-1790) aka Levy Neck, near Smithfield.
94. Peniel Friends Church begun 1921. Mathews Co.
95. Pisquinoqy Swamp (1719-1775) aka Grassy Swamp and Swamp.
96. Pine Creek (1882-1889) Wythe Co.
97. Portsmouth-First Evangelical Friends Church begun 1893.
98. Providence Friends Church begun 1953. Virginia Beach.
99. Providence (1736-1758) aka Beeson's nr Martinsburg, now WVa. Later reconstituted as Tuscarora.
100. Quaker Lake Preparative Meeting begun 1988 nr Farmville.
101. Reedy Island (1792-1812) Pittsylvania Co.
102. Rescue Friends Church begun 1913. Nr Smithfield.
103. Reston Monthly Meeting begun 1982. Fairfax Co.

104. <u>Richmond Monthly Meeting</u> begun 1795.
105. <u>Richmond-Hanover Friends Church</u> begun 1963.
106. Ridge (1777-1830) aka Hackney's and Lower Ridge. Whitehall, Frederick Co.
107. Ridge (1735-1920) aka Apple Pie Ridge, Upper Ridge and Lupton's. Frederick Co.
108. Road Creek (1802-1810) Carroll Co.
109. <u>Roanoke Monthly Meeting</u> begun 1966.
110. <u>Rockingham Monthly Meeting</u> begun 1978 nr Harrisonburg.
111. Sandy Creek (1792-1865) Monongalia Co., now WVa.
112. Seacock (1788-1817) Southampton Co.
113. Seneca (1781-1810) Campbell Co.
114. <u>Shenandoah Allowed Meeting</u> begun 1990. Woodstock, Shenandoah Co.
115. Silcott Springs (1889-1924) nr Purcellville, Loudoun Co.
116. Skimino (1698-1827) York Co.
117. Smith's Creek (1736-1810) aka Broadway, Shenandoah and New Market, held first in Rockingham and later Shenandoah Co.
118. <u>Somerton Monthly Meeting</u> begun 1672. Suffolk.
119. South Fork (1750-1890) Unison, Loudoun Co.
120. Southland (1772-1805) aka Mount Pony. Nr Stevensburg, Culpeper Co.
121. South River (1757-1839). Lynchburg.
122. Stafford (1769-1807) aka Potomac Creek. Stafford Co.
123. Stanton's (1760-1829) Sussex Co.
124. Sugar Loaf Mountain (1747-1754) Keswick, Albemarle Co.
125. Swansqut (1736-1790) Accomack Co.
126. Terrasco Neck (1672-1772) Isle of Wight Co.
127. <u>Trinity Friends Church</u> begun 1947. Martinsville.
128. Tuscarora (1760-1796) replaced Providence Meeting. Nr Martinsville, now WVa.
129. Upper Machodoc (1681-1689) Westmoreland Co.
130. Vick's (1768-1825) Southampton Co.
131. <u>Virginia Beach Monthly Meeting</u> begun 1954.
132. <u>Wakefield Friends Church</u> begun 1990. Portsmouth.
133. Ward's (1770-1790) aka Sadler's. Brunswick Co.
134. Ward's Gap (1795-1825) Hillsville, Carroll Co.
135. Warwick (1696-1720) aka Denby and York. York Co.
136. <u>Washington Worship Group</u> begun 1980. Washington, Rappahannock Co.
137. <u>West End Friends Church</u> begun 1987. Richmond.
138. Western Branch (1672-1844) aka Lower. Isle of Wight County.
139. Weyanoke (1699-1841) formerly known as James Howard's or Old Man's Neck. Charles City County.
140. Wheeling (1789-1823) aka Head of Wheeling now WVa.
141. White Oak Swamp (1722-1807) aka Henrico or Chickahominy Swamp. Henrico Co.
142. <u>Williamsburg Monthly Meeting</u> begun 1983.
143. <u>Woodlawn</u> begun 1846, now known as Alexandria Monthly Meeting. Fairfax Co.

Started in late 1992.

144. <u>Floyd Monthly Meeting</u>, Floyd Co.
145. <u>Lynchburg Worship Group</u>

## ACKNOWLEDGEMENTS

Gathering material for *The Friendly Virginians* has been a thirty-year adventure, from Friends House in London to the great Huntington Library in Pasadena. I harvested facts and ambiance from thirty-five history repositories and troubled more than a hundred guardians of manuscripts and rare books to delve into their collections. Virtually every one of these kind professionals treated me courteously.

I am most grateful to certain individual librarians: Elizabeth Potts Brown and Diana Peterson of Haverford College's Quaker Collections; Nancy Speers and Mary Ellen Chijioke of the Friends Historical Library at Swarthmore College; Carole Treadway of Guilford College's Friends Historical Collection; and Mabel Talley of the Charlottesville-Albemarle Historical Society. Staff members of the University of Virginia's Alderman Library, the State Library of Virginia and the Library of Congress were especially helpful.

My creative wife, Carolyn, made many timely suggestions. Brother Scott and daughter Laura accompanied me on photo-gathering trips around Virginia which were good times. Gail and Emilie Worrall and Jackie Fitzgerald did the word-processing, and showed me some things about computers in the process. Chic Moran and Ben Branch, my fellow Quakers, were consistently encouraging.

Finally, seven knowledgeable friends read and mended the manuscript *in toto*. Beside Ben Branch, these are Werner Janney, Editorial Staff, retired, *National Geographic Magazine*; Herbert Tucker of the University of Virginia's English faculty, Arnold Ricks and Marilyn Dell Brady, professors of history at Bennington and Virginia Wesleyan Colleges respectively; Charles Fager, editor of *A Friendly Letter*, and Marie Tyler-McGraw, former Senior Historian of the Valentine Museum.

Thank you all, dear friends.

# BIBLIOGRAPHY.

This listing is arranged alphabetically as follows: *books* by last name of author; *Periodicals and newspapers* by the title of the publication; and *manuscripts* by name of the preserving institution.

Adams, Nancy. *Report to the American Friends Service Committee*, not published, 10-30-1965.
Alderman Library of the University of Virginia. Manuscripts.
Alderson, William T. *The Freedman's Bureau in Virginia*. (a doctoral thesis of Vanderbilt University, Nashville), 1951.
Alley, Robert S. *James Madison on Religious Liberty*. Buffalo: Prometheus Books, 1985.
American Antiquarian Society Proceedings.
American Historical Association Annual Reports.
American Philosophical Society, Philadelphia. Manuscript.
Ames, Susie M. *Studies of the Virginia Shore in the 17th Century*, Richmond, 1940.
Anderberg, Lorna A. *Comparison of Alexandria Quakers to the Population of White Alexandria*, Alexandria, VA, ca 1986.
Andrews, Matthew P. *Virginia. the Old Dominion*, Richmond, 1949.
Anscombe, Francis A. *I Have Called You Friends: The Story of Quakerism in North Carolina*. Boston, 1959.
Anthony, Katherine. *Dolly Madison, Her Life and Times*, Garden City, NY: Doubleday, 1949.
Asbury, Francis. *Journal and Letters*, Nashville: Abingdon Press, 1958.
Ashmead, Henry G. *Historical Sketch of Chester on Delaware*, 1883.
Augusta County Historical Society. *Great Valley Patriots: Western Virginia's Struggle for Liberty*, Staunton, VA, 1976.

Backhouse, James. *Life and Correspondence of William and Alice Ellis*. London, 2nd Edition, 1850.
Bacon, Margaret H. *Rebellion at Christiana*, New York / Crown, 1975.
Bacon, Margaret H. *As the Way Opens: The Story of Quaker Women in America*, Richmond, IN.: Friends United Press, 1980.
Bailey, James H. *A History of the Diocese of Virginia: The Formative Years*, Richmond, 1956.
Baltimore Evening Sun newspaper.
Baltimore Yearly Meeting Indian Committee. *Report on a Mission to The Indians*, 1804.

Baltimore Yearly Meeting (Hicksite). *Memorials Concerning Several Ministers and Others Deceased of the Religious Society of Friends within the Limits of Baltimore Yearly Meeting*, Baltimore, 1875.

Baltimore Yearly Meeting (Orthodox). *Minutes of Pastoral Committee*, not published, 1877 et seq.

Barclay, Abram R. *Letters. Etc. of Early Friends*, London, 1841.

Barclay, Robert. *An Apology for the True Christian Divinity: Being an Explanation and Vindication of the Principles and Doctrines of the People Called Quakers*. Philadelphia: Friends Book Store, 1906 (first ed. 1675).

Barnard, Ella K. *Dorothy Payne. Quakeress*, Philadelphia, 1909.

Barnes, Gilbert H. *The Anti-Slavery Impulse, 1830-1844*. New York: Harcourt Brace and World, 1964 (second edition).

Bassuk, Daniel. *Abraham Lincoln and The Quakers*, Wallingford, PA (Pendle Hill Pamphlet #275), 1987.

Bates, Onward. *Bates et al of Virginia and Missouri*. Chicago, 1914.

Bauman, Richard. *For The Reputation of Truth: Politics. Religion and Conflicts Among the Pennsylvania Quakers. 1750-1800*, Baltimore: Johns Hopkins Press, 1971.

Beeman, Richard. *The Evolution of the Southern Back Country: A Case Study of Lunenberg County. Virginia. 1746-1852*, Philadelphia: University of Pennsylvania Press, 1984.

Bell, James P. *Our Quaker Friends of Ye Olden Time*, Lynchburg, VA, 1905.

Benezet, Anthony. *Memoir* (revised with additions by Wilson Armistead), London, 1859 (reprinted Westport, NY, 1971).

Benjamin, Philip S. *The Philadelphia Quakers in the Industrial Age. 1865-1920*. Philadelphia: Temple University Press, 1976.

Berlin, Ira. *Slaves Without Masters: The Free Negro in the Ante Bellum South*, New York: Pantheon, 1974.

Besse, Joseph. *Sufferings of the People Called Quakers for the Testimony of a Good Conscience, 1650 to 1680*. London, 1753.

Bill, J. Brent. *David Updegraff, Quaker Holiness Preacher*, Richmond IN: Friends United Press, 1983.

Bishop, George. *New England Judged by the Spirit of the Lord*, London, 1703 (2nd edition).

Blackburn, Joyce. *George Wythe of Williamsburg*, New York: Harper & Row, 1975.

Blacksburg (VA) News Messenger newspaper.

Blake, W. A. *History of Slavery and the Slave Trade*, Columbus, OH, 1860.

Blanton, Wyndham B. *Medicine in Virginia in the 17th century*: Richmond, 1930.

Bliven, Bruce, Jr. *The American Revolution. 1760-1783*, New York: Random House, 1958.

Blockson, Charles L. *The Underground Railroad*, New York: Berkley, 1989.

Blum, John M. et al. *The National Experience: A History of the United States*, New York: Harcourt, Brace and World, 1963.

Boddie, John B. *17th Century Isle of Wight. Virginia*, Chicago, 1938.

Bohannan, Aurelius W. *Old Surry*, Petersburg, VA, 1927.

Bond, James O. *Walk Cheerfully over the Earth*, Baltimore: Gateway, 1985.

Bowden, James. *History of the Society of Friends in America*, London, 1854.

Bowen, L. P. *Days of Makemie: or The Vine Planted. 1680-1700*, Philadelphia: Presbyterian Board of Publication, 1885.

Boyd, Percival. *Boyd's Marriage Index*, London: Society of Genealogists, ca 1930.

Boyle, Sarah Patton. *The Desegregated Heart*, New York: Morrow, 1962.

Brailsford, Mabel R. *Quaker Women. 1650-1690*, London, 1915.

Braithwaite, William C. *Beginnings of Quakerism*, London, 1970 (2nd edition).

Braithwaite, William C. *Tho Second Period of Quakerism*, London, 1961 (2nd edition).

Branch, Benjamin H. Miscellany, not published, 1983 et seq.

Branch, Benjamin H., comp. Extracts from the *Interchange*, beginning Twelfth month, 1884.

Branch, Benjamin H. *A Historical Travel Among Quakers*, not published, 1985.

Brandt, Francis B. *The Wissahickon Valley*, Philadelphia, 1927.

Brawley, Benjamin. *Doctor Dillard of the Jeanes Fund*, New York, 1930.

Breault, Judith C. *The World of Emily Howland--Odyssey of a Humanitarian*, Millbrae, CA: Les Femmes, 1976.

Brinton, Howard H. *Quaker Journals: Varieties of Religious Experience Among Friends*, Wallingford, PA, 1972.

Brisbane, Robert H. *The Black Vanguard*, Valley Forge: Judson Press, 1970.

Brissot, Jacques-Pierre, *New Travels in The United States of America*, London, 1792 (reprinted 1964).

Brock, Peter. *Pacifism in the United States: from the Colonial Era to the First World War*, Princeton, 1968.

Brookes, Anthony S. *Friend Anthony Benezet*, Philadelphia, 1937.

Brown, Douglas S. *History of Lynchburg's Pioneer Quakers. 1754-1936*, Lynchburg, 1936.

Brown, Robert E. and B. Katherine. *Virginia 1705-1786: Democracy or Aristocracy?*, East Lansing, MI, 1964.

Brown, Stuart E., Jr. *Virginia Baron: The Story of Thomas. Sixth Lord Fairfax*, Berryville, VA, 1965.

Bruce, Philip A. *Institutional History of Virginia in the 19th Century*, New York: Putnam, 1910.

Bruce, Philip A. *Virginia Plutarch*, Chapel Hill: University of North Carolina Press, 1929.

Bruce, William C. *John Randolph of Roanoke*, New York: Putnam, 1922.

Bruns, Roger E. *Am I Not a Man and Brother: The Anti-Slavery Crusade of Revolutionary America, 1688-1788*, New York: Chelsea House, 1977.

Brydon, George M. *Virginia's Mother Churches*, Richmond, Virginia Historical Society, 1952.

Budge, Frances Anne. *Annals of the Early Friends*, Philadelphia, 1908.

Burk, John D. *The History of Virginia from the First Settlement to the Present Day*, Petersburg, VA, 4 volumes, 1804-16.

Burke, James L. and Donald E. Bensch. *Mount Pleasant and the Early Quakers of Ohio*, Columbus: Ohio Historical Society, 1975.

Burrough, Edward. *The Memorable Works of a Son of Thunder and Consolation*, London (?), 1672.

Byrd, William, II. *Dividing Line Histories*, William K. Boyd ed., Raleigh: North Carolina Historical Commission, 1929.

Byrd, William, II. *Secret Diary. 1709-12*, Louis B. Wright and Marion Tinling ed., Richmond, 1941.

Cabell, Margaret C.A. *Sketches and Recollections of Lynchburg by the Oldest Inhabitant*, Richmond, 1858.

Cadbury, Henry J. *Friendly Heritage: Letters from the Quaker Past*, Norwalk, CT: Silvermine, 1972.

Cady, Edwin H. *John Woolman*, New York: Washington Square Press, 1963.

Caldwell, J. A. *History of Belmont and Jefferson Counties, Ohio*, Wheeling, 1880.

Callahan, North. *Daniel Morgan, Ranger of the Revolution*, New York: Holt Rinehart, 1961.

Campbell, Thomas E. *Colonial Caroline: A History of Caroline County. Virginia*, Richmond, 1954.

Canter, Bernard comp. *The Quaker Bedside Book*, New York: McKay, 1952.

Carroll, Joseph C. *Slave Insurrections in the United States. 1800-1865*, New York: Negro Universities Press, third edition, 1970.

Carroll, Kenneth L. *John Perrot: Early Quaker Schismatic*, London: Friends Historical Society, 1971.
Cartland, Fernando G. *Southern Heroes*, Cambridge, MA, 1895.
Catterall, Helen T. ed. *Judicial Cases Concerning American Slavery and the Negro*, Washington, DC: Carnegie Institution, five volumes, 1926-37.
Chace, Elizabeth B. and Lucy B. Lovell. *The Quaker Sisters*, New York: Liveright, 1937.
Charles, Helen W. ed. *Quaker Chuckles*, Oxford, OH, 1961.
Charlottesville (VA) Daily Progress newspaper.
Child, L. Maria. *Isaac T. Hopper: A True Life*, Boston, 1854.
Child, L. Maria. *Memoir of Benjamin Lay*, New York: American Anti-Slavery Society, 1842.
Chitwood, Oliver P. *History of Colonial America*, New York: Harper, third edition, 1937.
Christian, W. Asbury. Richmond: *Her Past and Present*, Spartanburg, SC, 1973 (reprint of 1912 edition).
Churchman, John. *Journal*, Philadelphia, 1779.
Clark, Allen C. *Life and Letters of Dolly Madison*, Washington, DC, 1914.
Clement, Maud C. *History of Pittsylvania County. Virginia*, Lynchburg, 1953 (reprint of 1929 edition).
Cocke, William R., III, comp. *Hanover County Chancery Wills and Notes*, Columbia, VA, 1940.
Coffin, Addison. *Early Settlement of Friends in North Carolina: Traditions and Reminiscences*, not published and undated (in Guilford College Library).
Coffin, Addison. *Life and Travels*, Cleveland, 1897.
Coffin, Levi. *Reminiscences*, Cincinnati, 1876.
Columbia Historical Society of Washington, D.C. Records.
Comly, John. *Journal*, Philadelphia, 1853.
Comly, John. *Grammar and Spelling Book*, Philadelphia, Ninth edition, 1818.
Comly, John and Isaac ed. *Friends' Miscellany*, Byberry, PA, 12 volumes, 1831-39.
Comstock, Elizabeth L. *Life and Letters*, completed by her sister, C. Hare, Philadelphia: Winston, 1895.
Cook, Ebenezer. *The Sot Weed Factor*, Bernard C. Steiner ed., 1708 edition, Baltimore: Maryland Historical Society, 1900.
Craven, Avery. *The Coming of the Civil War*, Chicago, 1942.
Cregar, William F. *Ancestry of Samuel Stockton White. D.D.S.*, Philadelphia, 1888.
Crosfield, Helen G. *Margaret Fox of Swarthmoor Hall*, London, 1951.

Crouch, Kenneth E. *Lower Goose Creek Meeting and Quaker Baptist Church. 1757-1957*, Bedford, VA, 1957.
Cummings, Charles M. *Yankee Quaker. Confederate General: The Curious Career of Bushrod Rust Johnson*, Rutherford NJ: Fairleigh Dickinson University Press, 1971.
Cunliffe, Marcus et al. *The Story of America-Manifest Destiny*, New York: Torstar, 1975.
Current, Richard N. et al. *United States History*, Glenview, IL: Scott Foresman, 1967.
Cutts, Lucia B. *Letters of Dolly Madison*. New York, 1986.

Dabney, Virginius. *Virginia, the New Dominion*, Charlottesville: University Press of Virginia, 1983.
Daniels, Jonathan. *The Randolphs of Virginia*, Garden City, NY: Doubleday, 1972.
Davidson, Marshall B. *Life in America*, Boston: Houghton Mifflin, 1951.
Davis, Anna H. *James and Lucretia Mott*, Boston: Houghton Mifflin, 1884.
Davis, Eliza T. comp. *Surry County Records, 1652-1684*, Baltimore: Genealogical Publishing Company, 1980.
Davis, Harry A. *Davis Family of Wales and America*, Washington, DC, 1927.
Day, Sherman. *Historical Collections*, Philadelphia, 1843.
Dewsbury, William. *Works*.
Dinwiddie, Robert. *Official Records When Lieutenant Governor of the Colony of Virginia, 1751-1758*, Richmond: Virginia Historical Society, 1883
District of Columbia History Curriculum Project. *City of Magnificent Intentions: A History of the District of Columbia*.
Doherty, Robert W. *The Hicksite Separation--A Sociological Analysis*, New Brunswick, NJ: Rutgers University Press, 1967.
Dorman, John F. comp. *Caroline County. Virginia. Order Book. 1740-46*, Washington, DC, 1971.
Drake, Thomas E. *Quakers and Slavery in America*, New Haven, CT, 1950.
Drinker, Elizabeth. *Extracts from the Journal of Elizabeth Drinker*, Henry D. Biddle ed., Philadelphia: Lippincott, 1889.
Dunlap, William C. *Quaker Education in Baltimore and Virginia Yearly Meetings*, Philadelphia, 1936.

Early, Ruth H. *Campbell Chronicles and Family Sketches. 1782-1926*, Lynchburg, 1927.

Easley, S. C. and S. Emmett Lucas, Jr., ed. *Virginia Colonial Aristocrats*, ca 1929.

Eaton, Clement. *Freedom of Thought in the Old South*, New York, 1964.

Eaton, Clement. *A History of the Old South*, New York: MacMillan, second edition, 1964.

Eckenrode, Hamilton J. *The Political History of Virginia During the Reconstruction*, Baltimore: Johns Hopkins Press, 1904 (numbers 6-8 of Series 22 of Johns Hopkins University Studies in Historical and Political Science).

Eckenrode, Hamilton J. *The Revolution in Virginia*, Boston: Houghton Mifflin, 1916.

Edmondson, William. *Journal*, Dublin, 1715.

Elliott, Errol T. *Quaker Profiles from the American West*, Richmond, IN: Friends United Press, 1972.

Evangelical Friends Church Eastern Region, *175th Anniversary Book*, Canton, OH, 1987.

Evans, Charles comp. *American Bibliography*, Worcester, MA: American Antiquarian Society, 1959.

Evans, William. *Journal*, Philadelphia, 1870.

Evans, William and Thomas. *Friends Library*, Philadelphia, 14 volumes, 1837-50.

Evans, William Bacon comp. *Dictionary of Quaker Biography*, maintained and interleaved with a Dictionary of English Quaker Biography by the Quaker Collection staffs of Haverford and Swarthmore Colleges.

Evans, Willis F. *History of Berkeley County. West Virginia*, Martinsburg, WV, 1928.


Fabre, Emile ed. *God's Underground*, St. Louis: Bethany Press, 1970.

Fager, Charles E. *A Man Who Made a Difference--the Life of David H. Scull*, McLean, VA: Langley Hill Friends Meeting, 1985.

Farrar, Emmie F. and Emilee H. Cantieri. *Old Virginia Houses Along the Fall Line*, New York, 1971.

Fisher, Sydney G. *The True William Penn*, Philadelphia, 1900.

Fiske, John. *The Dutch and English Colonies in America*, Boston: Houghlin Mifflin, 1927.

Flake, Carol. *Redemptorama: Culture. Politics and the New Evangelicalism*, Garden City, NY: Doubleday, 1984.

Fleet, Beverly and Margaret M. Ayres comp. *Charles City County Orders, 1655-1696*, 5 volumes, 1941-1968.

Follmer, Don ed. *The Virginia Horse Country* Middleburg, VA 3rd edition, 1976.

Fontaine, John. *Journal* (Edward D. Alexander ed.), Williamsburg: Colonial Williamsburg Foundation, 1972.
Foote, William H. *Sketches of Virginia, Historical and Biographical*, Richmond: John Knox Press, 1966 (reprint of 1850 edition).
Forbush, Bliss. *Elias Hicks. Quaker Liberal*, New York: Columbia University Press, 1956.
Forbush, Bliss. *History of Baltimore Yearly Meeting of Friends*, Sandy Spring, MD, 1972.
Forbush, Bliss. *Moses Sheppard. Quaker Philanthropist of Baltimore*, Philadelphia: Lippincott, 1968.
Ford, Alice. *Edward Hicks. His Life and Art*, New York: Abbeville, 1985.
Fox, Early L. *The American Colonization Society, 1817-1840*, Baltimore: Johns Hopkins Press, 1919.
Fox, George. *Journal*, John Nickalls ed., London: Religious Society of Friends, 1975.
Franklin, Benjamin. *Autobiography*, New York: Washington Square Press, 1966.
Freeman, Douglas S. *George Washington*, New York: Scribners, 1948.
*Friend, The* (London).
*Friend, The* (Philadelphia, 1828-1941).
*Friendly Letter, A*, newsletter.
Friends Association of Philadelphia and Vicinity for the Relief of Colored Freedmen. *Fourth Annual Report*, Philadelphia, 1867.
Friends General Conference pub. *Quaker Torch Bearers*, Philadelphia, 1943.
Friends Historical Association of Philadelphia periodicals, 1906 to date with titles as follows:
*Bulletin of Friends Historical Society*, 1906-1921
*Bulletin of Friends Historical Association*,. 1922-1961
*Quaker History*, 1962 to date
Friends Historical Society of London periodicals.
Friends House, London, Manuscripts.
*Friends Journal* (formerly *Friends Intelligencer*)
Friends World Committee for Consultation, *Friends Directory of Meetinys and Churches* in the Section of the Americas, 1992.
Friends World Committee for Consultation pub. *Trends in American and Canadian Quakerism. 1925-1950*, London, 1951.
Frost, J. William. *The Quaker Family in Colonial America*, New York: St. Martin's, 1973.
Fry, Harold E. and D'Arcy McNickle. *Indians and Other Americans*, New York: Harper, 1970.
Frysinger, Catherine T., A Conversation in 1980.

Futhey, John S. and Gilbert Cope. *History of Chester County, Pennsylvania*, Philadelphia, 1881.

Gardiner, Mabel H. and Ann H. *Chronicles of Old Berkeley*, Durham, NC, 1938.
Gardner, Anna. *Harvest Gleanings*, New York, 1881.
*Genius of Universal Emancipation*, newspaper 1821-1839.
Gewehr, Wesley M. *The Great Awakening in Virginia*, Durham: Duke University Press, 1930.
Gill, Harold B., Jr., and Ann Finlayson. *Colonial Virginia*, Nashville: Thomas Nelson, 1973.
Gillingham, Chalkley. *Journal*, not published, 1861-1870.
Gilpin, Thomas. *Exiles in Virginia*, Philadelphia, 1848.
Ginther, Herman. *Captain Staunton's River*, Richmond, 1968.
Givens, Lula P. *Christiansburg. Montgomery County, Virginia*, Pulaski, VA, 1981.
Good, Donald G. *Elisha Bates, American Quaker Evangelical*, Ann Arbor, MI, 1976.
Good, James M. *A Brief History of Virginia State Penitentiary*, not published, 1973.
Goodell, William. *Slavery and Anti-Slavery*, New York, 1852.
Goodhart, Briscoe. *History of the Independent Loudoun Rangers*, Washington, DC, 1896.
Grave, John. *A Song of Sion*, London, 1662.
Gregg, John W. *William Gregg. Quaker Immigrant, and his Descendants*, Middleton, WI, 1979.
Gregg, Pauline. *Freeborn John*, London: Harrap, 1961.
Grellet, Stephen. *Memoirs*, Benjamin Seebohm ed., Philadelphia, 1860.
Guilday, Peter. *The Catholic Church in Virginia*, New York: U.S. Catholic Historical Society, 1924.
Guilford College Quaker Collection, Manuscripts.
Gummere, Amelia M. *The Quaker: a Study in Costume*, New York, 2nd edition, 1968.
Gurko, Miriam. *The Ladies of Seneca Falls*, New York: Schocken, 1976.
Gurney, Joseph John. *A Letter to the Followers of Elias Hicks in the City of Baltimore and Vicinity* (a pamphlet), 1839.
Gurney, Joseph John. *Extracts from The Journals. Letters. etc. of Joseph John Gurney*, not published, 1847.
Gurney, Joseph John. *Memoirs*, Joseph B. Braithwaite ed., Philadelphia: Lippincott, 1854.
Gurney, Joseph John. *A Journey in North America*, Norwich, 1841 (reprint by Da Capo Press, 1973).

Hadley, Sarah. Six items re Woodlawn Friends Meeting, received 1985.
Hadley, Sarah. Conversation, 8-15-1986.
Hallowell, Benjamin. *Autobiography*, Philadelphia, 2nd edition, 1884.
Hamm, Thomas D. *The Transformation of American Quakerism: Orthodox Friends 1800-1907*, Garden City, NY: Doubleday, 1984.
Harford County (MD) Historical Society, *The Little Falls Meeting of Friends, 1738-1988*, Belair, MD: 1988.
Harrison, Fairfax. *The Harrisons of Skimino*, Richmond, 1910.
Harrison, Fairfax. *Landmarks of Old Prince William*, Richmond, 1924.
Harrison, Samuel A. *Wenlock Christison and the Early Friends of Talbot County, Maryland*, Baltimore, 1875.
Hart, Freeman H. *The Valley of Virginia in the American Revolution (1763-1789)*, Chapel Hill: University of North Carolina Press, 1942.
Harvey, Henry. *History of The Shawnee Indians. 1681-1854*, Cincinnati, 1855 (Kraus reprint 1971).
Haverford College Quaker Collection, Manuscripts.
Havighurst, Walter. *Alexander Spottswood: Portrait of a Governor*, Williamsburg, 1967.
Haviland, Laura S. *A Woman's Life Work*, Cincinnati, 1884.
Hedman, Kathryn P. *The Pierpoint-Pierpont Family*, 1973.
Hemphill, William E., Marvin W. Schlegel and Sadie E. Engelberg. *Cavalier Commonwealth: History and Government of Virginia*, New York: McGraw-Hill, 1957.
Hening, William W. *Virginia Statutes at Large 1619-1791*, Richmond and Philadelphia, 13 volumes, 1809-23.
Henrico County Records, 1677-1692.
Hickin, Patricia E. P. *Anti Slavery in Virginia, 1831-1861*, a University of Virginia Ph.D. thesis, three volumes, 1968.
Hicks, Elias, *Journal*, New York, 1832.
Hillsboro (VA) Bicentennial Committee. *Hillsboro: Memories of a Mill Town*, Leesburg,
Hinshaw, Seth B. and Mary E. *Carolina Quakers, 1672-1972*, Greensboro, NC, 1972.
Hinshaw, William W. *Encyclopedia of American Quaker Genealogy*, Ann Arbor, MI, 6 volumes, 1950.
Hixson, Robert. *Laurie Tatum. Indian Agent*, Wallingford, PA: Pendle Hill Pamphlet #238, 1981.
Hoffman, Daniel. *Brotherly Love*, New York: Vintage, 1981.
Holme, Benjamin. *Epistles and Works*, London, 1754.
Hopewell Friends Joint Committee assisted by John W. Wayland, *Hopewell Friends History, 1734-1934*, Strasburg, VA, 1936.

Horst, Samuel. *Mennonites in the Confederacy* Scottsdale PA: Herald Press, 1967.
Howe, Henry. *Howe's Historical Collections of Ohio*, Norwalk, OH, 1896.
Howgill, Francis. *The Dawnings of the Gospel Day and Its Light and Glory Discovered*, London (?), 1676.
Hughes-McIntire, Mary Frances. *History of Richmond Friends Meeting, 1795-1962*, Richmond, 1979.
Hunt, William and Nathan. *Memoirs*, Philadelphia, 1858.
Hunter, W. H. *The Pathfinders of Jefferson County, Ohio*, (supplement to Volume VI of Ohio Archaeological and Historical Society Publications) Columbus, OH, 1900.
Huntington Library, Brock and Ellesmere Manuscript Collections.

Ianniello, Lyne ed. *Milestones along the March*, New York: Praeger, 1965.
Ingle, H. Larry. *Quakers in Conflict: the Hicksite Reformation*, Knoxville: University of Tennessee Press, 1986.
Interdiocesan Bicentennial Committee of the Virginias. *Up from Independence: The Episcopal Church in Virginia*, Orange, VA, 1976.
Irwin, Inez H. *The Story of Alice Paul and the National Woman's Party*, Fairfax VA: Denlinger's, 3rd edition, 1977.
Isaac, Rhys. *The Transformation of Virginia, 1740-1790*, Chapel Hill: University of North Carolina Press, 1982.

Jackson, Homer U. *From Dixie to Canada*, Westport, CT: Negro Universities Press, 1970 (reprint).
Jackson, Luther P. *Free Negro Labor and Property Holding in Virginia, 1830-60*, New York: Appleton-Century, 1942.
Jacob, Norma. *Quaker Roots: The Story of Western Quarterly Meeting of Philadelphia Yearly Meeting*, Kennett Square, PA, 1980.
Jacobson, Phebe R. *Quaker Records in Maryland*, Annapolis, MD, 1966.
James, Edward W. ed. *Lower Norfolk County Virginia Antiquary*, Baltimore, 1899.
James, Sydney V. *A People Among Peoples: Quaker Benevolence in Eighteenth Century America*, Cambridge, MA, 1963.
Janney, Samuel M. *History of the Religious Society of Friends to 1828*, Philadelphia, 1861.
Janney, Samuel M. *Virginia, Her Past, Present and Future*, 1865.
Janney, Samuel M. *Memoirs*, Philadelphia, 1881.
Janney, Werner and Asa Moore. *The Composition Book. Stories from the Old Days in Lincoln. Virginia*, Bethesda, MD, 1973.
Janney, Werner and Asa Moore. *Ye Meetg Hous Smal: A Short Account of Friends in Loudoun County. Virginia*, Lincoln, VA, 1980.

Janney, Werner and Asa Moore ed. *John Jay Janney's Virginia*, McLean, VA, 1978.
Jay, Allen. *Autobiography*, Philadelphia, 1910.
Jefferson, Thomas. *Papers*, Julian P. Boyd ed., 15 volumes, Princeton, NJ, 1950.
Johnson, Allen and Dumas Malone ed. *Dictionary of American Biography*, New York: Scribners, 1927-36.
Johnson, Eddis. *The Johnson Family of Isle of Wight County and Later of Indiana*, Martinsville, IN, 2nd edition, 1968.
Johnson, William P. ed. *Hiatt-Hiett Genealogy and Family History*, 1699-1949, Provo, UT, 1951.
Jolliffe, William. *The Jolliffe Family of Virginia, 1652 to 1893*, Philadelphia: Lippincott, 1893.
Jones, Lance G. E. *The Jones Teacher in the United States, 1908-33*, Chapel Hill: University of North Carolina Press, 1937.
Jones, Louis T. *The Quakers of Iowa*, Iowa City, 1914.
Jones, Mary Hoxie. *Swords into Ploughshares: An Account of the American Friends Service Committee. 1917-1931*, New York: MacMillan, 1931.
Jones, Rufus M. *Eli and Sibyl Jones: Their Life and Work*, Philadelphia, 1889.
Jones, Rufus M. *Quakers in The American Colonies*, London: MacMillan, 1921.
Jones, Rufus M. *The Later Periods of Quakerism*, London: MacMillan, 1921.
Jones, Rufus M. *A Service of Love in Wartime: American Friends' Relief Work in Europe, 1917-1919*, New York: MacMillan, 1920.
Jones, Rufus M. *A Call to What is Vital*, New York: MacMillan, 1949.
Journal of Friends Historical Society (London).
Journal of Negro History
Journal of Southern History
Joyner, Peggy S., *Jordan Denson: Some of His Ancestors and Descendants and "Beechwood"*, Portsmouth, VA, 1978.
Judge, Hugh. *Memoir and Journal*, Philadelphia, 1841.
Justice, Hilda. *Life and Ancestry of Warner Mifflin*, Philadelphia, 1905.

Kangas, M. N. and D. E. Payne. *Frederick County, Virginia, Wills and Administrations, 1795-1816*, Baltimore: Genealogical Publishing Company, 1983.
Kegley, F. B. *F. B. Kegley's Virginia Frontier...1740-1783*, Roanoke: Southwest Virginia Historical Society, 1938.
Keim, Albert N. *The CPS Story*, Intercourse, PA: Good Books, 1990.

Kelly, J. Reaney. *Quakers in the Making of Anne Arundel County, Maryland*, Baltimore: Maryland Historical Society, 1963.
Kelpius, Johannes. *Diarium*, Lancaster, PA, 1917.
Kelsey, Rayner W. *Friends and The Indians. 1655-1917*, Philadelphia, 1917.
Kercheval, Samuel. *A History of the Valley of Virginia*, Winchester, 4th edition, 1925.
Ketcham, Ralph ed. *The Anti-Federalist Papers and Constitutional Convention Papers*, New York: Mentor, 1986.
Keve, Paul W. *The History of Corrections in Virginia*, Charlottesville: University Press of Virginia, 1986.
Khan, Lurey. *One Day, Levin*, New York, 1972.
Kimber, Emmor. *Account of the Time of Holding the Yearly, Quarterly and Monthly Meetings of Friends [in] America*, Philadelphia, 1812.
Kirby, Ethyn W. *George Keith*, New York, 1942.

Land, Aubrey C. *Law, Society and Politics in Early Maryland*, Baltimore: Johns Hopkins Press, 1974.
Lasley, Elizabeth H. *Somerton Friends Meeting: Three Hundred Years of Witness*, Greensboro, NC, 1972.
Levering, Miriam. A conversation, 5-27-1991.
Lewis, Orlando F. *The Development of American Prisons and Prison Customs, 1776-1845*, Montclair, NJ, 2nd edition, 1967.
Lippincott, Mary S. *Life and Letters*, Philadelphia, 1893.
Little, Lewis P. *Imprisoned Preachers and Religious Liberty in Virginia*, Lynchburg, 1938.
Littrell, Mary P., Mary E. Outland and Janie O. Sams. *History of Rich Square Monthly Meeting of Friends, 1760-1960*, Woodland, NC, 1960.
Lloyd, Arnold. *Quaker Social History, 1669-1738*, London, 1950.
Locke, Amy A. *The Hanbury Family*, London, 1916.
London Yearly Meeting Aborigines Committee. *Some Account of the Conduct of...Friends toward the Indian Tribes...to 1843*, London, 1849.
*Los Angeles Times* newspaper.
Lundy, Benjamin. *Life, Travels and Opinions*, Thomas Earle ed., Philadelphia, 1847.
Lutz, Francis E. *The Prince George-Hopewell Story*, Richmond, 1957.
Lynchburg (VA) *News* newspaper.
Lynd, Staughton. *Intellectual Origins of American Radicalism*, New York: Vintage, 1969.
Lyons, Eugene. *Herbert Hoover*, Garden City, NY: Doubleday, 1948.

MacMaster, Richard K., with Samuel L. Horst and Robert F. Ulle, *Conscience in Crisis: Mennonites and Other Peace Churches in America, 1739-1789*, Scottdale, PA: Herald Press, 1979.

Maddox, William A. *The Free School Idea in Virginia Before The Civil War*, New York, 1918.

Madison, James. *Papers*, William T. Hutchinson and William M. E. Rachel ed., Chicago: University of Chicago Press, 1962.

*Magazine of Albemarle County (VA) History*.

Magdol, Edward. *A Right to the Land: Essays on the Freedmens' Community*, Westport, CT: Greenwood Press, 1977.

Malone, Dumas. *Jefferson and His Time*, Boston: Little Brown, 5 volumes, 1948 et seq.

Manarin, Louis H. and Clifford Dowdey. *History of Henrico County*, Charlottesville: University Press of Virginia, 1984.

Manners, Emily. *Elizabeth Hooton, First Quaker Woman Preacher*, London: Headley Brothers, 1914.

Mardock, Robert W. *The Reformers and the American Indian*, Columbia: University of Missouri Press, 1971.

Marschean, Amy L. *Glory in the Flower: The Impact of Woman Suffrage in Virginia*, a history thesis of the University of Virginia, 1988.

Maryland Historic Society, Matthews Papers.

May, Ernest. *Life History of The United States*, New York: Time Life, 1976.

McClellan, Woodford. *Russia: A History of The Soviet Period*, Englewood, NJ.

McColley, Robert. *Slavery and Jeffersonian Virginia*, Urbana: University of Illinois Press, 1964.

McIlwaine, Henry R. ed. *Journals of the House of Burgesses of Virginia, 1619-1776*, Richmond, 13 volumes, 1905-15.

McIlwaine, Henry R. ed. *Executive Journals of the Council of Colonial Virginia, 1630-1775*, Virginia State Library, 6 volumes, 1925 et seq.

McIlwaine, Henry R. ed. *Journals of The Council of The State of Virginia. 1776-1791*, RichmondNirginia State Library, 5 volumes, 1931-82.

Mead, Frank S. *See Those Banners Go*, Indianapolis: Bobbs-Merrill, 1936.

Meade, William. *Old Churches. Ministers and Families in Virginia*, Philadelphia: Lippincott, 1857.

Mekeel, Arthur J. *The Relation of The Quakers to the American Revolution*, Washington, DC: University Press of America, 1979.

Middleton, Arthur P. *Tobacco Coast: A Maritime History of Chesapeake Bay in the Colonial Era*, Newport News, 1953.

Miller, Warwick. *Reminiscences of Alexandria, Virginia*, 1875.

Minear, Mark. *Richmond 1877*, Richmond IN: Friends United Press, 1987.
Moore, Virginia. *The Madisons*, New York: McGraw-Hill, 1978.
Moran, Charles E. Interview with Mary Elizabeth Pidgeon, Alderman Library Tape #RG 21-21, 1977.
Moran, Charles E. *Four Quaker Presences in Albemarle County*, not published, 1990.
Mordecai, Samuel. *Virginia. Especially Richmond in Bygone Days*, Richmond, 1860.
Morrison, Norman, Memorial of Service Minutes, not published, 1965.
Morse, Kenneth S. P. *Gleanings from the Records of Baltimore Yearly Meeting, 1672-1830*, Barnesville, OH: 1961.
Morton, Frederick. *The Story of Winchester, Virginia*, Strasburg, VA, 1925.
Morton, Richard L. *Colonial Virginia*, Chapel Hill University of North Carolina Press, 1960.
Muir, Dorothy T. *Potomac Interlude: Woodlawn and the Mount Vernon Neighborhood, 1846-1943*, Washington, DC, 1943.
Munford, Beverly B. *Virginia's Attitude Toward Slavery and Secession*, Richmond, 3rd edition, 1915.

*National Gazette* newspaper.
*National Geographic Magazine*.
Neave, Joseph J. *Leaves from His Journal*, London, 1911.
Neill, Edward D. *Virginia Carolorum*, Albany, NY, 1886.
Netherton, Nan, Donald Sweig, Janice Artemel, Patricia Hickin and Patrick Reed. *Fairfax County, Virginia: A History*, Fairfax, 1978.
Newlin, Algie L. *Charity Cook, a Liberated Woman*, Richmond, IN: Friends United Press, 1981.
Newman, Daisy. *A Procession of Friends: Quakers in America*, Garden City, NY: Doubleday, 1972.
Newport News *Daily Press*, newspaper.
New York *Times*, newspaper.
*Non-Slaveholder*, The, monthly journal 1846-50, reprint by Negro Universities Press, 1970.
Norfolk *Virginian-Pilot*, newspaper.
Norris, J. E. *History of the Lower Shenandoah Valley*, Chicago, 1890 (reprint by Virginia Book Company, Berryville, 1972).
Northampton County (VA) Court Orders.
Nuttall, Gregory F. *Early Quaker Letters*, London, 1952.

Ohio Archaeological and Historical *Quarterly*.

Olmsted, Frederick L. *The Cotton Kingdom*, Arthur M. Schlesinger ed., New York, 1953.
O'Neall, John B. and John A. Chapman. *Annals of Newberry*, 1859 (reprint by Genealogical Publishing Company, Baltimore, 1974).
Osborne, Charles. *Journal*, Cincinnati, 1854.

Padover, Saul K. *A Jefferson Profile, as Recalled by His Letters*, New York: Day, 1956.
Palmer, William P. et al ed. *Calendar of Virginia State Papers...1652-1869* Richmond, 11 volumes, 1875-1893.
Pemberton, John C. *John C. Pemberton, Defender of Vicksburg*, Chapel Hill: University of North Carolina Press, 1942.
Penney, Norman ed. *The First Publishers of Truth*, London, 1907.
Pennsylvania Historical Society Manuscripts.
Pennsylvania *Magazine of History and Biography*.
Pennypacker, Samuel W. *Historical and Biographical Sketches*, Philadelphia, 1883.
Pepys, Samuel. *Diary, 1660-1669*.
Perdue, Charles L., Thomas E. Burden and Robert K. Phillips ed. *Weevils in the Wheat: Interviews with Virginia Ex-Slaves*, Charlottesville: University Press of Virginia, 1976.
Perdue, Gershom. *Memorandum of the Early Settlement of Friends in the Northwest Territory*, 1871 (reprint by Willard Heiss, Indianapolis, 1974).
Perry, William A. *Historical Collections Relating to the American Colonial Church*, Hartford, CT, 1870.
Philadelphia Yearly Meeting Book Committee. *Quaker Biographies*, not dated.
Philips, Edith. *The Good Quaker in French Legend*, Philadelphia: University of Pennsylvania Press, 1932.
Pickett, Clarence. *For More Than Bread*, Boston: Little Brown, 1953.
Pidgeon, Mary Elizabeth. Letter to Jay Worrall, 10-4-1979.
*Pioneer, The* (Quarterly journal of the Pioneer Historical Society of Bedford County, PA)
Poland, Charles P., Jr. *From Frontier to Suburbia*, Marceline, MO, 1976.
Poley, Irvin and Ruth. *Friendly Anecdotes*, New York: Harper, 1950.
Pollock, John. *George Whitefield and the Great Awakening*, Garden City: Doubleday,1972.
Powell, Esther W. *Tombstone Inscriptions and Family Records of Belmont County, Ohio*, Akron, 1969.
Powell, Mary G. *History of Old Alexandria. Virginia, 1749-1861*, Richmond, 1928.

Pringle, Cyrus G. *Civil War Diary*, Wallingford, PA, 1962 (Pendle Hall Pamphlet #122).

Pugh, Mary Jane. Conversation at Strawberry Hill, 7-18-1985.

*Quaker Life*, monthly magazine.

*Quaker Religious Thought* journal.

Quaker Universalist Fellowship, Reader Number One, Landenberg, PA, 1986.

Randolph, Edmund. *History of Virginia*, Charlottesville: University Press of Virginia, 1970.

Ratcliff, Mildred. *Memorandum and Correspondence*, Philadelphia, 1890.

Ratcliff, Richmond P. *Our Special Heritage: Sesqui-Centennial History of Indiana Yearly Meeting of Friends. 1822-1971*, New Castle, IN, 1970.

Rawick, George P. ed. *The American Slave...Narratives*, Westport, CT: Greenwood, 1972.

Reckitt, William. *Life and Gospel Labors*, London, 1783.

Redpath, James. *The Public Life of Captain John Brown*, Boston, 1860.

Remini, Robert V. *The Revolutionary Age of Andrew Jackson*, New York: Harper and Row, 1976.

Rhodes, Phillip W. ed. *Campbell County, Virginia Deed Book I*, Rustburg, VA, 1976.

Richardson, John. *Account of His Life*, London, 1756.

Richmond *Times Dispatch*, newspaper.

Ricks, R. Arnold, *Strawberry Hill, Hanover County, Virginia*, not published, not dated.

Ricks, R. Arnold, Letter to Jay Worrall, 1-9-1991.

Ross, Isabel. *Margaret Fell, Mother of Quakerism*, London: Longmans Green, 1949.

Rouse, Parke, Jr. *Planters and Pioneers- Life in Colonial Virginia*, New York: Hastings, 1968.

Rouse, Parke, Jr. *James Blair of Virginia*, Chapel Hill: University of North Carolina Press, 1971.

Rouse, Parke, Jr. *The Great Wagon Road from Philadelphia to the South*, New York, 1973.

Russell, Elbert. *The History of Quakerism*, New York: MacMillan, 1942.

Russell, John H. *The Free Negro in Virginia, 1619-1865*, Baltimore: Johns Hopkins Press, 1913.

Russell, William G. *What I Know About Winchester*, Winchester-Frederick County Historical Society, 1953.

Ryland, Garnett. *The Baptists of Virginia, 1699-1926*, Richmond, VA, Baptist Board of Missions, 1954.

Sandburg, Carl. *Abraham Lincoln*, New York: Harcourt Brace, 1925 et seq.
Sappington, Roger E. *The Brethren in Virginia*, Harrisonburg, 1973.
Savery, William. *Journal*, Jonathan Evans Ed., Philadelphia, 1873.
Scattergood, Thomas. *Journal*, Philadelphia, 1841.
Scheel, Eugene M. *Culpeper: A Virginia County's History through 1920*, Culpeper: Culpeper Historical Society, 1982.
Scheel, Eugene M. *The Story of Purcellville. Loudoun County, Virginia*, Purcellville, 1977.
Scheel, Eugene M. *The Guide to Loudoun*, Loudoun County Chamber of Commerce, 1975.
Schooley, William. *Journal*, Zanesville, OH, 1977.
Scott, Daniel. *History of the Early Settlement of Highland County, Ohio*, Hillsborough, OH, 1890.
Scott, Job. *Life and Travels*, Dublin, 1798.
Scott, Mary W. *Old Richmond Neighborhoods*, Richmond, 1951.
Scott, William W. *History of Orange County, Virginia*, Richmond, 1907.
Selleck, George A. *The Quakers in Boston. 1656-1964*, Cambridge, MA, 1969.
Sessions, William H. *Laughter in Quaker Grey*, York, England, 3rd edition, 1974.
Sewell, William. *History of the Rise, Increase and Progress of the Christian People Called Quakers*, London, 4th edition, 1799.
Seymour, Flora W. *Indian Agents of the Old Frontier*, New York: Appleton-Century, 1941.
Shelton, Charlotte J. *Woman Suffrage and Virginia Politics, 1909-1920*, Charlottesville, 1969 (Master's Thesis of the University of Virginia).
Shepherd, Samuel. *The Statutes at Large in Virginia from 1792-1806*, Richmond, three volumes, 1835-36.
Sheppard, Walter L. Jr., ed. *Penn's Colony: Passengers and Ships Prior to 1684*, Baltimore: Genealogical Publishing Company, 1970.
Sheridan, Philip H. *Personal Memoirs*, New York, 1888.
Shillitoe, Thomas. *Journal*, London, 1839.
Shomette, Donald G. *Pirates on the Chesapeake*, Centerville, MD, 1985.
Siebert, Wilbur H. *The Underground Railroad from Slavery to Freedom*, New York, 1898 (reprint 1967).
Siebert, Wilbur H. *The Mysteries of Ohio's Underground Railroads*, Columbus, OH, 1951.
Simkins, Francis B. Spotswood H. Jones and Sidman P. Poole. *Virginia: History, Government, Geography*, New York: Saunders, 1964.
Simler, Lucy L. *Marple Township, 1684-1784*, 1984.
Smedley, R. C. *History of The Underground Railroad in Chester and the Neighboring Counties of Pennsylvania*, Lancaster, PA, 1883 (reprinted 1968 by Negro Universities Press).

Smith, Bob. *They Closed Their Schools: Prince Edward County, Virginia, 1951-64*, Chapel Hill: University of North Carolina Press, 1965.
Smith, George. *History of Delaware County, Pennsylvania*, Philadelphia, 1862.
Smith, Hannah W. *Philadelphia Quaker: The Letters of Hannah Whitall Smith*, New York: Harcourt Brace, 1950.
Smith, John. *A Collection of Memorials Concerning...Quakers...to the Year 1787*, Philadelphia, 1787.
Smith, Joseph. *Bibliotheca Anti-Quakeriana*, London, 1873 (Kraus reprint 1968).
Smith, Lizzie B. Her autograph book while at Lincoln Academy, 1881.
*Southern Friend, The*, published by John B. Crenshaw in Richmond, 1864-1866.
*Southern Friend, The*, journal of North Carolina Friends Historical Society.
Spotswood, Alexander. *Official Letters*, Richmond: Virginia Historical Society, 1885.
Spraker, Hazel A. *The Boone Family*, Baltimore: Genealogical Publishing Company, 1977.
Stabler, Harold B. *Some Recollections, Anecdotes and Tales of Olden Time*, not published, 1962.
Stabler, Harold B. *Some Further Recollections*, not published, 1963.
Stabler, William. *Memoir of the Life of Edward Stabler*, Philadelphia, 1846.
Stanard, Mary N. *Colonial Virginia, Its People and Customs*, 1917.
Stevenson, Gertrude S. *Charles I in Captivity*, New York: Appleton, 1927.
Stewart, R. A. ed. *Abstracts of York County Wills*.
Still, William. *Still's Underground Railroad Records*, Philadelphia, 1886.
Stone, Helen. *Pages from the Past*, Washington, DC: Alexandria Monthly Meeting, not dated.
Sturge, Joseph. *A Visit to the United States in 1841*, Boston, 1842.
Sutcliff, Robert. *Travels in Some Parts of North America in the Years 1804, 1805 and 1806*, Philadelphia, 1812.
Swarthmore College Quaker Collection Manuscripts.
Swayne, Norman W. *Chester County Swaynes*, Philadelphia, 1955.
Sweet, William W. *Virginia Methodism: A History*, Richmond, 1960.
Swift, David E. *Joseph John Gurney. Banker, Reformer and Quaker*, Middletown, CT, Wesleyan University Press, 1962.
Swint, Henry L. ed. *Dear Ones at Home: Letters from Contraband Camps*, Nashville: Vanderbilt University Press, 1966.
Swint, Henry L. *The Northern Teacher in the South*, New York: Octagon, 2nd edition, 1967.

Tanner, Edwin P. *The Province of New Jersey, 1664-1738*.
Taylor, John. *Journal*, London, 1710.

Terrell, Clayton C. *Quaker Migration to Southwestern Ohio*, 1967.
Thomas, Anna B. *The Story of Baltimore Yearly Meeting*, Baltimore, 1938.
Thomas, Edward. *Quaker Adventures*, New York: Reveli, 1928.
Thomas, Charles G. A Letter to Fannie Pretlow, 1-25-1916.
Thomas, Stanton B. *Nathan M. Thomas: An Account of His Life*, Cassapolis, MI, 1925.
Thompson, Ernest T. *Presbyterians in the South*, Richmond: John Knox Press, 1963.
Thorburn, Grant. *Laurie Todd's Notes on Virginia*, New York, 1848.
Thwaites, Reuben G. *Daniel Boone*, New York: Appleton-Century, 1935.
Time-Life Books Editors. *The Life History of the United States*, Alexandria, VA, Time-Life Books, 12 volumes, 1946-1977.
Tolles, Frederick B. *Emerson and Quakerism*, in volume 10 #2 of *American Literature*, 1938.
Tolles, Frederick B. *Quakers and the Atlantic Culture*, New York: MacMillan, 1965.
Tolles, Frederick B. *George Logan of Philadelphia*, New York, 1953.
Torrence, Clayton. *Old Somerset on the Eastern Shore of Maryland*, Richmond, 1935.
Townsend, William. *Life of Jacob Lindley*, Philadelphia, 1893.
Tract Association of Friends. *Biographical Sketches and Anecdotes*, Philadelphia, 1871.
Tract Association of Friends. *American Annual Monitor...for 1858*, New York, 1859.
Trevelyan, George Macaulay. *History of England*, New York: Longman Green.
Trollope, Frances. *Domestic Manners of the Americans*.
Trueblood, D. Elton. *The Life We Prize*, New York: Harper, 1951.
Tucker, Rob W. *Springfield Meeting: The First Hundred Years*, Springfield, PA, 1986.
Turner, Fitzhugh. *Loudoun County and The Civil War*, Leesburg, VA, 1961.
Tyler-McGraw, Marie and Gregg D. Kimball. *In Bondage and Freedom: Antebellum Life in Richmond, Virginia*, Richmond, 1988.
*Tyler's Quarterly Historical and Genealogical Magazine*, issued 1920-52.

Valentine, Edward Pleasants. *Papers*, Richmond, 1927.
Vining, Elizabeth G. *Friend of Life: The Biography of Rufus M. Jones*, Lippincott: Philadelphia, 1958.
Virginia Association of Realtors, *State Historical Markers*, Richmond, 1975.
*Virginia Cavalade* magazine.
Virginia Council on Human Relations *Observer*, newsletter.
*Virginia Gazette*, newspaper, 1736-1780.

*Virginia Genealogist*, journal, 1957-1982.
*Virginia Magazine of History and Biography*.
Virginia Quarterly Meeting, newsletter.
*Virginia Weekly*, newspaper.
Virginia Writers Project of the U. S. Works Progress Administration, *Virginia--A Guide to the Old Dominion*, New York: Oxford, 1941.

Walker, Williston. *A History of The Christian Church*, New York, 1959.
Walthall, William B. *A Biographical Sketch of My Life*, 14 typewritten pages, 1890.
Wamsley, James S. with Anne M. Cooper. *Idols, Victims, Pioneers: Virginia's Women from 1607*, Richmond: Virginia State Chamber of Commerce, 1976.
Ward, Harry M. *Richmond. An Illustrated History*, Northridge, CA: Windsor, 1985.
Ward, Harry M. and Harold E. Greer, Jr. *Richmond During The Revolution, 1775-83*, Charlottesville: University of Virginia Press, 1977.
Warfield, J. D. *The Founders of Anne Arundel and Howard Counties, Maryland*, Baltimore, 1905.
Warner, Stafford A. *Yardley Warner--the Freedman's Friend*, Didcot, England: Wessex Press, 1957.
Washington, George. *Diaries*, John C. Fitzpatrick ed., Boston: Houghton Mifflin, 1925.
Washington, George. *Diaries*, Donald Jackson and Dorothy Twohig ed.
Washington Post, newspaper.
Watson, J. F. *Annals of Philadelphia and Pennsylvania*, 1857.
Wayland, John W. *A History of Rockingham County*, Dayton, VA, 1912.
Wayland, John W. *A History of Shenandoah County*, Strasburg, VA, 1927.
Wayland, John W. *Virginia Valley Records*, Strasburg, VA, 1930.
Weddell, Alexander W. *Richmond Virginia in Old Prints*, Richmond, 1932.
Weeks, Stephen B. *Southern Quakers and Slavery*, Baltimore: Johns Hopkins Press, 1896.
Weigle, Luther A. *American Idealism*, (volume 10 of *The Pageant of America*, Ralph H. Gabriel ed.), 1928.
Wertenbaker, Thomas J. *Norfolk: Historic Southern Port*, Durham, NC: Duke University Press, 1931.
*Western Work*, magazine.
Westtown Boarding School, *A Brief History with a General Catalogue*, Philadelphia, 3rd edition, 1884.
Wheeling (WV) *News-Register*, newspaper.
Whichard, Rogers D. *History of Lower Tidewater Virginia*, New York, 1958.

White, Miles, Jr. *Early Quaker Records in Virginia*, Baltimore: Genealogical Publishing Company, 1977 (reprint).
White, Miles, Jr. *The Quaker Janneys of Cheshire and Their Progenitors*, Harrisburg, PA, 1904.
Whitefield, George. *Journals*, London: The Banner of Truth Trust, 1960.
Whitelaw, Ralph T. *Virginia's Eastern Shore*, Gloucester, MA, 1968.
Whitman, Walt. *Collected Writings*, Floyd Stovall ed., New York,: New York University Press, 1964.
Whittier, John G. *Complete Poetical Works*, Boston: Houghton Mifflin, 1894.
Wilbur, John. *Journal*, Providence, RI, 1859.
*William and Mary Quarterly Historical Magazine*.
Williams, Harrison. *Legends of Loudoun*, Richmond, 1938.
Willison, George F. *Behold Virginia: The Fifth Crown*, New York, 1952.
Wilson, Raymond. *Uphill for Peace*, Richmond, IN: Friends United Press, 1975.
Wilson, Robert H. *The Philadelphia Quaker, 1681-1981*, Philadelphia: Philadelphia Yearly Meeting, 1981.
Wise, Jennings C. *History of The Eastern Shore of Virginia*, Lynchburg, VA, 1911.
Wistar, Isaac J. *Autobiography*, Philadelphia: Wistar Institute, 1937.
Woolman, John. *Journal*, John Greenleaf Whittier ed., Secaucus, NJ, 1972.
Wright, Edward N. *Conscientious Objectors in the Civil War*, Philadelphia: University of Pennsylvania Press, 1931.
Writers Program of the Works Progress Administration in Virginia, *Prince William: The Story of Its Places and People*, Richmond, 1941.
Wust, Klaus. *The Virginia Germans*, Charlottesville: University of Virginia Press, 1969.

York County, Virginia, Records, 1657-1662.

Zigler, D. H. *A History of the Brethren in Virginia*, Elgin, IL: Brethren Publishing House, 1908.

# END NOTES.

These end notes indicate last name of author, or title of periodical or newspaper, or name of preserving institution; followed by page number (Penney 163). For multi-volume sources, volume and page number are given (Friends House Swarthmore 3/127). See Bibliography (pages 541-562 above) for full title of each source.

CHAPTER I
(pages 1-18)
1  Penney 163
2  Burrough 29ff
   Howgill 5, 549
   Dewsbury 154-65
3  Russell, Elbert 34-35
   Braithwaite, Beginnings 182
   Gregg, Pauline 229, 347
4  Fox, George 263
5  Barclay, Abram 33
6  Jones, RM Quakers in American Colonies 27
7  Ibid 219
8  Warmer 35
9  Friends House, Swarthmore Mss 3/127
10 Bishop 12
11 Boddie 288
   Meade 221
   VA Mag Hist & Biog 37/77-9
12 Boddie 66-7
13 Boyd (St. Mary's Abchurch Record)
14 Braithwaite, Beginnings 517-9
15 Braithwaite, Beginnings 426
   Kelly 14
16 Friends Hist Soc, London 8/51
17 Boddie 78
   Kelly 14-7, 20, 91-2
   Warfield 11, 155
   Newport News Daily Press 8-18 & 9-24-1974
18 Jones, RM Quakers in American Colonies 237-8
19 Crosfield 59-60
20 Braithwaite 380
21 Besse 2/40
22 Kelly 78
   Friends House, Crosfield Ms
23 Braithwaite, Beginnings 517
24 Friends Hist Soc. (London) 8/51
25 Kelly 78
26 Besse 1/533, 537
27 Kelly 78
28 Ibid 80
29 Tanner 686
30 Brailsford 114
31 Ross 57
32 Va Mag. Hist. & Biog 8/166
33 Bruce, PA Institutional History 1/226
34 Friends Hist Asso (Phila) Vol 62
35 Barclay, AR Letter 13
   Bishop 28
36 Bishop 28
37 Ibid
38 Friends Hist Asso (Phila) Vol 62
39 Barclay, AR Letter 1
   Jones, RM, Quakers in American Colonies 50-1
40 Jones, RM, Quakers in American Colonies 46 ff
41 Budge 210
42 Ames 231-2
   Bruce, PA, Institutional History 1/220, 226
43 Bowden 1/170
44 Ross 57
45 Bowden 1/370
   Barclay, AR Letter 44
   Friends House, Crosfield Ms
46 Va Mag Hist & Bio 24/83
47 Ricks Letter w/copy of Northumberland Co court records for 6-26, 6-29 & 9-18-1660
48 Boddie 117
   White, Early Quaker Records 42
49 James, EW 3/103
50 Fleet 3/81-5
51 Torrence 91
   Whitelaw 499
52 William and Mary Qrly Series 1 Vol 1/89-94
   York Co. Records, 1657-1662
53. Weigle 100

CHAPTER II
(pages 19-42)
1  Wise 25
2  Perry 1
   Ames 218
   Burk 124-5
3  Bruce, PA, Institutional History 1/132, 149, 221, 255
4  Bruce, PA, Institutional History 1/253
   Boddie 57, 72
5  Bruce, PA, Institutional History 1/252
6  Ibid 1/255
7  Bruce, PA, Institutional History 1/252
   Boddie 59,67
8  VA Mag Hist & Biog 11/35-41
9  Hening 1/384
10 Davis, ET 35
   Simkins? 113
11 Bruce, PA, Institutional History 1/231
   James EW 3/103, 4/73
12 Smith, Joseph
13 Hening 1/530-3
14 Boddie 101
15 Boddie 448, 491
16 Weeks 23
   Hening 2/198
17 James, EW 3/102-3
   Va Mag Hist & Biog 25/77
18 Bancroft 2/ch 16
19 James, EW 4/73
20 Ibid 3/146, 4/78
21 Ibid 3/105
22 Ibid 3/79-110 ff
23 Wm & Mary Qrly Ser 1, Vol 1/90-4
   Bruce, PA, Institutional History 1/229-33
   York Co Records 163
24 Stewart 11
25 Wamsley 35
   Hening 1/370 ff
26 Fleet 85
27 Ibid 3/75

28 Ibid 1/37
29 Ibid 3/75,81,85
30 Lutz 41, 103
31 Va Mag Hist & Biog 74/180-9
32 Bowden 11/347
33 Cadbury 194
34 Bowden 1/265, 268,348
35 Jones, RM , Quakers in American Colonies 274 Harrison, S.A.
36 Weeks 29
37 Bowden 1/227-8
38 Wm & Mary Qrly Series 3 Vol 33/131-2
39 VA Mag Hist & Biog 3/33
40 Bowden 1/344-6
Kelly 45-7
Besse 2/381
Bishop 351
41 Bowden 1/344-6
42 Bishop 422,439-40
Friends House, Swarthmore Mss 4/239
43 Va Mag Hist & Biog 74/170-89
44 Valentine 740
45 Neill 286
46 Va Mag Hist & Biog 74/170-89
Whitelaw 499
47 Wise 632, 1151
48 Bowen 332
49 Neill 221
Hening 1/380
50 Ames 232-3
51 Northampton Co Court Orders 89
52 Whitelaw 662
53 Neill 303
Torrence 388-91
54 Jones, RM, Quakers In American Colonies 337
55 Va Mag Hist & Biog 8/169
56 Wise 87
57 Neill 418
Wise 146-52
58 Bruce, PA. Institutional History 1/239
59 Fox, George 651
60 Friends Hist Asso (Phila) Bulletin 3/132
61 Hening 2/49-50
62 Ibid 2/48, 165
63 Ibid 2/181-3
64 Fox, George 41-3,159-70
65 Braithwaite, Beginnings 445
66 Fox, George xix
Braithwaite, Beginnings 465
67 Braithwaite, Beginnings 404

CHAPTER III
(pages 43-66)
1 Carroll KL 48
2 Ibid 76-7
3 Taylor
4 Sewel 1/491
5 Evans, W & T Vol 11 (Life of John Burnyeat)
6 Haverford College Journals, Diaries, etc (Ms Collection 975 C)
7 Braithwaite. Beginnings 58
8 Braithwaite. Second Period 25
9 Jones, R M Quakers in American Colonies 109
10 Whittier 121
11 Jones, RM Quakers in American Colonies 108
12 Bruce, PA. Institutional History 1/277
13 Hening, Vol III
14 Evans, W & T, Vol 11 (Life of John Burnyeat) 188-9
15 Fox, George, preface
16 Smith, Joseph 412-3
17 Braithwaite, Beginnings
18 Fox, George 578-80
19 Ibid 590
20 Ibid 602-6
21 Drake 5-6
22 Fox, George 616
23 Edmondson, 66 et seq
24 Fox, George 639-648
25 Weeks 43-4
26 Valentine 733
Boddie 345
27 Fox, George, 651
28 Manners, 43
29 Friends Hist Soc, London 11/28-31
30 Ibid 9/194
31 Ibid 11/203
32 Hinshaw, William 6/29
33 Drake 9-10

CHAPTER IV
(pages 67-90)
1 Hening 2/511-17
Neill 337
2 Davis, ET 87
3 Edmondson 79-80
4 Brydon 166
5 Va Mag Hist Biog 74/170-89
Whitelaw 1402
6 Henrico Co. Records 191-95
7 Friends Hist Soc, London 21/43
Sheppard, WL 147, 209
8 Barclay, Robert
9 Va Genealogist, Vol 17 #2, (1973) 135
10 Russell, Elbert 131-2

11 Braithwaite, Second Period 58
12 Fisher
13 Sheppard, WL
14 Fiske 2/157-9
15 Bruce, PA, Institutional History 1/274
VA Mag Hist & Biog 26/41
16 Fox, George 316-7
17 Kirby 53
18 Jones, RM. Quakers in American Colonies 445-50
19 Johnson, Allen 5/289
Janney, SM, History 3/71-91
Wm & Mary Quarterly, 3rd Series, Vol 38/431-52 20
Bowen 198
21 Ibid 217
22 Pa Mag Hist & Biog. Vol 18 (1894)
23 Stevenson 19
24 Neill 292-3
25 Brydon 246
26 Braithwaite, Second Period 130-4
Brydon 208
27 Braithwaite, Second Period 154
28 Trevelyan 475-6
29 Brydon 279-87
30 Manarin 66
31 Evans, W & T 12/369-412 (Jnl of James Dickinson)
32 Ibid 2/325 ff (Life of Thomas Wilson)
33 McIlwaine, Jnls of Burgesses (1659-93) 431-3
34 Manarin 49-52
35 McIlwaine, Jones of Burgesses (1659-93) 431-3
36 Manarin 67
37 Swarthmore, Oliver E. Janney Ms
38 White. Early Quaker Records
39 Wm & Mary Quarterly 2d Series, Vol 6/88-93
40 Huntington Library. Ellesmore Mss, # 9599, 1-17
41 Rouse, James Blair 236, 245
42 McIlwaine, Executive Jnls of Council 1/427
43 Brown, R.E. & B.K. 126
44 McIlwaine, Executive Jnls of Council 1/441
45 Ibid 1/456

CHAPTER V
(pages 91-122)
1 Valentine 211
White, Early Quaker Records 30-1
Joyner 17

2 American Antiquarian Proceedings 70(1960)/269-70
3 Russell, Elbert 125
4 Tolles, Quakers & Atlantic Culture 31-2
5 Morse 5
6 James, EW 1/65
7 Braithwaite, Second Period 492-3
8 Jones, RM, Quakers in American Colonies 455
9 Richardson 96-118
10 Kirby 141
11 Va Mag Hist & Biog 35/187, 72/332
Kelpius 64-9
12 Brandt 85-8
13 Ibid
14 Va Mag Hist & Biog 35/187
15 Hemphill 87
16 Va Mag Hist & Biog 21/72-4
17 Evans, W&T, Vol 4 (Life of John Richardson)
18 Friends Hist Soc, London, 6/68
19 Ibid
20 Evans, W & T, Vol 10 (Life of Thomas Story)
21 Ibid
22 Ashmead 139
23 Backhouse 155
24 Evans, W & T 4/100 (Life of John Richardson)
25 Haverford Journals Diaries, etc. Mss # 975 B/16
26 Wm & Mary Quarterly, Series 1 Vol 7/310
Evans, W & T Vol 10 (Life of Thomas Story)
27 Fox, George 7
28 Jones, RM Quakers in American Colonies 538
29 Haverford. Journals, Diaries, etc Mss # 975 C
Richardson 143-170
Evans, W & T Vol 4 (Life of John Richardson)
30 Richardson 239
31 Backhouse 155
32 Drake 18
33 White, Early Quaker Records 51
34 Evans, W & T Vol 10 (Life of Thomas Story)
35 Smith, John 46-7
36 Evans, W & T Vol 13 ( Life of John Fothergill)
37 Thompson 1/15
38 Braithwaite, Second Period 594
39 Brydon 271
40 Brydon 261-5
Thompson 1/16-7

41 Evans, W & T Vol 10 (Life of Thomas Story)
42 Morton RL 391
Ryland 3
43 Fox, George 4
44 Byrd, Secret Diary
45 Evans, W & T 4/77-8
46 Hinshaw, WW 6/166, 204-5,211
Valentine 1128,1140,1191
47 Hinshaw, WW 6/166,204
48 American Antiquarian Proceedings 53/82
49 Spotswood 1/120
50 Valentine 1983
51 Spotwood 1/99
52 Wm & Mary Quarterly Series 1 Vol 21/252
53 Holme 25
54 Spotswood 337-40
Shomette 218-23
55 Braithwaite, Second Period 183
Hening 3/298
56 Braithwaite, Second Period 203
57 McIlwaine, Executive Jnls of Council 13
58 Valentine 727-9
59 Havighurst 16
60 McIlwaine Jnls of Council 150
61 Evans, W & T Vol 10 (Life of Thomas Story)
62 Lloyd 38
63 Haverford, Virginia Yearly Meeting Archives Mss # 1116, Item 153/32
64 Forbush, History 40
65 Lloyd 73
Penney 377-81
Selleck 37
Bacon 16
66 Trueblood
67 Fox, George 169
68 Tolles, Quakers & Atlantic Culture 58
69 Cook 28
70 Byrd, Dividing Line Histories 68
71 Brydon 363-8
72 Chitwood 388
Middleton 65
73 Bohannan 66

CHAPTER VI
(pages 123-144)
1 Fontaine 106 Hemphill 92
Rouse, Great Wagon Rd 12-13 Simkins, 146-7
2 Wayland, Va Valley Records 315

3 Wayland, Hist Shenandoah Co 645
4 Dorman 2/62
5 Brown, SE 68
6 Ibid 42
7 Norris 52 Brown, SE 71-2
8 Hopewell 185 Norris 55
Brown, SE 71-2
9 Ibid Harrison, F, Landmarks 613-6
10 Va Mag Hist & Bio 1/75
Janney, SM, Va Her Past 27
Kegley, map op 43
11 Rouse, Great Wagon Rd, Chapter 1
12 Wayland, Hist Shenandoah Co 57 Clement 25 Poland 26
13 Hopewell 180 Newlin 23
14 Va Asso Realtors 268
15 Churchman 66
16 Rouse, Great Wagon Rd 21
17 Ibid 29
18 Wust 48
19 MacMaster 42
20 Hopewell 202-06
21 Thompson 1/48
22 Jolliffe 148-9
23 American Antiquarian 10-31-1959, p 114
24 Clement 14
25 Kercheval 45,53 Morton 39
26 Wayland, Hist Shenandoah Co 55
27 Gardiner 10
28 Kercheval 56
29 Norris 740
30 Kercheval 37
31 Hopewell 39
32 Kercheval 45-47
33 Janney, W & AM, Ye Meetg Hous Smal 8-9
34 Janney, JJ 3
35 Janney, W & AM, Ye Meetg Hous Smal 17
36 Va Mag Hist & Bio 86/8
37 Andrews 174-5
38 Valentine 246,1226
McIlwaine, Jnls of Burgesses 1727-406/445
39 Fox, George 292
40 Daniels 57
41 Stanard 241-15
42 Daniels 119
43 Valentine 1341
44 Haverford Quaker Mss 1116 153/53 Morse 11
46 Freeman 1/416 Dinwiddie, Vols 1,2
47 American Antiquarian Proceedings Vol 58 Part 1 p 178
48 Locke 251
49 Va Gazette Nov 1738 p 24

# END NOTES

50 Perry 360
51 Campbell 96
52 Pollock 8
53 Franklin 133
54 Pollock 112
55 Whitefield 201, 237
56 Ibid 335
57 Tolles, Quakers & Atlantic Culture 97
58 Whitefield 341
59 Franklin 129-32
60 Chitwood 447
61 Whitefield 372
62 Chitwood 449
63 Willison 120-28
64 Manarin 94
65 Ibid 145, 209, 298
66 Kercheval 62-3
67 Sweet 36
68 Ibid 38
69 Little 32
70 Sweet 40

## CHAPTER VII
*(pages 145-162)*
1 Haverford Quaker Mss 1116
2 Ibid
3 Woolman 19-21
4 Jones RM, Quakers in Am Colonies xxix
5 Drake 52
6 Woolman 22
7 Cady 79
8 Woolman 52
9 Ibid 53-59
10 Ibid 60-61
11 James SV 2
12 Ibid 316-17
13 Brookes 23
14 Hinshaw WW 6/12-13
15 Haverford Quaker Mss 1116 163/8
16 Hoffman 84
17 Kercheval Wayland, Hist Shenandoah Co 55 Norris 104
18 Gardiner 10
19 Va Asso Realtors 162
20 Kelsey 49
21 Brown SE 125
22 Freeman 1/236 Dinwiddie 1/17 American Antiquarian Proceedings Vol 58 Part 1/17-190 Locke 249
23 Gill 106-7
24 Dinwiddie 257 American Antiquarian Proceedings Vol 58 Part 1/178
25 Brown SE 136
26 Kercheval 72 Brown SE 140
27 Hopewell 58 Gardiner 12
28 Kercheval 73
29 Hopewell 119

30 Hoffman
31 Hopewell 117-20
32 Pa Hist Society James Kenny Jnls Ms 109/31, 46-7
33 Brown, DS 52 Early 45 Haverford Quaker Mss 1116 160/74
34 Hopewell 58, 71
35 Reckitt 77
36 Va Mag Hist & Bio 86/9
37 Hopewell 187-8
38 Va Mag Hist & Bio 86/13
39 Friends Hist Society (Phila) Bulletin 53/12ff
40 Friend, The (Philadelphia) vol 34 (1861)/44
41 Jones RM Quakers in American Colonies 503-4 MacMaster 134-56
42 MacMaster 146
43 Brookes 147 Bauman 11,62
44 Pa Hist Society James Kenny Jnls Ms 109
45 Kercheval 97-102
46 Brown SE 98
47 Ibid 27-28
48 Hopewell 549
49 Wayland, Hist Shenandoah Co 663
50 Wayland, Hist Rockingham Co 248 Wayland, Hist Shenandoah Co, 3
51 Rouse, Great Wagon Rd 99
52 Wayland, Hist Shenandoah Co 648
53 Wayland, Hist Rockingham Co 48 Wayland, Va Valley Records 57
54 Evans, Willis 23
55 Howe, Hist Collections 2/104 Kercheval 113 Caldwell 60, 134
56 Rouse, Great Wagon Rd ix

## CHAPTER VIII
*(pages 163-190)*
1 Hemphill 139-40 Simkins 228-30
2 Foote 319
3 Meade 18
4 Little xviii-xix
5 Ibid 46-7
6 Ibid
7 Little 134,235 Gewehr 123,127
8 Hinshaw WW 6/232
9 Evans, W&T 11/81
10 Haverford Quaker Mss 1116/168
11 Little 210
12 Haverford Quaker Mss 975C
13 Mekeel 15-19

14 Hemphill 142
15 Gill 114-15
16 Mekeel 20
17 Ibid 321-24
18 Hemphill 116
19 Mekeel 36-7
20 Jones RM, Quakers in American Colonies 559
21 Mekeel 35
22 Gill 144
23 Mekeel 46-7, 69-70
24 Bowden 383-87
25 Mekeel 47-8
26 Ibid 68-70
27 Chitwood
28 Dabney 121
29 Hopewell 167
30 Daniels 111
31 Haverford Quaker Mss 1116/168
32 Valentine 237
33 Haverford Quaker Mss 975C
34 Janney SM, History of Friends 3/434-5
35 Wm & Mary Qrly Series 2 Vol 1/108
36 Valentine 2272 Harrison F, Harrisons of Skimino 34-5
37 Johnson, Allen ed
38 Johnson, Allen ed Munford 42
39 Evans W&T 13/381
40 Freeman 1/38 Scott WW 96-7 Harrison F, Landmarks 420
41 Washington, Diaries (Jackson) 9
42 Cadbury 66
43 Watson 165
44 Campbell 128
45 Freeman 1/245
46 Valentine 1128-29
47 Wm & Mary Qrly Ser 2 Vol 1/107
48 Benezet 73
49 Washington, Diaries (Fitzpatrick) 2/165
50 Washington, Diaries (Jackson)
51 Malone 195
52 Johnson, Allen ed
53 Benezet 78 Brookes 321
54 Brookes 72 Bauman 146
55 Chitwood 537
56 Mekeel 95
57 Ibid 96
58 Ibid 98-9
59 Huntington Library Brock Mss 7/239
60 Mekeel 241-2
61 Ibid 102 Manarin 127
62 Mekeel

63 Haverford Quaker Mss 1116 153/138
64 Ibid 153/146
65 Ibid 153/148
66 Brookes 103
67 Drake 37
68 Mekeel 6 Tucker 34
69 Bell 163-4
70 Ibid 145-7
71 Hinshaw WW 6/214
72 Jones RM, Quakers in American Colonies 254
73 Haverford Quakers Mss 1116 153/2-4
74 Ibid 154/151-5
75 Jolliffe 77 Va Mag Hist & Bio 86/13 McIlwaine, Jnls of Burgesses 1766-69/ 101
76 Va Mag Hist & Bio 59/359-61
77 Ibid 63/404
78 Huntington Library Brock Mss Box 42
79 Day 340
80 Caldwell 60, 131-2
81 Hopewell 88, 223
82 Malone 170
83 Gill 130-1
84 Caldwell 78
85 Chitwood 505
86 Gill 135
87 Ibid 138-9

CHAPTER IX
*(pages 191-224)*
1 Dabney 131-33 Gill 142 Eckenrode, Revolution 67
2 Haverford Quaker Mss 1116/168
3 Huntington Library Brock Mss 7/253-7
4 Mekeel 135
5 Eckenrode, Revolution 261-2
6 Gill 143-3 Eckenrode, Revolution 110
7 Eckenrode, Revolution 164
8 Isaac 279 Alley 147-8
9 Isaac 278
10 Hemphill 160 Sweet 139
11 Mekeel 131
12 Haverford Quaker Mss 1116/168
13 Mekeel 131-2
14 Mekeel 150-1 MacMaster 370 Huntington Library Brock Mss Box 12/25
15 Mekeel 162 MacMaster 370
16 Mekeel 170
17 Ibid 162-3
18 Ohio Arch & Hist Qrly 53/56 Perdue G 3
19 Terrell 34
20 White, Early Quaker Rcds 52
21 James SV 80-1, 89-90 Hopewell 122
22 Brookes 114
23 Wm & Mary Qrly Ser 1 vol 2/174-5
24 Wm & Mary Qrly Ser 1 vol 2/175
25 Blackburn 45
26 Ibid 33
27 Eckenrode, Revolution 19,25
28 Hening 9/471
29 Hemphill 161
30 Joyner 161-2 Isaac 280
31 Hening 9/34-5
32 MacMaster 38-9
33 Hemphill 161
34 Hening 9/139
35 Ibid 10/261-2, 314-5, 334-5, 360-1, 417-8
36 Haverford Quaker Mss 1116 Item 153/157
37 MacMaster 494-5 Hening 11/252-3 Eckenrode, Revolution 118
38 Augusta Co Hist Society 123
39 Mekeel 266-7
40 Charles 91
41 Evans, W & T 11/441-80
42 Clement 144 Va Gazette 8-11 & 10-13-1775
43 Clement 178-9 Hening 12/512
44 Eckenrode, Revolution 73
45 Rouse, Planters & Pioneers 96 Early 195 Augusta Co Hist Society 117 Clement 178-9
46 Ginther 22
47 Hening 11/134-5
48 Augusta Co Hist Society 117
49 Philips 9-10
50 Ibid 65-6
51 Justice 56
52 Johnson, Allen ed 6/608-9
53 Brissot,165-7
54 Pa Mag Hist & Bio 29/439-50
55 Mekeel 176
56 McIlwaine, Jnls of Council 1/499-500
57 Bliven 81
58 Gilpin 35-6 Pa Mag Hist & Bio 29/302 Mekeel 173
59 Wilson, RH 54
60 Pa Mag Hist & Bio 29/301
61 Wilson, RH 56
62 Friends Hist Asso, Quaker History vol 75 #1 (Spring 1986)
63 Mekeel 176
64 Pa Mag Hist & Bio 96/305
65 Gilpin 36
66 Wilson RH 56
67 Gilpin 143 Pa Mag Hist & Bio 96/307
68 Pa Mag Hist & Bio 96/309
69 Gilpin 160, 171
70 Ibid 171-2, 177
71 McIlwaine, Jnls of Council 9
72 Gilpin 172
73 Hopewell 85, 123 Haverford Quaker Mss 854 Swarthmore Quaker Mss-Wharton Papers
74 Jones RM, Later Periods 10
75 Gilpin 208 Pa Mag Hist & Bio 96/312 Swarthmore Quaker Mss Wharton Papers
76 Mekeel 178
77 Ibid 182
78 Ibid 182-3
79 Swarthmore Quaker Mss Wharton Papers
80 Gilpin 213
81 Ibid 279-80
82 Drinker
83 Ibid 97-102
84 Pa Mag Hist & Bio 96/323-4
85 Gill 145
86 Callahan 18 Norris 128 Russell WG 17
87 Hopewell 127-9 Haverford Quaker Mss Box 14 Mekeel 264 Swarthmore Quaker Mss Wharton Papers 88 Tract Asso Bio Sketches 61
89 Mekeel 264
90 MacMaster 380-2
91 Augusta Co Hist Soc 218
92 Hopewell 184
93 Alderman Library Univ of Va Ms 38-160
94 Savery 19
95 Mekeel 192
96 Weeks 189
97 Haverford Quaker Mss 851 & 1116/168
98 Mekeel 265-6
99 Manarin 141
100 Haverford Quaker Mss 1116/168/65
101 Ward & Greer 161
102 Haverford Quaker Mss 1116/168/65
103 Ward & Greer 161
104 Wm & Mary Qrly Ser 2 Vol 1/181
105 Ward & Greer 85, 92 Haverford Quaker Mss 1116/168/67
106 Maryland Hist Soc Matthews Papers

END NOTES

　　　Swarthmore Quaker Mss
　　　Epistles
107　Friend The Phila 35/51
108　Bruns 466
109　Philips 92, 118
110　Ibid 177-9
111　Comly J & I 2/253
112　Howe 1/314 Augusta Co
　　　Hist Soc 109 Caldwell
　　　126-7
113　Eckenrode, Revolution
　　　276-83

CHAPTER X
*(pages 225-264)*
1　Blake 177 Brown RE & BK
　　284 Randolph 329
　　Eckenrode, Revolution 19-
　　20
2　Haverford Quaker Mss 851
3　McColley 90
4　Brookes 436
5　Friend, The 17/172-80
6　Haverford Quaker Mss
　　1116-125
7　Blake 389 Brookes 109
8　Blake
9　Friends Hist Asso 44/77-83
10　Blake 170-1 Jones RM
　　Later Periods 322
11　Ward and Greer 125
12　Goodell 110 Munford 41
13　Munford 41
14　James SV 298
15　Haverford Quaker Mss
　　1116/168
16　Ibid
17　Haverford Quaker Mss 851
18　Haverford Quaker Mss
　　1116/168 103-4
19　Bruns 508
20　Russell E 248 Forbush 40,44
　　Dunlap 450-62 Janney SM,
　　History 3/428-39 Littrell 17
　　Bauman 196 Goodell 38
21　Drake 83 Ward & Greer
　　125 Russell JH 56
22　Hughes-McIntire 11
23　Hinshaw WW 6/115
24　Padover 61
25　Haverford Quaker Mss
　　1116/168
26　Scattergood 125, 137
27　Catterall 109 Huntington
　　Library Brock Mss 7/297-
　　307
28　Huntington Library Mss Box
　　13/Letters 21,28,45
29　Dabney 162-3
30　Sweet 139
31　Isaac 282-6
32　Isaac 287 Alley 55-60
33　Isaac 233-4

34　Friendly Letter 11th Mo
　　1983
35　Bailey 27
36　Guilday xxiv
37　Ward 50
38　Sweet 46-7, 60-2
39　Ibid 134
40　Meade 17
41　Isaac 313
42　Rouse, Planters 111-2
43　Walker 485
44　Bruns 76
45　Brookes 84-5
46　Ibid 105
47　McColley 150-1 Asbury 2/33

48　Munford 102
49　Bruns 493-501
50　Blake 391 Friend, The
　　(Phila) 17/181
51　Lynd 165 Ketcham 46
52　Drake 161
53　Ibid 102
54　Davidson 2/318
55　Wilson RH 68
56　Drake 102
57　Blake 407-21 Drake 103-06
58　Madison 13/109
59　Drake 106
60　Madison 13/176
61　Drake 107
62　Blake 424
65　Cartland 50 Brissot xvi
　　Bruns 384-5 Goodell 95
66　Huntington Library Brock
　　Mss Box 12/3
67　Brissot 238
68　Haverford Quaker Mss
　　1116/168/160
69　Evans, Charles 29803
70　Haverford Quaker Mss
　　1116/168/179
71　Ibid 1116/168/169
72　Ibid 1116/168/202
73　Ibid 851
74　MacMaster 533 Madison
　　13/330-1
75　Madison 14/30-1, 70
76　Ibid 14/91-2
77　Haverford Quaker Mss
　　1116/168/229
78　Berlin 82
79　Hening 1/363-5
80　Netherton 210
81　Swarthmore Quaker Mss
　　Misc
82　Johnson WP
83　Swarthmore Quaker Mss
　　Stabler Papers
84　Ibid Mss Miscellaneous
85　Mordecai
87　Weeks 128

88　Jones RM, Quakers in Am
　　Colonies 311
89　Haverford Quaker Mss
　　1116/153
90　Russell 56
91　Bell 98,104 Valentine 1648
　　Pa Mag Hist & Bio 29/279
　　Barnard 17ff Haverford
　　Quaker Mss 851 Huntington
　　Library Brock Mss 7/237-8
　　& Box 43/2
92　Jones RM, Later Periods
93　Haverford Quaker Mss
　　1116/168
94　Stabler Wm 17
95　Haverford Quaker Mss
　　1116/153/164-5
96　Hopewell 155
97　Janney JJ 57 Judge 4
98　Dunlap 179,181
99　Comly, J&I 10/139- 86
100　Westtown 17-23
101　Dunlap 173  James SV
　　393
102　Powell M 217
103　Haverford Quaker Mss
　　1116/168/223
104　Scattergood 20
105　Ibid 40, 190
106　Ibid 458
107　Ingle 8-9
108　Ibid
109　Haverford Quaker Mss
　　1116/168/159
110　Ibid
111　Asbury 1/46, 1/197-
　　8,2/460,  3/85
112　James SV 6
113　Scott, Job 191-2
114　Savery 156-7
115　Swarthmore Quaker Mss
　　Samuel Smith Collection
116　James SV 315
117　Weeks 195-7 Palmer ed
　　5/370-1 Hening 11/389-91,
　　13/44 Shepard 2/141
　　McIlwaine, Jnls of Council
　　5/ 318-9
118　Brissot 415
119　Swarthmore Quaker Mss
　　Misc
120　Drinker 185
121　Townsend 11-12
122　Janney SM, History 4/149
　　Bauman 206-7
123　Savery 28-87
124　Baltimore YM Indian
　　Committee  134
125　Ibid 142-3
126　Hopewell 124
127　Balto YM Comtee 137
128　Ibid 142-3
129　Thompson 191

# THE FRIENDLY VIRGINIANS

130 Ohio Arch & Hist Qrly - Supplement to Vol 6 (1900)
131 Jones RM Later Periods 397
132 Perdue G 5
133 Howe 1/588, 2/328-9
134 Comly J&I 10/162
135 Weddell 102 Christian 35
136 National Gazette 10-30-1791
137 Valentine 1271 Weddell 38
138 Jacobson 50
139 Hicks 68
140 Haverford Quaker Mss 1116/153/178
141 Ibid 1116/168
142 Valentine 1238 Tyler's Qrly 2/166 Haverford Quaker Mss 1116/153/196 475-7 Haverford Quaker Mss 1116/168/133 206,216
143 Ibid
144 Haverford Quaker Mss 1116/168/87
145 Ibid 1116/168/205
146 Cocke 73

CHAPTER XI
(pages 265-330)
1 Comly, J & I 12/217-19
2 Jones RM, Later Periods 408-9
3 Haverford Quaker Mss 975C
4 Ibid
5 Walthall 1-2
6 Weeks 246-7
7 Johnson WP 59
8 Wheeling News- Register 8-31-1986
9 Walthall 3
10 Friends Hist Asso (Phila) Vol 12 (Spring 1923)
11 Bond 183
12 Terrell 31
13 Bond 180-1
14 Ohio Arch & Hist Soc 37/45
15 Hunter 201
16 Daniels 111 Malone 1/4
17 Daniels 57
18 Malone 1/15
19 Valentine 1138, 1189
20 American Philos Society Jefferson Farm Book Ms
21 Jefferson 2/174-5
22 Ibid 6/160
23 Blum 155
24 Haverford Quaker Mss 851
25 Jefferson 10/254
26 Stabler, Some Recollections 10
27 Hadley Conversation
28 American Philos Society Jefferson Farm Book Ms
29 Ibid
30 Sutcliff 190
31 Tolles, George Logan 257
32 Swarthmore Quaker Mss Misc
33 Cadbury 39
34 Jefferson 12/75-80, 345-46
35 Haverford Quaker Mss 851
36 Padover 318-9
37 Jefferson 15/374
38 Ibid 15/433-4
39 Anthony 16
40 Madison 13/330
41 Anthony 79
42 Moore 91
43 Johnson, Allen 6/182
44 Sutcliff 90
45 Tolles, George Logan 224-5
46 Anthony 97 Moore 164
47 Anthony 119-20
48 Moore 188-9
49 Cutts 72 Moore 164
50 Grellet 145
51 Cutts 521
52 Ibid 132
53 Hubbs 24ff
54 Cutts 121
55 Jnl of Negro Hist 21/199
56 Kersey 74
57 Swarthmore Quaker Mss Record Group 5
58 Anthony 217
59 Forbush, History
60 Clark 143
61 Blum 208-9
62 Carroll JC 48
63 Carroll JC 51 Jnl of Southern Hist Vol 56 #2/191-214
64 Carroll JC 53
65 Ibid 56
66 Ibid 57
67 McColley 105
68 Catterall 63-73
69 Hinshaw WW 6/163-7 Weeks 215-17 Dunlap 58,458 Drinker 386 Haverford Quaker Mss 1116/153/239
70 Kangas 61
71 Weeks 217
72 Tolles, George Logan 243-8
73 Va Mag Hist & Bio 75/297
74 Blake 438 Munford 35
75 Blake 447
76 Russell JH 79
77 Columbia Hist Society 3/240
78 Sweet 200
79 Blake 450
80 Tolles, George Logan 307
81 Bruce WC 2/486-7
82 Lundy 273
83 Hinshaw WW 6/378
84 Swarthmore Quaker Mss Record Group 5
85 Fox EL 42 Drake 125
86 Goodell 248
87 Fox EL 89
88 Ricks RA, Shrubbery Hill
89 Lundy 14-15 Shotwell 254
90 Drake 17
91 Lundy 20-22
92 Ibid 199
93 Shotwell 267 Powell EW 280
94 Lundy 206
95 Dunlap 460-1 Valentine 1244
96 Dunlap 497-8
97 Haverford Quaker Mss 116/165/26
98 Johnson, Allen 8/6-7
99 Scheel, Culpeper 161
100 Russell E 360
101 Siebert, Underground 33
102 Drake 96 Bruns 508
103 Child 196
104 Smedley 27
105 Coffin L 34-38
107 Interdiocesan 85-6
108 Jones RM Later Periods 299-307 Friends Hist Asso (Phila) Vol 78 #2/62-67
109 Grellet 63
111 Harrison F, Landmarks 450
112 National Geog Mag Jun 1987
113 Jones RM Later Periods 787-8
114 Janney W & AM, Ye Meetg Hous Smal 34
115 Harrison F, Landmarks 579
116 Hening 11/571, 12/479
117 Jacob 58-9 Davidson 249
118 Columbia Hist Society 1957-59/28
119 Fox G 520
120 Tolles, Quakers 460
121 Ibid 470
122 Doherty 218
123 Forbush, Moses Sheppard 123
124 Ibid 107
125 Comly J, Journal 449
126 Schooley 12-13
127 Hinshaw WW 6/622ff
128 Scattergood 78
129 Bell 146
130 Thorburn 12
131 Hinshaw WW 6/129-50
132 Comly J & I 7/212-13
133 Brock 337-9, 719

134 Weeks 196
135 Palmer ed 10/210
136 Ibid 10/331-2
137 Dabney 206-7
138 Netherton 228
139 Stabler W 55-6
140 Huntington Library Brock Mss Box 43 Folder 36
141 Howe 301 Dunlap 410 Janney SM, History 4/161 Ohio Arch & Hist Qrly vol 54 Morse 29-32, 37 Keslsey 124-37 Baltimore YM Indian Committee Burke 28
142 Haverford Quaker Mss 1116/164/17
143 Dunlap 403
144 Jones RM, Later Periods 676-8
145 Va Writers Project 121 Scott MW 105
146 Swift 50-2
147 Poland 151 Janney W & AM, Ye Meetg Hous 67-71
148 Hedman 280
149 Hallowell
150 Bruce PA, Va Plutarch 2/171
151 Hallowell 123
152 Good 4
153 Netherton 296
154 Jones RM, Later Periods 363
155 Lewis 34
156 Ibid 29
157 Keve 23-4
158 Hughes-McIntire 14 Wm & Mary Qrly Ser 1 18/289-91
159 Mordecai 36
160 Va Mag Hist & Bio 59/178 Scott MW 121
161 Hughes-McIntire 14
162 Smith G 480
163 Hinshaw WW 6/201-2
164 Keve 17
165 Ibid 24-9
166 Lewis 213
167 Genius
168 Keve 35
169 Ibid 58
170 Ibid 38
171 Lewis 215
172 Keve 241
173 Good JM 8
174 Lewis 212

CHAPTER XII
*(pages 331-350)*
1 Guilford Quaker Ms 74
2 Hunt W & N 52-4

3 Whitman 637-8
4 Forbush, Elias Hicks 135-6
5 Ibid 34
6 Grellet 142-3
8 Hicks 69
9 Grellet 61
10 Hicks 70
11 Grellet 148
12 Forbush, Elias Hicks 419-20 Grellet 151,635
13 Grellet 69
14 Morse 392
15 Ingle 17-18
16 Jones RM, Later Periods 460 Hicks 372
17 Ingle 84-5
18 Jones RM, Later Periods 460-1
19 Forbush, Elias Hicks 224
20 Whitman 683
21 Ingle 41
22 Ibid 128
23-26 Ibid 146
27 Ibid 44
28 Ibid 100, 271 Note 32
29 Ibid 101
30 Ibid 102
31 Ibid 111-12
32 Whitman 645
33 Ibid
34 Ingle 8
35 Ibid 33
36 Ibid 163,187,192-3
37 Shillitoe 2/91
38 Good DG 154 Ingle 238-40
39 Jones, Later Periods 477
40 Hicks 426 Thomas AB 72
41 Haverford Quaker Mss 1116/153
42 Forbush, History 58-9
43 Forbush, Elias Hicks 274
44 Haverford, Quaker Mss 1020 Ibid Mss 1106/15/23 Janney, W & AM, Ye Meetg Hous 87 Branch, Miscellany
46 Stabler, HB, Further Recollections 325
47 Shillitoe 2/261-2 Barnes 128-9 Ingle 35
48 Smith John 89-96 Stone Ingle 152
49 Hinshaw WW 6/200 Lundy 237
50 Valentine 1260 Dunlap 173
51 Hinshaw WW 6/169-71
52 Drake 130
53 Lundy 18 Poland 145 Janney W & AM, Ye Meetg Hous 62
54 Eaton 234 Jnl of Southern Hist 37/162

55 Lundy 213 Fox EL 212 Hughes-McIntire 12
56 Swarthmore Quaker Mss-Journals
57 Lundy 22
58 Christian 18-19 Carroll JC 131-2
59 Remini 100 Carroll JC 134-5
60 Janney JJ 94
61 Jackson LP 8 Carroll JC 152-3
62 Drake 136
63 Carroll JC 155-6
64 Writers Program 45 Hickin, Antislavery 131-54 Munford 46-8, 91-5 Carroll JC 156-9 Beeman 221-3
65 Swarthmore Quaker Mss Emlen Collection,Ltrs 31,32
66 Tyler-McGraw 68
67 Drake 137 Munford 51-2
68 Columbia Hist Society 3/244
69 Fox EL 10 Dabney 228,278 Cabell 97 Munford 132
70 Haverford Quaker Mss 851
71 Swarthmore Quaker Mss Emlen Collection, Letter 31,1-11-1832

CHAPTER XIII
*(pages 351-396)*
1 Coffin A, Life 94
2 Jones LT 38-9 Quaker Life 10th Mo 1986/6
3 Western Work Jan 1908
4 Huntington Library Brock Mss 15 Item 18
5 Lynchburg News 6-8- 1919
6 Friend, The (Phila) 6/172
7 Friend, The (London) 7th Mo 1845/142
8 Thomas OG, to Fannie Pretlow 1-25-1916
9 Huntington Library Brock Mss 15 Item 12
10 Hadley, Six Items
11 Va Cavalcade Vol 26 #3/27
12 Va Mag Hist & Bio 76/57
13 Muir 27
14 Ibid 52
15 Va Mag Hist & Bio 76/56-7
16 Netherton 284
17 Pugh, Conversation
18 Janney, SM, Memoirs
19 Huntington Library Brock Mss 12 Item 31
20 Fox EL 212
21 Lundy 213
22 Janney SM, Memoirs 28 Hallowell 109-10 Swarthmore Quaker Mss Truman Collection
23 Jnl Southern Hist 37/163

24  Hickin 478
25  Hinshaw SB & ME 138-9
26  Gurney, Memoirs 116 Haverford Quaker Mss 851
27  Wilson RH 34-5 Ford 78-188
28  Russell E 343
29  Jones RM, Later Periods 513-17
30  Russell E 343-4
31  Jones RM, Later Periods 506-8
32  Good, DG 219-26
33  Ibid 294
34  Jones RM, Later Periods 506-7 Gurney, Extracts 415
35  Swift 44
36  Swift 131-5 Smith, Joseph 75
37  Jones RM, Later Periods 513 Wilbur 158
38  Swift 173
39  Ibid 213-4
40  Ratcliff 183-4
41  Swift 190
42  Wright Guilford Quaker Mss Crenshaw Papers
43  Gurney, Journey 70
44  Gurney, Journey 58-9
45  Gurney, Extracts 411
46  Swift 200
47  Gurney, Journey 75
48  Gurney, Letter
49  Gurney, Journey 51
50  Gurney, Memoirs 117 Gurney, Journey 81, 385-92 Gurney, Extracts 412 Swift 200
51  Jones RM, Later Periods 520 Wilbur 276
52  Wilbur 137-40, 286
53  Russell E 351-2
54  Ibid 353-6
55  Ratcliff 19-20
56  Poley 53
57  Ratcliff xi
58  Osborn 144
59  Good DG 65
60  Friends Hist Asso 61/91-106
61  Drake 209 Brock 346,350 Good DG 82
62  O'Neall & Chapman 10-15-1825
63  Caldwell 530
64  Gurney, Journey 97
65  Ibid Sessions 68
66  Blake 365
67  Russell E 336-7
68  Gurney, Journey 18,142
69  Swift 200
70  Gurney, Journey 108
71  Wilbur 54-5, 117, 119
72  Gurko 88-9
73  Johnson, Allen (Grimke)

74  Blockson 211-12
75  Davis AH 92
76  Davis AH 299 Gurko 2ff
77  Davis AH 68-9, 103, 233-9 Swarthmore Quaker Mss Dugdale Collection
78  Gurko 103
79  Cunliffe 50
80  Haverford Quaker Mss 1116 172/20-50
81  Dunlap 97-185
82  Chace 23
83  Comly, John Grammar
84  Gregg JW 23
85  Branch, Miscellany
86  Jones RM, Later Periods 687-98
87  Dunlap 131
88  Janney SM, Memoirs 93-5 Janney SM, Virginia 39 Dabney 249-50 Poland 150-1 Maddox 149-52
89  Harvey 291
90  London YM 174-94
91  Forbush, History 61 Forbush, Moses Sheppard 112-29 Dunlap 396-404
92  Jones RM, Later Periods 569ff Howe 2/769-72 Coffin L 525 Drake 137-8 Blockson 236-7
93  Mead 125,240 Goodell 411 Christian 133-4 Sturge 184 Wust 126 Sweet 209 Hickin 347
94  Craven 120 Southern Friend (Richmond)
95  Haverford Quaker Mss 1111.5
96  Ibid 1116/161/249
97  Jackson LP 19
98  Dunlap 195-7 Drake 169
99  Hughes-McIntire 12
100 Ricks, Shrubbery Hill
101 Hughes-McIntire 11-12
102 Ricks, Shrubbery Hill
103 Swarthmore Quaker Mss Misc
104 Janney SM, Memoirs 52 Hickin 617-93
105 Swarthmore Quaker Mss Truman Collection
106 Jnl Southern Hist 37/167-83
107 Swarthmore Quaker Mss Truman Collection
108 Ibid Janney Collection
109 Dabney 236
110 Janney SM Memoirs 189 Dunlap 125-6 Forbush, Moses Sheppard 179
111 Jnl Southern Hist 37/183
112 Poland 158-61

113 Goodell 243 Va Writers Project 79 Tyler-McGraw 63
114 Sturge 75
115 Jackson HU 9
116 Natl Geog Mag Vol 166 #1(July 1984)
117 Jones RM, Later Periods 580-93 Cartland 106, 110-11 Anscombe 168-9 Siebert, Underground 40 Ratcliff RP 67
118 Siebert, Underground 68
119 Ibid Map op page 113
120 Siebert, Mysteries 126-33
121 Siebert, Underground 46-8
122 Siebert, Underground 424 Drake 122 Caldwell 157,161 Haverford Quaker Mss 851
123 Olmsted 321-2
124 Hopewell 489 Branch, Miscellany
125 Siebert, Underground 280 Coffin L 272ff Jolliffe 96ff Blockson 187 Siebert, Mysteries 53
126 Janney, W & AM, Composition Bk 20 Poland 163
127 Coffin A, Early Settlement
128 Ibid
129 Southern Friend (Greensboro) Vol 2 #1 (Spring 1980) Haverford Quaker Mss 851
130 Powell MG 342
131 Washington Post 2-25-1991
132 Non Slaveholder 3/66
133 Chace 136-63
134 Siebert, Underground 177-89
135 Cartland 404
136 Weeks 242ff
137 Cartland 380
138 Tract Association, Monitor 64 Frysinger
139 Perdue CL 110
140 Ibid 234
141 Remini 5
142 Hemphill 265-6 Hillsboro 18 Poland 74 Davidson 1/412
143 Norris 783
144 Jolliffe 206
145 Hopewell 173
146 Ibid 171
147 Harrison F, Landmarks 578, 596
148 Va Asso Realtors 61,267

149  Haverford Quaker Mss 975B
150  Tolles, Emerson 146-8
151  Blum 241-2
152  Tolles, Emerson 146ff
153  Hemphill 253
154  Ward HM
155  Dabney 257,265 Wamsley 125-32
156  Dabney 222 Ward HM 90
157  Swift 140
158  Walker 510
159  Tyler-McGraw 36-44,61
160  Bailey 25
161  Wust 146-8

CHAPTER XIV
*(pages 397-438)*
1   Eaton 470
2   Blake 532-63
3   Smedley 126, 216-7 Still 348-68 Bacon, Rebellion Blockson 215
4   Janney SM, Memoirs
5   Poland 103-4
6   Coffin A, Life 110-15 Va Mag Hist & Bio 81/259-79 Janney W & AM, Ye Meetg Hous 30
7   Hinshaw WW 6/556 Jones LT 147 Jacobson 57 Swarthmore Quaker Mss Record Group 5
8   Jones RM, Later Periods 903
9   Swarthmore Quaker Mss Jnls
10  Jones RM, Later Periods 592-3
11  Jay 140 Non-Slaveholder 6/100 Evans Wm 597-8
12  Still 170-1
13  Poland 163
14  Bell 103-4
15  Redpath 240-64
16  Washington Post 9-16-1973/C3
17  Jones RM, Later Pds 851-2 Swarthmore Quaker Mss Misc
18  Redpath 348-9
19  Chace 166-78
20  Lippincott 121-7
21  Rawick ed
22  Janney W & AM, Composition Bk 25
23  White, Quaker Janneys 37
24  Turner 15 Miller 17
25  Swarthmore Quaker Mss Record Group 5
26  Christian 218-9
27  Turner 15 Williams 198-9 Haverford Quaker Mss 950 Munford 302-3
28  Thomas AB 65
29  Janney W & AM Composition Bk 25 Janney W & AM Ye Meetg Hous 35
30  Gillingham 3-5
31  Ibid 7
32  Jones RM, Later Pds 740 Wright 92-7 Brock 764
33  Hinshaw SB & ME 190-3
34  Janney SM, Memoirs 94,222 Hopewell 131, 201, 335 Hughes-McIntire 5 Haverford Quaker Mss 1106/15/15 Gillingham 5
35  Cartland 334 Muir 107-8, 122 Gillingham 7-8
36  Gillingham 15-16
37  Jay 198-200 Janney SM, Memoirs 103-6 Swarthmore Quaker Mss Misc
38  Wright 64, 100
39  Bell 269
40  Cartland 126-7
41  Wright 106 Cartland 358
42  Davis HA 16
43  Rouse Great Wagon Rd 99 Hopewell 186 Thwaites 194 Wayland, Hist Shenandoah Co 647 Spraker 536-7 Haverford Quaker Mss 1005E Wayland, Va Valley Records 57 Newport News Daily Press 11-10-1974 Bassuk
44  Comstock 186, 206 Bates 25, 29 American Hist Reports 30/415-25
45  Pringle 62, 85 Comstock 206 Friend, The (Phila) 114,297-9 Jones RM, Eli & Sibyl 179 Swarthmore Quaker Mss Jnls Elliott 14 American Hist Reports 30/415-25
46  Wright 126-30 Weeks 280 Cartland 129 Ohio Arch & Hist Qrly 37/33 Thomas SB 8
47  Hopewell 185, 495 Swayne Swarthmore Quaker Mss Janney Collection Futhey & Cope 733
48  Janney SM, Memoirs Jolliffe 338 Poland 216 Swarthmore Quaker Mss Janney Collection Ibid Pidgeon Papers Ser 4/R65
49  Bassuk 7-8
50  Wright 112 Bassuk 8-9
51  Bassuk 9-10 Cadbury 269 Smedley 244
52  Haverford Quaker Ms 1026
53  Cartland 132
54  Cadbury, Essays 122, 198 Ketcham 9-10 Terrell 43-4 Davidson 390
55  Cartland 223
56  Hinshaw WW 6/404,510, 665,711
57  Cartland 363
58  Ibid 369
59  Wright Guilford Quaker Mss Crenshaw Papers
60  Cartland 366 Guilford Quaker Mss Crenshaw Papers
61  Hinshaw WW 6/452 Walker 406 Swarthmore Quaker Mss Misc
62  Hopewell 130-1 Swarthmore Quaker Mss Misc
63  Cartland 224, 356
64  Ibid 226,355,358
65  Ibid 231-53
66  Ibid 355
67  Ibid 195-200
68  Pemberton 275
69  Cartland 336-8
70  Hillsboro 22
71  Bell 276
72  Cartland 342-3
73  Comstock 206
74  Gillingham 35
75  Haverford Quaker Mss 1116 Item G Guilford Quaker Mss Crenshaw Papers
76  Swarthmore Quaker Mss Misc
77  Pringle 162-93
78  Wright 72-76
79  Guilford Quaker Mss Crenshaw Papers
80  Wright 116-18 Horst 88
81  Cartland 191-3 Evans WF Goodhart 8
82  Cartland 145,189- 91
83  Hinshaw WW 1/750 Cartland 216
84  Janney, SM Memoirs 218-23
85  Horst 108
86  Hinshaw WW 6/731 Hopewell 35-6 Sheridan 3-9, 28
87  Cartland 343-4 Comstock 217 Elliott 109-11
88  Janney, SM Memoirs 229-31 Janney, W & AM, Ye Meetg Hous 45-7 Swarthmore, Thomas R Smith Mss
89  Janney W & AM, Comp Bk 26 Follmer 71

90  Bell 276 Thomas AB 31-2 Neave 59-60

CHAPTER XV
*(pages 439-478)*
1   Janney, W & AM, Composition Bk 28
2   Janney SM, Memoirs 235
3   Sandburg 4/309-10
4   Jones RM, Eli & Sibyl 179-81
5   Cartland 366 Janney SM, Memoirs 230-2
6   Jones RM, Later Pds 330 Hopewell 137-8 Scott MW 240
7   Janney SM Memoirs 232
8   Mag Albemarle Co Hist 37/26-48
9   Janney SM Virginia 42
10  Netherton 366-8 Eckenrode, Political Hist 18
11  Eckenrode, Political Hist 41-6
12  Ibid 27
13  Va Mag Hist & Bio 80/360
14  Christian 304-8
15  Phila YM Book Committee 190
16  Dunlap 498-500
17  Jacobson 128 Scott MW
18  Russell E 408 Jones RM, Later Pds 499 Davis AH 411
19  Swint, Dear Ones 5-131 Davis AH 411 Haverford Quaker Mss 975B
20  Wistar 417-54
21  Magdol 268 Swint, Dear Ones 100 Wistar 417-44
22  Jones RM, Later Pds 601-2
23  Swint, Dear Ones 109-20
24  Warner 64-5
25  Swint, Northern Teacher 20
26  Swint, Dear Ones 154-5
27  Haviland 40 Lasley 615 Southern Friend (Richmond) 109
28  Hinshaw WW 6/207 Weeks 313 Benjamin 129 Southern Friend (Richmond) 117
29  Warner 216
30  Weeks 408 Friends Asso for Freedmen 167
31  Jones RM, Later Pds 602-3 Warner 216
32  Benjamin 133 Blacksburg News- Msgr 7-1-1976 Alderson 73
33  Jones RM, Later Pds 613 Blacksburg News- Msgr 7-1-1976 Alderson 73
34  Va Mag Hist 61/432-8 Gardner 37 Alderson 84, 94 Swint, Northern Teacher 85-6
35  Breault Richmond Times-Dispatch 4-4-1985
36  Janney SM, Memoirs 243 Scheel, Purcellville 11 Netherton 369 Follmer 109 Swarthmore Quaker Mss Misc
37  Haviland 401
38  Tyler-McGraw 17
39  Alderson 18
40  Neave 64 Lasley 13
41  Forbush, History 192 Lasley 15 Southern Friend (Richmond) 192
42  Alderson 54
43  Alderson 56 Swint, Northern Teacher 95-8
44  Gardner 51
45  Alderson 135
46  Jones RM, Later Pds 603
47  Richmond Times- Dispatch 5-17-1981 Charlottesvl Dly Progress 1986
48  Jones RM, Later Periods 946-51 Benjamin 3
49  Dunlap 498-500 Hughes-McIntire 12 Phila YM Bk Committee 190
50  Phila YM Bk Committee 200 Alderson 210
51  Hughes-McIntire 15 Bacon 112
52  Gillingham
53  Ibid
54  Eaton, Old South
55  Simkins
56  Forbush, History 50-6 Dunlap 137,170 Follmer 109 Branch, Interchange 6-7,22
57  Thomas AB 110, 132 Poland 246-8
58  Jones RM, Later Pds 709 Stone
59  Jones RM, Later Pds 704-5
60  Janney W & AM, Ye Meetg Hous 74-6
61  Ibid 78
62  Comstock 502
63  Jones RM, Later Pds 179
64  Swarthmore Quaker Mss Samuel Janney Collection Branch Interchange
65  Swarthmore Quaker Mss Samuel Janney Collection
66  Forbush, History 38 Morton 49 Swarthmore Quaker Mss Samuel Janney Collection Gillingham 49
67  Janney W & AM, Comp Bk 92
68  Smith, LB
69  Mardock 22,86-7
70  Dunlap 408-9
71  Mardock 35
72  Kelsey 167-8 Mardock 52
73  Hallowell 261-2
74  Kelsey 170
75  Dunlap 411-2 Mardock 50
76  Southern Friend (Greensboro) Vol 10 #2/32
77  Hallowell 163
78  Janney SM, Memoirs 254 Swarthmore Quaker Mss Samuel Janney Collection
79  Swarthmore Quaker Mss, Green Coll
80  Janney SM, Memoirs 272
81  Fry 51
82  Janney SM, Memoirs 272-4
83  Mardock 3
84  Janney SM, Memoirs 271-2
85  Hixson 19
86  Swarthmore Quaker Mss Green Coll
87  Dunlap 415-6 Mardock 38
88  Ibid 239
89  Janney SM, Memoirs 283 Swarthmore Quaker Mss Baltimore YM (Hicksite) Collection
90  Swarthmore Quaker Mss Green Coll
91  Dunlap 414
92  Mardock 82
93  Janney SM, Memoirs 283
94  Johnson, Allen Dist of Columbia Hist 99-100,114, 329-30
95  Mardock 144
96  Mead 136
97  Benjamin 91
98  Thomas AB 99
99  Branch, Interchange Vol 1#3(2-15-1885)
100 VA Qrly Mtg Jan-Feb 1962
101 Branch, Hist Travel Baltimore YM Pastoral Comtee 1886/27
102 Guilford Quaker Ms 182 Branch, Hist Travel Southern Friend (Greensboro) Vol 2 (Autumn 1979)
103 Thomas AB 102
104 Trollope
105 Russell E 426-7 Hamm 75, 84
106 Scheel, Purcellville 10
107 Branch, Interchange 11th Mo 1898, 2nd Mo 1899
108 Thomas AB 110
109 Branch, Interchange 4th Mo 1899

110 Good DG 304 Hamm 78
111 Janney SM, Memoirs 294-5
112 Russell E 428 Hamm 84
113 Jones RM, Later Periods 924-5
114 Bill Minear 40,82
115 Phila YM Book Comtee 206
116 Janney SM, Memoirs 305 Stone
117 Forbush, History 84-5 Janney SM, History 4/343-5
118 Branch, Interchange
119 Vining, 38-9, 249
120 Smith HW
121 Jones RM, Later Periods 927-8
122 Ibid 929
123 Jones RM, Later Pds 929-30
124 Minear 114,131-3
125 Elliott 157-8
126 Branch, Interchange
127 Russell E 496 Forbush, History 108 Janney W & AM, Ye Meetg Hous 90-1 Swarthmore Quaker Mss Misc

CHAPTER XVI
(pages 479-506)
1 Dabney 429-30, 434
2 Ibid 436-7
3 Wilson RH 109
4 Russell E 510-15 Jones RM, Service of Love 28-35
5 Current 517
6 Forbush, History 110-11
7 Jones RM, Service of Love 12
8 Jones RM, Service of Love 248-50 Jones MH, Swords 6, 42-4, 51-64,320,322
9 Jones RM, Service of Love 267-82 Jones MH, Swords 312
10 Jones RM, Service of Love 239-40
11 Russell E 525-6 Jones RM, Service of Love 123
12 Bacon 95,101 Columbia Hist Society 1971-72 Records/657-78
13 Alderman Library, Equal Suffrage League Papers
14 Bacon 107-8
15 Moran, Interview
16 May 150
17 Irwin 217-8
18 Bacon 107 Irwin 271-86
19 Irwin 429

20 Shelton 26,32,51-2 Clare 35-7 Marschean 40
21 Marschean 55
22 Moran, Interview
23 Bacon 109-10
24 Jones MH, Swords 80-1
25 Jones RM, Service of Love 250-1
26 Thomas AB 132-3 Thomas E 15
27 Thomas, E 117
28 Ibid 118-9
29 Canter 156-7
30 Thomas E 110
31 McClellan 68
32 Thomas E 111-2
33 Russell E 492-5
34 Ibid 495-7
35 Russell E 524 Jones MH, Swords 128-32
36 Quaker Religious Thought Vol 13#1 (Autumn 1971)
37 Va Qrly Mtg Lasley 25
38 Anscombe 349-52
39 Thomas AB 117
40 Jacobson 128 Haverford Quaker Mss 918 Scott MW 240
41 Muir 171 Netherton 505 Hadley, Six Items
42 Friends World Comtee, Trends Benjamin 217-8
43 Jones RM, A Call
44 Benjamin 215
45 Hughes-McIntire
46 Thomas AB 134-5
47 Anscombe 243 Branch, Miscellany Norfolk Virginian- Pilot 3-13-1958
49 Branch, Miscellany Friends World Comtee, Trends 7-10
50 Lyons 144,174
51 Lyons 287 Pickett 43,56
52 Forbush, History 131
53 Moran, Four Quaker Presences
54 Vining 291
55 Fabre 71-2
56 Keim

CHAPTER XVII
(pages 507-536)
1 Evangelical Friends' Anniversary Bk
2 Moran, Four Quaker Presences
3 Fager 22-3
4 Ibid 61
5 Fager 48-9 Ianniello 39-48
6 Washington Star 2- 15-1977
7 Brisbane 237-45 Ianniello 49-58
8 Dabney 530-8

10 Fager 64-77
11 Friends Jnl 7-15-1985
12 Newman 306-15
13 Newman 333-4 Friends Jnl 11-1- 1960
14 Smith B Adams N
15 Wilson Raymond 236
16 Ibid 175-88
17 Time-Life Books 12/140-6
18 Ibid 12/143, 152-3
19 Forbush, History 149-55
21 Washington Post 12-2-1985 New York Times 11- 7-1965 Baltimore Eve Sun 11-25-1965
22 Morrison 2-3
23 Washington Post 6-5-1965, 6-29-1965 Los Angeles Times 6-12-1969
24 Charlottesville Dly Progress 5-6-1969
25 Va Ccl Human Relations 1966- 69
26 Friends Jnl 11-15-1965
27 Richmond Times Dispatch 6-3-1968 to 11-30-1969 Charlottesville Daily Progress 6-3-68 to 11-30-1969 Va Weekly 6-3-1968 to 11-3-1969
28 Va Ccl Human Relations Jan 1970
29 Flake 7
30 Washington Post 8-4-1988
31 Friends World Comtee, Directory 1992
32 Anscombe 355-6 Newman 412 Wilson, Raymond 173-4 Friendly Ltr #34 (1st Mo 1984) Levering
33 Flake 7-8, 50
34 Quaker Univ Flshp 2-10
35 Friendly Ltr #120 (4th Mo 1991)
36 Quaker Univ Flshp 23

# INDEX

Adams
  Bob 204
  Frank 519, 522, 525, 526
  John 179, 208, 274, 278
  John Quincy 297, 343, 366
  Robert 203
  Robert (Jr) 204
  Samuel 179
Akehurst
  Daniel 97
Alcott
  Bronson 392
Alexander
  (Czar of Russia) 358
Allen
  Benjamin 130
  Mary Ann Marriage 471
  William 363
Allinson
  Samuel 178
Ambrose
  Alice 31
Ames
  William 10
Anderson
  Naomi 76
Andrews
  Isaac 146, 147
Andros
  Edmund 87, 88
Anthony
  Joseph 165, 166
  Susan 487, 488, 490, 491
  Susan B. 486
Archdale
  John 93, 101
Arnold
  Benedict 219
Asbury
  Francis 236, 254
Atkinson
  Roger 174
Audland
  John 11
Austin
  Ann 3, 4
  Charles 428
  Elizabeth 4, 40
Aylmer
  Justinian 27

Babb
  Herbert 485
  Howard 485
  Nancy 391, 485, 493, 494, 500
Bache
  Elizabeth 7
  Humphrey 8, 9
Bacon
  Nathaniel (Jr) 68
Bagby
  Arthur 322
Bailey
  Anselm 192
  David 270
  J. 229
  M. 229
  Michael 261
  Samuel 244
Baily
  Joshua 451
Baker
  Helen 516
Bakker
  Jim 526, 527
  Tammy 526
Ballinger 355
  D. Walton 460
Bancroft
  Edward 230
Banister
  Mary 99
Banneker
  Benjamin 231, 274
Barbour
  James 313
Barclay
  David 169, 180
  Robert 70, 71, 76, 118, 169, 255, 302, 362
  William 56
Barker
  Cyrus 424
  Jacob 283
  Nathan 424
Barnard
  Hannah Jenkins 298
Barnes
  John 68
Barnett
  Walter 530
Bartlett
  Claude 497
  Fred 497
  James 497

Bartram
  John 272
Bates 486
  Benjamin 251, 310, 312, 417
  Edward 417, 434
  Elijah 310
  Elisha 292, 340, 341, 361, 364, 367, 369, 472, 474, 475
  Fleming 310, 347, 364, 365
  James 104
  John 101
  Micajah 251
  Thomas Fleming 261
Beals 486
  Thomas 197, 198
Beare
  Edward 64, 119
Beckerdite
  John R. 430
Beeson
  Charity 127
  Henry 188, 189
  Jane 246, 247
  Mary 188
  Richard 127
Behre
  Ed 502, 515, 520
  Vernice 502, 515
Bell
  Nathan 294
  Sally 294
  William F. 430
Benbricke
  Robert 1, 9
Benezet
  Anthony 137, 159, 172, 174, 177, 178, 182, 226, 236, 237, 242
Bennett
  Anne 7
  Philip 21
  Richard 6, 7, 11, 21, 22, 28, 34, 56-58, 173
Bentley
  Caleb 283
Benton
  William 400
Bergson
  Henri 392

# INDEX

Berkeley
  John 56
  Norborne 169, 187
  William 5, 8, 19, 23, 24, 25, 26, 28, 29, 31, 34, 35, 37, 39, 47, 54, 56, 58, 61, 67, 68, 70, 80
Berry
  Fanny 405
Bettle
  Samuel 342
Beverly
  William 126
Biddle
  Clement 214
Bigelow
  Joshua 388, 402
Biglow
  Robert W. 402
Billing
  Edward 10
Binford
  Oliver 373
  William 228
Bishop
  George 12, 16, 32
Black
  Eileen 509
Blair
  James 82, 83, 88, 89, 95, 97, 107, 115
Blake
  John 33
Bland
  Anne 28
  Richard 173, 177, 195, 225
  Theodorick 28
Boddie
  Anna 62
  William 62
Bolling
  Richard A. 347
  Robert 198
Bolon
  Buck 439
Bonaparte
  Napoleon 359
Bond
  Abel 400
  Asa Moore 417
  John 25
  Joseph 258
  Sarah Alice 417
Bonger
  Thomas 107

Boone
  Daniel 161, 265, 269
  George 124
  Raymond 525
  Sarah 124, 161
Booth
  John Wilkes 440
Borden
  Benjamin 126
Boston
  Henry 36, 37
Boukley
  Joseph 401
Bowater
  John 38, 65
Bradbury
  Emilie 485
Bradby
  James 523
Braddock
  Edward 154
Bradshaw 468
  Anne Elizabeth 468
  Evelyn 514
Braithwaite
  Anna 340, 342, 361
  Isaac 340, 361
Branson
  Ann 367
  Billy 246
  Joseph 258
  W. 247
Bray
  Thomas 94
Brayton
  Patience Greene 203
Brend
  William 14
Brewster
  Margaret 48
Brickhouse
  George 38
Bridger
  Joseph 61
  William 102
Bridle
  Francis 92
Briggs
  Isaac 274
  Thomas 52
Brissot-de-Warville
  Jacques-Pierre 243
  Jean-Pierre 205
British Monarchs (House of Hanover)
  George I 113, 123
  George III 163, 168, 169, 170, 171, 180, 181, 182, 183, 194, 200, 202, 225, 320

British Monarchs (House of Stuart)
  Anne 109, 112
  Charles I 2, 6, 19, 20, 22, 79
  Charles II 23, 31, 34, 36, 44, 46, 52, 54, 58, 61, 67, 73, 79, 80, 124, 153, 154
  Henrietta Maria 79
  James II 79, 80
  Mary II and William 81, 84, 193
  Mary, Queen of Scots 75
British Monarchs (House of Tudor)
  Elizabeth I 20
  Henry VIII 2
Broadnax
  William 347
Brown 355
  Barratt 479
  Charles Brockden 209
  David 258
  Elijah 209
  Geneva 509
  Herbert 520
  Jesse 400
  John 403, 404, 406, 421
  Joshua 220
  Judith 184
  Lydia Janney 458
  Moses 239, 302
  Orlando 449
  William 300
Browne
  John 45, 46
Bryan
  Morgan 125, 161
  Morgan (Jr) 161
  William Jennings 471
Bryant
  Anita 529
Buchanan
  James 406
Buffum
  Elizabeth 404
Bufkin
  Levin 92, 117
Bundy
  Sarah 385
Burns
  Lucy 487

Burnyeat
  John 47-49, 54, 55
Burr
  Aaron 279
  Henry 147
Burrough
  Edward 1, 2, 43, 94
Burruss
  John 166
  Rachel 166
Burtell
  James 102, 103
Bushrod
  Mary 27
  Thomas 27, 28
Butcher
  Ann 260
  John 258, 260
Butler
  Ben 447
  Joseph 341
Byrd
  William 28, 70, 108, 109, 119-121, 125
  William (II) 108
Cadwalader
  John 195
Cadwallader
  Rees 258
Calhoun
  John C. 297
Callaway
  James 203, 204
Calthorpe
  Christopher 27
Calvert
  (Governor of Maryland) 37
Calvin
  John 24, 75
Camm
  John 11
Campbell
  David 365
  Hugh 93
  John A. 418, 430
Canby
  Samuel 196
  William 277
Candler
  Daniel 352
Cant
  William 100
Carmichael
  Stokely 524
Carroll
  Coleman 529
  John 234

Carter
  Charles 227, 243
  Jimmy 526
  Joseph 130
  Robert 228, 243
  Robert "King" 125, 126
  Shirley 243
  Sydney 43
Cartwright
  John 38, 52, 62
Cary
  Archibald 166
Caton
  William 10
Catt
  Carrie 489, 490
  Carrie Chapman 488
Cayton
  Nathan 510
Chalkley
  Thomas 99, 123, 131
Champion
  William 187
Chandlee 486
Chandler
  John A. 347
Chapman
  Thomas 11, 12, 15
Chappell
  Jeremiah 373
Charles 486
Chase
  Jeremiah T. 238
  Lucy 447, 448, 450
  Pliny Earle 474
  Salmon P. 420
  Sarah 447, 448, 450
Cheadle
  John 219
Cheesman
  George 244
Chetwynd
  William 175
Chiles
  James 165-167
Chisman
  Edmund 27, 28
  Mary 27
Christison
  Wenlock 30
Claiborne
  William 22
Clark 273
  Christopher (Kit) 166, 167
  Mary 14
  Robert 520

Clarkson
  Robert 8
Clay
  Henry 291, 343, 366, 373, 397, 407
Cloud
  Red 466
Coale
  Josiah 8, 11, 12, 15, 16, 17
Cochran
  Fred 418
  Frederick 417
Cocke
  Thomas 70
Codrington
  Christopher 52
Coffin
  Addison 295, 351
  Catherine 398
  Levi 295, 384, 398, 449
  Vestal 295
Coggeshall
  Elizabeth 298, 335
Coke
  Thomas 236
Cole
  William 31
Coleridge
  Samuel Taylor 392
Coles
  Edward 283
Collier
  George 218
Collins 355
  Elizabeth 279
Colvin
  Fermine 508
Comfort
  Henry 451
Comly
  John 373
Compton
  Henry 74
Comstock
  Elizabeth 432, 434, 459
Congdon
  Eunice 448
  Gilbert 377, 378, 402
Connelley
  John 189
Conquest
  Richard 26
Cook
  Ebenezer 119
  Priscilla 341

# INDEX

Cooley
  Victoria 523
Coolidge
  Calvin 501
Cooper
  Thomas 276
Cope
  Joshua 385
  Marmaduke 447
  Regina 447
Copeland
  Dolly 389
  Henry 389
  Jesse 267
  John 101
  Will 313
Copeman
  Nancy 493
  Tom 493
Copperthwaite
  Joseph 196
Coppock
  Barclay 404
  Edwin 404
Cornell
  Ezra 457
Cornwallis
  Charles Lord 221
Cowart
  Elizabeth 8
Cramp
  William 354
Crandall
  Prudence 377
Crawford
  Robert 511
Crenshaw
  Charles 356
  Deborah Anne 436
  Eliza Kate 499
  Elizabeth 402
  John 387, 402, 410, 414, 415, 416, 418, 422, 423, 426, 430, 436, 440, 445, 446, 450, 455, 456, 473, 499
  John Bacon 356, 374
  Margaret 499
  Mary 436
  Nathaniel 291, 344, 353, 355-358, 365, 374, 379, 387, 402, 410, 414, 416
  Willie 436
Cresap
  Michael 189

Crew 344
  Andrew 111
  Anna 353
  Benjamin 344
  Chappell 344
  David 344
  Deborah 309, 356
  Galley 111
  Henry 344, 385
  Jacob 344
  James 344
  John 111, 192, 220, 243, 261
  Lemuel 309, 342, 353, 356
  Margaret 309, 310, 379, 402
  Micajah 187, 188, 243, 281, 309, 310, 353
  Robert 111, 310
  Terrell 344
Crewdson
  Isaac 361, 362, 475
Crey
  John 43
Cromwell
  Oliver 2, 5, 6, 22, 23
  Richard 23
Cross
  Mildred A. 482
Cuffey
  Paul 282, 290
Cuffin
  David 16
Culpeper
  (1680's Virginia Governor) 74
Curry
  James 388
Custer
  George 441, 467
Custis
  Martha 134
  Nellie 354
D'Aubigne
  Francoise 106
D'Yrujo
  Sally McKean 281
Dabney
  George 188
Dakin
  Peter 427
Dana
  C. A. 432
Darby
  Deborah 333

Darwin
  Charles 474
David
  Catherine 416
  Morgan 416
Davies
  Samuel 141
Davis
  Evan 416
  Gressey 244
  Jackson 481
  Jefferson 404, 406, 414, 415, 416, 436, 455
  Ken 524
  Mary 217
  Phineas 301
  Susanna 252
  Thomas 26
  William 215
  William (Jr) 352
Dearborn
  Henry 316
Dempsey
  Joseph 476
Dennis
  Philip 316, 317
Denny
  William 159
Denson
  Frances 92
  James 92
  John 92
  Will 92
  William 26
Denwood
  Levin 34, 38, 234
  Mary 38, 234
Dew
  Joseph 266
  Thomas 57, 58, 62
  Thomas R. 349
Dick
  Elisha 245, 290, 313
Dickinson
  James 83, 84
  John 170, 178, 228, 237, 239, 252
Dicks
  Zachariah 266
Digges
  Edward 11, 12, 16, 23
Diggs
  Charles 470
Dillon
  James 251
  Moses 258
  Rebecca 251

Dillwyn
  George 237
Dinwiddie
  Robert 134, 153, 158
Dixon
  Ambrose 36, 37
Dorland 355
Dorsey
  Ann 8
  Edward 8
Doudney
  Richard 14
Douglas
  John 278
Douglass
  Frederick 524, 525
Dowell
  Richard 64
Doyle
  Zachariah 373
Draper
  Thomas 197
Drayton
  Fenny 49
Drinker
  Elizabeth 212
  Henry 209
Drummond
  John 77
Drysdale
  Hugh 115
Dubois
  Abbe Jean 234
  W. E. B. 524
Duer
  William 208
Duff
  William 92, 129
Duryea 467
Dyer
  Mary 41
Eccles
  Solomon 48, 52
Eddy
  Thomas 325, 326
Edmonds
  Howell 29
Edmondson
  William 54, 56, 58, 59, 62, 65, 68, 80
Edmundson
  William 52
Effingham
  Howard of 82
Einstein
  Alfred 503

Elam
  Joseph 207
Elgar
  John 301
Ellicott 231
  Andrew 274
  Nathaniel 276, 300
  Thomas 318
Elliott
  Joseph 414
Ellis
  William 99, 100, 104
Ellyson
  John 157
  William 158
Embree
  Elihu 292
Emerson
  Ralph Waldo 391, 392, 474
Emlen
  Sarah 348, 349
Emperor
  Francis 26, 27
  Mary 26, 27
Endicott
  (Governor of Massachusetts) 41
England
  Isaac 210
  John 175
Evans
  Ernestine 489
  Evan 271
  John 155, 157
  Jonathan 336, 337, 339, 358-360, 363, 376
  Joshua 259
  Nathan "Shanks" 412
  William 358
Evers
  Medgar 524
Fairfax
  Thomas 22, 125
Fairlamb
  John 288
Falwell
  Jerry 526, 529
Farrar
  John 70
Faulkner
  Charles James 348
Featherstone
  Henry 244
Fell
  Margaret 3, 9-11, 16
  Margaret (Jr) 9

Ferris
  Benjamin 337, 338, 342
Fillmore
  Millard 398
Finney
  John 243
Fisher
  Martha 52
  Mary 3, 4, 40
Fleming
  Charles 85, 108
Fletcher
  Elizabeth 48
Fontaine
  John 123
  Peter 120
Forby
  Benjamin 26
Forstall
  Richard 52, 53
Forster
  Joseph 401
  William 401
Fothergill
  John (Jr) 168-170, 175, 180, 214, 323
Fowler
  Robert 13
Fox
  George 1, 2, 4, 9, 10, 15, 38, 40, 43-45, 47, 49-54, 57, 59-63, 67, 71, 75, 80, 86, 93, 99, 102, 103, 107, 117, 118, 120, 134, 152, 205, 251, 255, 272, 301, 302, 336, 360, 361, 365, 392, 454, 474, 498, 532
  Margaret 117, 458
Franklin
  Benjamin 136, 137, 148, 182, 221, 235, 239, 241, 242
Frazer
  Emmet 500
Freeze
  Ed 29
French
  Paul 504
Frissell
  Hollis 480, 481
Fry
  Elizabeth 290, 370
  Elizabeth Gurney 363

Fuller
  Margaret 392
  William 45
Furbush
  C. A. 441
Gabriel
  (of Gabriel's
    Rebellion) 285,
    286, 288, 345
Gage
  D. T. 441
  Thomas 172
Galloway
  Joseph 178
Gandhi
  Mahatma 533
Gardner
  Anna 451
Garner
  J. D. 457
Garrett
  Thomas 388, 419
Garrison
  W. L. 348
  William Lloyd 344,
    345, 377
Garwood 354
Gavin
  Anthony 136
Gawthrop
  Hannah 247
  Patience 247
George
  Lloyd 487
Gerrard
  John 142
Gerry
  Elbridge 274
Gibbons
  Sarah 14
Gibbs 355
  Edward 413
  Elizabeth 413
Gifford
  Hannah 374
Gilbert
  Eliphalet W. 337
Gill
  Joseph 129
  Roger 101
Gillingham
  Chalkley 409, 413,
    455, 473
  Elizabeth 355
  Keziah 409
  Lucas 354, 355

Gilpin
  George 211
  Thomas 209, 211,
    212
Glaister
  Joseph 102, 103
Glass
  Carter 479, 480
Godwin
  Elizabeth 61
  Thomas 33, 61
Goldsmith
  Mary 69
Gooch
  William 116, 124,
    125, 136, 138, 141
Goodall
  Mary 188
Goode
  William O. 347
Gordon
  C.W.B. 389
Gorsuch
  Dickinson 398
  Edward 398
Gosney
  Mary 215
Gotby
  Richard 64
Gover
  Henry 418
  Miriam 413, 414
Grant
  Ulysses S. 425, 431,
    432, 461, 462, 466,
    467
Grave(s)
  John 33
Graves
  Richard 244
Green 355
  Albert 463, 465, 466
Greene
  Nathanael 203, 228
Gregg 304
  Israel 300
  John William 476
  Thomas 313
Gregory
  John 68
Grellet
  Stephen 281, 298,
    332, 333, 334, 337,
    340, 342, 363
Griffin
  Francis 510

Griffith
  Aaron 413, 433, 434,
    440
  Hatty 433
  John 391, 427
  Rachel 391
Grimke
  Angelina 371, 372
  John Faucheraud 371
  Sarah 371
Groom
  Samuel 36, 70
Grubb
  Sarah 363
Guggenheim
  Daniel 501
Gurney
  Eliza Kirkbride 419,
    420
  John 363
  Joseph John 358,
    362, 363-366, 370,
    371, 408, 419
Hague
  Francis 132
  Jane 132
Haight 355
Haines 355
  Anna 485
  Nathan 409
Hale
  John 35, 38, 234
Halkett
  Peter 154
Hall
  John 52, 298
Hallowell
  Benjamin 284, 321,
    374, 378, 387, 457,
    462, 465, 466
  Henry 387
Hamlin
  Hannibal 447
  Stephen 28
Hanbury
  Capel 169
  John 134, 153, 154,
    169, 176, 272
  Richard 134
Hancock
  John 208
Hanway
  Castner 398
Harding
  Warren Gamaliel 501
Hare 486
  Robert 373
  William 373

Hargrave
  James 321
  Samuel 197, 231
Harlan
  Ezekiel 125
  James 461
Harris
  Cornelius 158
  Edward 422, 437, 447
  Eliza 398
  Elizabeth 1-12, 17, 19, 25, 43, 48, 57, 72, 119, 173, 398, 400, 528
  James 243, 422
  John 158, 196
  Matthew 391, 422, 471
  Rebecca 309
  Robert 471
  Sarah 471
  Thomas 262
  Tilman 422
  William 3, 7, 9, 373, 422
  William the Younger 7
Harrison
  B. 177
  Benjamin 173, 175, 178
  Elizabeth 9
  Jesse Burton 349
  Sarah 229, 254, 361
  Thomas 20, 21
  William 175, 192
  William Henry 407
Harriss
  Samuel 165
Harrod
  Catherine 271
Hartley
  Thomas 240
Hartshorne
  Susanna 260
  William 252, 257, 260, 300
Harvey 269
  Ann 376
  Henry 376
  Isaac 269, 318, 420, 421
  J. 424
  John 101
  Sarah 420
  Thomas 97

Hauxhurst
  Job 442, 488
  John 442-446, 456
  Mrs. George 488
Hawthorne
  Nathaniel 392
Hay
  George 312
Hayes
  Rutherford P. 467
Hedgepeth 468
Henry
  Patrick 163, 165, 168, 173, 174, 177-179, 187, 190, 193, 199-201, 207, 210, 214, 219, 222, 226, 232, 237, 243, 272, 279
  Patrick (Jr) 174
  William 453
Hershey
  Lewis 504
Hewes
  Deborah 213
Hicks
  Edward 359, 360
  Elias 253, 261, 303, 331, 332-341, 358, 359, 361, 364, 365, 391
  Thomas Holliday 408
Hill
  Frank 470
Hillary
  William 175
Himmler
  Heinrich 503
Hinshaw 486
  Amos 424
  Thomas 424
Hirst 304
Hite
  Jost 161
  Yost 125
Hitler
  Adolf 502
Hoag
  Enoch 464
  Joseph 335
Hobson
  John 423, 437
  Stephen 423
Hockett
  Stephen 351
  William 423, 424

Hodgson
  Robert 14, 15
Hoffman
  Daniel 152, 351
Hoge 385
  Asa 391
  Hannah 342
  Isaac C. 468
  James 342
  Jesse 400
  Joshua 385
  Lewis Neill 471
  Susanna 471
  William 241
Holder
  Christopher 15, 41
Holley
  Sallie 452
Holliday
  Rachel 398
  Simeon 398
Hollingsworth
  Abraham 124, 127, 129
  Anne 124, 127
  George 129, 157
  Isaac 158
  Robert Isaac 417
  Thomas 128
Hollowell 486
  Alice 72
Holme
  Benjamin 113
Holmes 486
  Elmina 374
  Jesse 509
  Joseph 300, 456
  William 411
Holway
  Edward 428, 448, 450
Hooker
  Thomas 31
Hooton
  Elizabeth 50, 52, 53, 72
Hoover
  Herbert 491, 492, 494, 495, 501
  Lou Henry 501
Hopkins
  Elizabeth 356
  Johns 88, 356, 457
  Stephen 168, 178
Hopper
  Isaac T. 294
Horsey
  Stephen 36, 37

582　　　　　　　　　　　　　　INDEX

Houdon
  Jean-Antoine 260
Hough
  David 421
  Henry 421
  John 132, 196, 211, 300
  Mary 248
  Sarah 132
  Will 426
Houghton
  Anne 502
  Daniel 501, 502
Howard
  Francis 80
  James 100
  John 323
  Oliver O. 449
  Sarah 161
Howe
  Elias 390
  William 202
Howell
  David 238, 405, 421
  John 421
Howgill
  Francis 1-3, 43
Howland
  Emily 452, 457
Hubbs
  Rebecca 281, 282
Humphreys
  Charles 178
Hunnicutt 486
  Glaister 231
  John 243, 262
  Thomas 341
Hunt
  Jane 372
  John 209, 212, 242
  Nathan 331
Hunter 355
Hutchins
  Francis 92
Ingledue
  Hannah 132
Jackson
  Andrew 343, 375, 390
  James 240
  Joseph 423
  Stonewall 433
James
  Joseph 436
  Thomas 21
  William 51
Janney 304
  Abel 259
  Abijah 356
  Alcinda 420
  Amos 132

  Anne 459
  Asa 386, 452, 463
  Asa Moore 304, 380, 441, 458, 463, 466, 467, 508, 520
  Elisha 303
  Elizabeth 356, 452, 466
  Hannah 356
  Henry 418
  Israel 258, 300, 301
  Jacob 132, 356
  James C. 426
  John 314, 406, 407, 420
  John Jay 304-306, 308, 346
  Joseph 196, 211, 300
  Mahlon 196
  Mary 132
  Micajah 314
  Nathaniel 303
  O. Edward 459
  Phineas 300, 356, 391
  Rachel 173
  Richard 303, 358
  Samuel 357, 374, 375, 378, 379-381, 386, 399, 402, 406, 410, 412, 417, 418, 422, 432, 439, 441, 452, 462, 463-466, 472
  Samuel Hopkins 303
  Samuel McPherson 293, 303, 344, 356, 439
  Werner 304, 386, 501, 502, 505, 508
Jarratt
  Devereaux 235
Jay 486
  Antoine 221
  John 38, 62
Jeanes
  Anna 480
Jefferson
  Peter 272
  Thomas 111, 164, 194, 198, 200, 201, 219, 225, 230-233, 235, 237, 238, 253, 260, 272, 273, 274-278, 280, 286, 288, 290, 297, 300, 316, 335, 338, 341, 348, 358, 452

Jehle
  Herbert 503, 508
Jernagin
  W. H. 509
Johns
  Richard 87, 97
Johnson
  Andrew 443, 444, 449, 461
  Bushrod Rust 435
  Christopher 228, 231
  George 36, 37, 69
  Gerard 352
  James 228
  John 317
  Joseph 401
  Lyndon B. 517, 518, 524
  Marmaduke 407
  Robin 352
  William 228
Jolliffe
  John 418
  John J. 386
  Joseph 426
  Joseph N. 386
  William 186
Jones
  Ann 340, 342
  Edward 45
  Eli 440
  George 244, 340, 342
  Norris 229
  Rufus 473, 474, 484, 495, 498, 499, 503
  Sibyl 440
  Susanna 212
Jordan
  Joseph 114
  Margaret 32, 38, 46, 175, 234
  Matthew 100
  Robert 114-116
  Samuel 129
  Thomas 32, 34, 38, 46, 59, 65, 80, 86, 87, 114, 234
  Thomas (III) 102
  Thomas (IV) 103
  Thomas (Jr) 102
Judge
  Hugh 334, 335
Kant
  Immanuel 235
Keats
  John 458

Keesee
  Charles  195
Keith
  George  70, 76-79, 94, 95, 96, 112, 200, 325, 337
Kelpius
  Johannes  95, 96
Kennedy
  Bobby  516
  John F.  517
  Walter  113
Kenny
  James  156, 160
Kent
  Mrs. William  487
Kersey
  Jesse  282, 290, 335
Key
  Francis Scott  291
Kilpatrick
  James J.  511
King
  Francis T.  408
  Martin Luther  513, 524
  Martin Luther (Jr)  507
Kirk
  William  317
Kite
  James  377
Knight
  Jonathan  301
Knott
  Luke  113
Knowles
  John  21
Knox
  John  75
Krebser
  Marian  517
Lacey
  John  203
Lacy
  Robert  68
Ladd
  Amos  197, 219
  Benjamin  341, 358, 385, 386
  Benjamin W.  340, 349, 354
  James  197, 243, 262
  Thomas  325
  William  419
Lafayette
  Marquis de  277

LaFollette
  Mrs. Robert  487
Lamb
  Charles  265
Lancaster
  James  52, 57, 58
  Joseph  319
Lang
  John  376
Langdale
  John  160
Langley
  Robert  230
Larrabee
  Kent  530
Laughlin
  Sarah  431
  Seth  431
Lawrence
  Robert  26, 32
Leatherbury
  Thomas  34
Leddra
  William  41
Lee
  Arthur  175
  Charles  192
  Elizabeth Collins  284
  Fitzhugh  459
  R.H.  177
  Richard Henry  173, 175, 207-209, 232
  Robert E.  321, 403, 407, 425, 431, 437, 444
Leeds
  Morris  451
Lemmon
  Bill  439
Lerber
  Maria Elisabet  95
Letcher
  John  406
Levering
  Miriam  528
  Samuel  528
Lewis  355
  Elijah  398
  Esther  292
  Lawrence  354
Liddal
  Jane  30
Lightfoot
  Mary  463
  Samuel  160
  Thomas  463

Lilburne
  John  272
Lincoln
  Abraham  406-408, 416, 418, 420, 427, 429, 434, 440, 442, 443, 449
  John  161
  Mary  434, 440
  Rebecca  161, 416
  Virginia John  416
Linsey
  David  16
Linton
  John  532
Lippincott
  Mary  405
Lloyd
  Cornelius  21
Loe
  Thomas  74
Logan
  Charles  273
  George  273, 280, 290
  James  273
London
  Ambrose  38
Long
  Jack  70
Love
  John  43, 44
Lownes
  Caleb  323-325
  Hugh  325
  James  325
Luce
  Marquis de la  106
Lumpkin
  Robert  382
Lundy
  Benjamin  291, 292, 327, 343-345, 357, 369
  Esther  292, 293
Lupton
  Joel  391
  Jonah  427
  Joseph  130, 157, 161
  Lewis  391
  Lydia  427
  Mary  157, 161
  William  130
Luther
  Martin  40, 141
Lynch  273
  Charles  172, 203, 204, 232
  Charles (Jr)  273
  John  228, 300

# INDEX

Mackie
  Josiah 106
Macomber
  Lindley 427
Macon
  Ahijah 431, 437
  Isaiah 430, 437
Madison
  Dolley 272, 276, 280,
    281, 282, 284, 290
  Dolley Payne 283
  James 193, 194, 225,
    232, 237, 239, 241,
    242, 244, 245, 272,
    277, 278-282, 284,
    290
Maeterlinck
  Maurice 392
Makemie
  Francis 76, 77, 88,
    89, 106
Mallory
  Philip 27, 28
Malone
  Emma 476
  Walter 476
Marchant
  Henry Clay 441
Marks
  Matthew 107
Marmaduke
  Alcinda 407
Marshall
  John 232
Martin
  Mary 188
  Thomas 490
Mason
  George 193, 198,
    413, 452
  James 397, 404
Matthews
  Samuel 16, 23, 35
Maury
  James 163, 272
Mazzei
  Filippo 253
McClintock
  Mary Anne 372
McCormick
  Cyrus 390
McDiarmid
  Dorothy 514
McDowell
  James 375
McGrew
  James 258

McIlhany
  James 348
McKay 486
  Andrew 288
  Hannah 129
  Robert 125-127, 129,
    131, 161
McKinley
  William (Jr) 459
McMasters
  David 370
McNamara
  Robert 521
McPherson 486
  Aimee Semple 498
Meade
  Bishop 291, 297
Megear
  Michael 278, 338
Mendenhall
  James 258, 316
  Nereus 415, 422
  Richard 404
Mercer
  George 168
Meredith
  Reese 176
Merritt
  Wesley 435
Merry
  Anthony 280
Michener
  Sarah Janney 391
Michie
  John 227
Miege
  Guy 205
Miers
  Elizabeth 52
Mifflin
  Daniel 237
  Nancy 281
  Thomas 178, 203
  Walter 206
  Warner 204-206, 211,
    221, 226, 228, 237,
    242, 281
Mildred
  Daniel 169
Miles
  William P. 415
Millard
  Jane 30
Miller
  Adam 123
  Robert H. 391

Milliken
  Clark 430
Mills
  Henry 129
  Hur 129
  John 129, 142
  Thomas 129
Milner
  Beverly 197
Minh
  Ho Chi 515
Mitchell
  John 525
  Robert 231
Modyford
  Thomas 46
Monro
  Andrew 102
Monroe
  James 284, 286
Moody
  Dwight L. 468, 469,
    476
Moon 486
Moore
  Asa 318
  Martha 488
  Samuel M. D. 347
Moorman 273
  Charles 231
  Clark 231
  Rachel 231
Moran
  Charles E. (Chic)
    502, 505, 508, 511
  Fermine 508
Morgan
  Charles 328
  Daniel 213
Morris
  Anthony 284
  Elliston Perot 451
  Mildred 367
  Robert 192, 294
  Samuel 141
Morrison
  Anne 521
  Ben 521
  Emily 521
  Norman 521, 522
  Tina 521
Morse
  Samuel F. B. 390
Moryson
  Francis 31
Mosby
  John S. 435

Mott
  Lucretia 371, 372, 392, 486
  Richard 267, 277, 335, 358
Murray
  John 172, 189, 190
  Lindley 373
Naftel
  Mary 335
Native Americans (Shawnee Tribe)
  Big Snake 317
  Black Hoof 317
  Tecumseh (The Shooting Star) 317
  Yellow Feathers (Little Chief) 317
Native Americans (Sioux Tribe)
  Chief Red Cloud 466
Nayler
  James 44
Neale
  Samuel 166
Neall
  Daniel 384
Neave
  Joseph James 436
  William 169
Newby
  Nathan 105
Newhall
  Mary 335
Newhouse
  Thomas 47, 48, 56, 62
Newlin 486
Newport
  Elizabeth 400, 401
Newton
  Isaac 417, 428, 434, 442
Nichols 304, 385
  Eli 385
  Joseph 439
Nicholson
  Francis 82, 83, 87, 88, 93, 95, 97, 99, 106, 112
  Joseph 30, 45
  Thomas 218
  William 414
Nietszche
  Friedrich 392
Niles
  Hezekiah 291

Nixon
  Barnaby 254, 261
  Hannah 524
  Richard M. 524, 528
Norden
  Robert 107
Norman
  Lucy 417
North
  Frederick 181
Norton 486
  Humphrey 13
Ochs
  Johan Rudolph 95, 97
  Johan, the Younger 125
Olmsted
  Frederick Law 386
Ong
  Jacob 271, 340
Osborn
  Jesse 437
Osborne
  Charles 292, 369
  Jesse 423
  Matthew 423
Osgood
  Anna 134
  John 109, 134
Outland 486
Owen
  Thomas 26
Page
  John 241
  Thomas 104
Paine
  Thomas 253, 359
  Tom 193, 208, 235
Painter
  Edward 463
Palmer
  Esther 99
Pancoast
  Tacy 400
Pankhurst
  Emmeline 487
Parker
  Charlie 524
  Ely Samuel 461, 462, 467
  Isaac 389
  Jane 389
  Josiah 241
Parkins
  Isaac 127, 157

Parrish
  John 226
  Joseph 290, 447
Parsons
  Elizabeth Ladd 326
  Samuel 197, 228, 325, 326, 327, 328
  Samuel Pleasants 326, 328
  Sarah 310
Pattison
  George 52, 57
Paul
  Alice 487-491
Payne
  Dolley 250, 279
  John 199, 207, 250, 279
  Mary Coles 199, 250, 279, 280
Pearson
  Angelina 269
  Lazarus 388
Pease
  Edward 301, 353
  John 353
Peebles
  Stephen 214
Pemberton
  Ann 425
  Hannah 212
  Israel 159, 160, 171, 178, 179, 195, 199, 207, 208, 274, 425
  James 169, 171, 179, 180, 209, 237, 242, 243, 244
  John 159, 171
  John C. 425
  Joseph 425
  Molly 435
Pendleton
  Edmund 173, 175, 177, 178, 193, 200
Penn
  Thomas 153
  William 73, 76, 78, 87, 88, 127, 129, 131, 153, 178, 273, 301, 319, 363, 388, 461, 522
Pennington
  Isaac 175
Perkins
  Joseph 255
Perrot
  John 10, 30, 43-47, 51, 58, 76, 77

# 586 INDEX

Perry
  John 317
Petty
  Peter 401
Peyton
  Francis 211
Phillips
  Henry 55
  William 220
Pickering
  Timothy 257, 258
Pickett
  Samuel 497
Pidgeon
  Isaac 351
  Mary Elizabeth 488, 489, 490, 491
  Ruth 351
Pierce
  Franklin 401
Pierpont
  Francis 441, 443, 444
  John 374, 441
  John R. 321
Piggott
  Isaac 400
Pike 486
Pinder
  Richard 30
Pleasants
  Henry 435
  Isaac 219
  Israel 210
  James 272, 293, 327
  Jane 104
  John 85, 86, 108, 195, 219
  John Hampden 380, 381
  Jonathan 195, 272
  Joseph J. 354
  Margaret 176
  Mary 212
  Matthew 219
  Molly. 273
  Philip. 219
  Robert 111, 166, 173, 174, 176, 181, 182, 191, 192, 195, 197, 198, 199, 210, 218, 219, 220, 221, 223, 225, 226-228, 231, 243, 244, 253, 261, 273, 310, 435, 523
  Robert (Jr) 219
  Samuel 174, 195, 209, 219, 287, 435
  Thomas 243

Polk
  James K. 366, 372
Pope
  Martha 271
  Nathaniel 271
Porter
  John 26, 399, 442
  John (Jr) 27, 60, 326
  William 341
Pownall
  Levi 398
Preston
  George 30
  James 57, 291
  Richard 7, 22
  William 204
Pretlow
  John 422
  John D. 468
  Joseph 373
  Robert 373
  Thomas 310
Price
  Rachel 335
  Thomas 36, 37
Pringle
  Cyrus 427
Prosser
  Tom 285
Pugh
  Achilles 377
Purcell
  John 390
Putnam
  Carrie 452
Pyatt
  Jane 389
Pyron
  Jane 522
Raiford
  Edward 500, 501, 505
Randolph
  Anne 272
  Dorothy 272
  Edmond 290
  Isham 134, 272
  Jane 272
  John 134, 289, 291
  Martha 275
  Peyton 141, 172, 173, 177, 178
  Ryland 220
  Thomas Jefferson 348, 375, 382
  Virginia Estelle 481, 482

Ratcliff
  Harrison 367
  Mildred 341, 364, 367, 397
Ratliff 486
Rawson
  Arthur 492
Reagan
  Ronald 526, 529
Reckitt
  William 157
Reid
  William Ferguson 522
Rhoads
  Charles 501
  James 448, 450, 457, 501
  Margaret 448
  Samuel 178
Richards
  Lydia 270
  Mary 270
  Rowland 270
Richardson
  John 94, 98, 100, 104, 110
Ricks
  Abraham 92
  Arnold 499
  Hoge 499, 500
  Isaac 91
  James Hoge 499
  Katherine 499
  Richard 485
  Richard Arnold 499
  Robert 92
Ridgeway 355
Riley
  Janet 530
Ritchie
  Thomas (Jr) 381
Rives
  William C. 347
Roane
  William H. 347
Roberts 355
  Abigail 442
  Gerard 1, 3, 4, 8
  Hugh 78
  Jonathan 442-444
  Robert 413
  Ruth Ann 413
Robertson
  Pat 526
Robinson
  Will 12, 14, 15, 17, 34, 35, 41
  William 141

Robson
    Elizabeth 340, 343, 361
Roemer
    John 521
Rofe
    George 30
Rogers
    Edward 157
Roosevelt
    Teddy 479, 483
Ross
    Alexander 125-127, 131, 161
    Catherine 127
Rotch
    Francis 171
    Mary 392
    William 171, 239
Rous
    John 41, 52
Ruffner
    Henry 377
Rumsey
    James 299, 301
Rush
    Benjamin 242
    Richard 283
Russell
    Benjamin 251
    John 259
    Richard 26
Rye
    George 399, 445
Sailer
    Agnes 509
Sainte-Beuve
    Charles 146
Salkeld
    John 99
Salter
    Hannah 52
Sampson
    David 469
Sanbourne
    Daniel 91
Sankey
    Ira D. 468, 469
Savery
    William 256, 257, 262
Scarburgh
    Charles 34
    Edmund 15, 34, 35, 38
Scarlett
    Joseph 398

Scattergood
    Henry 451, 501
    Thomas 231, 253, 261, 262, 307
Schaeffer
    Charles 450
Schooley 400
    Will 307
Scott
    Job 253, 256, 339
    Joseph 192
    Thomas 241
    Winfield 321
Scull
    David 502, 509-512, 522
    Laurel 502, 509
    Susan 281
Sears
    Huldah 341
Sedgwick
    Theodore 241
Sewel
    William 46
Shearman
    Julia 453
Sheppard
    John 68
    Mosby 286
Sheridan
    Philip 432-434
Shillitoe
    Thomas 340, 343
Shoemaker
    Daniel 514
    Isaac 275
    John 267, 335
    Jonathan 275, 300
    Joseph 220
Shreve
    Benjamin 249, 300
    Isaac 249
Slater
    Samuel 302
Small
    Elizabeth 105
Smiley
    Sarah 448, 450
Smith
    Gerrit 379
    James 243
    John 184, 210
    Lizzie B. 460
    Samuel 256
    William L. 240, 294
Snake
    Big 317

Snead
    Robert 87
Socrates 247
Souder
    Theodate 520
Southall
    James 451
Spangenthal
    Peggy 523
Spotswood
    Alexander 111-114, 123
Spring
    Isabel 26
    Rebecca Buffum 405, 421
    Robert 26
St.Clair
    John 154
St.John-de-Crevecoeur
    Hector 205
Stabler
    Deborah Pleasants 283
    Edward 151, 158, 173, 176, 182, 183, 191, 192, 195, 197, 199, 210, 237, 248, 262, 392, 474
    Edward (III) 283, 459
    Edward (Jr) 248, 314, 318, 342, 391, 393
    Henry 485
    Mary 151
    Thomas 405
    William 248
Stanley
    John 158
    Seth 295
    Thomas 188, 511, 512
    William 158, 184
Stanton
    Edwin 429, 434, 442, 443, 449
    Edwin M. 417
    Elizabeth Cady 372, 486
Starbuck
    Mary 104
Stearns
    Shubael 142, 165
Steer
    Sarah 452
Steere 486

Stephen
  Adam 212, 242
Stephens
  Frances Culpeper 67
  Nathaniel 49
Stephenson 468
  Marmaduke 41
Steptoe
  George 280
Stevens
  Thaddeus 398, 442
Stiles 355
  Levi 427
Stone
  Michael Jenifer 240
Story
  Thomas 99-103, 107
Stover
  Daniel 124
  Jacob 123-125
  Sarah 123
Stowe
  Harriet Beecher 398
Strawbridge
  Robert 235
Stringer
  Colonel 35
  John 15
Stuart
  David 242
  Henry 430
Stubbs
  John 9, 10, 52
Sullivan
  John 208
Sumner
  Charles 442
Sunday
  Billy 471, 498
Sutcliff
  Robert 276, 280
Sutton 355
Swaggart
  Jimmy 527
Swann
  Samuel 85
Swayne
  Noah Haines 417
Taberer
  Margaret 62
  Thomas 56, 62
Tacitus 235
Tagore
  Rabindranath 508
Talbot
  John 95

Tappan
  Arthur 345
Tate
  William 439
Tauler
  John 474
Tavenner
  Lot 439
Taylor 304
  Benjamin Franklin
    321, 376
  Emma 459
  George Keith 324
  Henry S. 439, 531
  Jacob 318
  John 46, 288, 291
  John Marshall 421
  Jonathan 340, 341,
    358
  Jonathan K. 457, 459
  Joseph 457
  Mahlon 304
  Mary 304
  Robert Barraud 313
  Rodney 408
  Samuel 376
  Thomas 31
  Thomas E. 446, 456
  Yardley 387, 400,
    402, 411
Terrell 273
  Joseph 349
  Mary Church 509
  Rachel 166
Thomas
  Edward 101
  Evan 301
  James Carey 468
  John 199, 223, 226
  Mary Snowden 469
  Philip 377
  Philip E. 301, 303,
    318, 342, 376
  Richard H. 469
Thompson
  Israel 252, 300
Thomson
  James 512
Thoreau
  Henry David 392
Thornton
  Anna Maria 280, 290
  William 275, 280,
    290, 291, 354
Throckmorton
  James 421
  Job 411, 422, 437
  Leah 422

Thurston
  Thomas 8, 11, 12, 15,
    16, 17, 32
Tinling
  Marian 108
Todd
  Dolley 250
  Dolley Payne 279
  John 250, 279, 284
  Laurie 310
Toft
  Ann 34
Toler
  Burwell 445
Tomkins
  Mary 31
Tompson
  William 21
Toms
  Francis 55
Tooke
  William 68
Torrey
  Charles 388
Townshend
  Charles 169
Travers
  Benjamin 29
Trevelyan
  George Macaulay 67
Trollope
  Frances 470
Troth 354
  Anne 466
  Hillman 413
  Jacob 388, 463, 465,
    466
Trueblood
  Elton 117
Truitt
  George 38
Tucker
  Beverly 397
  Jane Larcome 85
  St. George 231
Turner
  Albert 514
  Nat 345, 349, 352,
    404
Twain
  Mark 163
Tyler
  John 407
  John (Sr) 284
Tyndale
  William 40

Tyson 355
  Elisha 388
Underwood
  John 417, 445, 455
  John C. 399
Updegraff 472
  David 362, 472, 474, 475
  David Brainerd 472
  Rebecca 362
Valentine
  Lila Meade 490
Van Blarcom
  James 450
Van Buren
  Martin 366, 370, 376
Van Yahres
  Mitchell 524
Vaux
  Ann 15
  Henry 15, 35, 38, 234
Vernon
  Mabel 488
Vestal
  John 175
Vinson
  Frederick 510
Vogt
  G. A. 524
Voltaire 178, 191, 205
Von Jehle
  Julius 503
von Kotzebue
  August 206
von Steuben
  Baron 221
Votaw 486
Walcott
  Mary Vaux 502
Walker
  Anne 95
  Eliza 489, 490
  George 95, 97, 112, 200
  Gilbert C. 446, 456
Wall
  J. Barry 511
Walthall
  William B. 267, 269, 289
Walton 355
  David 408
  Ella 466
  George 503
  Jemima Ann 409
  Samuel 466
  Walter 413

Warner
  James 10
  Yardley 450, 451
Warren
  Earl 510
Washington
  Augustine 153, 175, 176
  Bushrod 291
  George 134, 153, 158, 173, 175, 177, 178, 203, 206, 208, 209, 211, 212, 221, 228, 232, 237, 240, 241, 242, 243, 256, 260, 272, 273, 279, 283, 294, 299, 300, 354, 355
  Jane 355
  John 175
  John A. 355
  John Augustus 211
  Laurence 153, 176
  Lucy Payne 280
  Martha 213, 260, 354
Watkins
  Elizabeth 70
  Henry 70
  Katherine 70
  Thomas 141
Watson
  Moses 439
Waugh
  Dorothy 14
Wawillay
  Chief 271
Way 486
Wayne
  Anthony 221, 257, 259, 314
Webb
  Elizabeth 100
  Thomas 188
Webster
  Daniel 291, 366, 390, 397
Weld
  Isaac 235
Wellons
  Lucy 520
Wesley
  Charles 136
  John 136, 234, 236, 253, 296, 298, 331, 333, 360, 368
West
  Benjamin 154, 260
  John (Jr) 154
  Joseph 93

Wetherald
  Thomas 342, 343
Wetherhead
  Mary 14
Wetherill
  Samuel 179
Wharton
  Isaac 171
  Thomas 171, 213
Wheeler
  Daniel 358
Whitacre
  Thornton 439
Whitall
  John 419
White
  Alexander 241
  Catherine 384
  Edward 486
  Howard 463
  Lee 435
  Lige 417
  Oswin 422
Whitefield
  George 136-140, 142, 164, 234, 236, 254, 296, 297, 331, 360, 368, 468, 526
Whitehead
  George 141
Whitlock
  Jane 436
Whitman
  Walt 332, 339
Whitney
  Eli 245
Whittemore
  Thomas 278
Whittier
  John Greenleaf 138, 297, 360, 397, 472
Whittington
  Francis 28
  Louise 515
Widders
  Robert 52, 57
Wilbur
  John 361, 363, 366, 369, 371
  Lucy 502
Wiley
  Keith 508
  Mary 508
Wilks
  Colman 259
Will 355

Willcockes
  Henry 31
Williams
  Elizabeth 40
  Mary Elizabeth 417
  William 417, 418
Willoughby
  Sara 60
Wilson 304
  George 30, 31, 38, 234, 423
  Henry 404
  Louise Brown 508
  Martha Ann 373
  Rachel 166, 173
  Robert. 508
  Thomas 83, 84
  Woodrow 483, 487, 489, 491, 492
Winsor
  Ellen 489
  Mary 489
Winston 486
  Ann 348
  George 260
  James 348
  Sarah 173
Winthrop
  John 21
Wirt
  William 312
Wise
  George 496
  Henry Alexander 404, 406
  Katherine 496
Wistar
  Isaac 448
  Richard 323
Wood
  James 326
Woodson
  Charles 195
  Frederick 219
  Isham. 219
  John 85, 272
  Samuel 219
Woolman
  John 145-150, 178, 186, 367, 523
Woory
  Joseph 62
Wordsworth
  William 392
Worrall
  Peter 159

Worthington
  Robert 175
Wren
  Christopher 97
Wright 354, 486
  Amos 423, 433
  Jesse 426
  Joe 523
  Johnny 426
  Jonathan 258
  Lydia 426
  Martha 372
  Mary 58, 59, 61
  Patience 170
  Rebecca 432-434
  Sarah 355
  Thomas 354, 355
  William 56, 58, 295
Wynne
  Robert 28
Wythe
  George 199, 200, 232, 237, 273, 324
  Margaret Walker 200
X
  Malcolm 524
Yarnall
  Robert 503
Yarrett
  Margaret 72
  William 45
Yarrow
  William 58
Yevtushenko
  Yevgeny 531
Zane
  Betty 222
  Ebenezer 189, 222
  Isaac 162, 172, 203, 204, 232, 274
  Isaac (Jr) 160, 210, 256, 273, 281
  Isaac (Sr) 210, 211, 274
  Sally 281
  Sarah 274, 372
  William 161, 188, 189, 222
Wyandot Isaac 172

www.ingramcontent.com/pod-product-compliance
Lightning Source LLC
Chambersburg PA
CBHW071216290426
44108CB00013B/1190